Other Kaplan Books for Students in High School

High School 411

Learning Power

AP Biology

Yale Daily News Guide to Summer Programs

Essential Review: High School Chemistry

Essential Review: High School Biology

Essential Review: High School Mathematics I

Essential Review: High School Mathematics II

Essential Review: High School Mathematics III

Upper Level
SSAT/ISEE*

By Joanna Cohen, Ed.M.; Darcy L. Galane, J.D.;
and the Staff of Kaplan, Inc.

Simon & Schuster

NEW YORK · LONDON · SINGAPORE · SYDNEY · TORONTO

* SSAT is a registered trademark of the Secondary School Admission Test Board, and ISEE is a registered trademark of the Educational Records Bureau. Neither organization endorses this book.

Kaplan Publishing
Published by Simon & Schuster
1230 Avenue of the Americas
New York, NY 10020

For bulk sales to schools, please contact: Order Department, Simon & Schuster, 100 Front Street, Riverside, NJ 08075. Phone: 1-800-223-2336. Fax: 1-800-943-9831.

Project Editor: Ruth Baygell

Contributing Editors: Marc Bernstein, Marcy Bullmaster

Cover Design: Cheung Tai

Interior Page Design and Layout: Lori Stepat

Production Editor: Maude Spekes

Production Manager: Michael Shevlin

Managing Editor: Dave Chipps

Executive Editor: Del Franz

Special thanks to: Marcy Bullmaster, Susanne Rust, Robert Reiss, and Rudy Robles

Manufactured in the United States of America

October 2000
10 9 8 7 6 5 4 3 2 1

ISBN: 0-7432-0180-9

Table of Contents

About the Authors

Joanna Cohen received her B.S. in Human Development and Family Studies from Cornell University and her Ed.M. from Harvard University. As an educator, she has taught, conducted research, and written educational materials for students and teachers. Ms. Cohen has developed curriculum for Kaplan's SAT, PSAT, SSAT/ISEE, GRE, GMAT, and LSAT programs and is currently the Manager of Pre-College Curriculum.

Darcy L. Galane is the Associate Director of Pre-College Curriculum at Kaplan's Corporate Office. She received a B.A. from UCLA and began teaching SAT and LSAT classes for Kaplan while earning her J.D. at the University of Connecticut School of Law. Having taught and written curriculum for most of Kaplan's courses, Ms. Galane has helped thousands of students to raise their scores on standardized tests.

Preface

Welcome to Kaplan!

In your hands, you have the best test prep available for the SSAT or ISEE. Kaplan's 62 years of test prep experience went into creating the most up-to-date, comprehensive study material you'll find anywhere. Before you get started, take a quick look to make sure you've purchased the right book for your testing needs. You should use this book if you:

- Are applying to a private or independent school

- Need to take the upper level of the SSAT or ISEE for your application

- Are currently in grades 8–11

Please note that this book is designed to prepare you for the **upper** level SSAT or ISEE only. Much of the material contained in this book may prove useful to students taking the **lower** level SSAT or **lower** or **middle** level ISEE, but there are differences between the different levels of the tests. This book has been specially designed for the **upper** level tests, so the material will be less directly applicable to other levels.

Every year, close to 100,000 students take either the SSAT or ISEE for admission to nearly 2,000 independent (private) schools. Although the components of the two tests are remarkably similar, there are some critical differences. In order to organize your studies effectively, you should contact the school(s) to which you are applying to determine which test you need to take. Also, don't forget to register for your test!

And remember, to get the latest tips, test information, and advice, log on to **www.kaptest.com** any time of the day or night. Kaplan has the answers to all of your questions.

How to Use This Book: The Classic Plan

Ideally, you should take a couple of months to work through this book, though it's certainly possible to read it in far less time. Here's how you should go about training with it:

1. Read through each chapter completely, learning from the example problems and trying the practice problems. In the "Study Aids" section, you'll find a list of over 200 SSAT/ISEE vocabulary words, complete with vocabulary-building exercises, a root list, and a word families list, as well as a review of the most important math concepts to know for the SSAT/ISEE.

2. At the beginning of each chapter, there is a Highlights box containing the most important concepts in the chapter. At the end of many chapters, you'll find a Checklist that allows you to check off the concepts as you master them.

3. Read the stress management section at the end of chapter 1 to set the stage for your training and testing success.

4. Take Practice Test One under strictly timed conditions.

5. Score your Practice Test. Find out where you need help and then review the appropriate chapters.

6. Reread all the Highlights boxes once more before trying your luck at the other Practice Tests. Repeat the process of reviewing your areas of weakness.

7. Give yourself a day of rest right before the real exam.

If you have time, do just two or three chapters a week, and let the material sink in slowly. Don't hesitate to take some time off from your SSAT/ISEE preparation when you need to. Nobody can take this stuff day in and day out for weeks at a time without a break.

How to Use This Book: The Emergency Plan

Maybe you have only two or three weeks—or even less time than that. Don't freak! *SSAT/ISEE* has been designed to work for students in your situation, too. If you go through a chapter or two every day, you can finish this book in a couple of weeks. If you have limited time to prepare for the SSAT/ISEE (fewer than six weeks), we suggest you do the following:

1. Take a slow, deep breath. Read the stress management section at the end of chapter 1 to maximize your study and testing time.

2. Read the "SSAT/ISEE Mastery" chapter.

3. Read the "SSAT/ISEE Emergency" sidebars throughout the book. The suggestions in these sidebars can really streamline your study strategy as well as ensure that you cover the really vital concepts before Test Day.

4. Take as many of the Practice Tests as you can—*under timed conditions.*

5. Review your results, with special attention to the questions you missed.

6. Give yourself the day before the test off.

Scattered throughout the text you'll find "hints"—special points that we feel deserve emphasis. Pay special attention to these hints, which spotlight some very important test prep information, key strategies, and fun facts.

SSAT/ISEE Emergency FAQs

Q. It's two days before the SSAT/ISEE and I'm clueless. What should I do?

A. First of all, don't panic. If you have only a day or two to prepare for the test, then you don't have time to prepare thoroughly. But that doesn't mean you should just give up. There's still a lot you can do to improve your potential score. First and foremost, you should become familiar with the test. Read chapter 1, "SSAT/ISEE Mastery." And if you don't do anything else, take one of the full-length practice tests at the back of this book under reasonably testlike conditions. When you finish the practice test, check your answers and look at the explanations to the questions you didn't get right.

Q. Math is my weak spot. What can I do to get better at math in a big hurry?

A. Review the "Math Foundations Workshop," which highlights the Key Math Concepts for the SSAT/ISEE. Then do as many of the sample problems in the Question Bank as you have time for. If you don't have time, just read the sidebars in the math chapters. They contain helpful facts and tips.

Q. I'm great at Math, but Verbal scares me. How can I improve my Verbal score right away?

A. Go straight to the Vocabulary Reference and make sure to hit the Verbal sections in the Question Bank, too. Much of the SSAT/ISEE Verbal depends on your ability to work with unfamiliar words. Then do as many of the sample problems in the Verbal chapters as you have time for. If you don't have time to do the sample problems, just read the sidebars in those chapters. These strategies can help boost your score.

Q. My parents are upset with me for waiting till the last minute to study, and now I can't concentrate. Help!

A. Take a deep breath! Anxiety and stress are the enemies of all test takers—no matter how much time they have to prepare. Read through the stress management section at the end of chapter 1. Do the exercises. And don't forget to think positively!

Q: The SSAT/ISEE is tomorrow. Should I stay up all night studying geometry formulas?

A: The best thing to do right now is to try to stay calm. Read the "What Do I Do Now?" chapter to find out the best way to survive, and thrive, on Test Day. And get a good night's sleep.

Q: I don't feel confident. Should I just guess?

A: This depends on whether you are taking the SSAT or the ISEE. The SSAT does have a wrong-answer penalty, but that doesn't mean you should never guess. If you can rule out even ONE answer choice, you should guess, because you have significantly increased your chances of guessing correctly. Also, on questions that appear early in a section, more obvious answers will tend to be correct, so you can guess more confidently on those questions. Finally, always guess on Grid-Ins, since there is no wrong-answer penalty on that question type. If you're taking the ISEE, you should ALWAYS guess, since there is no wrong-answer penalty.

Q: What's the most important thing I can do to get ready for the SSAT/ISEE quickly?

In addition to basic math and verbal skills, the SSAT/ISEE mainly tests your ability to take the test. Therefore, the most important thing you can do is to familiarize yourself with the directions, the question types, the answer grid, and the overall structure of the test. Make sure you feel comfortable with the logistics—how to get to your testing location, how to fill in Grid-Ins, and so forth. Read every question carefully—many mistakes are the result of simply not reading thoroughly.

Q. So it's a good idea to panic, right? RIGHT?

A. No! No matter how prepared you are for the SSAT/ISEE, stress will hurt your performance, and it's really no fun. Stay confident, and don't cram. So . . . breathe. Stay calm, and remember, it's just a test.

A Special Note for International Students

The population of international students and students whose native language is not English attending secondary schools in the United States is steadily increasing. In addition, approximately 500,000 international students pursue academic degrees in the United States at the undergraduate, graduate, or professional level each year. Most competitive programs use standardized exams, such as the SSAT or ISEE, as part of their admissions process. These exams often are challenging for students whose native language is not English. Kaplan's programs for international students and professionals can help you meet this challenge.

Kaplan International Programs

Kaplan International Programs are designed to help non-native speakers of English reach their educational goals. Kaplan provides English language instruction to students of all levels, in addition to test preparation programs, at locations throughout the United States. These programs help students to improve their academic and conversational English skills, raise their scores on the TOEFL, SSAT, ISEE, SAT, ACT, and other standardized exams, and gain admission to the schools of their choice. Our staff and instructors give international students the individualized attention they need to succeed. Here's a brief description of some of the programs:

General Intensive English

These classes are designed to help you improve your skills in all areas of English and to increase your fluency in spoken and written English. Classes are available for beginning to advanced students, and the average class size is 12 students.

English for TOEFL and University Preparation

This course provides you with the skills you need to improve your TOEFL score and succeed in an American university or graduate program. It includes advanced reading, writing, listening, grammar, and conversational English, plus university admissions counseling. You will also receive training for the TOEFL using Kaplan's exclusive computer-based practice materials.

SAT Test Preparation Course

The SAT is an important admission criterion for American colleges and universities. A high score can help you stand out from other applicants. This course includes the skills you need to succeed on each section of the SAT, as well as access to Kaplan's exclusive practice materials.

English & SAT

This course includes a combination of English instruction and SAT test preparation. Our English & SAT course is for students who need to boost their English skills while preparing for the SAT and admission to an American university.

Other Kaplan Programs

Since 1938, more than 3 million students have come to Kaplan to advance their studies, prepare for entry to American universities, and further their careers. In addition to the above programs, Kaplan offers courses to prepare for the ACT, GMAT, GRE, MCAT, DAT, USMLE, NCLEX, and other standardized exams at locations throughout the United States.

Applying to Kaplan International Programs

To get more information, or to apply for admission to any of Kaplan's programs for international students and professionals, contact us at:

Kaplan International Programs
370 Seventh Avenue, New York, NY 10001 USA
Telephone: (212) 492-5990 Fax: (917) 339-7505
E-mail: world@kaplan.com Web: www.studyusa.kaplan.com

Kaplan is authorized under federal law to enroll nonimmigrant alien students.
Kaplan is authorized to issue Form IAP-66 needed for a J-1 (Exchange Visitor) visa.
Kaplan is accredited by ACCET (Accrediting Council for Continuing Education and Training).
Test names are registered trademarks of their respective owners.

The Basics

SSAT/ISEE Mastery

- How to take advantage of the structure of the test

- How to approach test questions systematically

To perform your best on the SSAT/ISEE, there are some key things you need to know that have nothing to do with vocabulary words or isosceles triangles. Namely, you need to know how to be a good test taker.

Acquiring the skills and building the confidence you need to ace the SSAT/ISEE is what this book is all about.

To get a great score on a private school admissions test, you need to do three simple things:

- You need to have a basic understanding of the nature of the test.

- You need to hone your math and verbal skills.

- You need to develop strategies and test-taking techniques.

Having a solid grasp of the content on the test is obviously important. Simply put, you can't do well if you don't know the material. However, understanding the nature of your private school admissions test, including its setup, its structure, and traps it commonly sets for you, will allow you to gain many more points on your test that you might not otherwise earn.

Emergency Plan

If you have only a few weeks to prep for the test, don't panic. The first thing you should do, regardless of how much time you have, is become familiar with the test. This chapter is the place to start.

USING THE STRUCTURE OF THE TEST TO YOUR ADVANTAGE

Whether you're taking the SSAT (Secondary School Admission Test) or the ISEE (Independent School Entrance Exam), you'll notice pretty quickly that it is very different from the tests you're used to taking in school. On a school test, you're often told to show your work, to spend more time on tough questions (since they're worth more points), and to work thoroughly, even if it means taking extra time.

None of these things applies in the world of standardized testing. On your private school admissions test, it won't matter how you answer a question; it only matters what your final answer is. Also, all questions are worth the same number of points, so it's always to your advantage to answer easier questions first, to get them out of the way.

Both the SSAT and ISEE are given to students in a range of grades, so if you're in 8th grade, you're not expected to get as many questions right as someone in 11th grade. Keep that in mind as you take the test so you won't get discouraged if you find a lot of questions that you can't answer!

To succeed in this unique testing environment, you need to know some fundamentals about the structure of your test. Both the SSAT and ISEE have some quirks about them, so read carefully.

A Different Kind of Test

The SSAT and ISEE are not like the tests you take in school. In school, you usually need to get about 85 or 90 percent of the questions right to get a decent score. On the SSAT/ISEE, you're graded against students nationwide and in other grades, which means that you might get only 75 percent of the questions right, but still have what's considered a great score.

The SSAT/ISEE Are Highly Predictable

Because the format and directions of the SSAT and ISEE remain relatively unchanged from year to year, you can learn the setup in advance. Then on test day, all you'll have to worry about will be answering each question, not learning how a Synonym question works.

One of the easiest and most useful things you can do to boost your performance on your private school admissions test is to learn and understand the directions before taking the test. Since the instructions are always exactly the same, there's no reason to waste your time on the day of the test reading them. Get them straight in your head beforehand, while you go through this book, and you'll be able to skip them during the test.

Jump Around

You're allowed to skip around as much as you'd like within each section of the SSAT/ISEE. High scorers know this and use it to their advantage. They move through the test efficiently, quickly marking and leaving questions they can't answer immediately, racking up points on questions they do know, then coming back to the tough ones later. They don't dwell on any questions, even a hard one, until they've tried every question at least once.

When you see questions that look tough, circle them in your test booklet and skip them for later. Gather points on other questions first. On a second look, some tricky-looking questions can turn out to be much easier than they initially looked. And remember, if you're on the younger side of the testing group, expect to see several questions that you won't be able to answer. The test is intentionally set up this way, so don't let it discourage you.

Guessing—Know Your Test

When should you guess? That's a question we hear from students all the time. It depends which test you're taking. Read the information below and follow the instructions for your test. Guessing is one of the few areas in which the SSAT and ISEE operate differently, so read carefully!

SSAT: There is a wrong answer penalty on the SSAT. For each answer you get right, you get one point. For each answer you get wrong, 1/4 of a point is deducted from your total score. Does this mean you shouldn't guess? No, not at all. What it means is that you need to be smart about it. Essentially, if you can eliminate even ONE answer choice, it's to your advantage to guess, because you've tipped the odds of guessing correctly in your favor. If you can't eliminate anything, however, you're better off leaving the question blank.

ISEE: There is NO wrong-answer penalty on the ISEE. That means you should answer every single question on the test, even if you have no idea what it's asking you. The ISEE calculates your score simply by adding up your right answers, so you might as well fill in all those ovals completely. You never know what you might get right by luck!

Kaplan Rules

On the SSAT, guess only if you can eliminate at least one answer choice.

On the ISEE, ALWAYS guess, even if you can't eliminate anything.

The Answer Grid Has No Heart

Misgridding. It sounds so basic, but it happens all the time: When time is short, it's easy to get confused going back and forth between your test book and your answer grid. If you know the answer, but misgrid, you won't get any points, so be careful. Don't let it happen to you. Here are some tips to help you avoid making mistakes on the answer grid:

Always Circle the Questions You Skip

Put a big circle in your test book around any question numbers you skip. When you go back, these questions will be easy to locate. Also, if you accidentally skip a box on the grid, you can check your grid against your book to see where you went wrong.

Always Circle the Answers You Choose

Circling your answers in the test book makes it easier to check your grid against your book.

Grid Five or More Answers at Once

Don't transfer your answers to the grid after every question. Transfer your answers after every five questions, or at the end of each reading passage. That way, you won't keep breaking your concentration to mark the grid. You'll save time and you'll gain accuracy.

Circle Before You Skip

A common cause of major test disasters is filling in all of the questions with the right answers—in the wrong spots.

Every time you skip a question, circle it in your test book and make sure that you skip it on the answer grid, too.

Be careful at the end of a section, when time may be running out. You don't want to have your answers in the test booklet and not be able to transfer them to your answer grid because you have run out of time. Make sure to transfer your answers after every five questions or so.

APPROACHING SSAT/ISEE QUESTIONS

Apart from knowing the setup of the SSAT or ISEE, you need to have a system for attacking the questions. You wouldn't travel around a foreign city without a map and you shouldn't approach your private school admissions test without a plan, either. Now that you know some basics about how each test is set up, you can approach each section a little more strategically. What follows is the best method for approaching all test questions systematically.

Think about the Question Before You Look at the Answer

The people who make the test love to put distracters among the answer choices. Distracters are answer choices that look like the right answer, but aren't. If you jump right into the answer choices without thinking first about what you're looking for, you're more likely to fall for one of these traps.

Use Backdoor Strategies If the Answer Doesn't Come to You

There are usually a number of ways to get to the right answer on an SSAT/ISEE question. Most of the questions are multiple-choice. That means the answer is right in front of you—you just have to find it. This makes SSAT/ISEE questions open to a lot of ways of finding the answer. If you can't figure out the answer in a straightforward way, try other techniques. We'll talk about specific Kaplan methods such as backsolving, picking numbers, and eliminating wrong answers in later chapters.

Pace Yourself

The SSAT/ISEE gives you a lot of questions in a short period of time. In order to get through an entire section, you can't spend too much time on any one question. Keep moving through the test at a good speed; if you run into a hard question, circle it, skip it, and come back to it later if there's time.

The questions get harder as you move through a problem set. Ideally, you can work through the easy problems at a brisk, steady clip, and use a little more of your time for the harder ones that come at the end of the set.

One caution: Don't completely rush through the easy problems just to save time for the harder ones. These early problems are points in your pocket, and you're better off not getting to the last couple of problems than losing these easy points.

Locate Quick Points If You're Running Out of Time

Some questions can be done quickly; for instance, some reading questions will ask you to identify the meaning of a particular word in the passage. These can be done at the last minute, even if you haven't read the passage. When you start to run out of time, locate and answer any of the quick points that remain.

When you take the SSAT/ISEE, you have one clear objective in mind: to score as many points as you can. It's that simple. The rest of this book will help you do that.

MANAGING STRESS

The countdown has begun. Your date with the test is looming on the horizon. Anxiety is on the rise. The butterflies in your stomach have gone ballistic. Your thinking is getting cloudy. Maybe you think you won't be ready. Maybe you already know your stuff, but you're going into panic mode anyway. Don't freak! It's possible to tame that anxiety and stress—*before* and *during* the test.

Remember, a little stress is good. Anxiety is a motivation to study. The adrenaline that gets pumped into your bloodstream when you're stressed helps you stay alert and think more clearly. But if you feel that the tension is so great that it's preventing you from using your study time effectively, here are some things you can do to get it under control.

Take Control

Lack of control is a prime cause of stress. Research shows that if you don't have a sense of control over what's happening in your life, you can easily end up feeling helpless and hopeless. Try to identify the sources of the stress you feel. Which ones of these can you do something about? Can you find ways to reduce the stress you're feeling about any of these sources?

Focus on Your Strengths

Make a list of areas of strength you have that will help you do well on the test. We all have strengths, and recognizing your own is like having reserves of solid gold at Fort Knox. You'll be able to draw on your reserves as you need them, helping you solve difficult questions, maintain confidence, and keep test stress and anxiety at a distance. And every time you recognize a new area of strength, solve a challenging problem, or score well on a practice test, you'll increase your reserves.

Imagine Yourself Succeeding

Close your eyes and imagine yourself in a relaxing situation. Breathe easily and naturally. Now, think of a real-life situation in which you scored well on a test or did well on an assignment. Focus on this success. Now turn your thoughts to the SSAT/ISEE, and keep your thoughts and feelings in line with that successful experience. Don't make comparisons between them; just imagine yourself taking the upcoming test with the same feelings of confidence and relaxed control.

Set realistic goals

Facing your problem areas gives you some distinct advantages. What do you want to accomplish in the time remaining? Make a list of realistic goals. You can't help feeling more confident when you know you're actively improving your chances of earning a higher test score.

Exercise Your Frustrations Away

Whether it's jogging, biking, pushups, or a pickup basketball game, physical exercise will stimulate your mind and body, and improve your ability to think and concentrate. A surprising number of students fall out of the habit of regular exercise, ironically because they're spending so much time prepping for exams. A little physical exertion will help to keep your mind and body in sync and sleep better at night.

Avoid Drugs

Using drugs (prescription or recreational) specifically to prepare for and take a big test is definitely self-defeating. (And if they're illegal drugs, you may end up with a bigger problem than the SSAT/ISEE on your hands.) Mild stimulants, such as coffee or cola can sometimes help as you study, since they keep you alert. On the down side, too much of these can also lead to agitation, restlessness, and insomnia. It all depends on your tolerance for caffeine.

Eat Well

Good nutrition will help you focus and think clearly. Eat plenty of fruits and vegetables, low-fat protein such as fish, skinless poultry, beans, and legumes, and whole grains such as brown rice, whole wheat bread, and pastas. Don't eat a lot of sugar and high-fat snacks, or salty foods.

Keep Breathing

Conscious attention to breathing is an excellent way to manage stress while you're taking the test. Most of the people who get into trouble during tests take shallow breaths: They breathe using only their upper chests and shoulder muscles, and may even hold their breath for long periods of time. Conversely, those test takers who breathe deeply in a slow, relaxed manner are likely to be in better control during the session.

Stretch

If you find yourself getting spaced out or burned out as you study or take the test, stop for a brief moment and stretch. Flex your feet and arms. Even though you'll be pausing on the test for a moment, it's a moment well spent. Stretching will help to refresh you and refocus your thoughts.

"Managing Stress" adapted from "The Kaplan Advantage Stress Management System" by Dr. Ed Newman and Bob Verini, © 1996 by Kaplan, Inc.

2

Inside the SSAT and ISEE

- Understand the structure of the tests

- Learn how the tests are scored

- How to time and pace yourself

As you know, both the SSAT and ISEE are standardized tests. That means that even though the specific questions will vary from test to test, the basic structure, contents, and even questions will be very similar to what you'll see as you work your way through this book. In this chapter, we'll walk you through the structure of the SSAT and the ISEE. That way, when you sit down to take your test, you'll already know exactly what to expect—what kinds of questions you'll find, what the instructions will say, how the test will be scored, and how you will be timed.

SSAT/ISEE Emergency

If you have only a week or two to prep for the SSAT/ISEE, you should spend time getting familiar with your test. Be sure to read this chapter.

STRUCTURE—SSAT

Here's the question breakdown for the SSAT:

Section	Number of Questions	Timing	Scoring
Verbal	30 Synonyms 30 Analogies	25 minutes	250–350
Math	25 Questions	25 minutes	250–350
Reading	40 Questions	25 minutes	250–350
Math	25 Questions	25 minutes	250–350
Experimental	25–40 Questions	25 minutes	unscored
Essay	1 Essay	25 minutes	unscored
Total		$2\frac{1}{2}$ hours	Math + Verbal (250–350)

TIMING/PACING

Timing is pretty tight on the SSAT, so it's important that you get accustomed to answering questions quickly, skipping questions that give you trouble, and knowing when to guess. Never fear, though; this book will help you master all of these strategies.

Give yourself a rough time limit for each question. If you haven't answered it within that time, move on. On Reading, don't spend more than one minute reading any passage. Just get the basic point and move on to the questions, which is where you'll net your points.

SCORING

On the SSAT, students in grades 8–11 take the *same test*. Don't worry, though. That doesn't mean that if you're in 8th grade you're expected to get as many questions right as someone in 11th grade. Schools will compare your score to the national and local averages for *your* grade level. National averages tend to be around 300 in grade 8, and increase 10 points or so for each higher grade level. What's most important, however, is to find out what kind of scores the school you're applying to looks for, and shoot to beat that.

Remember, you can expect to see questions on the test that may be too hard for you. You don't need to get every question right to get the score you need to get into the private school of your dreams!

STRUCTURE—ISEE

Here's the question breakdown for the ISEE:

Section	Number of Questions	Timing	Scoring
Verbal	20 Synonyms 20 Sentence Completions	20 minutes	800–950
Math	45 Regular Math	40 minutes	800–950
Reading	40 Questions	40 minutes	800–950
Math	20 Regular Math 15 Quantitative Comparisons	35 minutes	800–950
Experimental	25–40 Questions	25 minutes	unscored
Essay	1 Essay	30 minutes	unscored
Total		about 3 hours	(800–950)

HOW IS THE ISEE DIFFERENT FROM THE SSAT?

- The Verbal section contains Sentence Completions instead of Analogies.
- There are Quantitative Comparisons on the Math section (15 Questions).
- There is NO wrong answer penalty, so you should ALWAYS guess if you aren't sure of the answer.
- There are only four answer choices on all multiple-choice questions.

For tips on Timing/Pacing, see the SSAT section above.

Both the SSAT and ISEE include an unscored essay. Even though your essay will not be graded like the other sections of your test, you should still give it equal attention. Schools evaluate essays critically as evidence of your writing ability, so don't use the essay time to take a nap!

Scoring on the ISEE works similarly to the SSAT, in that you will be compared against students in grades other than your own, and to national and local averages. Understanding the scoring system for these two tests is probably more difficult than mastering any of the material on either of them! Just focus on performing your best, getting as many points as you can, and moving swiftly through each section. By working through this book thoroughly, you'll be in a great position to excel on your test.

How to Register

SSAT:

Call 1-609-683-4440

Log on to: http://www.ssat.org

Write to SSAT Registration, CN 5339, Princeton, NJ 08543

ISEE:

Call 1-800-446-0320

Log on to: http://www.erbtest.org/isee.html and download fax registration form. Then, fax to (919) 682-5775.

Write to ISEE Operations Office, 423 Morris Street, Durham, NC 27701

Verbal Skills Workout

3

Synonyms

Highlights

- Kaplan Three-Step Method for Synonyms

- Avoiding pitfalls

- How to think strategically about synonyms

INTRODUCTION

We all have a general idea of what a synonym is. At its most basic level, it's a word that is similar in meaning to another, already defined word. *Fast* is a synonym for *quick*. OK, that makes sense. Unfortunately, if Synonyms were that easy on the SSAT/ISEE, the tests wouldn't tell Admissions Officers very much. The synonyms you'll see on your actual test will be much trickier than the example above, but they'll all follow the same logic. You'll see a word in capital letters (we call this the *stem word*), and it will be followed by five other words (four on the ISEE). One of them will be the synonym to the given word, and the others will not.

EXAMPLE

AUTHENTIC:

(A) genuine

(B) valuable

(C) ancient

(D) damaged

(E) historical

KAPLAN 15

Which of these words means about the same thing as AUTHENTIC? What's the best way to approach this question efficiently? Maybe you "just knew" that the answer was (A) *genuine*, and maybe you didn't. What you need is a great method for tackling any Synonym question, one that will work for you on the easy ones and the hard ones. What you need is the . . .

KAPLAN THREE-STEP METHOD FOR SYNONYMS

Step 1. Define the stem word.

Step 2. Find the answer choice that best fits your definition.

Step 3. If no choice fits, think of other definitions for the stem word and go through the choices again.

Let's take another look at the example above, using the Three-Step Method.

Step 1:   Define the Stem Word.

What does *authentic* mean? Something authentic is something *real*, such as an authentic signature, rather than a forgery. Your definition might be something like this: Something authentic can be *proven* to be what it *claims* to be.

Walk the Walk

> What if WALK were your stem word. What part of speech is it? It could be the *act of* walking (a verb), or *to take* a walk (the noun). Just look at the answer choices. They'll always be the same part of speech as the stem word. So you'll always know whether to WAVE to Mom or ride the WAVE . . . though she'd probably prefer you do both at once!

Step 2:   Find the Answer Choice that Best Fits your Definition.

Go through the answer choices one by one to see which one fits best. Your options are: *genuine, valuable, ancient, damaged,* and *historical.* Something AUTHENTIC could be worth a lot or not much at all, old or new, in good shape or bad, or even recent or historical. The only word that really means the same thing as AUTHENTIC is (A) genuine.

Step 3:   If no choice fits, think of other definitions for the stem word and go through the choices again.

In this instance, one choice fits, but take a look at the following example:

EXAMPLE

GRAVE:

(F) regrettable

(G) unpleasant

(H) serious

(J) careful

(K) lengthy

Say you defined GRAVE as *a burial location*. You looked at the choices, and didn't see any words like *tomb* or *coffin*. What to do? Move to step 3, and go back to the stem word, thinking about other definitions. Have you ever heard of a "grave situation"? GRAVE can also mean *serious* or *solemn*, and you can see that (H) serious, now fits the bill perfectly. If none of the answer choices seem to work with your definition, there may be a secondary definition you haven't yet considered.

AVOIDING PITFALLS

OK, so we lied just a little bit. The Three-Step Method should always be the basis for tackling every question, but there are a few other things you need to know to perform your best on Synonyms. Fortunately, there are only two big pitfalls to watch out for.

Pitfall 1:   Running out of Time.

Pace yourself. You have a limited amount of time, so make sure you use it wisely. Never waste time on a question you don't know—circle it and come back to it later. Synonyms get harder as they go, so move through the early questions quickly, leaving more time for the tougher ones at the end.

Pitfall 2:   Choosing Tempting Wrong Answers.

The test maker chooses her wrong answer choices very carefully. Sometimes that means throwing in answers that will tempt you, but that aren't right. Be a savvy test taker; don't fall for these distracters!

What kinds of wrong answers are we talking about here? There are two types of wrong answers to watch out for: answers that are *almost right*, and answers that *sound like the stem word*. Let's illustrate both types to make it concrete.

Major Pitfalls

- Running out of time
- Choosing tempting wrong answers

EXAMPLE

REPUTE:

(A) renewal
(B) renown
(C) priority
(D) mutability
(E) reaction

Arduous, or Just Hard?

One other trap to watch out for is answer choices that sound hard. Particularly if the stem word is pretty tough, you might be tempted to pick an answer choice that sounds similarly difficult. Often, the correct answer is straightforward. When you see a tough word, keep your cool, and ask yourself, is this arduous, or just hard?

EXAMPLE

FAVOR:

(F) award

(G) recognize

(H) respect

(J) improve

(K) prefer

In the first example, choices (A), (B), and (E) might be tempting, because they all start with the prefix *re-*, just like the stem word, REPUTE. It's important that you examine all the answer choices, because otherwise you might choose (A) and never get to the correct answer, (B).

In the second example, you might look at the word FAVOR and think, oh, that's something positive. It's something you do for someone else. It sounds a lot like choice (F), award. Maybe you pick (F) and move on. If you do that, you would fall for a trap. The correct answer is (K) prefer, since FAVOR is being used as a verb, and to FAVOR someone or something is to like it better than something else, in other words, to prefer it. Like in the first example, if you don't read through all of the choices, you might be tricked into choosing a wrong answer.

At this point, you have a great set of tools for answering most Synonym questions. You know how to approach them and you know some traps to avoid. But what happens if you look at the word in capitals and you don't know what it means? Should you just give up and move on, fill out the rest of your test in crayon, or start waving your arms around, saying "They're after us!"? Well, probably not.

VOCABULARY TECHNIQUES

There are several things you can do to figure out the meaning of a tough vocabulary word and, thus, to answer a hard Synonym question. Here are four techniques that will help you when you don't know a stem word:

Technique 1. Look for familiar roots and prefixes.

Technique 2. Use your knowledge of foreign languages.

Technique 3. Remember the context.

Technique 4. Use Word Charge.

Let's examine each technique more closely.

Technique 1:   Look for familiar roots and prefixes.

Remember how we told you in the "Mastery" chapter to start working on your vocabulary skills? Well, having a good grasp of how words are put together will help you tremendously on Synonyms, particularly when you don't know a vocabulary word. If you can break a word into pieces that you do understand, you'll be able to answer questions that you might have thought too difficult to tackle.

Look at the words below. Circle any prefixes or roots that you know.

- BENEVOLENCE
- INSOMNIA
- INSCRIBE
- CONSPIRE
- VERITY

BENE means *good*; SOMN has to do with *sleep*; SCRIB has to do with *writing*; CON means doing something *together*; and VER has to do with *truth*.

Technique 2:   Use your knowledge of foreign languages.

Do you study a foreign language? If so, it can help you decode lots of vocabulary words on the SSAT/ISEE, particularly if it's one of the Romance languages (French, Spanish, Italian, Rumanian, Portuguese). Look at the example words below. Do you recognize any foreign language words in them?

- FACILITATE
- DORMANT
- EXPLICATE

Facile means *easy* in French and Italian; *dormir* means *to sleep* in French and Spanish; and *expliquer* means *to explain* in French.

Technique 3:   Remember the Context.

Sometimes a word might look strange sitting on the page by itself, but if you think about it, you realize you've heard it before in other phrases. If you can put the word into context, such as in a cliché, you're well on your way to deciphering its meaning.

EXAMPLE

GNARLED:

(A) fruitful
(B) dead
(C) twisted
(D) flowering
(E) drooping

What kind of a plant have you heard described as gnarled?

EXAMPLE

ALLEGATION:

(F) evidence

(G) accusation

(H) conservation

(J) foundation

(K) fabrication

What does "making an allegation" mean?

EXAMPLE

LAURELS:

(A) vine

(B) honor

(C) lavender

(D) cushion

(E) work

Have you heard the phrase "don't rest on your laurels"? What do you think it might mean?

- *Trees* are often described as gnarled, particularly old ones. They are knotty and twisted, the kind you think would appear in fairy tales.

- "*Making an allegation*" is accusing someone of committing a crime, a phrase you might have seen on the news or on a police-related TV show.

- The phrase "*don't rest on your laurels*" originated in ancient Greece, where heroes were given wreaths of laurel branches to signify their accomplishments. Telling someone to not rest on his laurels is the same thing as telling him to not get too smug, living off the success of one accomplishment, rather than striving for improvement.

Technique 4:   Use Word Charge.

Even if you know nothing about the word, have never seen it before, don't recognize any prefixes or roots, and can't think of any word in any language that it sounds like, you can still make a stab at a Synonym question. One useful strategy when you're stumped is Word Charge.

What do we mean by Word Charge? Are some words electric? Do they spend too much money on credit cards? No, and no. Word charge refers to the *sense* that a word gives you as to whether it's a positive word or a negative one.

VILIFY: this sounds like *villain*, a word most people would say is bad.

GLORIFY: this sounds like *glorious*, a word most people would say is good.

Let's say that VILIFY has a negative charge (–) and GLORIFY has a positive charge (+). On all Synonym questions, the correct answer will have *the same charge as the stem word*, so use your instincts about word charge to help you when you're stuck on a tough word.

Decide whether each of the following words has a positive (+) or negative (–) charge.

AUSPICIOUS _____

MALADY _____

NOXIOUS _____

AMIABLE _____

BOORISH _____

MELANCHOLY_____

HUMANE _____

Often words that sound harsh have a negative meaning, while smooth-sounding words tend to have positive meanings. If *cantankerous* sounds negative to you, you would be right. It means "difficult to handle."

You can also use prefixes and roots to help determine a word's charge. *Mal, de, dis, un, in, im, a,* and *mis* often indicate a negative, while *pro, ben,* and *magn* are often positives.

Not all words sound positive; some sound neutral. But if you can define the charge, you can probably eliminate some answer choices on that basis alone.

Now let's see how you did on identifying the charge of the words listed above.

Auspicious (+) means favorable; a *malady* (–) means an illness; *noxious* (–) means harmful; *amiable* (+) means agreeable; *boorish* (–) means rude; *melancholy* (–) means sadness; and *humane* (+) means kind.

Practice Makes Perfect

Now that you've been through all of the techniques to succeed on Synonym questions, it's time for some practice. Work through the following 20 questions, using the Kaplan Three-Step Method, avoiding Pitfalls, and employing Vocabulary techniques when you get stuck.

Practice Questions

1. DISMAL:

   (A) bleak
   (B) crowded
   (C) comfortable
   (D) temporary
   (E) typical

2. HUMID:

   (F) damp
   (G) windy
   (H) hot
   (J) stormy
   (K) hazy

3. DEPORT:

   (A) punish
   (B) banish
   (C) censor
   (D) jail
   (E) praise

4. PEDDLE:

   (F) assemble
   (G) steal
   (H) edit
   (J) deliver
   (K) sell

5. TERMINATE:

   (A) extend
   (B) renew
   (C) end
   (D) sell
   (E) finalize

6. DEARTH:

   (F) explosion
   (G) increase
   (H) shortage
   (J) change
   (K) surplus

7. OBSCURE:

   (A) tragic
   (B) dark
   (C) obligatory
   (D) ignored
   (E) legendary

8. MOURN:

   (F) inaugurate
   (G) celebrate
   (H) greet
   (J) oppose
   (K) grieve

9. RECLUSE:

   (A) artist
   (B) beggar
   (C) lunatic
   (D) scavenger
   (E) hermit

10. HOMAGE:

   (F) youth
   (G) wreath
   (H) respect
   (J) affection
   (K) household

11. HERBIVOROUS:

   (A) huge
   (B) warm-blooded
   (C) endangered
   (D) plant-eating
   (E) intelligent

12. SYNOPSIS:

   (F) summary
   (G) satire
   (H) paragraph
   (J) update
   (K) rebuttal

13. WANTON:

   (A) fantastic
   (B) repeated
   (C) lustful
   (D) careful
   (E) needy

14. IMPERIOUS:

   (F) royal
   (G) friendly
   (H) gusty
   (J) arrogant
   (K) insightful

15. HALLOW:

    (A) revere
    (B) dig
    (C) inhabit
    (D) discover
    (E) release

16. BLISS:

    (F) ecstasy
    (G) escape
    (H) prayer
    (J) terror
    (K) fun

17. INDECENT:

    (A) centralized
    (B) immortal
    (C) improper
    (D) incessant
    (E) recent

18. TANGIBLE:

    (F) unrelated
    (G) glib
    (H) touchable
    (J) tanned
    (K) incapable

19. FEROCITY:

    (A) hardness
    (B) humility
    (C) narrowness
    (D) scarcity
    (E) fierceness

20. TENACIOUS:

    (F) tender
    (G) determined
    (H) temporary
    (J) talkative
    (K) discouraged

Practice Question Answers

1.   (A)

2.   (F)

3.   (B)

4.   (K)

5.   (C)

6.   (H)

7.   (B)

8.   (K)

9.   (E)

10.   (H)

11.   (D)

12.   (F)

13.   (C)

14.   (J)

15.   (A)

16.   (F)

17.   (C)

18.   (H)

19.   (E)

20.   (G)

Analogies

- Kaplan Three-Step Method for Analogies

- How to build a bridge and use it to find the right answer

- Understanding three-term analogies

- What to do if you're stuck: backsolving and guessing

Analogies may seem frightening because they look pretty weird at first glance. You'll feel better about them as soon as you realize that you speak and think in analogies all the time. Any time you say "my sister is like a slug," you're drawing an analogy between your sister and slugs—perhaps your sister is as gross as a slug, or maybe she always falls asleep in her cereal. That may not be the kind of relationship that will appear on your test, but the thinking is the same.

Once you get familiar with their format, you'll find that Analogy questions are pretty straightforward, and very predictable. In fact, prepping often gains you more points on Analogies than on any other Verbal question type. With practice, you can even learn to get Analogy questions right when you don't know all of the vocabulary words involved.

Emergency Plan

If you don't have much time to prep for the SSAT/ISEE, here's the best way to spend your time:

- Learn the Kaplan Three-Step Method for Analogies.

- Do the practice set in this chapter.

- If you miss an answer, review the tips in this chapter.

THE FORMAT

1. Flake is to snow as

   (A) storm is to hail
   (B) drop is to rain
   (C) field is to wheat
   (D) stack is to hay
   (E) cloud is to fog

The two words in the beginning of the question are called the *stem words*. The instructions will tell you to select the pair of words that is related in the same way as this pair. In this example, the answer is (B). A flake is a small unit of snow, just as a drop is a small unit of rain.

Did you get the right answer? If so, how did you determine the right answer? Did you just *feel* that one choice was right, or did you try to figure out how the words in the stem were related, then go through the choices one by one? The Kaplan Three-Step Method will help you handle any Analogy question, even the toughest ones, because you'll be approaching every question systematically, rather than just using instincts. Let's see how it works.

KAPLAN THREE-STEP METHOD FOR ANALOGIES

Step 1. Build a bridge.

Step 2. Plug in the answer choices.

Step 3. Adjust your bride if necessary.

What does it mean to "build a bridge"? A suspension bridge? A steel bridge? No, we're not spanning oceans here; we're bubbling ovals on a piece of paper. Wait a minute and it will all make sense. A Bridge expresses the relationship between the words in the stem pair, and building a bridge helps you zone in on the correct answer quickly, and helps you avoid wrong-answer traps. Let's take a closer look to see how it works.

Step 1: Build a Bridge.

In every Analogy question, there's a strong, definite connection between the two stem words. Your task is to identify this relationship, and then to look for a similar relationship among the answer pairs.

What's a strong, definite relationship?

- The words *library* and *book* have a strong, definite connection. A library is defined as a place where books are kept. *Library is to book as* could be a question stem.

- The words *library* and *child* do not have a strong, definite connection. A child may or may not have anything to do with a library. *Library is to child* would never be a question stem.

In our original example, a good bridge would be "A flake is a small unit of snow." A bridge is a short sentence that relates the two words in the stem, and every pair of stem words will have a strong bridge that links them.

Step 2:   Plug in the Answer Choices.

You figured out how the words *flake* and *snow* are related. Now you need to determine which answer choice relates words in the same way. Don't just rely on your feeling about the words unless you don't know the vocabulary (more on that later). Go through the choices systematically, building bridges between each word pair as you go. Here's how it would work:

If a *flake* is a small unit of *snow*, then . . .

(A) A *storm* is a small unit of *hail*?

(B) A *drop* is a small unit of *rain*?

(C) A *field* is a small unit of *wheat*?

(D) A *stack* is a small unit of *hay*?

(E) A *cloud* is a small unit of *fog*?

Going through the choices, you can see that only one of them makes sense, (B). At this point, you would be done.

Step 3:   Adjust Your Bridge if Necessary.

If your bridge is very specific, you won't need to go to step 3, but sometimes you will. For example, if you had the question:

Fish is to gill as

(F) oyster is to shell

(G) penguin is to wing

(H) whale is to spout

(J) mammal is to lung

(K) dolphin is to flipper

Let's say you made the bridge "A fish has a gill." Then you went to the choices and plugged in that bridge:

(F) An oyster has a shell.

(G) A penguin has a wing.

(H) A whale has a spout.

(J) A mammal has a lung.

(K) A dolphin has a flipper.

Every choice fits! In this case, the bridge was too general, so you'll need to adjust your bridge.

What would a good adjustment be? Try to articulate to yourself the most specific relationship between the words, because the more specific your bridge is, the fewer choices will match it. A good bridge for this pair might be: *A fish uses a gill to breathe.* Now try plugging the bridge into the answer choices.

(F) An oyster uses a shell to breathe?

(G) A penguin uses a wing to breathe?

(H) A whale uses a spout to breathe?

(J) A mammal uses a lung to breathe?

(K) A dolphin uses a flipper to breathe?

It should now be easier to see the correct answer, (J), A mammal uses a lung to breathe.

STRONG BRIDGES & WEAK BRIDGES

Just to make sure you have your strong and weak bridges straight, try the following exercise. For each phrase, decide whether there is a strong relationship or a weak one.

1. dog is to canine   _____

2. dog is to friendly   _____

3. dog is to kennel   _____

4. dog is to mammal   _____

5. dog is to cat   _____

6. dog is to paw   _____

7. dog is to puppy   _____

8. dog is to hound   _____

9. dog is to bark   _____

10. dog is to biscuit   _____

SIX CLASSIC BRIDGES

There are some bridges that appear on the SSAT/ISEE over and over again. We call these *Classic Bridges* because no matter what other bridges come and go, these tend to stick around. By getting to know these bridges, you'll be able to identify them quickly, saving yourself a lot of time as you go through Analogy questions.

Bridge Type 1: CHARACTER

One word characterizes the other.

Quarrelsome is to argue [Someone quarrelsome tends to argue.]

Bridge Type 2: LACK

One word describes what someone or something is <u>not</u>.

Coward is to bravery [A coward lacks bravery.]

Bridge Type 3: FUNCTION

One word names an object; the other word defines its function.

Scissors is to cut [Scissors are used to cut.]

Bridge Type 4: DEGREE

One word is a greater or lesser degree of the other word.

Deafening is to loud [Something deafening is extremely loud.]

Bridge Type 5: EXAMPLE

One word is an example of the other word.

Measles is to disease [Measles are a type of disease.]

Bridge Type 6: GROUP

One word is made up of several of the other word.

Forest is to trees [A forest is made up of many trees.]

Answers to Strong/ Weak Bridges

1. strong

2. weak

3. strong

4. strong

5. weak

6. strong

7. strong

8. strong

9. strong

10. weak

I Am, By Definition, Confused

When making a bridge, a good rule of thumb is to relate the words in such a way that you'd be able to insert the phrase *by definition* and the relationship would hold true. A poodle, by definition, is a type of dog. However, a poodle does not, by definition, have a collar. If you can't use *by definition* in the sentence that relates the stem words, your bridge isn't strong and it needs to be reworked.

PREDICTING ON THREE-TERM ANALOGIES

Some analogies will have three terms in the stem and only one word in each answer choice. For example:

Delight is to grin as dismay is to:

(A) frown

(B) smile

(C) shrug

(D) stare

(E) giggle

Three-term analogies aren't very different from two-term analogies. The key difference is that you need to predict your answer *before* you look at the answer choices. Otherwise, the choices won't make much sense to you! Here's how it works.

First, make your bridge:

A grin shows delight and a —— shows dismay.

Now predict your answer. What might show *dismay*? *Tears*, perhaps, or a *frown*. Look at the answer choices. At this point, it should be easier than a two-term analogy, because you already have one of the two words in the answer.

Does a *frown* show dismay?

Does a *smile* show dismay?

Does a *shrug* show dismay?

Does a *stare* show dismay?

Does a *giggle* show dismay?

As you'll see, (A) is the correct answer: A frown shows dismay. That makes a lot of sense. Can you can see how much harder this would have been if you hadn't gone through the steps of building a bridge and predicting the answer? You would likely be staring blankly at five words. Always predict your answer on three-term analogies, and you'll whiz through them in no time.

Practice your skills of prediction on these stems:

1. Thicket is to bush as grove is to ——.

2. Mason is to brick as carpenter is to ——.

3. Enthusiast is to apathy as miser is to ——.

Now let's see how well you did on predicting:

1. Thicket is to bush as grove is to *tree*.

2. Mason is to brick as carpenter is to *wood*.

3. Enthusiast is to apathy as miser is to *generosity*.

Even with your arsenal of tools, you may run into Analogy questions where you don't know what to do. Perhaps you won't know what a word in the question stem means, or how the words relate to one another. What should you do?

There are a few strategies that will really up your chances of getting the question right, even if you're stuck. How cool is THAT?

What to Do if You're Stuck

- Backsolving

- Educated guessing

- Remembering context

- Using Word Charge

BACKSOLVING

What is backsolving? It may sound like an obscure form of chiropractic medicine, but it's actually just a nifty way of approaching analogies when you can't answer them directly. So how does it work?

Basically, you skip right past the question stem and head straight for the answer choices. You may be wondering, "How you can figure out the answer without knowing what the question is asking?" Well, you can't necessarily figure out the *answer* right away, but you can start to eliminate *clearly wrong* answer choices, leaving fewer options to choose from. When you rule out choices that you know can't be right, the odds are better that you'll pick the right choice from what's left.

Screwdriver is to tool as

(F) animal is to plant

(G) garden is to bed

(H) fertilizer is to soil

(J)   tree is to leaf

(K) rose is to flower

Even if you didn't know that a screwdriver is a type of tool, what could you rule out? Well, in (F), there's no logical connection between animal and plant, except that they're both living things. Choice (G), garden is to bed, also sounds somewhat off. You could make the argument that a garden has a bed, but does it have to? What about a hanging garden, or a rock garden? You could rule out (G) as having a weak bridge.

By eliminating even one illogical answer choice, you'll narrow down your choices and have a better chance of getting the question right. Always keep your eye out for *Both Are* traps and *Weak Bridges* as you work through the Analogy section, and you'll rack up lots of points on even the toughest questions.

Both Are . . . Wrong!

Watch out for the *Both Are* trap on Analogy questions. Choice (F) in the screwdriver example is a *Both Are* trap; both words (*animal* and *plant*) are part of a larger group, but there's no connection, by definition, between the words themselves. Similarly, bread and bananas are both types of food, but what exactly is their relationship? Bananas aren't a type of bread, a lack of bread, or a function of bread. Watch out for this trap, particularly on harder Analogy questions.

GUESSING

What if you reach the point where: You can't figure out the bridge for the stem words, you can't rule out wrong answer choices, and you want to cry? Well, first of all, don't cry. It's a waste of time and it makes it difficult to read the questions. You have a few options.

Technique 1:   Make an Educated Guess.

You know the Six Classic Bridges. You know they show up a lot on Analogy questions. So even if you don't know the exact definition of one (or both!) words, you could make an educated guess about the bridge. For example, say you saw the stem:

Word is to philologist as

(A) —————

(B) —————

(C) —————

(D) —————

(E) —————

What might the bridge be? Well, a *philologist* sounds like a type of person (since it ends in -ologist), and a *word* is a thing, so maybe a philologist does something with words. Philologist is a tricky word, but you could make a great guess by saying that a philologist studies words, which is exactly right!

Technique 2:   Remember the Context.

Sometimes a word sounds familiar, but you can't remember why. If that happens, try to think of a place where you may have heard it before. Putting words into context makes it easier to determine their meaning. For example,

Vote is to suffrage as

(F) —————

(G) —————

(H) —————

(J) —————

(K) —————

What does *suffrage* mean? Have you heard of the suffrage movement? Or the suffragists? Think about the word *suffrage* in the context of *voting*. What could the words have to do with each other? Well, suffrage is the right to vote, and the movement to give women the right to vote at the beginning of the 20th century was commonly known as the Suffrage Movement. Just looking at the word *suffrage* in isolation might have left you scratching your head, but putting it in context with the concept of voting could get you back on track and help you zone in on the right answer.

Technique 3:   Use Word Charge.

Some words give you the feeling that they're either positive or negative. Use this sense to help you figure out the bridge between words in the stem when you don't actually know what one of them means—or both!

Decide whether the following words are positive or negative:

1.   Cruel (+, −) is to clemency (+, −) as
2.   Boorish (+, −) is to polite (+, −) as
3.   Animated (+, −) is to ecstatic (+, −) as
4.   Annoyed (+, −) is to enraged (+, −) as

So how does Word Charge help you find the right answer? Once you determine the charge of the words in the stem pair, you can look for words in the answer choices that have the same charge relationship. When both words in the stem are either positive or negative, both words in the correct answer choice will have the same charge, too, though it may be the opposite charge from the words in the stem. If one stem word is positive and the other is negative, chances are that the right answer will have the same relationship.

So, what charge does each word above have?

1. (−, +); 2. (−, +); 3. (+, +); 4. (−, −)

PRACTICE MAKES PERFECT

You have a lot of strategies and skills at your disposal for the Analogy section of the SSAT/ISEE. You should be ready to handle any Analogy question that comes your way if you put your knowledge into practice. Speaking of practice, that's the only way to really solidify what you've learned, so try the following 20 questions. Make sure you use everything you learned in this lesson!

Practice Questions

1. Circumference is to circle as

   (A)   diameter is to sphere
   (B)   height is to width
   (C)   side is to hexagon
   (D)   perimeter is to square
   (E)   round is to oval

2. Write is to paper as paint is to

   (F)   board
   (G)   canvas
   (H)   brush
   (J)   palette
   (K)   can

3. Collar is to shirt as

   (A)   toe is to shoe
   (B)   cuff is to trousers
   (C)   waist is to belt
   (D)   hat is to head
   (E)   zipper is to button

4. Hysteria is to control as

   (F)   joke is to laughter
   (G)   feeling is to emotion
   (H)   absurdity is to sense
   (J)   calm is to serenity
   (K)   passion is to insanity

5. Square is to cube as

   (A)   dot is to point
   (B)   angle is to triangle
   (C)   rectangle is to parallelogram
   (D)   hexagon is to octagon
   (E)   circle is to sphere

6. Shark is to aquatic as

   (F)   world is to hungry
   (G)   camel is to terrestrial
   (H)   bird is to winged
   (J)   bat is to blind
   (K)   pig is to hairless

7. Admonish is to mild as castigate is to

   (A)   tepid
   (B)   sweet
   (C)   unbeatable
   (D)   uncertain
   (E)   harsh

8. Abrupt is to gradual as

   (F)   corrupt is to virtuous
   (G)   stirring is to sudden
   (H)   sneaky is to criminal
   (J)   remarkable is to alarming
   (K)   conspicuous is to extreme

9. Stanza is to poem as

   (A)   rhythm is to beat
   (B)   verse is to word
   (C)   movement is to symphony
   (D)   play is to theater
   (E)   column is to journal

10. Violin is to string as

    (F)   harp is to angelic
    (G)   drum is to stick
    (H)   score is to music
    (J)   oboe is to reed
    (K)   bass is to large

11. Canter is to horse as

    (A)   hop is to rabbit
    (B)   halt is to pony
    (C)   hunt is to lion
    (D)   beg is to dog
    (E)   chew is to cow

12. Baseball is to game as

    (F)   hurricane is to storm
    (G)   overcast is to cloud
    (H)   stadium is to sport
    (J)   wind is to tornado
    (K)   conflict is to violence

13. Rigid is to bend as

    (A)   tremulous is to sway
    (B)   incomprehensive is to think
    (C)   immortal is to die
    (D)   lazy is to perspire
    (E)   stiff is to divide

14. Canine is to wolf as feline is to

    (F)   panther
    (G)   pig
    (H)   monkey
    (J)   rat
    (K)   vulture

15. Rind is to melon as

    (A) skin is to mammal
    (B) armor is to shield
    (C) shell is to claw
    (D) peel is to core
    (E) pod is to vine

16. Mile is to length as

    (F) acre is to land
    (G) inch is to foot
    (H) kilometer is to race
    (J) yard is to fabric
    (K) fathom is to depth

17. Truthful is to dishonest as arid is to

    (A) sublime
    (B) aloof
    (C) innocent
    (D) moist
    (E) clear

18. Tarnish is to silver as

    (F) streak is to glass
    (G) dirt is to car
    (H) rust is to iron
    (J) dull is to wax
    (K) dust is to wood

19. Delay is to hasten as

    (A) misunderstand is to dislike
    (B) undermine is to improve
    (C) sink is to descend
    (D) remove is to indict
    (E) facilitate is to impede

20. Think is to daydream as walk is to

    (F) stagger
    (G) crawl
    (H) meander
    (J) run
    (K) prance

Practice Question Answers

1. (D)
2. (G)
3. (B)
4. (H)
5. (E)
6. (G)
7. (E)
8. (F)
9. (C)
10. (J)
11. (A)
12. (F)
13. (C)
14. (F)
15. (A)
16. (K)
17. (D)
18. (H)
19. (E)
20. (H)

KAPLAN

Critical Reading

- Reading strategies for the ISEE and the SSAT

- Kaplan Four-Step Method for Critical Reading

- Explanation of all question types

OVERVIEW

The Reading section presents you with seven or eight passages and 40 questions. The passages will be in the form of serious articles, stories, and poems. For each passage, you'll be asked a variety of questions about the main idea and details presented. You'll only get points for answering questions correctly, not for reading the text thoroughly, so keep your attention on reading as quickly as possible and answering as many questions as you can.

However, remember that if you are an 8th grader, you DON'T need to answer all of the questions—in fact, you don't even need to read all of the passages. You can get a great score even if you don't answer all the questions, so don't kill yourself.

Read, Don't Learn

On the SSAT/ISEE, you'll have to read quickly and efficiently. Your goal is not to learn the information presented, or even to think about it very much. Rather, you need to figure out the main point and where to look for any details you might be asked about.

READING STRATEGIES

On the one hand, it's a good thing that you're inherently prepared for this section because you already know how to read. On the other hand, your previous reading experience has the

What NOT to Do

DON'T not read too slowly.

DON'T continually reread things you don't understand.

DON'T spend more time on the passage than on the questions.

potential to get you into a bit of trouble on this section of the test. Reading habits that may serve you well in school can get in the way on the test. There are three big reading traps that you need to avoid on the SSAT/ISEE.

Common Reading Traps

Trap 1: Reading too slowly.

Trap 2: Continually rereading things you do not understand.

Trap 3: Spending more time on the passages than on the questions.

SSAT/ISEE READING IS DIFFERENT FROM EVERYDAY READING!!!

So that wasn't exactly subtle. It's an important point. You already know how to read, but the way that you read normally may not help you maximize your points on the SSAT/ISEE. There are three main skills you'll need to employ to ace the Reading section:

1. **Summarizing:** You'll need to be able to sum up what the passage is all about.

2. **Researching:** You'll need to be able to find facts, figures, and names in the passage.

3. **Making Inferences:** You'll need to be able to piece together information that isn't directly stated.

How can you make sure you do all of these very official-sounding things? Here are some solid strategies for SSAT/ISEE Reading Success:

1. Look for the Big Idea.

Don't read as if you're memorizing everything. Aim to pick up just the gist of the passage—the author's main idea.

2. Pay attention to language.

The author's choice of words can tell you everything about his or her point of view, attitude and style.

3. Be a critical reader.

As you read, ask yourself critical questions: "What's the author's main point? What message is the author trying to get across?"

4. Make it simple.

Despite the fancy language, Reading passages are usually about pretty simple topics. Don't get bogged down by technical language; translate the author's ideas into your *own words*.

5. Keep moving.

Aim to spend no more than one minute reading each passage; remember, just reading the passage won't score you points.

6. Don't sweat the details.

Don't waste time reading and rereading parts you don't understand. Move swiftly through the passage to answer the questions, which is what really counts.

You've probably realized by now that Kaplan has a multistep method for all the question types on the SSAT/ISEE. It's in your best interest to approach the test as a whole and the individual sections systematically. If you approach every passage the same way, you'll work your way through the Reading section efficiently.

KAPLAN FOUR-STEP METHOD FOR CRITICAL READING

Step 1. Read the passage.

Step 2. Decode the question.

Step 3. Research the details.

Step 4. Predict the answer and check the answer choices.

Like the other multistep methods, the Kaplan Four-Step Method for Critical Reading requires you to do most of your work before you attempt to answer the questions. It's very tempting to read the questions and immediately jump to the answer choices. Don't do this. The work you do up front will not only save you time in the long run, it will increase your chances of avoiding the tempting wrong answers.

Step 1:   Read the Passage.

The first thing to do is to read the passage. This shouldn't come as a big surprise. And although you don't want to memorize or dissect the passage, you **do** need to read it. If you try to answer the questions without doing so, you're likely to make mistakes. Although you'll learn more about *how* to read the passages later, keep in mind that the main things you want to look for are the **Big Idea**, and the **Paragraph topics**. Additionally, you'll want to note where the passage seems to be going.

For example, if you saw the following passage (which, admittedly, is a little shorter than the average SSAT/ISEE passage), these are some of the thing you might want to note . . .

The first detective stories, written by Edgar Allen Poe and Arthur Conan Doyle, emerged in the mid-nineteenth century, at a time when there was an
Line enormous public interest in scientific progress. The
(5) newspapers of the day continually publicized the latest scientific discoveries, and scientists were acclaimed as the heroes of the age. Poe and Conan Doyle shared this fascination with the step-by-step, logical approach used by scientists in their experiments, and instilled
(10) their detective heroes with outstanding powers of scientific reasoning.

This passage is basically about detective stories . . . and science.

The character of Sherlock Holmes, for example, illustrates Conan Doyle's admiration for the scientific mind. In each case that Holmes investigates, he is able
(15) to use the most insubstantial evidence to track down his opponent. Using only his restless eye and ingenious reasoning powers, Holmes pieces together the identity of the villain from such unremarkable details as the type of cigar ashes left at the crime scene,
(20) or the kind of ink used in a hand-written letter. In fact, Holmes' painstaking attention to detail often reminds the reader of Charles Darwin's On the Origin of the Species, published some twenty years earlier.

Holmes is an <u>example</u> of a detective hero with a brilliant scientific mind . . .

← ———— **Poe and Conan Doyle seem to be important.**

← ———— **Comparison between Holmes and Darwin.**

Again, you'll spend more time later learning how to read the passage. The point here is that the first thing you want to do is read through the entire passage noting the major themes and a few details.

Step 2: Decode the Question.

Several questions will follow the passage. And *before* you can answer each question, you'll have to figure out exactly what's being asked. You need to make the question make sense to you.

Kaplan Rules

Make the question make sense to you. Take a moment to figure out what's really being asked.

Which of the following is implied by the statement that Holmes was able to identify the villain based on "unremarkable details"?

(A) Holmes' enemies left no traces at the crime scene.

(B) The character of Holmes was based on Charles Darwin.

(C) Few real detectives would have been capable of solving Holmes' cases.

(D) Holmes was particularly brilliant in powers of detection.

(E) Criminal investigation often involves tedious, time-consuming tasks.

Step 3: Research the Details.

This does *not* mean that you should start rereading the passage from the beginning to find the reference to "unremarkable details." Focus your research. Where does the author mention Holmes? You should have noted when you read the passage that the author discusses Holmes in the second paragraph. So scan that paragraph for the reference to "unremarkable details." (Hint: the reference can be found in line 18.)

Additionally, don't answer questions based on your memory. Go back and do the research. In other words, if you can answer questions based on your memory, you have spent too much time on the passage.

Kaplan Rules

Don't try to answer questions just from your memory.

Step 4: Predict the Answer and Check the Answer Choices.

When you find the detail in the passage, think about the *purpose* that it serves. Why does the author mention the "unremarkable details"? If you read the lines surrounding the phrase, you'll see that the author talks about how amazing it is that Holmes can solve mysteries based on such little evidence. Therefore, the *reason* the author mentions "unremarkable details" is to show how impressive Holmes is. Now scan your answer choices.

(A) Holmes's enemies left no traces at the crime scene.

(B) The character of Holmes was based on Charles Darwin.

(C) Few real detectives would have been capable of solving Holmes's cases.

(D) Holmes was particularly brilliant in powers of detection.

(E) Criminal investigation often involves tedious, time-consuming tasks.

Answer choice (D) should leap out at you.

CRITICAL READING SKILLS IN ACTION

Remember earlier in the lesson when we discussed the three key critical reading skills: Summarizing, Researching, and Making Inferences? Let's look at how these skills can help you not only to read the passage, but also to answer the questions.

Summarizing

For the purposes of the SSAT/ISEE, **summarizing** means capturing in a single phrase what the *entire* passage is about. Most passages will be followed by a question that deals with the passage as a whole. Wrong answers will include choices that cover only one paragraph or some other subset of the passage. You'll need to recognize the answer choice that deals with the passage as a whole. If you've thought about the Big Picture ahead of time, you're more likely to home in on the correct answer.

Line

(5)

(10)

(15)

The four brightest moons of Jupiter were the first objects in the solar system discovered with the use of the telescope. Their proven existence played a central role in Galileo's famous argument in support of the Copernican model of the solar system, in which the planets are described as revolving around the Sun.

For several hundred years after their discovery by Galileo in 1610, scientific understanding of these moons increased fairly slowly. Observers on earth succeeded in measuring their approximate diameters, their relative densities, and eventually some of their light-reflecting characteristics. However, the spectacular close-up photographs sent back by the 1979 Voyager missions forever changed our impressions of these bodies.

EXAMPLE

Which of the following best tells what this passage is about?

(F) Galileo's invention of the telescope

(G) the discovery of the Galilean moons

(H) scientific knowledge about Jupiter's four
     brightest moons

(J) the Copernican model of the solar system

(K) the early history of astronomy

Which choice sums up the entire passage?

There is only one answer choice here that sums up the contents of both paragraphs. (G) is just a detail. (F) cannot be correct because Galileo's telescope is not even mentioned. (J) is mentioned only in the first paragraph and is a distortion of the author's point. (K) is too broad in scope.

Only (H) summarizes the entire passage. The passage deals with scientific knowledge about Jupiter's four brightest moons. The four moons are the first thing mentioned in the first paragraph, and the rest of the first paragraph discusses the role they played for Galileo. The second paragraph deals with how the moons were perceived by scientists throughout history. In sum, both paragraphs deal with scientific knowledge about these moons.

Researching

Researching essentially means knowing *where* to look for the details. Generally, if you note your paragraph topics, you should be in pretty good shape to find the details. Once you know where to look, just scan for key phrases found in the question.

A human body can survive without water for
several days and without food for as much as several
weeks. If breathing stops for as little as three to six
Line minutes, however, death is likely. All animals require a
(5) constant supply of oxygen to the body tissues, and
especially to the heart or brain. In the human body, the
respiratory system performs this function, by
delivering air containing oxygen to the blood.

Breathing is the most urgent human bodily function.

But respiration in large animals possessing lungs
(10) involves more than just breathing. It is a complex
process that delivers oxygen to internal tissues while
eliminating waste carbon dioxide produced by cells.
More specifically, respiration involves two processes
known as bulk flow and diffusion. Oxygen and carbon
(15) dioxide are moved in bulk through the respiratory and
circulatory systems; gaseous diffusion occurs at
different points across thin tissue membranes.

Respiration in large animals is a complex process.

Take a look at the passage and paragraph topics above. The paragraph topics are very general; they just note the gist of the paragraphs. If you saw the following questions, would you know where to find the answers?

EXAMPLE

Which bodily function, according to the passage, is least essential to the survival of the average human being?

(A) eating

(B) drinking

(C) breathing

(D) blood circulation

(E) the oxygen supply

The first paragraph deals with bodily functions. Lines 2–3 note that food is most expendable.

EXAMPLE

Which part of an animal's body is responsible for producing waste carbon dioxide?

(F) the internal tissues

(G) the circulatory systems

(H) the tissue membranes

(J) the bloodstream

(K) the cells

The second paragraph deals with the complex details of respiration. Carbon dioxide is mentioned in lines 14–15.

Making Inferences

Making an Inference means looking for something that is strongly implied, but not stated explicitly. In other words, making an inference means *reading between the lines*. What did the author *almost* say, but not say exactly?

Inferences will not stray too far from the language of the text. Wrong answers on inference questions will often fall beyond the subject matter of the passage.

Children have an amazing talent for learning vocabulary. Between the ages of one and seventeen, the average person learns the meaning of about 80,000
Line words—about 14 per day. Dictionaries and traditional
(5) classroom vocabulary lessons only account for part of this spectacular knowledge growth. More influential are individuals' reading habits and their interaction with people whose vocabularies are larger than their own. Reading shows students how words are used in
(10) sentences. Conversation offers several extra benefits that make vocabulary learning engaging—it supplies visual information, offers frequent repetition of new words, and gives students the chance to ask questions.

EXAMPLE

When is a child most receptive to learning the meaning of new words?

(A) when the child reaches high school age

(B) when the child is talking to other students

(C) when the child is assigned vocabulary exercises

(D) when the child is regularly told that he or she needs to improve

(E) when vocabulary learning is made interesting

This short passage discusses how children learn vocabulary. The question asks when children are **most** receptive to learning new words. No sentence in the passage states that "Children are **most** receptive to learning new words . . ." However, in lines 6–8, the author mentions that reading and conversation are particularly helpful. Lines 10–13 note how conversation makes vocabulary engaging. This is consistent with (E). There is nothing in the passage to suggest that children learn more at high school age, (A). (B) might be tempting, but it is too specific: There's no reason to believe that talking to students is more helpful than talking to anyone else. (C) contradicts the passage and (D) is never mentioned at all.

Now it's time to put some of this together. Take about three minutes to read the following passage, and then another four minutes to answer the questions that follow.

The poems of the earliest Greeks, like those of other ancient societies, consisted of magical charms, mysterious predictions, prayers, and traditional songs
Line of work and war. These poems were intended to be
(5) sung or recited, not written down, since they were created before the Greeks began to use writing for literary purposes. All that remains of them are fragments mentioned by later Greek writers. Homer, for example, quoted an ancient work-song for
(10) harvesters, and Simonides adapted the ancient poetry of ritual lamentation, songs of mourning for the dead, in his writing.

The different forms of early Greek poetry all had something in common: they described the way of life
(15) of a whole people. Poetry expressed ideas and feelings that were shared by everyone in a community—their folktales, their memories of historical events, their religious speculation. The poems were wholly impersonal, with little emphasis on individual
(20) achievement. It never occurred to the earliest Greek poets to tell us their names or to try to create anything completely new.

In the "age of heroes," however, the content and purpose of Greek poetry changed. By this later period,
(25) Greek communities had become separated into classes of rulers and ruled. People living in the same community therefore had different, even opposed, interests; they shared fewer ideas and emotions. The particular outlook of the warlike upper class gave
(30) poetry a new content, one that focused on the lives of individuals. Poets were assigned a new task: to celebrate the accomplishments of outstanding characters, whether they were real or imaginary, rather than the activity and history of the community.
(35) In the heroic age, poets became singers of tales who performed long poems about the fates of warriors and kings. One need only study Homer's *Iliad* and *Odyssey*, which are recorded examples of the epic poetry that was sung in the heroic age, to understand
(40) the influence that the upper class had on the poet's performance. Thus, the poetry of the heroic age can no longer be called a folk poetry. Nor was the poetry of the heroic age nameless, and in this period it lost much of its religious character.

What's the passage about?

What subject is mentioned repeatedly throughout paragraph 1?

What's paragraph 2 about?

What's paragraph 3 about?

(Did you see keyword at the start of paragraph 3?)

What's paragraph 4 about?

Exercises

i. Which of the following best tells what this passage is about?
    (A) how the role of early Greek poetry changed
    (B) how Greek communities became separated into classes
    (C) the superiority of early Greek poetry
    (D) the origin of the *Iliad* and the *Odyssey*
    (E) why little is known about early Greek poets

ii. The earliest Greek poems were probably written in order to
    (F) bring fame to kings.
    (G) bring fame to poets.
    (H) express commonly held beliefs.
    (J) celebrate the lives of warriors.
    (K) tell leaders how they should behave.

iii. The term "folk poetry" (line 42) refers to poetry whose contents mainly depict
    (A) the adventures of warriors.
    (B) the viewpoint of a ruling class.
    (C) the problems of a new lower class.
    (D) the concerns of a whole culture.
    (E) the fates of heroes.

iv. Which of the following did poetry of the heroic age primarily celebrate?
    (F) community life
    (G) individuals
    (H) religious beliefs
    (J) the value of work
    (K) common people

v. The passage suggests that, compared to communities in an earlier period, Greek communities during the heroic period were probably
    (A) less prosperous.
    (B) less unified.
    (C) better organized.
    (D) more peaceful.
    (E) more artistic.

vi. Which of the following situations is most like the one involving poets in the heroic age as it is presented in the passage?
    (F) A school of artists abandons portrait painting in favor of abstract art.
    (G) A sports team begins to rely increasingly on the efforts of a star player.
    (H) A species of wolf is hunted to the verge of extinction.
    (J) A group of reporters publicize the influence of celebrities on historical events.
    (K) A novelist captures the daily lives of a rural community.

At this point, you have a lot of tools to help you read passages and approach questions. It's a good idea to have a solid understanding of what the questions are, what types of questions you'll see, and how to best approach each one. There are three basic question types in the Reading Section, **Main Idea**, **Detail**, and **Inference** questions.

Since you can't exactly deal with questions unless you have an accompanying passage, take 3 or 4 minutes to read the following passage. As usual, mark it up. Read it with the goal of answering questions afterwards.

The first truly American art movement was formed by a group of landscape painters that emerged in the early nineteenth century called the Hudson
Line River School. The first works in this style were created
(5) by Thomas Cole, Thomas Doughty and Asher Durand, a trio of painters who worked during the 1820s in the Hudson River Valley and surrounding locations. Heavily influenced by European Romanticism, these painters set out to convey the remoteness and splendor
(10) of the American wilderness. The strongly nationalistic tone of their paintings caught the spirit of the times, and within a generation the movement had mushroomed to include landscape painters from all over the United States. Canvases celebrating such
(15) typically American scenes as Niagara Falls, Boston Harbor, and the expansion of the railroad into rural Pennsylvania were greeted with enormous popular acclaim.

One factor contributing to the success of the
(20) Hudson River School was the rapid growth of American nationalism in the early nineteenth century. The War of 1812 had given the United States a new sense of pride in its identity, and as the nation continued to grow, there was a desire to compete with
(25) Europe on both economic and cultural grounds. The vast panoramas of the Hudson River School fitted the

bill perfectly by providing a new movement in art that was unmistakably American in origin. The Hudson River School also arrived at a time when writers in the
(30) United States were turning their attention to the wilderness as a unique aspect of their nationality. The Hudson River School profited from this nostalgia because they effectively represented the continent the way it used to be. The view that the American
(35) character was formed by the frontier experience was widely held, and many writers were concerned about the future of a country that was becoming increasingly urbanized.

In keeping with this nationalistic spirit, even the
(40) painting style of the Hudson River School exhibited a strong sense of American identity. Although many of the artists studied in Europe, their paintings show a desire to be free of European artistic rules. Regarding the natural landscape as a direct manifestation of God,
(45) the Hudson River School painters attempted to record what they saw as accurately as possible. Unlike European painters who brought to their canvases the styles and techniques of centuries, they sought neither to embellish nor to idealize their scenes, portraying
(50) nature with the care and attention to detail of naturalists.

Hopefully, you understood that this passage was about why the Hudson River School became so successful. You should have also noted that the second paragraph addresses how American nationalism contributed to the success of the Hudson River School and the third paragraph discusses how nationalist sentiment was evident in the Hudson River School painting style.

Main Idea Questions

A **Main Idea** question asks you to summarize the topic of the passage.

EXAMPLE

Which of the following best tells what this passage is about?

(A) the history of American landscape painting

(B) why an art movement caught the public imagination

(C) how European painters influenced the Hudson River School

(D) why writers began to romanticize the American wilderness

(E) the origins of nationalism in the United States

Main idea questions are pretty easy to recognize. They will always ask something general about the passage.

Look for the answer choice that summarizes the entire passage. Rule out choices that are too broad or too narrow.

Do you see which one of these answers describes the entire passage without being too broad or too narrow?

(A) is too broad, as is (E). The passage is not about all American landscape painting; it's about the Hudson River School. Nationalism in the United States is much larger than the role of nationalism in a particular art movement. (H) and (D) are too narrow. European painters did influence the Hudson River School painters, but that wasn't the point of the whole passage. Similarly, writers are mentioned in paragraph 2, but the passage is about an art movement. Only (B) captures the essence of the passage—it's about an art movement that caught the public imagination.

Detail Questions

A **Detail** question asks you to research information that is directly stated in the passage.

EXAMPLE

Which of the following is not mentioned as one of the reasons for the success of the Hudson River School?

(F) American nationalism increased after the War of 1812.

(G) Americans were nostalgic about the frontier.

(H) Writers began to focus on the wilderness.

(J) The United States wanted to compete with Europe.

(K) City-dwellers became concerned about environmental pollution.

Note how the detail question asks about what is specifically mentioned—or not mentioned.

Scan the passage words or phrases in the answer choices. When you find the references, cross out the answer choices that do appear in the passage. The one left over will be the correct answer.

Four of the five answer choices are mentioned explicitly in the passage. (F) is mentioned in lines 20–25. (G) appears in line 32. (H) shows up in line 30. (J) is mentioned in line 24. Only (K) does not appear in the passage.

Inference Questions

An **Inference** question, like a **Detail** question, asks you to find relevant information in the passage. But once you've located the details, you have to go one step further: you have to figure out the underlying point of a particular phrase or example.

Strategy

Use your **inference** skills to figure out what the author's point is. The answer will not be stated, but it will be *strongly implied*.

EXAMPLE

Which of the following best describes what is suggested by the statement that the Hudson River School paintings "fitted the bill perfectly" (line 26)?

(A) The paintings depicted famous battle scenes.

(B) The paintings were very successful commercially.

(C) The paintings reflected a new pride in the United States.

(D) The paintings were favorably received in Europe.

(E) The paintings were accurate in their portrayal of nature.

"Suggested" is a classic inference clue. If something is "suggested," it is not stated outright.

Read the lines surrounding the quote. Summarize the author's point in your mind before you check the answer choices.

First, read the lines surrounding the quote to put the quote in context. Paragraph 2 talks about American pride; that's why Hudson River School paintings "fitted the bill." Hudson River School paintings were about America. (C) summarizes the point nicely. Note how this question revolves around the interplay between main idea and details. This detail strengthens the topic of the paragraph, the growing sense of nationalism in America. (A) superficially relates to the War of 1812, but doesn't answer the question. (B), (D), and (E) are way off base.

A Reminder about Timing

Plan to spend approximately three minutes reading the passage and roughly a minute to a minute and a half on each question. When you first start practicing, you'll probably find yourself spending more time than that on the passages. That's OK. However, you need to pay attention to your timing and cut the time down to around three minutes. If you don't, it will hurt you in the long run.

A Word about Science Passages

You may see at least one reading passage that deals with a science or technical topic. You will NOT be tested on any outside science knowledge, so do not answer the questions based on anything other than the information contained in the passage.

Exercise Answers

Greek Poetry Passage

Big Idea: What the poems of the ancient Greeks were like.

Paragraph 2: Ancient Greek poetry was an expression of the community, not individuals

Paragraph 3: How later ancient Greek poetry (in the "age of heroes") became more individualistic. (Note contrast keyword "however" in line 23)

Paragraph 4: More changes in later Greek Poetry

   i. (A) Main Idea. Only (A) captures paragraphs 1–4. (B) is beyond the scope of this passage. (C) expresses an extreme view that the author never takes. (D) mentions the *Iliad* and the *Odyssey*, which are discussed only in paragraph 4. (E) again does not address the purpose of the entire passage.

   ii. (H) Paragraph Topic. Refer to the topic of paragraph 2. (F), (G), (J), and (K) are never mentioned in this paragraph.

   iii. (D) Inference. You need to use your inference skills to answer this question. The reference to line 42 leads you to paragraph 4. Here "folk poetry" refers to the age before the "heroic age" when poetry was about the entire community, and not just the warriors and kings. (A), (B), and (E) do not refer to the "folk" at all and are therefore incorrect. (C) mentions class conflict, which is not discussed in this paragraph.

   iv. (G) Paragraph Topic. The answer is clearly stated in paragraph 3. "In the heroic age, poets became singers of tales who performed long poems about the fates of warriors and kings" (i.e., individuals).

   v. (B) Inference. Paragraph 3 talks about social changes. "Greek communities had become separated into classes of rulers and rules" (i.e. communities were now stratified, not united).

   vi. (J) Inference. Here you are asked to apply the ideas of the passage to a hypothetical situation. Paragraphs 3 and 4 discuss the portrayal of individual heroes in later Greek poetry such as Homer's *Iliad*. Journalism focusing on celebrities is analogous.

Practice Questions

The painter Georgia O'Keeffe was born in Wisconsin in 1887, and grew up on her family's farm. At seventeen she decided she wanted to be an artist
Line and left the farm for schools in Chicago and New
(5) York, but she never lost her bond with the land. Like most painters, O'Keeffe painted the things that were most important to her, and nearly all her works are simplified portrayals of nature.

O'Keeffe became famous when her paintings
(10) were discovered and exhibited in New York by the photographer Alfred Stieglitz, whom she married in 1924. During a visit to New Mexico in 1929, O'Keeffe was so moved by the bleak landscape and broad skies of the Western desert that she began to
(15) paint its images. Cows' skulls and other bleached bones found in the desert figured prominently in her paintings. When her husband died in 1946, she moved to New Mexico permanently and used the horizon lines of the desert, colorful flowers, rocks, barren hills,
(20) and the sky as subjects for her paintings. Although O'Keeffe painted her best-known works in the 1920s,

'30s, and '40s, she continued to produce tributes to the western desert until her death in 1986.

O'Keeffe is widely considered to have been a
(25) pioneering American modernist painter. While most early modern American artists were strongly influenced by European art, O'Keeffe's position was more independent. She established her own vision and preferred to view her painting as a private endeavor.
(30) Almost from the beginning, her work was more identifiably American than that of her contemporaries in its simplified and idealized treatment of color, light, space, and natural forms. Her paintings are generally considered "semiabstract" because even though they
(35) depict recognizable images and objects, the paintings don't present those images in a very detailed or realistic way.

Rather, the colors and shapes in her paintings are often so reduced and simplified that they begin to take
(40) on a life of their own, independent of the real-life objects from which they are taken.

1. Which of the following best tells what this passage is about?

   (A) O'Keeffe was the best painter of her generation.
   (B) O'Keeffe was a distinctive modern American painter.
   (C) O'Keeffe liked to paint only what was familiar to her.
   (D) O'Keeffe never developed fully as an abstract artist.
   (E) O'Keeffe used colors and shapes that are too reduced and simple.

2. Which of the following is not mentioned as an influence on O'Keeffe's paintings?

   (F) her rural upbringing
   (G) her life in the west
   (H) the work of Mexican artists
   (J) the appearance of the natural landscape
   (K) animal and plant forms

3. The passage suggests that Stieglitz contributed to O'Keeffe's career by

   (A) bringing her work to a wider audience
   (B) supporting her financially for many years
   (C) inspiring her to paint natural forms
   (D) suggesting that she study the work of European artists
   (E) requesting that she accompany him to New Mexico

4. Which of the following is most similar to O'Keeffe's relationship with nature?

   (F) a photographer's relationship with a model
   (G) a writer's relationship with a publisher
   (H) a student's relationship with a part-time job
   (J) a sculptor's relationship with an art dealer
   (K) a carpenter's relationship with a hammer

5. Why have O'Keeffe's paintings been described as "semiabstract" (line 34)?

   (A) They involve a carefully realistic use of color and light.
   (B) They depict common, everyday things.
   (C) They show familiar scenes from nature.
   (D) They depict recognizable things in an unfamiliar manner.
   (E) They refer directly to real-life activities.

6. Why was O'Keeffe considered an artistic pioneer?

   (F) Her work became influential in Europe.
   (G) She painted the American Southwest.
   (H) Her paintings had a definite American style.
   (J) She painted things that were familiar to her.
   (K) Her work was very abstract.

Practice Question Explanations

1. (B) A main idea question. (A) is wrong because it's simply never stated that O'Keeffe was the best painter of her generation. (B) is accurate and may be the best choice, so keep it in mind. (C) is a bit tricky. It's true that O'Keeffe liked to paint things that were familiar to her—primarily certain nature images—but this is just one point covered in the passage. The broader, more important idea is that O'Keeffe was an important modern American painter. (D) is never suggested by the passage. (E) focuses too much on a detail, and also distorts the "message" of the passage. The author never says that O'Keeffe's colors and shapes are "too" reduced and simple. O'Keeffe is never criticized. That leaves (B), which is both accurate and general enough without being so general that the meaning of the passage is lost.

2. (H) A factual detail question. You're looking for the factor that did not influence O'Keeffe. The third paragraph describes O'Keeffe's work as distinctly American in style. Mexican influences are never even mentioned, so (H) is correct here. The four wrong choices are all true. As for (F), the passage makes clear that her rural childhood had a lasting influence. (G), (J), and (K) are supported in the second paragraph: her work was greatly affected by her life in the West, particularly by its natural landscape with bleached animal bones, hills, and colorful flowers.

3. (A) Paragraph 2 states that O'Keeffe "became famous" when Stieglitz "discovered and exhibited" her work in New York City. You can infer, then, that Stieglitz helped O'Keeffe by bringing her work to a wider audience. Whatever financial arrangement, if any, existed between them (B) is not mentioned in the passage. Paragraph 1 strongly implies that O'Keeffe was inspired to paint natural forms (C) long before she met Stieglitz. (D) contradicts paragraph 3, and (E), the circumstances leading to O'Keeffe's visit to New Mexico are not described.

4. (F) First ask yourself what O'Keeffe's relationship to nature was. O'Keeffe painted from nature—it was the subject of her work. Which choice is most similar to the relationship between a painter and her subject? (F) is best, because a model is the subject of a photographer's work. (G) is wrong because a publisher is not the subject of a writer's work. Similarly, (H) is out because a part-time job is not a student's subject. It is not what a student bases her work on. Same with (J): an art dealer buys and sells a sculptor's work. Finally, a hammer is simply a carpenter's tool; it doesn't provide a carpenter with a subject or model, so (K) is out.

5. (D) O'Keeffe's "semiabstract" style is discussed in the passage's last two sentences. Was "semiabstract" confusing to you? Hopefully not, because, as always, everything you need to know will be stated or clearly suggested. The next-to-last sentence states that O'Keeffe's paintings are thought of as semi-abstract because they depict recognizable images in a way that is not very detailed or realistic. (D) simply restates this. (A) and (E) are wrong because they refer to "realistic" qualities, which contradict the passage's explanation of "semiabstract." While (B) and (C) both describe O'Keeffe's work accurately, they are not reasons for her work being called "semiabstract." They describe subjects of her paintings, but not the semiabstract style in which they were painted.

6. (H) The third paragraph states that O'Keeffe is considered a pioneering modern American painter and why—because her style was independent and identifiably American, and not strongly influenced by European art. (H) restates the idea. (F) is never suggested. (G) and (J) are true of O'Keeffe's work, but are not the reasons she was considered an artistic pioneer. (K) is not true of O'Keeffe's work, which is considered semiabstract, not very abstract. Furthermore, (K) does not address the question of why O'Keeffe is considered an artistic pioneer.

6

Writing Mechanics/
The Essay

- Kaplan Four-Step Method for Writing

- Common pitfalls to avoid in essay writing

- How to pace yourself on the essay sections of the tests

INTRODUCTION

On both the SSAT and ISEE, you'll be required to write an essay, but on neither one is your essay graded. So why do you need to write it? Well, the essay is a great way for schools to see how you express yourself, particularly how well you present and argue your opinions. The rest of the test tells them how well you perform on a series of standard tasks, but the essay is the one part of the exam where you get to shine through. Schools look closely at your essay, so think of it as part of your application and take it seriously.

So, what do you need to know to write an essay that will stand out? Really, only a few key things. First and most important, answer the question. No other aspect about your essay will matter if you don't answer the question. Second, write clearly and logically. And finally, proofread your essay before you finish. Even if you think you have been very careful, you'll undoubtedly find things that you'll want to fix or change.

There are five important things to know about the Essay:

1. You'll need to organize your thoughts quickly (you'll have 25 minutes on the SSAT and 30 minutes on the ISEE to write a complete essay).

2. Your essay is limited to two pages.

3.   Essay topics will be easy to grasp.

4.   What you say is more important than using perfect grammar.

5.   Your essay will not be graded.

Please just answer the question, ma'am.

The Golden Rule of essay writing is to answer the question. That means you need to decide whether you agree or disagree with the statement, think of a few reasons why, and lay them out for the reader. You don't need to be very creative; all you need to do is stick to the topic and write clearly. Before you write a word, though, decide what your opinion is.

What's Wrong with This Picture?

Writing a good essay means following a few key rules about writing. Take a look at the paragraph below and think about what's wrong with it. Use the space below to jot down the problems you notice.

Sample Topic: No good deed goes unpunished.

It always bothers me when people talk about punishment. It's not fair. I mean, there are some kids out there who do really good things, even though people don't notice them. In my opinion, everyone spends too much time talking about whether or not there is enough punishment in the world. We should really be talking about more important things like the environment . . .

_____

_____

_____

_____

_____

_____

Common Pitfalls in Essay Writing

What did you notice in the paragraph you just read? The biggest problem with it is that it fails to answer the question. Granted, you're only seeing the beginning of the essay, but you can tell from the way it ends that the author is about to go off on a tangent about the environment instead of discussing the topic. Remember, *always* answer the question.

What else is wrong with the sample paragraph? You might have noticed that it sounds very casual, almost like a conversation. Phrases such as "I mean" and "In my opinion" give the essay a tone that's too familiar and too emotional. While you always want to present your opinion, you should do it in a detached, formal way, like a newspaper article. Try to avoid "I" statements in your essay writing.

How can you avoid making these types of mistakes? How can you make sure you don't get sidetracked while you write, arguing rather than defending, or being redundant? Kaplan has an easy method that you should follow when you write your essay. By following each and every step, you'll be guaranteed to create an organized, clear essay.

KAPLAN FOUR-STEP METHOD FOR WRITING

Step 1. Brainstorm.

Step 2. Make an outline.

Step 3. Write your essay.

Step 4. Proofread.

This might sound pretty general, a lot like the essays you've written for school. In fact, the essay is the part of the test that most closely resembles the work you do in school. However, the essay follows a much more specific format than other essays, and you don't have a lot of time to do it, so it's very important that you follow all four steps. Let's break them down.

STEP 1:   Brainstorm

When you start to brainstorm for ideas, ask yourself, "Do I agree or disagree with the topic?" With the sample topic <u>No good deed goes unpunished,</u> your thinking might go like this: I believe that people are rewarded for good deeds, not punished. Okay, what examples can I use to support this point of view?

It's important that you're clear in your head about what your stance is *before* you start to organize your essay. Once you start to put your examples together, you don't want to have to go back and figure out what you're trying to show. It doesn't matter what position you take, as long as you support it well. So don't stress too much about what you really think—just choose a position that will be easy for you to argue.

STEP 2:   Make an Outline

Once you've decided your opinion, the next step is to write an outline. You should always come up with three examples to support your opinion. Your examples should serve to argue why your opinion is right, so make sure they all support the point of view that you're presenting.

Next, decide the best order in which to present your examples. Is there a logical order to lay out your ideas? How do you want to start your essay? How do you want to end it? Make some notes on your scratch paper so when you start to write, you can glance at them to keep you on track and writing quickly.

STEP 3:   Write Your Essay

The next thing you have to do is actually write the essay. Follow your outline carefully, but be flexible. Maybe you'll think of another great idea midway through your writing. Should you ignore it, or should you substitute it for the third example you had planned to include? If you think it's better than what you originally came up with, go ahead and write about it instead. Just make sure that any deviation you make from your outline is in fact an improvement over the original idea.

STEP 4:   Proofread

Wrap up your writing five minutes before the end of your allotted time. Give your essay a good read-through, making sure you haven't made any spelling mistakes, written run-on sentences, or forgotten to capitalize a proper name. You won't be able to make any huge changes at this point—after all, you only have five minutes left—but you do want to make sure that you haven't made any egregious errors.

PACING

How much time should you spend on each step? Use your watch and this guideline as you write. You want to give yourself sufficient time for each step, because planning and proofreading will make your essay much stronger. Use the following guidelines for timing:

	SSAT	ISEE
Outlining/Planning	5 minutes	5 minutes
Writing	15 minutes	20 minutes
Rereading/Correcting	5 minutes	5 minutes
Total time:	**25 minutes**	**30 minutes**

BRAINSTORMING IN ACTION

When you get to the essay section, the last thing you want to happen is a *brain freeze*. You know the feeling: You look at the page, you see the words, your brain doesn't register, you stare into space . . . you can't think of a thing to write about.

What Was I Thinking?

Even if you're feeling rushed, don't skip the Outlining/Planning step. Planning your essay will make the entire writing process easier and faster, and will ensure that your writing is well organized. Remember, wear a watch on test day so you can keep a handle on your pacing.

How do you avoid such a situation? One of the best ways to make sure your brain is in gear and ready to brainstorm on the spot is to practice doing it. Take a look at the statements below. For each one, decide what position you would take and think of three examples you would present in support of your opinion. Give yourself about five minutes to do each one.

Remember, for each topic, ask yourself the following two questions:

• Do you agree or disagree?

• What examples could you use to support your opinion?

Sample Topic 1: Free speech on the Internet should be protected at all costs.

_____

_____

_____

_____

_____

_____

Sample Topic 2: We learn more from our mistakes than our successes.

_____

_____

_____

_____

_____

_____

Sample Topic 3: Thanks to technological advances, the world is getting smaller every day.

_____

_____

_____

_____

_____

_____

Sample Topic 4: Schools should teach values, not just skills.

_____

_____

_____

_____

_____

_____

Sample Topic 5: The more things change, the more they stay the same.

_____

_____

_____

_____

_____

_____

SHOW, DON'T TELL

You've probably heard the saying that good writing _shows_ rather than _tells_. What does that mean, and what do examples have to do with it?

Take the statement "You can't teach an old dog new tricks." Say you wanted to disagree with it. You could explain why you believe the statement isn't true, what you think about teaching and age, and so forth. Or, you could use examples that _illustrate_ the same point. For example, you could discuss the number of retired persons currently using the Internet on a regular basis. The fact that people generally considered _old_ by society are adapting to a new technology in large numbers serves to show that you can, in fact, teach an old dog new tricks.

What makes a good example? A good example illustrates the point you want to make. In addition, a good example comes out of the world at large, rather than from your personal life. While it may be true that your grandmother e-mails you, it's more powerful to say that many retired persons use the Internet every day.

If you're not doing so already, try reading the newspaper on a regular basis. Not only will you know more about what's going on in the world and be ready with great examples for your essays, you'll also improve your vocabulary, which will improve your performance on all of the verbal sections of your test.

JUST THE FACTS

Aside from answering the question with supporting examples, what do you need to remember as you write your essay? Here are some basics things that you should always do when you write an essay for the SSAT/ISEE:

ALWAYS . . .

- Develop and organize your ideas.
- Use three paragraphs.
- Use appropriate examples.
- Write in standard English.
- Stick to the topic.
- Use proper spelling, grammar and punctuation.

Reading Tips

What makes good reading material? Well-written articles that present views in a clear, logical manner will provide good examples, and will show you how strong essays are written. When you read the newspaper, look at the Editorial page. You'll see how writers argue their opinions on a variety of topics and what kinds of examples they use. And you might learn something interesting in the process, too.

WRITE ON

Okay, it's time to practice putting things together. Here are two essay topics that you should work through as though they were the real thing. Look at the topic, brainstorm your ideas, make an outline, write, and proofread. Time yourself (remember to give yourself 25 minutes if you're taking the SSAT and 30 minutes if you're taking the ISEE).

Essay Topic: Voting is such an important responsibility that all citizens should be required to vote in every election.

Step 1. Brainstorm.

Brainstorm in the space provided below. Do you agree or disagree? What examples might you use to support your argument? (Remember, give yourself only a few minutes to do this!)

Step 2. Make an Outline.

Write your outline here. Keep your essay to three paragraphs. Paragraph 1 gives your introduction and an example. Paragraph 2 gives another example, and Paragraph 3 gives your final example and your conclusion.

Paragraph 1

_____

_____

_____

Paragraph 2

_____

_____

_____

Paragraph 3

_____

_____

_____

_____

Step 3. Write your Essay.

Write your essay below. Give yourself 15 minutes if you're taking the SSAT and 20 minutes if you're taking the ISEE.

_____

_____

_____

_____

_____

_____

_____

Step 4. Proofread.

Go back to your essay and read through it again. Does it make sense? Have you made any spelling or grammar errors? Fix them. Get used to making corrections clearly on your page, since that's how you will do it the day of the test.

Essay Topic: Good things come to those who wait.

Step 1. Brainstorm.

Brainstorm in the space provided below. Do you agree or disagree? What examples might you use to support your argument? (Remember, give yourself only a few minutes to do this!)

_____

_____

_____

_____

_____

_____

_____

_____

_____

_____

_____

_____

_____

_____

_____

_____

_____

Step 2. Make an Outline.

Write your outline here. Keep your essay to three paragraphs. Paragraph 1 gives your introduction and an example. Paragraph 2 gives another example, and Paragraph 3 gives your final example and your conclusion.

Paragraph 1

_____

_____

_____

Paragraph 2

_____

_____

_____

Paragraph 3

_____

_____

_____

Step 3. Write your essay.

Write your essay below. Give yourself 15 minutes if you're taking the SSAT and 20 minutes if you're taking the ISEE.

_____

_____

_____

_____

_____

_____

Step 4. Proofread.

Go back to your essay and read through it again. Does it make sense? Have you made any spelling or grammar errors? Fix them. Get used to making corrections clearly on your page, since that's how you will do it the day of the test.

Math Skills Workout

7

Algebra

Highlights

- How to approach SSAT/ISEE math problems

- Backdoor methods to solving problems

- Tips on solving different types of algebra problems

OVERVIEW

Algebra problems will appear in two forms on the SSAT/ISEE: as regular math problems and as word problems. Word problems will be dealt with in the following section. This section will give you a chance to review the basic algebra concepts that you'll see on the test. The Word Problems section will build on these concepts and introduce word problem-specific skills.

HOW TO APPROACH SSAT/ISEE MATH

Before we dive into the actual math, let's take a step back and think about how to approach math problems in general. You've done math before. You've most likely already been exposed to most of the math concepts you'll see on your private school admissions test. This begs the question as to why you need to approach SSAT/ISEE math differently than you approach any other math.

Helpful Hint

The SSAT/ISEE Test is not math class. No one is going to check your work. Choose the fastest method to solve the problem, even if your math teacher would not approve.

The answer to this question is that it's not that you have to do the math *differently*, it's just that you have to do it very *deliberately*. You'll be under a lot of time pressure when you take your test, so you need to use your time well.

Ultimately, the best way to take control of your testing experience is to approach every SSAT/ISEE math problem the same way. This doesn't mean that you'll *solve* every problem the same way. Rather, it means that you'll use the same process to *decide* how to solve, or even whether to solve, each problem.

Read Through the Question

Okay, this may seem a little too obvious. Of course, you're going to read the question. How else can you solve the problem? In reality, this isn't quite as obvious as it seems. The point here is that you need to read the entire question carefully before you start solving the problem. When you don't read the question carefully, it's incredibly easy to make careless mistakes. Consider the following problem:

EXAMPLE

For what positive value of x does $\frac{4}{3} = \frac{x^2}{27}$?

(A) 3

(B) 6

(C) 12

(D) 18

(E) 36

It's crucial that you pay close attention to precisely what the question is asking. The question contains a classic trap that's very easy to fall into if you don't read it carefully. Did you notice how easy it would be to solve for x^2 instead of x ? Yes, this would be careless, but it's easy to be careless when you're working quickly.

There are other reasons to read the whole question before you start solving the problem. One is that you may save yourself some work. If you start to answer too quickly, you may assume that a problem is more difficult than it actually is. Similarly, you might assume that the problem is *less* difficult than it actually is and skip a necessary step or two.

Another reason to read carefully before answering is that you probably shouldn't solve every problem on your first pass. A big part of taking control of your test experience is deciding which problems to answer, which to save for later, and which to skip (unless you're taking the ISEE, in which case you should NEVER skip any problems).

Decide Whether to Do the Problem or Skip It for Now

Each time you approach a new math problem you have the option of answering it immediately or putting it aside. Therefore, you have to make a decision each time about how to best use your time. You have three options.

1. **If you can solve the problem relatively quickly and efficiently, do it! This is the best option.**

2. **If you think you can solve it, but that it will take you a long time, circle the number in your test booklet and go back to it later.**

   Remember that when you go back to the problems you have skipped the first time, you'll want to fill in an answer even if it's a random guess. Don't underestimate your ability to eliminate wrong answers even when you don't know how to solve a problem. Every time you rule out a wrong answer choice, you increase your chances of guessing correctly.

3. **If you have no idea what to do, skip the problem and circle it. Save your time for the problems you can do.**

   EXAMPLE

   Tamika, Becky, and Kym were investors in a new restaurant. Tamika and Becky each invested one half as much as Kym invested. If the total investment made by these three was $5,200, how much did Kym invest?

   (F) $900
   (G) $1,300
   (H) $1,800
   (J) $2,100
   (K) $2,600

Different test takers are will have different reactions to this question. Some students may quickly see the algebra—or the backdoor method for solving this problem—and do the math. Others may see a word problem and run screaming from the room. This approach is not recommended. However, if you know that you habitually have difficulty with algebra word problems, you may choose to save this problem for later or make an educated guess.

Here's the algebra, by the way. Kym, Tamika, and Becky contributed a total of $5,200. You can represent this algebraically as $K + T + B = \$5,200$. Since Tamika and Becky each contributed $\frac{1}{2}$ as much as Kym, you can represent these relationships as follows:

$$T = \frac{1}{2}K$$
$$B = \frac{1}{2}K$$

Now, substitute variables so that you can solve the equation.

$$K + T + B = 5,200$$
$$K + \frac{1}{2}K + \frac{1}{2}K = 5,200$$
$$2K = 5,200$$
$$K = 2,600 \text{ (Choice K)}$$

If you choose to tackle the problem, look for the fastest method.

EXAMPLE

Jenna is now x years old and Amy is 3 years younger than Jenna. In terms of x, how old will Amy be in 4 years?

(A) $x - 1$

(B) x

(C) $x + 1$

(D) $x + 4$

(E) $2x + 1$

Here is the algebraic solution. It Jenna is x years old, then Amy is $x - 3$ years old, since Amy is 3 years younger than Jenna. Therefore, in 4 years, Amy will be $(x - 3) + 4$, or $x + 1$.

Here is the picking numbers solution. Suppose that $x = 10$. Then Jenna is now 10 years old. Amy is now 7 years old because Amy is 3 years younger than Jenna. In 4 years, Amy will be 11. Now plug 10 for x into all of the answer choices and see which answer choices equal 11. You can eliminate any answer choice which does not equal 11. Since only choice (C), $x + 1$, equals 11, choice (C) must be correct.

With the method of picking numbers it sometimes happens that more than one answer choice gives you the correct result for the particular number or numbers that you choose. When that happens you must go back and pick another number or numbers to eliminate the remaining incorrect answer choices.

Here is the point: **Know your strengths and make decisions about how to approach Math problems accordingly!!!!**

Some people *see* algebra. Others have a harder time with it. The same is true for geometry, word problems, etc. There's often more than one way to do a particular problem. The *best* method is the method that will get you the correct answer accurately and quickly.

The lesson here is that you have to know your own strengths. Again, in case you missed the point, *know your strengths and use them to your advantage.*

Helpful Hint

When you skip a question, circle it in your test booklet so that it will be easy to spot if you have time to go back.

Remember, only guess on the SSAT if you can eliminate at least one answer. However, don't leave any answers blank on the ISEE. Since there's no penalty for wrong answers, there is no harm in guessing.

Of course, the fact that random guessing doesn't hurt you doesn't mean that you shouldn't guess strategically. Remember, every answer choice you rule out increases your odds of guessing correctly.

EXAMPLE

What is the greatest common factor of 95 and 114 ?

    (F)   1
    (G)   5
    (H)   6
    (J)   19
    (K)   38

If you couldn't remember how to find the greatest common factor or were running out of time on the test and wanted to save your time for other questions, you should be able to eliminate at least one answer choice pretty easily. Do you see which one?

Since all multiples of 5 end in 5 or 0, 5 cannot be a factor of 114. Therefore, choice (G) must be incorrect.

BACKDOOR METHODS

There are two backdoor methods that are likely to serve you well on the test: **Picking Numbers** and **Backsolving**. Use a backdoor method if it gets you the answer more quickly. After all, the timing on the test is tight, and no one is going to check your math.

Reminder

The SSAT/ISEE is not a math test; it's an admissions exam. You don't have to do the math the "right" way. You just need to get the right answer.

Picking Numbers

Sometimes a math problem can appear more difficult than it actually is because it's general or abstract. You can make a question like this more concrete—and easier—by temporarily substituting numbers for the variables in the question. This "picking numbers" strategy can help make the math easier.

EXAMPLE

$3a(2b + 2) =$

(A) $2b + 3a$

(B) $5ab + 2b$

(C) $5ab + 2a + 1$

(D) $6ab + 2a$

(E) $6ab + 6a$

The algebra in this question is pretty straightforward. According to the Distributive Property, $3a(2b + 2) = (3a)(2b) + (3a)(2) = 6ab + 6a$ or choice (E). Most test takers will probably do the algebra to solve the question.

However, if you have trouble with algebra, or simply find that it takes you a long time, you can approach the problem another way. Pick simple numbers for a and b and plug them into the expression $3a(2b + 2)$. If $a = 2$ and $b = 3$, then $3a(2b + 2) = (3)(2)[2(3) + 2] = 6(6 + 2) = 48$. Now you know that if $a = 2$ and $b = 3$, the expression equals 48.

Once you know this, simply plug 2 in for a and 3 in for b in each of the answer choices. Any answer choice that does not equal 48 can be eliminated. Since only choice (E) equals 48, choice (E) is the answer.

Pick easy numbers!

Pick small numbers that are easy to use. This method is supposed to make the problem *easier*.

(A) $2b + 3a = 2(3) + 3(2) = 12$

(B) $5ab + 2b = 5(2)(3) + 2(3) = 36$

(C) $5ab + 2a + 1 = 5(2)(3) + 2(2) + 1 = 35$

(D) $6ab + 2a = 6(2)(3) + 2(2) = 40$

(E) $6ab + 6a = 6(2)(3) + 6(2) = 48$

If two or more answer choices had come out to 48, then you would have to do a little more work. Under those circumstances you would have to pick new numbers for a and b, come up with a new value and then plug those numbers into the answer choices that came out the same the first time.

In other words, if choices (B) and (E) had both equaled 48, you could have made $a = 3$ and $b = 4$, discovered that the expression $3a(2b + 2)$ equals 90 and then plugged 3 and 4 into only choices (B) and (E) to determine which one equaled 90.

Word Problems

Picking numbers can be extremely helpful when the answer choices to a word problem contain variables. Remember this problem?

EXAMPLE

Be Wary of Picking 0 or 1

Even though 0 and 1 are small, easy numbers, avoid picking them. They often give several "possibly correct" answers.

Jenna is now x years old and Amy is 3 years younger than Jenna. In terms of x, how old will Amy be in 4 years?

(A) $x - 1$

(B) x

(C) $x + 1$

(D) $x + 4$

(E) $2x + 1$

As you saw earlier, there's more than one way to solve this problem. Some test takers will find it easier to solve this question by working with algebraic expressions. Others may feel that this will slow them down. Picking a number for x may be faster and easier.

If you say that $x = 10$, then Jenna is 10 years old and Amy is 7, since she's three years younger. In four years, Amy will be 11. Once you have this value, plug in 10 for x in each of the answer choices to see which ones equals 11. Those answer choices that don't equal 11 can be eliminated.

(A) $10 - 1 = 9$

(B) 10

(C) $10 + 1 = 11$

(D) $10 + 4 = 14$

(E) $2(10) + 1 = 21$

Only choice (C) equals 11, so (C) must be correct.

Percent Increase/Decrease Problems

If you see a problem on the SSAT/ISEE that deals with percents, picking 100 is the easiest and quickest way to solve the problem.

EXAMPLE

If the price of a stock decreases by 20 percent, and then by an additional 25 percent, by what percent has the price decreased from its original value?

(F) 40%

(G) 45%

(H) 50%

(I) 55%

(J) 60%

Kaplan Rules

Always pick 100 for percent problems. It will help you find the answer quickly and accurately!

Make the original price of the stock $100. The initial 20% decrease brings the price down to $80. (20% of 100 is 20.) 25% of 80 or $\frac{1}{4}$ of $80 is $20. Therefore the price of the stock is decreased by an additional $20, bringing the final price down to $60. Since the price dropped from $100 to $60, the total decrease is $40 or 40% of the original price. (F) is the correct answer.

You may have been able to solve this problem by setting up algebraic equations, but picking 100 is easier and faster here.

Backsolving

All of the questions in the Math section of the SSAT and ISEE are multiple-choice. One way that you can use this to your advantage is by **backsolving**. What this means is that you can work backwards from the answer choices.

You Can Only Backsolve If . . .

Backsolving will work only if your answer choices are all numbers (and they don't include variables.)

Here's how it works. When answer choices are numbers—i.e., not variables—you can expect them to be arranged from *small to large* or *large to small*. The testmaker does not get creative with the order of the answer choices. What you do is to start with the *middle* answer choice and plug it directly into the problem. If it works, you're set. If it doesn't, you can usually determine whether to try a larger or smaller answer choice. Look at the following problem and explanation.

EXAMPLE

Three consecutive multiples of 20 have a sum of 300. What is the greatest of these numbers?

(A) 60

(B) 80

(C) 100

(D) 120

(E) 140

Speed Tip

Always start with the middle answer choice when backsolving. If it's too small, move to the bigger ones.

Begin with the middle answer choice. If 100 is the greatest of the three numbers, the three numbers must be 100, 80, and 60. 100 + 80 + 60 = 240. The correct three numbers will add up to 300, so the greatest of these numbers must be greater than 100. Try answer choice (D). If 120 is the greatest, the three numbers must be 120, 100, and 80. 120 + 100 + 80 = 300. Answer (D) is correct.

It's worth noting that if (D) had also given you a sum less than 300, you would not have to check choice (E). Think about it. If the numbers are arranged from small to large and the second largest number gives you an answer that is too small, you know that the largest number has to be correct.

A Word about Calculators

No Calculators

Practice doing math without a calculator since you can't use one on the test.

This is an easy one. You *cannot* use a calculator on the SSAT or ISEE. Leave your calculator home. End of story.

The rest of the Math Section in this book deals with Math Content review. Some of this will be familiar; some may be less familiar. Take a look at all of it, but spend more time with the subjects that are less familiar. Even if you don't need to review a particular subject, make sure you do the practice set. There's no harm in practicing extra problems.

ALGEBRA CONCEPTS

If you feel lost at any point, turn to the Math Reference section and Math Foundations Workshops at the end of this book. They'll give you solid background and practice in the nitty-gritty math concepts, terms, and skills you'll need to have down pat. Then dive back into this lesson.

Expressions

A question about simplifying an algebraic **expression** on the SSAT or ISEE is likely to look something like this:

$$(11 + 3x) - (5 - 2x) =$$

It would, of course, be followed by five answer choices (four on the ISEE). In addition to algebra, this problem tests your knowledge of odds and evens, and the order of operations (PEMDAS). It's not uncommon for algebra problems to contain elements of arithmetic, but there are certain algebra concepts you'll need to know.

The main thing you need to remember about **expressions** on the SSAT/ISEE is that you can combine only "like terms."

For example, to combine monomials or polynomials, simply add or subtract the coefficients of terms that have the exact same variable. When completing the addition or subtraction, do not change the variables.

$$6a + 5a = 11a$$

$$8b - 2b = 6b$$

$$3a + 2b - 8a = 3a - 8a + 2b = -5a + 2b \text{ or } 2b - 5a$$

Remember, you cannot combine:

$$6a + 5a^2$$
or
$$3a + 2b$$

For Algebraic Expressions

Make sure you combine only "like terms."

Exercise
Now, try the following sample problem.

i. $(11 + 3x) - (5 - 2x) =$

   (A) $6 + x$
   (B) $6 + 5x$
   (C) $13 + 6x$
   (D) $14 + x$
   (E) $16 + 5x$

Multiplying and dividing monomials is a little different. In addition and subtraction, you can only combine like terms. With multiplication and division, you can multiply and divide terms that are different. When you multiply monomials, multiply the coefficients of each term. (In other words, multiply the *numbers that come before the variables.* Add the exponents of like variables. Multiply different variables together.)

$$(6a)(4b) = (6 \times 4)(a \times b)$$
$$= 24ab$$

$$(6a)(4ab) = (6 \times 4)(a \times a \times b)$$
$$= (6 \times 4)(a^{1+1} \times b)$$
$$= 24\, a^2 b$$

Use the FOIL method to **multiply binomials**. FOIL stands for <u>F</u>irst <u>O</u>uter <u>I</u>nner <u>L</u>ast.

$$(y + 1)(y + 2) = (y \times y) + (y \times 2) + (1 \times y) + (1 \times 2)$$
$$= y^2 + 2y + y + 2$$
$$= y^2 + 3y + 2$$

Exercise

  ii. $5a + 2b - 3(b + 3a)$
  iii. $-3a - (-2a)$
  iv. $6xy \div 2x$
   v. $(m + 2)(m + 8)$
  vi. $(n - 6)(n + 3)$

Equations

The key to **solving equations** is to do the same thing to both sides of the equation until you have your variable isolated on one side of the equation and all of the numbers on the other side.

$$12a + 8 = 23 - 3a$$

First, subtract 8 from each side so that the left side of the equation has only variables.

$$12a + 8 - 8 = 23 - 3a - 8$$
$$12a = 15 - 3a$$

Then, add 3a to each side so that the right side of the equation has only numbers.

$$12a + 3a = 15 - 3a + 3a$$
$$15a = 15$$

Finally, divide both sides by 15 to isolate the variable.

$$\frac{15a}{15} = \frac{15}{15}$$
$$a = 1$$

Sometimes you're given an equation with two variables and asked to **solve for one variable in terms of the other**. This means that you must isolate the variable for which you are solving on one side of the equation and put everything else on the other side. In other words, when you're done, you'll have x (or whatever the variable is) on one side of the equation and an expression on the other side.

Solve $7x + 2y = 3x + 10y - 16$ for x in terms of y.

Since you want to isolate x on one side of the equation, begin by subtracting $2y$ from both sides.

$$7x + 2y - 2y = 3x + 10y - 16 - 2y$$
$$7x = 3x + 8y - 16$$

Then, subtract $3x$ from both sides to get all the x's on one side of the equation.

$$7x - 3x = 3x + 8y - 16 - 3x$$
$$4x = 8y - 16$$

Finally, divide both sides by 4 to isolate x.

$$\frac{4x}{4} = \frac{8y - 16}{4}$$

$$x = 2y - 4$$

> **Treat Both Sides Equally**
>
> Always do the same thing to both sides to solve for a variable in an equation.

Exercise

vii. $5a - 6 = -11$

viii. $6y + 3 = y + 38$

ix. $18 = -6x + 4(3x - 3)$

x. If $5a = b$, what is a in terms of b.

xi. If $xy \neq 0$ and $2xy = 8y$, what is x in terms of y.

Substitution

If a problem gives you the value for a variable, just plug the value into the equation and solve. Make sure that you follow the rules of PEMDAS and are careful with your calculations.

> If $x = 15$ and $y = 10$, what is the value of $4x(x - y)$?
> Plug 15 in for x and 10 in for y.

$$4(15)(15 - 10) =$$

Then evaluate.

$$(60)(5) = 300$$

Picking Numbers

As described in the beginning of this chapter, picking numbers is a very useful strategy for avoiding lots of tedious calculations. Instead of solving the equation and figuring out which answer choice matches your answer, you plug choices back into the equation until one fits.

Some typical questions that can be solved by picking numbers are:

- Age stated in terms of variables
- Remainder problems
- Percentages or fractions of variables
- Even/odd variables calculations
- Questions with algebraic expressions as answers

Inequalities

Solve **inequalities** like you would any other equation. Isolate the variable for which you are solving on one side of the inequality symbol and everything else on the other side.

$$4a + 6 > 2a + 10$$
$$4a - 2a > 10 - 6$$
$$2a > 4$$
$$a > 2$$

The only difference here is that instead of finding a specific value for a, you get a range of values for a. The rest of the math is the same.

There is, however, one *crucial* difference between solving equations and inequalities. **When you multiply or divide both sides of an inequality by a *negative* number, you must change the direction of the sign.**

$$-5a > 10$$
$$a < -2$$

If this seems confusing, think about the logic. You're told that −5 times something is greater than 10. This is where your knowledge of positives and negatives comes into play. You know that negative × positive = negative and negative × negative = positive. Since −5 is negative and 10 is positive, −5 has to be multiplied by something negative to get a positive product. Therefore a has to be less than −2, not greater than it. If $a > -2$, then any value for a that is greater than −2 should make −5a less than 10. Say a is 20. −5a would be −100, which is certainly NOT greater than 10.

While it's a good idea to memorize the fact that you need to flip the sign if you multiply or divide both sides of an inequality by a negative, the math makes sense if you think about it.

Exercise

xii. Solve for y in each of the following inequalities:

$$y + 2 > 10$$
$$10 + 2y - 3 < 4 - y$$
$$6y < -20 + y$$
$$18 - 6y > 12$$
$$3(y + 10) - 4 > 2 + 5(2y - 3)$$

Exercise Answers

i.   (B) $(11 + 3x) - (5 - 2x) =$
$11 + 3x - 5 + 2x =$
$11 - 5 + 3x + 2x = 6 + 5x$

ii. $-4a - b$

iii. $-a$

iv. $3y$

v. $m2 + 10m + 16$

vi. $n2 - 3n - 18$

vii. $a = -1$

viii. $y = 7$

ix. $x = 5$

x. $a = \dfrac{b}{5}$

xi. $x = 4$

xii. $y > 8$
$y < -3$
$y < -4$
$y < 1$
$y < \dfrac{39}{7}$

Practice Questions

1. What is the value of $a(b-1) + \frac{bc}{2}$ if $a = 3$, $b = 6$, and $c = 5$?

   (A)   0
   (B)   15
   (C)   30
   (D)   45
   (E)   60

2. If $\frac{c}{d} = 3$ and $d = 1$, then $3c + d =$

   (F)   3
   (G)   4
   (H)   6
   (J)   7
   (K)   10

3. What is the value of x in the equation $5x - 7 = y$, if $y = 8$?

   (A)   −1
   (B)   1
   (C)   2
   (D)   3
   (E)   70

4. What is the value of $x(y - 2) + xz$, if $x = 2$, $y = 5$, and $z = 7$?

   (F)   12
   (G)   20
   (H)   22
   (J)   28
   (K)   32

5. If $x = \sqrt{3}$, $y = 2$, and $z = \frac{1}{2}$, then $x^2 - 5yz + y^2 =$

   (A)   1
   (B)   2
   (C)   4
   (D)   7
   (E)   8

6. If $x + y = 7$, what is the value of $2x + 2y - 2$?

   (F)   5
   (G)   9
   (H)   12
   (J)   14
   (K)   16

7. What is the value of a in the equation $3a - 6 = b$, if $b = 18$?

   (A)   4
   (B)   6
   (C)   8
   (D)   10
   (E)   18

8. If $\frac{x}{y} = \frac{2}{5}$ and $x = 10$, $y =$

   (F)   4
   (G)   10
   (H)   15
   (J)   20
   (K)   25

9. $-5n(3m - 2) =$

   (A) $-15mn + 10n$
   (B) $15mn - 10n$
   (C) $-8mn + 7n$
   (D) $8mn + 7n$
   (E) $-2mn - 7n$

10. What is the value of $(a + b)^2$, when $a = -1$ and $b = 3$?

    (F)   2
    (G)   4
    (H)   8
    (J)   10
    (K)   16

11. If $s - t = 5$, what is the value of $3s - 3t + 3$?

    (A)   2
    (B)   8
    (C)   11
    (D)   12
    (E)   18

12. $(3d - 7) - (5 - 2d) =$

    (F) $d - 12$
    (G) $5d - 2$
    (H) $5d + 12$
    (J) $5d - 12$
    (K) $8d + 5$

13. What is the value of $xyz + y(z - x) + 2x$ if $x = -2$, $y = 3$ and $z = 1$?

    (A)   −13
    (B)   −7
    (C)   −1
    (D)   7
    (E)   19

14. If $3x + 7 = 14$, then $x =$

    (F)   −14
    (G)   0
    (H) $\frac{7}{3}$
    (J)   3
    (K)   7

15. If x is an integer, which of the following expressions is always even?

  (A) $2x + 1$
  (B) $3x + 2$
  (C) $4x + 3$
  (D) $5x + 4$
  (E) $6x + 2$

16. If $4z - 3 = -19$, then $z =$

  (F) -16
  (G) $-5\frac{1}{2}$
  (H) -4
  (J) 0
  (K) 4

17. If $3ab = 6$, what is the value of a in terms of b?

  (A) 2
  (B) $\frac{2}{b}$
  (C) $\frac{2}{b^2}$
  (D) $2b$
  (E) $2b^2$

18. If x and y are integers, in which equation must x be negative?

  (F) $xy = -1$
  (G) $xy^2 = -1$
  (H) $x^2y = -1$
  (J) $x^2y^2 = 1$
  (K) $xy^2 = 1$

19. If n is an odd number, which of the following expressions is always odd?

  (A) $2n + 4$
  (B) $3n + 2$
  (C) $3n + 5$
  (D) $5n + 5$
  (E) $5n + 7$

20. If $5p + 12 = 17 - 4(\frac{p}{2} + 1)$, what is the value of p?

  (F) $\frac{1}{7}$
  (G) $\frac{1}{3}$
  (H) $\frac{6}{7}$
  (J) $1\frac{2}{7}$
  (K) 2

21. If $\frac{2x}{5y} = 6$, what is the value of y, in terms of x?

  (A) $\frac{x}{15}$
  (B) $\frac{x}{2}$
  (C) $\frac{15}{x}$
  (D) $15x$
  (E) $\frac{30}{x}$

22. If x is an odd integer and y is an even integer, which of the following expressions MUST be odd?

  (F) $2x + y$
  (G) $2(x + y)$
  (H) $x^2 + y^2$
  (J) $xy + y$
  (K) $2x + y^2$

23. If $100 \div x = 10n$, then which of the following is equal to nx?

  (A) 10
  (B) $10x$
  (C) 100
  (D) $10xn$
  (E) 1000

24. For what value of y is $4(y - 1) = 2(y + 2)$?

  (F) 0
  (G) 2
  (H) 4
  (J) 6
  (K) 8

25. $$\frac{3}{4} + x = 8.3$$

  What is the value of x in the equation above?

  (A) 4.9
  (B) 6.75
  (C) 7.55
  (D) 8.0
  (E) 9.05

26. If $2(a + m) = 5m - 3 + a$, what is the value of a, in terms of m?

  (F) $\frac{3m}{2}$
  (G) 3
  (H) $5m$
  (J) $4m + 33$
  (K) $3m - 3$

Practice Question Explanations

1. (C) Plug in $a = 3$, $b = 6$, and $c = 5$.

   $3(6 - 1) + \dfrac{6 \times 5}{2}$

   $= 3(5) + \dfrac{30}{2}$

   $= 15 + 15$

   $= 30$

2. (K) Since we're told the value of d, we can plug it into the equation $\dfrac{c}{d} = 3$ to find the value of c. We are told that $d = 1$, so $\dfrac{c}{d} = 3$ can be rewritten as $\dfrac{c}{1} = 3$. Since $\dfrac{c}{1}$ is the same as c, we can rewrite the equation again as $c = 3$. Now we can plug the values of c and d into the expression: $3(3) + 1 = 10$.

3. (D) We are told that $y = 8$, so first we'll replace the y in the equation with 8, and then we can solve for x.

   $5x - 7 = y$

   $5x - 7 = 8$

   Now we can add 7 to both sides:

   $5x - 7 + 7 = 8 + 7$

   $\qquad 5x = 15$

   Next we divide both sides by 5:

   $\dfrac{5x}{5} = \dfrac{15}{5}$

   $\quad x = 3$

4. (G) Here we have three values to plug in. Remember, xz means x times z. After we plug in the values of x, y, and z, we will do the operations in PEMDAS order—Parentheses, Exponents, Multiplication and Division, Addition and Subtraction.

   $x(y - 2) + xz = 2(5 - 2) + 2 \cdot 7$

   $\qquad\qquad\quad = 2(3) + 2 \cdot 7$

   $\qquad\qquad\quad = 6 + 14$

   $\qquad\qquad\quad = 20$

5. (B) This is another "plug in" question. Remember, $5yz$ means $5 \cdot y \cdot z$. First we will replace x, y, and z with the values given. Then we will carry out the indicated operations using the PEMDAS order of operations—Parentheses, Exponents, Multiplication and Division, Addition and Subtraction.

   $x^2 - 5yz + y^2 = (\sqrt{3})^2 - 5 \cdot 2 \cdot \dfrac{1}{2} + 2^2$

   $\qquad\qquad\quad = 3 - 5 \cdot 2 \cdot \dfrac{1}{2} + 4$

   $\qquad\qquad\quad = 3 - 5 + 4$

   $\qquad\qquad\quad = -2 + 4$

   $\qquad\qquad\quad = 2$

6. (H) If you look carefully at the expression $2x + 2y - 2$, you should see some similarity to $x + y = 7$. If we ignore the -2 for a moment, $2x + 2y$ is really just twice $x + y$. If it helps to make it clearer, we can factor out the 2, making $2x + 2y$ into $2(x + y)$. Since $x + y = 7$, $2(x + y)$ must equal $2(7)$, or 14. If we replace $2x + 2y$ with 14, the expression $2x + 2y - 2$ becomes $14 - 2$, which equals 12, or choice (H)

7. (C) Plug in 18 for b in the equation:

   $3a - 6 = 18$

   Isolate a on one side of the equation:

   $3a = 18 + 6$

   $3a = 24$

   Divide both sides by 3 to find the value of a:

   $a = 8$

8. (K) Substitute 10 for x in the equation:

$\frac{10}{y} = \frac{2}{5}$

Cross multiply:

$(10)(5) = (2)(y)$

$50 = 2y$

Divide both sides by 2 to find the value of y:

$\frac{50}{2} = \frac{2y}{2}$

$25 = y$

9. (A) Distribute $-5n$ to each term within the parentheses:

$-5n(3m - 2) = (-5n)(3m) + (-5n)(-2)$

Multiply through:

$= -15mn + 10n$

Note that $(-5n)(-2) = +10n$, because -1 times -1 is $+1$.

10. (G) Plug $a = -1$ and $b = 3$ into the expression:

$(-1 + 3)^2 =$

$\quad (2)^2 = 4$

11. (E) The expression can be rewritten as:

$3(s - t) + 3$

Plug in 5 for $s - t$:

$3(5) + 3$

$15 + 3$

18

12. (J) Perform the operations:

$3d - 7 - 5 - (-2d)$

Combine like terms:

$3d - (-2d) - 7 - 5$

$5d - 12$

Note that $3d$ minus $-2d$ equals $+5d$, because -1 times -1 is $+1$.

13. (C) Plug in $x = -2$, $y = 3$, and $z = 1$:

$(-2)(3)(1) + 3[(1 - (-2)] + 2(-2)$

$-6 + 3(3) - 4$

$-6 + 9 - 4$

$3 - 4$

-1

14. (H) To solve this problem, we have to rearrange the equation until the x is alone on one side of the $=$ sign. Remember that when you do something to one side of the equation, you must do the same thing to the other side.

First we will take away the 7 from both sides:

$3x + 7 = 14$

$3x + 7 - 7 = 14 - 7$

$3x = 7$

$\frac{3x}{3} = \frac{7}{3}$

$x = \frac{7}{3}$

15. (E) This is another question for which we have to try each answer choice until we find one that represents an even number. Notice that the question asks which expression is always even. (E), $6x + 2$, is correct. Since 6 is even, the product of 6 and any integer is even. The sum of two even numbers is an even number, so $6x + 2$ is even.

16. (H) In this question, we must rearrange the equation until the z is alone on one side of the = sign. Anything we do to one side of the equation we must also do to the other side.

First we'll add 3 to both sides:

$$4z - 3 = -19$$
$$4z - 3 + 3 = -19 + 3$$
$$4z = -16$$

Next we'll divide both sides by 4:

$$\frac{4z}{4} = -\frac{16}{4}$$
$$z = -4$$

17. (B) To solve this problem, we have to rearrange the equation until we have the variable a alone on one side of the = sign.

$$3ab = 6$$
$$\frac{3ab}{3} = \frac{6}{3}$$
$$ab = 2$$
$$\frac{ab}{b} = \frac{2}{b}$$
$$a = \frac{2}{b}$$

18. (G) For this question we will have to try each answer choice until we find the correct one.

(F) $xy = -1$. If the product of two integers is negative, then one of the two integers must be negative. In this case x could be negative, but it's possible that y is negative and x is positive. We're looking for an equation where x will always have to be negative, so this isn't the answer.

(G) $xy^2 = -1$. The exponent here applies only to the y, not to the x. The square of any non-zero number is positive, so whatever y is, y^2 must be positive. (We know that y isn't zero; if it were, then the product xy^2 would also be zero.) Since y^2 is positive and the product of y^2 and x is negative, x must be negative. (G) is the answer.

19. (B) We're told that n is odd, so we don't have to check to see what happens if n is even. We do have to try each answer to see which one represents an odd number. Let's say $n = 3$ and replace all the n's with 3's.

(A) $2n + 4$. $2(3) + 4 = 6 + 4 = 10$. 10 is even,

(B) $3n + 2$. $3(3) + 2 = 9 + 2 = 11$. 11 is odd, so (B) is the answer.

20. (F) This equation takes a few more steps than the previous ones, but it follows the same rules.

First we multiply using the distributive law:

$$5p + 12 = 17 - 4(\tfrac{p}{2} + 1)$$
$$5p + 12 = 17 + (-4) \cdot \left(\frac{p}{2}\right) + (-4) \cdot (1)$$
$$5p + 12 = 17 + \left(-\frac{4p}{2}\right) + (-4)$$

$\frac{4p}{2}$ is equal to $2p$, so

$$5p + 12 = 17 - 2p - 4$$

Now we can combine the integers on the right side:

$$5p + 12 = 13 - 2p$$

We can add $2p$ to each side to get all the ps on one side:

$$5p + 2p + 12 = 13 - 2p + 2p$$
$$7p + 12 = 13$$

Now we will subtract 12 from both sides:

$$7p + 12 - 12 = 13 - 12$$
$$7p = 1$$

And lastly, we divide both sides by 7:

$$\frac{7p}{7} = \frac{1}{7}$$
$$p = \frac{1}{7}$$

21. (A) We want to rearrange the equation until y is alone one side of the = sign. There's more than one way to do this, but here's one way:

$$\frac{2x}{5y} = 6$$
$$(5y)\frac{2x}{5y} = 6(5y)$$
$$2x = 30y$$
$$\frac{x}{15} = y$$

22. (H) This is another "try each answer" problem. We know that x is odd and y is even. Let's say that $x = 3$ and $y = 4$.

    (F) $2x + y$. $2(3) + 4 = 6 + 4 = 10$. 10 is even, so this isn't correct.

    (G) $2(x + y)$. $2(3 + 4) = 2(3 + 4) = 2(7) = 14$. 14 is even.

    (H) $x^2 + y^2$. $3^2 + 4^2 = 9 + 16 = 25$. 25 is odd, so (H) is correct.

23. (A) This problem looks harder than it really is. If

$$100 \div x = 10n \text{ then}$$
$$10n \bullet x = 100 \text{ or}$$
$$10nx = 100$$
$$nx = 10, \text{ choice (A)}$$

24. (H) Multiply through and solve for y by isolating it on one side of the equation:

$$4(y - 1) = 2(y + 2)$$
$$4y - 4 = 2y + 4$$
$$2y - 4 = 4$$
$$2y = 8$$
$$\frac{2y}{2} = \frac{8}{2}$$
$$y = 4$$

25. (C) Isolate x on one side of the equation:

$$\frac{3}{4} + x = 8.3$$
$$\frac{3}{4} + x - \frac{3}{4} = 8.3 - \frac{3}{4}$$
$$x = 8.3 - \frac{3}{4}$$

$\frac{3}{4}$ can be rewritten as 0.75, so subtracting 0.75 from 8.3 gives you 7.55.

26. (K) Multiply through and then find a in terms of m by isolating a on one side of the equation:

$$2(a + m) = 5m - 3 + a$$
$$2a + 2m = 5m - 3 + a$$
$$2a = 3m - 3 + a$$
$$a = 3m - 3$$

8

Arithmetic

- Review of SSAT/ISEE arithmetic concepts: fractions, percents, ratios, probability, etc.

- Tips for solving SSAT/ISEE arithmetic problems

OVERVIEW

On the SSAT/ISEE, **Arithmetic** means more than addition and subtraction. **Arithmetic** is the umbrella term for a wide range of math concepts, including **number properties**, **factors**, **divisibility**, **fractions**, **decimals**, **exponents**, **radicals**, **percents**, **averages**, **ratios**, **proportions**, **rates**, and **probability**. These concepts are summarized in your Math Reference at the end of the book. This section will go over these important concepts and give you a chance to practice problems dealing with these subjects.

First, take a look at a few definitions:

Number Type:	Definition:	Examples:
Integers	*Whole numbers, including 0 and negative whole numbers*	$-900, -3, 0, 1, 54$
Fractions	*A **fraction** is a number that is written in the form $\frac{A}{B}$ where A is the numerator and B is the denominator.*	$-\frac{5}{6}, -\frac{3}{17}, \frac{1}{2}, \frac{899}{901}$
	*An **improper fraction** is a number that is greater than 1 (or less than -1) that is written in the form of a fraction. Improper fractions can be converted to a **mixed number**.*	$-\frac{65}{64}, \frac{9}{8}, \frac{57}{10}$ $-1\frac{1}{64}, 1\frac{1}{8}, 5\frac{7}{10}$
Positive/Negative	*Numbers greater than 0 are positive numbers; numbers less than 0 are negative. 0 is neither positive nor negative.*	Positive: $\frac{7}{8}, 1, 5, 900$ Negative: $-64, -40, -11, -\frac{6}{13}$
Even/Odd	*An even number is an integer that is a multiple of 2.*	Even numbers: $-8, -2, 0, 4, 12, 188$
	An odd number is an integer that is not a multiple of 2.	Odd numbers: $-17, -1, 3, 9, 457$
Prime Number	*An integer greater than 1 that has no factors other than 1 and itself.* *2 is the only even prime number.*	$2, 3, 5, 7, 11, 59, 83$
Consecutive Numbers	*Numbers that follow one after another, in order, without skipping any.*	Consecutive integers: $3, 4, 5, 6$ Consecutive even integers: $2, 4, 6, 8, 10$ Consecutive multiples of 9: $9, 18, 27, 36$
Factor	*A positive integer that divides evenly into a given number with no remainder.*	The complete list of factors of 12: $1, 2, 3, 4, 6, 12$
Multiple	*A number that a given number will divide into with no remainder.*	Some multiples of 12: $0, 12, 24, 60$

Odds and Evens

Even ± Even = Even

Even ± Odd = Odd

Odd ± Odd = Even

Even × Even = Even

Even × Odd = Even

Odd × Odd = Odd

Positives and Negatives

There are few things to remember about positives and negatives. You will not see many problems that focus specifically on positives and negatives, but you must know the basics because these concepts will show up as part of harder problems.

Adding a negative number is basically subtraction.

6 + (−4) is really 6 − 4 or 2.

4 + (−6) is really 4 − 6 or −2.

Subtracting a negative number is basically addition.

6 − (−4) is really 6 + 4 or 10.

−6 − (−4) is really −6 + 4 or −2.

Multiplying and **Dividing** positives and negatives is like all other multiplication and division, with one catch. To figure out whether your product is positive or negative, simply count the number of negatives you had to start. If you had an odd number of negatives, the product is negative. If you had an even number of negatives, the product is positive.

6 × (−4) = −24 (1 negative → negative product)

(−6) × (−4) = 24 (2 negatives → positive product)

(−1) × (−6) × (−4) = −24 (3 negatives → negative product)

Similarly,

−24 ÷ 6 = −4 (1 negative → negative quotient)

−24 ÷ (−4) = 6 (2 negatives → positive quotient)

Negative × or ÷ negative = positive

Positive × or ÷ negative = negative

To find the absolute value of a number, simply strip it of its sign.

Absolute Value

To find the **absolute value** of a number, simply strip the number within the vertical lines of its sign.

$$|4| = 4$$
$$|-4| = 4$$

When absolute value expressions contain different arithmetic operations, perform the operation and then strip the sign from the result.

$$|-6 + 4| = |-2| = 2$$
$$|(-6) \times 4| = |-24| = 24$$

Exercise

   i. $\ |-11.8| = $ ____

   ii. $\ |5 - 6| = $ ____

   iii. $\ |-3.5 + 1| - |-15 - 17| = $ ____

Factors and Multiples

To find the **prime factorization** of a number, keep breaking it down until you are left with only prime numbers.

To find the prime factorization of 168:

$$168 = 4 \times 42$$
$$= 4 \times 6 \times 7$$
$$= 2 \times 2 \times 2 \times 3 \times 7$$

To find the **greatest common factor (GCF)** of two integers, break down both integers into their prime factorizations and multiply all prime factors they have in common.

If you're looking for the greatest common factor of 40 and 130, first identify the prime factors of each integer.

$$40 = 4 \times 10$$
$$= 2 \times 2 \times 2 \times 5$$
$$140 = 10 \times 14$$
$$= 2 \times 5 \times 2 \times 7$$
$$= 2 \times 2 \times 5 \times 7$$

Next, see what prime factors the two numbers have in common and then multiply these common factors.

Both integers share two 2's and 5, so the GCF is $2 \times 2 \times 5$ or 20.

If you need to find a **common multiple** of two integers, you can always multiply them. However, you can use prime factors to find the **least common multiple (LCM)**. To do this, multiply all of the prime factors of each integer as many times as they appear. This may sound confusing, but it becomes pretty clear once it's demonstrated. Take a look at the example to see how it works.

Common multiple of 20 and 16:
$20 \times 16 = 320$

320 is a common multiple of 20 and 16, but it is not the least common multiple.

Least common multiple of 20 and 16:
$20 = 2 \times 2 \times 5$
$16 = 2 \times 2 \times 2 \times 2$

Least common multiple $= 2 \times 2 \times 2 \times 2 \times 5 = 80$

The Order of Operations

You need to remember the order in which arithmetic operations must be performed. PEMDAS (or Please Excuse My Dear Aunt Sally) may help you remember the order.

Please = Parentheses
Excuse = Exponents
My Dear = Multiplication and Division (from left to right)
Aunt Sally = Addition and Subtraction (from left to right)

$3^3 - 8(4 - 2) + 60 \div 4$
$= 3^3 - 8(2) + 60 \div 4$
$= 27 - 8(2) + 60 \div 4$
$= 27 - 16 + 15$
$= 11 + 15$
$= 26$

Divisibility Rules

If you've forgotten—or never learned—divisibility rules, spend a little time with this chart. Even if you remember the rules, take a moment to refresh your recollection. Remember, there are no easy divisibility rules for 7 and 8.

> **When Performing Multiple Operations, Remember This**
>
> Make sure you use the right order of operations: Parentheses, Exponents, Multiplication and Division, Addition and Subtraction (PEMDAS). You may find it easier to remember as Please Excuse My Dear Aunt Sally.

> **Kaplan Rules**
>
> Don't confuse the divisibility tests. To test for 2, 4, 5, or 10, just look at the last digit or two. To test for 3 or 9, add all the digits.

Divisible by:	The Rule:	Example: 558
2	The last digit is even.	a multiple of 2 because 8 is even
3	The sum of the digits is a multiple of 3.	a multiple of 3 because $5 + 5 + 8 = 18$, which is a multiple of 3
4	The last 2 digits comprise a 2-digit multiple of 4.	NOT a multiple of 4 because 58 is not a multiple of 4
5	The last digit is 5 or 0.	NOT a multiple of 5 because it doesn't end in 5 or 0
6	The last digit is even AND the sum of the digits is a multiple of 3.	a multiple of 6 because it's a multiple of both 2 and 3
9	The sum of the digits is a multiple of 9.	a multiple of 9 because $5 + 5 + 8 = 18$, which is a multiple of 9
10	The last digit is 0.	not a multiple of 10 because it doesn't end in 0

Exercise

iv. What are the following numbers divisible by?

1,455 _____

50,022 _____

0 _____

Fractions and Decimals

Generally, it's a good idea to **reduce fractions** when solving math questions. To do this, simply, cancel all factors that the numerator and denominator have in common.

$$\frac{28}{36} = \frac{4 \times 7}{4 \times 9} = \frac{7}{9}$$

To **add fractions**, get a common denominator and then add the numerators.

$$\frac{1}{4} + \frac{1}{3} = \frac{3}{12} + \frac{4}{12} = \frac{3+4}{12} = \frac{7}{12}$$

To **subtract fractions**, get a common denominator and then subtract the numerators.

$$\frac{1}{4} - \frac{1}{3} = \frac{3}{12} - \frac{4}{12} = \frac{3-4}{12} = -\frac{1}{12}$$

To **multiply fractions**, multiply the numerators and multiply the denominators.

$$\frac{1}{4} \times \frac{1}{3} = \frac{1 \times 1}{4 \times 3} = \frac{1}{12}$$

To **divide fractions**, invert the second fraction and multiply. In other words, multiply the first fraction by the **reciprocal** of the second fraction.

$$\frac{1}{4} \div \frac{1}{3} = \frac{1}{4} \times \frac{3}{1} = \frac{1 \times 3}{4 \times 1} = \frac{3}{4}$$

To **compare fractions**, multiply the numerator of the first fraction by the denominator of the second fraction to get a product. Then, multiply the numerator of the second fraction by the denominator of the first fraction to get a second product. If the first product is greater, the first fraction is greater. If the second product is greater, the second fraction is greater.

Compare $\frac{2}{3}$ and $\frac{5}{8}$.

16 is greater than 15, so $\frac{2}{3}$ is greater than $\frac{5}{8}$.

To **convert a fraction to a decimal**, divide the denominator into the numerator.

To convert $\frac{8}{25}$ to a decimal, divide 25 into 8.

$$\frac{8}{25} = 0.32$$

To **convert a decimal to a fraction**, first set the decimal over 1. Then, move the decimal over as many places as it takes until it is immediately to the right of the digit furthest to the right. Count the number of places that you moved the decimal. Then add that many 0's to the 1 in the denominator.

$$0.3 = \frac{0.3}{1} = \frac{3.0}{10} \text{ or } \frac{3}{10}$$

$$0.32 = \frac{0.32}{1} = \frac{32.0}{100} \text{ or } \frac{8}{25}$$

Exercise

v. Reduce the following fractions and expressions to lowest terms:

$$\frac{39}{72} = \underline{\qquad}$$

$$\frac{248}{504} = \underline{\qquad}$$

$$\frac{5}{9} + \frac{2}{6} = \underline{\qquad}$$

$$\frac{1}{2} - \frac{3}{7} = \underline{\qquad}$$

$$\frac{5}{21} \times \frac{7}{25} = \underline{\qquad}$$

$$\frac{13}{4} \div \frac{39}{12} = \underline{\qquad}$$

vi. Convert the following fractions to decimals:

$$\frac{11}{16} = \underline{\qquad}$$

$$\frac{5}{8} = \underline{\qquad}$$

vii. Convert the following decimals to fractions:

$$0.15 = \underline{\qquad}$$

$$0.64 = \underline{\qquad}$$

Common Percent Equivalencies

Familiarity with the relationships among percents, decimals, and fractions can save you time on test day. Don't worry about memorizing the following chart. Simply use it to refresh your recollection of relationships you already know (e.g., $50\% = 0.50 = \frac{1}{2}$) and to familiarize yourself with some that you might not already know. To convert a fraction or decimal to a percent, multiply by 100%. To convert a percent to a fraction or decimal, divide by 100%.

Fraction	Decimal	Percent
$\frac{1}{20}$	0.05	5%
$\frac{1}{10}$	0.10	10%
$\frac{1}{8}$	0.125	12.5%
$\frac{1}{6}$	$0.16\overline{6}$	$16\frac{2}{3}\%$
$\frac{1}{5}$	0.20	20%
$\frac{1}{4}$	0.25	25%
$\frac{1}{3}$	$0.33\overline{3}$	$33\frac{1}{3}\%$
$\frac{3}{8}$	0.375	37.5%

Fraction	Decimal	Percent
$\frac{2}{5}$	0.40	40%
$\frac{1}{2}$	0.50	50%
$\frac{3}{5}$	0.60	60%
$\frac{2}{3}$	$0.6\overline{66}$	$66\frac{2}{3}\%$
$\frac{3}{4}$	0.75	75%
$\frac{4}{5}$	0.80	80%
$\frac{5}{6}$	$0.8\overline{33}$	$83\frac{1}{3}\%$
$\frac{7}{8}$	0.875	87.5%

Exponents and Roots

Exponents are the small raised numbers written to the right of a variable or number. They indicate the number of times that variable or number is to be used as a factor. On the SSAT/ISEE, you'll usually deal with numbers or variables that are squared, but you could see a few other concepts involving exponents.

To **add** or **subtract** terms consisting of a coefficient (the number in front of the variable) multiplied by a power (a power is a base raised to an exponent), both the base and the exponent *must* be the same. As long as the bases and the exponents are the same, you can add the coefficients.

$x^2 + x^2 = 2x^2$
$3x^4 - 2x^4 = x^4$
$x^2 + x^3$ cannot be combined.
$x^2 + y^2$ cannot be combined.

To **multiply** terms consisting of coefficients multiplied by powers having the same base, multiply the coefficients and add the exponents.

$2x^5 \times 8x^7 = (2 \times 8)(x^{5+7}) = 16x^{12}$

To **divide** terms consisting of coefficients multiplied by powers having the same base, divide the coefficients and subtract the exponents.

$6x^7 \div 2x^5 = (6 \div 2)(x^{7-5}) = 3x^2$

Kaplan Rules

To multiply powers with the same base, add exponents. To raise a power to an exponent, multiply exponents.

To **raise a power to an exponent**, multiply the exponents.

$$(x^2)^4 = x^{2 \times 4} = x^8$$

A **square root** of a nonnegative number is a number that, when multiplied by itself, produces the given quantity. The radical sign "$\sqrt{}$" is used to represent the positive square root of a number, so $\sqrt{25} = 5$, since $5 \times 5 = 25$.

To **add** or **subtract** radicals, make sure the numbers under the radical sign are the same. If they are, you can add or subtract the coefficients outside the radical signs.

$$2\sqrt{2} + 3\sqrt{2} = 5\sqrt{2}$$
$$\sqrt{2} + \sqrt{3} \text{ cannot be combined.}$$

To **simplify** radicals, factor out the perfect squares under the radical, unsquare them, and put the result in front of the radical sign.

$$\sqrt{32} = \sqrt{16 \times 2} = 4\sqrt{2}$$

To **multiply** or **divide** radicals, multiply (or divide) the coefficients outside the radical. Multiply (or divide) the numbers inside the radicals.

$$\sqrt{xy} = \sqrt{x} \times \sqrt{y}$$
$$3\sqrt{2} \times 4\sqrt{5} = 12\sqrt{10}$$

$$\sqrt{\frac{x}{y}} = \frac{\sqrt{x}}{\sqrt{y}}$$

$$12\sqrt{10} \div 3\sqrt{2} = 4\sqrt{5}$$

To **take the square root of a fraction**, break the fraction into two separate roots and take the square root of the numerator and the denominator.

$$\sqrt{\frac{16}{25}} = \frac{\sqrt{16}}{\sqrt{25}} = \frac{4}{5}$$

Exercise

viii. Simplify the following expressions.

$$x^5 + 2x^5 = \underline{\hphantom{xxx}}$$

$$2x(x^2 + 3y) = \underline{\hphantom{xxx}}$$

$$(x^4)^3 = \underline{\hphantom{xxx}}$$

$$\sqrt{49} - \sqrt{16} = \underline{\hphantom{xxx}}$$

$$\sqrt{2} \times \sqrt{10} = \underline{\hphantom{xxx}}$$

$$\sqrt{\frac{25}{64}} = \underline{\hphantom{xxx}}$$

Scientific Notation

The exponent of a power of 10 indicates how many zeros the number would contain if it were written out. For example, $10^4 = 10,000$ (4 zeros) since the product of 4 factors of 10 is equal to 10,000.

When multiplying a number by a power of 10, move the decimal point to the right the same number of places as the number of zeros in that power of 10.

$$0.0123 \times 10^4 = 123$$

When dividing by a power of 10, move the decimal point, to the left.

$$43.21 \div 10^3 = 0.04321$$

Multiplying by a power with a negative exponent is the same as dividing by a power with a positive exponent. Therefore, when you multiply by a number with a positive exponent, move the decimal to the right. When you multiply by a number with a negative exponent, move the decimal to the left.

Percents

Remember this formula Part = Percent × Whole or Percent = $\dfrac{\text{Part}}{\text{Whole}}$

To find **part, percent**, or **whole** plug the values you have into the equation and solve.

$$44\% \text{ of } 25 = 0.44 \times 25 = 11$$

42 is what percent of 70 ?

$$42 \div 70 = 0.6$$
$$0.6 \times 100\% = 60\%$$

To **increase or decrease a number by a given percent**, take that percent of the original number and add it to or subtract it from the original number.

To increase 25 by 60%, first find 60% of 25.

$$25 \times 0.6 = 15.$$

Then add the result to the original number.

$$25 + 15 = 40.$$

To decrease 25 by the same percent, subtract the 15.

$$25 - 15 = 10.$$

Exercise

ix. 16 of the 64 cookies on the tray are chocolate chip. What percent are NOT chocolate chip? _____

x. 3% of 42 equals 42% of _____.

Average, Median, and Mode

$$\text{Average} = \frac{\text{Sum of the terms}}{\text{Number of terms}}$$

The average of 15, 18, 15, 32, and 20 $= \frac{15 + 18 + 15 + 32 + 20}{5} = \frac{100}{5} = 20$

When there are an odd number of terms, the Median of a group of terms is the value of the middle term, with the terms arranged in increasing order.

Suppose that you want to find the median of the terms 15, 18, 15, 32, and 20. First, put the terms in order from small to large. 15, 15, 18, 20, 32.

Then, identify the middle term. The middle term is 18.

When there are an even number of terms, the Median is the average of the two middle terms with the terms arranged in increasing order.

Suppose that you want to find the mode of the terms 15, 18, 15, 32, and 20. The Mode is the value of the term that occurs most. 15 occurs twice, so it is the mode.

Exercise

xi. There are five children whose ages are 11, 5, 8, 5, and 6.

What is the average age? _____

What is the median age? _____

Which age is the mode? _____

Ratios, Proportions, and Rates

Ratios can be expressed in two forms.

The first form is $\frac{a}{b}$.

If you have 15 dogs and 5 cats, the ratio of dogs to cats is $\frac{15}{5}$. (The ratio of cats to dogs is $\frac{5}{15}$.) Like any other fraction, this ratio can be reduced. $\frac{15}{5}$ can be reduced to $\frac{3}{1}$. In other words, for every three dogs, there's one cat.

The second form is **a:b**.

The ratio of dogs to cats is 15:5 or 3:1. The ratio of cats to dogs is 5:15 or 1:3.

Pay attention to what ratio is specified in the problem. Remember that the ratio of dogs to cats is different from the ratio of cats to dogs.

To solve a **proportion**, cross-multiply and solve for the variable.

$$\frac{x}{6} = \frac{2}{3}$$

$$3x = 12$$

$$x = 4$$

A **rate** is a ratio that compares quantities measured in different units. The most common example is *miles per hour*. Use the following formula for such problems:

Distance = Rate $\times$ Time

Remember that although not all rates are speeds, this formula can be adapted to any rate.

Exercise

xii. There are 18 white marbles and 6 red marbles in a bag. What is the ratio of red marbles to white marbles? _____

xiii. $\frac{36}{8} = \frac{9}{y}$. What is the value of y ? _____

xiv. If it took Michael three hours to bike 48 miles, what was his average speed in miles per hour?

_____

Probability

An **event** is a collection or set of outcomes.

For example, suppose that a die with faces numbered 1, 2, 3, 4, 5, and 6 is rolled. All the possible outcomes are 1, 2, 3, 4, 5, and 6. Let A be the event that a 1, 3, or 5 is rolled. The event A is made up of the outcomes 1, 3, and 5. Thus A can also be described by saying that the number rolled is odd. A possible outcome is the elementary building block from which events are made up.

An event is a set of possible outcomes. Of course, it is possible for an event to consist of a single possible outcome. For example, suppose that $B = \{4\}$, that is, the event B is the result that a 4 is rolled. An event consisting of a single possible outcome is called an elementary event. Thus, B, which is $\{4\}$, is an elementary event.

However, in general, an outcome is more elementary than an event, with an event being a set of possible outcomes. For example, the event $C = \{1, 2, 4, 6\}$ is the event that one of the possible outcomes 1, 2, 4, and 6 results. Note that C is not an elementary event.

To find the **probability** that an event will occur, use the formula

$$\text{Probability} = \frac{\text{Number of desirable outcomes}}{\text{Number of possible outcomes}}$$

If there are 12 books on a shelf and 9 of them are mysteries, what is the probability of picking a mystery?

$\frac{9}{12} = \frac{3}{4}$. This probability can also be expressed as 0.75 or 75%.

To find the probability that two **events** will occur, find the probability that the first event occurs and multiply this by the probability that the second event occurs given that the first event occurs.

If there are 12 books on a shelf and 9 of them are mysteries, what is the probability of picking a mystery first and a non-mystery second if exactly two books are selected?

Probability of picking a mystery: $\frac{9}{12} = \frac{3}{4}$.

Look Out

> If it's a symbol you've never seen before, you can be sure the Testmaker just made it up.

Probability of picking a nonmystery: $\frac{3}{11}$. (Originally there were 9 mysteries and 3 nonmysteries. After the mystery is selected, there are 8 mysteries and 3 nonmysteries, i.e., 11 books remaining.)

Probability of picking both books: $\frac{3}{4} \times \frac{3}{11} = \frac{9}{44}$.

Strange Symbolism and Terminology

Some math problems will be confusing because you're unfamiliar with the math concept being tested. Other problems will seem confusing because the math has literally been made up just for the purposes of the Test. The Test makers make up math symbols and terminology to test your ability to deal with unfamiliar concepts.

Kaplan Rules

> Made up terminology will most likely be in quotes.

These problems aren't as hard as they sound. When a strange symbol appears in a math problem, the problem will **always** indicate what the symbol means. Similarly, if you see strange terminology, it will **always** be defined. The problems are essentially about following directions, so don't panic when you see them. All you have to do is slow down, read the problem and follow the directions.

If $x<<>>y = \sqrt{x + y}$, what is $9<<>>16$?

All you have to do here is to plug $9<<>>16$ into the defining equation: $\sqrt{9+16} = \sqrt{25} = 5$.

To "chomp" a number, take the sum of the digits of that number and divide this value by the number of digits. What value do you get when you "chomp" 43,805 ?

$4 + 3 + 8 + 0 + 5 = 20$

$20 \div 5 = 4$

Exercise Answers

i. 11.8

ii. 1

iii. −29.5

iv. 3, 5
2, 3, 6, 9
0 is divisible by every nonzero integer.

v. $\frac{13}{24}, \frac{31}{63}, \frac{8}{9}, \frac{1}{14}, \frac{1}{15}, 1$

vi. 0.6875, 0.625

vii. $\frac{3}{20}, \frac{16}{25}$

viii. $3x^5, 2x^3 + 6xy, x^{12}, 3, 2\sqrt{5}, \frac{5}{8}$

ix. 75%

x. 3

xi. 7, 6, 5

xii. 1:3

xiii. $y = 2$

xiv. 16 mph

Practice Questions

1. Which of the following is not even?

    (A) 330
    (B) 436
    (C) 752
    (D) 861
    (E) 974

2. What is the least prime number greater than 50 ?

    (F) 51
    (G) 53
    (H) 55
    (J) 57
    (K) 59

3. Which of the following is a multiple of 2 ?

    (A) 271
    (B) 357
    (C) 463
    (D) 599
    (E) 756

4. $\dfrac{15 \times 7 \times 3}{9 \times 5 \times 2} =$

    (F) $\dfrac{2}{7}$

    (G) $\dfrac{3}{5}$

    (H) $3\dfrac{1}{2}$

    (J) 7

    (K) $7\dfrac{1}{2}$

5. What is the least common multiple of 18 and 24 ?

    (A)   6
    (B) 54
    (C) 72
    (D) 96
    (E) 432

6. Which of the following is a multiple of 3 ?

    (F) 115
    (G) 370
    (H) 465
    (J) 589
    (K) 890

7. $-6(3 - 4 \times 3) =$

    (A) −66
    (B) −54
    (C) − 12
    (D) 18
    (E) 54

8. Which of the following is a multiple of 10 ?

    (F)   10,005
    (G)   10,030
    (H)   10,101
    (J) 100,005
    (K) 101,101

9. Which of the following is a multiple of both 5 and 2 ?

    (A) 2,203
    (B) 2,342
    (C) 1,005
    (D) 7,790
    (E) 9,821

10. Which of the following is a multiple of both 3 and 10 ?

    (F) 103
    (G) 130
    (H) 210
    (J) 310
    (K) 460

11. Which of the following is a multiple of 2, 3, and 5 ?

    (A) 165
    (B) 235
    (C) 350
    (D) 420
    (E) 532

12. Which of the following is an even multiple of both 3 and 5 ?

    (F) 135
    (G) 155
    (H) 250
    (J) 350
    (K) 390

13. Professor Jones bought a large carton of books. She gave 3 books to each student in her class and there were no books left over. Which of the following could be the number of books she distributed?

    (A) 133
    (B) 143
    (C) 252
    (D) 271
    (E) 332

14. Two teams are having a contest. The prize is a box of candy that the members of the winning team will divide evenly. If team *A* wins, each player will get exactly 3 pieces of candy and if team *B* wins, each player will get exactly 5 pieces. Which of the following could be the number of pieces of candy in the box?

    (F) 153
    (G) 325
    (H) 333
    (J) 425
    (K) 555

15. Three consecutive multiples of 4 have a sum of 60. What is the greatest of these numbers?

    (A)   8
    (B) 12
    (C) 16
    (D) 20
    (E) 24

16. Sheila cuts a 60 foot wire cable in equal strips of $\frac{4}{5}$ of a feet each. How many strips does she make?

    (F) 48
    (G) 51
    (H) 60
    (J) 70
    (K) 75

17. Which of the following is NOT odd?

    (A) 349
    (B) 537
    (C) 735
    (D) 841
    (E) 918

18. Which of the following can be the sum of two negative numbers?

    (F)   4
    (G)   2
    (H)   1
    (J)   0
    (K) −1

19. Which of the following is NOT a prime number?

    (A)   2
    (B)   7
    (C)   17
    (D)   87
    (E) 101

20. All of the following can be the product of a negative integer and positive integer EXCEPT

    (F)   1
    (G) −1
    (H) −2
    (J) −4
    (K) −6

21. Susie and Dennis are training for a marathon. On Monday, they both run 3.2 miles. On Tuesday, Susie runs $5\frac{1}{5}$ miles and Dennis runs 3.6 miles. On Wednesday, Susie runs 4.8 miles and Dennis runs $2\frac{2}{5}$ miles. During those 3 days, how many more miles does Susie run than Dennis?

    (A) 4.8
    (B) 4.0
    (C) 3.2
    (D) 3.0
    (E) 2.4

22. Which number is a multiple of 60 ?

    (F)   213
    (G)   350
    (H)   540
    (J)   666
    (K) 1,060

23. Two odd integers and one even integer are multiplied together. Which of the following could be their product?

    (A)   1.5
    (B)   3
    (C)   6
    (D)   7.2
    (E) 15

24. If the number 9,899,399 is increased by 2,082, the result will be

   (F)   9,902,481
   (G)   9,901,481
   (H)   9,901,471
   (J)   9,891,481
   (K)   901,481

25. What is the sum of five consecutive integers if the middle one is 13 ?

   (A)   55
   (B)   60
   (C)   65
   (D)   70
   (E)   75

26. $\frac{4x^5}{2x^2} =$

   (F) $2x^2$
   (G) $2x^3$
   (H) $2x^4$
   (J) $4x^2$
   (K) $4x^3$

27. $-2^3 (1-2)^3 + (-2)^3 =$

   (F) -12
   (G) -4
   (H)   0
   (J)   4
   (K)   12

28. n is an odd integer and $10 < n < 19$. What is the mean of all possible values of n ?

   (F)   13
   (G)   13.5
   (H)   14
   (J)   14.5
   (K)   15.5

29. $a \Delta b = \frac{3a}{b}$. What is $\frac{14}{32} \Delta 1\frac{3}{4}$?

   (A) $\frac{1}{4}$
   (B) $\frac{1}{3}$
   (C) $\frac{1}{2}$
   (D) $\frac{3}{4}$
   (E) $\frac{49}{64}$

30. Jon works 4.5 hours a day, 3 days each week after school. He is paid $4.25 per hour. How much is his weekly pay (rounded to the next highest cent)?

   (F) $12.75
   (G) $13.50
   (H) $19.13
   (J) $54.00
   (K) $57.38

31. Zim buys a calculator that is marked 30% off. If he pays $35, what was the original price?

   (A) $24.50
   (B) $45.50
   (C) $47.00
   (D) $50.00
   (E) $62.50

32. A museum records 16 visitors to an exhibit on Monday, 21 on Tuesday, 20 on Wednesday, 17 on Thursday, 19 on Friday, 21 on Saturday, and 17 on Sunday, what is the median number of visitors for the week?

   (F)   18.50
   (G)   18.75
   (H)   19
   (J)   19.50
   (K)   19.75

33. A bag contains 8 white, 4 red, 7 green and 5 blue marbles. 8 marbles are withdrawn randomly. How many of the withdrawn marbles were white if the chance of drawing a white marble is now $\frac{1}{4}$?

   (A)   0
   (B)   3
   (C)   4
   (D)   5
   (E)   6

34. $\sqrt{1,500} =$

   (F) $10 + \sqrt{15}$
   (G) $10\sqrt{15}$
   (H)   25
   (J) $100 + \sqrt{15}$
   (K) $10\sqrt{150}$

35. $2(3 \times 2)^2 - 27(6 \div 2) + 3^2 =$

   (A)   72
   (B)   9
   (C)   3
   (D)   0
   (E) -24

36. Which of the following numbers is closest to the product 48.9×21.2 ?

    (F)   10,000
    (G)   8,000
    (H)   1,000
    (J)   100
    (K)   70

37. $|16 - 25| + \sqrt{25 - 16} =$

    (A)   –12
    (B)   –6
    (C)   0
    (D)   6
    (E)   12

38. Which of the following is 81,455 rounded to the nearest 100 ?

    (F)   81,000
    (G)   81,400
    (H)   81,500
    (J)   82,000
    (K)   90,000

39. If 35% of x is 7, what is x% of 35 ?

    (A)   7
    (B)   20
    (C)   28
    (D)   35
    (E)   42

40. A number is considered "blue" if the sum of its digits is equal to the product of its digits. Which of the following numbers is "blue"?

    (F)   111
    (G)   220
    (H)   321
    (J)   422
    (K)   521

41. When you "fix" –3, you get

    (A)   –13
    (B)   4
    (C)   5
    (D)   13
    (E)   14

To "fix" a number, you must perform the following four steps:

Step 1: Raise the number to the 3rd power.

Step 2: Divide the result by 2.

Step 3: Take the absolute value of the result of Step 2.

Step 4: Round off this result to the nearest whole number.

42. When D is divided by 15 the result is 6 with a remainder of 2. What is the remainder when D is divided by 6 ?

    (F)   0
    (G)   1
    (H)   2
    (J)   3
    (K)   4

43. For any two numbers a and b, a ? $b = (a + b)(a - b)$. For example, 10 ? 5 = (10 + 5)(10 – 5) = (15)(5) = 75. The value of 7 ? 5 is

    (A)   2
    (B)   12
    (C)   24
    (D)   36
    (E)   48

44. What is the greatest integer less than $\frac{71}{6}$?

    (F)   9
    (G)   10
    (H)   11
    (J)   12
    (K)   1345.Which of the following is NOT less than 0.25 ?

    (A) $\frac{2}{9}$

    (B) $\frac{3}{14}$

    (C) $\frac{16}{64}$

    (D) $\frac{19}{80}$

    (E) $\frac{4}{17}$

46. If the average of 5 consecutive odd numbers is 11, then the largest number is

    (F)   17
    (G)   15
    (H)   13
    (J)   11
    (K)   9

Practice Question Explanations

1. (D) The way to tell if an integer is even is to look at the last digit to the right—the ones' digit. If that digit is divisible by 2, or is 0, the number is even. Looking at the choices, only (D) ends in a number that isn't 0 and isn't divisible by 2, so only it is not even.

2. (G) A prime number is an integer greater than 1 that is divisible by only two different positive integers, itself and 1. Of the choices, only (G), 53 and (K), 59 are prime. You want the least prime number greater than 50, so (G) is correct. Using the divisibility rules would quickly show you that 51 and 57 are divisible by 3, while 55 is divisible by 5.

3. (E) If the ones digit of a number can be divided by 2, the number is divisible by 2. All of the answer choices except (E) end in an odd number, so only choice (E) is a multiple of 2.

4. (H) Before you do the multiplication, see which common factors in the numerator and denominator can be canceled. Canceling a 3 from the 3 in the numerator and the 9 in the denominator leaves $\frac{15 \times 7 \times 1}{3 \times 5 \times 2}$. Canceling a 5 from the 15 in the numerator and the 5 in the denominator leaves $\frac{3 \times 7 \times 1}{3 \times 1 \times 2}$. Canceling the 3 in the numerator and the 3 in the denominator leaves $\frac{7 \times 1}{1 \times 2} = \frac{7}{2} = 3\frac{1}{2}$, (H).

5. (C) The least common multiple (LCM) of two integers is the product of their prime factors, each raised to the highest power with which it appears. The prime factorization of 18 is $2 \cdot 3^2$ and that of 24 is $2^3 \cdot 3$. So their LCM is $2^3 \cdot 3^2 = 8 \cdot 9 = 72$. You could also find their LCM by checking out the multiples of the larger integer until you find the one that's also a multiple of the smaller. Check out the multiples of 24: 24 ? No. 48 ? No. 72 ? Yes, $72 = 4 \times 18$.

6. (H) If a number is divisible by 3, the sum of its digits will be divisible by 3. Checking the answer choices, only (H), 465 works, since $4 + 6 + 5 = 15$, which is divisible by 3.

7. (E) According to PEMDAS, start in the parentheses. As per PEMDAS, perform multiplication before subtraction: $-6(3 - 12)$. After the subtraction: $-6(-9)$. Since a negative times a negative is a positive, the answer is 54, (E).

8. (G) If a number is divisible by 10, its last digit will be a 0. Only G fits this criterion.

9. (D) If a number is divisible by both 5 and 2, then it must also be divisible by $5 \cdot 2$ or 10. Since a number divisible by 10 must have a 0 as its last digit, (D) is correct.

10. (H) For a number to be divisible by 3 and 10, it must satisfy the divisibility rules of both: its last digit must be 0 (which automatically eliminates (F), and the sum of its digits must be divisible by 3. Checking the rest of the answer choices, only (H) is also divisible by 3, since $2 + 1 + 0 = 3$.

11. (D) For a number to be a multiple of both 2 and 5 it must also be a multiple of $2 \cdot 5 = 10$. This means it must have a 0 as its last digit, which eliminates all but (C) and (D). To be a multiple of 3, the number's digits must sum to a multiple of 3. (D) is the only of the remaining two choices that fits this requirement, since $4 + 2 + 0 = 6$.

12. (K) Since an even number is divisible by 2, the question is asking for a number that is divisible by 2, 3, and 5. If the number is divisible by 2 and 5, it must also be divisible by 10, so its last digit must be 0. To be a multiple of 3, its digits must sum to a multiple of 3. Eliminate (F) and (G) since they don't end in 0. Of the remaining choices, only (K) is a multiple of 3, since $3 + 9 + 0 = 12$.

13. (C) If Professor Jones was able to distribute all the books in groups of 3 without any left over, the number of books she started with was divisible by 3. Whichever choice is divisible by 3 must therefore be correct. For a number to be divisible by 3, the sum of its digits must also be divisible by 3. Only (C) fits this requirement: $2 + 5 + 2 = 9$.

14. (K) The problems tells you that the number of pieces of candy in the box can be evenly divided by 3 and 5. So the correct answer is the choice that has a 0 or 5 as its last digit, and the sum of whose digits is divisible by 3. Eliminate (F) and (H) since they don't end in either 0 or 5. Of the remaining choices, only (K) is also divisible by 3, since $5 + 5 + 5 = 15$.

15. (E) Use the answer choices to help find the solution. When backsolving, start with the middle choice, since it will help you determine if the correct answer needs to be greater or less than it. In this case the middle choice is 16. The sum of 16 and 2 numbers that are each smaller than 16 has to be less than $3 \cdot 16$ or 48, so it is obviously too small. Therefore, (A) and (B) must also be too small and you can eliminate all three. Try (D), 20. Again, 20 plus two numbers smaller than 20 will be less than $3 \cdot 20$ or 60, so it's not correct. The only choice remaining is (E), 24, so it must be correct. To prove it, 24 plus the two preceding consecutive multiples of 4, which are 16 and 20, do indeed sum to 60: $16 + 20 + 24 = 60$.

16. (K) When you're asked how many strips $\frac{4}{5}$ of a foot long can be cut from a 60 foot piece of wire, you're being asked how many times $\frac{4}{5}$ goes into 60, or what is $60 \div \frac{4}{5}$. Before you even do the division, you can eliminate some unreasonable answer choices. Since $\frac{4}{5}$ is less than 1, $\frac{4}{5}$ must go into 60 more than 60 times. Eliminate (F), (G), and (H) because they're all less than or equal to 60. Dividing by a fraction is the same as multiplying by its reciprocal, so $60 \div \frac{4}{5} = 60 \cdot \frac{5}{4} = 75$.

17. (E) If a number is odd, its last digit must be odd. (E) ends in an even digit, so it is not odd.

18. (K) The sum of two negative numbers is always negative. (K) is the only negative choice, so it must be correct. If you're wondering how two negative numbers can add up to –1, remember, "number" doesn't necessarily mean "integer." It can also mean "fraction." For example, $(-\frac{1}{4}) + (-\frac{3}{4}) = -1$. Always read the questions carefully to see what types of numbers are involved.

19. (D) A prime number has only two different positive factors, 1 and itself. 2, 7, and 17 are obviously prime, so eliminate them. Use the divisibility rules to check out the two remaining choices. Both end in an odd number, so neither is divisible by 2. But the digits of 87 sum to 15 which is a multiple of 3, so 87 is divisible by 3 and is therefore not prime.

20. (F) The product of a positive integer and a negative integer is always negative. (F) is positive, so it couldn't be the product of a negative and a positive.

21. (B) The simplest way to solve this problem is to convert the numbers so that they're all decimals or all fractions. $5\frac{1}{5} = 5\frac{2}{10} = 5.2$. $2\frac{2}{5} = 2\frac{4}{10} = 2.4$. Now you can more easily compare the distances. On Monday, they ran the same number of miles. On Tuesday, Susie ran 5.2 miles and Dennis ran 3.6 miles. The difference between the two amounts is $5.2 - 3.6$, or 1.6, so on Tuesday Susie ran 1.6 more miles than Dennis did. On Wednesday, Susie ran 4.8 miles and Dennis ran 2.4. $4.8 - 2.4 = 2.4$, so on Wednesday Susie ran 2.4 miles more than Dennis. The total difference for the three days is $1.6 + 2.4 = 4.0$ more miles.

22. (H) A number that is a multiple of 60 must be both a multiple of 10 and a multiple of 6. A number that is a multiple of 10 ends in a 0, so you can eliminate (F) and (J). A multiple of 6 meets the requirements for multiples of 2 and 3. All of the

remaining choices are even, so they're all divisible by 2. The one that is divisible by 3, that is, the one whose digits sum to a multiple of 3, is the correct answer. Only (H) fits this requirement, since $5 + 4 + 0 = 9$.

23. (C) The product of three integers must be an integer, so eliminate (A) and (D). A product of integers that has at least one even factor is even, so the product of two odd integers and one even integer must be even. The only even choice is 6, (C).

24. (G) This question is simply asking for the sum of 9,899,399 and 2,082, which is 9,901,481, choice (G).

25. (C) If the middle of five consecutive integers is 13, the first two are 11 and 12 and the last two are 14 and 15. So the sum is
$11 + 12 + 13 + 14 + 15 = 65$. You could get to this answer more quickly if you knew that the middle term in a group of consecutive numbers is equal to the average of the group of numbers. In other words, the average of these five integers is 13, so their sum would be $13 \cdot 5 = 65$.

26. (G) To divide powers with the same base, subtract exponents. So $\dfrac{4x^5}{2x^2} = \dfrac{4}{2}x^{5-2} = 2x^3$.

27. (C) A negative number raised to an odd power is negative. Using PEMDAS,
$-2^3(1 - 2)^3 + (-2)^3$
$= -2^3(-1)^3 + (-2)^3$
$= -8(-1) + (-8)$
$= 8 + (-8)$
$= 8 - 8$
$= 0$

28. (H) The mean (or average) is the sum of the terms divided by the number of terms. The numbers included are 11, 13, 15, and 17. Note that 19 is not in the set, since n is less than 19. The average is
$\dfrac{11+13+15+17}{4} = \dfrac{56}{4} = 14$. The average is an even

number although the numbers in the set are all odd.

29. (D) Stay calm, and simply substitute the number on the left for a and the number on the right for b in the formula given for the strange symbol. First convert b to an improper fraction: $\dfrac{7}{4}$. So the numerator is 3 times $\dfrac{14}{32}$, or (simplifying the fraction) 3 times $\dfrac{7}{16}$, or $\dfrac{21}{16}$. Dividing by $\dfrac{7}{4}$ is the same as multiplying by $\dfrac{4}{7}$. So we have
$\dfrac{21}{16} \times \dfrac{4}{7}$ or $\dfrac{3}{4} \times \dfrac{1}{1} = \dfrac{3}{4}$.

30. (K) Multiply the number of hours per day, times the number of days, times the rate per hour. Wrong answer (F) results if you skip the first factor, 4.5. Wrong answer (G) results if you skip the third factor, 4.25. Wrong answer (H) results if you skip the second factor, 3.

31. (D) Let's say the original price is x dollars. The price paid is 70 percent of the original price (100% minus 30%). So,
$0.7x = 35$, $70x = 3{,}500$, $x = 50$.

32. (H) The numbers for the week are: 16, 21, 20, 17, 19, 21, 17. Listing them in ascending order, we have: 16, 17, 17, 19, 20, 21, 21. There are an odd number of numbers, so the median is the number in the middle of the set: 19.

33. (C) By adding the 8 white, 4 red, 7 green, and 5 blue marbles, we have a total of 24 marbles. If 8 are withdrawn, 16 remain in the bag. If the chance of drawing a white marble is now $\dfrac{1}{4}$, 4 white marbles remain in the bag, so $8 - 4$, or 4 must have been drawn out.

34. (G) To simplify the square root of a large number, break the number down into two or more

factors, and write the number as the product of the square roots of those factors. This is especially useful when one of the factors is a perfect square. In this case, break 1,500 down into two factors. $1,500 = 15 \cdot 100$, and 100 is a perfect square. So $1,500 = \sqrt{100 \cdot 15} = \sqrt{100} \cdot \sqrt{15} = 10\sqrt{15}$.

35. (D) This is a basic arithmetic problem and if you remember PEMDAS, it will be a breeze. PEMDAS tells you the order in which you need to do the different calculations: Parentheses, Exponents, Multiplication and Division, Addition and Subtraction. Take the expression and solve the parts in that order:

$$2(3 \times 2)^2 - 27(6 \div 2) + 3^2$$
$$= 2(6)^2 - 27(3) + 3^2$$
$$= 2(36) - 27(3) + 9$$
$$= 72 - 81 + 9$$
$$= -9 + 9$$
$$= 0$$

36. (H) Obviously, one way to solve this one would be to do the calculation. But this is really a test to see if you understand how to approximate a calculation by rounding off numbers. You could round off both numbers to the nearest whole number, but that wouldn't make the calculation much easier. And besides, the answer choices you're choosing between are pretty far apart, so you can probably round both numbers to the nearest ten. 48.9 is close to 50.0, so round it up to 50. 21.2 is close to 20, so round it down to 20. Now the multiplication is $50 \cdot 20$ or 1,000, choice (H).

37. (E) First find the absolute value of $16 - 25$. $16 - 25 = -9$; the absolute value of a negative number is the same number part without the negative sign. So the part of the expression to the left of the plus sign is 9. Now consider what's to the right of the plus sign. Remember the convention that if x is positive, $\sqrt{x}$ means the positive square root of x. On the right you have $\sqrt{25 - 16}$. $25 - 16 = 9$ and the

positive square root of 9 is 3. So $\sqrt{25 - 16} = 3$. So the expression becomes $9 + 3$, or 12, choice (E).

38. (H) To round a number off to the nearest hundred, consider the tens digit. If the tens digit is 5 or greater, round the hundreds digit up 1. If the tens digit is 4 or smaller, keep the same hundreds digit. Here the tens digit is 5, so round the hundreds digit up to 5. To the nearest 100, 81,455 is 81,500, choice (H).

39. (A) This problem is a snap if you remember that $a\%$ of $b = b\%$ of a. In this case, 35% of $x = x\%$ of 35, so $x\%$ of 35 is 7.

If you didn't remember that $a\%$ of $b = b\%$ of a, you could also have solved the question by solving the statement that 35% of x is 7 for x and then found $x\%$ of 35. Percent $\cdot$ Whole = Part, so

$$\frac{35}{100}x = 7$$
$$35x = 700$$
$$x = 20$$

So $x\%$ of 35 is 20% of 35, which is 7, choice (A).

40. (H) In this type of problem you're given a rule or definition you've never heard before and then asked a question involving that new rule. In this example, you're given a definition of the term *blue*: a number is blue if the sum of its digits is equal to the product of its digits. To solve, simply try each answer until you find the one that fits the definition of blue. When you do so, you see that only (H) is blue, because $3 + 2 + 1 = 3 \cdot 2 \cdot 1 = 6$.

41. (E) This is another invented rule question. This time all you have to do is follow directions. To "fix"–3, you first raise it to the 3rd power: $(-3)^3 = -27$. Then divide this result by 2: $-27 \div 2 = -13.5$. Next take the absolute value of -13.5, which is just 13.5. Finally, round off this

result to the nearest integer: 13.5 rounds up to 14, choice (E).

42. (H) First figure out what D is. You're told that $D \div 15 = 6$ with a remainder of 2. This means that $D = (15 \cdot 6) + 2$. So $D = 90 + 2$, or 92. Now that you know the value of D, just divide it by 6 and see what the remainder is. $92 \div 6 = 15$ with a remainder of 2, so (H) is correct.

43. (C) This is another follow the instructions problem. Just replace a with 7 and b with 5. So $7 ? 5 = (7 + 5)(7 - 5) = (12)(2)$, or 24, choice (C).

44. (H) $\frac{71}{6} = 11\frac{5}{6}$, so the greatest integer less than $\frac{71}{6}$ is 11.

45. (C) $0.25 = \frac{1}{4}$, so just find which choice is NOT less than $\frac{1}{4}$. Choice (C), $\frac{16}{64}$, reduces to $\frac{1}{4}$ so it is equal to, not less than, 0.25.

46. (G) The average of an odd number of consecutive numbers is equal to the middle term. Since 11 is the average of these five consecutive odd numbers, 11 is the third and middle term. So the five numbers are 7, 9, 11, 13, and 15. The largest number is 15.

9

Geometry

Highlights

- Review of geometry content on the tests including the Pythagorean Theorum, coordinate geometry, etc.

- Tips on solving geometry problems

OVERVIEW

You'll definitely see some geometry on the SSAT/ISEE. Like the rest of the math you'll see on your private-school admissions test, SSAT/ISEE Geometry will range from straightforward to difficult and tricky. You can count on seeing questions that test your knowledge of lines and angles, triangles, circles, and other assorted geometric figures. Additionally, you'll see a little coordinate geometry. Remember that diagramless geometry can also show up in the form of word problems.

The most helpful thing you can do is review geometry content and practice a whole bunch of geometry problems. If you're concerned about your math readiness, take some time now to go through the Math Foundations Workshop at the end of this book. Next, read through this chapter, spending more time with the subjects that are less familiar to you. Make certain that you do all of the problems in the practice set even if you feel comfortable with the geometry problems presented.

It's important to know that unless it's specified, diagrams are not drawn to scale. Keep this in mind so that you don't carelessly eyeball diagrams and reach false conclusions. In other words, don't judge the size of the answer just by looking at the size of the diagram.

Remember

> A straight angle contains 180º.

GEOMETRY CONTENT REVIEW

Lines and Angles

Line Segments

Some of the most basic geometry problems deal with line segments. A **line segment** is a piece of a line, and it has an exact measurable length. A question might give you a segment divided into several pieces, provide the measurements of some of these pieces, and ask you for the measurement of a remaining piece.

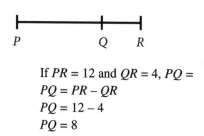

If $PR = 12$ and $QR = 4$, $PQ =$
$PQ = PR - QR$
$PQ = 12 - 4$
$PQ = 8$

Kaplan Rules

> Figures are drawn to scale unless otherwise indicated, so you can usually eyeball the measurements of a figure.

The point exactly in the middle of a line segment, halfway between the endpoints, is called the **midpoint** of the line segment. To bisect means to cut in half, so the midpoint of a line segment bisects that line segment.

M is the midpoint of AB, so $AM = MB$.

Exercise

i. If points A, D, B, and C lie on a line in that order, and $AB = 8$, $DC = 16$, and D is the midpoint of AB, then $AC = ?$

Angles

And the Midpoint Is . . .

The midpoint of a line segment bisects that line segment.

A **right angle** measures 90 degrees and is usually indicated in a diagram by a little box. The figure above is a right angle. Lines that intersect to form right angles are said to be **perpendicular.**

Angles that form a straight line add up to 180 degrees. In the figure above, $a + b = \mathbf{180}$.

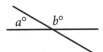

When two lines intersect, **adjacent angles are supplementary**, meaning they add up to 180 degrees. In the figure above, $a + b = 180$.

Kaplan Rules

Angles around a point add up to 360°.

Angles around a point add up to 360 degrees. In the figure above, $a + b + c + d + e = 360$.

When lines intersect, angles across the vertex from each other are called **vertical angles** and **are equal to each other.** Above, $a = c$ and $b = d$.

Exercise

In the following figures, find *x*:

ii.

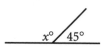

iii.

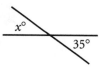

iv.

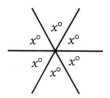

Parallel Lines

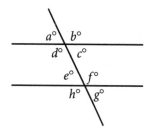

When parallel lines are crossed by a transversal:

- Corresponding angles are equal (for example, *a* = *e*).

- Alternate interior angles are equal (*d* = *f*).

- Same side interior angles are supplementary (*c* + *f* = 180).

- All four acute angles are equal, as are all four obtuse angles.

Triangles

Triangles in General

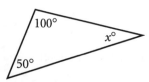

The three interior angles of any triangle add up to 180°. In this figure, *x* + 50 + 100 = 180, so *x* = 30.

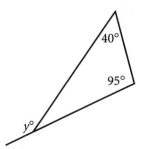

An exterior angle of a triangle is equal to the sum of the remote interior angles. In this figure, the exterior angle labeled $y°$ is equal to the sum of the remote interior angles: $y = 40 + 95 = 135$.

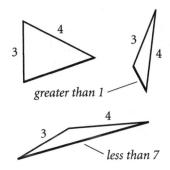

The length of one side of a triangle must be greater than the positive difference and less than the sum of the lengths of the other two sides. For example, if it is given that the length of one side is 3 and the length of another side is 4, then the length of the third side must be greater than $4 - 3 = 1$ and less than $4 + 3 = 7$.

Triangle Tip

The length of one side of a triangle must be greater than the positive difference and less than the sum of the lengths of the other two sides.

Exercise

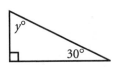

v. $y =$

vi. If two sides of a triangle are 5 and 8, which of the following could be the length of its third side? (circle all that are possible)

3   5   9   13   15

Triangles—Area and Perimeter

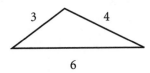

The **perimeter** of a triangle is the sum of the lengths of its sides.

The perimeter of the triangle in the figure above is: 3 + 4 + 6 = 13

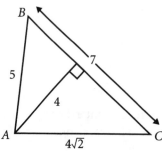

Area of triangle $= \frac{1}{2}$ (base)(height)

The height is the perpendicular distance between the side that's chosen as the base and the opposite vertex. In this triangle, 4 is the height when the 7 is chosen as the base.

Area $= \frac{1}{2}bh = \frac{1}{2}(7)(4) = 14$

Exercise

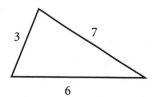

vii.

Perimeter =

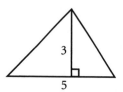

viii.

Area =

Similar Triangles

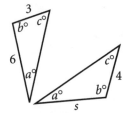

Similar triangles have the same shape: **corresponding angles are equal and corresponding sides are proportional**. These triangles are similar because they have the same angles. The 3 corresponds to the 4 and the 6 corresponds to the *s*.

$$\frac{3}{4} = \frac{6}{s}$$

$$3s = 24$$

$$s = 8$$

Special Triangles

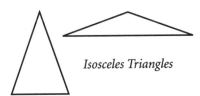

Isosceles Triangles

An isosceles triangle is a triangle that has two equal sides. Not only are two sides equal, but the angles opposite the equal sides, called base angles, are also equal.

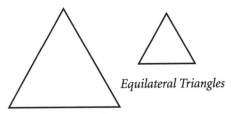

Equilateral Triangles

Equilateral triangles are triangles in which all three sides are equal. Since all the sides are equal, all the angles are also equal. All three angles in an equilateral triangle measure 60 degrees, regardless of the lengths of the sides.

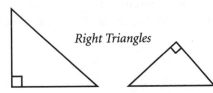

Right Triangles

A right triangle is a triangle with a right angle. Every right triangle has exactly two acute angles. The sides opposite the acute angles are called the legs. The side opposite the right angle is called the hypotenuse. Since it's opposite the largest angle, the hypotenuse is the longest side of a right triangle.

Right Triangles

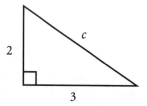

The Pythagorean theorem:

$$(\text{leg}_1)^2 + (\text{leg}_2)^2 = (\text{hypotenuse})^2$$

If one leg is 2 and the other leg is 3, then:

$$2^2 + 3^2 = c^2$$
$$c^2 = 4 + 9$$
$$c = \sqrt{13}$$

Exercise

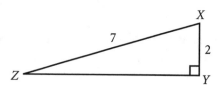

ix. In right triangle *XYZ*, what is the length of *YZ* ?

Pythagorean "Triplets"

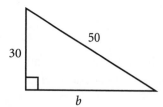

If a right triangle's leg-to-leg ratio is 3:4, or if the leg-to-hypotenuse ratio is 3:5 or 4:5, it's a 3-4-5 triangle and you don't need to use the Pythagorean theorem to find the third side. Just figure out what multiple of 3-4-5 it is. In this right triangle, one leg is 30 and the hypotenuse is 50. This is 10 times 3-4-5. The other leg is 40.

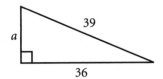

If a right triangle's leg-to-leg ratio is 5:12, or if the leg-to-hypotenuse ratio is 5:13 or 12:13, then it's a **5-12-13 triangle** and you don't need to use the Pythagorean theorem to find the third side. Just figure out what multiple of 5-12-13 it is. Here one leg is 36 and the hypotenuse is 39. This is 3 times 5-12-13. The other leg is 15.

Exercise

Find the missing side in each of the following triangles:

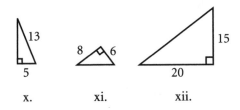

x.   xi.   xii.

Side-Angle Ratios

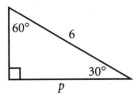

The sides of a 30-60-90 triangle are in a ratio of $x : x\sqrt{3} : 2x$. You don't need to use the Pythagorean theorem. If the hypotenuse is 6, then the shorter leg is half that, or 3; and then the longer leg is equal to the short leg times $\sqrt{3}$, or $3\sqrt{3}$.

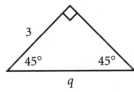

The sides of a 45-45-90 triangle are in a ratio of $x : x : x\sqrt{2}$. If one leg is 3, then the other leg is also 3, and the hypotenuse is equal to a leg multiplied by $\sqrt{2}$, or $3\sqrt{2}$.

Quadrilaterals

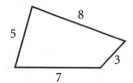

The **perimeter** of a polygon is the sum of the lengths of its sides.

The perimeter of the quadrilateral in the figure above is: $5 + 8 + 3 + 7 = 23$

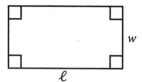

A **rectangle** is a parallelogram containing four right angles. Opposite sides are equal.

The formula for the area of a rectangle is:

Area = (length)(width)

In the figure above, ℓ = length and w = width, so Area = ℓw. Perimeter = $2(\ell + w)$

A **square** is a rectangle with four equal sides.

The formula for the area of a square is:

Area = (side)^2

In the figure above, s = the length of a side, so Area = s^2. Perimeter = $4s$.

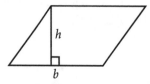

A **parallelogram** is a quadrilateral with two sets of parallel sides. Opposite sides are equal, as are opposite angles. The formula for the area of a parallelogram is:

Area = (base)(height)

In the diagram above, h = height and b = base, so Area = bh

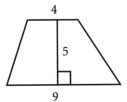

A **trapezoid** is a quadrilateral with one pair of parallel sides.

The formula for the area of a trapezoid is:

Area = $\frac{1}{2}$ (sum of the lengths of the parallel sides)(height)

In the figure above, the area of the trapezoid is $\frac{1}{2}(4 + 9)(5) = 32.5$

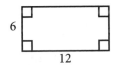

If two polygons are similar, then corresponding angles are equal and corresponding sides are in proportion.

The two rectangles above are similar because all the angles are right angles, and each side of the larger rectangle is $1\frac{1}{2}$ times the corresponding side of the smaller.

Exercise

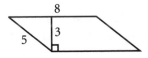

xiii. What is the area of the parallelogram above?

xiv. What is the area of the trapezoid above?

xv. The rectangles above are similar. If the area of the larger rectangle is 300, what is the area of the smaller rectangle?

Circles

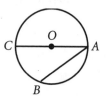

A **circle** is a figure each point of which is an equal distance from its center. In the diagram, O is the center of the circle.

The **radius** of a circle is the straight line distance from its center to any point on the circle. All radii of one circle have equal lengths. In the figure above, OA is a radius of circle O.

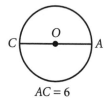

A **chord** is a line segment that connects any two points on a circle. Segments AB and AC are both chords. The largest chord that may be drawn in a circle will be a diameter of that circle.

A **diameter** of a circle is a chord that passes through the circle's center. All diameters are the same length and are equal to twice the radius. In the figure above, AC is a diameter of circle O.

$AC = 6$

The **circumference** of a circle is the distance around it. It is equal to πd, or $2\pi r$. In this example: Circumference $= \pi d = 6\pi$

The **area** of a circle equals π times the square of the radius, or πr^2. In this example, since AC is the diameter, $r = \frac{6}{2} = 3$, and Area $= \pi r^2 = \pi(3^2) = 9\pi$

Exercise

xvi. Radius = 3
Diameter =

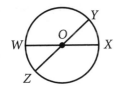

xvii. $OZ = 4$
$WX =$
$OX =$

What's π?

π is approximately 3.14, but all you need to remember is that it's a little more than 3.

xviii. Radius = 8
Circumference =

xix. Area = 16π
Radius =

Coordinate Geometry

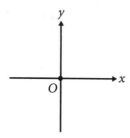

The diagram above represents the **coordinate axes**—the perpendicular "number lines" in the coordinate plane. The horizontal line is called the **x-axis**. The vertical line is called the **y-axis**. In a coordinate plane, the point O at which the two axes intersect is called the **origin**.

The pair of numbers, written inside parentheses, which specifies the location of a point in the coordinate plane, are called **coordinates**. The first number is the x-coordinate and the second number is the y-coordinate. The origin is the zero point on both axes, with coordinates $(0, 0)$.

Starting at the origin:

to the right:	x is positive
to the left:	x is negative
up:	y is positive
down:	y is negative

The two axes divide the coordinate plane into 4 quadrants. When you know what quadrant a point lies in, you know the signs of its coordinates. A point in the upper left quadrant, for example, has a negative x-coordinate and a positive y-coordinate.

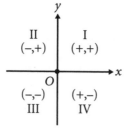

Plotting Points

If you were asked to graph the point $(2, -3)$ you would start at the origin, count 2 units to the right and 3 down. To graph $(-4, 5)$ you would start at the origin, go 4 units to the left and 5 units up.

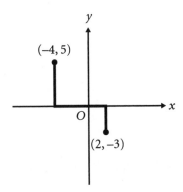

Slope of a Line

To use two points to find the slope of a line, use the following formula:

$$\text{Slope} = \frac{\text{change in } y}{\text{change in } x} = \frac{\text{rise}}{\text{run}}$$

In general, the slope of a line connecting the points (x_1, y_1) and (x_2, y_2) is

$$\frac{y_2 - y_1}{x_2 - x_1}.$$

The slope of a line that contains the points $A(4, 6)$ and $B(0, -3)$

$$\frac{y_2 - y_1}{x_2 - x_1} = \frac{-3 - 6}{0 - 4} = \frac{-9}{-4} = \frac{9}{4}$$

To use an equation of a line to find the slope, put the equation into the slope-intercept form:

$y = mx + b$ where the slope is m.

To find the slope of the equation $5x + 3y = 6$, rearrange it:

$$5x + 3y = 6$$
$$3y = -5x + 6$$
$$y = -\frac{5}{3}x + 2$$

The slope is $-\frac{5}{3}$.

Figuring Lengths

To find the length of a line segment **parallel to the x-axis** in the coordinate plane, its length is the absolute value of the difference of its x-coordinates.

To find the length of a line segment **parallel to the y-axis** in the coordinate plane, its length is the absolute value of the difference of its y-coordinates.

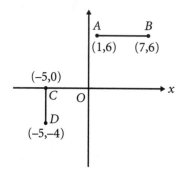

In the figure above, the length of AB is $|7 - 1| = 6$. The length of CD is $|0 - (-4)| = 4$.

Exercise

xx. Find the slopes of the lines that contain the following points:

   $(0, 3)$ and $(4, 5)$

   $(-1, 2)$ and $(9, 8)$

xxi. Find the slopes of the following lines:

   $y = 2x - 3$

   $y = -\dfrac{1}{5}x + 2$

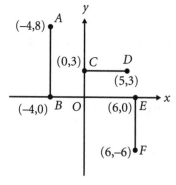

xxii. Find the lengths of the line segments graphed above:

1. $AB =$

2. $CD =$

3. $EF =$

Exercise Answers

    i. $AC = 20$

    ii. $x = 135$

    iii. $x = 35$

    iv. $x = 60$

    v. $y = 60$

    vi. 5, 9 (The third side must be greater than 3 and less than 13.)

    vii. 16

    viii. $\frac{15}{2}$

    ix. $\sqrt{45}$ or $3\sqrt{5}$

    x. 12

    xi. 10

    xii. 25

    xiii. 24

    xiv. 24

    xv. 75

    xvi. Diameter = 6

    xvii. $WX = 8$, $OX = 4$

    xviii. Circumference = 16π

    xix. Radius = 4

    xx. $\frac{1}{2}, \frac{3}{5}$

    xxi. $2, -\frac{1}{5}$

    xxii. $AB = 8$, $CD = 5$, $EF = 6$

Practice Questions

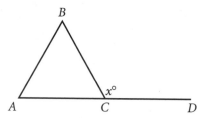

1. In the figure above, segments *AB*, *BC*, *CD*, and *AC* are all equal. What is the value of **x**?

    (A)   30
    (B)   45
    (C)   60
    (D)   90
    (E)   120

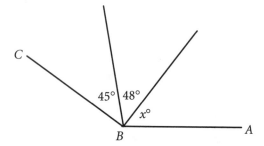

2. If the measure of angle *ABC* is 145°, what is the value of *x* ?

    (F)   39
    (G)   45
    (H)   52
    (J)   55
    (K)   62

3. If the perimeter of a square is 32 meters, what is the area of the square, in square meters?

    (A)   16
    (B)   32
    (C)   48
    (D)   56
    (E)   64

4. In triangle *XYZ* the measure of angle *Y* is twice the measure of angle *X*, and the measure of *Z* is three times the measure of angle *X*. What is the degree measure of angle *Y* ?

    (F)   15
    (G)   30
    (H)   45
    (J)   60
    (K)   90

5. The perimeter of triangle *ABC* is 24. If *AB* = 9 and *BC* = 7, then *AC* =

    (A)   6
    (B)   8
    (C)   10
    (D)   15
    (E)   17

6. If the perimeter of an equilateral triangle is 150, what is the length of one of its sides?

    (F)   35
    (G)   35
    (H)   50
    (J)   75
    (K)   100

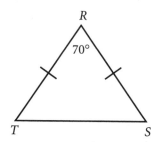

7. In triangle *RST*, if *RS* = *RT*, what is the degree measure of angle *S* ?

    (A)   40
    (B)   55
    (C)   70
    (D)   110
    (E)   It cannot be determined from the information given.

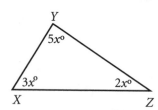

8. In triangle *XYZ*, what is the degree measure of angle *YXZ* ?

    (F)   18
    (G)   36
    (H)   54
    (J)   72
    (K)   90

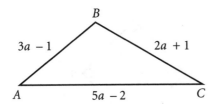

9. If the perimeter of triangle *ABC* is 18, what is the length of *AC*?

    (A)   2
    (B)   4
    (C)   5
    (D)   6
    (E)   8

10. What is the area, in square units, of a square that has the same perimeter as the rectangle above?

    (F)   25
    (G)   36
    (H)   49
    (J)   64
    (K)   81

11. What is the value of *a* in the figure above?

    (A)   20
    (B)   40
    (C)   60
    (D)   80
    (E)   140

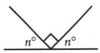

12. In the figure above, what is the value of *n*?

    (F)   30
    (G)   60
    (H)   45
    (J)   90
    (K)   135

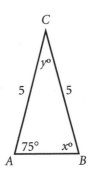

13. In the figure above, what is the value of $x - y$?

    (A)   30
    (B)   45
    (C)   75
    (D)   105
    (E)   150

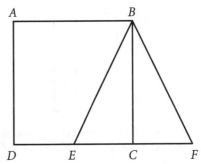

14. A square and a triangle are drawn together as shown above. The perimeter of the square is 64 and *DC = EF*. What is the area of triangle *BEF*?

    (F)   32
    (G)   64
    (H)   128
    (J)   256
    (K)   It cannot be determined from the information given.

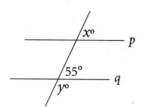

15. If line p is parallel to line q, what is the value of $x + y$?

    (A)   90
    (B)   110
    (C)   125
    (D)   180
    (E)   250

$2\sqrt{2}$

16. What is the area of the square above?

    (F)   4
    (G)   8
    (H) $4\sqrt{2}$
    (J)   16
    (K)   24

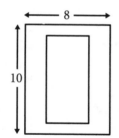

17. What is the area of the frame in the figure above if the inside picture has a length of 8 and a width of 4?

    (A)   4
    (B)   8
    (C)   16
    (D)   24
    (E)   48

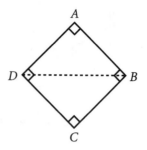

18. In the figure above, $ABCD$ is a square and the area of triangle ABD is 8. What is the area of square $ABCD$?

    (F)   2
    (G)   4
    (H)   8
    (J)   16
    (K)   64

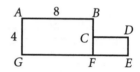

Note: Figure not drawn to scale.

19. In the figure above, $ABFG$ and $CDEF$ are rectangles, C bisects BF, and EF has a length of 2. What is the area of the entire figure?

    (A)   4
    (B)   16
    (C)   32
    (D)   36
    (E)   72

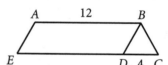

20. In the figure above, $ABDE$ is a parallelogram and BCD is an equilateral triangle. What is the perimeter of $ABCE$?

    (F)   12
    (G)   16
    (H)   24
    (J)   32
    (K)   36

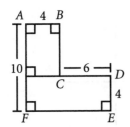

21. In the figure above, what is the perimeter of *ABCDEF*?

(A)   14
(B)   24
(C)   28
(D)   38
(E)   40

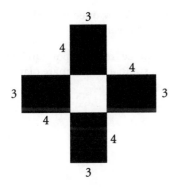

22. If the shaded regions are 4 rectangles, what is the area of the unshaded region?

(F)   9
(G)   12
(H)   16
(J)   19
(K)   20

Note: Figure not drawn to scale.

23. In the figure above, *AB* is twice the length of *BC*, *BC* = *CD* and *DE* is triple the length of *CD*. If *AE* = 49, what is the length of *BD*?

(A)   14
(B)   21
(C)   28
(D)   30
(E)   35

8 inches

24. In the figure above, circle *P* is inscribed in a square with sides of length 8 inches. What is the area of the circle?

(F)   4π square inches
(G)   16 square inches
(H)   8π square inches
(J)   16π square inches
(K)   32π square inches

25. What is the radius of a circle whose circumference is 36π?

(A)   3
(B)   6
(C)   8
(D)   18
(E)   36

26. If the perimeter of the square is 36, what is the circumference of the circle?

(F)   6π
(G)   9π
(H)   12π
(J)   15π
(K)   18π

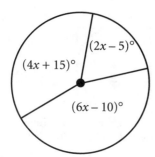

27. In the figure above, what is the value of *x*?

    (A)   15
    (B)   30
    (C)   55
    (D)   70
    (E)   135

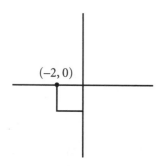

28. In the figure above, a square is graphed on the coordinate plane. If the coordinates of one corner are (−2, 0), what is the area of the square?

    (F) $\frac{1}{4}$
    (G)   1
    (H)   2
    (J)   4
    (K)   16

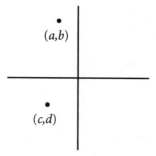

29. Points (*a*, *b*) and (*c*, *d*) are graphed in the coordinate plane as shown above. Which of the following statements must be true?

    (A)   *bd* > *ac*
    (B)   *c* > *ad*
    (C)   *b* > *acd*
    (D)   *bc* > *ad*
    (E)   It cannot be determined from the information given.

30. What is the distance from the point (0, 6) to the point (0, 8) in a standard coordinate plane?

    (F)   2
    (G)   7
    (H)   10
    (J)   12
    (K)   14

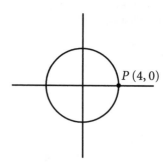

31. Circle *O* above has its center at the origin. If point *P* lies on circle *O*, what is the area of circle *O* ?

    (A) 4π
    (B) 8π
    (C) 10π
    (D) 12π
    (E) 16π

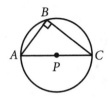

32. In the figure above, right triangle *ABC* is inscribed in circle *P*, with *AC* passing through center *P*. If *AB* = 6, and *BC* = 8, what is the area of the circle?

    (F) 10π
    (G) 14π
    (H) 25π
    (J) 49π
    (K) 100π

33. In the figure above, a circle is inscribed within a square. If the area of the circle is 25π, what is the perimeter of the shaded region?

    (A) $40 + 5\pi$
    (B) $40 + 10\pi$
    (C) $100 + 10\pi$
    (D) $100 + 25\pi$
    (E) $40 + 50\pi$

34. What is the slope of the line that contains points $(3, -5)$ and $(-1, 7)$?

    (F) -3
    (G) $-\dfrac{1}{3}$
    (H) $-\dfrac{1}{4}$
    (J) $\dfrac{1}{3}$
    (K) 3

35. If the circumference of a circle is 16π, what is its area?

    (A) 8π
    (B) 16π
    (C) 32π
    (D) 64π
    (E) 256π

36. What is the area of the square above with diagonals of length 6?

    (F)   9
    (G)   12
    (H) $9\sqrt{2}$
    (J)   15
    (K)   18

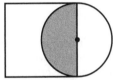

37. A square and a circle are drawn as shown above. The area of the square is 64. What is the area of the shaded region?

    (A) 4π
    (B) 8π
    (C) 16π
    (D) 32π
    (E)   It cannot be determined from the information given.

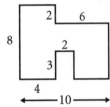

38. What is the area of the polygon above if each corner of the polygon is a right angle?

    (F)   40
    (G)   62
    (H)   68
    (J)   74
    (K)   80

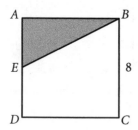

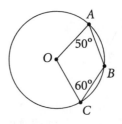

39. *ABCD* is a square. If *E* is the midpoint of *AD*, what is the area of the shaded region?

    (A)   8
    (B)   12
    (C)   16
    (D)   24
    (E)   32

40. Circle *A* has radius *r* + 1. Circle *B* has radius *r* + 2. What is the positive difference between the circumference of circle *B* and the circumference of circle *A*?

    (F)   1
    (G) 2π
    (H) $2\pi + 3$
    (J) $2\pi r + 3$
    (K) $2\pi(2r + 3)$

41. Erica has 8 squares of felt, each with area 16. For a certain craft project she cuts the largest circle possible from each square of felt. What is the combined area of the excess felt left over after cutting out all the circles?

    (A) $4(4 - \pi)$
    (B) $8(4 - \pi)$
    (C) $8(\pi - 2)$
    (D) $32(4 - \pi)$
    (E) $8(16 - \pi)$

42. In the figure above, points *A*, *B*, and *C* lie on the circumference of the circle centered at *O*. If $\angle OAB$ measures 50° and $\angle BCO$ measures 60°, what is the degree measure of $\angle AOC$?

    (F)   110
    (G)   125
    (H)   140
    (J)   250
    (K)   It cannot be determined from the information given.

Practice Question Explanations

1. (E) Since $AB = BC = AC$, triangle ABC is equilateral. Therefore, all of its angles are 60°. Since angle BCD or x is supplementary to angle BCA, a 60° angle, the value of x is $180 - 60$ or 120.

2. (H) Since the degree measure of angle ABC is 145, $45 + 48 + x = 145$, $93 + x = 145$, and $x = 52$.

3. (E) A square has four equal sides, so its perimeter is equal to $4s$, where s is the length of a side of the square. Its perimeter is 32, so its side length is $\frac{32}{4} = 8$. The area of a square is equal to s^2, so the area of the square is 8^2 or 64.

4. (J) In any triangle, the measures of the three interior angles sum to 180°, so $X + Y + Z = 180$. Since the measure of angle Y is twice the measure of angle X, $Y = 2X$. Similarly, $Z = 3X$. So $X + 2X + 3X = 180$, $6X = 180$ and $X = 30$. Since $Y = 2X$, the degree measure of angle Y is $2 \cdot 30 = 60$.

5. (B) The perimeter of a triangle is the sum of the lengths of its sides, in this case, $AB + BC + AC$. The perimeter of triangle ABC is 24, so plugging in the given values, $9 + 7 + AC = 24$, $16 + AC = 24$, and $AC = 8$.

6. (H) In an equilateral triangle, all three sides have equal length. The perimeter of a triangle is equal to the sum of the lengths of its three sides. Since all three sides are equal, each side must be $\frac{1}{3}$ of 150, or 50.

7. (B) Since RS and RT are equal, the angles opposite them must be equal. Therefore, angle T = angle S. Since the three angles of a triangle sum to 180, $70 + \text{angle } S + \text{angle } T = 180$ and angle S + angle $T = 110$. Since the two angles, S and T, are equal, each must be half of 110, or 55.

8. (H) The three interior angles of a triangle sum to 180 degrees, so $2x + 3x + 5x = 180$, $10x = 180$ degrees and $x = 18$. Angle YXZ has a degree measure of $3x = 3(18) = 54$.

9. (E) The perimeter of triangle ABC is 18, so $AB + BC + AC = 18$. Plugging in the algebraic expressions given for the length of each side, you get:

$$(3a - 1) + (2a + 1) + (5a - 2) = 18$$
$$10a - 2 = 18$$
$$10a = 20$$
$$a = 2$$

The length of AC is represented by the expression $5a - 2$, so $AC = 5(2) - 2 = 8$.

10. (H) The perimeter of a rectangle is $2(\ell + w)$, where ℓ represents its length and w its width. The perimeter of this rectangle is $2(9 + 5) = 28$. A square has four equal sides, so a square with a perimeter of 28 has sides of length 7. The area of a square is equal to the length of a side squared, so the area of a square with a perimeter of 28 is 7^2 or 49.

11. (B) An exterior angle of a triangle is equal to the sum of the measures of the two remote interior angles. So $7x = 4x + 60$, $3x = 60$, and $x = 20$. So the angle marked $7x°$ has a degree measure of $7(20) = 140$. The angle marked $a°$ is supplementary to this angle, so its measure is $180 - 140 = 40$.

12. (H) The angle between the two angles of measure n degrees is a right angle, so it contains 90°. A straight angle contains 180°, so $2n + 90 = 180$, $2n = 90$, and $n = 45$.

13. (B) Since $AC = CB$, the angles opposite these sides are equal as well. So angle CAB = angle CBA, and $x = 75$. The three interior angles of a triangle sum to 180 degrees, so $2(75) + y = 180$ and $y = 30$. The question asks for the value of $x - y$, or $75 - 30 = 45$.

14. (H) The area of a triangle is equal to $\frac{1}{2}bh$. In triangle BEF, the height is BC and the base is EF. The square's perimeter is 64, so each of its sides is a fourth of 64, or 16. Therefore $BC = 16$. The question also states that $DC = EF$, so $EF = 16$ as well. Plugging into the formula, the area of triangle BEF is $\frac{1}{2}(16 \times 16)= 128$.

15. (D) When parallel lines are crossed by a transversal, all acute angles formed are equal, and all acute angles are supplementary to all obtuse angles. So in this diagram, obtuse angle y is supplementary to the acute angle of 55°. Angle x is an acute angle, so it is equal to 55°. Therefore, angle x is supplementary to angle y, and the two must sum to 180°.

16. (G) The area of a square is equal to one of its sides squared. In this case, the square has a side length of $2\sqrt{2}$, so its area is $(2\sqrt{2})^2$ or $2 \cdot 2 \cdot \sqrt{2} \cdot \sqrt{2}$ or $4 \cdot 2 = 8$.

17. (E) To find the area of the frame, find the area of the frame and picture combined (the outer rectangle) and subtract from it the area of the picture (the inner rectangle). The outer rectangle has area $10 \cdot 8 = 80$, the inner rectangle has area $8 \cdot 4 = 32$, so the area of the frame is $80 - 32 = 48$.

18. (J) Diagonal BD divides square $ABCD$ into two identical triangles. If the area of triangle ABD is 8, the area of the square must be twice this, or 16.

19. (D) The area of the entire figure is equal to the area of rectangle $ABFG$ plus the area of rectangle $CDEF$. The area of $ABFG$ is $8 \cdot 4 = 32$. So the area of the entire figure must be greater than 32, and at this point you can eliminate (A), (B), and (C). Since BF has length 4, and C bisects BF, CF has length 2. The question states that EF has length 2, so $CDEF$ is actually a square, and its area is 2^2 or 4. So the area of the entire figure is $32 + 4 = 36$, choice (D).

20. (K) The perimeter of $ABCE$ is equal to $AB + BC + CD + DE + EA$. Since triangle BCD is equilateral, $BC = CD = BD = 4$. Because $ABDE$ is a parallelogram, $AB = DE = 12$ and $BD = EA = 4$. Therefore the perimeter of $ABCE$ is $12 + 4 + 4 + 12 + 4 = 36$, choice (K).

21. (E) Simply add the six sides of the L-shaped figure. Four of them are labeled, and you can use these to figure out the remaining two. The length of side EF must be $4 + 6 = 10$. The length of side BC is $10 - 4 = 6$. This makes the perimeter: $10 + 10 + 4 + 6 + 6 + 4 = 40$.

22. (F) Each of the shaded segments has a side of length 3 as its segment contributing to the inside region. Hence, the unshaded region, a square, has an area of $3^2 = 9$.

23. (A) Let $BC = x$. AB has twice the length of BC, so it is $2x$. $BC = CD$, so $CD = x$. DE is three times the length of CD, or $3x$. Since $AE = 49$, $2x + x + x + 3x = 49$, $7x = 49$, and $x = 7$. BD is composed of segments BC and CD, so its length is $7 + 7 = 14$.

24. (J) Since circle P is inscribed within the square, you can see that its diameter is equal in length to a side of the square. Since the circle's diameter is 8, its radius is half this, or 4. Area of a circle = πr^2, where r is the radius, so the area of circle P is $\pi(4)^2 = 16\pi$.

25. (D) Circumference of a circle = $2\pi r$, where r is the radius of the circle. So a circle with a circumference of 36π has a radius of $\frac{36\pi}{2\pi} = 18$.

26. (G) The perimeter of the square is 36, and since all four sides are equal, one side has length 9. Since the circle is inscribed in the square, its diameter is equal in length to a side of the square, or 9. Circumference is πd, where d represents the diameter, so the circumference of the circle is 9π.

27. (B) A circle contains $360°$, so

$$(4x + 15) + (2x - 5) + (6x - 10) = 360$$
$$4x + 2x + 6x + 15 - 5 - 10 = 360$$
$$12x = 360$$
$$x = 30$$

28. (J) The area of a square is equal to the length of one of its sides squared. Since one of the vertices (corners) of the square lies on the origin at $(0, 0)$ and another vertex lies on the point $(-2, 0)$, the length of a side of the square is $|-2 - 0| = |-2| = 2$. Therefore, the area of the square is $2^2 = 4$.

29. (C) While there's no way to determine the numerical values of a, b, c, or d, from their positions on the coordinate plane, you do know that a is negative, b is positive, c is negative, and d is negative. Bearing in mind that a negative times a negative is a positive, consider each answer choice. (C) is indeed true: b, which is positive, is greater than the product acd, which is negative.

30. (F) The points $(0, 6)$ and $(0, 8)$ have the same x-coordinate. That means that the segment that connects them is parallel to the y-axis and that all you have to do to figure out the distance is subtract the y-coordinates. $|8 - 6| = 2$, so the distance between the points is 2.

31. (E) OP is the radius of the circle. Since O has coordinates $(0, 0)$, the length of OP is $|4 - 0| = |4|$ $= 4$. The area of a circle is πr^2 where r is the radius, so the area of circle O is $\pi(4)^2 = 16\pi$.

32. (H) Right triangle ABC has legs of 6 and 8, so its hypotenuse must be 10. Notice that the hypotenuse is also the diameter of the circle. To find the area of the circle, we need its radius. Radius is half the diameter, so the radius of circle P is 5. The area of a circle is πr^2 where r is the radius, so the area of circle P is $\pi(5)^2 = 25\pi$.

33. (B) Note that the perimeter of the shaded region is in fact equal to the perimeter of the square, plus the perimeter—or circumference—of the circle. The area of a circle is πr^2 where r is the radius, and since the area of the circle is 25π, its radius is 5. Circumference is equal to $2\pi r$, or $2\pi(5) = 10\pi$. Only (B) and (C) contain 10π, so you can eliminate choices (A), (D), and (E). Since the circle is inscribed within the square, its diameter is equal to a side of the square. The diameter of the circle is $2r$ or 10, so a side of the square is 10 and its perimeter is $4(10) = 40$. Therefore the perimeter of the shaded region is $40 + 10\pi$, choice (B).

34. (F) Slope of a line is defined by the formula $\frac{y_2 - y_1}{x_2 - x_1}$, where (x_1, y_1) and (x_2, y_2) represent two points on the line. Plug the given points into the formula (it doesn't matter which you designate as point 1 or point 2):

$$\text{slope} = \frac{y_2 - y_1}{x_2 - x_1} = \frac{7 - (-5)}{-1 - 3} = \frac{12}{-4} = -3$$

35. (D) The circumference of a circle is $2\pi r$, where r is the radius, so a circle whose circumference is 16π has a radius of $\frac{16\pi}{2\pi} = 8$. The area of a circle is πr^2, so in this case the area is $\pi(8)^2 = 64\pi$, choice (D).

36. (K) It might help to sketch a diagram:

Since all sides of a square are equal, notice that the diagonal of the square is also the hypotenuse of an isosceles right triangle. Use this information to determine the length of a side of the square, marked s in the figure. The ratio of the sides in such a triangle is $1:1:\sqrt{2}$. Since the hypotenuse is 6, each leg is $\frac{6}{\sqrt{2}}$ (because $\frac{6}{\sqrt{2}} \cdot \sqrt{2} = 6$). The area of a square is equal to the length of one side squared, or $\left(\frac{6}{\sqrt{2}}\right)^2 = \frac{36}{2} = 18$.

37 (B) The shaded region represents one half the area of the circle. Find the length of the radius to determine this area. Notice that the diameter of the circle is equal to a side of the square. Since the area of the square is 64, it has a side length of 8. So the diameter of the circle is 8, and its radius is 4. The area of the circle is πr^2, or $\pi(4)^2 = 16\pi$. This isn't the answer though; the shaded region is only half the circle, so its area is 8π.

38 (G) Think of the figure as a rectangle with two rectangular bites taken out of it. Sketch in lines to make one large rectangle (see diagram below):

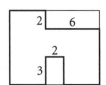

The area of a rectangle is length times width. If we call the length of the large rectangle is 10, then its width is 8, so its area is $10 \cdot 8 = 80$. The rectangular bite taken out of the top right corner has dimensions 6 and 2, so its area is $6 \cdot 2$ or 12. The bite taken out of the bottom has dimensions 2 and 3, so its area is $2 \cdot 3 = 6$. To find the area of the polygon, subtract the areas of the two bites from the area of the large rectangle: $80 - (12 + 6) = 80 - 18 = 62$, choice (G).

39. (C) Since $ABCD$ is a square, all four sides have the same length, and the corners meet at right angles. The area you're looking for is that of a triangle, and since all corners of the square are right angles, angle EAB is a right angle, which makes triangle EAB a right triangle. The area of a right triangle is $\frac{1}{2}(\text{leg}_1)(\text{leg}_2)$. The diagram shows that BC has length 8, so $AB = AD = 8$. Point E is the midpoint of AD, so AE is 4. Now that you have the lengths of both legs, you can plug into the formula: $\frac{1}{2}(AB)(AE) = \frac{1}{2}(8)(4) = 16$, choice (C).

40. (G) The circumference of a circle is equal to $2\pi r$, where r is the radius. The circumference of circle A is $2\pi(r + 1) = 2\pi r + 2\pi$. The circumference of circle B is $2\pi(r + 2) = 2\pi r + 4\pi$. So the positive difference between the two circumferences is simply 2π, choice (G).

41. (D) A square with area 16 has sides of length 4. Therefore the largest circle that could possibly be cut from such a square would have a diameter of 4.

Such a circle would have a radius of 2, making its area $\pi(2)^2 = 4\pi$. So the amount of felt left after cutting such a circle from one of the squares of felt would be $16 - 4\pi$, or $4(4 - \pi)$. There are 8 such squares, so the total area of the left over felt is $8 \cdot 4(4 - \pi) = 32(4 - \pi)$, choice (D).

42. (H) The key to solving this problem is to draw in *OB*:

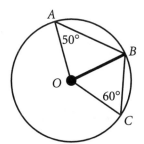

Because *OA*, *OB*, and *OC* are all radii of the same circle, triangle *AOB* and triangle *BOC* are both isosceles triangles, each therefore having equal base angles:

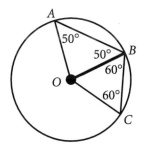

Using the fact that the 3 interior angles of a triangle add up to 180°, you can figure out that the vertex angles measure 80° and 60° as shown:

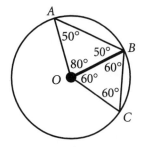

Angle *AOC* measures $80 + 60 = 140$, choice (H).

10

Word Problems

- How to translate word problems

- Backdoor strategies for solving word problems

- Explanation of the types of word problems you'll encounter on the SSAT/ISEE

- Roman numeral problems

OVERVIEW

Word Problems. Two simple words that evoke more fear and loathing than most other math concepts and question types combined.

When the subject of word problems arises, you might envision the following nightmare:

> Two trains are loaded with equal amounts of rock salt and ball bearings. Train *A* leaves Frogboro at 10:00 A.M. carrying 62 passengers. Train *B* leaves Toadville at 11:30 A.M. carrying 104 passengers. If Train *A* is traveling at a speed of 85 mph and makes four stops and Train *B* is traveling at an average speed of 86 mph and makes three stops and the trains both arrive at Lizard Hollow at 4:30 P.M., what is the average weight of the passengers on Train *B* ?

The good news is that you won't see anything this ugly. SSAT/ISEE word problems are pretty straightforward. Generally, all you have to do is translate the prose to math and solve.

The bad news is that you can expect to see a lot of word problems on your test. Keep in mind that, while word problems are generally algebra problems, they can contain other math concepts.

TRANSLATION

Many word problems seem tricky because it's hard to figure out what they're asking. It can be difficult to translate English into math. The following table lists some common words and phrases that turn up in word problems, along with their mathematical translations.

When you see:	Think:
sum, plus, more than, added to, combined total	+
minus, less than, difference between, decreased by	−
is, was, equals, is equivalent to, is the same as, adds up to	=
times, product, multiplied by, of, twice, double, triple	×
divided by, over, quotient, per, out of, into	÷
what, how much, how many, a number	x, n, etc.

Now, try translating the following phrases from English to math.

English   **Math**

1. y is 5 more than x _____

2. r equals half of s _____

3. x is twice as great as y _____

4. 2 less than m is equal to n _____

5. the product of a and b is 3 more than their sum   _____

Translate the Story

In some questions, the translation will be embedded within a "story." Don't be put off by the details of the scenario—it's the numbers that matter. Focus on the math and translate.

Now lets look at how you did:

1. $y = x + 5$
2. $r = \frac{1}{2}s$ or $2r = s$
3. $x = 2y$
4. $n = m - 2$
5. $ab = (a + b) + 3$

Exercise

i. In a certain class there are twice as many boys as girls. If the total number of students in the class is 36, how many boys are there?

(A)   9
(B)   12
(C)   18
(D)   24
(E)   27

ii. Paul developed a roll of film containing 36 pictures. If he made 2 prints each of half of the pictures, and 1 print of each of the rest, how many prints did he make in all?

(F)   18
(G)   27
(H)   36
(J)   54
(K)   72

Symbolism Word Problems

Word problems, by definition, require you to translate English to math. Some word problems contain an extra level of translation. *Symbolism word problems* are like any other word problem; just translate the English and the symbols into math and then solve.

Assume that the notation □ (w, x, y, z) means "Divide the sum of w and x by y and multiply the result by z." What is the value of

□ $(10, 4, 7, 8)$ + □ $(2, 6, 4, 5)$?

First, translate the English / symbols into math.

□ (w, x, y, z) means $\dfrac{w + x}{y} \times z$

Next, plug the values into the equation.

$$\square\, (10, 4, 7, 8) + \square\, (2, 6, 4, 5) = \left(\frac{10 + 4}{7} \times 8\right) + \left(\frac{2 + 6}{4} \times 5\right) = 16 + 10 = 26$$

Now try a couple of testlike questions.

Exercise

iii. Assume that the notation $a \bullet b$ means "Subtract 12 from the product of ab and then round the result to the nearest 10." What is the value of $14 \bullet 10$?

(A) 120

(B) 128

(C) 125

(D) 130

(E) 140

iv. Assume that for positive x, y, and z the notation $\bullet (x, y, z)$ means "Add the product of x and y to z and then take the positive square root of the result." If $\bullet (9, n, 13) = 11$ and $n > 0$, what is the value of n ?

(F)   10

(G)   11

(H)   12

(J)   13

(K)   14

Word Problems with Formulas

Some of the more difficult word problems may involve translations with mathematical formulas. For example, you might see questions dealing with averages, rates, or areas of geometric figures. Since the SSAT/ISEE does *not* provide formulas for you, you'll have to know these going in.

> If a truck travels at 50 miles per hour for $6\frac{1}{2}$ hours, how far will the truck travel?

To answer this question, you need to remember the Distance Formula (Distance = Rate × Time). Once you note the formula, you can just plug in the numbers.

$$D = 50 \times 6.5$$
$$D = 325 \text{ miles}$$

Exercise

v. If the average weight of a group of six children is 71 pounds, what is the total weight, in pounds, of the children?

(A)   331

(B)   348

(C)   366

(D)   396

(E)   426

vi. If a machine produces 150 widgets in 30 minutes, how many widgets will the machine produce in 4 hours?

(F)   500

(G)   600

(H)   750

(J)   900

(K)   1,200

Backdoor Strategies

Word problems are extraordinarily susceptible to the backdoor strategies detailed in chapter 7. Here's a quick recap of Kaplan's **Picking Numbers** and **Backsolving** Strategies.

Kaplan Three-Step Method for Picking Numbers

Step 1. Pick simple, easy to use numbers for each variable.

Step 2. Solve the problem using the numbers you pick.

Step 3. Plug your numbers into each answer choice. The choice that gives you the same numerical solution you arrived at in Step 2 is correct.

A few things to remember are:

- You can pick numbers only when the answer choices contain variables.

- Pick easy numbers rather than realistic numbers. Keep the numbers small and manageable.

- Remember that you have to try all the answer choices. If more than one works, pick another set of numbers.

- Don't pick the same number for more than one variable.

- When picking a number for a remainder problem, add the remainder to the number you're dividing by.

- Always pick 100 for percent questions.

Try Picking Numbers for the following problem.

Exercise

vii. The average of four numbers is n. If three of the numbers are $n + 3$, $n + 5$, and $n - 2$, what is the value of the fourth number?

(A) $n - 6$

(B) $n - 4$

(C) n

(D) $n + 2$

(E) $n + 4$

Backsolving

- You can backsolve when the answer choices are only numbers.

- Always start with the middle answer choice, (C) or (H).

- If the middle answer choice is not correct, you can usually eliminate two more choices simply by determining whether the value must be higher or lower.

Exercise

viii. Mike has n Hawaiian shirts and Adam has 3 times as many Hawaiian shirts. If Adam gives Mike six Hawaiian shirts, both boys would have an equal number of Hawaiian shirts. How many Hawaiian shirts does Mike have?

   (F)   3
   (G)   6
   (H)   9
   (J)   15
   (K)   18

Roman Numeral Problems

You might see a Roman numeral problem on your test. If you do, keep a few things in mind. Keeping with the problem style, let's lay them out in Roman numerals . . .

   I.   You don't have to work with the statements in the order they are given. Deal with them in whatever order is easiest for you.

   II.   If you find a statement that is true, eliminate all of the choices that *don't* include it.

   III.   If you find a statement that is false, eliminate all of the choices that *do* include it.

Try this out on the following problem:

Exercise

ix. If the product of the positive numbers x and y is 20 and x is less than 4, which of the following must be true?

   I. y is greater than 5.
   II.   The sum of x and y is greater than 10.
   III.   Twice the product of x and y is equal to 40.

   (A)   I only
   (B)   II only
   (C)   I and III only
   (D)   II and III only
   (E)   I, II, and III

Now it's time to put all of your skills into play with some practice questions. Remember to translate the English to math, don't get intimidated, and keep your cool. Off you go!

Exercise Answers

i. (D) $\quad 2g = b$
$$g + b = 36$$
$$g + 2g = 36$$
$$3g = 36$$
$$g = 12$$
$$12 + b = 36$$
$$b = 24$$

ii. (J) $\qquad 36 \div 2 = 18$
$$(18 \times 2) + (18 \times 1) =$$
$$36 + 18 = 54$$

iii. (D) $14 \cdot 10 = (14)(10) - 12$
$$= 140 - 12$$
$$= 128$$
128 rounded to the nearest 10 is 130.

iv. (H) The product of x and y is xy. "Add the product of x and y to z" means $xy + z$. "Take the positive square root of the result" means $\sqrt{xy + z}$. So when x, y, and z are all positive, $\bullet(x,y,z) = \sqrt{xy + z}$. To write down what $\bullet$ (9, n, 13) is replace x with 9, y with n, and z with 13. So $\bullet$ (9, n, 13) $= \sqrt{9n + 13}$. We know that $\bullet$ (9, n, 13) = 11, so $\sqrt{9n + 13} = 11$. Now solve this for n.
$$\sqrt{9n + 13} = 11$$
$$(\sqrt{9n + 13})^2 = 11^2$$
$$9n + 13 = 121$$
$$9n = 108$$
$$n = \frac{108}{9}, \text{ so } n = 12$$

v. (E) Average $= \dfrac{\text{Sum of the terms}}{\text{Number of terms}}$
$$71 = \frac{x}{6}$$
$$x = 71 \times 6, \text{ so } x = 426$$

vi. (K) Total widgets = Rate $\times$ Time

Total widgets $= \dfrac{150 \text{ widgets}}{30 \text{ min}} \times 4 \text{ hours}$

Total widgets $= \dfrac{150 \text{ widgets}}{\frac{1}{2} \text{ hr.}} \times 4 \text{ hours}$

$$= 1{,}200$$

vii. (A) Pick an easy number for n, such as 10. If the average of four numbers is 10, the sum of the four numbers is 40 ($4 \times 10 = 40$). If three of the numbers are $n + 3$, $n + 5$, and $n - 2$, then those three numbers are $10 + 3$, $10 + 5$ and $10 - 2$ or 13, 15, and 8. $13 + 15 + 8 = 36$. The sum of the four numbers must equal 40, so the remaining number is 4. If you plug 10 in for n in each of the answer choices, only (A) gives you 4.

viii. (B) Start with the middle answer choice, 9. If Mike has 9 shirts, then Adam has three times as many, or 27. If Adam gives Mike 6 shirts, Adam now has 21 and Mike has 15. This is not equal, so (H) is not correct. Since Adam was left with too many shirts when Mike had 9, Mike must have fewer than 9. Try (G). If Mike has 6 shirts, then Adam has 18. If Adam gives Mike 6, then they both have 12 shirts.

ix. (C) We're told that $xy = 20$ and $x < 4$. Now let's look at the statements. Statement I says that $y > 75$. Since $xy = 20$, $y = \frac{20}{x}$. When $x = 4$, $y = 5$. If we replace x with a smaller number than 4 in $\frac{20}{x}$, then $\frac{20}{x}$, which is y, will be greater than 5. Statement I must be true. Statement I must be part of the correct answer. Eliminate choices (B) and (D). Statement II says that $x + y > 10$. Try picking some values such that $xy = 20$ and x, 4. If $x = 3$, then $y = \frac{20}{x} = \frac{20}{3} = 6\frac{2}{3}$. The sum of x and y is not greater than 10. Statement II does not have to be true. it will not be part of the correct answer. Eliminate (E). Statement III says that $2(xy) = 40$, or $2xy = 40$. The question stem says that $xy = 20$. Multiplying both sides of the equation $xy = 20$ by 2, we have that $2(xy) = 2(20)$, or $2xy = 40$. Statement III must be true. (C) is correct.

Practice Questions

1. After the announcement of a sale, a bookstore sold $\frac{1}{2}$ of all its books in stock. On the following day, the bookstore sold 4,000 more books. Now only $\frac{1}{10}$ of the number of books in stock before the sale remain in the store. How many books were in stock before the announcement of the sale?

   (A)   8,000
   (B)   10,000
   (C)   12,000
   (D)   15,000
   (E)   20,000

2. Brad bought a radio on sale at a 20% discount from its regular price of $118. If there is an 8% sales tax that is calculated on the sale price, how much did Brad pay for the radio?

   (F) $23.60
   (G) $86.85
   (H) $94.40
   (J) $101.95
   (K) $127.44

3. Sheila charges $5.00 per haircut during the weekdays. On Saturday, she charges $7.50 per haircut. If Sheila has 6 customers each day of the week except Sunday, how much money does she earn in five weekdays and Saturday?

   (A) $150.00
   (B) $175.00
   (C) $180.00
   (D) $195.00
   (E) $210.00

4. The original price of a television decreases by 20 percent. By what percent must the price increase to reach its original value?

   (F)   15%
   (G)   20%
   (H)   25%
   (J)   30%
   (K)   40%

5. Ed has 100 dollars more than Robert. After Ed spends 20 dollars on groceries, Ed has five times as much money as Robert. How much money does Robert have?

   (A) $20
   (B) $30
   (C) $40
   (D) $50
   (E) $120

6. A worker earns $15.00 an hour for the first 40 hours he works each week, and one and a half times this much for every hour over 40 hours. If he earned $667.50 for one week's work, how many hours did he work?

   (F)   40
   (G)   41
   (H)   42
   (J)   43
   (K)   44

7. Liza has 40 less than three times the number of books that Janice has. If B is equal to the number of books that Janice has, which of the following expressions shows the total number of books that Liza and Janice have together?

   (A) $3B - 40$
   (B) $3B + 40$
   (C) $4B - 40$
   (D) $4B$
   (E) $4B + 40$

8. If $a \bullet b = \frac{ab}{a-b}$, which of the following does $3 \bullet 2$ equal?

   (F) $2 \bullet 3$
   (G) $6 \bullet 1$
   (H) $6 \bullet 2$
   (I) $6 \bullet 3$
   (J) $8 \bullet 4$

9. If William divides the amount of money he has by 5, and he adds $8, the result will be $20. If X is equal to the number of dollars that William has, which of the following equations shows this relationship?

   (A) $(X \div 8) + 5 = 20$
   (B) $(X \div 5) + 8 = 20$
   (C) $(X + 8) \div 5 = 20$
   (D) $(X + 5) \div 8 = 20$
   (E) $8(X + 5) = 20$

10. If a six-sided pencil with a trademark on one of its sides is rolled on a table, what is the probability that the side with the trademark is <u>not</u> touching the surface of the table when the pencil stops?

    (F) $\frac{1}{6}$

    (G) $\frac{1}{3}$

    (H) $\frac{1}{2}$

    (J) $\frac{2}{3}$

    (K) $\frac{5}{6}$

11. Team *A* had four times as many losses as it had ties in a season. If Team *A* won none of its games, which could be the total number of games it played that season?

    (A) 12
    (B) 15
    (C) 18
    (D) 21
    (E) 26

12. 587 people are travelling by bus for a field trip. If each bus seats 48 people and all the buses are filled to capacity except one, how many people sit in the unfilled bus?

    (F) 37
    (G) 36
    (H) 12
    (J) 11
    (K)   7

13. Rose has finished $\frac{5}{6}$ of her novel after one week of reading. If she reads an additional tenth of the novel during the next two days, what part of the novel will she have read?

    (A) $\frac{1}{10}$

    (B) $\frac{7}{15}$

    (C) $\frac{4}{5}$

    (D) $\frac{14}{15}$

    (E) $\frac{29}{30}$

14. A farmer has $4\frac{2}{3}$ acres of land for growing corn, and $2\frac{1}{2}$ times as many acres for growing wheat. How many acres does she have for wheat?

    (F) $2\frac{2}{3}$

    (G) $4\frac{1}{2}$

    (H) $8\frac{1}{6}$

    (I) $10\frac{1}{2}$

    (J) $11\frac{2}{3}$

15. Joyce baked 42 biscuits for her 12 guests. If six biscuits remain uneaten, what's the average number of biscuits that the guests ate?

    (A)   2
    (B)   3
    (C)   4
    (D)   6
    (E) 12

16. The average weight of Jake, Ken, and Larry is 60 kilograms. If Jake and Ken both weigh 50 kilograms, how much, in kilograms, does Larry weigh?

    (F) 40
    (G) 50
    (H) 60
    (I) 70
    (J) 80

17. If 3 added to 4 times a number is 11, the number must be

    (A) 1
    (B) 2
    (C) 3
    (D) 4
    (E) 5

18. The sum of 8 and a certain number is equal to 20 minus the same number. What is the number?

    (F)   2
    (G)   4
    (H)   6
    (J) 10
    (K) 14

Word Problems

19. Liz worked 3 hours less than twice as many hours as Rachel did. If W is the number of hours Rachel worked, which of the following expressions shows the total number of hours worked by Liz and Rachel together?

    (A) $2W - 3$
    (B) $2W + 3$
    (C) $3W - 3$
    (D) $3W + 3$
    (E) $4W - 2$

20. The area of a circle is πr^2 where r is the radius. If the circumference of a circle is $h\pi$, what is the area of the circle, in terms of h ?

    (F) $h^2 r^2$

    (G) $\dfrac{h^2 \pi}{4}$

    (H) $\dfrac{h^2 \pi}{2}$

    (J) $h^2 \pi$

    (K) $4h^2 \pi$

21. If $m \neq 0$ and $m \neq 1$, $m\ddagger = \dfrac{m}{m^2 - m}$. What is the value of $6\ddagger - (-5)\ddagger$?

    (A) $\dfrac{1}{30}$

    (B) $\dfrac{1}{20}$

    (C) $\dfrac{1}{4}$

    (D) $\dfrac{11}{30}$

    (E) $\dfrac{9}{20}$

22. Five less than 3 times a certain number is equal to twice the original number plus 7. What is the original number?

    (F) 2
    (G) $2\frac{2}{5}$
    (H) 6
    (J) 11
    (K) 12

23. The volume of a sphere is $\frac{4}{3}\pi r^3$ where r is the radius. What is the volume of a sphere with a radius of 3 ?

    (A) 4π
    (B) 8π
    (C) 16π
    (D) 36π
    (E) 72π

Practice Question Explanations

1. (B) After two days of the sale, $\frac{1}{10}$ of the original number of books in stock is left. This means that altogether, $\frac{9}{10}$ of the original number of books have been sold. $\frac{1}{2}$ of the books were sold on the first day. $\frac{1}{2}$ can also be called $\frac{5}{10}$. If $\frac{9}{10}$ were sold in two days, and $\frac{5}{10}$ were sold on the first day, then on the second day $\frac{4}{10}$ must have been sold. You're told that 4,000 books were sold on the second day, so 4,000 must be $\frac{4}{10}$ of the original number of books. Now you must determine what number 4,000 is $\frac{4}{10}$ of. Call the number N. If $\frac{4}{10}N = 4{,}000$, then $N = \frac{10}{4}(4{,}000) = 10(1{,}000) = 10{,}000$.

2. (J) This problem needs to be done in several steps. First find out the sale price of the radio. The discount was 20%, so the sale price was 80% of the original price.

   Percent • Whole = Part

       80% • $118 = Sale Price

       .80 • $118 = Sale Price

          $94.40 = Sale Price

   Now figure out how much tax Brad paid. The tax was 8% of the sale price.

   Percent • Whole = Part

       8% • $94.40 = Tax

       .08 • $94.40 = Tax

         $7.5520 = Tax

          $7.55 = Tax

   Now just add the tax to the sale price.

       $94.40 + 7.55 = $101.95

3. (D) Each weekday Sheila earns: $5.00 • 6 haircuts = $30. Each Saturday Sheila earns $7.50 • 6 haircuts = $45. In five weekdays she earns 5 • $30 = $150. In one Saturday she earns $45. So in five weekdays plus one Saturday she earns $150 + $45, or $195.

4. (H) The key is that while the value of the television decreases and increases by the same amount, it doesn't increase and decrease by the same percent. Let's pick $100 for the price of the television. If the price decreases by 20%, then since 20% of $100 is $20, the price decreases by $20. The new price is $100 − $20, or $80. For the new price to reach the original price ($100), it must be increased by $20. $20 is $\frac{1}{4}$ of 80, or 25% of $80. The new price must be increased by 25%, choice (H).

5. (A) Translate to get two equations. Let E be the amount Ed has and R be the amount Robert has. "Ed has $100 more than Robert" becomes $E = R + 100$. "Ed spends $20" means he'll have $20 less, or $E - 20$. "Five times as much as Robert" becomes $5R$. Therefore, $E - 20 = 5R$.
   Substitute $R + 100$ for E in the second equation and solve for R:

   $$(R + 100) - 20 = 5R$$
   $$R + 80 = 5R$$
   $$80 = 4R$$
   $$20 = R, \text{ so Robert has } \$20.$$

6. (J) Run the answer choices through the information in the stem to see which one gives a total of $667.50. Since the answer choices are in numerical order, start with the middle choice, (H). If he works for 42 hours, he earns $15 per hour for the first 40 hours, or $600, and he earns $1\frac{1}{2}$ times his normal rate for the two extra hours. $\frac{3}{2}$ times $15 is $22.50 per hour, and since he worked 2 hours at that rate, he made an additional $45. The total is $645, which isn't enough. So (H) is too small, as are (F) and (G). Now try (J). He still earns $600 for the first 40 hours, but now you have to multiply the overtime rate, $22.50, by 3,

which gives you $67.50. The total is $667.50, which means that (J) is correct.

7. (C) This is a simple translation problem. You're told that Janice has B books. Liza has 40 less than three times the number of books Janice has, which you can translate as $L = 3B - 40$. The total number they have together equals $B + (3B - 40)$, or $4B - 40$.

8. (J) Plug in the given values to solve. Then try the values in each answer choice until you find the one that produces the same result. Plugging in 3 and 2 gives you $\frac{(3)(2)}{3-2} = \frac{6}{1} = 6$. So you're looking for the answer choice that produces a result of 6. Only (J) does, so it is correct.

9. (B) This problem asks you to translate from English sentences into math.

The amount of money William has is X.
This amount divided by 5: $X \div 5$.
Add 8 dollars: $X \div 5 + 8$.
The result is 20 dollars: $(X \div 5) + 8 = 20$, choice (B).
Since division comes before addition in the order of operations, the parentheses aren't really necessary.

10. (K) The probability of an event happening is the ratio of the number of desired outcomes, to the number of possible outcomes or

$\text{Probability} = \frac{\text{Number of desired outcomes}}{\text{Number of possible outcomes}}$

If one side of the pencil has the trademark on it, then the other 5 sides are blank. When any one of the 5 blank sides is touching the surface of the table, the marked side cannot be touching the table. So there are 5 different ways for the pencil to lie on the table without the markd side touching the surface. The total number of possible sides for the pencil to lie on is 6. The proba-

bility that the trademark will not be touching the surface of the table when the pencil stops rolling is $\frac{5}{6}$, choice (K).

11. (B) Let the number of ties Team A had equal x. It lost 4 times as many games as it tied, or $4x$ games. It had no wins so the total number of games played by Team A is $x + 4x = 5x$. So the number of games played must be a multiple of 5; the only choice that is a multiple of 5 is (B), 15.

12. (J) There are 587 people traveling and each bus holds 48 people. $587 \div 48 = 12$ with a remainder of 11. So 12 buses are full and 11 people remain to ride in the unfilled bus.

13. (D) Rose read $\frac{5}{6}$ of the novel and plans to read another $\frac{1}{10}$, which will result in her having read $\frac{5}{6} + \frac{1}{10}$ of the novel. Add these two fractions, using 30 as the common denominator: $\frac{5}{6} + \frac{1}{10} = \frac{25}{30} + \frac{3}{30} = \frac{28}{30} = \frac{14}{15}$

14. (K) The farmer has $4\frac{2}{3} \cdot 2\frac{1}{2}$ acres for growing wheat. Change these mixed numbers to fractions in order to multiply: $\frac{14}{3} \times \frac{5}{2} = \frac{35}{3} = 11\frac{2}{3}$

15. (B) If 6 biscuits remained, $42 - 6 = 36$ were eaten by the 12 guests.

$\text{Average} = \frac{\text{Sum of the terms}}{\text{Number of terms}}$, so the average number of biscuits eaten by the guests was $\frac{36}{12} = 3$.

16. (E)

$\text{Average} = \frac{\text{Sum of the terms}}{\text{Number of terms}}$, so

$60 = \frac{\text{Total weight}}{3}$

$60 \times 3 = \text{Total weight}$

$180 = \text{Total weight}$

Jake and Ken each weigh 50 kilograms, so 50 + 50 + Larry's weight = 180 kilograms. Doing the math, Larry must weigh 80 kilograms.

17. (B) Let the number be x. Translating gives you $3 + 4x = 11$. Therefore, $4x = 8$ and $x = 2$.

18. (H) Translate from English to math. The sum of 8 and b is simply $8 + b$. The question states that this is equal to 20 minus the same number, or $20 - b$. So your equation is $8 + b = 20 - b$, and you can solve for b:

$$8 + b = 20 - b$$
$$8 + 2b = 20$$
$$2b = 12$$
$$b = 6$$

19. (C) Rachel worked W hours, and Liz worked 3 hours less than twice as many hours as Rachel, or $2W - 3$. Add these expressions to find the total number of hours worked by Liz and Rachel together:

$W + 2W - 3 = 3W - 3$, choice (C).

20. (G) Circumference of a circle is π times diameter, so a circumference of $h\pi$ means a diameter of h. The radius is half the diameter, or $\frac{h}{2}$. Plug $\frac{h}{2}$ into the area formula:

$$\pi\left(\frac{h}{2}\right)^2 = \pi\left(\frac{h^2}{4}\right) = \frac{h^2\pi}{4}$$

21. (D) Just plug into the expression that defines the symbol ‡:

$$6‡ - (-5)‡ =$$
$$= \frac{6}{6^2 - 6} - \frac{-5}{(-5)^2 - (-5)}$$
$$= \frac{6}{36 - 6} - \frac{-5}{25 + 5}$$
$$\frac{6}{30} - \frac{-5}{30}$$
$$\frac{6}{30} + \frac{5}{30} = \frac{11}{30}$$

Note that at two points in your calculation it is crucial to remember that subtracting a negative is the same as adding a positive.

22. (K) Call the unknown number x. Five less than 3 times the number, or $3x - 5$, equals twice the original number plus 7, or $2x + 7$. So $3x - 5 = 2x + 7$. Solve for x:

$$3x - 5 = 2x + 7$$
$$x - 5 = 7$$
$$x = 12$$

23. (D) All you need to do is plug the value of $r = 3$ into the formula you're given and simplify:

$$\text{volume} = \frac{4}{3}\pi(3)^3$$
$$= \frac{4}{3}\pi(27)$$
$$= 36\pi$$

ISEE Workshop

by Susanne L. Rust

Quantitative Comparisons

Highlights

- Understand the directions for Quantitative Comparisons

- Kaplan's five stategies for Quantitative Comparisons

- Avoiding the traps of Quantitative Comparisons

THE FORMAT

Where They Appear

Quantitative Comparisons, or QCs, appear **only on the ISEE**. Of the 40 math questions in the Quantitative Ability section, 20 are QCs. They are arranged in order of increasing difficulty.

The Questions

In QC's, instead of solving for a particular value, you need to compare two quantities.

In each question, you'll see two mathematical expressions; one in Column A, the other in Column B. Your job is to compare them.

Some questions include additional information about one or both quantities. This information is centered, unboxed, and essential to making the comparison.

Direction Box:

In questions 1–10, note the given information, if any, and then compare the quantity in Column A to the quantity in Column B. Next to the number of each question write

(A) if the quantity in Column A is greater

(B) if the quantity in Column B is greater

(C) if the two quantities are equal

(D) if the relationship cannot be determined from the information given

Three Rules for Choice (D)

Choice (D) is the only choice that represents a relationship that cannot be determined. (A), (B), and (C) all mean that a definite relationship can be found between the quantities in Columns A and B.

Three Things to Remember About Choice (D):

Rule 1: (D) is **rarely** the correct answer for the first few QC questions.

Rule 2: (D) is **never** the correct answer if both boxed quantities contain **only numbers.**

Rule 3: (D) **is** the correct answer if you can find more than one possible relationship between the two columns.

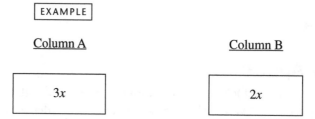

EXAMPLE

Column A

Column B

$3x$

$2x$

If x is a positive number, then Column A is larger. If x is equal to zero, then the quantities in Columns A and B are equal. If x is a negative number, then Column B is larger.

There is more than one possible relationship between Columns A and B in the previous example. Therefore, according to Rule 3, (D) is the correct choice. Of course, unlike the case above where we demonstrated three different possible relationships, as soon as you realize that there is **more than one** possible relationship, choose (D) and move on.

COMPARE, DON'T CALCULATE: KAPLAN'S FIVE STRATEGIES

The following is a list of five strategies that will help you to make quick comparisons on test day.

Strategy 1: Compare Piece by Piece

Strategy 2: Make One Column Look Like the Other

Strategy 3: Do the Same Thing to Both Columns

Strategy 4: Pick Numbers

Strategy 5: Avoid QC Traps

Let's look at each strategy in detail.

Kaplan Rules

There's usually an easier way to solve a QC question than to calculate it out.

Strategy 1: Compare Piece by Piece

This applies to QC's that compare two sums or two products.

EXAMPLE

Column A	Column B
$a > b > c > d$	
$a + c$	$b + d$

We're given four variables, or "pieces," in the above example, as well as the relationship between these pieces. We're told that a is greater than all of the other pieces, while c is greater only than d, etc. The next step is to compare the value of each "piece" in each column. If every "piece" in one column is greater than the corresponding "piece" in the other column, and if addition is the only mathematical operation involved, the column with the greater individual values ($a > b$, and $c > d$) will have the greater total value ($a + c > b + d$).

To recap, we knew from the information given that $a > b$, and $c > d$. Therefore, the first term in Column A, a, is greater than its corresponding term in Column B, b. Likewise, the second term in Column A, c, is greater than d, its corresponding term in Column B. Since each individual "piece" in Column A is greater than its corresponding "piece" in Column B, the total value of Column A must be greater. The answer is (A).

Strategy 2: Make One Column Look Like the Other

Use this strategy when the quantities in the two columns look so different that a direct comparison would be impossible.

If the quantities in Column A and B are expressed differently, or if one looks more complicated than the other, try to make a direct comparison easier by changing one column to look more like the other.

Let's try an example in which the quantities in Column A and Column B are expressed differently.

EXAMPLE

Column A

$2(x + 1)$

Column B

$2x + 2$

In the example above, it's difficult to make a direct comparison as the quantities are written. However, if you get rid of the parentheses in Column A so that the quantity more closely resembles that in Column B, you should see right away that a comparison can be made. So, if you get rid of the parentheses in Column A, you'll end up with $2x + 2$ in both columns. Therefore, the columns are equal in value, and the answer is (C).

This strategy is also useful when one column looks more complicated than the other.

EXAMPLE

Column A

$\dfrac{2\sqrt{3}}{\sqrt{6}}$

Column B

$\sqrt{2}$

Try simplifying Column A, since it is the more complicated looking quantity of the two.

1) $\dfrac{2\sqrt{3}}{\sqrt{6}} = \dfrac{2\sqrt{3}}{\sqrt{6}}$

2) $\dfrac{2\sqrt{3}}{\sqrt{6}} = \dfrac{2}{\sqrt{2}}$

3) $\dfrac{2}{\sqrt{2}} = \dfrac{2}{\sqrt{2}} \times \dfrac{\sqrt{2}}{\sqrt{2}} = 2\sqrt{2}$

4) $\dfrac{2\sqrt{2}}{} = \sqrt{2}$

By simplifying Column A, we are able to make a direct and easy comparison between the two columns. Column A, when simplified, is equivalent to $\sqrt{2}$, which is the quantity in Column B. Therefore, (C) is the correct answer.

Strategy 3: Do the Same Thing to Both Columns

By adding or subtracting the same amount from both columns, you can often unclutter a comparison, and make it more apparent. You can also multiply or divide both columns by the same positive number. This keeps the relationship between the columns the same. If the quantities in both columns are positive, you can square both columns. This keeps the relationship between the columns the same.

Changing the values, and not just the appearances of the quantities in both columns is often helpful in tackling QC questions. Set up the problem as an inequality, with the two columns as opposing sides of the inequality.

Kaplan Rules

> Do not multiply or divide both QC columns by a negative number.

To change the values of the columns, add or subtract the same amount from both columns and multiply or divide by a positive number without changing the absolute relationship. But **be careful**. Remember that the direction of an inequality sign will be reversed if you multiply or divide by a negative number. Since this reversal will alter the relationship between the two columns, avoid multiplying or dividing by a negative number. You can also square the quantities in both columns when both columns are positive. But **be careful**. Do not square both columns unless you know for certain that both columns are positive.

You can only square both columns when both are positive. Remember these two things when squaring the quantities in both columns: (1) the direction of an inequality sign can be reversed if one or both quantities are negative, and (2) the inequality sign can be changed to an equals sign if one quantity is positive and the other quantity is negative, with one quantity being the negative of the other. For example, $4 > -5$, yet $4^2 < (-5)^2$, since $16 < 25$. $2 > -2$, yet $2^2 = (-2)^2$, since $2^2 = (-2)^2 = 4$.

In the QC below what could you do to both columns?

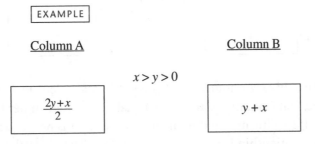

EXAMPLE

Column A	Column B
$x > y > 0$	
$\dfrac{2y+x}{2}$	$y + x$

Try multiplying both columns by 2 to get rid of that fraction in Column A. You're left with $2y + x$ in Column A and $2y + 2x$ in Column B. We know that $2y = 2y$. But what about the relationship between x and $2x$? The centered information tells us that $x > 0$, therefore, $2x > x$, and Column B is greater than Column A. Choice (B) is the right answer.

In the next QC, what could you do to both columns?

EXAMPLE

Column A	Column B
$\frac{1}{4} + \frac{1}{5} - \frac{1}{3}$	$\frac{1}{2} - \frac{1}{3} + \frac{1}{20}$

In this example, try adding $\frac{1}{3}$ to both sides. If you do this, you'll be left with $\frac{1}{4} + \frac{1}{5}$ in Column A and $\frac{1}{2} + \frac{1}{20}$ in Column B. Now treat this QC question like a standard fraction problem. To find the sums in each column, you must find the lowest common denominator. You're left with $\frac{9}{20}$ in Column A and $\frac{11}{20}$ in Column B. Column B is greater than Column A, and the answer is (B).

Strategy 4: Pick Numbers

Substitute numbers into those abstract algebra QC's. Try using a positive, a negative, and zero.

If a QC question involves variables, pick numbers to clarify the relationship. Here's what to do:

- Pick numbers that are easy to work with

- Plug in the numbers and calculate the values. What's the relationship between the columns?

- Pick a different number for each variable and recalculate.

Column A	Column B
$x > 0$	
x	$\frac{1}{x}$

Try choosing a relatively easy number like 1. Plug it in and calculate. If you have calculated correctly, you'll find that Columns A and B are equal, $1 = \frac{1}{1}$. Remember to try another number. Let's try $x = \frac{1}{2}$. If we plug in $\frac{1}{2}$ and recalculate, Column A is now equal to $\frac{1}{2}$, and Column B is equal to 2. The relationship is not the same as before. Therefore, the answer is (D).

Pick Different Kinds of Numbers

Never assume that all variables represent positive integers. Unless you're told otherwise, as in the case above, variables can be positive or negative, they can be zero or fractions. Because different kinds of numbers behave differently, you should always choose a different kind of number the second time around. In the example above, we knew that x wasn't a negative number, nor was it zero, so we tried a fraction, and discovered that the relationship between the columns did not remain the same.

In the next three examples, we'll choose different kinds of numbers, and observe the results. Remember that if there's more than one possible relationship between the two columns, the answer is (D).

Kaplan Rules

- Not all numbers are positive.
- Not all numbers are integers.

EXAMPLE

Column A | Column B

x | $-x$

If $x = 1$, Column A = 1 and Column B = −1.
In this case, Column A is greater

If $x = -1$, Column A = −1 and Column B = 1.
In this case, Column B is greater.

EXAMPLE

Column A | Column B

$x > 0$

x | $\frac{1}{x}$

If $x = 2$, Column A = 2 and Column B = $\frac{1}{2}$.

In this case, Column A is greater.

If $x = \frac{1}{2}$, Column A = $\frac{1}{2}$ and Column B = 2.

In this case, Column B is greater.

EXAMPLE

Column A	Column B
x	x^2

If $x = \frac{1}{2}$, Column A $= \frac{1}{2}$ and Column B $= \frac{1}{4}$.

In this case, Column A is greater.

If $x = 2$, Column A $= 2$ and Column B $= 4$.
In this case, Column B is greater.

Strategy 5: Avoid QC Traps!

Keep your eyes open for those trick questions designed to fool you into the obvious, but wrong answer.

To avoid these nasty traps, always be on your toes. Never assume anything. Be particularly careful towards the end of a QC set.

Don't Be Tricked by Misleading Information

EXAMPLE

Column A	Column B
Frank weighs more than Hector.	
Frank's height in meters	Hector's height in meters

The tests makers are hoping that you'll make some faulty logic, and think "If Frank is heavier, he must be taller." But that's not necessarily so. The answer in this case would be (D). If you keep your eyes open for these kinds of things, you'll spot them immediately.

Don't Assume

| EXAMPLE |

| Column A | Column B |

$$1 + x^2 = 10$$

| x | 3 |

A common mistake on QC questions is to assume that variables represent positive integers. We already dealt with these kinds of problems in the Picking Numbers strategy. Remember that positive and negative numbers, as well as fractions and zeros, behave differently.

In the example above, the test makers are hoping you'll assume that $x = 3$, since the square of $3 = 9$. But x could also be equal to -3. Because x could be 3 or -3, (D) is the correct answer.

Don't Fall for Look-Alikes

| EXAMPLE |

| Column A | Column B |

| $\sqrt{4} + \sqrt{4}$ | $\sqrt{8}$ |

Now, $4 + 4 = 8$, **but** $\sqrt{4} + \sqrt{4} > \sqrt{8}$! Don't forget the rules of radicals. The test makers are counting on you to rush and look for the obvious choice, (C). Be aware, and don't let them fool you. If $a > 0$ and $b > 0$, then $\sqrt{a+b} \neq \sqrt{a} + \sqrt{b}$.

Remember the convention that if x is positive, $\sqrt{x}$ means the positive square root. So $\sqrt{4} + \sqrt{4} = 2 + 2 = 4$. Now we have 4 in Column A and $\sqrt{8}$ in Column B. Since $\sqrt{8} < \sqrt{9}$ and $\sqrt{9} = 3$, $\sqrt{8} < 3 < 4$. Thus, $4 > \sqrt{8}$ and Column A is greater. Because 4 and $\sqrt{8}$ are both positive, you could also show that $4 > \sqrt{8}$ by squaring both 4 and $\sqrt{8}$. $4^2 = 16$ and $(\sqrt{8})^2 = 8$. $16 > 8$, so $4 > \sqrt{8}$. Choice (A) is correct.

Practice Questions

> **Directions:** In questions 1–9, note the given information, if any, and then compare the quantity in Column A to the quantity in Column B. Next to the number of each question write:
>
> **A** if the quantity in Column A is greater
>
> **B** if the quantity in Column B is greater
>
> **C** if the two quantities are equal
>
> **D** if the relationship cannot be determined from the information given

	Column A	Column B
1.	The average of 106, 117, 123, and 195	The average of 110, 118, 124, and 196

$$2x - 6 = 2x + 3x$$

	Column A	Column B
2.	x^2	4

$x > 0$

$y > 0$

	Column A	Column B
3.	$x - y$	$y - x$

$x \neq 0$

	Column A	Column B
4.	$\dfrac{x+2}{3}$	$x + 5$

	Column A	Column B
	\multicolumn{2}{c}{x is an even integer.}	
5.	x^2	x^3
6.	$\dfrac{6 + \sqrt{3}}{2}$	$\dfrac{3 + \sqrt{6}}{\sqrt{4}}$
7.	$6 + 10$	$\sqrt{36} + \sqrt{100}$
8.	25% of 65	$65 \times \sqrt{\dfrac{1}{4}}$

$a > b > c > d$

	Column A	Column B
9.	$a^2 + c$	$b^2 + d$

Practice Question Explanations

1. (B) The corresponding numbers in Column B are greater than those in Column A. Therefore, the average in Column B must be greater.

2. (C) Solve for x in the centered equation. First, subtract $2x$ from both sides. This will leave you with $-6 = 3x$. Divide both sides by 3. Now, $x = -2$. Plug in -2 for x to find the value of x^2 in Column A. Then $x^2 = (-2)^2 = 4$. The quantities in both columns are equal.

3. (D) From the centered information, you know only that the variables x and y must be positive. So plug in some positive integers. If $x = 5$ and $y = 3$, then Column A is $x - y = 5 - 3 = 2$ and Column B is $y - x = 3 - 5 = -2$. In this case, Column A is greater. Now plug in some different numbers. Notice that you have not been given any information about the relationship between x and y. If you were to switch the values that you used on the first try, so that now $x = 3$ and $y = 5$, then in this case Column A is $x - y = 3 - 5 = -2$ and Column B is $y - x = 5 - 3 = 2$. In this case, Column B is greater. Since more than one relationship between the columns is possible, choice (D) is correct.

4. (D) This problem appears to be an obvious candidate for the Pick-A-Number strategy. However, be careful with the numbers you choose. Let's plug in a number like 2 for x. In this case, Column A is $\frac{2 + 2}{3}$, or $\frac{4}{3}$, and Column B is $2 + 5$, or 7. In this case, Column B is greater. You next likely step would be to switch your plug-in number from a positive to a negative. Here's where the test makers trick you if you aren't careful. By letting $x = -2$, you find that Column A is $\frac{-2 + 2}{2}$, or 0, while Column B is $-2 + 5$, or 3. In this case, once again, Column B is greater.

Nonetheless, trust your instinct—your original anticipation about this question was right-on! What happens if you plug in a negative number which is considerably further away from 0 ? If you let $x = -100$, then Column A is $\frac{-100 + 2}{3} = \frac{-98}{3}$, or $-32\frac{2}{3}$, and Column B is $-100 + 5$, or -95. In this case, Column A is greater. Since more than one relationship between the columns is possible, choice (D) is correct.

5. (D) The centered information is actually not very helpful in this QC question. This is a classic Pick a Number type of problem. Let's begin by plugging in a positive value for x that is consistent with the centered information. Let $x = 2$. Then in this case, Column A is $2^2 = 2 \times 2$, or 4, and Column B is $2^3 = 2 \times 2 \times 2$, or 8. In this case, Column B is greater. Now pick a negative value for x which is consistent with the centered information. Let $x = -2$. Then in this case Column A is $(-2)^2 = (-2) \times (-2) = 4$ and Column B is $(-2)^3 = (-2) \times (-2) \times (-2) = -8$. In this case, Column A is greater. Since more than one relationship between the columns is possible, choice (D) is correct.

6. (A) Remember the convention that if x is positive, $\sqrt{x}$ means the positive square root of x. While it is true that every positive number has two square roots, a positive square root and a negative square root, the convention with the symbol $\sqrt{}$ is that if x is positive, $\sqrt{x}$ means the positive square root of x. For example 16 has the two square roots 4 and -4, while $\sqrt{16}$ means the positive square root of 16, which is 4. Thus, $\sqrt{16} = 4$.

First notice that the denominator $\sqrt{4}$ of Column B is equal to 2. So we're comparing $\frac{6 + \sqrt{3}}{2}$ in

Quantitative Comparisons

Column A with $\dfrac{3+\sqrt{6}}{2}$ in Column B. Now try doing the same thing to both columns. Multiplying both columns by 2 leaves us with $6 + \sqrt{3}$ for Column A and $3 + \sqrt{6}$ for Column B. Next, subtracting 3 from both columns leaves us with $3 + \sqrt{3}$ for Column A and $\sqrt{6}$ for Column B. Now $3 = \sqrt{9}$ and $\sqrt{9}$ is greater than $\sqrt{6}$. So 3 is greater than $\sqrt{6}$. Surely $3 + \sqrt{3}$ which is what we now have for Column A is greater than 3. Also 3 is greater than $\sqrt{6}$, with $\sqrt{6}$ being what we have for Column B. So $3 + \sqrt{3}$ for Column A must be greater than $\sqrt{6}$ for Column B. Choice (A) is correct.

7. (C) Remember the convention that if x is positive, $\sqrt{x}$ means the positive square root of x. Now look at the two columns. In Column A, $6 + 10 = 16$. In Column B we have $\sqrt{16} + \sqrt{36}$. By convention, $\sqrt{16} = 4$ and $\sqrt{36} = 6$. So $\sqrt{16} + \sqrt{36} = 4 + 6 = 10$. The quantities in both columns are equal to 10.

8. (B) Change one of the columns so you can make a direct comparison. A percentage can be written as a fraction and vice-versa. It's generally easier to work with fractions, so convert 25% in Column A to a fraction. The fractional equivalent of 25% is $\dfrac{1}{4}$. If you do not remember a percent equivalent, you convert a percent to a fraction (or decimal) by dividing the percent by 100%. Let's convert 25% to a fraction just for the sake of the discussion.

$25\% = \dfrac{25\%}{100\%} = \dfrac{25}{100} = \dfrac{1}{4}$. So Column A is $\dfrac{1}{4}$ of 65, or $\dfrac{65}{4}$. Column B is $65 \times \sqrt{\dfrac{1}{4}}$. Let's first simplify $\sqrt{\dfrac{1}{4}} \cdot \sqrt{\dfrac{1}{4}} = \dfrac{\sqrt{1}}{\sqrt{4}} = \dfrac{1}{2}$. So Column B is $65 \times \dfrac{1}{2}$, or $\dfrac{65}{2}$. Since $\dfrac{65}{2}$ is greater than $\dfrac{65}{4}$, Column B is greater.

9. (D) Since the variables could be positive or negative, pick different kinds of numbers for the variables to see if different relationships between the columns are possible. Remember that the values you pick must be consistent with the centered information, which is that $a > b > c > d$.

If $a = 4$, $b = 3$, $c = 2$, and $d = 1$, then the value of Column A is $a^2 + c = 4^2 + 2 = 16 + 2 = 18$ and the value of Column B is $b^2 + d = 3^2 + 1 = 9 + 1 = 10$. In this case, Column A is greater. If you only pick positive numbers for the variables which are consistent with the centered information, then it will always be true that $a^2 + c > b^2 + d$. You could fall for the trap here of thinking that $a^2 + c$ is always greater than $b^2 + d$ if you don't let some or all of the variables be negative. Now let $a = -1$, $b = -2$, $c = -3$, and $d = -4$. These values are consistent with the centered information. This time the value of Column A is $a^2 + c = (-1)^2 + (-3) = 1 - 3 = -2$ and the value of Column B is $b^2 + d = (-2)^2 + (-4) = 4 - 4 = 0$. So in this case Column B is greater. Since more than one relationship between the columns is possible, choice (D) is correct.

12

Sentence Completions

by Susanne L. Rust

Highlights

- Kaplan Four-Step Method for Sentence Completions

- How to pick up on clue Words

- How to avoid tricky wrong answers

- How to break down tough sentences

Sentence Completions are probably the easiest of all the verbal question types. Unlike Analogies, they give you some context in which to think about vocabulary words, and unlike Critical Reading, they only require you to focus on a single sentence at a time.

THE FORMAT

Sentence Completions appear only on the ISEE. Of the 40 questions in the Verbal Ability section, 15 are Sentence Completions. They're arranged in order of increasing difficulty.

Sentence Completions are "fill-in-the-blank" questions. Each question will have one or two blanks, and you must select the best fit from the four choices provided.

The instructions for the Sentence Completion Section will look something like this:

Panic Plan

If you have less than one month to study for the ISEE, here's the best way to spend your time:

- Learn the Kaplan Four-Step Method for Sentence Completions.

- Do the practice problems. If you miss an answer, scan the chapter and look at the examples.

Select the word(s) that best fit the meaning of each sentence.

> EXAMPLE
>
> Although the tomato looked sweet and _____, it tasted more like a very sour, dried out old sponge.
>
> (A) arid
> (B) juicy
> (C) enormous
> (D) cloying

In the example above, a contrast is presented about the way the tomato looked and tasted. We're told that the tomato tasted sour and had the texture of dry sponge. Since we already know that it looked *sweet* (the opposite of *sour*), we can infer that we need to find the opposite of *dry*. Therefore the tomato must have looked juicy, so (B) is the answer.

KAPLAN FOUR-STEP METHOD FOR SENTENCE COMPLETIONS

Step 1: Read the sentence carefully, looking for clues.

Step 2: Predict the answer.

Step 3: Pick the best match.

Step 4: Plug in your selection.

Let's take a closer look at each step.

Kaplan Rules

> Clue Words like *and, but, such as, however,* and *although* can indicate where a sentence is heading. Keep your eyes open for these kinds of helpful words.

1. Read the Sentence Carefully, Looking for Clues.

Think carefully about the sentence before looking at the answer choices. What does the sentence mean? Are there any clue words?

2. Predict the Answer.

Take a look at the following examples:

"They say that M&M's do not melt in your hands, but last summer . . . "

"Despite the fact that it was 50° below zero, we were . . . "

"I am so hungry I could . . . "

You could probably fill in the rest of these sentences using words similar to the speaker's own. It's often easy to see the direction in which a sentence is going; that's because the structure and the tone of a sentence can clue you in to its meaning.

Your job for the ISEE Sentence Completion questions is to fill in the missing pieces. One way to do this is to anticipate the answer before looking at the answer choices. Clue words and sentence structure (construction and punctuation) can help you determine where a sentence is headed.

Making an exact prediction isn't necessary. If you can even identify the missing word as just positive or negative, that will often be sufficient.

3. Pick the Best Match.

Make sure to scan every choice before deciding.

4. Plug in Your Selection.

Only one of the four possible answer choices will make sense. If you've gone through the four steps and more than one choice still seems possible, though, don't dwell on it. Try to eliminate at least one choice, guess and move on. Remember, on the ISEE, a wrong answer will not affect your score.

Using some examples, let's see how the four-step method works.

EXAMPLE

Most North American marsupials are ____; at night they forage for food and during the day they sleep.

(A) fastidious

(B) amiable

(C) monolithic

(D) nocturnal

Read the sentence carefully, looking for clues. The semicolon (;) is a big clue. It tells you that the first part of the sentence follows the direction of second first part. In other words, you're looking for a word that means nighttime activity and daytime rest.

Predict which word should go into the blank

Compare the answer choices with your prediction. Pick the best match. (A) *fastidious*, has nothing to do with being active at night. Neither does (B), *amiable*, or for that matter (C) *monolithic*. (D) *nocturnal*, however, means to be active at night, so that seems correct.

Check your choice by plugging it into the sentence. Try it out: "Most North American marsupials are nocturnal; at night they forage for food and during the day they sleep." Sounds pretty good. Finally, scan the other choices to make sure that (D) is indeed the best choice. No other choice works in the sentence, so (D) is right.

EXAMPLE

Juniper skated with such ____, that no one could ____ her talent any longer.

(A) speed . . ascertain

(B) melancholy . . deny

(C) agility . . question

(D) grace . . affirm

Read the sentence carefully, looking for clue words. A major clue here is *such … that*. You know that Juniper's skating ability, whether good or bad, has led to everybody agreeing about her talent. So whatever words go into the two blanks, they must agree. The second blank must support the first blank.

Predict the words that go into the blanks, making sure that whatever goes in the second blank supports the meaning of the first. If Juniper skated well, no one would deny that she has a lot of talent. If she skated terribly, everyone would agree that she had no talent. Don't let the negative structure of the second part of the sentence fool you: It's written as "no one could ____," as opposed to "everyone could ____." Make some predictions about the two missing pieces.

Compare your predictions with each answer choice, and pick the best fit. Which two words, when in context, will agree and support each other?

In (A), *speed* and *ascertain* don't make much sense together. In (B), *melancholy* and *deny* don't support one another. It doesn't make sense that "no one could *deny* her talent" because she skated sadly, mournfully, or with *melancholy*. In (C), *agility* and *question* do fit together well. Juniper skates with *agility*, so who could question her ability? In (D), *grace* and *affirm*, initially seem to support one another. But remember the negative in the second part of the sentence: " … *no one* could ____ her talent." It's illogical to say that she skated with such *grace* that "no one could *affirm* her talent." (C) is the answer.

PICKING UP ON CLUES

You need to be able to show how a sentence fits together in order to do well on Sentence Completions. Clue words will help you do that. The more clues you can find, the clearer the sentence will become. The clearer the sentence, the better your prediction.

What are clue words? There are a variety of clue words. Some will indicate **cause-and effect**, others a **contrast**, and some others will **define the missing word**.

EXAMPLES

• **Clues that indicate cause-and-effect**:

<u>Because</u> he was so scared of the dark, we were
_____ to find him sleeping without a night light.

<u>As a result</u> of her constant lying, Sheila was _____
_ to trust anyone else.

• **Clues that indicate contrast**:

Rita is funny and light-hearted; her twin,
Wendy, <u>however</u> is _____ and _____.

<u>Following</u> the wonderful news, Harry's visage
changed <u>from</u> an expression of _____ to one of
_____.

• **Clues that define the missing word**:

A <u>loud and tiresome child</u>, he acted particularly
_____ during the long car trip.

Smart and witty, Roger was the most _____
student in the class.

> **Be Careful**
>
> A single word can change the meaning of the entire sentence, so make sure to read the sentence carefully.

EXAMPLE

Fiona's bedroom still looks like a _____, despite
her efforts to keep it tidy.

Whatever goes into the blank must complete the contrast implied by the word *despite*. You know then, that it must describe the *opposite of tidy*. *Mess* or *sty* would be good predictions.

Exercises

Try using clue words to anticipate the answers to the questions below. Look at the sentences below, but *before* you look at the answers:

- Circle clue words.
- Think of a word or phrase that would best complete the sentence.
- Write your prediction below each sentence.

i. Although the dog had been through obedience class five times, it was still _____.

_____

ii. The scuba diver was _____ to have survived after her oxygen tank operated _____.

_____   _____

iii. The newspaper column _____ the senator's recent actions, in spite of his overall _____ and good will.

_____ _____

iv. Although Greg was a drivers education instructor, he drove _____.

_____

Here are the same questions with their answer choices. Now find the right answer to each, referring to the predictions you just made.

i. Although the dog had been through obedience class five times, it was still _____.
   (A) dutiful
   (B) unruly
   (C) candid
   (D) prostrate

ii. The scuba diver was _____ to have survived after her oxygen tank operated _____.
   (A) unable ... perfectly
   (B) anxious ... instinctively
   (C) surprised ... adequately
   (D) fortunate ... improperly

iii. The newspaper column _____ the senator's recent actions, in spite of his overall _____ and good will.
   (A) praised ... behavior
   (B) lauded ... neglect
   (C) parodied ... salute
   (D) denounced .. integrity

iv. Although Greg was a drivers education instructor, he drove _____.
   (A) harmlessly
   (B) precisely
   (C) impressively
   (D) recklessly

TACKLING HARD QUESTIONS

Sentence Completions will get increasingly harder as you go through them, so the last few will be the most difficult. If you get stuck, here are a few tips to help you through:

- Avoid tricky wrong answers.
- Take apart tough sentences.
- Work around tough vocabulary.

Avoiding Tricky Wrong Answers

Toward the end of a set, keep your eyes open for tricky answer choices. Avoid:

Hint

Questions tend to go from *easiest* to *hardest*—so, in general, the higher the question number, the harder the question.

- Opposites of the correct answer.

- Words that may sound right because they are tough.

- Questions with two missing pieces, where one word sounds right but the other doesn't.

The following would be the twelfth question out of a fifteen-problem set.

> EXAMPLE

> At first the house seemed frightening with all its cobwebs and creaking shutters, but we soon realized that it was quite _____.

> (A) benign
> (B) deceptive
> (C) affluent
> (D) haunted

Read this sentence carefully or you may get tricked. If you read it too quickly, it may sound like "The house was really scary with all of those cobwebs and creaking shutters, and we soon realized … it was!" So, you would pick (D) *haunted*, or maybe (B) *deceptive*.

Pick Up the Clues

There are two major clue words here, and you should have picked them up right away. The first one, *At first*, indicates that the author perceived something to be one way *at first*—but after taking a second look, realized it was different. That leads us to the second clue word, *but*. Just as we predicted, the author thought the house was creepy at first, *but* then felt differently. We know, therefore, that the word in the blank must be the *opposite*, or at least not the same, as *creepy*, or *haunted*.

Don't Pick an Answer Just Because it Sounds Hard

Affluent means wealthy. You might be tempted to choose it because looks or sounds impressive. But it's thrown in there to trick you. Don't choose a word without good reason.

Let's look at a two-blank sentence. The following example is the fifteenth of a fifteen-problem set.

EXAMPLE

Screaming and laughing, the students were __
by their ___ experience on the white-water
raft.

(A) amused .. tepid

(B) irritated .. continued

(C) exhilarated .. first

(D) frightened .. secure

Two-Blank Sentences

Sentences with two blanks can be
easier than those with one blank.

- Try the easier blank first.

- Save time by eliminating all
  choices that won't work for
  that blank.

Look At All the Choices

Check out the first blank first. Sometimes you can eliminate one or more
answer choices right away if some possibilities don't fit. *Irritated* and/or
frightened students do not scream and laugh. So, eliminate (B) and (D).

Now check the second blank. A tepid (or half-hearted) experience wouldn't
make a bunch of students scream and laugh, either, so (A) is out. Only (C)
fits both of the blanks: The students would laugh and scream of exhilaration
on their first white water rafting experience.

Taking Apart Tough Sentences

Look at the following example, another fifteenth of a fifteen-problem set.

EXAMPLE

The ___ argument had never been written
down but was understood and upheld by the
governments of both countries.

(A) tacit

(B) public

(C) distinguished

(D) illegal

What if you were stumped. What if you had no idea which word to pick? Try this method; it
goes something like this:

Tacit, hmmm, sounds familiar.

Public, nope. It doesn't sound right in this context.

Distinguished—if it was so distinguished, why was it never written down?

Illegal, nope. Do governments uphold and support illegal arguments? That doesn't sound
    right.

Choice (A) sounds the best. As it turns out, it's also correct. *Tacit* arguments are unspoken or silent ones; they're not expressed or declared openly, but *implied*. This makes sense here.

Let's try a complex sentence with two blanks. Remember the rules:

- Try the easier blank first.
- Save time by eliminating all choices that won't work for that blank.

EXAMPLE

The old _____ hated parties and refused to _____ in the festivities.

(A) actor .. direct

(B) curmudgeon .. partake

(C) mediator .. take

(D) surgeon .. place

Well, the easier of the two blanks here is the first one, but it's impossible to rule out any choices, because an actor, a curmudgeon (especially), a mediator, and a surgeon all have the potential of hating parties.

Try the second blank, and see what can be ruled out. (A) doesn't make any sense; what does *direct* in the festivities mean? It's nonsensical. (B) *partake* makes sense. (C) take in the festivities doesn't sound right, and neither does (D) *place* in the festivities. That leaves choice (B) as the best and only fit. A *curmudgeon* is, by definition, an ornery or grumpy person, so it makes sense that he wouldn't want to *partake* in the festivities.

Exercise Answers

i. (B) Clue: *although*. *Although* indicates that
        there was something the dog hadn't
        learned, even after five classes. Because we
        know that the dog was at obedience class,
        the only choice that makes sense is (B)
        unruly.

ii. (D) *After* is the clue word. Try the first blank.
        What works? They all do: The scuba diver
        could be *unable*, *anxious*, *surprised*, or *for-
        tunate* to have survived. But only one
        choice creates a contrast between what her
        tank *did*, and how she was *after* the inci-
        dent. The scuba diver was *fortunate* to
        survive *after* her tank operated *improperly*.

iii. (D) Clue: *in spite of*, which means despite, or
        even though. So, the newspaper column
        negatively displayed the senator, in spite
        of his positive qualities, i.e., good will.
        Therefore, we need a negative word in the
        first blank and a positive one in the sec-
        ond blank. (A) and (B) can be eliminated,
        since they both have positive first blanks.
        Now, if you compare (C) and (D), you'll
        see that only (D) makes sense.

iv. (D) The clue word is *although*. So, *although*
        Greg was a drivers education instructor,
        he drove in a manner unlike one. We can
        infer that a drivers education instructor
        would be a safe, reliable driver, so the
        answer must be the *opposite* of these qual-
        ities. Only one choice makes the match,
        and that's (D), *recklessly*.

Practice Questions

1. The firm employed many lackadaisical employees, who had a ___ approach to their work.

    (A) creative
    (B) independent
    (C) unproductive
    (D) discontented

2. Due to ___ weather, the school closed and ___ all classes.

    (A) cold . . continued
    (B) severe . . cancelled
    (C) humid . . relieved
    (D) frosty . . alleviated

3. Many paleontologists believe that modern birds and crocodiles are the ___ of the ancient dinosaurs.

    (A) descendants
    (B) ancestors
    (C) neologisms
    (D) reptiles

4. Her eyes were wide with ___, as the ship ___ with gold, jewels, and precious metals sailed into port.

    (A) amazement . . arrived
    (B) reason . . purged
    (C) wonder . . laden
    (D) purpose . . meandered

5. It was Mt. Vesuvius that erupted and ___ the city of Pompeii in the year 79 A.D.

    (A) desiccated
    (B) decimated
    (C) erected
    (D) detected

6. The determined young cadet ___ every character that the ideal soldier should have.

    (A) embodied
    (B) created
    (C) secluded
    (D) vaporized

Practice Question Answers

1. (C) *Lackadaisical* means showing a lack of interest or spirit, listless or languid. If the firm employed lackadaisical workers, these workers probably had an *unproductive* approach to their work.

2. (B) If you tried each of the choices in the first blank, you'd see that they all fit. As for the second blank, only one choice makes sense, because of *severe* weather, all classes were *cancelled*.

3. (C) Her eyes could well have been wide with *amazement, reason, wonder,* and *purpose* as the ship sailed in. But the only choice that makes sense when you try to fill in the second blank is that "her eyes were wide with *wonder*, as the ship *laden* with gold, jewels and precious metals sailed into port." The other combinations just don't make sense.

4. (A) This question is filled with elements that the test makers hopes to fool you with. Both the answer choices and the question itself contain difficult vocabulary, i.e., *neologisms* and *paleontologists*. In addition, the antonym for the correct answer is thrown in as a curve ball. However, the only choice that makes sense is (A) *descendents*. Many paleontologists believe that birds and crocodiles are *descended* from dinosaurs.

5. (B) It's possible to infer from the information in the sentence that Mt. Vesuvius is a volcano. Regular hills and mountains don't erupt, only volcanoes do. And volcanoes don't *erect* cities, nor do they *detect* or *desiccate* cities. Indeed, volcanoes are very dangerous because they have the potential to *decimate* cities.

6. (A) *To embody* means *to personify*. (A) is the only choice that works here. The cadet doesn't *create* the characters of an ideal soldier, nor does he *seclude* or for that matter *vaporize* those characters.

Summing Up

13

What Do I Do Now?

Highlights

- Tips for managing your time just before the test

- Tips for handling stress during the test

Is it starting to feel like your whole life is a build-up to the SSAT/ISEE? You really want to go to a certain school and you know your parents want you to as well. You have worried about the test for months, and spent at least a few hours in solid preparation for it. As the test gets closer, you may find your anxiety is on the rise. Don't worry. After the preparation you've received from this book, you're in good shape for the test.

ITINERARY

To calm any pretest jitters you may have, this chapter leads you through a sane itinerary for the last week.

The Week Before the Test

- Focus on strategy and backup plans.

- Practice strategies you had the best success rate with.

- Decide and know **exactly** how you're going to approach each section and question type.

- Sit down and do practice problems in the Question Bank or complete extra drills you might have skipped the first time through.

- Practice waking up early and eating breakfast so that you'll be alert in the morning on Test Day.

Quick Tips For the Days Just Before the Exam

- The best test takers do less and less as the test approaches. Taper off your study schedule and take it easy on yourself. Give yourself time off, especially the evening before the exam. By that time, if you've studied well, everything you need to know is firmly stored in your memory bank.

- Positive self-talk can be extremely liberating and invigorating, especially as the test looms closer. Tell yourself things such as "I will do well" rather than "I hope things go well"; "I can" rather than "I cannot." Replace any negative thoughts with affirming statements that boost your self-esteem.

- Get your act together sooner rather than later. Have everything (including choice of clothing) laid out in advance. Most important, make sure you know where the test will be held and the easiest, quickest way to get there. You'll have great peace of mind by knowing that all the little details—gas in the car, directions, etcetera—are set before the day of the test.

- Go to the test site a few days in advance, particularly if you are especially anxious. If at all possible, find out what room your part of the alphabet is assigned to, and try to sit there (by yourself) for a while. Better yet, bring some practice material and do at least a section or two.

- Forego any practice on the day before the test. It's in your best interest to marshal your physical and psychological resources for 24 hours or so. Even race horses are kept in the paddock and treated like princes the day before a race. Keep the upcoming test out of your consciousness; go to a movie, take a pleasant hike, or just relax. Don't eat junk food or tons of sugar. And, of course, get plenty of rest the night before—just don't go to bed too early. It's hard to fall asleep earlier than you're used to, and you don't want to lie there worrying about the test.

Two Days Before the Test

Do your last studying—a few more practice problems, a few more vocabulary words—and call it quits.

The Night Before the Test

Don't study. Get together the following items:

- Your admission/registration ticket

- Photo ID

- A watch (choose one that is easy to read)

- Slightly dull No. 2 pencils (so they fill in the ovals faster)

- Pencil sharpener

- Erasers

- Clothes you'll wear (Dress in layers! The climate at the test location may vary, as may your body temperature. Make sure you can warm up or cool down easily.)

- Snacks (easy to open or partially unwrapped)

- Money

- Packet of tissues

Know exactly where you're going and exactly how you're getting there.

Relax the night before the test. Read a good book, take a bubble bath, watch TV. Get a good night's sleep. Go to bed at a reasonable hour and leave yourself extra time in the morning.

Things Not to Do the Night Before the Test

- Try to copy the dictionary onto your fingernails.

- Stay up all night watching all the *Friday the 13th* movies.

- Eat a large double anchovy, sausage, and pepper pizza with a case of chocolate soda.

- Send away for brochures from clown school.

- Start making flashcards.

- Tattoo yourself.

The Morning of the Test

Eat breakfast. Make it something substantial and nutritious, but don't deviate too much from your everyday pattern.

Dress in layers so that you can adjust to the temperature of the test room.

Read something to warm up your brain with a newspaper or a magazine before the test starts.

Be sure to get there early. Leave enough time to allow for traffic, mass transit delays, your Dad getting lost en route, and any other snag that could slow you down.

During the Test

Don't be shaken. If you find your confidence slipping, remind yourself how well you've prepared. You know the structure of the test; you know the instructions; you've studied for every question type.

Even if something goes really wrong, don't panic. If the test booklet is defective—two pages are stuck together or the ink has run—try to stay calm. Raise your hand, tell the proctor you need a new book. If you accidentally misgrid your answer page or put the answers in the wrong section, again don't panic. Raise your hand, tell the proctor. He or she might be able to arrange for you to regrid your test after it's over, when it won't cost you any time.

Don't think about which section is experimental. Remember, you never know for sure which section won't count. Besides, you can't work on any other section during that section's designated time slot.

Handling Stress During the Test

The biggest stress monster will be the test itself. Fear not; there are methods of quelling your stress during the test.

- Keep moving forward instead of getting bogged down in a difficult question. You don't have to get everything right to achieve a fine score. So, don't linger out of desperation on a question that is going nowhere even after you've spent considerable time on it. The best test takers skip difficult material temporarily in search of the easier stuff. They mark the ones that require extra time and thought.

- Don't be thrown if other test takers seem to be working more busily and furiously than you are. Don't mistake the other people's sheer activity as signs of progress and higher scores.

- *Keep breathing!* Weak test takers tend to share one major trait: They don't breathe properly as the test proceeds. They might hold their breath without realizing it, or breathe erratically or arrhythmically. Improper breathing hurts confidence and accuracy. Just as important, it interferes with clear thinking.

- Some quick isometrics during the test—especially if concentration is wandering or energy is waning—can help. Try this: Put your palms together and press intensely for a few seconds. Concentrate on the tension you feel through your palms, wrists, forearms, and up into your biceps and shoulders. Then, quickly release the pressure. Feel the difference as you let go. Focus on the warm relaxation that floods through the muscles.

Now you're ready to return to the task.

- Here's another isometric that will relieve tension in both your neck and eye muscles. Slowly rotate your head from side to side, turning your head and eyes to look as far back over each shoulder as you can. Feel the muscles stretch on one side of your neck as they contract on the other. Repeat five times in each direction.

What Are "Signs of a Winner," Alex?

Here's some advice from a Kaplan instructor who won big on *Jeopardy!*™ In the green room before the show, he noticed that the contestants who were quiet and "within themselves" were the ones who did great on the show. The contestants who didn't perform as well were those who were cramming facts and talking a lot before the show. Lesson: Spend the final hours before the test getting sleep, meditating, and generally relaxing.

With what you've just learned here, you're armed and ready to do battle with the test. This book and your studies will give you the information you'll need to answer the questions. It's all firmly planted in your mind. You also know how to deal with any excess tension that might come along, both when you're studying for and taking the exam. You've experienced everything you need to tame your test anxiety and stress. You're going to get a great score.

Good luck!

After the Test

Once the test is over, put it out of your mind. Start thinking about more interesting things. You might walk out of the SSAT/ISEE thinking that you blew it. You probably didn't. You tend to remember the questions that stumped you, not the many that you knew.

If you want more help, want to know more about the SSAT/ISEE, or want to find out about Kaplan prep courses for the PSAT, SAT, and ACT, give us a call at 1-800-KAP-TEST. We're here to answer your questions and to help you in any way that we can. You can also check out our Web site at www.kaptest.com.

Practice Tests
and
Explanations

SSAT TEST OVERVIEW

Total Time

Approximately $2\frac{1}{2}$ hours.

Questions

Aside from the essay, all questions are multiple-choice in format. Questions alternate between answer choices labeled A–E and choices labeled F–K.

Content

The SSAT tests Math and Verbal skills. There are two scored Math sections, two scored Verbal sections, one unscored Experimental section (which may be either Math or Verbal), and one unscored Essay section.

Pacing

You are not expected to complete all items on the SSAT. This is particularly true if you are at the low end of the age range of test takers (8th or 9th grade). The best approach to pacing is to work as quickly as you can without losing accuracy. Further, if a question is giving you difficulty, circle it and move on. You can always come back to it later, but you shouldn't waste time on a question that is stumping you when you could be gaining valuable points elsewhere.

Guessing

On the SSAT, you receive 1 point for each question answered correctly. For those questions you answer incorrectly, you lose $\frac{1}{4}$ point. As a result, guess *only* when you can do so intelligently. In other words, don't guess wildly, but *do* guess if you can eliminate at least one answer choice as clearly wrong.

14

SSAT Upper Level
Practice Test 1

HOW TO TAKE THIS PRACTICE TEST

Before taking this practice test, find a quiet room where you can work uninterrupted for two-and-a-half hours. Make sure you have a comfortable desk, your calculator, and several No. 2 pencils.

Use the answer sheet provided to record your answers. (You can cut it out or photocopy it.)

Once you start this practice test, don't stop until you've finished. Remember—you can review any questions within a section, but you may not go back or forward a section.

You'll find an answer key, score conversion charts, and explanations following the test.

Good luck.

SSAT Practice Test 1
Answer Sheet

Remove (or photocopy) this answer sheet and use it to complete the practice test.

Start with number 1 for each section. If a section has fewer questions than answer spaces, leave the extra spaces blank.

SECTION 1

1 Ⓐ Ⓑ Ⓒ Ⓓ Ⓔ	13 Ⓐ Ⓑ Ⓒ Ⓓ Ⓔ	25 Ⓐ Ⓑ Ⓒ Ⓓ Ⓔ	37 Ⓐ Ⓑ Ⓒ Ⓓ Ⓔ	49 Ⓐ Ⓑ Ⓒ Ⓓ Ⓔ
2 Ⓕ Ⓖ Ⓗ Ⓙ Ⓚ	14 Ⓕ Ⓖ Ⓗ Ⓙ Ⓚ	26 Ⓕ Ⓖ Ⓗ Ⓙ Ⓚ	38 Ⓕ Ⓖ Ⓗ Ⓙ Ⓚ	50 Ⓕ Ⓖ Ⓗ Ⓙ Ⓚ
3 Ⓐ Ⓑ Ⓒ Ⓓ Ⓔ	15 Ⓐ Ⓑ Ⓒ Ⓓ Ⓔ	27 Ⓐ Ⓑ Ⓒ Ⓓ Ⓔ	39 Ⓐ Ⓑ Ⓒ Ⓓ Ⓔ	51 Ⓐ Ⓑ Ⓒ Ⓓ Ⓔ
4 Ⓕ Ⓖ Ⓗ Ⓙ Ⓚ	16 Ⓕ Ⓖ Ⓗ Ⓙ Ⓚ	28 Ⓕ Ⓖ Ⓗ Ⓙ Ⓚ	40 Ⓕ Ⓖ Ⓗ Ⓙ Ⓚ	52 Ⓕ Ⓖ Ⓗ Ⓙ Ⓚ
5 Ⓐ Ⓑ Ⓒ Ⓓ Ⓔ	17 Ⓐ Ⓑ Ⓒ Ⓓ Ⓔ	29 Ⓐ Ⓑ Ⓒ Ⓓ Ⓔ	41 Ⓐ Ⓑ Ⓒ Ⓓ Ⓔ	53 Ⓐ Ⓑ Ⓒ Ⓓ Ⓔ
6 Ⓕ Ⓖ Ⓗ Ⓙ Ⓚ	18 Ⓕ Ⓖ Ⓗ Ⓙ Ⓚ	30 Ⓕ Ⓖ Ⓗ Ⓙ Ⓚ	42 Ⓕ Ⓖ Ⓗ Ⓙ Ⓚ	54 Ⓕ Ⓖ Ⓗ Ⓙ Ⓚ
7 Ⓐ Ⓑ Ⓒ Ⓓ Ⓔ	19 Ⓐ Ⓑ Ⓒ Ⓓ Ⓔ	31 Ⓐ Ⓑ Ⓒ Ⓓ Ⓔ	43 Ⓐ Ⓑ Ⓒ Ⓓ Ⓔ	55 Ⓐ Ⓑ Ⓒ Ⓓ Ⓔ
8 Ⓕ Ⓖ Ⓗ Ⓙ Ⓚ	20 Ⓕ Ⓖ Ⓗ Ⓙ Ⓚ	32 Ⓕ Ⓖ Ⓗ Ⓙ Ⓚ	44 Ⓕ Ⓖ Ⓗ Ⓙ Ⓚ	56 Ⓕ Ⓖ Ⓗ Ⓙ Ⓚ
9 Ⓐ Ⓑ Ⓒ Ⓓ Ⓔ	21 Ⓐ Ⓑ Ⓒ Ⓓ Ⓔ	33 Ⓐ Ⓑ Ⓒ Ⓓ Ⓔ	45 Ⓐ Ⓑ Ⓒ Ⓓ Ⓔ	57 Ⓐ Ⓑ Ⓒ Ⓓ Ⓔ
10 Ⓕ Ⓖ Ⓗ Ⓙ Ⓚ	22 Ⓕ Ⓖ Ⓗ Ⓙ Ⓚ	34 Ⓕ Ⓖ Ⓗ Ⓙ Ⓚ	46 Ⓕ Ⓖ Ⓗ Ⓙ Ⓚ	58 Ⓕ Ⓖ Ⓗ Ⓙ Ⓚ
11 Ⓐ Ⓑ Ⓒ Ⓓ Ⓔ	23 Ⓐ Ⓑ Ⓒ Ⓓ Ⓔ	35 Ⓐ Ⓑ Ⓒ Ⓓ Ⓔ	47 Ⓐ Ⓑ Ⓒ Ⓓ Ⓔ	59 Ⓐ Ⓑ Ⓒ Ⓓ Ⓔ
12 Ⓕ Ⓖ Ⓗ Ⓙ Ⓚ	24 Ⓕ Ⓖ Ⓗ Ⓙ Ⓚ	36 Ⓕ Ⓖ Ⓗ Ⓙ Ⓚ	48 Ⓕ Ⓖ Ⓗ Ⓙ Ⓚ	60 Ⓕ Ⓖ Ⓗ Ⓙ Ⓚ

right in section 1

wrong in section 1

SECTION 2

1 Ⓐ Ⓑ Ⓒ Ⓓ Ⓔ	6 Ⓕ Ⓖ Ⓗ Ⓙ Ⓚ	11 Ⓐ Ⓑ Ⓒ Ⓓ Ⓔ	16 Ⓕ Ⓖ Ⓗ Ⓙ Ⓚ	21 Ⓐ Ⓑ Ⓒ Ⓓ Ⓔ
2 Ⓕ Ⓖ Ⓗ Ⓙ Ⓚ	7 Ⓐ Ⓑ Ⓒ Ⓓ Ⓔ	12 Ⓕ Ⓖ Ⓗ Ⓙ Ⓚ	17 Ⓐ Ⓑ Ⓒ Ⓓ Ⓔ	22 Ⓕ Ⓖ Ⓗ Ⓙ Ⓚ
3 Ⓐ Ⓑ Ⓒ Ⓓ Ⓔ	8 Ⓕ Ⓖ Ⓗ Ⓙ Ⓚ	13 Ⓐ Ⓑ Ⓒ Ⓓ Ⓔ	18 Ⓕ Ⓖ Ⓗ Ⓙ Ⓚ	23 Ⓐ Ⓑ Ⓒ Ⓓ Ⓔ
4 Ⓕ Ⓖ Ⓗ Ⓙ Ⓚ	9 Ⓐ Ⓑ Ⓒ Ⓓ Ⓔ	14 Ⓕ Ⓖ Ⓗ Ⓙ Ⓚ	19 Ⓐ Ⓑ Ⓒ Ⓓ Ⓔ	24 Ⓕ Ⓖ Ⓗ Ⓙ Ⓚ
5 Ⓐ Ⓑ Ⓒ Ⓓ Ⓔ	10 Ⓕ Ⓖ Ⓗ Ⓙ Ⓚ	15 Ⓐ Ⓑ Ⓒ Ⓓ Ⓔ	20 Ⓕ Ⓖ Ⓗ Ⓙ Ⓚ	25 Ⓐ Ⓑ Ⓒ Ⓓ Ⓔ

right in section 2

wrong in section 2

SECTION 3

1 Ⓐ Ⓑ Ⓒ Ⓓ Ⓔ	9 Ⓐ Ⓑ Ⓒ Ⓓ Ⓔ	17 Ⓐ Ⓑ Ⓒ Ⓓ Ⓔ	25 Ⓐ Ⓑ Ⓒ Ⓓ Ⓔ	33 Ⓐ Ⓑ Ⓒ Ⓓ Ⓔ
2 Ⓕ Ⓖ Ⓗ Ⓙ Ⓚ	10 Ⓕ Ⓖ Ⓗ Ⓙ Ⓚ	18 Ⓕ Ⓖ Ⓗ Ⓙ Ⓚ	26 Ⓕ Ⓖ Ⓗ Ⓙ Ⓚ	34 Ⓕ Ⓖ Ⓗ Ⓙ Ⓚ
3 Ⓐ Ⓑ Ⓒ Ⓓ Ⓔ	11 Ⓐ Ⓑ Ⓒ Ⓓ Ⓔ	19 Ⓐ Ⓑ Ⓒ Ⓓ Ⓔ	27 Ⓐ Ⓑ Ⓒ Ⓓ Ⓔ	35 Ⓐ Ⓑ Ⓒ Ⓓ Ⓔ
4 Ⓕ Ⓖ Ⓗ Ⓙ Ⓚ	12 Ⓕ Ⓖ Ⓗ Ⓙ Ⓚ	20 Ⓕ Ⓖ Ⓗ Ⓙ Ⓚ	28 Ⓕ Ⓖ Ⓗ Ⓙ Ⓚ	36 Ⓕ Ⓖ Ⓗ Ⓙ Ⓚ
5 Ⓐ Ⓑ Ⓒ Ⓓ Ⓔ	13 Ⓐ Ⓑ Ⓒ Ⓓ Ⓔ	21 Ⓐ Ⓑ Ⓒ Ⓓ Ⓔ	29 Ⓐ Ⓑ Ⓒ Ⓓ Ⓔ	37 Ⓐ Ⓑ Ⓒ Ⓓ Ⓔ
6 Ⓕ Ⓖ Ⓗ Ⓙ Ⓚ	14 Ⓕ Ⓖ Ⓗ Ⓙ Ⓚ	22 Ⓕ Ⓖ Ⓗ Ⓙ Ⓚ	30 Ⓕ Ⓖ Ⓗ Ⓙ Ⓚ	38 Ⓕ Ⓖ Ⓗ Ⓙ Ⓚ
7 Ⓐ Ⓑ Ⓒ Ⓓ Ⓔ	15 Ⓐ Ⓑ Ⓒ Ⓓ Ⓔ	23 Ⓐ Ⓑ Ⓒ Ⓓ Ⓔ	31 Ⓐ Ⓑ Ⓒ Ⓓ Ⓔ	39 Ⓐ Ⓑ Ⓒ Ⓓ Ⓔ
8 Ⓕ Ⓖ Ⓗ Ⓙ Ⓚ	16 Ⓕ Ⓖ Ⓗ Ⓙ Ⓚ	24 Ⓕ Ⓖ Ⓗ Ⓙ Ⓚ	32 Ⓕ Ⓖ Ⓗ Ⓙ Ⓚ	40 Ⓕ Ⓖ Ⓗ Ⓙ Ⓚ

right in section 3

wrong in section 3

SECTION 4

1 Ⓐ Ⓑ Ⓒ Ⓓ Ⓔ	6 Ⓕ Ⓖ Ⓗ Ⓙ Ⓚ	11 Ⓐ Ⓑ Ⓒ Ⓓ Ⓔ	16 Ⓕ Ⓖ Ⓗ Ⓙ Ⓚ	21 Ⓐ Ⓑ Ⓒ Ⓓ Ⓔ
2 Ⓕ Ⓖ Ⓗ Ⓙ Ⓚ	7 Ⓐ Ⓑ Ⓒ Ⓓ Ⓔ	12 Ⓕ Ⓖ Ⓗ Ⓙ Ⓚ	17 Ⓐ Ⓑ Ⓒ Ⓓ Ⓔ	22 Ⓕ Ⓖ Ⓗ Ⓙ Ⓚ
3 Ⓐ Ⓑ Ⓒ Ⓓ Ⓔ	8 Ⓕ Ⓖ Ⓗ Ⓙ Ⓚ	13 Ⓐ Ⓑ Ⓒ Ⓓ Ⓔ	18 Ⓕ Ⓖ Ⓗ Ⓙ Ⓚ	23 Ⓐ Ⓑ Ⓒ Ⓓ Ⓔ
4 Ⓕ Ⓖ Ⓗ Ⓙ Ⓚ	9 Ⓐ Ⓑ Ⓒ Ⓓ Ⓔ	14 Ⓕ Ⓖ Ⓗ Ⓙ Ⓚ	19 Ⓐ Ⓑ Ⓒ Ⓓ Ⓔ	24 Ⓕ Ⓖ Ⓗ Ⓙ Ⓚ
5 Ⓐ Ⓑ Ⓒ Ⓓ Ⓔ	10 Ⓕ Ⓖ Ⓗ Ⓙ Ⓚ	15 Ⓐ Ⓑ Ⓒ Ⓓ Ⓔ	20 Ⓕ Ⓖ Ⓗ Ⓙ Ⓚ	25 Ⓐ Ⓑ Ⓒ Ⓓ Ⓔ

right in section 4

wrong in section 4

Section 1
Time—25 Minutes
60 Questions

This section consists of two different types of questions. There are directions and a sample question for each type.

Each of the following questions consists of one word followed by five words or phrases. You are to select the one word or phrase whose meaning is closest to the word in capital letters.

Sample Question:

CHILLY: (A) lazy (B) nice (C) dry
(D) cold (E) sunny
Ⓐ Ⓑ Ⓒ ● Ⓔ

1. PLEAD: (A) strike (B) cry (C) tease
   (D) beg (E) try

2. PROWL: (F) growl (G) sneak (H) scrub
   (J) leave (K) fight

3. VESSEL: (A) blood (B) decoration (C) car
   (D) account (E) container

4. APPROVE: (F) withhold information
   (G) regard innocently (H) watch attentively
   (J) judge favorably (K) consider carefully

5. SEEP: (A) ooze (B) gurgle (C) liquefy
   (D) stick (E) fall

6. VEX: (F) scribble (G) locate (H) scream
   (J) play (K) irritate

7. DOZE: (A) graze (B) sleep
   (C) refresh (D) bore (E) ignore

8. BOUNTY: (F) outside border (G) new harvest
   (H) woven basket (J) upper limit
   (K) generous gift

9. COARSE: (A) sifted (B) sticky (C) unpopular
   (D) difficult (E) rough

10. MEEK: (F) submissive (G) old (H) tiny
    (J) worried (K) quick

11. SATURATE: (A) anger (B) measure (C) soak
    (D) boil (E) pour

12. GENTEEL: (F) timid (G) loud (H) stupid
    (J) harmless (K) refined

13. WINSOME: (A) athletic (B) charming
    (C) critical (D) small (E) shy

14. REPROACH: (F) retreat (G) blame
    (H) insist (J) complain (K) whine

15. DEMONSTRATE: (A) object (B) show
    (C) require (D) renew (E) imply

16. CAMOUFLAGE: (F) jewelry (G) outfit
    (H) disguise (J) outlook (K) helmet

17. AGHAST: (A) shocked (B) swollen
    (C) irritated (D) nasty (E) rude

18. RECOLLECT: (F) invent (G) remove
    (H) discover (J) reject (K) remember

19. INITIATE: (A) gather (B) try (C) start
    (D) command (E) celebrate

20. SUFFOCATE: (F) give instruction
    (G) pull out (H) make willing
    (J) surround completely (K) deprive of air

21. PREVAIL: (A) triumph (B) predict
    (C) entrust (D) cover (E) enlighten

22. PRANCE: (F) boast (G) lead (H) strut
    (J) pry (K) sing

23. OBNOXIOUS: (A) objective (B) playful
    (C) sorry (D) embarrassing (E) offensive

24. LIMBER: (F) supple (G) wooden (H) skinny
    (J) sober (K) sociable

25. TERMINATE: (A) escape from
    (B) give freedom to (C) cause to relax
    (D) invite to enter (E) bring to an end

GO ON TO THE NEXT PAGE ➡

26. CONTEMPLATE: (F) ponder (G) reject
    (H) founder (J) dominate (K) deserve

27. CAPRICE: (A) idea (B) mistake
    (C) whim (D) decision (E) guess

28. ADAGE: (F) permission (G) disdain
    (H) humor (J) prevention (K) proverb

29. DIN: (A) outline (B) clamor
    (C) improvement (D) demonstration
    (E) pressure

30. EXPUNGE: (F) erase (G) handle (H) label
    (J) assault (K) keep

GO ON TO THE NEXT PAGE ➡

The following questions ask you to find relationships between words. For each question, select the choice that best completes the meaning of the sentence.

> Sample Question:
>
> Kitten is to cat as
>
> (A) fawn is to colt
>
> (B) puppy is to dog
>
> (C) cow is to bull
>
> (D) wolf is to bear
>
> (E) hen is to rooster
>
>
>
> Choice B is the best answer because a kitten is a young cat just as a puppy is a young dog. Of all the answer choices, (B) states a relationship that is most like the relationship between kitten and cat.

31. Pilot is to airplane as

(A) team is to players
(B) horse is to cart
(C) captain is to ship
(D) passenger is to train
(E) army is to country

32. Snake is to python as dog is to

(F) terrier (G) canine (H) pet
(J) mammal (K) quadruped

33. Mayor is to city as

(A) governor is to state
(B) member is to union
(C) board is to district
(D) secretary is to committee
(E) citizen is to legislature

34. Paper is to novel as

(F) person is to poll
(G) paint is to brush
(H) canvas is to portrait
(J) back is to chair
(K) color is to palette

35. Refined is to vulgar as

(A) calm is to placid
(B) submissive is to recalcitrant
(C) happy is to ecstatic
(D) helpful is to victorious
(E) tranquil is to forgivable

36. Whip is to lash as

(F) stick is to throw
(G) shoe is to walk
(H) saddle is to sit
(J) food is to eat
(K) club is to beat

37. Migrate is to swallow as

(A) hibernate is to ground hog
(B) pet is to dog
(C) reproduce is to fish
(D) sting is to bee
(E) pounce is to cat

38. Weather is to meteorologist as vegetation is to

(F) driver (G) artist (H) oceanographer
(J) hunter (K) botanist

39. Track is to horse racing as

(A) circus is to elephant
(B) court is to tennis
(C) net is to basketball
(D) goal is to football
(E) air is to bird

40. Director is to actor as coach is to

(F) executive (G) player (H) chorus
(J) airplane (K) officer

41. Dessert is to meal as

(A) finale is to performance
(B) lunch is to breakfast
(C) fork is to spoon
(D) plate is to table
(E) ocean is to river

42. Confirm is to deny as

(F) accept is to reject
(G) assert is to proclaim
(H) contend is to imply
(J) pull is to tug
(K) simplify is to organize

43. Tower is to airport as lighthouse is to

(A) museum (B) jet (C) park
(D) farm (E) shoreline

GO ON TO THE NEXT PAGE ➡

44. Fidelity is to unfaithfulness as

 (F) loyalty is to honor
 (G) friendship is to gossip
 (H) honesty is to deceit
 (J) laziness is to slothfulness
 (K) intelligence is to unconcern

45. Widespread is to limited as

 (A) encompassed is to surrounded
 (B) enlarged is to big
 (C) broad is to narrow
 (D) unusual is to strange
 (E) provincial is to international

46. Saw is to carpenter as plow is to

 (F) banker (G) surveyor (H) farmer
 (J) physician (K) steelworker

47. Sword is to fence as glove is to

 (A) box (B) soccer (C) hockey
 (D) baseball (E) golf

48. Encourage is to demand as

 (F) insinuate is to hint
 (G) fire is to dismiss
 (H) suggest is to order
 (J) motivate is to undermine
 (K) condemn is to reprimand

49. Grin is to delight as

 (A) anxiety is to confusion
 (B) frown is to dismay
 (C) perspiration is to exhaustion
 (D) laugh is to happiness
 (E) resignation is to uncertainty

50. Mysterious is to understandable as

 (F) unknown is to indefinable
 (G) doubtful is to incredulous
 (H) skillful is to swift
 (J) clouded is to warm
 (K) obscure is to clear

51. Injury is to heal as malfunction is to
 (A) repair (B) bandage (C) misinterpret
 (D) throw (E) disassemble

52. Jog is to sprint as trot is to
 (F) ramble (G) gallop (H) roam
 (J) saunter (K) soar

53. Bone is to body as

 (A) floor is to house
 (B) motor is to boat
 (C) driver is to car
 (D) knob is to door
 (E) beam is to building

54. Amorphous is to shape as odorless is to

 (F) appearance (G) weight
 (H) worth (J) scent (K) anger

55. Vain is to humble as

 (A) anxious is to boisterous
 (B) cantankerous is to thoughtless
 (C) judicious is to lenient
 (D) authoritative is to discursive
 (E) extroverted is to shy

56. Test is to study as

 (F) job is to apply
 (G) train is to practice
 (H) play is to rehearse
 (J) office is to employ
 (K) income is to work

57. Smile is to frown as cheer is to

 (A) jeer (B) wince (C) laugh
 (D) extricate (E) leap

58. Banana is to peel as

 (F) egg is to crack
 (G) carrot is to uproot
 (H) apple is to core
 (J) bread is to slice
 (K) corn is to husk

59. Touch is to tactile as

 (A) sound is to noise
 (B) smell is to olfactory
 (C) mouth is to oral
 (D) eye is to visual
 (E) taste is to sense

60. Articulateness is to speech as

 (F) etiquette is to society
 (G) music is to note
 (H) ballet is to form
 (J) legibility is to handwriting
 (K) painting is to palette

IF YOU FINISH BEFORE TIME IS CALLED, YOU MAY CHECK YOUR WORK ON THIS SECTION ONLY. DO NOT TURN TO ANY OTHER SECTION IN THE TEST. **STOP**

Section 2
Time—25 Minutes
25 Questions

In this section, there are 5 possible answers after each problem. Look at each answer and choose which one is best. You may use the blank space at the right of the page for scratchwork.

<u>Note:</u> Figures provided with the problems are drawn with the greatest possible accuracy, UNLESS a specific problem states that its figure is not drawn to scale.

USE THIS SPACE FOR FIGURING.

Sample Problem:

$12 \times 9 =$

(A) 21   (B) 24   (C) 48   (D) 108   (E) 129

1. Each member of a club sold the same number of raffle tickets. If the club sold a total of 120 tickets, which of the following CANNOT be the number of tickets sold by each member?

    (A) 2   (B) 8   (C) 10   (D) 12   (E) 16

2. According to the graph in Figure 1, about how many students are art majors?

    (F) 200   (G) 225   (H) 280   (J) 300   (K) 360

3. Sean arrives home 14 minutes before midnight and his sister gets home 25 minutes later. When does Sean's sister arrive home?

    (A) 11 minutes before midnight
    (B) 11 minutes after midnight
    (C) 14 minutes after midnight
    (D) 25 minutes after midnight
    (E) 39 minutes after midnight

4. Which of the following is closest to 0.52×78 ?

    (F) $\frac{1}{5}$ of 70   (G) $\frac{1}{5}$ of 80   (H) $\frac{2}{5}$ of 70

    (J) $\frac{1}{2}$ of 70   (K) $\frac{1}{2}$ of 80

MAJORS OF 900 STUDENTS

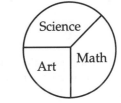

Figure 1

GO ON TO THE NEXT PAGE ➡

Questions 5-6 refer to the graph in Figure 2.

5. Brian's summer savings is greater than James's summer savings by how many dollars?

   (A) 3   (B) 4   (C) 100   (D) 150   (E) 200

6. The amount of money saved by Andy is how many times the amount of money saved by James?

   (F) 3   (G) 4   (H) 6   (J) 300   (K) 400

7. How many students are in a class if 30 percent of the class is equal to 30 students?

   (A) 10   (B) 90   (C) 100   (D) 900
   (E) It cannot be determined from the information given.

8. Each of the following is less than 2 EXCEPT

   (F) $\frac{15}{8}$ (G) $\frac{45}{22}$ (H) $\frac{99}{50}$

   (J) $\frac{180}{100}$ (K) $\frac{701}{400}$

9. The sides and angles of triangles ABC, BDE, BCE, and CEF in Figure 3 are all equal. Which of the following is the longest path from A to F?

   (A) A – C – B – D – F
   (B) A – B – E – C – F
   (C) A – B – C – E – F
   (D) A – C – E – F
   (E) A – B – D – F

10. Which of the following is closest to 80.08?

    (F) 80   (G) 80.01   (H) 80.1   (J) 81   (K) 90

11. If $\frac{1}{3}$ of a number is less than 12, then the number must be

    (A) less than 36
    (B) equal to 4
    (C) greater than 4
    (D) equal to 36
    (E) greater than 36

USE THIS SPACE FOR FIGURING.

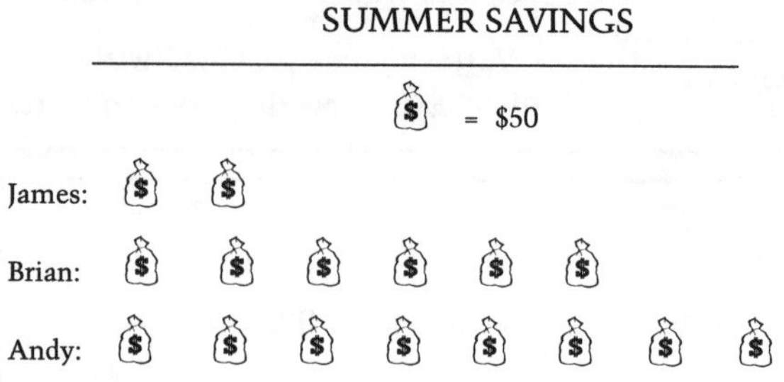

SUMMER SAVINGS

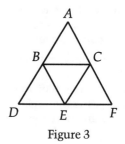

Figure 2

Figure 3

GO ON TO THE NEXT PAGE ➡

USE THIS SPACE FOR FIGURING.

12. In a basketball game, Team *A* scored 39 points and Team *B* scored more points than Team *A*. If Team *B* has 5 players, the average score of the players on Team *B* must have been at least how many points?

(F) 1   (G) 5   (H) 6   (J) 8   (K) 12

13. In the triangle shown in Figure 4, what is the value of *a* ?

(A) 4   (B) 6   (C) 8   (D) 9
(E) It cannot be determined from the information given.

14. A man bought a piece of land for 40 thousand dollars. Then he spent 2 million dollars to build a house on it. The cost of the house is how many times the cost of the land?

(F) 5   (G) 20   (H) 50   (J) 200   (K) 500

15. If $(x - y) + 2 = 6$ and *y* is less than 3, which of the following CANNOT be the value of *x* ?

(A) –3   (B) 0   (C) $1\frac{1}{2}$ (D) 4   (E) 8

16. In Figure 5, the distance from *A* to *D* is 55 and the distance from *A* to *B* is equal to the distance from *C* to *D*. If the distance from A to B is twice the distance from *B* to C, how far apart are *B* and *D* ?

(F) 11   (G) 30   (H) 33   (J) 44   (K) 45

17. A book is placed on a flat table surface, as shown in Figure 6. Which of the following best shows all of the points where the book touches the table?

(A)   (B)   (C)

(D)   (E)

18. Which of the following can be expressed as $(J + 2) \times 3$ where *J* is a whole number?

(F)   40
(G)   52
(H)   65
(J)   74
(K)   81

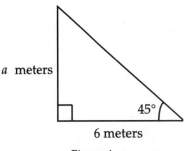

a meters

45°

6 meters

Figure 4

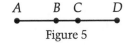

A   *B* *C*   *D*

Figure 5

Figure 6

GO ON TO THE NEXT PAGE ➡

19. If $a - 7 = 3b + 4$, what does $a + 5$ equal?

    (A) $b - 1$
    (B) $4b - 1$
    (C) $3b + 9$
    (D) $3b + 16$
    (E) It cannot be determined from the information given.

20. According to a census report for Country A, 21.5 out of every 100 families live in rural areas. Based on this report, how many of the 2 million families in Country A live in rural areas?

    (F) 430,000 (G) 215,000 (H) 43,000
    (J) 4,300 (K) 430

21. Bob is x years old and Jerry is 7 years older. In terms of x, what was the sum of their ages, in years, 5 years ago?

    (A) $2x + 3$ (B) $2x + 2$ (C) $2x - 3$
    (D) $x - 3$ (E) $x - 10$

22. A game show contestant answered exactly 20 percent of the questions correctly. Of the first 15 questions, he answered 4 correctly. If he answered only one of the remaining questions correctly, which of the following must be true?

    I. There were a total of 20 questions.
    II. He answered 10 percent of the remaining questions correctly.
    III. He didn't answer 9 of the remaining questions correctly.

    (F) I only (G) II only (H) I and II only
    (J) II and III only (K) I, II, and III

USE THIS SPACE FOR FIGURING.

GO ON TO THE NEXT PAGE ➡

23. If C is the product of consecutive integers A and B, then C must be

    (A) greater than $A + B$
    (B) a negative integer
    (C) a positive integer
    (D) an even integer
    (E) an odd integer

24. A 20 percent discount is offered on all sweaters at Store S. If a cotton sweater is on sale for \$48.00 and a wool sweater is on sale for \$64.00, what was the difference in price of the sweaters before the discount?

    (F) \$16.00   (G) \$19.20   (H) \$20.00
    (J) \$24.00   (K) \$32.00

25. The maximum load that a railway car can carry is $17\frac{1}{3}$ tons of freight. If a train has 36 railway cars, and each of these carries $\frac{5}{9}$ of a ton less than its maximum load, how many tons of freight is the train carrying?

    (A) 604   (B) $612\frac{7}{9}$ (C) $640\frac{5}{9}$

    (D) 648   (E) 660

USE THIS SPACE FOR FIGURING.

IF YOU FINISH BEFORE TIME IS CALLED, YOU MAY CHECK YOUR WORK ON THIS SECTION ONLY. DO NOT TURN TO ANY OTHER SECTION IN THE TEST.   **STOP**

Section 3
Time—25 Minutes
40 Questions

Read each passage carefully and then answer the questions about it. For each question, decide on the basis of the passage which one of the choices best answers the question.

The reading passages in this test are brief excerpts or adaptations of excerpts from published material. To make the text suitable for testing purposes, we may in some cases have altered the style, contents or point of view of the original. The passages do not necessarily reflect the opinions of Kaplan, Inc.

Line

Typical lemurs are primates with bodies similar to those of monkeys but with pointed muzzles and large eyes; most have long, bushy tails. Their fur is woolly and may be colored red, gray, brown or black.
(5) The name of the lemur stems from the Latin *lemures*, the Roman name for vampire-like ghosts of the dead which these large-eyed creatures were thought to resemble. Found only off the east coast of Africa on the island of Madagascar and neighboring
(10) islands, lemurs spend some time on the ground but most often are in the trees, building nests high in the branches. Besides leaves, lemurs eat eggs, fruit, insects, and small animals. They are active throughout the day and night and are reputed to be
(15) gentle, friendly creatures. Besides typical lemurs, the lemur family includes avahi, aye-aye, loris and galogo. However, contrary to popular belief, the so-called flying lemur is not even a primate, much less a true lemur; it is, in fact, a member of an altogether
(20) different order of mammals known as *Dermoptera*.

1. The style of the passage is most like that found in a

   (A) biology textbook
   (B) novel about Madagascar
   (C) zoologist's diary
   (D) tourist's guidebook
   (E) personal letter

2. Which of the following would be the best title for this passage?

   (F) The Lemur: Friend or Foe?
   (G) Madagascar's Loneliest Hunters
   (H) Facts About Lemurs
   (J) African Vampires
   (K) The Diet of the Lemur

3. According to the passage, all of the following are true about lemurs EXCEPT

   (A) they spend much of their time in trees
   (B) most have long, bushy tails
   (C) the flying lemur is not a true lemur
   (D) they eat only fruits and leaves
   (E) the body of the lemur resembles the body of the monkey

4. The passage suggests that

   (F) the lemur is a member of an order of mammals known as Dermoptera
   (G) flying lemurs are only active during the night
   (H) the lemur is not an aggressive animal
   (J) lemurs spend most of their time on the ground
   (K) flying lemurs can only be found on Madagascar and neighboring islands

GO ON TO THE NEXT PAGE ➡

Line   Eleanor Roosevelt was the niece of the 26th president of the United States, Theodore Roosevelt, and the wife of the 33rd president, Franklin D. Roosevelt. It would be doing her a great injustice,

(5)   however, to describe her only in terms of her relationship to men in powerful and important positions. She was, in her own right, an important figure in twentieth-century American history who strongly supported a variety of social causes and

(10) simply used her political position to further these causes.

      A dedicated worker for humanitarian causes before her marriage, and prior to her husband's election to the presidency, she simply expanded

(15) her role when she became the First Lady. She took a more powerful voice on behalf of a broad range of social issues, which included employment of youths and civil rights for women and blacks. She conducted press conferences, had her own radio

(20) program, and wrote a nationally syndicated column in a daily newspaper. After her husband died, she served as the United States delegate to the United Nations and played a role in the drafting of the UN Declaration of Human Rights.

(25) In short, she clearly proved to be an important and influential figure, above and beyond her political connections.

5. All of the following are true about Eleanor Roosevelt EXCEPT

(A) she was the First Lady of the United States

(B) she served as the United States delegate to the United Nations

(C) she was a dedicated supporter of many social causes

(D) she began to work for humanitarian causes only after her marriage

(E) she had her own radio program

6. When discussing Eleanor Roosevelt, the author's tone in this passage could best be described as

(F) critical

(G) admiring

(H) bitter

(J) serene

(K) neutral

7. The passage is mainly about

(A) the success of the Roosevelt family

(B) Eleanor Roosevelt's background and accomplishments

(C) the various social causes that Eleanor Roosevelt supported

(D) Eleanor Roosevelt's role in the United Nations

(E) important figures in twentieth-century American history

8. The author of the passage describes Eleanor Roosevelt's accomplishments in order to show that

(F) she should have been elected to the presidency

(G) she could have done more with her life if she had used her political connections to a greater extent

(H) her greatest achievement was marrying a man who later became president

(J) she was more successful than either her uncle or husband in gaining public support

(K) she deserves recognition beyond her family and marital connections

GO ON TO THE NEXT PAGE ➡

Line   Before a joint session of Congress in January
        1918, President Woodrow Wilson outlined his plan
        for a post–World War I peace settlement. Known as
        the Fourteen Points, Wilson's plan is best
(5)   remembered for its first point, which declared that
        international diplomacy should be conducted in
        the open and that quiet, unpublicized diplomacy
        should be made illegal. Wilson believed that public
        diplomacy would end the threat of war by
(10)   preventing immoral national leaders from secretly
        plotting aggressive actions against others.
            Although Wilson was a highly intelligent and
        well-meaning man, he lacked insight into the
        complexities of international politics. Contrary to
(15)   Wilson's belief, war rarely results from the behind-
        the-scenes plotting of unscrupulous national
        leaders. Rather, war usually stems from
        unresolved disagreements among nations—
        disagreements over territory, access to resources,
(20)   and so forth. Even if quiet diplomacy could be
        eliminated, these disagreements would still
        remain, as would the
        threat of war.

9. The second paragraph of this passage is
   primarily about

   (A) a post–World War I peace settlement
   (B) diplomacy's role in international
        politics
   (C) disagreements among nations
   (D) the actual causes of war
   (E) the first point in Wilson's Fourteen
        Points

10. The attitude of the writer toward the subject is

    (F) calculating
    (G) suspicious
    (H) opinionated
    (J) cheerful
    (K) apologetic

11. The author would most likely agree that war
    between country *A* and country *B* would
    result from which of the following
    situations?

    (A) A dispute over ownership of a piece of
         land bordering both countries
    (B) An agreement by a leader in country *A*
         to tax imports from a third country
    (C) The capture of a spy from country *A* in
         country *B*
    (D) An unpublicized agreement by country
         A to sell weapons to country *B*
    (E) A secret alliance made between
         country *A* and another country

12. Why does the author say that open diplomacy
    would not prevent war?

    (F) Quiet diplomacy will always be a part
         of international relations.
    (G) War breaks out because immoral rulers
         make decisions in secret.
    (H) Open diplomacy is not a solution to
         the problems which lead to war.
    (J) Disagreements over territory and
         resources rarely lead to conflict.
    (K) International relations are too complex
         to be conducted in the public eye.

13. Which of the following is the author most
    likely to discuss next?

    (A) Wilson's domestic policies in the post–
         World War I period
    (B) The impact of import taxes on foreign
         trade relations
    (C) An example of a war that resulted from
         a territorial or resource dispute
    (D) The events leading up to World War I
    (E) Other examples of Wilson's
         intelligence

GO ON TO THE NEXT PAGE ➡

Line Live thy Life,
     Young and old,
   Like yon oak,
     Bright in spring,
(5)   Living gold;

   Summer-rich
     Then: and then
   Autumn-changed,
   Soberer-hued
(10)   Gold again.

   All his leaves
     Fall'n at length,
   Look, he stands,
   Trunk and bough,
(15)   Naked strength.

"The Oak," by Alfred, Lord Tennyson.

14. In this poem, the seasons represent different

  (F) kinds of trees
  (G) times of day
  (H) stages of life
  (J) styles of dress
  (K) periods of history

15. The "he" mentioned in line 13 refers to

  (A) the poet
  (B) life
  (C) the oak
  (D) autumn
  (E) the reader

16. What does "Gold again" in line 10 signify?

  (F) The arrival of autumn
  (G) The richness of summer
  (H) The increased wealth of the narrator
  (J) The color of oak trees
  (K) The revival of the past

17. During which season is the oak referred to as "Living gold"?

  (A) Spring
  (B) Summer
  (C) Autumn
  (D) Winter
  (E) This description does not refer to a season.

18. With which of the following statements about life would the speaker be most likely to agree?

  (F) People should live every period of their lives to the fullest.
  (G) It is important to try to accomplish something during one's lifetime.
  (H) Life is too short to spend time doing unpleasant things.
  (J) The seasons are unpredictable.
  (K) Trees are an integral part of the enjoyment of life.

GO ON TO THE NEXT PAGE ➡

Line   Tea is consumed by more people and in greater amounts than any other beverage in the world, with the exception of water. The tea plant, from whose leaves tea is made, is native to India, China,

(5) and Japan and was first cultivated for use by the Chinese in prehistoric times. The plant, which is characterized as an evergreen, can reach a height of about thirty feet but is usually pruned down to three or four feet for cultivation. It has dark green

(10) leaves and cream-colored, fragrant blossoms.

    Cultivation of the tea plant requires a great deal of effort. The plant must grow in a warm, wet climate, in a carefully protected, well-drained area. Its leaves must be picked by hand.

(15) (Cultivation in North America has been attempted, but was found to be impractical because of a shortage of cheap labor.) Today, the plant is cultivated in the lands to which it is native, as well as in Sri Lanka, Indonesia, Taiwan,

(20) and South America.

    Tea was probably first used as a vegetable relish and for medicinal purposes. In the 1400's Chinese and Japanese Buddhists developed a semi-religious ceremony surrounding tea-drinking. It was not

(25) until after 1700, however, that it was first imported into Europe. Today, the United Kingdom imports more tea than does any other nation— almost one third of the world's production. The United States is also a large importer, but

(30) Americans have seemed to prefer coffee ever since the famous Boston Tea Party in 1773.

19. This passage is mainly about

    (A)   the tea plant
    (B)   the uses of the tea plant
    (C)   tea-drinking throughout history
    (D)   the tea trade
    (E)   the cultivation of the tea plant

20. According to the passage, the tea plant

    (F)   was first cultivated in Japan in prehistoric times
    (G)   requires well-drained soil to grow properly
    (H)   is the largest import of the United Kingdom
    (J)   has odorless flowers
    (K)   is native to South America

21. Why is a large supply of cheap labor important for the cultivation of tea?

    (A)   Since the tea plant can reach a height of thirty feet, several workers are required to harvest each plant.
    (B)   Since tea is exported all over the world, a lot of people are needed to handle the trade complications that arise.
    (C)   Since tea has been around since prehistoric times, many workers are employed to protect it and ensure that it doesn't die out.
    (D)   Since England and China are far away from each other, many workers are required to coordinate tea shipments and deliveries.
    (E)   Since the tea plant is hand picked, many laborers are needed at harvest time.

22. The style in the passage is most like that found in a

    (F)   newspaper article
    (G)   passage in an encyclopedia
    (H)   cookbook
    (J)   journal entry
    (K)   history textbook

23. Which of the following is the author most likely to discuss next?

    (A)   The details and aftermath of the Boston Tea Party
    (B)   Other major imports of the United Kingdom and United States
    (C)   Current trends in tea consumption
    (D)   Other examples of plants that have a medicinal value
    (E)   A description of what China was like in prehistoric times

24. The purpose of the second paragraph is to

    (F)   describe the role of tea in religious ceremonies
    (G)   explain why Americans prefer coffee
    (H)   discuss historical uses of tea
    (J)   describe the cultivation of tea
    (K)   question the importance of tea

GO ON TO THE NEXT PAGE ➡

Line   There were moments of waiting. The youth
thought of the village street at home before the
arrival of the circus parade on a day in the spring.
He remembered how he had stood, small thrillful
(5)   boy, prepared to follow the band in its faded
chariot. He saw the yellow road, the lines of
expectant people, and the sober houses. He
particularly remembered an old fellow who used to
sit upon a cracker box in front of the store and
(10)   pretend to despise such exhibitions. A thousand
details of color and form surged in his mind.

    Someone cried, "Here they come!" There was
rustling and muttering among the men.

    They displayed a feverish desire to have every
(15)   possible cartridge ready to their hands. The boxes
were pulled around into various positions, and
adjusted with great care.

    The tall soldier, having prepared his rifle,
produced a red handkerchief of some kind. He was
(20)   engaged in knitting it about his throat with
exquisite attention to its position, when the cry
was repeated up and down the line in a muffled
roar of sound.

    "Here they come! Here they come!" Gun locks
(25)   clicked.

    Across the smoke-infested fields came a brown
swarm of running men who were giving shrill
yells. They came on, stooping and swinging their
rifles at all angles. A flag, tilted forward, sped near
(30)   the front.

25. In the first paragraph, the youth is primarily
    concerned with

    (A)   reliving a fond childhood memory
    (B)   describing a turning point in his life
    (C)   preparing for the upcoming battle
    (D)   planning his day at the circus
    (E)   watching a soldier tie a handkerchief

26. What is meant by the exclamation "Here
    they come!" in line 13?

    (F)   A band in a chariot is approaching.
    (G)   The circus is coming to town.
    (H)   The enemy soldiers are advancing.
    (J)   A group of men selling handkerchiefs
           is on its way.
    (K)   The youth's family is arriving to save
           him.

27. The tone of the passage undergoes a change
    from the first to the second paragraph that
    can best be described as a movement from

    (A)   anger to amusement
    (B)   reminiscence to anticipation
    (C)   informality to formality
    (D)   reluctance to fear
    (E)   respect to indifference

28. According to the passage, all of the following
    are ways the soldiers prepare for battle
    EXCEPT

    (F)   gathering cartridges
    (G)   positioning ammunition
    (H)   priming their guns
    (J)   tying handkerchiefs
    (K)   saddling horses

29. Why are the men in the last paragraph
    carrying a flag?

    (A)   It is going to be raised in the youth's
           village.
    (B)   It needs to be protected from gunfire.
    (C)   It is going to be burned in a public
           demonstration.
    (D)   It represents the side they are fighting for.
    (E)   It has been damaged and needs to be
           mended.

GO ON TO THE NEXT PAGE ➡

Line   Acupuncture is a type of medical therapy that has been part of Chinese medicine since ancient times. It involves the insertion of thin, solid needles into specific sites on the body's
(5)   surface. The belief is that the application of a needle at one particular point produces a specific response at a second point. It is based on the ancient Chinese philosophy that human beings are miniature versions of the universe and that the
(10) forces that control nature also control health. These forces are divided between two main principles called the yin and the yang, which have an opposite but complementary effect on each other. For example, one force keeps the body's
(15) temperature from rising too high and the other keeps it from dropping too low. When they are in balance, the body maintains a constant, normal state. Disease occurs when these forces get out of balance.
(20)   Although acupuncture had been used in Western countries during many periods, it was not until the 1970s that it gained widespread interest, when it was determined that it could be used to control pain during surgery. The mechanism for its
(25) effectiveness is still a mystery, but it has become a very popular technique in many countries in the treatment of various diseases and medical problems.

30. Which of the following is true about acupuncture?

   I.   Although originally only a part of Chinese medicine, it is now practiced in many Western countries.
   II. It has been used to control pain during surgery since ancient times.
   III. The mechanism for its effectiveness was discovered during the 1970s.

   (F) I only
   (G) I and II only
   (H) I and III only
   (J) II and III only
   (K) I, II, and III

31. This passage is primarily about

   (A) various diseases that are particularly common among the Chinese
   (B) the meaning and use of the yin and the yang
   (C) different types of medical therapies and their relative effectiveness
   (D) the historical and philosophical background to acupuncture
   (E) modern uses of acupuncture both in China and in Western countries

32. According to the passage, acupuncture is based on

   (F) the idea that the human body is a model of the universe and is therefore controlled by the forces of nature
   (G) a firm belief in the Chinese gods known as the yin and the yang
   (H) an ancient Chinese religious ceremony that involves the insertion of needles into the body
   (J) a philosophy of health and disease that originated in China but has been totally changed by Western countries
   (K) the ideas of an astronomer who was attempting to study the universe in ancient times

33. According to the passage, the yin and the yang are principles that represent

   (A) high and low extremes of temperature
   (B) states of health and disease
   (C) similar treatments for different diseases
   (D) competing, balancing forces within the body
   (E) the ideas of comfort and pain

34. The author includes the example of the yin and the yang controlling the extremes of body temperature in order to

   (F) back up her claim that the forces within the body mirror the forces of the universe
   (G) clarify how these forces have a complementary effect on each other
   (H) provide proof that acupuncture is an effective medical therapy
   (J) suggest a possible explanation for why people sometimes run high fevers
   (K) highlight a feature of the body that acupuncture has not yet been shown to influence

GO ON TO THE NEXT PAGE ➡

Line   The painter Georgia O'Keeffe was born in Wisconsin in 1887 and grew up on her family's farm. At seventeen she left for Chicago and New York but she never lost her bond with the land.
(5)   Like most painters, O'Keeffe painted the things that were most important to her, and she became famous for her simplified paintings of nature. During a visit to New Mexico in 1929, O'Keeffe was moved by the desert's stark beauty, and she
(10)   began to paint many of its images. From about 1930 until her death in 1986, her true home was in the western desert, and bleached bones, barren hills, and colorful flowers were her characteristic subjects.
(15)   O'Keeffe is widely considered to have been a pioneering American modernist painter. While most early modern American artists were strongly influenced by European art, O'Keeffe's position was more independent.
(20)   Almost from the beginning, her work was more identifiably American—in its simplified and idealized treatment of color, light, space, and natural forms. Her paintings are generally considered "semiabstract," because, while they
(25)   often depict recognizable images and objects, they don't present those images in a very detailed or realistic way. Rather, the colors and shapes in her paintings are often so reduced and simplified that they begin to take on a life of their own,
(30)   independent from the real-life objects they are taken from.

35. According to the passage, all of the following strongly influenced O'Keeffe's paintings EXCEPT

(A) her rural upbringing
(B) her life in the West
(C) the work of artists in other countries
(D) the appearance of the natural landscape
(E) animal and plant forms

36. O'Keeffe's relationship to nature is most similar to

(F) a photographer's relationship to a model
(G) a writer's relationship to a publisher
(H) a student's relationship to a part-time job
(J) a sculptor's relationship to an art dealer
(K) a carpenter's relationship to a hammer

37. O'Keeffe's paintings have been called "semiabstract" because they

(A) involve a carefully realistic use of color and light
(B) depict common, everyday things
(C) show recognizable scenes from nature
(D) depict familiar things in an unrealistic way
(E) refer directly to real-life activities

38. According to the passage, O'Keeffe is considered an artistic pioneer because

(F) her work became influential in Europe
(G) she painted the American Southwest
(H) her paintings had a definite American style
(J) she painted things that were familiar to her
(K) her work was very abstract

39. The passage's main point about O'Keeffe is that she

(A) was the best painter of her generation
(B) was a distinctive modern American painter
(C) liked to paint only what was familiar to her
(D) never developed fully enough as an abstract artist
(E) used colors and shapes that are too reduced and simple

40. It can be inferred from the passage that modern European art of the time

(F) did not depict images of the desert
(G) was extremely abstract
(H) did not portray natural shapes in a simple, idealistic manner
(J) was not influenced by rural landscapes
(K) approached colors in a semiabstract manner

Section 4	In this section, there are 5 possible answers after each problem. Look at each answer and choose which one is best. You may use the blank space at the right of the page for scratchwork.
Time—25 Minutes 25 Questions	**Note:** Figures provided with the problems are drawn with the greatest possible accuracy, UNLESS a specific problem states that its figure is not drawn to scale.

USE THIS SPACE FOR FIGURING.

Sample Question:

$12 \times 9 =$

(A) 21   (B) 24   (C) 48

(D) 108   (E) 129

Ⓐ Ⓑ Ⓒ ● Ⓔ

1. The crown in Figure 1 is made up of toothpicks that each have the same length. If each toothpick is 2 meters long, what is the perimeter of the crown in meters?

(A) 5   (B) 7   (C) 10   (D) 12   (E) 14

Figure 1

2. D is an odd number between 4 and 11. If D is also between 7 and 18, what is the value of D ?

(F) 5   (G) 7   (H) 8   (J) 9   (K) 11

3. Gary has a collection of 16 different operas and his roommate Paul has a collection of 18 different operas. If Paul and Gary have 4 operas common to both record collections, how many different operas do they have between them?

(A) 18   (B) 30   (C) 34   (D) 36   (E) 38

4. If $\frac{1}{9} G = 18$, then $\frac{1}{3} G =$

(F) 6   (G) 9   (H) 36   (J) 54   (K) 63

5. A model sailboat floating on the water is attached to a string 1 meter long, as shown in Figure 2. If the string is tied to a post on the dock, which of the following best shows the area of water on which the sailboat can float?

(A)   (B)   (C)

(D)   (E)

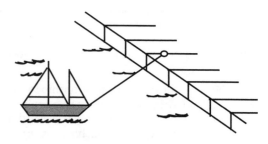

Figure 2

6. At a party, there are exactly 4 times as many adults as children. Which of the following could be the total number of people at this party?

(F) 14   (G) 16   (H) 21   (J) 25   (K) 29

GO ON TO THE NEXT PAGE ➡

7. Using a pair of scissors, which of the following can be made from a 20 cm by 28 cm rectangular sheet of paper by 1 straight cut?

   I. Triangle
   II. Square
   III. Rectangle

(A) I only   (B) II only   (C) III only
(D) I and II only   (E) I, II, and III

8. According to the graph in Figure 3, the average number of students taking the swimming class during the four months of March through June was

(F) 50   (G) 55   (H) 60   (J) 65   (K) 70

Questions 9–11 refer to the following definition.

For all real numbers n and r, $n \clubsuit r = (n - 1) - \frac{n}{r}$.

Example: $5 \clubsuit 3 = (5 - 1) - \frac{5}{3} = 4 - \frac{5}{3} = 2\frac{1}{3}$.

9. What is the value of $4 \clubsuit 2$?

(A) 1   (B) 2   (C) 6   (D) 8   (E) 16

10. If $Q \clubsuit 2 = 4$, then $Q =$

(F) 10   (G) 8   (H) 6   (J) 4   (K) 2

11. If $n \neq 0$ and $r \neq 0$, which of the following must be true?

   I. $n \clubsuit 1 = -1$
   II. $1 \clubsuit n = 0$
   III. $n \clubsuit n = r \clubsuit r$

(A) I only   (B) II only   (C) I and II only
(D) II and III only   (E) I, II, and III

12. Robert wants to leave a 15 percent tip for a dinner that costs $20.95. Which of the following is closet to the amount of tip he should leave?

(F) $2.70   (G) $3.00   (H) $3.15
(J) $3.50   (K) $3.75

USE THIS SPACE FOR FIGURING.

NUMBER OF STUDENTS TAKING SWIMMING CLASS

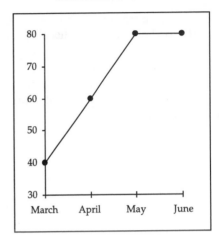

Figure 3

GO ON TO THE NEXT PAGE ➡

USE THIS SPACE FOR FIGURING.

13. Juan studied from 4:00 P.M. to 6:00 P.M. and finished $\frac{1}{3}$ of his assignments. He is taking a break and wants to finish his homework by 10:30 P.M. If he plans to continue working at the same rate, what is the latest time that he can return to his studies?

    (A) 6:30 P.M.   (B) 7:00 P.M.   (C) 7:30 P.M.
    (D) 8:00 P.M.   (E) 8:30 P.M.

14. Mrs. Brown and her z children each ate 2 peaches. What's the total number of peaches they ate?

    (F) $z + 1$ (G) $z + 2$ (H) $2z$
    (J) $2z + 1$ (K) $2z + 2$

15. Which figure can be drawn WITHOUT lifting the pencil or retracting?

    (A)   (B)   (C)

    (D)   (E)

16. If 0.59 is about $\frac{N}{5}$, then N is closest to which of the following?

    (F) 0.3   (G) 1   (H) 2   (J) 3   (K) 30

17. If the largest of 7 consecutive integers is 25, what is the average of the 7 integers?

    (A) 24   (B) 22   (C) 21   (D) 20   (E) 16

18. The price of a box of raisins increased from $0.93 to $1.08. The increase in price is closest to what percent?

    (F) 1%   (G) 14%   (H) 15%
    (J) 16%   (K) 20%

$$21\overline{)Q}\ ^{15}$$

$$15\overline{)S}\ ^{21\ \text{remainder}\ 8}$$

19. In the division problems shown above, $S - Q =$

    (A) 6   (B) 8   (C) 15   (D) 18   (E) 21

20. What is the least number of square tiles with side 6 cm needed to cover a rectangular floor 72 cm long and 48 cm wide?

    (F) 14   (G) 72   (H) 96   (J) 144   (K) 192

GO ON TO THE NEXT PAGE ➡

21. It takes Craig 5 minutes to type n pages. At this rate, how many minutes will it take him to type 20 pages?

(A) $\dfrac{n}{100}$ (B) $\dfrac{4}{n}$ (C) $\dfrac{100}{n}$

(D) $4n$ (E) $100n$

22. The width of a rectangular swimming pool is one quarter of its length. If the length is 60 meters, what is the perimeter of the pool?

(F) 60 m   (G) 120 m   (H) 150 m
(J) 180 m   (K) 240 m

23. The price of a dress at a department store decreases by 20 percent every month it is not sold. After 3 months, the current price of the unsold dress is approximately what percent of the original price?

(A) 40%   (B) 50%   (C) 60%
(D) 70%   (E) 80%

24. If p is a positive integer and n is a negative integer, which of the following is greatest?

(F) $\dfrac{p}{n}$ (G) $\dfrac{n}{p}$ (H) $\dfrac{1}{p-n}$ (J) $\dfrac{1}{n-p}$

(K) It cannot be determined from the information given.

25. In a yoga school, $\dfrac{1}{9}$ of the men and $\dfrac{1}{3}$ of the women are vegetarians and twice as many men as women are vegetarians. If there are 84 people in the yoga school, how many of the men are vegetarians?

(A) 4   (B) 8   (C) 12   (D) 27   (E) 72

IF YOU FINISH BEFORE TIME IS CALLED, YOU MAY CHECK YOUR WORK ON THIS SECTION ONLY. DO NOT TURN TO ANY OTHER SECTION IN THE TEST.

STOP

Section 5	Write an essay on the following prompt on the paper provided. Your essay should NOT
Time—25 Minutes	exceed 2 pages and must be written in ink. Erasing is not allowed.

Prompt: <u>Capital punishment serves no purpose and should be ended.</u>

Do you agree or disagree with this statement? Use examples from history, literature, or your own personal experience to support your point of view.

DO NOT TURN THE PAGE UNTIL TIME IS CALLED. ANSWER EXPLANATIONS
ARE AVAILABLE ON THE FOLLOWING PAGES.

STOP

KAPLAN   217

Answer Explanations

Section 1: Verbal

Synonyms

1. **D** To plead is to appeal earnestly, desperately—to beg, choice D.

2. **G** To prowl is to move around secretly, stealthily—in other words, to sneak, choice G.

3. **E** A vessel, such as a bowl or glass, is a container for holding something, so E is correct.

4. **J** To approve means to judge favorably, choice J.

5. **A** To seep means to flow through little cracks, or to ooze, choice A.

6. **K** To vex means to anger, or irritate, choice K.

7. **B** To doze is to sleep lightly, choice B. You might doze because someone bores you, but the two words are not synonymous.

8. **K** Bounty is a reward, or a generous gift, choice K.

9. **E** Something coarse is harsh, or rough, choice E. Something like sand that's been sifted, choice A, has had its larger, coarser grains screened out.

10. **F** Meek means to be patient and long-suffering, or submissive, choice F.

11. **C** To saturate is to wet something thoroughly, or to soak it, choice C. You saturate a sponge in water, for example.

12. **K** The word "genteel" describes something elegant, aristocratic, stylish, or refined, choice K.

13. **B** Winsome means pleasing, or charming, choice B.

14. **G** To reproach means to express disapproval of, to rebuke, or to blame someone, choice G. The closest wrong choice is probably complain J, but you can complain in general without blaming anything or anyone specific.

15. **B** To demonstrate means to explain clearly, or to show, choice B.

16. **H** To camouflage means to hide or disguise, choice H. An outfit G may or may not be camouflage.

17. **A** Aghast is an adjective that means to be struck with amazement or horror—in other words, to be shocked, choice A.

18. **K** To recollect means to remember, choice K.

19. **C** To initiate means to begin, or to start, choice C.

20. **K** To suffocate is to choke, or deprive of air, choice K.

21. **A** To prevail means to win, overcome, or triumph, choice A.

22. **H** To prance is to walk in a cocky way, to swagger, or to strut, choice H. The closest wrong choice, in attitude at least, is boast, choice F. But boasting is not a way of walking.

23. **E** Obnoxious means repugnant, repulsive, or offensive, choice E. Someone else's obnoxious behavior may cause you embarrassment, choice D, but obnoxious and embarrassing are not synonyms.

24. **F** Limber means flexible, lithe, nimble, or supple, choice F. Wooden G is a good antonym or opposite for limber.

25. **E** Terminate means to finish, to complete, or bring to an end, choice E.

26. **F** Contemplate means to consider, to think about, or to ponder, choice F.

27. **C** A caprice is a sudden fancy, or a whim, choice C. Idea A is tempting, but not all ideas are whims or caprices.

28. **K** An adage is a saying, an axiom, or a proverb, choice K.

29. **B** A din is a loud, confused mixture of noises—in other words, a clamor, choice B.

30. **F** To expunge is to get rid of, obliterate, or erase, choice F.

Analogies

31. **C** A pilot directs a plane. A captain directs a ship.

32. **F** One breed of snake is a python. One breed of dog is a terrier. A dog is a type of canine G, pet H, mammal J, and quadruped K; but all these relationships are in the opposite order as snake and python. Quadruped, by the way, simply means 4-legged.

33. **A** A mayor is the highest official in a city. A governor is the highest official in a state. The suggested bridge easily eliminates choices B, C, and E. A secretary D is not usually the highest official on a committee—the chairperson is.

34. **H** Paper is the material a novel is written on. Similarly, canvas is the material a portrait is painted on.

35. **B** Refined is the opposite of vulgar. In correct choice B, submissive is the opposite of recalcitrant, which means stubbornly defiant. Calm and placid A are synonyms, not opposites. Ecstatic in C is an extreme state of happiness. The word pairs in D and E bear no obvious relationship to each other.

36. **K** You use a whip to lash someone. You use a club to beat someone. As for choice F, you may throw a stick at someone, but the more common association with stick is that it's used to hit or beat someone, and that's not what we have here.

37. **A** Migrate is a seasonal, adaptive action taken by a swallow (it's a kind of bird). In the winter, swallows migrate. In the winter, groundhogs hibernate, a kind of long sleep. Petting is something a person does to a dog B. Choices C, D, and E are all things that these animals do, but none is done specifically in winter.

38. **K** Flip the words: a meteorologist studies weather. Similarly, a botanist studies plants, or vegetation.

39. **B** Again, flip the pairs: horse racing is done, or played, on a track. In the same way, tennis is played on a court.

40. **G** A director tells an actor what to do. A coach tells a player what to do.

41. **A** Here the relationship is one of order or sequence. A dessert is eaten at the end of a meal. A finale is played at the end of a performance. Lunch is eaten after breakfast, but it's a different meal, not part of the same one.

42. **F** The words in the stem are opposites. The only pair of opposites among the choices is in F: to accept is the opposite of reject, just as to confirm is the opposite of to deny.

43. **E** A tower is the tall structure that enables planes to navigate safely at an airport. In the same way, a lighthouse is the tall structure that enables ships to navigate safely at the shoreline.

44. **H** Fidelity is the opposite or absence of unfaithfulness. Honesty is the opposite or absence of deceit. Choices F and J feature synonymous word-pairs. There's no clear relationship between the words in G and K.

45. **C** If something is widespread, it's not limited. If something is broad, it's not narrow. Encompassed and surrounded A are synonyms; so are the words in choices B and D. The toughest wrong choice is E: international means, involving many countries; it has the connotation of meaning sophisticated, which is the opposite of provincial. But the words in E are in the opposite order as those in the stem and correct choice C, which have the "larger" word first.

46. **H** A saw is a tool used by a carpenter. A plow is a tool used by a farmer. None of the occupations in the other choices require the use of a plow.

47. **A** A sword is to used against an opponent in fencing, just as a glove is used in boxing.

48. **H** Here the relationship is one of degree, with the second word being much stronger than the first. You can encourage or suggest that someone do something, and they may or may not do it. But if you demand or order them to do it, then they must. The pairs in F and G are synonyms. The pair in J are opposites, and to condemn in K is stronger than to reprimand, not the other way around.

49. **B** A grin is a facial expression showing delight. A frown is a facial expression showing dismay. (Dismay is a mixture of fear and discouragement.) A laugh in D expresses happiness, but it isn't a facial expression.

50. **K** Something mysterious is not understandable. Something obscure is not clear.

51. **A** When an injury heals, it disappears. When a malfunction is repaired, it disappears. In both cases, the thing that heals or is repaired gets better; that's why disassemble E is not as good as repair.

52. **G** A jog is a slow run; a sprint is a fast run. In the same way, a trot is, for a horse, a slow run, while a gallop is a fast run. To roam H is to wander about—not at a great speed. To saunter J has the same problem: it means to stroll. And soaring K is flying, not running.

53. **E** A bone is one part of the structural system of the body—the system that holds it up. Similarly, a beam—a long piece of timber or steel—is one part of the structural system that holds up a building. A may have been tempting, but notice in your mind's eye the similar shapes of most bones, on the one hand, and beams or girders on the other. Within the body, bones connect to other bones like girders connect to girders within a building. Floors don't generally connect to other floors. A motor, choice B, is part of the structure of a boat, but not the part that "holds it up."

54. **J** Amorphous means "without shape." So amorphous is to shape as odorless is to odor, or scent, choice J.

55. **E** Another relationship of opposites. A vain person is, by definition, not humble. Similarly, an extroverted or outgoing person is, by definition, not shy. A may have been tempting: boisterous means noisy, exuberant. But anxious people aren't by definition quiet; one may be anxious and act boisterously, by talking too much out of nervousness, for example. Cantankerous B means bad-tempered, quarrelsome; discursive D means to talk in a rambling way.

56. **H** You study for a test, just as you rehearse for a play. In both cases, the second word is preparation for the first. Applying for a job F is a close second here, but not as good as H. Studying for a test involves going over the same material again and again, in order to demonstrate during the test that you've learned it. In the same way, actors rehearsing a play work through the same material—the script—again and again, in order to learn it for the performance.

57. **A** You smile when you're happy, and frown when you're sad or angry. In the same way, you cheer to signal your approval and jeer your disapproval of a sports team, for example. To wince B is to express pain, more on the private scale of a smile or frown. To extricate D means to get oneself out of; you extricate yourself from a trap, or a predicament.

58. **K** To peel a banana is to pull off its outer covering. In the same way, to husk an ear of corn is to pull off its outer covering (also called a husk). To crack an egg F is to break its outer covering, not pull it off. To uproot a carrot G is to pull it out of the ground. To core an apple H is to remove its center.

59. **B** Tactile refers to anything perceptible through the sense of touch, just as olfactory refers to anything perceptible through the sense of smell. In order to be correct (which they're not), choice D should read "sight is to visual," and choice C should read "taste is to oral."

60. **J** Articulateness is the quality of speaking or writing in a clear and easily understood manner. Similarly, legibility is handwriting that's clear and easily understood. Etiquette F isn't society that's easily understood, it's good manners, the accepted way of behaving decently, politely and with dignity.

Section 2: Math

1. **E** We need an answer here which is not a factor of 120. In other words, a number which is not evenly divisible into 120. Only choice E, 16, is not a factor of 120.

2. **G** Recall that all figures on the SSAT are always drawn to scale unless stated otherwise. Extending the vertical line segment boundary of the art slice upward and extending the horizontal line segment boundary of the art slice to the right shows that the art slice is about 25% of the pie. 25% or $\frac{1}{4}$ of 900 (the total number of students) is 225 art students.

3. **B** Sean's sister must arrive $(25 - 14)$ or 11 minutes after midnight because it takes 14 minutes to reach midnight and 11 more minutes to add up to 25 minutes.

4. **K** The key here is to make what you are given look like the answer choices. No calculation is needed here. Round off .52 to .5 or $\frac{1}{2}$ and round 78 to 80.

5. **E** Careful! The question asks for dollars. Each piggy bank = $50 as is noted in the table. Brian has 4 more banks than James, so the amount more than James that Brian saved is 4 times $50 which equals $200.

6. **G** We must determine how much was saved by Andy and how much was saved by James and compare the two. Andy saved 8 banks which is 8 times $50 or $400 and James saved 2 banks which is 2 times $50 or $100. Thus, Andy's $400 is 4 times James's $100.

7. **C** Using the formula Part = Percent × Whole, 30 = 30% × N (total number of students). We need to isolate the total number of students (N). 30% = $\frac{30}{100}$ so the equation can be written as 30 = $\frac{30}{100}$ × N. Now multiply both sides of this equation by $\frac{100}{30}$; the N is now by itself once $\frac{30}{100}$ and $\frac{100}{30}$ cancel out to 1. Multiplying 30 × $\frac{100}{30}$ gives a value of 100 for N.

8. **G** Because of the word except, we need to determine which fraction is not less than 2. So we are looking for a fraction which is greater than or equal to 2. In order to determine this, make all of the fractions improper: With choice F, $\frac{15}{8}$ = 1 $\frac{7}{8}$ The only fraction where the denominator can be divided into the numerator with a result of at least 2 is choice G: $\frac{45}{22}$ = 2 $\frac{1}{22}$

9. **A** We are told all the sides are equal, thus set each segment = 1 and add. With choice A, $A - C - B - D - F$ = 1 (A to C) + 1 (C to B) + 1 (B to D) + 2 (D to E and then E to F) = 5. Choice B counts to 4, hence cross it out. Choice C counts to 4 also so cross it out. Choice D counts to 3 and Choice E counts to 4. The longest path is 5, so Choice A is correct.

10. **H** Scan the answer choices. Choice F, 80, is 80.08 – 80 = 0.08 away from 80.08. Choice G, 80.01, is 80.08 – 80.01 = 0.07 away from 80.08. Choice H, 80.1, is 80.1 –80.08 = 0.02 away from 80.08. Choice J, 81, is 0.92 away from 80.08 and choice K, 90, is more than 9 away from 80.08. The question asks for the choice closest to 80.08, and thus H, 80.1, is correct.

11. **A** Call the number N. Write an inequality using the information given. Remember, "of" means multiply. $\frac{1}{3}$ × N < 12. We need to isolate N, our unknown value. Multiplying both sides by the reciprocal of $\frac{1}{3}$ which is 3 produces a result of N < 12 × 3, and thus N < 36. Choice A is correct.

12. **J** The minimum number of points Team B could have scored is one more than Team A or 40. Using the average formula, Average = $\frac{\text{Sum of the terms}}{\text{Number of terms}}$ we can plug in our given information: Average = $\frac{40 \text{ points}}{5 \text{ players}}$. Thus the average score of the players on Team B must have been at least 8 points per player.

13. **B** The sum of the 3 interior angles of any triangle is 180 degrees. Figure 4 indicates that two of the angles have degree measures of 90 and 45. So the degree measure of the third angle is 180 – 90– 45 = 45. So this is a 45-45-90 triangle. In any triangle, the sides opposite two equal angles must be equal. Hence, a = 6.

14. **H** Here, we need to divide 40,000 into 2,000,000: $\frac{2,000,000}{40,000}$. Simply cancel out 4 zeros from the bottom and 4 zeros from the top. We now have $\frac{200}{4}$ which equals 50.

15. **E** The question states that y is less than 3, and we want the value which x cannot equal, so let's solve the equation for x in terms of y and see if we can conclude something about x. The equation is $(x – y)$ + 2 = 6. First subtract 2 from both sides. Then $(x – y)$ = 6 – 2, or $(x – y)$ = 4. The parentheses are not needed, so $x – y$ = 4. Adding y to both sides, we have that $x = y + 4$. Since y is less than 3, $y + 4$ must less than 7. Now $x = y + 4$, so x must be less than 7. Now look for a choice which is not less than 7. Only choice E, 8, is not less than 7. So x cannot be 8 and choice E is correct.

16. **H** Segment AD = 55. Because the length of AB is 2 times the length of BC, let $BC = x$ and let $AB = 2x$. Since $AB = CD$, let $CD = 2x$ also.

The total length of $AD = AB + BC + CD = 2x + x + 2x = 5x = 55$. Hence, $x = 11$ and $BD = BC + CD = x + 2x = 3x = 3 \times 11 = 33$.

17. **E** The question asks for all the points. Choice A is incorrect because it only includes the rectangular boundary of the set of all the points that touch the table; it does not include the points inside this rectangle which also touch the surface of the table. Choice E indicates all the points and is correct.

18. **K** The question is not asking for a value of J. Indeed, J could be any whole number. The question is asking for the answer choice which can be written in the form $(J + 2) \times 3$, where J is an integer. Since 3 is a factor of $(J + 2) \times 3$, the choice we're looking for must be a multiple of 3. A integer is a multiple of 3 if and only if the sum of its digits is a multiple of 3. Looking at the answer choices, only the sum if the digits of choice K, 81, is a multiple of 3. That is, the sum of the digits of 81 is $8 + 1 = 9$, which is a multiple of 3. So choice K is correct.

19. **D** Using the information given, isolate a: $a = 3b + 4 + 7 = 3b + 11$. Thus, $a = 3b + 11$. Next add 5 to both sides of this equation: $a + 5 = 3b + 11 + 5 = 3b + 16$.

20. **F** They give us 21.5 out of 100 which is easily translated into 21.5%. Hence, 21.5% of (multiplication) 2,000,000 is $\frac{21.5}{100} \times 2,000,000$. Cancel out two zeros from the 100 in the denominator and from the 2,000,000 in the numerator to get $21.5 \times 20,000 = 430,000$.

21. **C** Translate from English into math. Let Bob's current age = x and let Jerry's current age = $x + 7$. To find their ages 5 years ago, subtract 5 years from each current age: 5 years ago Bob was $x - 5$ and Jerry was $x + 7 - 5 = x + 2$. The sum of Bob and Jerry's ages 5 years ago was: $x - 5 + x + 2 = 2x - 3$.

22. **J** The contestant answered a total of 5 questions correctly. Using our Percent Formula, Percent × Whole = Part, 20% × total number of questions = 5.

Multiply both sides of the equation by $\frac{100}{20}$, (the reciprocal of 20%) and the total number of questions = 25. Thus, statement I is incorrect so eliminate choices F, H and K. For statement II, there were $25 - 15 = 10$ questions remaining and 1 of these 10 questions

was answered correctly. So he answered $\frac{1}{10}$, or 10% of the remaining questions correctly, so statement II is true. (Also, both remaining answer choices, G and J, contain this Roman numeral.) Finally, statement III is true because 1 of the remaining 10 was answered correctly so 9 of these 10 were not answered correctly. Eliminate choice G. Choice J remains and is correct.

23. **D** This problem is perfect for our Picking Numbers Strategy. $C = A \times B$. Pick two consecutive numbers for A and B such as 2 and 3. Their product is 6 and positive. However, if we selected 1 and 0, the product would be 0 which is neither positive nor negative. Because the integers are consecutive, one of the integers must be even, or a multiple of 2, and hence the product of any two consecutive integers must be even. Choice D.

24. **H** Be careful here. The question asks for the difference before the discount. The sweaters were sold for 100% − 20% of their old price. Using our Percent Formula, Part = Percent × Whole, we have that $48 = 80\% \times$ old price. Convert 80% to $\frac{80}{100}$ and multiply both sides by $\frac{100}{80}$. We now have $\frac{100}{80} \times 48 =$ old price. Canceling yields $60. Use the Percent Formula for the wool sweater and you have the equation $64 = 80\% \times$ old price. You'll find that its original price was $80. The difference is $80 − $60 = $20.

25. **A** The maximum load that a car can carry is $17\frac{1}{3}$ tons. If each car carries the maximum load minus $\frac{5}{9}$ of a ton then each car carries $17\frac{1}{3} - \frac{5}{9} = \frac{52}{3} - \frac{5}{9} = \frac{52}{3} \times \frac{3}{3} - \frac{5}{9} = \frac{156 - 5}{9} = \frac{151}{9}$ tons. Next multiply this amount carried in each car by 36 cars and we get $\frac{151}{9} \times 36$ tons. Cancel the 9 into the 36 and we get $151 \times 4 = 604$.

Section 3: Reading Comp

Lemurs passage

First up is a fact-based scientific passage about the lemur, a monkeylike animal that lives chiefly on Madagascar. The lone paragraph gives a variety of information about lemurs: their physical characteristics, the origin of their name, where they're found, what they do and eat, etcetera. Don't sweat the details on a passage like this; just read and try to keep a clear image of the Big Idea—in this case, information about lemurs.

1. **A** The author's style is straightforward and informative, like the style of a biology textbook. There's no evidence that this passage is a work of fiction B; a zoologist's diary C would more likely be in the first-person ("June 20: saw two lemurs in a jungle in Southern Madagascar"). A tourist's guidebook D might describe lemurs, but probably would go into less scientific detail and would place them in a specific location ("Be sure to check out the lemurs in Avahi National Park"). And there's simply no evidence for E: nothing subjective or personal.

2. **H** Summarize the passage in your own mind; you might have come up with something like, "Things to Know about Lemurs." H restates this idea: the passage is a group of facts about lemurs. F, J, and K are too narrow, each touching on only one of the details you're given about lemurs. The passage doesn't mention whether lemurs hunt alone or in groups G.

3. **D** You're looking for the detail that's false. The passage states that lemurs "most often are in the trees" A; that "most have long, bushy tails" B; that "the so-called flying lemur is not even a primate, much less a true lemur" C; and that lemurs have "bodies similar to those of monkeys" E. This leaves D as correct: the author states that lemurs eat "leaves...eggs, fruit, insects, and small animals."

4. **H** At the beginning of the second half of the paragraph, the author states that lemurs "are reputed to be gentle, friendly creatures." If they're "gentle" and "friendly," then you can infer that they're not very aggressive, choice H. F is contradicted in the final sentence of the passage. G and J are refuted when the author says that lemurs "are active throughout the day and night" and are "most often are in the trees." Not enough information is given about the flying lemur K to infer that it can only be found in and around Madagascar.

Roosevelt passage

We move on to a history passage about Eleanor Roosevelt, niece of one American President and wife to another. The author says "it would be an injustice" to reduce her to an historical footnote, because she accomplished many things in her own right working for humanitarian causes.

5. **D** The beginning of paragraph 2 states that Eleanor Roosevelt worked for humanitarian causes "before her marriage," so D is the false detail here.

6. **G** The author calls Eleanor Roosevelt "in her own right, an important figure," "dedicated" and "influential." Strongly positive words such as this signal that "admiring" G correctly sums up the author's opinion of Roosevelt. F and H are too negative, and J and K too neutral to be accurate here.

7. **B** Try to summarize the passage in your own words. It's about Eleanor Roosevelt, her life and achievements; B restates this idea best. Other Roosevelts A are only mentioned briefly. C and D focus too narrowly on details from paragraph 2. And E is way too broad, not even mentioning Eleanor Roosevelt.

8. **K** According to the second and third sentences of paragraph 1, it would be unjust to say that Eleanor Roosevelt was only related or married to famous, powerful men. To the author, she was, "in her own right, an important figure in . . . American history" who used her position to further various social causes. K correctly restates this opinion. F and G speculate on what Roosevelt could or might have done, while the author simply tells you what she did do. H takes the opposite view of the author, who thinks that Roosevelt's accomplishments went far beyond marrying the President. And the passage doesn't say which Roosevelt was most successful at gaining public support J.

Woodrow Wilson passage

Next up is another historical passage, this one about President Woodrow Wilson and his post-World War I peace settlement. The author focuses on the first of Wilson's Fourteen Point plan, which called for the abolition of secret diplomacy. Wilson considered open negotiations vital for peace, but in paragraph 2 the author disagrees, arguing that Wilson's view was too simplistic and that the things nations fight over are not curable by open diplomacy.

9. **D** The first and second sentences of each paragraph usually reveal the paragraph's topic. In this case, it's the second sentence: Wilson was wrong—war stems not from secret deals by national leaders, but from "unresolved disagreements among nations." Therefore, D is best: the second paragraph is primarily about what actually causes most wars. Choices A and E summarize the topic of paragraph 1, not paragraph 2. B is too general; the paragraph mainly discusses why one form of diplomacy usually fails to avert wars. Not all disagreements among nations lead to war, so C is also too broad.

10. **H** The author tells you that Wilson called for an end to secret negotiations as a way to end war, then argues that Wilson was wrong, that "he lacked insight into the complexities of international politics." Clearly, the author disagrees with Wilson, and isn't afraid to express this opinion. Her attitude can therefore be described as "opinionated," choice H. F is tempting, given the author's "realpolitik" attitude. But the author isn't being Machiavellian; she simply tells you what Wilson tried to do and why she thinks it was a bad idea. G and J are too emotional, and K is wrong because the author doesn't apologize for criticizing Wilson.

11. **A** The scenario in choice A—two countries fighting over land ownership—is the closest parallel to the author's thinking. As the next-to-last sentence of the passage puts it, "war usually stems from unresolved disagreements among nations . . . over territory." Choice B's scenario is an economic trade agreement involving a third country—not very likely to lead to war. C, D, and E all involve secret deals or covert activity of the kind that Wilson—not the author—thought would lead to war.

12. **H** Look again at the last two sentences of the passage. According to the author, war stems from disputes between nations over territory or access to resources; even if secret diplomacy were discontinued, these disputes "would still remain, as would the threat of war." In other words, open diplomacy can't solve the kinds of problems that lead to war, and choice H is correct. F's assertion that quiet diplomacy will always be with us doesn't explain why open diplomacy won't prevent war. Similarly, G merely echoes Wilson's argument, that secret diplomacy causes wars. J flatly contradicts the author, and K distorts a detail from the beginning of paragraph 2, where the author argues that Wilson didn't understand "the complexities of international politics." This is not the same as explaining why open diplomacy cannot prevent wars.

13. **C** In order to imagine where the author might go next, retrace the steps of the argument: 1) Wilson offered a peace proposal that argued for open diplomacy, which Wilson thought would end wars; 2) Wilson failed to grasp that secret diplomacy is not the cause of most wars, which occur because of unresolved disputes among nations over such things as territory and resources. Having disagreed with Wilson, it's most likely that the author will try to illustrate this last point, by giving an example of a war or wars that occurred because of a territorial or resource dispute, C. A, D and E suggest that the author will return to the subjects of President Wilson or World War I. But the author has moved beyond Wilson, to discuss what really causes wars.

Poetry passage

Passage 4 is a poem; you'll see one poem in every reading comprehension section of the SSAT, and when you do, be alert for tone and the use of metaphor. Here, the poet uses the oak tree as a metaphor—we should live our lives as an oak tree does, in accordance with nature and the change of seasons. The first three lines of the poem generate its central metaphor: "Live thy life, young and old, like yon oak." ("Yon" is short for "yonder," meaning "that oak over there.") In other words, "live your life, at all ages, like that oak tree does."

14. **H** This question asks you to infer the poem's central metaphor. What do the seasons represent? The successive stages of life, choice H: spring is youth, summer is maturity, autumn is middle age, and winter is old age.

15. **C** Who is the "he" of line 13? The entire stanza provides clues: "he" has lost his leaves, "he" stands, "trunk and bough, naked strength." "He," then, is the oak tree, choice C.

16. **F** The second stanza shows the oak tree in summer and in autumn; "gold again" refers to the seasonally changed color of the oak tree's leaves, so F is best here. G, H and K are pretty easily eliminated. The problem with J is that the arrival of autumn signals a change in foliage—and the quoted phrase refers to the latter, not the former.

17. **A** An easy detail question. The oak is referred to as "living gold" in line 5 of the poem; the

previous line says, "bright in spring," so A is correct.

18. **F** This question is basically asking for the statement that mirrors the poem's Big Idea, which is that we should be like the oak tree, living each season of our lives as well as we can; F restates this idea best. G is wrong because its "something" can apparently be accomplished at any point in one's life; what about the other "seasons"? H makes little sense: the tree in the poem lives a full life span (the four seasons). J contradicts the poem, which lists the very predictable succession of the seasons. And K dispenses with the poem's central metaphor altogether; it's not that a good life includes the enjoyment of trees, it's that a good life is lived as a tree lives its life.

Tea passage

Here's a passage about tea—the plant, and the history of its cultivation and uses. Paragraph 1 describes the plant's universal popularity, where it originated, and what it looks like in nature and when being cultivated. Paragraph 2 describes the difficulties of cultivating tea, and where the plant is currently grown. And the final paragraph briefly summarizes the history of tea—how it was used in ancient times, in the 1400s, and since 1700 in Europe and the United States.

19. **A** The Big Idea question. The choice that best sums up the passage is A. B, C, D, and E each touch on only one aspect of the passage.

20. **G** A detail question; correct answer G is a restatement of the second sentence of paragraph 2. F is wrong because lines 5-6 say that tea was first cultivated in China. H distorts lines 25–27: the author states that the U.K. is the world's largest importer of tea, not that tea is the U.K.'s largest import. Line 10 says that the plant has "fragrant blossoms," not odorless ones J. And tea, though now cultivated in South America K, is native only to "India, China and Japan" (lines 4-5).

21. **E** The key phrase in the question stem, "cheap labor," is also found in paragraph 2, which states that, since tea leaves "must be picked by hand," cultivation in North America "was found to be impractical because of a shortage of cheap labor." In other words, tea cultivation requires a supply of cheap labor because the leaves must be hand-picked, choice E. A contradicts paragraph 1, which says that tea plants are "usually pruned down" to heights of "three or four feet for cultivation." B's

"trade complications," and C's notion that tea plants might become extinct without a large labor force, are never mentioned in the passage. And E incorrectly reduces the world's cultivation and consumption of tea to two countries, England and China.

22. **G** A style inference question. The author's style is informative, offering an encyclopedic summary of the cultivation and uses of tea G. A newspaper article F implies news, not history. A cookbook H would probably be limited to recipes; it wouldn't mention other uses of tea or the history and practical details of its cultivation. The passage lacks any subjective or personal references such as might be found in a journal J, and a history textbook K, if it even mentioned tea, would probably only feature the information found in paragraph 3, not the rest of the passage.

23. **C** Again, you're looking to guess where the author's headed. Since paragraph 3 summarizes the historic uses of tea, beginning with ancient times and ending with consumption today in the U.K. and the U.S., it's most likely that the author will continue to discuss current consumption trends, choice C. A temptingly mentions the very last detail in the passage, but the Boston Tea Party is really only a footnote, a lighthearted explanation of why consumption of tea in the U.S. today lags behind that of coffee. B, D, and E incorrectly suggest that the author's main focus is, respectively, imports B, the medicinal uses of plants in general D, or a description of China, the birthplace of tea use E.

24. **J** Paragraph 2 describes the difficulties of cultivating tea, and where it is currently cultivated. So J is correct here. Religious ceremonies F, the American preference for coffee G, and the historical uses of tea H are mentioned only in paragraph 3. And the author never questions the importance of tea K.

Fiction passage

Next we have a fiction passage, about the thoughts going through one soldier's mind and the preparations going on around him in the final moments before a battle. Notice how the two lines of dialogue are used to increase the tension of the imminent attack. As with the Tennyson poem, you should be alert for shifts of tone and perspective, and the use of metaphor.

25. **A** After the teaser of its brief opening sentence (moments of waiting for what?), the first para-

graph details the youth's childhood memory of a circus coming to town, choice A. The remembered arrival of the circus was not a "turning point" (choices B and D), and while the upcoming battle C may well be one, it's not mentioned in the first paragraph. The handkerchief E is not mentioned until line 22.

26. **H** The quoted exclamation, which signals the end of the youth's reverie and leads to feverish last-minute preparations, is intended to warn that the enemy is advancing, choice H. F and G wrongly assume that the exclamation is part of the youth's memory. J and K are completely unwarranted inferences.

27. **B** In the first paragraph, the youth remembers a good time from childhood. This is followed by the soldiers' final preparations, so the tone changes from reminiscence, or remembering, to anticipation of battle, making choice B correct.

28. **K** An easy detail question. Horses are never mentioned in the passage; all the soldiers are on foot. So K is correct. Each of the other choices is mentioned from lines 16–22.

29. **D** An easy inference question. Why do soldiers carry a flag? Like the American flag raised at Iwo Jima, or the Star-spangled Banner, it's meant to represent the side they're fighting for, choice D. A is tempting, but only true if the enemy wins. B makes no sense, since the flag is carried at the front of a charging line of soldiers. And there's no evidence for C or E.

Acupuncture passage

Next up is a modified science passage about acupuncture, an ancient Chinese form of medical therapy. There's very little science in the passage; the author mainly describes the thinking behind acupuncture and gives a brief history of its use in Western countries.

30. **F** A Roman Numeral question. The only true statement, according to the passage, is statement I: the first sentences of paragraphs 1 and 2 tell you that acupuncture was first practiced in China, but is now practiced in many Western countries as well. Statement II is false: according to that first sentence of paragraph 2, acupuncture was not used to control pain during surgery until the 1970s. And the final sentence of the passage disputes statement III: the mechanism for its effectiveness "is still a mystery."

31. **D** The Big Idea question. The author of this passage tells you what acupuncture involves, what ancient Chinese philosophy it's based on, and how it recently spread to the West. Therefore, the passage is primarily about the historical and philosophical background of acupuncture, choice D. No particularly Chinese diseases A are mentioned. B focuses too narrowly on paragraph 1. C is too general—acupuncture is one type of medical therapy. And E leaves out the history and the philosophy detailed in paragraph 1.

32. **F** The fourth sentence of paragraph 1 states that acupuncture is based on the ancient Chinese belief that "human beings are miniature versions of the universe" and that the same forces control nature and health. So choice F is correct here. Yin and yang are not Chinese gods G; they're principles. No mention is made of ancient Chinese religious ceremonies H, or ancient astronomers K. And contrary to J, Western countries have not "totally changed" the Chinese philosophy of health and disease. They may have ignored it, or failed to understand it, but the passage doesn't state that they "changed" it.

33. **D** A detail question based in paragraph 1. Yin and yang have "an opposite but complementary effect on each other....When they are in balance, the body maintains a constant, normal [i.e., healthy] state." So D is correct: yin and yang are competing, balancing forces within the body. A names an example of how the two principles operate, not what they represent. B wrongly states that one principle is healthy, and the other unhealthy. But it's a balance of both that maintains health, and an imbalance that results in sickness. Yin and yang are principles, not treatments C or ideas of comfort and pain E.

34. **G** Lines 10-13 state that yin and yang represent "opposite but complementary" forces controlling body temperature, right? When yin and yang are in balance, the body is healthy, but when they're out of balance, disease occurs. What you're learning here is how these two forces, yin and yang, work together or complement each other as correct choice G puts it. The "author's claim" in F was made by ancient Chinese philosophy. No actual proof that acupuncture works H is given in the passage. J follows plausibly from the temperature control example, but the author doesn't actually speculate as to the cause of high fevers. Nor does she mention any part of the body that isn't influenced by acupuncture K.

O'Keeffe passage

The final passage of this section is about the American painter Georgia O'Keeffe. Paragraph 1 introduces O'Keeffe—her life, her fame, and the subjects of her paintings. The passage's main point is summed up in the opening sentence of paragraph 2, which claims that O'Keeffe is "widely considered to have been a pioneering American modernist painter." The rest of the passage goes on to explore this claim.

35. **C** Basically a hunt-down-the-fake detail question. Correct choice C is contradicted by the second sentence of paragraph 2, which states that O'Keeffe was "more independent" than most other early modern American artists, who were "strongly influenced by European art." Each of the other choices can be found in the passage as influences on O'Keeffe, who "never lost her bond with the land." O'Keeffe "grew up on her family's farm" A, and made her home for more than fifty years in the "western desert" B. We also learn that "bleached bones . . . and colorful flowers were her characteristic subjects" (choices D and E).

36. **F** O'Keeffe was the artist, and nature was her favorite subject. Do this one like an analogy. The relationship of artist to subject is repeated in choice F—a photographer and a model; the model is the photographer's subject. A publisher G and a dealer J represent writers and artists. A part-time job H provides a student with income, it's not necessarily the subject of her studies. And a hammer K is a carpenter's tool; you might say that wood is the carpenter's subject.

37. **D** Why are the paintings "semiabstract" (second paragraph)? Because although they often show "recognizable images and objects," they "don't present those images in a very detailed or realistic way." Choice D correctly restates this idea. O'Keeffe's use of color and light wasn't carefully realistic A, it was "simplified and idealized." She did depict common, everyday things B, and show recognizable scenes from nature C, but each of these is only half an answer. It was her treatment of these objects and scenes—the way she painted them—that makes them "semiabstract." And it's never stated that O'Keeffe's paintings refer to activities E.

38. **H** This takes us back to the beginning of paragraph 2. Why was she considered a "pioneering American modernist"? Because she was, unlike her contemporary American painters, "independent," not influenced by European art. Her work was "identifiably American," which makes choice H correct. We don't learn that her painting became influential in Europe F. G and J are factually true, but they're not why she's considered a pioneer. And her work was considered "semiabstract," not very abstract K.

39. **B** Paragraph 1 introduces O'Keeffe—her life, fame, and the subjects of her paintings. The passage's main point is summed up in the opening sentence of paragraph 2, which claims that she is "widely considered to have been a pioneering American modernist painter." The rest of the passage goes on to explore this claim, and choice B, which more or less restates it, is correct here. The author never claims that O'Keeffe was the best painter of her generation A, and never complains that she didn't develop a fully abstract style D, or that her simplified colors and shapes were "too reduced and simple" E. C is a plausible statement (although we never learn that O'Keeffe painted only familiar subjects), but it's not the main point of the passage.

40. **H** We're told that European art strongly influenced most American artists of O'Keeffe's time. Unlike European art, however, O'Keeffe's paintings offered a "simplified and idealized treatment of color, light, space, and natural forms." Since it was different from O'Keeffe's art, we can infer that European art did not portray natural shapes in a simple, idealistic way, and choice H is correct. None of the other choices can be inferred. As for F, we're only told that O'Keeffe painted images of the desert, not whether anyone else also painted it. And we don't know to what extent European art was abstract (choices G and K), or whether it was influenced by rural landscapes J.

Section 4: Math

1. **E** The perimeter of a polygon is the sum of the lengths of its sides. Label each of the sides with a value of 2 and add.

2. **J** Choice H can be immediately eliminated because it is an even integer and we are looking for an odd. Since D is an odd integer between 4 and 11, D must be one of the integers 5, 7, or 9. Since D is also between 7 and 18, D must be one of the integers 9, 11, 13,

15, or 17. The only choice which meets both requirements is choice J, 9. Choice J is correct. Notice that choice K, 11, is not between 4 and 11.

3. **B** Gary and Paul have a total of $16 + 18 = 34$ operas put together. This number is equal to the number of operas that only Gary has plus the number of operas that only Paul has plus twice the number of operas that they both have in common. The number that they have in common was counted twice. It was counted once in the number of operas that Gary has and once in the number of operas that Paul has. Since the number of operas that they have in common should only be counted once, subtract the 4 they have in common from 34 and our result is 30 different operas.

4. **J** Solve for G by multiplying both sides by the reciprocal of $\frac{1}{9}$: $G = 18 \times \frac{9}{1} = 162$. Substitute 162 for G into the expression $\frac{1}{3}G$ and you will get $\frac{1}{3}G = \frac{1}{3} \times 162 = 54$.

5. **A** The boat can swing out and around as far as the line extends or the wind can push it anywhere within this semicircle. If you chose B, you assumed the boat could float onto the dock. You want the choice indicating all the points of the semicircle shaded, which is choice A.

6. **J** Let x = the number of children. Hence, $4x$ = the number of adults. The total number of people is then $x + 4x = 5x$. The key to solving this is keeping in mind that x must be an integer. It is because of this that $5x$ must be a multiple of 5. Therefore the correct answer choice must be a multiple of 5. Choice J, 25, is correct.

7. **E** Draw a figure! With a diagonal cut, triangles can be created. By cutting to decrease the length 28 of the rectangle by 8 with a cut parallel to the sides of length 20, a square can be created, and cutting anywhere parallel to any side of the original rectangle, a rectangle with new dimensions can be created.

8. **J** We must note how many students were in the swimming class during each month. March = 40, April = 60, May = 80, and June = 80. Use the formula: Average = $\frac{\text{Sum of the terms}}{\text{Number of terms}}$. Here, the average is $\frac{40 + 60 + 80 + 80}{4} = \frac{260}{4} = 65$.

9. **A** The value of n is 4 and the value of r is 2. Simply substitute these values into the equation which defines the symbol: $4 \clubsuit 2 = (4 - 1) - \frac{4}{2} = 3 - \frac{4}{2} = 3 - 2 = 1$. Choice A.

10. **F** Here, you are given $n = Q$ and $r = 2$. Use the equation given in the definition to set $Q \clubsuit 2$ equal to 4 and solve for Q: $(Q - 1) - \frac{Q}{2} = 4$. First, eliminate the denominator by multiplying both sides by 2: $2(Q - 1) - Q = 8$. Then, distribute the 2 through the parentheses: $2Q - 2 - Q = 8$. Third, isolate the Q: $Q = 10$, Choice F.

11. **A** In statement I, $n = n$ and $r = 1$. So $n \clubsuit 1 = (n - 1) - \frac{n}{1} = n - 1 - n = -1$. So $n \clubsuit 1 = -1$ and statement I is true. Eliminate B and D. Statement II: $n = 1$ and $r = n$. According to the definition, $1 \clubsuit n = (1 - 1) - \frac{1}{n} = -\frac{1}{n}$, and $-\frac{1}{n}$ is not equal to 0. Thus $1 \clubsuit n$ is not equal to 0, so eliminate C and E. The answer must be A. There is no need to go any further but for argument's sake, $n \clubsuit n = (n - 1) - \frac{n}{n} = n - 1 - 1 = n - 2$ and $r \clubsuit r = (r - 1) - \frac{r}{r} = r - 1 - 1 = r - 2$. So $n \clubsuit n = n - 2$ and $r \clubsuit r = r - 2$. Since nothing in the question indicates that n must equal r, n could very well not be equal to r and statement III does not have to be true.

12. **H** Using our Percent Formula, Part = Percent ×
Whole. Here, tip = 15% of $20.95 = 15% ×
$20.95. Round the $20.95 to $21.00 and eval-
uate: $\frac{15}{100} \times 21 = \frac{3}{20} \times 21 = \frac{63}{20} = 3\frac{3}{20} = \$3.15$.

13. **A** Break down the problem into steps. Juan 0
finishes $\frac{1}{3}$ of his homework in 2 hours, thus
he has $\frac{2}{3}$ still left to do. If it takes 2 hours to
do $\frac{1}{3}$, it must take 4 hours to do $\frac{2}{3}$ (twice as
much). Finally, subtract 4 hours from 10:30
P.M. and we are left with 6:30 P.M.

14. **K** Mrs. Brown ate 2 peaches plus each child ate
2 peaches and she has z children so 2 for each
of z children and 2 for Mrs. Brown = $2z + 2$.

15. **D** Recall Kaplan's strategy for this type of problem; count the number of intersections in the
given diagram. If there are exactly 0 or 2
points where an odd number of lines intersect, then it can be drawn without lifting the
pencil or retracing, otherwise, it cannot. Here,
Choice A has 4 points with 3 lines intersecting and 1 point with 4 lines intersecting. D
has only two points where an odd number of
lines intersect; thus it is the answer.

16. **J** Round .59 to .6. Now, $.6 = \frac{N}{5}$. Isolate the N
by multiplying both sides by 5. Then $N = 3.0$.
(Be careful in placing the decimal point).

17. **B** The consecutive integers must be 19, 20, 21,
22, 23, 24, 25. The average of an odd number
of equally spaced numbers is always the middle one. Consecutive integers are an instance
of equally spaced numbers. The answer is 22.

18. **H** The percent increase can be found using this
formula: $\frac{\text{new price} - \text{old price}}{\text{old price}}$. Here, $\frac{1.08 - .93}{.93} =$
$\frac{.15}{.93} = \frac{15}{93} = \frac{5}{33}$. To the nearest percent, $\frac{5}{33}$ is
15%.

19. **B** The question is looking for $S - Q$. To find Q,
use the first division problem. $Q = 15 \times 21 =$
315. To find S, use the second division problem. Then $S = 21 \times 15 + 8$. We already know
that $15 \times 21 = 315$, so add 8 to the value 315

of Q to get 323. Finally, $S - Q = 323 - 315 = 8$.
Notice that this is also the remainder of the
second division problem.

20. **H** The area of the floor is found by multiplying
72×48. Dividing this result by the area of a
single tile, which is 6×6, gives us the num-
ber of tiles needed. In the fraction $\frac{72 \times 48}{6 \times 6}$ cancel the 6's leaving $12 \times 8 = 96$.

21. **C** Set up a ratio here. n pages is to 5 minutes as
20 pages is to how many minutes? Call x is
the number of minutes it will take to type 20
pages. Then $\frac{n}{5} = \frac{20}{x}$. Cross multiplying we
get: $xn = 100$. Finally, isolate the x by dividing
each side by n: $x = \frac{100}{n}$, choice C.

22. **H** Draw a figure. The length is 60 and the width
is $\frac{1}{4}$ of 60 or $\frac{1}{4} \times 60 = 15$. The perimeter is
simply the sum of the lengths of all the sides:
$60 + 60 + 15 + 15 = 150$ meters.

23. **B** Pick 100 when dealing with percent problems. If the dress was $100 the first month,
the second month it costs 80% of 100 or $80
and the third month it costs 80% of 80 which
is $64. After 3 months it costs 80% of 64
which is about $51. So, after 3 months, the
cost of it is about 50% of the original price.

24. **H** Picking numbers is your best option here. If
$p = 4$ and $n = -2$, then the results are: F, -2; G,
$-\frac{1}{2}$; H, $-\frac{1}{6}$; J, $-\frac{1}{6}$. The greatest value is thus $\frac{1}{6}$,
making H the correct choice. This question
can also be solved by realizing that for any
positive integer p and any negative integer n,
choices F, G, and J will be negative, while
choice H will be positive.

25. **B** This is a challenging problem. Call the number of men in the school m and the number of
women in the school w. The first statement

can be translated into $\frac{1}{9}m = 2\left(\frac{1}{3}m\right)$. We also know that the men and the women total 84. So $m + w = 84$. Solving the first equation for w in terms of m gives us $w = \frac{3}{2} \times \frac{1}{9}m = \frac{3}{18}m = \frac{1}{6}m$. Substituting $\frac{1}{6}m$ for w in the equation $m + w = 84$ gives us $m + \frac{1}{6}m = 84$. Then, $\frac{7}{6}m = 84$. Multiplying both sides by $\frac{6}{7}$, which is the reciprocal of $\frac{7}{6}$, we get that $m = 84 \times \frac{6}{7} = 12 \times 6 = 72$. Hence, there are 72 men in the school and $\frac{1}{9}$ of these 72 men, or 8 men, are vegetarians.

15

SSAT Upper Level
Practice Test 2

HOW TO TAKE THIS PRACTICE TEST

Before taking this practice test, find a quiet room where you can work uninterrupted for two-and-a-half hours. Make sure you have a comfortable desk, your calculator, and several No. 2 pencils.

Use the answer sheet provided to record your answers. (You can cut it out or photocopy it.)

Once you start this practice test, don't stop until you've finished. Remember—you can review any questions within a section, but you may not go back or forward a section.

You'll find an answer key, score conversion charts, and explanations following the test.

Good luck.

SSAT Practice Test 2
Answer Sheet

Remove (or photocopy) this answer sheet and use it to complete the practice test.

Start with number 1 for each section. If a section has fewer questions than answer spaces, leave the extra spaces blank.

SECTION 1

1 (A) (B) (C) (D) (E)   6 (F) (G) (H) (J) (K)   11 (A) (B) (C) (D) (E)   16 (F) (G) (H) (J) (K)   21 (A) (B) (C) (D) (E)

2 (F) (G) (H) (J) (K)   7 (A) (B) (C) (D) (E)   12 (F) (G) (H) (J) (K)   17 (A) (B) (C) (D) (E)   22 (F) (G) (H) (J) (K)

3 (A) (B) (C) (D) (E)   8 (F) (G) (H) (J) (K)   13 (A) (B) (C) (D) (E)   18 (F) (G) (H) (J) (K)   23 (A) (B) (C) (D) (E)

4 (F) (G) (H) (J) (K)   9 (A) (B) (C) (D) (E)   14 (F) (G) (H) (J) (K)   19 (A) (B) (C) (D) (E)   24 (F) (G) (H) (J) (K)

5 (A) (B) (C) (D) (E)   10 (F) (G) (H) (J) (K)   15 (A) (B) (C) (D) (E)   20 (F) (G) (H) (J) (K)   25 (A) (B) (C) (D) (E)

right in section 1

wrong in section 1

SECTION 2

1 (A) (B) (C) (D) (E)   9 (A) (B) (C) (D) (E)   17 (A) (B) (C) (D) (E)   25 (A) (B) (C) (D) (E)   33 (A) (B) (C) (D) (E)

2 (F) (G) (H) (J) (K)   10 (F) (G) (H) (J) (K)   18 (F) (G) (H) (J) (K)   26 (F) (G) (H) (J) (K)   34 (F) (G) (H) (J) (K)

3 (A) (B) (C) (D) (E)   11 (A) (B) (C) (D) (E)   19 (A) (B) (C) (D) (E)   27 (A) (B) (C) (D) (E)   35 (A) (B) (C) (D) (E)

4 (F) (G) (H) (J) (K)   12 (F) (G) (H) (J) (K)   20 (F) (G) (H) (J) (K)   28 (F) (G) (H) (J) (K)   36 (F) (G) (H) (J) (K)

5 (A) (B) (C) (D) (E)   13 (A) (B) (C) (D) (E)   21 (A) (B) (C) (D) (E)   29 (A) (B) (C) (D) (E)   37 (A) (B) (C) (D) (E)

6 (F) (G) (H) (J) (K)   14 (F) (G) (H) (J) (K)   22 (F) (G) (H) (J) (K)   30 (F) (G) (H) (J) (K)   38 (F) (G) (H) (J) (K)

7 (A) (B) (C) (D) (E)   15 (A) (B) (C) (D) (E)   23 (A) (B) (C) (D) (E)   31 (A) (B) (C) (D) (E)   39 (A) (B) (C) (D) (E)

8 (F) (G) (H) (J) (K)   16 (F) (G) (H) (J) (K)   24 (F) (G) (H) (J) (K)   32 (F) (G) (H) (J) (K)   40 (F) (G) (H) (J) (K)

right in section 2

wrong in section 2

SECTION 3

1 (A) (B) (C) (D) (E)   6 (F) (G) (H) (J) (K)   11 (A) (B) (C) (D) (E)   16 (F) (G) (H) (J) (K)   21 (A) (B) (C) (D) (E)

2 (F) (G) (H) (J) (K)   7 (A) (B) (C) (D) (E)   12 (F) (G) (H) (J) (K)   17 (A) (B) (C) (D) (E)   22 (F) (G) (H) (J) (K)

3 (A) (B) (C) (D) (E)   8 (F) (G) (H) (J) (K)   13 (A) (B) (C) (D) (E)   18 (F) (G) (H) (J) (K)   23 (A) (B) (C) (D) (E)

4 (F) (G) (H) (J) (K)   9 (A) (B) (C) (D) (E)   14 (F) (G) (H) (J) (K)   19 (A) (B) (C) (D) (E)   24 (F) (G) (H) (J) (K)

5 (A) (B) (C) (D) (E)   10 (F) (G) (H) (J) (K)   15 (A) (B) (C) (D) (E)   20 (F) (G) (H) (J) (K)   25 (A) (B) (C) (D) (E)

right in section 3

wrong in section 3

SECTION 4

1 (A) (B) (C) (D) (E)   13 (A) (B) (C) (D) (E)   25 (A) (B) (C) (D) (E)   37 (A) (B) (C) (D) (E)   49 (A) (B) (C) (D) (E)

2 (F) (G) (H) (J) (K)   14 (F) (G) (H) (J) (K)   26 (F) (G) (H) (J) (K)   38 (F) (G) (H) (J) (K)   50 (F) (G) (H) (J) (K)

3 (A) (B) (C) (D) (E)   15 (A) (B) (C) (D) (E)   27 (A) (B) (C) (D) (E)   39 (A) (B) (C) (D) (E)   51 (A) (B) (C) (D) (E)

4 (F) (G) (H) (J) (K)   16 (F) (G) (H) (J) (K)   28 (F) (G) (H) (J) (K)   40 (F) (G) (H) (J) (K)   52 (F) (G) (H) (J) (K)

5 (A) (B) (C) (D) (E)   17 (A) (B) (C) (D) (E)   29 (A) (B) (C) (D) (E)   41 (A) (B) (C) (D) (E)   53 (A) (B) (C) (D) (E)

6 (F) (G) (H) (J) (K)   18 (F) (G) (H) (J) (K)   30 (F) (G) (H) (J) (K)   42 (F) (G) (H) (J) (K)   54 (F) (G) (H) (J) (K)

7 (A) (B) (C) (D) (E)   19 (A) (B) (C) (D) (E)   31 (A) (B) (C) (D) (E)   43 (A) (B) (C) (D) (E)   55 (A) (B) (C) (D) (E)

8 (F) (G) (H) (J) (K)   20 (F) (G) (H) (J) (K)   32 (F) (G) (H) (J) (K)   44 (F) (G) (H) (J) (K)   56 (F) (G) (H) (J) (K)

9 (A) (B) (C) (D) (E)   21 (A) (B) (C) (D) (E)   33 (A) (B) (C) (D) (E)   45 (A) (B) (C) (D) (E)   57 (A) (B) (C) (D) (E)

10 (F) (G) (H) (J) (K)   22 (F) (G) (H) (J) (K)   34 (F) (G) (H) (J) (K)   46 (F) (G) (H) (J) (K)   58 (F) (G) (H) (J) (K)

11 (A) (B) (C) (D) (E)   23 (A) (B) (C) (D) (E)   35 (A) (B) (C) (D) (E)   47 (A) (B) (C) (D) (E)   59 (A) (B) (C) (D) (E)

12 (F) (G) (H) (J) (K)   24 (F) (G) (H) (J) (K)   36 (F) (G) (H) (J) (K)   48 (F) (G) (H) (J) (K)   60 (F) (G) (H) (J) (K)

right in section 4

wrong in section 4

SSAT Practice Test 2
Answer Sheet

Section 1

Time—25 Minutes
25 Questions

In this section, there are 5 possible answers after each problem. Look at each answer and choose which one is best. You may use the blank space at the right of the page for scratchwork.

<u>Note:</u> Figures provided with the problems are drawn with the greatest possible accuracy, UNLESS a specific problem states that its figure is not drawn to scale.

USE THIS SPACE FOR FIGURING.

Sample Question:

$12 \times 9 =$
(A) 21　　(B) 24　　(C) 48
(D) 108　　(E) 129

1. The polygon in Figure 1 has a perimeter of 30. If each side of the polygon has the same length, what is the length of one side?

   (A) 3　(B) 4　(C) 5　(D) 6　(E) 7

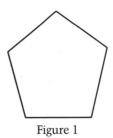

Figure 1

2. Mr. Stuart sold peppermint candy to 25 customers and caramel candy to 17 customers. If 4 of these customers bought both types of candy, how many bought only caramel candy?

   (F) 29　(G) 25　(H) 21　(J) 17　(K) 13

3. In a bag of 24 balloons, there is an equal number of balloons of each color. Which of the following CANNOT be the number of different colors in the bag?

   (A) 2　(B) 3　(C) 4　(D) 5　(E) 6

4. Which of the following is a whole number less than 13 and also a whole number between 11 and 18?

   (F) 11　(G) 12　(H) 12.5　(J) 13　(K) 14

5. According to the graph in Figure 2, Susan spent about how many hours watching movies?

   (A) 2　(B) 3　(C) 4　(D) 6　(E) 9

6. If $\frac{1}{2}R = 16$, then $\frac{3}{4}R =$

   (F) 24　(G) 20　(H) 16　(J) 12　(K) 8

HOW SUSAN SPENT 12 HOURS
WATCHING TV

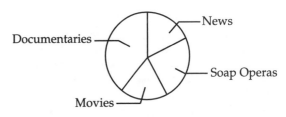

Figure 2

GO ON TO THE NEXT PAGE ➡

USE THIS SPACE FOR FIGURING.

7. Which of the following is closest to $\frac{1}{4}$ of 59?

(A) 0.26×50 (B) 0.41×50 (C) 0.26×60

(D) 0.41×60 (E) 41×60

8. According to the graph in Figure 3, the average sales of Company *M* from 1983 to 1987 was

(F) $250,000   (G) $260,000   (H) $265,000

(J) $270,000   (K) $275,000

<u>Questions 9-10</u> refer to the following definition.

For all real numbers u and v, $u \oslash v = u - \left(1 - \frac{1}{v}\right)$

    (Example: $3 \oslash 2 = 3 - \left(1 - \frac{1}{2}\right) = 3 - \frac{1}{2}$.)

9. Which of the following is equal to $5 \oslash 5$?

(A) 0   (B) 1   (C) $4\frac{1}{5}$ (D) $4\frac{4}{5}$ (E) 25

10. If $a \oslash 3 = 4\frac{1}{3}$, then $a =$

(F) $\frac{2}{3}$ (G) 3   (H) 4   (J) $4\frac{2}{3}$ (K) 5

11. Twenty percent of 64 is equal to 5 percent of what number?

(A) 16   (B) 20   (C) 64

(D) 128   (E) 256

12. During the 4 fishing trips that Rich and Andy made, Rich caught a total of 35 fish. If Andy caught more fish than Rich, Andy must have caught an average of a least how many fish per trip?

(F) $8\frac{3}{4}$ (G) 9   (H) 36   (J) 140   (K) 144

13. Jeff, Todd, and Lee were hired by their father to work on the yard, and each was paid at the same hourly rate. Jeff worked 4 hours, Todd worked 6 hours, and Lee worked 8 hours. If the 3 boys together earned $27, how much did Lee earn?

(A) $8   (B) $12   (C) $15   (D) $16   (E) $27

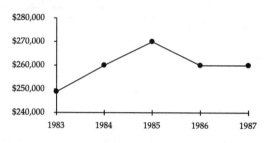

SALES OF COMPANY M: 1983–1987

Figure 3

GO ON TO THE NEXT PAGE ➡

USE THIS SPACE FOR FIGURING.

14. Johnny picked apples from 9:00 a.m. to 11:30 a.m. and gathered 200 apples. He wants to pick at least 600 apples before 7:15 p.m. If he plans to pick apples at the same rate, what is the latest time that he can start picking apples again?

(F) 1:15 p.m.   (G) 1:45 p.m.   (H) 2:15 p.m.
(J) 2:45 p.m.   (K) 3:15 p.m.

15. If 0.88 equals 8W, what is the value of W?

(A) 0.11   (B) 0.9   (C) 1.1   D) 9   (E) 11

16. In the triangle shown in Figure 4, what is the value of r ?

(F) 50   (G) 60   (H) 70   (J) 80

(K) It cannot be determined from the information given.

Figure 4

17. A company's income increased from 9 thousand dollars in 1958 to 4.5 million dollars in 1988. Its income in 1988 was how many times greater than its income in 1958?

(A)   200
(B)   500
(C)   2,000
(D)   5,000
(E)   20,000

18. Which of the following can be expressed as $(5 \times R) + 2$, where R is a whole number?

(F) 25   (G) 33   (H) 47   (J) 56   (K) 68

19. Which of the following can be drawn without lifting the pencil or retracing?

(A)   (B)   (C)

(D)   (E)

GO ON TO THE NEXT PAGE ➡

USE THIS SPACE FOR FIGURING.

20. If the population of Country X increased by 10 percent each year over a 2-year period, what was the total percent increase in the population over the entire period?

(F) 2% (G) 10% (H) 11% (J) 20% (K) 21%

21. If $z = y + 2$, what does $2z + 1$ equal?

(A) $y + 3$
(B) $2y + 3$
(C) $2y + 5$
(D) $2y + 6$
(E) It cannot be determined from the information given.

22. If x is greater than 0 but less than 1, and y is greater than x, which of the following is the LEAST?

(F) $\frac{y}{x}$ (G) $\frac{x}{y}$ (H) xy   (J) $\frac{1}{x-y}$

(K) It cannot be determined from the information given.

23. In a restaurant, there are x tables that can each seat 6 people and there are y tables that can each seat 5 people. What is the maximum number of people that may be seated?

(A) $5x + 6y$ (B) $6x + 5y$ (C) $11x + 11y$

(D) $11xy$ (E) $30xy$

24. Mrs. Smith bought 3 square pieces of fabric. A side of the largest piece is 3 times as long as a side of the middle one, and a side of the middle one is 3 times as long as a side of the smallest one. The area of the largest piece is how many times the area of the smallest piece?

(F) 112   (G) 81   (H) 27   (J) 9   (K) 3

25. Mr. Dali's car uses $\frac{3}{4}$ gallons of gas each time he drives to work. If his gas tank holds exactly 9 gallons of gas, how many tanks of gas does he need to make 18 trips to work?

(A) $1\frac{1}{2}$ (B) $2\frac{1}{2}$ (C) 4   (D) 6   (E) 9

IF YOU FINISH BEFORE TIME IS CALLED, YOU MAY CHECK YOUR WORK ON THIS SECTION ONLY. DO NOT TURN TO ANY OTHER SECTION IN THE TEST. STOP

Section 2
Time—25 Minutes
40 Questions

Read each passage carefully and then answer the questions about it. For each question, decide on the basis of the passage which one of the choices best answers the question.

The reading passages in this test are brief excerpts or adaptations of excerpts from published material. To make the text suitable for testing purposes, we may in some cases have altered the style, contents, or point of view of the original. The passages do not necessarily reflect the opinions of Kaplan, Inc.

Line   Scott Joplin composed approximately 60 works during his lifetime, including 41 piano pieces called "rags," many songs and marches, Line and an opera entitled Treemonisha. His most significant
(5)   creative contribution was to the development of ragtime, a type of instrumental music marked by its distinctive, choppy rhythm. Joplin's rhythmic diversity was very important to the development of ragtime as a genre, a unique musical form. In
(10)   1899, his "Maple Leaf Rag" became the most popular piano rag of the time and he was dubbed the "King of Ragtime." Despite all of those accomplishments, he was not considered a serious composer during his lifetime. It was not until 59
(15)   years after his death that he was properly recognized: In 1976, he was awarded the Pulitzer Prize for music, at last receiving the praise he deserved.

1. The term "rag," as it is used in the passage refers to

   (A) a specific piece of operatic music
   (B) a genre of dance music
   (C) a piece of piano music known for its unique rhythm
   (D) a kind of instrumental music played by marching bands
   (E) a style of songs invented by Joplin

2. This passage deals primarily with

   (F) the fact that Joplin was not taken seriously during his lifetime
   (G) the history and development of ragtime music
   (H) the diversity of styles in which Joplin composed
   (J) how Joplin came to win the Pulitzer Prize
   (K) Joplin's contributions to and accomplishments in the world of music

3. According to the passage, Joplin died in

   (A) 1899
   (B) 1917
   (C) 1941
   (D) 1959
   (E) 1976

4. When discussing Scott Joplin, the author's tone in this passage could best be described as

   (F) indifferent
   (G) amused
   (H) envious
   (J) resentful
   (K) appreciative

5. It can be inferred from the passage that a genre is

   (A) a particular type of ragtime music
   (B) a distinct category or style
   (C) a term that Joplin coined when he created ragtime
   (D) a rhythmic style characteristic of Joplin's period
   (E) an early form of "rag"

GO ON TO THE NEXT PAGE ➡

Line   John Podgers was broad, sturdy, short, and a
very hard eater, as men of his figure often are.
Being a hard sleeper likewise, he divided his time
pretty equally between these two recreations,
(5)   always falling asleep when he had done eating, and
always taking another turn at the feeding trough
when he had done sleeping, by which means he
grew more obese and more drowsy every day of his
life. Indeed, it used to be currently reported that
(10)   when he strolled up and down the sunny side of
the street before dinner (as he never failed to do in
fair weather), he enjoyed his soundest nap; but
many people held this to be a fiction, as he had
several times been seen to look after fat oxen on
(15)   market days, and had even been heard, by persons
of good credit and reputation, to chuckle at the
sight, and say to himself with great glee, 'Live beef,
live beef!'

It was upon this evidence that the wisest
(20)   people in Windsor (beginning with the local
authorities, of course) held that John Podgers was a
man of strong, sound sense, not what is called
smart, perhaps, and might be of a rather lazy turn,
but still a man of solid parts and one who meant
(25)   much more than he cared to show.

6. John Podgers is described as being all of the
   following EXCEPT

   (F)   intelligent
   (G)   stocky
   (H)   lazy
   (J)   sensible
   (K)   solid

7. The author of the passage is primarily
   concerned with

   (A)   explaining why people think John
         Podgers is smarter than he lets on
   (B)   questioning why John Podgers
         comments on the oxen in the
         marketplace
   (C)   discussing John Podgers's reasons for
         eating so much
   (D)   providing the details of John Podgers's
         daily stroll up the street
   (E)   describing John Podgers's physical and
         mental qualities

8. John Podgers spent the majority of his time
   doing which of the following pairs of things?

   (F)   Drinking and eating
   (G)   Strolling and resting
   (H)   Chuckling and walking
   (J)   Eating and sleeping
   (K)   Napping and thinking

9. The tone of the writer toward the subject is

   (A)   cautious
   (B)   formal
   (C)   respectful
   (D)   angry
   (E)   humorous

GO ON TO THE NEXT PAGE ➡

Line   Thousands of species of birds exist today, and nearly every species has its own special courtship procedures and "identification checks." Identification checks are important, because if
(5) birds of different species mate, any offspring will usually be sterile or badly adapted to their surroundings.

    Plumage often plays a key role in both identification and courtship. In breeding season,
(10) male birds often acquire distinctive plumage which they use to attract females who will, in turn, only respond to males with the correct markings. In some species, the females are more brightly colored, and the courtship roles are
(15) reversed. Distinctive behavioral changes can also be important aspects of courtship and breeding activity. Aggressiveness between males, and sometimes between females, is quite common. Some birds, like whooping cranes and trumpeter
(20) swans, perform wonderfully elaborate courtship dances in which both sexes are enthusiastic participants.

    Bird sounds are often a very central part of identification and courtship behavior between
(25) individuals in a given species. When a female migrates in the spring to her breeding region, she often encounters numerous birds of different species. By its singing, the male of a species both identifies itself and communicates to females of
(30) that species that it is in breeding condition. This information allows a female to predict a male's response to her approach. Later, after mating has taken place, the note patterns of a particular male's song enable a nesting female to continue to
(35) identify her own partner.

10. The author implies that a bird engages in identification and courtship procedures mainly in order to

(F) find a better nesting spot
(G) find the most colorful partner it can
(H) attract a mate of its own species
(J) increase its control over its nesting partner
(K) try to dominate the bird population of a given area

11. According to the passage, a feature of the male song bird is its ability to

I. attract a female of its own species
II. intimidate rival males
III. communicate its identity to its mate

(A) I only
(B) III only
(C) I and II only
(D) I and III only
(E) I, II, and III

12. The author uses the whooping crane as an example of a bird that

(F) seldom participates in courtship procedures
(G) acquires a distinctive breeding plumage
(H) behaves in an unusual and noteworthy way during courtship
(J) reverses the normal male and female courtship roles
(K) displays unusual aggressiveness while courting

13. According to the passage, matings between birds of different species

(A) are quite common
(B) produce more sturdy offspring
(C) may help to establish a permanent new species
(D) do not usually result in healthy offspring
(E) have never happened

14. The passage is primarily about

(F) causes of aggression between male birds
(G) several courtship and identification methods used by birds
(H) the breeding season of birds
(J) the role of bird sounds in courtship identification
(K) why birds migrate to particular breeding regions

Line   More than 1,500 Native American languages
have thus far been discovered by linguists. Edward
Sapir, a pioneer in the field of Native American
linguistics, grouped these languages into six
(5)   "families" more than three-quarters of a century
ago. Ever since that time, the classification of
Native American languages has been a source of
controversy. A small group of linguists has
recently argued that all Native American
(10)   languages fit into three linguistic families. These
scholars believe that similarities and differences
among words and sounds leave no doubt about the
validity of their classification scheme. The vast
majority of linguists, however, reject both the
(15)   methods and conclusions of these scholars,
arguing that linguistic science has not yet
advanced far enough to be able to group Native
American languages into a few families. According
to these scholars, Native American languages have
(20)   diverged to such an extent over the centuries that
it may never be possible to group them in distinct
language families.

15. This passage is primarily about

(A)   the classification of Native American
languages
(B)   the six families of Native American
languages
(C)   scholars' views about language
(D)   the similarities and differences
between words of Native American
languages
(E)   linguistic debates about how to group
languages

16. The scholars who believe that Native American languages can be classified into three
families apparently believe that

(F)   these languages have diverged
significantly over the last 75 years
(G)   languages can be classified according to
the degree of similarities and
differences between words
(H)   linguistic science has not advanced far
enough to safely classify languages so
narrowly
(J)   languages are all related by their
common origins
(K)   distinct language families have their
own peculiar grammatical rules

17. The style of the passage is most like that
found in a

(A)   personal letter written by a linguistics
student
(B)   textbook about linguistics
(C)   novel about Native American tribes
(D)   diary of a linguist
(E)   biography of Edward Sapir

18. It can be inferred that the classification of
Native American languages has been a
source of controversy because

(F)   scholars do not agree on the method
for classifying languages
(G)   languages have split in several
directions
(H)   linguistics is a very new field
(J)   there is not enough known about
Native American vocabulary
(K)   Native Americans dislike such
classifications

19. Which of the following questions is
answered by the passage?

(A)   Did Edward Sapir study languages
other than Native American
languages?
(B)   How many languages are in a typical
linguistic family?
(C)   How many Native American languages
are yet to discovered?
(D)   In what ways have Native American
languages changed over time?
(E)   Into how many families did Edward
Sapir classify Native American
languages?

GO ON TO THE NEXT PAGE ➡

Line   Hope is the thing with feathers
That perches in the soul,
And sings the tune without the words
And never stops at all,

(5)   And sweetest in the gale is heard;
And sore must be the storm
That could abash[1] the little bird
That kept so many warm.

(10)   I've heard it in the chillest land,
And on the strangest sea;
Yet, never, in extremity,
It asked a crumb of me.

[1] discourage
"Hope" by Emily Dickinson.

20. In this poem, hope is compared to which of the following?

(F)   a gale
(G)   a sea
(H)   a storm
(J)   a bird
(K)   a song

21. What is the poet saying in the last stanza of the poem?

(A)   It is terrible to imagine a world without hope and we must therefore do everything possible to preserve our hopes.
(B)   The bird continues to sing through all conditions.
(C)   Hope can be found anywhere and never asks anything in return for its loyalty.
(D)   The bird is very hungry because it is constantly singing and never takes any time to eat.
(E)   The potential for hope is always present but it takes a great effort to make it a reality.

22. The lines "the little bird/That kept so many warm" in the second stanza refers to the fact that

(F)   the feathers of birds have traditionally provided protection against the cold
(G)   hope has comforted a great many people over the years
(H)   the bird provided protection before it was destroyed in a storm
(J)   hope has often proven useless in the face of real problems
(K)   hope is a good last resort when faced with a difficult situation

23. The attitude of the speaker in this poem can best be described as

(A)   angry
(B)   unconcerned
(C)   respectful
(D)   nervous
(E)   grateful

GO ON TO THE NEXT PAGE ➡

Line   Although recycling has taken place in various forms for some time, today we are being asked to regard recycling as not only an important, but even a necessary measure.

(5)   Recycling, in its broadest sense, refers to the remaking of waste products and other used materials for practical purposes. For example, an old soda bottle can be returned, washed, and used as a bottle again, or it can be ground down and its

(10)   glass can be employed for another useful purpose. Since fixing up old things is often cheaper than making brand new ones, this often saves money. More importantly, it saves resources and reduces the amount of waste produced.

(15)   Businesses have been performing large-scale recycling for some time, based primarily on the goal of saving money. However, the amount of residential waste, that is, the waste produced at home, has been steadily increasing, and the role of the individual in

(20)   the recycling campaign has been seriously underemphasized. Although it is true that we, as individuals, cannot reduce the overall amount of waste significantly or save large amounts of money and resources on our own, taken collectively, we can

(25)   have an important impact. Our increased efforts towards recycling can have a dramatic effect on the future availability of resources and the condition of the environment. It is our duty to ourselves and to our fellow human beings to pitch in and help protect

(30)   what remains of it.

24. According to the passage, which of the following is true?

    I.   Recycling increases the amount of waste produced.

    II.   Re-using waste products can be very economical.

    III. The amount of waste produced in the home has been continuously growing.

    (F)   II only
    (G)   I and II only
    (H)   I and III only
    (J)   II and III only
    (K)   I, II, and III

25. The author would most likely agree that

    (A)   recycling is a good idea for big businesses but, on an individual level, it makes very little difference

    (B)   although businesses recycle to save money, individuals are motivated to recycle by a desire to serve the general good of society

    (C)   recycling is extremely important and everyone has a responsibility to contribute to the overall effort to preserve our environment

    (D)   although our natural resources are limited, we only live once and we shouldn't concentrate on conservation to such a degree that it interferes with our enjoyment of life

    (E)   recycling is a very expensive process and should be left to the owners of big businesses

26. All of the following are examples of recycling EXCEPT

    (F)   turning old newspapers into cardboard

    (G)   melting down scraps of metal and recasting them

    (H)   washing out empty soda bottles and using them as vases

    (J)   selling a piece of jewelry and using the money to buy a car

    (K)   crushing old cans and reusing the aluminum to make new ones

27. The tone of the writer of this passage is

    (A)   insistent
    (B)   relaxed
    (C)   formal
    (D)   amused
    (E)   disinterested

GO ON TO THE NEXT PAGE ➡

28. Which of the following is the author most likely to discuss next?

    (F) The current problem of toxic waste disposal

    (G) The negative side to recycling and the many problems that can develop when it is done too much

    (H) Different ways that an old bottle can be either reused or remade into an entirely different object

    (J) Other important differences between the way businesses and residences are run

    (K) Examples of ways in which people can recycle their own waste and help out on an individual basis

29. What can be said about the author based on lines 15-17?

    (A) She is only interested in the economic aspects of recycling.

    (B) She believes that businesses are motivated to recycle primarily for monetary gain.

    (C) She knows little about the possible financial savings of recycling.

    (D) She is more concerned with the environmental benefits of recycling than the economic rewards.

    (E) She values recycling even though it results in the production of greater amounts of waste.

GO ON TO THE NEXT PAGE ➡

Line   Most of us who live in relatively mild climates rarely view bad weather as more than an inconvenience, but in certain, less fortunate parts of the world a change in weather can have
(5)   disastrous consequences for an entire society. Weather fluctuations along the northwest coast of South America, for instance, can periodically have a dramatic effect on the area's fishing villages. Under normal circumstances, the cold, steadily
(10)   flowing waters of the Humboldt Current bring nutrients up from the sea floor along the coast, providing a dependable food supply for fish and squid. For centuries, the fishing villages have depended on this rich ocean harvest for food and
(15)   trade. Occasionally, however, global weather patterns cause the current to fail, setting off a deadly chain reaction. Without nutrients, the fish and squid die, depriving the villagers of their livelihood. This destructive weather phenomenon,
(20)   called "El Niño" (The Christ Child) because it occurs at Christmastime, has sometimes forced entire villages to disband and move elsewhere merely to avoid starvation.

30. According to the passage, the Humboldt Current flows

(F)   only at Christmastime
(G)   without fail
(H)   east to west
(J)   along the northwest coast of South America
(K)   through warm water

31. This passage is mainly about

(A)   how the economy of South American villages depends exclusively on fishing
(B)   the importance of fish and squid in the food chain
(C)   the advantages of living in a mild climate
(D)   the undependable nature of the Humboldt Current
(E)   how changes in weather patterns can have a dramatic effect on the way people live

32. According to the passage, all of the following are true EXCEPT

(F)   the actions of the Humboldt Current help provide nutrients for fish and squid
(G)   the Humboldt Current affects the survival of fishing on the northwest coast of South America
(H)   the warm waters of the Humboldt Current affect the climate of nearby land masses
(J)   the failure of the Humboldt Current can set off a deadly chain reaction
(K)   the Humboldt Current sometimes fails as a result of global weather patterns

33. Which of the following would be the best title for this passage?

(A)   An Example of Weather's Social Impact
(B)   Fishing Villages of South America
(C)   El Niño: A Christmas Occurrence
(D)   Fish and Squid: A Rich Ocean Harvest
(E)   The Impact of Fishing to Coastal Villages

34. The author's attitude toward the villagers along the northwest coast of South America can best be described as

(F)   sympathetic
(G)   unconcerned
(H)   condescending
(J)   angry
(K)   emotional

35. Which of the following is an example of a chain reaction?

(A)   Forest fires kill off thousands of acres of land, destroying valuable resources.
(B)   When temperatures start to fall, many birds fly south to spend winter in warm climates.
(C)   Earthquakes cause extensive damage to property and often result in the loss of human life.
(D)   Global warming causes glaciers to melt, resulting in rising water levels, which reduce the amount of habitable land.
(E)   The moon revolves around the Earth and the Earth revolves around the sun.

GO ON TO THE NEXT PAGE ➡

Line World War II left much of Western Europe deeply scarred in many ways. Economically, it was devastated. In early 1948, as the Cold War developed between the United States and the
(5) Soviet Union and political tensions rose, U.S. policymakers decided that substantial financial assistance would be required to maintain a state of political stability. This conclusion led the Secretary of State, George C. Marshall, to
(10) announce a proposal: the European countries were advised to draw up a unified plan for reconstruction, to be funded by the U. S.

  This European Recovery Program, also known as the Marshall Plan, provided economic and
(15) technical assistance to 16 countries. Between 1948 and 1952, participating countries received a combined total of 12 billion dollars in U.S. aid. In the end, the program was seen as a great success; it revived the economies of Western Europe and set
(20) them on a course for future growth.

36. Which of the following would be the best title for this passage?

 (F) The Aftermath of World War II
 (G) The Marshall Plan: A Program for European Reconstruction
 (H) The Economic Destruction of Europe
 (J) George C. Marshall: The Man Behind the Plan
 (K) Western European Recovery

37. The tone of the author toward the Marshall Plan is

 (A) objective
 (B) excited
 (C) insistent
 (D) anxious
 (E) unfavorable

38. All of the following are true about the Marshall Plan EXCEPT

 (F) it provided economic assistance to 16 countries
 (G) it went into action in 1948
 (H) it supplied economic aid for a period spanning four years
 (J) it gave each of the participating countries 12 billion dollars
 (K) it was considered a great long-term success

39. The passage suggests that the driving force behind the Marshall Plan was

 (A) a formal request for aid by European leaders
 (B) fear of economic repercussions for the U.S. economy
 (C) George C. Marshall's desire to improve his political career and public image
 (D) a joint U.S.-Soviet agreement to assist the countries of Western Europe
 (E) the increase in tension between the United States and the Soviet Union

40. Which of the following would the author be most likely to discuss next?

 (F) Developments in the Cold War during and after the years of the Marshall Plan
 (G) The events leading up to Western Europe's economic collapse
 (H) The detailed effects of the Marshall Plan on specific countries
 (J) Other successful economic recovery programs employed throughout history
 (K) How George C. Marshall became the U.S. Secretary of State

IF YOU FINISH BEFORE TIME IS CALLED, YOU MAY CHECK YOUR WORK ON THIS SECTION ONLY. DO NOT WORK ON ANY OTHER SECTION IN THE TEST.

STOP

Section 3

Time—25 Minutes
25 Questions

In this section, there are 5 possible answers after each problem. Look at each answer and choose which one is best. You may use the blank space at the right of the page for scratchwork.

Note: Figures provided with the problems are drawn with the greatest possible accuracy, UNLESS a specific problem states that its figure is not drawn to scale.

Sample Question:

$12 \times 9 =$
(A) 21   (B) 24   (C) 48
(D) 108   (E) 129

Ⓐ Ⓑ Ⓒ ● Ⓔ

USE THIS SPACE FOR FIGURING.

1. Justine bought a comic book at $5 above the cover price. A year later she sold the book for $9 less than she paid. At what price did Justine sell the book?

    (A) $14 below the cover price
    (B) $4 below the cover price
    (C) the cover price
    (D) $4 above the cover price
    (E) $14 above the cover price

Questions 2-3 refer to the graph in Figure 1.

2. How many fewer boxes of cereal were sold in February than in March?

    (F) 2   (G) 3   (H) 20   (J) 40   (K) 60

3. The number of boxes sold in January was how many times the number of boxes sold in February?

    (A) 2   (B) $2\frac{1}{2}$ (C) 3   (D) 40   (E) 60

CEREAL SALES AT STORE X

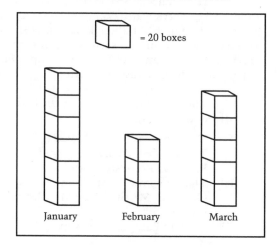

= 20 boxes

January   February   March

Figure 1

GO ON TO THE NEXT PAGE ➡

USE THIS SPACE FOR FIGURING.

4. Team *A* has 4 times as many losses as it had ties in a season. If Team *A* won none of its games, which could be the total number of games it played that season?

   (F) 12   (G) 15   (H) 18   (J) 21   (K) 26

5. Figure 2 contains rectangles and a triangle. How many different rectangles are there in Figure 2?

   (A) 5   (B) 7   (C) 9   (D) 10   (E) 12

6. Which of the following is NOT less than $\frac{1}{4}$?

   (F) $\frac{2}{9}$ (G) $\frac{3}{14}$ (H) $\frac{14}{64}$ (J) $\frac{19}{70}$ (K) $\frac{27}{125}$

7. In Figure 3, the sides of triangles *ABC* and *FGH*, and of squares *BCFE* and *CDGF*, are all equal in length. Which of the following is the longest path from *A* to *H*?

   (A)   *A – B – C – F – H*
   (B)   *A – B – E – F – H*
   (C)   *A – C – D – G – H*
   (D)   *A – B – E – G – H*
   (E)   *A – C – F – G – H*

8. If $5\frac{1}{3} \times (14 - x) = 0$, then what does *x* equal?

   (F) 0   (G) 1   (H) $5\frac{1}{3}$ (J) 14

   (K) It cannot be determined from the information given.

9. Which of the following is closest to 1.18?

   (A) 12   (B) 2.2   (C) 1.9   (D) 1.1   (E) 1

10. If *X* is greater than 15, then $\frac{1}{3}$ of *X* must be

    (F)   less than 5
    (G)   equal to 5
    (H)   greater than 5
    (J)   equal to 45
    (K)   less than 45

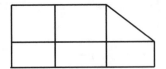

Figure 2

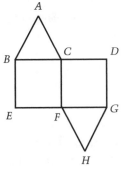

Figure 3

GO ON TO THE NEXT PAGE ➡

11. Of the following, 35 percent of $26.95 is closest to

(A) $7.00   (B) $9.45   (C) $10.50
(D) $11.15   (E) $12.25

12. If a factory can make 600 nails every 3 minutes, how long would it take to make 27,000 nails?

(F) 45 minutes
(G) 1 hour
(H) 1 hour, 45 minutes
(J) 2 hours, 15 minutes
(K) 3 hours, 15 minutes

13. Sally has x dollars and receives $100 for her birthday. With all this money, she buys a bicycle that costs $125. How many dollars does Sally have remaining?

(A) $x + 125$
(B) $x + 100$
(C) $x + 25$
(D) $x - 25$
(E) $x - 100$

14. If $\frac{A + B}{3} = 4$ and A is greater than 1, which of the following could NOT be the value of B ?

(F) –3   (G) 0   (H) 1   (J) 2   (K) 12

15. The average of 5 numbers is 10. If 2 of the 5 numbers are removed, the average of the remaining 3 numbers is 9. What is the sum of the 2 numbers that were removed?

(A) 17   (B) 18   (C) 21   (D) 22   (E) 23

USE THIS SPACE FOR FIGURING.

GO ON TO THE NEXT PAGE ➡

16. The bottom of the shopping bag shown in Figure 4 is placed flat on a table. Except for the handles, this shopping bag is constructed with rectangular pieces of paper. Which of the following diagrams best represents all the points where the shopping bag touches the table?

(F) ☐   (G) ▧   (H) △

(J) ◠   (K) ◖

17. The number of students in a certain school is expected to increase from 1,078 students in 1990 to 1,442 students in 1991. The expected increase is closest to what percent?

(A) 20%   (B) $33\frac{1}{3}\%$ (C) 37%

(D) 40%   (E) 45%

18. In Figure 5, the distance between W and Y is three times the distance between W and X, and the distance between X and Z is twice the distance between X and Y. If the distance from W to X is 2, how far apart are W and Z?

(F) 10   (G) 12   (H) 14   (J) 16   (K) 18

19. A fence surrounds a rectangular field whose length is 3 times its width. If the fence is 240 meters long, what is the width of the field?

(A) 30 m   (B) 40 m   (C) 60 m
(D) 80 m   (E) 90 m

20. Ms. Kirschner receives $50 for every $900 she collects from stock sales. How much does she receive if she collects $18,000 from stock sales?

(F) $100   (G) $180   (H) $1,000
(J) $1,200   (K) $1,800

USE THIS SPACE FOR FIGURING.

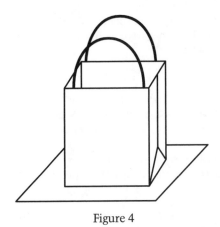

Figure 4

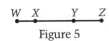
Figure 5

GO ON TO THE NEXT PAGE ➡

21. What is the greatest number of rectangles 4 centimeters wide and 6 centimeters long that can be cut from a square piece of paper with a side of 24 centimeters?

   (A) 2   (B) 10   (C) 24   (D 36   (E) 48

22. R is the sum of consecutive integers S and T. If S and T are negative, which of the following is always true?

   (F) $R = -4$
   (G) $R = -1$
   (H) R is less than either S or T.
   (J) R is greater than either S or T.
   (K) $R + S + T$ is positive.

23. Initially, Greg had a total of 60 records and cassettes in his music collection. He then sold $\frac{1}{8}$ of his cassettes and $\frac{1}{2}$ of his records. If the number of records he sold is twice the number of cassettes he sold, how many records did he sell?

   (A) 4   (B) 5   (C) 8   (D 10   (E) 20

24. Mary saved exactly 60 percent of the total allowance she received in the last two weeks, and spent the rest. If she received $20 for allowance each week and spent $12 of her first week's allowance, which of the following must be true?

   I.   She saved a total of $24.
   II.   She spent $6 of her second week's allowance.
   III. She saved 80 percent of her second week's allowance.

   (F)   None
   (G)   I only
   (H)   II only
   (J)   I and III only
   (K)   I, II, and III

25. Paul and Bill each received a raise of 20 percent. If Paul now earns $4.50 per hour while Bill earns $5.40 per hour, Bill earned how much more per hour than Paul before their raises?

   (A) $0.70
   (B) $0.73
   (C) $0.75
   (D) $0.80
   (E) $0.90

IF YOU FINISH BEFORE TIME IS CALLED, YOU MAY CHECK YOUR WORK ON THIS SECTION ONLY. DO NOT WORK ON ANY OTHER SECTION IN THE TEST. **STOP**

Section 4

Time—25 Minutes

60 Questions

This section consists of two different types of questions. There are directions and a sample question for each type.

Each of the following questions consists of one word followed by five words or phrases. You are to select the one word or phrase whose meaning is closest to the word in capital letters.

Sample Question:

CHILLY: (A) lazy (B) nice (C) dry
(D) cold (E) sunny

Ⓐ Ⓑ Ⓒ ● Ⓔ

1. HARSH: (A) cold (B) angry
   (C) poor (D) useless (E) severe

2. INDICATE: (F) meet with (G) look at
   (H) help with (J) point out (K) search for

3. BLEAK: (A) unknown (B) quiet
   (C) cheerless (D) trembling (E) timid

4. SECURE: (F) unseen (G) aware
   (H) secret (J) safe (K) knotty

5. ALIEN: (A) strange (B) futile
   (C) valuable (D) brutal (E) unclear

6. CHRONIC: (F) persistent (G) difficult
   (H) doubtful (J) legal (K) elaborate

7. QUENCH: (A) complete (B) compare
   (C) demean (D) satisfy (E) withdraw

8. SEVERE: (F) frozen (G) extreme
   (H) long (J) limited (K) essential

9. RANSACK: (A) search thoroughly
   (B) act quickly (C) cover completely
   (D) make secure (E) denounce publicly

10. SUMMIT: (F) plateau (G) landscape
    (H) slope (J) island (K) peak

11. TUMULT: (A) annoyance (B) commotion
    (C) insignificance (D) disagreement
    (E) blockage

12. RETARD: (F) turn around (G) push apart
    (H) slow down (J) change position
    (K) see through

13. ANTIDOTE: (A) fantasy (B) remedy
    (C) substitute (D) award (E) decoration

14. SOLITARY: (F) mindful (G) careless
    (H) friendly (J) alone (K) troubled

15. CAMOUFLAGE: (A) obstacle (B) range
    (C) emergency (D) disguise (E) amount

16. EXPEL: (F) finish off (G) teach
    (H) question (J) scold (K) cast out

17. LUNGE: (A) pursue (B) turn (C) thrust
    (D) restore (E) startle

18. BREVITY: (F) ambition (G) consistency
    (H) conflict (J) imagination (K) shortness

19. MARVEL: (A) discard (B) usurp
    (C) confuse (D) point (E) wonder

20. CANDOR: (F) majesty (G) daring
    (H) honesty (J) perception (K) fatigue

21. CONVENE: (A) clarify (B) serve
    (C) assemble (D) elect (E) dignify

22. CATASTROPHE: (F) illusion (G) disaster
    (H) indication (J) warning (K) estimate

23. GREGARIOUS: (A) sloppy (B) sociable
    (C) happy (D) intelligent (E) talented

24. DEXTERITY: (F) secrecy (G) equality
    (H) reserve (J) nimbleness
    (K) determination

GO ON TO THE NEXT PAGE ➡

25. IMMINENT: (A) intense (B) impressive
    (C) proper (D) observable (E) forthcoming

26. ANIMOSITY: (F) doubt (G) hatred
    (H) sadness (J) illness (K) guilt

27. AMEND: (A) create (B) address
    (C) observe (D) exclude (E) improve

28. DESPONDENT: (F) depressed
    (G) unintended (H) artificial (J) literary
    (K) unconcerned

29. UNFLINCHING: (A) uncommitted
    (B) distinct (C) uncompromising
    (D) transitory (E) invalid

30. REPUDIATE: (F) renounce (G) impede
    (H) provoke (J) divert (K) submit

GO ON TO THE NEXT PAGE ➡

The following questions ask you to find relationships between words. For each question, select the choice that best completes the meaning of the sentence.

Sample Question:

Kitten is to cat as
(A) fawn is to colt
(B) puppy is to dog
(C) cow is to bull
(D) wolf is to bear
(E) hen is to rooster

Choice B is the best answer because a kitten is a young cat just as a puppy is a young dog. Of all the answer choices, (B) states a relationship that is most like the relationship between kitten and cat.

31. Sun is to solar as

   (A) earth is to terrestrial
   (B) pond is to marine
   (C) ground is to subterranean
   (D) tower is to architectural
   (E) planet is to lunar

32. Botany is to plants as meteorology is to

   (F) weather   (G) flora   (H) health
   (J) language   (K) style

33. Hammer is to nail as

   (A) axe is to wood
   (B) lathe is to molding
   (C) chisel is to marble
   (D) nut is to bolt
   (E) screwdriver is to screw

34. Bone is to mammal as girder is to

   (F) skyscraper
   (G) steel
   (H) rivet
   (J) crane
   (K) concrete

35. Human is to primate as

   (A) kangaroo is to vegetarian
   (B) snake is to reptile
   (C) disease is to bacterium
   (D) bird is to amphibian
   (E) dog is to pet

36. Tremor is to earthquake as

   (F) eye is to hurricane
   (G) desert is to sandstorm
   (H) faucet is to deluge
   (J) wind is to tornado
   (K) flood is to river

37. Amusing is to uproarious as

   (A) silly is to serious
   (B) dead is to immortal
   (C) interesting is to mesmerizing
   (D) humorous is to dull
   (E) worthless is to valuable

38. Fickle is to steadfastness as tempestuous is to

   (F) worthlessness   (G) openness
   (H) inspiration   (J) peacefulness   (K) ire

39. School is to fish as

   (A) fin is to shark
   (B) library is to student
   (C) flock is to bird
   (D) leg is to frog
   (E) college is to mascot

40. Cartographer is to map as chef is to

   (F) flower   (G) silverware   (H) table
   (J) meal   (K) ingredient

41. Throne is to monarch as

   (A) miter is to pope
   (B) bench is to judge
   (C) lobby is to doorman
   (D) armchair is to general
   (E) ship is to captain

42. Canal is to river as

   (F) boat is to driftwood
   (G) puddle is to lake
   (H) hammer is to mallet
   (J) mine is to cavern
   (K) telephone is to computer

43. Milk is to sour as bread is to

   (A) bent   (B) stale   (C) folded
   (D) baked   (E) hot

GO ON TO THE NEXT PAGE ➡

44. Ore is to mine as

    (F) apple is to peel
    (G) water is to purify
    (H) batter is to stir
    (J) grain is to plow
    (K) oil is to drill

45. Weight is to scale as

    (A) distance is to speedometer
    (B) number is to slide rule
    (C) length is to thermometer
    (D) reading is to gauge
    (E) altitude is to altimeter

46. Porcupine is to quill as

    (F) bat is to wing
    (G) horse is to tail
    (H) skunk is to odor
    (J) oyster is to pearl
    (K) tiger is to stripe

47. Jar is to contain as pillar is to

    (A) stand (B) ascend (C) prepare
    (D) support (E) swing

48. Irrigate is to dry as

    (F) soften is to uneven
    (G) smooth is to coarse
    (H) purify is to distasteful
    (J) depend is to supportive
    (K) ferment is to salty

49. Electricity is to wire as

    (A) sound is to radio
    (B) water is to aqueduct
    (C) music is to instrument
    (D) light is to bulb
    (E) river is to bank

50. Contempt is to sneer as

    (F) shame is to shrug
    (G) anger is to laugh
    (H) enjoyment is to groan
    (J) agreement is to grimace
    (K) displeasure is to frown

51. Building is to foundation as plant is to

    (A) pane (B) grotto (C) primer
    (D) floor (E) root

52. Nose is to olfactory as ear is to

    (F) beautiful (G) edible (H) auditory
    (J) raspy (K) allergic

53. Irk is to soothing as support is to

    (A) conciliating (B) elevating
    (C) undermining (D) irritating
    (E) vilifying

54. Illegible is to read as

    (F) invisible is to see
    (G) illegal is to act
    (H) broken is to fix
    (J) irreparable is to break
    (K) intense is to strain

55. Tact is to diplomat as

    (A) parsimony is to philanthropist
    (B) agility is to gymnast
    (C) vulnerability is to victim
    (D) training is to physician
    (E) bias is to judge

56. Ravenous is to hunger as

    (F) pliable is to obstinacy
    (G) agitated is to placidity
    (H) concerned is to apathy
    (J) smart is to tenacity
    (K) furious is to indignation

57. Amplify is to sound as bolster is to

    (A) smell (B) courage (C) insomnia
    (D) light (E) silence

58. Auditorium is to lecture as

    (F) theater is to concert
    (G) attic is to storage
    (H) temple is to religion
    (J) cafeteria is to food
    (K) target is to arrow

59. Philanthropic is to benevolence as

    (A) smooth is to surface
    (B) ostentatious is to reserve
    (C) miserly is to stinginess
    (D) devout is to malice
    (E) realistic is to plan

60. Spurious is to authenticity as

    (F) lavish is to expense
    (G) abject is to subjectivity
    (H) affluent is to character
    (J) laughable is to seriousness
    (K) totalitarian is to completeness

IF YOU FINISH BEFORE TIME IS CALLED, YOU MAY CHECK YOUR WORK ON THIS SECTION ONLY. DO NOT WORK ON ANY OTHER SECTION IN THE TEST. **STOP**

Section 5	Write an essay on the following prompt on the paper provided. Your essay should NOT
Time—25 Minutes	exceed 2 pages and must be written in ink. Erasing is not allowed.

Prompt: <u>Tougher restrictions should be imposed on buying handguns.</u>

Do you agree or disagree with this statement? Use examples from history, literature, or your own personal experience to support your point of view.

GO ON TO THE NEXT PAGE ➡

DO NOT TURN THE PAGE UNTIL TIME IS CALLED. ANSWER EXPLANATIONS
ARE AVAILABLE ON THE FOLLOWING PAGES.

STOP

258   KAPLAN

Answer Explanations

Section 1: Math

1. **D** With a perimeter of 30 and 5 sides of equal length, the length of one side is $\frac{30}{5}$, or 6.

2. **K** There were a total of 17 customers who bought caramel candy. Subtract from these the 4 who bought both and we are left with the 13 who bought only caramel.

3. **D** Only factors of 24 (numbers which are evenly divisible into 24) can be the number of different colors in the bag. Since 5 is not a factor of 24, choice D, 5, is our correct choice.

4. **G** The question states a whole number so 12.5 is out. The integer must be less than 13, so 13 and 14 are out. 11 is not between 11 and 18, so 11 is out Hence, choice G, 12, is the correct choice.

5. **A** If we extend the vertical line between documentaries and news downward to the circle, we have a vertical diameter. One half the circle is 6 hours and choices D and E are too large. Drawing a horizontal line through the center of the circle which will be perpendicular to the vertical diameter that we drew in bisects the diameter, and allows us to eyeball that the movies are less than $\frac{1}{4}$ of 12 or 3. Hence, the correct choice is A.

6. **F** To solve for R, multiply both sides of the equation by 2, hence $R = 32$. Plug 32 for R into the expression $\frac{3}{4}R$, and you find that $\frac{3}{4}R = \frac{3}{4} \times 32 = 24$.

7. **C** The fraction $\frac{1}{4}$ has a decimal value of 0.25; thus choices B, D, and E can be eliminated. 59 rounded to the nearest ten is 60; indeed, 59 is much closer to 60 than to 50, so choice C is correct.

8. **G** There is no calculation necessary on this problem. Three of the five points lie on the horizontal $260,000 line and the only other two points are the identical distance above and below the line, thus $260,000 is the correct answer.

9. **C** This problem calls for substitution. $u = 5$ and $v = 5$. Plugging these values in yields $5 \phi 5 = 5 - \left(1 - \frac{1}{5}\right) = 5 - \frac{4}{5} = 4\frac{1}{5}$; choice C is correct.

10. **K** This problem calls for substitution. $u = a$, $v = 3$, and $a \phi 3 = 4\frac{1}{3}$. Using the definition for the left side of this equation, which is $a \phi 3$, we have $a - \left(1 - \frac{1}{3}\right) = 4\frac{1}{3}$; then $a - \frac{2}{3} = 4\frac{1}{3}$ and $a = 5$.

11. **E** Call the unknown number x and translate the information in the question into math. Remember that "of" means "times." 20% of 64 means $\frac{20}{100}(64)$ and 5% of x means $\frac{5}{100}x$. Then 20% of 64 is equal to 5% of x means that $\frac{20}{100}(64) = \frac{5}{100}x$. Reducing $\frac{20}{100}$ and $\frac{5}{100}$ yields $\frac{1}{5}(64) = \frac{1}{20}x$. Isolate the x by multiplying both sides by 20. Then $x = \frac{1}{5}(64) \times 20 = \frac{64}{5} \times 20 = 64 \times 4 = 256$.

12. **G** The minimum number of fish Andy could have caught was 36 or 1 more than Rich caught. Use the Average Formula, Average $= \frac{\text{Sum of the terms}}{\text{Number of terms}}$. Sum of the terms = 36 and Number of terms (or number of fishing trips) = 4. Hence, Andy must have caught an average of at least $\frac{36}{4} = 9$ fish per trip.

13. **B** We need to set up an equation here. We know all the boys earned the same amount per hour, so: 4Rate + 6Rate + 8Rate = 27. Thus, 18Rate = 27 and the Rate = $\frac{27}{18}$ = $1.50 per hour. Lee worked 8 hours so 8 × $1.50 = $12.00.

14. **H** Johnny has already picked 200 apples in 2.5 hours. He must pick an additional 600 − 200 = 400 apples. Call the number of additional hours that Johnny must spend picking apples x. To find x, set up a ratio and solve for x: $\frac{200 \text{ apples}}{x \text{ hours}} = \frac{400 \text{ apples}}{.x \text{ hours}}$. Since the numerator of the fraction on the right is equal to twice the numerator of the fraction on the left, the denominator of the fraction on the right must also be equal to twice the denominator of the fraction on the left. So $x = 2 \times 2.5 = 5$. Since Johnny must work an additional 5 hours, the latest time that he can begin picking apples again is 5 hours earlier than 7:15 PM. So 2:15 p.m. is the latest that Johnny can start picking apples again.

15. **A** Set up an equation: $8W = 0.88$. Isolate the W by dividing each side by 8. $W = \frac{0.88}{8} = 0.11$.

16. **J** Figure 4 indicates that the legs of two sides of the triangle are equal and thus the triangle is isosceles. Angles which are opposite equal sides must be equal. Thus, each of the two base angles is 50 degrees, and we know that the sum of the three interior angles of any triangle is 180 degrees, so $r = 180 − 50 − 50 = 80$.

17. **B** To determine how many times greater the income was in 1988, divide the 1988 income by the 1958 income. Then the number we are seeking is $\frac{4,500,000}{9,000}$. Dividing the numerator and the denominator by 1,000, we have that this number is $\frac{4,500}{9} = 500$.

18. **H** The correct answer choice, when 2 is subtracted from it, must be a multiple of 5. A number is a multiple of 5 only if its one's digit is a 5 or a 0. Looking at the choices, 25 − 2 =23 is not a multiple of 5, so eliminate choice F. 33 − 2 = 31 is not a multiple of 5, so eliminate choice G. 47 − 2 = 45, which is a multiple of 5. So choice H is correct.

19. **C** Recall Kaplan's strategy: A figure can be drawn without lifting the pencil or retracing if there are exactly 0 or 2 points where an odd number of lines intersect. Choice C has no points where an odd number of lines intersect, hence this is the correct answer.

20. **K** Pick 100 as the initial population of Country X. The increase for the first year was $\frac{10}{100}$ of 100 = 10 and the total at the end of the first year was 100 + 10 or 110 people. The increase for the second year was $\frac{10}{100}$ of 110 = 11 and the total at the end of the second year was 110 + 11 or 121 people. The population increased from 100 to 121 over the two-year period. The increase in the population was 121 − 100 = 21. Hence the percent increase in the population over the entire two-year period was $\frac{21}{100}$ or 21%.

21. **C** The value of z is given to us; we need to multiply this value by 2 and add 1. Hence, $2z + 1 = 2(y + 2) +1 = 2y + 4 + 1 = 2y + 5$, choice C.

22. **J** Picking numbers for x and y is a foolproof method for solving this problem. Pick a positive fraction for x which is less than 1, such as $\frac{1}{2}$. Then pick a positive value for y which is greater than x, which in this case means that the y that we pick must be greater than $\frac{1}{2}$. Remember, the question says that y is greater than x and the numbers you pick must always be consistent with the question stem. So let's pick 1 for y. So we're letting x

be $\frac{1}{2}$ and y be 1. With these values, choice F is 2, choices G and H are both $\frac{1}{2}$, and choice J is –2. Choice J is correct. Further examining choice J, we see that the denominator of choice J, $x - y$, has a larger positive number y subtracted from a smaller positive number x. So $x - y$ will always be negative. Therefore choice J, $\frac{1}{x - y}$, will also always be negative.

23. **B**   If 6 people can sit at each of x tables and 5 people can sit at each of y tables, then the maximum number of people that may be seated is $6x + 5y$.

24. **G**   Draw 3 squares: big, bigger, and biggest. Let the side of the middle fabric piece be 9. The side of the largest fabric piece must be three times this, or 27. Likewise, the side of the smallest square piece must be 3. The area of the largest piece is $27 \times 27 = 729$ and the area of the smallest piece is 9. How many times greater is 729 than 9: $\frac{729}{9} = 81$.

25. **A**   Begin by determining how many gallons of gas it takes to make the 18 trips: $\frac{3}{4} \times 18 = \frac{27}{2}$ = 13.5 gallons. If there are 9 gallons in a tank, Mr. Dali will need $\frac{13.5}{9} = 1.5$ tanks of gas.

Section 2: Reading Comp

Scott Joplin passage

First up is a brief history passage about Scott Joplin, a composer best known for his ragtime music. Don't try to absorb all the details even in a brief passage like this. Let them sort of wash over you as you strive to get a feel of the general thrust of the passage, the author's Big Idea, which is that Joplin was instrumental in developing the ragtime genre, but wasn't recognized as a serious composer until almost 60 years after his death.

1. **C**   Lines 2-3 note that Joplin composed 41 piano pieces known as "rags," the only time the word is used in the passage. C, then, must be correct. E's most tempting, but the genre or style of songs Joplin invented is described as "ragtime," not "rag." A's "operatic" is wrong; Joplin's TREEMONISHA was his only opera. B and D fail because ragtime is never described as "dance" music, or as played by marching bands.

2. **K**   Only K has the proper scope here. F and G focus too narrowly on details. It was Joplin's "rhythmic diversity," not his stylistic diversity H, that distinguished his composing. The passage doesn't say how Joplin finally won the Pulitzer J.

3. **B**   An easy detail question, unless the math threw you. The passage states that Joplin received the Pulitzer in 1976, "59 years after his death." Subtract 59 from 76 and you get 17, so Joplin died in 1917, choice B.

4. **K**   The author discusses Joplin's "significant creative contribution" to music, his great popularity, and how he "at last" received "the praise he deserved." Thus, K's "appreciative" best sums up the author's tone toward Joplin.

5. **B**   The passage states that Joplin was instrumental in developing ragtime "as a genre, a unique musical form." Therefore, B is the correct inference: a genre is a distinct category or style. While ragtime is an example of a musical genre, a genre is not an example of a particular type of ragtime A. There's no evidence that Joplin coined the term "genre" C.

John Podgers passage

Next up is a fiction passage describing a man named John Podgers, "hard eater" and "hard sleeper," a man who "grew more obese and more drowsy every day of his life." Now the author never actually says, "I'm making fun of this man," but hopefully, you sensed a humorous tone throughout the passage. This dry, "deadpan" humor comes out of the discrepancy between Podgers and the style in which he's described. They don't match. Podgers is lazy and a compulsive eater, but he's described in a style more befitting a hero, someone other people watch, admire and talk about.

6. **F**   Podgers is never described as intelligent F. The author describes Podgers as "broad, sturdy and short," in other words, stocky G. The people of Windsor describe him as "of a rather

lazy turn" H, of "good strong sense" J, and "of solid parts K, but "not what is called smart."

7. **E** A quick comparison of the verbs in the answer choices hints strongly at E, since the passage is composed of one descriptive sentence after another. A refers to the opinion of Podgers held by the "wisest people in Windsor," but the author doesn't explain why they hold this opinion. Similarly, Podgers's comments on the oxen B and his reasons for eating so much C are not explained; they're just reported. And his daily stroll D is just one detail in the descriptive portrait of Podgers, so choice E is in fact correct.

8. **J** A pretty easy detail question. As the second sentence of the passage states, Podgers spends all his time either eating or sleeping J. F leaves out Podgers's sleeping, G leaves out his eating. H names things Podgers is described as doing only at one point in the passage, and K's "thinking" is something Podgers rarely does.

9. **E** The writer depicts a man who is always either eating or sleeping, yet who is well thought of by the "smartest" people in his town. The writer's tone, then, is humorous, E. B and C may tempt, but their very similarity should make you suspicious of picking either one. Both fail to catch on that the author's making fun of Podgers while describing him in a superficially formal and respectful style.

Bird Courtship passage

Next up is a science passage, about the courtship procedures and "identification checks" used by birds during courtship and mating. Paragraph 1 introduces the topic; paragraph 2 details the roles of plumage and aggressive behavior, and paragraph 3 the role of sounds, in the birds' courting and mating rituals.

10. **H** An inference question answered in the opening paragraph. The author states that the bird's identification and courtship procedures are important "because if birds of different species mate, any offspring" will be sterile and have a low chance for survival. Thus, the procedures are important because they help a bird find a mate of its own species, H. F, J and K are not mentioned in the passage. G focuses too narrowly on a detail from paragraph 2.

11. **D** A Roman numeral detail question; the answer lies in paragraph 3, which states that a male's singing tells females of its species that "it is in breeding condition," I, and, after mating, enables

the nesting female "to continue to identify" her partner III. The passage does not mention that male birds use sound to intimidate male rivals II, so D, I and III only, is correct.

12. **H** This detail question focuses on the last sentence of paragraph 2. There we learn that whooping cranes "perform wonderfully elaborate courtship dances." So the whooping crane's an example of a bird that behaves in an unusual, noteworthy way during courtship, and H is correct. G, J and K incorrectly mention other details from paragraph 2—plumage, reversed roles, and aggressiveness. No species is described in the passage as seldom participating in courtship rituals F.

13. **D** The answer here is taken from the same sentence—the last of paragraph 1—that answered question 10. If birds of different species mate, "any offspring will usually be sterile or badly adapted to their surroundings." This point is restated in choice D. B is the opposite of the correct choice. The frequency of interspecies mating A is not mentioned in the passage, but it must happen occasionally, contrary to choice E, or the author wouldn't warn against its dangers. The idea of a new species evolving C is not discussed.

14. **G** This time the Big Idea question comes at the end of the set. The passage is about the various courtship behaviors and "identification checks" used by birds, which makes choice G correct. F and K raise issues not debated in the passage. H and J focus too narrowly on details from paragraphs 2 and 3, respectively.

Native American passage

Next up is a brief passage about the 1500 Native American languages that have been discovered by linguists. The Big Idea here is simple: a pioneering linguist originally divided these 1500 languages into six main groups; a recent group of scholars thinks they can all be divided into three broader groups, but other scholars disagree with this new theory.

15. **A** Choice A is the most specific and accurate, and it's correct here. B leaves out the recent debate over the revised classification of Native American languages into three groups. C and E are too broad; they could be talking about any group of languages, not just Native American languages. And D focuses too narrowly on a detail from the second sentence of paragraph 2.

16. **G** According to that second sentence of paragraph 2, scholars believe Native American languages can be classified into only three families because of "similarities and differences among words and sounds." Correct choice G can be inferred from this statement. F distorts a detail from paragraph 1, that Sapir grouped Native American languages into six families "three-quarters of a century"—or 75 years—ago. H is the argument of those who think Native American languages can't be classified into three families. J is too broad; it suggests that all languages—not just Native American ones—are related. K is beyond the scope of the passage.

17. **B** Where would you be likely to come upon this passage? In a discussion of Native American languages, or a linguistics textbook B. A, C, and D are wrong because there's nothing either personal or fictional in the text of this passage; it's just a series of factual statements. And while Sapir E pioneered the field of Native American linguistics, the passage doesn't contain any significant biographical information about his life.

18. **F** Why is classifying Native American languages controversial? Those who group them into three families have "no doubt about the validity" of their theory. But "the vast majority of linguists" argue that "linguistic science has not yet advanced far enough" to group 1500 languages into only three families. So the controversy exists because scholars do not yet agree on how to classify languages, and F is correct. G is a point argued by linguists who think Native American languages might never be properly grouped into families, but it's not the source of the controversy. We don't know when the field of linguistics was founded, but even though it hasn't "advanced far enough" it is not a "very new" field, as H suggests. There's no evidence for J or K.

19. **E** Paragraph 1 states that Sapir classified Native American languages into six families. None of the other questions is answered in the passage.

Poetry passage

Next up is a famous poem by Emily Dickinson. The first stanza seems to create a metaphor of hope as a bird that lives inside us and never stops singing. The second stanza says that the bird of hope sings even in bad weather, i.e., bad times. And in the final stanza the poet claims that, while she has heard the bird of hope singing in distant places, "it never asked a crumb of me."

20. **J** Hope is "the thing with feathers" in stanza 1, and "the little bird" in stanza 2, so J is correct. F, G, and H are trials and dangers that the bird/hope faces; K is what the bird sings.

21. **C** Paraphrase the final stanza: "I've heard the bird of hope in far-off places, and it never asked me for anything." This points to choice C as correct. A's wrong because the poem says nothing about a world without hope, or preserving hope at all costs. B summarizes the second stanza, not the third. D takes the poem literally to the point of absurdity; the "crumb" line doesn't mean that the bird is always hungry, but rather that it gives its song of hope freely. And E fails because, according to the poet, hope is always present; no great effort is required to make it so.

22. **G** Remember you're dealing with metaphor. This poem isn't about a bird; it's comparing hope to a bird that never stops singing. The statement that it "kept so many warm" means that hope has given comfort to a lot of people, and G is correct. F and H take the poem literally. J is pessimistic where the poet is optimistic about hope, and K's problem is that phrase "last resort," which implies that hope only works in the worst of situations. But the poet is saying that hope is helpful even in the worst of situations.

23. **E** The poet likens hope to a bird that, thankfully, is always there to help people, never asking anything in return. Her tone is one of gratitude, making choice E correct. C is the closest wrong choice, but "respectful" is too formal, too distancing. Hope in this poem isn't a great person or awesome display of nature, it's a little bird "that perches in the soul."

Recycling passage

The next passage is about recycling, the remaking of waste products and materials for practical purposes. In paragraph 1, we learn that recycling is now considered a necessity, that it saves money and resources and reduces wasted. In paragraph 2, the author focuses on residential recycling—what we as private citizens can do to reduce waste.

24. **J** Statement I is false: recycling "reduces the amount of waste produced (lines 14-15). This eliminates choices G, H, and K. Since statement II is included in both of the remaining answer choices, it must be true, and it is: we're told twice that recycling can save money. Statement III, then, is the crucial

one. And it's true: lines 19-20 state that "the amount of...waste produced at home has been steadily increasing." So only Statements II and III are true, and choice J is correct.

25. **C** This question offers five statements about recycling, and asks which one the author would agree with. A is easily eliminated: the author thinks the individual's role in recycling "has been seriously underemphasized." The first half of B is correct: businesses do recycle to save money. But the second half is wrong: the author doesn't think individuals are motivated to recycle by a sense of the greater good; but the author does think that we should be so motivated. This point is restated in correct choice C. As for D and E, D says we shouldn't recycle, which the author would certainly disagree with, and E claims that recycling is only the responsibility of businesses, which goes against the thrust of paragraph 2. So it's C for question 25.

26. **J** You're looking for the choice that is not an example of recycling, which the author defines at lines 5-7 as "the remaking of waste products and other used materials for practical purposes." Using this definition, choices F, G, and K are easily checked off as examples of recycling. Choice H involves a second use for empty soda bottles, as does the author's example in lines 8-11. This leaves correct choice J: selling jewelry to buy a car is not recycling, because the jewelry is not a waste product that's being remade.

27. **A** The author argues that recycling is "important...even necessary," that "it is our duty to ourselves and to our fellow human beings." These and similar signals throughout the passage reveal the author's tone as insistent, choice A. By the same token, choices B, D, and E are easy to eliminate. Choice C's formal may have been tempting, since the author tells us that the future of humanity is at stake. But A remains the best choice, because more than being formal, the author is trying to motivate us, to get us to do something (recycle).

28. **K** Paragraph 2 argued that individuals can and must learn to recycle their waste products. You can predict, then, that the author will go on to suggest one or more ways in which individuals can pitch in to help the recycling effort, a point restated in correct choice K. There's no evidence to suggest F or G. H wrongly suggests the author will return to a

detail from paragraph 1. And J doesn't even mention recycling.

29. **B** In lines 15-17, the author states that businesses recycle "based primarily on the goal of saving money." So you can infer that the author believes that businesses recycle primarily for financial gain, choice B. A is wrong because the economics of recycling are of greatest interest to businesses, not to the author. Nor can it be inferred from the passage that the author's knowledge of the financial aspects of recycling C is limited. And while D is probably true, it can't be inferred from lines 15-17 of the passage, on which this question is based. As for choice E, nothing in the passage suggests that recycling results in greater amounts of waste.

El Niño passage

The passage begins with a statement that, although bad weather is usually only an "inconvenience" for us, it can have "disastrous consequences" for communities in other parts of the world. The remainder of the passage describes an example of this disastrous bad weather: El Niño, a change in the Humboldt current (an ocean current, not an air current) that disrupts marine life and can thereby threaten villagers on the northwest coast of South America with starvation.

30. **J** The Humboldt Current flows off the northwest coast of South America, making J correct. Each of the other choices contradicts the passage. El Niño occurs only at Christmastime F, not the Humboldt Current, which otherwise flows all year long. The Humboldt Current does fail G when El Niño occurs. The passage does not state the directional flow of the Humboldt Current H, but does state that it is a cold-water current, not a hot-water current K.

31. **E** The bulk of the passage concerns what happens when the Humboldt Current fails, which makes D very tempting, but the Big Idea of the passage is really stated in the first sentence: changes in weather patterns can dramatically affect the way people live, making choice E correct here. Remember, the Humboldt Current-El Niño information is only there to back up this claim by the author. A, B, and C focus on details, and should have been easier to eliminate.

32. **H** Here you're looking for the one choice that isn't true. F is confirmed at lines 10-12; G at lines 16-18. J and K are restated in lines 15-17. Only

choice H is not confirmed in the passage, and it's correct here. As we noted in question 30, choice K, the Humboldt Current carries cold water, not warm; the passage also never states that the current affects "the climate of nearby land masses." So H is best for question 32.

33. **A** If you got question 31 correct, you probably answered this one too. If you got question 31 wrong, you probably also stumbled here. As we said before, this passage is not about El Niño; the El Niño is discussed in order to prove the author's larger point: that bad weather can harm communities. This means that A, not C, is the correct answer. B, D, and E should have been much easier to eliminate.

34. **F** We're told that bad weather can have a "dramatic effect" on these villages, "depriving" them "of their livelihood." The author's attitude toward the villagers, then, is—what? Not condescending H, angry J, or emotional K. And though the author doesn't express undue alarm, you wouldn't say she was simply unconcerned about the villagers, as G has it. No, the author's attitude is best described as sympathetic, choice F. The villagers occasionally have this awful problem, and the author expresses concern about it.

35. **D** The "chain reaction" described in the passage is as follows: the current fails, stopping the flow of nutrients to the fish and squid, which die, thereby harming the villagers. A chain reaction then, is not a pair but a series of causally-linked occurrences. This eliminates choices A, B, and C, each of which basically concerns only a pair—not a chain—of occurrences. The best example of a chain reaction in the choices is therefore choice D, where global warming leads to melted glaciers, which leads to higher water levels and then less available land for people. E gives two phenomena which basically occur at the same time.

Marshall Plan passage

The final passage is a history passage about the Marshall Plan, an American scheme to help rebuild Europe after World War II. Paragraph 1 sets the scene, explaining that The U.S. was worried that Europe's economic devastation needed to be cured in order to keep it from falling under the domination of the Soviet Union. Paragraph 2 explains that in 1948, U.S. Secretary of State George Marshall instituted the Marshall Plan, which distributed 12 billion dollars among 16 different European countries over the next four years.

36. **G** The "best title" question; the correct answer choice will probably mention the Marshall Plan and how it helped Europe; choice G fits this bill nicely. F is way too broad. H describes what happened during World War II that made the Marshall Plan so necessary, but says nothing about the Plan itself. J suggests that the passage is about Marshall himself, when the author actually tells you nothing more than Marshall's name and job— Secretary of State. And K, like F, is too broad, too vague.

37. **A** The author's tone is not noticeably positive B or negative E. It betrays no personal feelings such as insistence C or anxiety D. Instead, it's objective, choice A; the author deals with facts without interjecting personal feelings into the account.

38. **J** A relatively easy detail question, for careful readers. Paragraph 2 states that the Marshall Plan doled out "a combined total of $12 billion" to the 16 "participating countries." So each country did not get $12 billion, and J is correct. All of the other statements are substantiated in the passage.

39. **E** What was the driving force behind the Marshall Plan? Early in Paragraph 1, we learn that post–World War II Western Europe was economically devastated, and that when tensions between the U.S. and the Soviet Union escalated, U.S. policymakers felt that "substantial financial assistance" was needed in Western Europe "to maintain a state of political stability." This points to choice E: the driving force behind the Marshall Plan was rising tension between the U.S. and the Soviet Union. None of the other choices draws a correct inference from the passage. No formal aid request A by European leaders is mentioned, nor is any direct threat to the U.S. economy B. We learn nothing of Marshall's private ambitions C, and given the development of the Cold War, a U.S.-Soviet agreement D of any kind is highly unlikely.

40. **H** The first paragraph describes the post-war economic and political problems that the Marshall Plan was intended to solve, and paragraph 2 describes, in general terms, how much money was distributed and how well the plan worked. You can infer, then, that the author will go on to talk about specifics— how the Plan's money was put to work in some or all of the 16 participating countries; this makes H correct. F wrongly sees the Cold War, not the Marshall Plan, as the focus

of the passage. G goes back in time, to events before the Marshall Plan was ever dreamed up. No other economic recovery plans J are mentioned in the passage, so you can't infer that the author would go on to discuss them. And Marshall, though the brain behind the Plan, is a footnote in this passage, so a depiction of his rise to Secretary of State K is also unwarranted.

Section 3: Math

1. **B** Begin with $5 + cover price – $9 and simplify it. This can be simplified to cover price – $4, which means $4 below the cover price. Choice B is correct.

2. **J** Note here that each cube = 20 boxes. February has two cubes less than March, hence 2(20) = 40 boxes less.

3. **A** In January, 6 cubes were sold and in February, 3 cubes were sold. Thus, in January, the number of boxes sold was $\frac{6}{3}$ = 2 times the number of boxes sold in February. It is not necessary to perform calculation based on the 20 boxes within each cube.

4. **G** Let x = the number of ties for Team A; keep in mind that x is an integer here. Thus, Team A had $4x$ losses. Adding the losses and ties (there were no wins), the number of games the team played was $x + 4x = 5x$. Thus, the correct answer choice must be a multiple of 5 (because x is an integer). Only choice G, 15, is a multiple of 5.

5. **E** In order to make the discussion simpler, the five rectangles which are in the figure to begin with have been labeled.

A	B	
C	D	E

Systematically count the different rectangles in the figure. There are the 5 rectangles in the figure to begin with, which we will call basic rectangles. Next, let's count the number of rectangles that are made up of 2 basic rectangles. Rectangles made up of 2 basic rectangles can be formed from basic rectangles A and B, C and D, D and E, A and C, and B and D. There are 5 rectangles made up of 2 basic rectangles. Next, let's count the number of rec-

tangles that can be made up of 3 basic rectangles. There is just one such rectangle. This is the rectangle which is made up of the 3 basic rectangles at the bottom, rectangles C, D, and E. Next, let's count the number of rectangles which can be made up of 4 basic rectangles. There is just one such rectangle. This is the rectangle which is made up of basic rectangles A, B, C, and D. There are no other rectangles which can be made up of basic rectangles. There is a total of 5 + 5 + 1 + 1 = 12 different rectangles in the figure.

6. **J** We are looking for the fraction which is NOT less than $\frac{1}{4}$, that is, a fraction which is greater than or equal to $\frac{1}{4}$. Choice J is correct because $\frac{1}{4} = \frac{19}{19 \times 4} = \frac{19}{76}$ is less than $\frac{19}{70}$ because $\frac{19}{70}$ has a smaller denominator than $\frac{19}{76}$. Looking at the other choices, since $\frac{2}{8} = \frac{1}{4}$, $\frac{2}{9}$ must be less than $\frac{1}{4}$ (since 9 is a greater denominator). Since $\frac{3}{12} = \frac{1}{4}$, $\frac{3}{14}$ must be less than $\frac{1}{4}$ (due to the greater denominator 14). Reducing $\frac{14}{64}$, we get $\frac{7}{32}$ and since $\frac{8}{32} = \frac{1}{4}$, $\frac{14}{64} = \frac{7}{32}$ is less than $\frac{1}{4}$. Since $\frac{25}{125} = \frac{1}{5}$, $\frac{27}{125}$ must also be about $\frac{1}{5}$.

7. **D** Begin by labeling each side 1. Using the answer choices, count the lengths of 1 in the path: choice A = 4, choice B = 4, choice C = 4, choice D = 5, and choice E = 4. Choice D is the longest path.

8. **J** No long calculation is needed here. Choice J is correct. In order for a product of numbers to equal 0, at least one of the numbers must equal zero. Since $5\frac{1}{3}$ is not 0, the other factor, $14 - x$, must equal 0. So $14 - x = 0$, and $x = 14$.

9. **D** Since 1.18 has 2 places after the decimal point, write each answer choice with 2 places after the decimal point. Choices A and B are more than 1.00 away from 1.18. Choice C, 1.90 is more than 0.7 away from 1.18, choice D, 1.10, is 0.08 away from 1.18, and choice E, 1.00, is 0.18 away from 1.18. Choice D is the closest to 1.18 and is therefore correct.

10. **H** Write out the given inequality: $X > 15$. Next multiply both sides by $\frac{1}{3}$ (or divide both sides by 3). We now have $\frac{1}{3}X > \frac{15}{3}$ and $\frac{1}{3}X > 5$, choice H. You should remember that when both sides of an inequality are multiplied or divided by a positive number, the direction of the inequality sign stays the same. However, if both sides of an inequality are multiplied or divided by a negative number, the direction of the inequality sign is reversed.

11. **B** Round \$26.95 to 27.00. Then we have $\frac{35}{100} \times 27 = ?$. Canceling yields $\frac{7}{20} \times 27 = \frac{189}{20}$ = 9.45.

12. **J** Let T be the number of minutes. Set up a ratio: $\frac{600}{3} = \frac{27,000}{T}$. Reduce $\frac{600}{3}$ to $\frac{200}{1}$. Then $\frac{200}{1} = \frac{27,000}{T}$. Next cross multiply: $200T = 27,000$. Divide both sides by 100: $2T = 270$, and thus $T = 135$. Put this into the time format of hours and minutes by dividing 135 minutes by 60 minutes per hour and we have $2\frac{1}{4}$ hours, which is 2 hours and 15 minutes.

13. **D** Translate what is stated in the question step by step. To begin with, Sally has x dollars. After she receives 100 dollars she has $x + 100$ dollars. She spends 125 dollars so she has $(x + 100) - 125$ dollars left. Now simplify $(x + 100) - 125$. $(x + 100) - 125 = x + 100 - 125 = x - 25$. Sally has $x - 25$ dollars left, so choice D is correct.

14. **K** Begin by multiplying both sides by 3 to eliminate the denominator. Then $A + B = 12$. If A is greater than 1, then B must be less than 11, thus choice K, 12, could not be the value of B.

15. **E** Use the average formula, which is Average = $\frac{\text{Sum of the terms}}{\text{Number of terms}}$. Call X the sum of all 5 numbers. Then $\frac{X}{5} = 10$, so $X = 50$. Call Y the

sum of the 3 remaining numbers. Then $\frac{Y}{3} = 9$, so $Y = 27$. Subtracting from the sum of all 5 numbers the sum of the three numbers that remain leaves the sum of the 2 numbers that were removed. So the sum of the 2 numbers that were removed is $X - Y = 50 - 27 = 23$.

16. **G** The bottom surface of the bag is a rectangle and all points touch the surface so choice F can be eliminated. Choice G is correct.

17. **B** Recall our formula: $\frac{\text{New Amount} - \text{Old Amount}}{\text{Old Amount}}$.

Here, $\frac{1,442 - 1,078}{1,078} = \frac{364}{1,078}$. This fraction is approximately $\frac{1}{3}$, or $33\frac{1}{3}\%$, choice B.

18. **F** Label the length of WX a. Then the length of WY is $3a$. The length of XY must be $3a - a = 2a$. Then, the length of XZ must be $2 \times 2a = 4a$. If $WX = a = 2$, then $WZ = WX + XZ = a + 4a = 5a = 5(2) = 10$.

19. **A** Draw a rectangle. Label its width w and its length $3w$. The perimeter is 240, thus $3w + w + 3w + w = 240$, so $8w = 240$ and $w = 30$.

20. **H** For every indicates a ratio is needed. Call the amount she receives from the \$18,000 collection x. Here set up $\frac{50}{900} = \frac{x}{18,000}$. After cancellation on the left we have $\frac{1}{18} = \frac{x}{18,000}$. Cross multiply and get $18x = 18,000$. Solve for x by dividing each side by 18 and $x = 1,000$.

21. **C** We need to find out how many 4×6 rectangles fit into a square with a side of 24. Use our area formula $A = L \times W$: $\frac{24 \times 24}{4 \times 6} = 24$.

22. **H** Pick numbers. Let $S = -2$ and $T = -3$. Thus we have $R = -5$. Taking this value for R through our choices, only choice H fits.

23. **D** Call the number of records Greg has r and the number of cassettes he has c. Our first equation is: $r + c = 60$. The second equation is $\frac{1}{2}r = (2)\frac{1}{8}c$. So $\frac{1}{2}r = \frac{1}{4}c$ and $c = 4 \times \frac{1}{2}r = 2r$. Now, substitute $2r$ for c in the first equation, $r + c = 60$. Then $r + 2r = 60$, $3r = 60$, and $r = \frac{60}{3} = 20$. The problem asks how many records he sold, which is $\frac{1}{2}(20) = 10$.

24. **J** Mary received $20 each week for 2 weeks and saved 60% of this or $\frac{60}{100}(\$40) = \$24$. Since she saved only $8 the first week, she must have saved $16 the second week. Looking at the roman numeral statements, I is true so eliminate choices F and H. Looking at statement II, $20 – $16 = $4 was spent during the second week, not $6, so statement II is not true. Eliminate choice K. Finally in III, the percent of the second week's allowance that she saved was $\frac{16}{20} \times 100\% = \frac{4}{5} \times 100\% = 80\%$, so statement III is true. Choice J is correct.

25. **C** First work with Paul: original wage + 20% of his original wage = $4.50. Convert this into the equation: $x + .20x = 4.50$, then $1.2x = 4.50$ and $x = \$3.75$. Set up a similar equation for Bill: $y + .20y = 5.40$ and $1.2y = 5.40$, so $y = \$4.50$. Hence, $4.50 – $3.75 = $0.75.

Section 4: Verbal

Synonyms

1. **E** Harsh means rough or overly demanding—in other words, severe, choice E. A harsh penalty, for example. One can be angry B without being harsh; these words are not synonyms.

2. **J** Indicate means to show, state, or point out, choice J.

3. **C** Bleak means desolate and barren, or cheerless, choice C. "We camped out in a bleak wilderness."

4. **J** Secure means free from danger, or safe, choice J.

5. **A** Alien means foreign, or strange, choice A.

6. **F** Chronic means frequently occurring, habitual, or persistent F, as in a "chronic cough."

7. **D** To quench a thirst means to slake or satisfy it, choice D.

8. **G** Severe, as we saw in question 1, means harsh, overly demanding, or extreme, choice G. Severe cold leaves you frozen, choice F, but severe and frozen are not synonyms. Don't just think associatively; look for the word that's closest in meaning to the stem word.

9. **A** When thieves ransack an apartment, they turn it upside down looking for things to steal. In other words, to ransack is to search thoroughly, choice A.

10. **K** The summit is the top of something, as in the summit of a mountain peak, which makes choice K correct.

11. **B** A tumult is a loud noise, an uproar or commotion, choice B.

12. **H** To retard means to delay the progress of, to hold back or slow down, choice H.

13. **B** An antidote is a cure or remedy B, such as an antidote for poison.

14. **J** Solitary is the state of being secluded, or alone, choice J.

15. **D** To conceal means to hide, or disguise, choice D. The closest wrong choice is E, which means to overthrow, or corrupt.

16. **K** To expel means to drive out, to reject, or to cast out, choice K.

17. **C** To lunge is to make a sudden forward stride or leap. A lunge—especially with a weapon—is also called a thrust, choice C. To pursue A means to chase, to follow with the intent of overtaking. Pursuit may begin with a lunge, but the two verbs are not synonyms. In similar fashion, a lunge may involve a turn B or startle someone E, but these words are not synonyms of lunge, either.

18. **K** Brevity is the quality of being brief, which means of short duration—so shortness, choice K, is correct.

19. **E** To marvel is to feel surprise, amazed curiosity, or wonder, choice E.

20. **H** Candor is truthfulness, or honesty, choice H. To be daring G is to be bold, but not necessarily honest.

21. **C** To convene is to meet, or to assemble, choice C. The closest wrong choices, B and D, are actions associated with meetings that are convened, but they're not synonyms.

22. **G** A catastrophe is a great misfortune, a terrible occurrence, or a disaster, choice G.

23. **B** Gregarious means talkative, outgoing, or sociable, choice B.

24. **J** Dexterity is mental or physical skill and quickness. The best synonym here is nimbleness, choice J.

25. **E** To say that something is imminent means that it's about to happen, that it is forthcoming, choice E.

26. **G** Animosity is hostility, ill-will, resentment. The best synonym here is hatred, choice G.

27. **E** To amend means to change, alter, or improve, choice E.

28. **F** Someone who feels despondent is very sad, or depressed, choice F.

29. **C** Unflinching means not flinching or shrinking from; it's the quality of being steadfast. The best synonym here is uncompromising, choice C. A and D are near-antonyms for unflinching.

30. **F** To repudiate means to cast off, disown, or refuse to have anything to do with. The choice with the closest meaning to repudiate is renounce, choice F. To impede G is to slow or interfere with someone's progress.

Analogies

31. **A** Anything having to do with the sun is solar. In the same way, anything having to do with the earth is terrestrial, choice A. Marine B refers a sea or ocean, not to a pond. Subterranean C refers to what is below the ground, not to the ground itself. Lunar E refers to anything have to do with the moon, not with planets.

32. **F** Botany is the study of plants. Similarly, meteorology is the study of weather, choice F. Flora G is the generic word for plant life or vegetation.

33. **E** You use a hammer to put in a nail. In the same way, you use a screwdriver to put in a screw, choice E. You use an axe to chop wood A; a lathe to smooth or shape molding B; a chisel to chip marble C; and a nut to secure a bolt D.

34. **F** A bone is part of the structural system that supports a mammal. A girder is part of the structural system that supports a skyscraper, choice F. The other choices are also part of the structural system that supports a skyscraper, not the skyscraper itself.

35. **B** A primate is an order of mammals that includes monkeys, apes and humans. So a human is one species of the primate order, just as a snake is one species of the order of reptiles, choice B. Vegetarians A are not an order in the same way as primates and reptiles. A disease is not necessarily bacterial in nature C. Birds are not amphibians D; amphibians are a cross between fishes and reptiles, such as frogs.

36. **J** A tremor is a quivering motion of the earth. A powerful tremor may be an earthquake. In the same way, wind is a motion of the air, and a powerful wind may be a tornado, choice J. The analogy isn't exact here, but it's better than the other choices. An eye is the calm center of a hurricane F; a powerful desert is not a sandstorm G. A faucet is a manmade object through which water flows; a deluge H is a great flood. And a powerful flood K is not a river.

37. **C** Something tremendously amusing is uproarious; similarly, something tremendously interesting is hypnotic, fascinating, or mesmerizing, choice C.

38. **K** Being fickle, or inconstant, is the opposite of steadfastness. In the same way, being tempestuous, or stormy, is the opposite of peacefulness, choice J. Ire, choice K, means anger.

39. **C** A group of fish is called a school, just as a group of birds is called a flock, choice C.

40. **J** A cartographer is a designer of maps, just as a chef is a designer of meals, choice J.

41. **A** A throne is the official chair for a monarch, just as a bench is the official chair for a judge, choice B. A miter A is the headdress worn by bishops.

42. **F** A canal is a manmade river. Just as a mine is a manmade cavern, choice J. It's stretching things to call a boat a manmade piece of driftwood F, even though both float.

43. **B** When milk goes bad it gets sour; when bread goes bad it gets stale, choice B.

44. **K** Ore is mined to bring it up out of the earth, just as oil is drilled to bring it up out of the earth, choice K. Grain is plowed, choice J, but it's not found buried in the earth.

45. **E** Weight is measured on a scale, just as altitude is measured on an altimeter, choice E. Speed, not distance, is measured on a speedometer A. Choice B's a little tricky: numbers are measured on a slide rule, but only special kinds of numbers called logarithms.

46. **H** A porcupine protects itself with quills. In similar fashion, a skunk protects itself with its odor, choice H. None of the other choices has a second word that protects the species named in the first word.

47. **D** The purpose of a jar is to contain, just as the purpose of a pillar is to support, choice D. A and B are also words used with pillar, but don't name its purpose.

48. **G** Irrigate means to flush with liquid. So you irrigate something dry, just as you smooth something that's coarse, choice G. F and H are tempting, but not as good. You soften something that's hard, not uneven. And you purify H something that's impure, or tainted. To ferment K something is to create a state of chemical agitation in it; this has nothing to do with saltiness.

49. **B** Electricity flows through a wire, just as water flows through an aqueduct. Sound is broadcast from a radio A, which is not the same thing. C and D have similar problems; in each case the music or light is emitted from the object, it doesn't flow through it. And a river is contained by its bank E.

50. **K** You can express contempt with a sneer. In the same way, you express displeasure with a frown, choice K. Each of the other actions is inappropriately matched to its emotion.

51. **E** The base of a building is its foundation. The base of a plant is its root, choice E. If you chose A, C, or D, you were probably confusing the vegetative meaning of "plant" with, say, a manufacturing plant. A grotto B is a cave.

52. **H** Olfactory refers to anything having to do with the sense of smell. So our bridge could be, the nose is the organ of the olfactory sense. Similarly, the ear is the organ of the sense of hearing or auditory sense, choice H.

53. **C** Irk means to annoy, disgust or irritate. So the relationship here is of opposites: something that irks is not soothing. In the same way, something that supports is not weakening or undermining, choice C. Irritating, choice D, is second-best here; it would go better with soothing than with support.

54. **F** Something illegible is impossible to read, just as something invisible is impossible to see, choice F. Something broken H is not by definition impossible to fix.

55. **B** Tact is sensitivity, skill at doing or saying the right thing with people. So tact is a necessary quality for a diplomat. In the same way, agility is a necessary quality for a gymnast, which makes choice B correct. Parsimony A, or

stinginess, is a quality a philanthropist had better not have, since a philanthropist is someone who gives generous amounts of money to charity. Similarly, a judge E should be unbiased, not biased, which means having a declared preference for one side or the other. Victims may be vulnerable C, but you wouldn't ordinarily say that vulnerability is a necessary quality for being a victim. And training in D is too vague; it's not a quality specific to the practice of medicine.

56. **K** Ravenous means extremely hungry. So to be ravenous is to be in an extreme state of hunger. In the same way, to be furious is to be in an extreme state of indignation, choice K. None of the other choices has a first word that's an extreme version of the second word. Pliable F means flexible, while obstinacy is stubbornness, so these words are opposites. The same is true for G and H. Tenacity J is stubborn persistence; being smart is not being in an extreme state of tenacity.

57. **B** To amplify sound is to make it stronger or louder. To bolster something means to strengthen it. In the same way, then, to bolster courage B is to make it stronger. Getting the right answer here depends a little on knowing common usage. You simply don't bolster a smell A, insomnia or sleeplessness C, or light or silence D, E.

58. **F** Reverse the order of the stem pair: you attend a lecture in an auditorium. In the same way, you attend a concert in a theatre, choice F. This bridge clearly doesn't work on G, J, or K. You attend religious services, not religion itself, in a temple H.

59. **C** Philanthropic means generous, giving; benevolence is the quality of generosity. So our bridge might be, a philanthropic act is evidence of benevolence. In the same way, a miserly act is evidence of stinginess, choice C. Ostentatious B means showy or extravagant.

60. **J** Spurious is simply a fancy word meaning fake. So we've got a relationship of opposites here: something spurious has no authenticity. Similarly, something laughable has no seriousness J. Lavish F means extravagantly expensive. Abject means miserable; subjectivity may or may not be miserable G. There's no obvious bridge between the words in H, and K makes wrong-headed use of the similarity between "total" and "complete." But "totalitarian" refers to a system of government, so these words, "totalitarian" and "completeness," are not closely related.

16

Scoring Your SSAT Practice Test

Your SSAT score is calculated by using a formula that cannot be directly applied to your practice tests. Therefore, it is impossible to provide a completely accurate score for your practice tests. Nevertheless, you'll understandably want to get an idea of how well you have performed on your practice tests.

Follow the steps described below to obtain a rough approximation of what your score on the actual SSAT might be. First, add up the number of questions you got right and the number of questions you got wrong. Questions left blank are worth 0 points. Then, do the math, based on the following:

	Verbal (60 questions total)	(Quantitative) Math (50 questions total)	Reading Comprehension (40 questions total)
+ 1 point for each right answer	_____	_____	_____
$-\frac{1}{4}$ point for each wrong answer	_____	_____	_____
TOTAL:	_____	_____	_____

This is called your **raw score**. Next, take your raw score and look at the following chart, which *approximates* a conversion to a **scaled score**. A scaled score takes into account the range in difficulty level of the various editions of the test.

Scoring Your SSAT Practice Test

Math (Quantitative)

If Your Raw Score Is . . .	Then Your Scaled Score Is:
0	250
1	252
2	254
3	256
4	258
5	260
6	262
7	264
8	266
9	268
10	270
11	272
12	274
13	276
14	278
15	280
16	282
17	284
18	286
19	288
20	290
21	292
22	294
23	296
24	298
25	300
26	302
27	304
28	306
29	308
30	310
31	312
32	314
33	316
34	318
35	320
36	322
37	324
38	326
39	328
40	330
41	332
42	334
43	336
44	338
45	340
46	342
47	344
48	346
49	348
50	350

Reading Comprehension

If Your Raw Score Is . . .	Then Your Scaled Score Is:
0	258
1	260
2	262
3	264
4	266
5	268
6	270
7	272
8	274
9	276
10	278
11	280
12	282
13	284
14	286
15	288
16	290
17	292
18	294
19	296
20	298
21	300
22	302
23	304
24	306
25	308
26	310
27	312
28	314
29	316
30	318
31	320
32	322
33	325
34	328
35	331
36	334
37	338
38	342
39	346
40	350

Verbal

If Your Raw Score Is . . .	Then Your Scaled Score Is:	If Your Raw Score Is . . .	Then Your Scaled Score Is:
0	252	31	309
1	254	32	311
2	256	33	313
3	258	34	315
4	260	35	317
5	262	36	318
6	264	37	320
7	266	38	322
8	268	39	324
9	270	40	326
10	272	41	327
11	273	42	329
12	275	43	331
13	277	44	333
14	279	45	335
15	281	46	336
16	282	47	338
17	284	48	340
18	286	49	342
19	288	50	344
20	290	51	345
21	291	52	347
22	293	53	349
23	295	54	350
24	297	55	350
25	299	56	350
26	300	57	350
27	302	58	350
28	304	59	350
29	306	60	350
30	308		

Once you have your scaled score, look up your corresponding percentile rank (by grade and gender), a value on a scale of 100%. Your percentile rank indicates the percentage of girls or boys in your grade who received the same score or below as you. If your percentile rank is 75 on Verbal, that means you performed equal or better than 75 percent of the other students in your grade on that section.

Note: The following do not reflect the actual percentiles used for the SSAT and are being provided for informational purposes only. Your percentile score as derived from these charts is only a general approximation of what your score on the test might actually be. The charts reflect the actual percentile ranks for the test administrations 1996–1999. However, these numbers can be misleading, as they do not take into account the group of students to whom you will be compared on your test administration. Also, remember that your performance will vary based on many contributing factors.

Percentile Ranks on the SSAT

| | BOYS | | | GRADE 8 | | GIRLS | | |

Scaled Score	SSAT Percentile				Scaled Score	SSAT Percentile		
	V	Q	R			V	Q	R
350	99	99	99		350	99	99	99
349	99	99	99		349	99	99	99
348	99	99	99		348	99	99	99
347	99	99	99		347	99	99	99
346	98	98	99		346	99	99	99
345	98	98	99		345	98	99	99
344	98	97	99		344	98	99	99
343	97	97	99		343	98	99	99
342	97	96	99		342	98	99	99
341	97	96	99		341	97	98	99
340	96	95	99		340	97	98	99
339	96	95	99		339	97	98	99
338	95	94	99		338	96	98	99
337	95	94	99		337	96	97	99
336	94	93	99		336	95	97	99
335	94	92	99		335	95	97	99
334	93	91	99		334	95	96	99
333	92	91	99		333	94	96	99
332	92	89	99		332	93	95	99
331	91	88	99		331	93	94	99
330	91	87	99		330	92	93	99
329	90	86	98		329	92	93	98
328	88	85	98		328	90	92	98
327	87	84	98		327	90	91	98
326	87	82	98		326	89	90	97
325	85	81	97		325	88	89	97
324	85	80	97		324	87	88	96
323	83	78	96		323	86	87	96
322	82	77	96		322	86	86	95
321	81	75	95		321	84	85	95
320	80	73	94		320	83	83	94
319	79	72	93		319	82	82	93
318	77	71	93		318	81	81	93
317	76	69	92		317	79	80	92
316	74	68	91		316	78	78	91
315	73	66	90		315	77	77	90
314	71	64	89		314	75	75	88
313	70	63	88		313	74	74	87
312	68	60	87		312	72	72	86
311	67	59	85		311	71	70	85
310	65	57	84		310	69	68	84
309	63	55	82		309	67	67	82
308	61	54	81		308	65	65	81
307	59	52	80		307	63	63	79
306	57	50	78		306	61	61	77
305	56	48	76		305	60	60	75
304	53	46	75		304	57	57	74
303	53	45	73		303	56	56	72
302	50	43	72		302	53	54	71
301	49	42	69		301	52	52	68
300	46	40	69		300	50	50	67
299	45	38	65		299	49	48	64
298	42	36	65		298	46	46	63
297	40	34	61		297	44	43	59
296	39	33	61		296	43	42	59
295	36	31	57		295	40	40	55
294	35	30	56		294	39	38	54
293	33	27	52		293	36	36	50
292	32	26	52		292	34	34	50
291	30	25	48		291	32	33	46
290	28	23	47		290	30	31	44
289	26	22	45		289	29	29	43
288	25	20	42		288	27	27	40
287	23	19	40		287	25	25	38
286	22	18	38		286	24	24	35
285	20	16	36		285	21	22	33
284	19	15	33		284	21	21	31
283	17	14	31		283	19	19	29
282	16	13	29		282	17	18	26
281	15	12	27		281	16	17	24
280	14	11	24		280	15	15	22
279	13	10	23		279	14	14	20
278	12	9	21		278	12	13	18
277	11	8	20		277	11	12	18
276	10	7	17		276	10	10	15
275	9	7	17		275	9	10	15
274	8	6	15		274	8	8	12
273	7	6	14		273	7	8	12
272	7	5	12		272	6	7	10
271	6	4	11		271	6	6	9
270	5	4	10		270	5	5	8
269	5	3	9		269	5	5	7
268	4	3	8		268	4	4	6
267	4	2	7		267	3	3	5
266	3	2	6		266	3	3	5
265	3	2	6		265	3	2	4
264	3	1	5		264	2	2	3
263	2	1	4		263	2	2	3
262	2	1	4		262	2	1	2
261	2	1	3		261	1	1	2
250-260	1	1	3		250-260	1	1	2

| | BOYS | | | GRADE 9 | | GIRLS | | |

Scaled Score	SSAT Percentile					Scaled Score	SSAT Percentile		
	V	Q	R				V	Q	R
350	99	99	99			350	99	99	99
349	98	98	99			349	98	99	99
348	98	98	99			348	98	99	99
347	97	98	99			347	98	99	99
346	97	97	99			346	97	99	99
345	97	96	99			345	97	98	99
344	96	96	99			344	96	98	99
343	96	95	99			343	96	98	99
342	95	93	99			342	95	97	99
341	95	93	99			341	95	96	98
340	94	91	99			340	94	96	98
339	93	91	99			339	93	95	98
338	92	90	99			338	92	94	98
337	92	89	99			337	92	94	98
336	91	87	98			336	91	93	98
335	90	87	98			335	90	93	97
334	89	85	98			334	90	91	97
333	88	84	98			333	89	91	97
332	87	82	98			332	88	89	97
331	87	81	98			331	87	89	97
330	86	79	98			330	86	87	97
329	85	78	97			329	85	86	96
328	83	76	97			328	83	85	96
327	82	75	97			327	82	84	96
326	81	73	96			326	81	82	95
325	80	72	95			325	80	81	94
324	79	70	95			324	79	79	93
323	77	69	94			323	78	78	92
322	77	67	93			322	77	77	92
321	75	65	92			321	75	75	90
320	74	62	92			320	74	73	89
319	72	61	90			319	72	72	88
318	70	59	90			318	70	70	87
317	69	58	89			317	69	69	86
316	67	56	87			316	67	67	84
315	66	55	86			315	66	65	83
314	64	52	85			314	64	62	81
313	63	51	83			313	62	61	80
312	61	49	83			312	60	59	78
311	60	47	81			311	59	58	76
310	58	46	80			310	57	56	75
309	56	44	78			309	55	54	73
308	54	43	76			308	54	52	71
307	52	41	75			307	52	50	68
306	51	39	73			306	50	49	68
305	49	38	71			305	48	47	65
304	47	36	70			304	46	44	64
303	47	35	68			303	45	44	61
302	44	33	67			302	43	42	61
301	43	32	64			301	42	40	58
300	41	30	64			300	39	38	57
299	40	29	60			299	38	36	53
298	38	27	60			298	36	34	53
297	36	25	56			297	34	32	49
296	35	24	55			296	33	31	49
295	33	22	51			295	31	29	45
294	32	21	51			294	30	28	45
293	31	20	47			293	28	26	41
292	30	19	47			292	27	25	41
291	28	18	44			291	26	23	38
290	27	17	42			290	25	22	36
289	26	16	41			289	23	21	35
288	25	14	38			288	22	19	32
287	23	13	37			287	21	18	31
286	22	13	34			286	20	16	28
285	20	12	33			285	18	15	27
284	20	11	30			284	18	14	24
283	19	10	29			283	16	13	23
282	18	9	27			282	15	12	21
281	17	8	26			281	14	11	20
280	16	8	24			280	14	10	18
279	15	7	22			279	13	9	17
278	14	6	20			278	12	8	16
277	14	6	20			277	11	7	15
276	13	5	17			276	10	6	13
275	12	4	17			275	10	6	13
274	11	4	15			274	9	5	11
273	11	4	15			273	8	5	11
272	10	3	13			272	7	4	10
271	9	3	12			271	7	4	9
270	9	2	11			270	6	3	8
269	8	2	10			269	6	3	8
268	7	2	9			268	5	2	7
267	7	2	9			267	5	2	6
266	6	1	7			266	4	2	6
265	5	1	7			265	4	1	5
264	5	1	6			264	3	1	5
263	4	1	5			263	3	1	4
262	4	1	5			262	3	1	3
261	3	1	4			261	2	1	3
250-260	3	1	4			250-260	2	1	2

Percentile Ranks on the SSAT

GRADE 10

	BOYS				GIRLS		
Scaled Score	SSAT Percentile			Scaled Score	SSAT Percentile		
	V	Q	R		V	Q	R
350	99	99	99	350	99	99	99
349	97	97	99	349	96	98	99
348	96	96	99	348	96	98	99
347	96	96	99	347	96	98	98
346	95	95	99	346	95	97	98
345	95	94	99	345	94	97	98
344	94	93	99	344	93	96	98
343	94	92	99	343	93	95	98
342	93	90	99	342	92	94	98
341	92	89	98	341	91	94	97
340	91	87	98	340	91	92	97
339	91	87	98	339	90	92	97
338	90	85	98	338	89	91	97
337	89	84	98	337	88	90	97
336	88	83	97	336	87	88	96
335	88	82	97	335	86	87	96
334	86	80	97	334	84	86	96
333	85	79	97	333	83	85	96
332	84	77	97	332	83	83	96
331	83	76	97	331	82	82	95
330	82	73	97	330	81	80	95
329	81	73	96	329	80	79	94
328	80	70	96	328	78	77	94
327	78	69	96	327	77	76	93
326	78	67	95	326	76	74	93
325	76	66	93	325	74	73	91
324	75	64	93	324	73	71	91
323	74	63	92	323	72	70	89
322	73	61	92	322	70	68	89
321	71	59	91	321	68	66	87
320	70	57	90	320	67	64	87
319	68	55	88	319	66	63	85
318	67	53	87	318	64	61	84
317	65	52	86	317	63	60	82
316	64	50	85	316	61	58	81
315	63	48	83	315	60	57	80
314	61	45	82	314	58	54	78
313	60	44	81	313	57	53	77
312	58	42	80	312	55	51	75
311	57	41	78	311	54	50	73
310	55	39	76	310	52	48	72
309	54	37	74	309	51	46	69
308	52	35	73	308	49	45	67
307	51	34	71	307	48	43	65
306	49	32	70	306	46	42	64
305	48	30	68	305	45	40	61
304	46	28	67	304	43	37	60
303	45	27	64	303	43	36	57
302	43	26	64	302	40	34	57
301	42	25	61	301	39	33	54
300	41	24	60	300	38	31	53
299	40	22	57	299	37	30	50
298	38	21	57	298	35	28	49
297	36	19	53	297	34	26	46
296	36	19	53	296	33	25	46
295	34	17	49	295	31	23	43
294	33	17	49	294	30	22	43
293	32	16	46	293	28	21	39
292	31	15	45	292	27	20	38
291	29	14	42	291	26	18	36
290	28	13	41	290	25	17	34
289	27	12	39	289	24	17	33
288	26	11	38	288	23	15	31
287	25	10	36	287	22	14	29
286	24	9	34	286	21	13	28
285	23	9	32	285	19	12	27
284	22	8	30	284	19	11	25
283	21	7	29	283	18	10	23
282	20	7	27	282	17	10	22
281	19	6	26	281	16	8	20
280	18	5	24	280	15	8	19
279	17	5	22	279	15	7	17
278	16	5	21	278	13	6	16
277	15	4	20	277	13	6	15
276	14	3	18	276	12	5	14
275	13	3	18	275	11	5	14
274	13	3	16	274	10	4	12
273	12	2	15	273	10	4	12
272	11	2	14	272	9	3	11
271	10	2	13	271	8	3	10
270	10	2	12	270	8	2	8
269	9	1	11	269	7	2	8
268	9	1	10	268	6	2	7
267	8	1	9	267	6	1	6
266	7	1	8	266	5	1	6
265	6	1	8	265	5	1	5
264	5	1	6	264	4	1	4
263	5	1	6	263	4	1	4
262	4	1	5	262	3	1	3
261	4	1	4	261	3	1	3
250-260	3	1	4	250-260	2	1	2

GRADE 11

BOYS Scaled Score	V	Q	R
350	99	99	99
349	97	96	99
348	97	96	99
347	96	95	99
346	95	94	99
345	95	93	99
344	94	92	99
343	94	92	99
342	93	91	99
341	93	90	99
340	93	88	99
339	92	88	99
338	91	87	99
337	90	86	99
336	90	85	99
335	90	84	99
334	88	82	99
333	87	80	99
332	86	78	98
331	85	77	98
330	84	74	98
329	84	74	97
328	82	71	97
327	81	69	96
326	80	69	96
325	79	67	95
324	79	65	94
323	78	63	94
322	77	61	93
321	76	57	92
320	75	56	91
319	74	55	90
318	73	52	90
317	71	52	89
316	70	50	88
315	69	49	87
314	68	46	86
313	67	44	84
312	64	42	83
311	63	41	81
310	61	39	80
309	60	38	79
308	57	36	78
307	55	34	76
306	53	33	75
305	52	31	73
304	50	30	72
303	50	28	70
302	48	27	69
301	48	27	66
300	45	25	66
299	44	24	63
298	43	22	62
297	41	20	57
296	40	19	57
295	38	19	57
294	37	18	54
293	36	16	51
292	35	16	50
291	34	15	48
290	33	14	47
289	31	13	46
288	30	11	42
287	29	10	40
286	28	9	38
285	27	8	36
284	26	8	35
283	24	8	33
282	23	7	31
281	22	6	30
280	21	6	28
279	20	5	25
278	18	5	23
277	18	4	23
276	17	4	20
275	16	4	20
274	14	3	17
273	14	3	17
272	13	3	16
271	12	2	15
270	11	2	13
269	9	1	12
268	9	1	10
267	8	1	10
266	8	1	9
265	7	1	8
264	7	1	7
263	6	1	6
262	5	1	6
261	5	1	5
250-260	4	1	4

GIRLS Scaled Score	V	Q	R
350	99	99	99
349	98	99	99
348	97	99	99
347	97	98	99
346	97	98	99
345	97	97	99
344	96	96	99
343	96	95	98
342	95	95	98
341	95	94	98
340	94	93	98
339	93	92	98
338	91	91	98
337	91	91	98
336	90	90	98
335	90	89	98
334	89	89	98
333	87	88	98
332	87	86	97
331	86	85	97
330	85	83	97
329	84	83	97
328	83	82	97
327	81	81	97
326	81	80	96
325	80	79	96
324	80	77	95
323	77	76	95
322	77	75	94
321	75	73	92
320	75	71	91
319	73	69	90
318	72	66	89
317	70	65	88
316	69	62	87
315	67	60	86
314	65	59	85
313	64	58	83
312	62	55	83
311	61	53	82
310	59	51	81
309	59	49	79
308	56	47	78
307	56	45	75
306	55	43	74
305	54	41	73
304	53	39	72
303	53	36	69
302	50	34	67
301	49	33	63
300	47	32	63
299	45	30	60
298	43	29	60
297	42	26	54
296	42	25	54
295	40	24	51
294	39	23	51
293	37	21	48
292	36	20	47
291	34	19	45
290	34	17	44
289	31	17	43
288	31	15	41
287	29	15	38
286	28	14	36
285	27	13	35
284	26	12	34
283	24	10	31
282	23	10	29
281	23	8	27
280	21	8	26
279	21	7	24
278	20	6	22
277	19	6	22
276	17	4	20
275	17	4	19
274	16	4	17
273	16	4	17
272	14	3	16
271	13	3	16
270	11	2	14
269	10	2	12
268	9	2	11
267	8	2	10
266	8	2	8
265	7	2	6
264	7	2	6
263	6	2	5
262	6	1	4
261	4	1	4
250-260	3	1	3

17

ISEE Upper Level
Practice Test 1

HOW TO TAKE THIS PRACTICE TEST

Before taking this practice test, find a quiet room where you can work uninterrupted for three hours. Make sure you have a comfortable desk, your calculator, and several No. 2 pencils.

Use the answer sheet provided to record your answers. (You can cut it out or photocopy it.)

Once you start this practice test, don't stop until you've finished. Remember—you can review any questions within a section, but you may not go back or forward a section.

You'll find an answer key and explanations following the test.

Good luck.

ISEE TEST OVERVIEW

Total Time

Approximately 3 hours.

Questions

Aside from the essay, all questions are multiple-choice in format, with all answer choices labeled A–D.

Content

The ISEE tests Math and Verbal skills. There are two scored Math sections, two scored Verbal sections, and one unscored Essay section.

Pacing

You are not expected to complete all items on the ISEE. This is particularly true if you are at the low end of the age range of testtakers (8th or 9th grade). The best approach to pacing is to work as quickly as you can without losing accuracy. Further, if a question is giving you difficulty, circle it and move on. You can always come back to it later, but you shouldn't waste time on a question that is stumping you when you could be gaining valuable points elsewhere.

Guessing

There is no guessing penalty on the ISEE. You receive 1 point for each question that you answer correctly. You don't lose any points for questions left blank or for questions answered incorrectly. As a result, it's always to your advantage to guess on questions you don't know. However, it's better to answer questions correctly, so only guess if you try to answer the question and can't figure it out, or if you are running out of time.

ISEE Practice Test 1
Answer Sheet

Remove (or photocopy) this answer sheet and use it to complete the practice test.

Start with number 1 for each section. If a section has fewer questions than answer spaces, leave the extra spaces blank.

SECTION 1

1 Ⓐ Ⓑ Ⓒ Ⓓ 9 Ⓐ Ⓑ Ⓒ Ⓓ 17 Ⓐ Ⓑ Ⓒ Ⓓ 25 Ⓐ Ⓑ Ⓒ Ⓓ 33 Ⓐ Ⓑ Ⓒ Ⓓ
2 Ⓐ Ⓑ Ⓒ Ⓓ 10 Ⓐ Ⓑ Ⓒ Ⓓ 18 Ⓐ Ⓑ Ⓒ Ⓓ 26 Ⓐ Ⓑ Ⓒ Ⓓ 34 Ⓐ Ⓑ Ⓒ Ⓓ
3 Ⓐ Ⓑ Ⓒ Ⓓ 11 Ⓐ Ⓑ Ⓒ Ⓓ 19 Ⓐ Ⓑ Ⓒ Ⓓ 27 Ⓐ Ⓑ Ⓒ Ⓓ 35 Ⓐ Ⓑ Ⓒ Ⓓ
4 Ⓐ Ⓑ Ⓒ Ⓓ 12 Ⓐ Ⓑ Ⓒ Ⓓ 20 Ⓐ Ⓑ Ⓒ Ⓓ 28 Ⓐ Ⓑ Ⓒ Ⓓ 36 Ⓐ Ⓑ Ⓒ Ⓓ
5 Ⓐ Ⓑ Ⓒ Ⓓ 13 Ⓐ Ⓑ Ⓒ Ⓓ 21 Ⓐ Ⓑ Ⓒ Ⓓ 29 Ⓐ Ⓑ Ⓒ Ⓓ 37 Ⓐ Ⓑ Ⓒ Ⓓ
6 Ⓐ Ⓑ Ⓒ Ⓓ 14 Ⓐ Ⓑ Ⓒ Ⓓ 22 Ⓐ Ⓑ Ⓒ Ⓓ 30 Ⓐ Ⓑ Ⓒ Ⓓ 38 Ⓐ Ⓑ Ⓒ Ⓓ
7 Ⓐ Ⓑ Ⓒ Ⓓ 15 Ⓐ Ⓑ Ⓒ Ⓓ 23 Ⓐ Ⓑ Ⓒ Ⓓ 31 Ⓐ Ⓑ Ⓒ Ⓓ 39 Ⓐ Ⓑ Ⓒ Ⓓ
8 Ⓐ Ⓑ Ⓒ Ⓓ 16 Ⓐ Ⓑ Ⓒ Ⓓ 24 Ⓐ Ⓑ Ⓒ Ⓓ 32 Ⓐ Ⓑ Ⓒ Ⓓ 40 Ⓐ Ⓑ Ⓒ Ⓓ

right in section 1

wrong in section 1

SECTION 2

1 Ⓐ Ⓑ Ⓒ Ⓓ 9 Ⓐ Ⓑ Ⓒ Ⓓ 17 Ⓐ Ⓑ Ⓒ Ⓓ 25 Ⓐ Ⓑ Ⓒ Ⓓ 33 Ⓐ Ⓑ Ⓒ Ⓓ
2 Ⓐ Ⓑ Ⓒ Ⓓ 10 Ⓐ Ⓑ Ⓒ Ⓓ 18 Ⓐ Ⓑ Ⓒ Ⓓ 26 Ⓐ Ⓑ Ⓒ Ⓓ 34 Ⓐ Ⓑ Ⓒ Ⓓ
3 Ⓐ Ⓑ Ⓒ Ⓓ 11 Ⓐ Ⓑ Ⓒ Ⓓ 19 Ⓐ Ⓑ Ⓒ Ⓓ 27 Ⓐ Ⓑ Ⓒ Ⓓ 35 Ⓐ Ⓑ Ⓒ Ⓓ
4 Ⓐ Ⓑ Ⓒ Ⓓ 12 Ⓐ Ⓑ Ⓒ Ⓓ 20 Ⓐ Ⓑ Ⓒ Ⓓ 28 Ⓐ Ⓑ Ⓒ Ⓓ 36 Ⓐ Ⓑ Ⓒ Ⓓ
5 Ⓐ Ⓑ Ⓒ Ⓓ 13 Ⓐ Ⓑ Ⓒ Ⓓ 21 Ⓐ Ⓑ Ⓒ Ⓓ 29 Ⓐ Ⓑ Ⓒ Ⓓ 37 Ⓐ Ⓑ Ⓒ Ⓓ
6 Ⓐ Ⓑ Ⓒ Ⓓ 14 Ⓐ Ⓑ Ⓒ Ⓓ 22 Ⓐ Ⓑ Ⓒ Ⓓ 30 Ⓐ Ⓑ Ⓒ Ⓓ 38 Ⓐ Ⓑ Ⓒ Ⓓ
7 Ⓐ Ⓑ Ⓒ Ⓓ 15 Ⓐ Ⓑ Ⓒ Ⓓ 23 Ⓐ Ⓑ Ⓒ Ⓓ 31 Ⓐ Ⓑ Ⓒ Ⓓ 39 Ⓐ Ⓑ Ⓒ Ⓓ
8 Ⓐ Ⓑ Ⓒ Ⓓ 16 Ⓐ Ⓑ Ⓒ Ⓓ 24 Ⓐ Ⓑ Ⓒ Ⓓ 32 Ⓐ Ⓑ Ⓒ Ⓓ 40 Ⓐ Ⓑ Ⓒ Ⓓ

right in section 2

wrong in section 2

SECTION 3

1 Ⓐ Ⓑ Ⓒ Ⓓ 9 Ⓐ Ⓑ Ⓒ Ⓓ 17 Ⓐ Ⓑ Ⓒ Ⓓ 25 Ⓐ Ⓑ Ⓒ Ⓓ 33 Ⓐ Ⓑ Ⓒ Ⓓ
2 Ⓐ Ⓑ Ⓒ Ⓓ 10 Ⓐ Ⓑ Ⓒ Ⓓ 18 Ⓐ Ⓑ Ⓒ Ⓓ 26 Ⓐ Ⓑ Ⓒ Ⓓ 34 Ⓐ Ⓑ Ⓒ Ⓓ
3 Ⓐ Ⓑ Ⓒ Ⓓ 11 Ⓐ Ⓑ Ⓒ Ⓓ 19 Ⓐ Ⓑ Ⓒ Ⓓ 27 Ⓐ Ⓑ Ⓒ Ⓓ 35 Ⓐ Ⓑ Ⓒ Ⓓ
4 Ⓐ Ⓑ Ⓒ Ⓓ 12 Ⓐ Ⓑ Ⓒ Ⓓ 20 Ⓐ Ⓑ Ⓒ Ⓓ 28 Ⓐ Ⓑ Ⓒ Ⓓ 36 Ⓐ Ⓑ Ⓒ Ⓓ
5 Ⓐ Ⓑ Ⓒ Ⓓ 13 Ⓐ Ⓑ Ⓒ Ⓓ 21 Ⓐ Ⓑ Ⓒ Ⓓ 29 Ⓐ Ⓑ Ⓒ Ⓓ 37 Ⓐ Ⓑ Ⓒ Ⓓ
6 Ⓐ Ⓑ Ⓒ Ⓓ 14 Ⓐ Ⓑ Ⓒ Ⓓ 22 Ⓐ Ⓑ Ⓒ Ⓓ 30 Ⓐ Ⓑ Ⓒ Ⓓ 38 Ⓐ Ⓑ Ⓒ Ⓓ
7 Ⓐ Ⓑ Ⓒ Ⓓ 15 Ⓐ Ⓑ Ⓒ Ⓓ 23 Ⓐ Ⓑ Ⓒ Ⓓ 31 Ⓐ Ⓑ Ⓒ Ⓓ 39 Ⓐ Ⓑ Ⓒ Ⓓ
8 Ⓐ Ⓑ Ⓒ Ⓓ 16 Ⓐ Ⓑ Ⓒ Ⓓ 24 Ⓐ Ⓑ Ⓒ Ⓓ 32 Ⓐ Ⓑ Ⓒ Ⓓ 40 Ⓐ Ⓑ Ⓒ Ⓓ

right in section 3

wrong in section 3

SECTION 4

1 Ⓐ Ⓑ Ⓒ Ⓓ 11 Ⓐ Ⓑ Ⓒ Ⓓ 21 Ⓐ Ⓑ Ⓒ Ⓓ 31 Ⓐ Ⓑ Ⓒ Ⓓ 41 Ⓐ Ⓑ Ⓒ Ⓓ
2 Ⓐ Ⓑ Ⓒ Ⓓ 12 Ⓐ Ⓑ Ⓒ Ⓓ 22 Ⓐ Ⓑ Ⓒ Ⓓ 32 Ⓐ Ⓑ Ⓒ Ⓓ 42 Ⓐ Ⓑ Ⓒ Ⓓ
3 Ⓐ Ⓑ Ⓒ Ⓓ 13 Ⓐ Ⓑ Ⓒ Ⓓ 23 Ⓐ Ⓑ Ⓒ Ⓓ 33 Ⓐ Ⓑ Ⓒ Ⓓ 43 Ⓐ Ⓑ Ⓒ Ⓓ
4 Ⓐ Ⓑ Ⓒ Ⓓ 14 Ⓐ Ⓑ Ⓒ Ⓓ 24 Ⓐ Ⓑ Ⓒ Ⓓ 34 Ⓐ Ⓑ Ⓒ Ⓓ 44 Ⓐ Ⓑ Ⓒ Ⓓ
5 Ⓐ Ⓑ Ⓒ Ⓓ 15 Ⓐ Ⓑ Ⓒ Ⓓ 25 Ⓐ Ⓑ Ⓒ Ⓓ 35 Ⓐ Ⓑ Ⓒ Ⓓ 45 Ⓐ Ⓑ Ⓒ Ⓓ
6 Ⓐ Ⓑ Ⓒ Ⓓ 16 Ⓐ Ⓑ Ⓒ Ⓓ 26 Ⓐ Ⓑ Ⓒ Ⓓ 36 Ⓐ Ⓑ Ⓒ Ⓓ 46 Ⓐ Ⓑ Ⓒ Ⓓ
7 Ⓐ Ⓑ Ⓒ Ⓓ 17 Ⓐ Ⓑ Ⓒ Ⓓ 27 Ⓐ Ⓑ Ⓒ Ⓓ 37 Ⓐ Ⓑ Ⓒ Ⓓ 47 Ⓐ Ⓑ Ⓒ Ⓓ
8 Ⓐ Ⓑ Ⓒ Ⓓ 18 Ⓐ Ⓑ Ⓒ Ⓓ 28 Ⓐ Ⓑ Ⓒ Ⓓ 38 Ⓐ Ⓑ Ⓒ Ⓓ 48 Ⓐ Ⓑ Ⓒ Ⓓ
9 Ⓐ Ⓑ Ⓒ Ⓓ 19 Ⓐ Ⓑ Ⓒ Ⓓ 29 Ⓐ Ⓑ Ⓒ Ⓓ 39 Ⓐ Ⓑ Ⓒ Ⓓ 49 Ⓐ Ⓑ Ⓒ Ⓓ
10 Ⓐ Ⓑ Ⓒ Ⓓ 20 Ⓐ Ⓑ Ⓒ Ⓓ 30 Ⓐ Ⓑ Ⓒ Ⓓ 40 Ⓐ Ⓑ Ⓒ Ⓓ 50 Ⓐ Ⓑ Ⓒ Ⓓ

right in section 4

wrong in section 4

Section 1
Time—20 Minutes
40 Questions

Each of the following questions consists of one word followed by four words or phrases. You are to select the one word or phrase whose meaning is closest to the word in capital letters.

1. EXCESS: (A) exit (B) surplus (C) disorder (D) end

2. REIMBURSE: (A) punish (B) divert (C) compensate (D) recollect

3. ASTOUND: (A) stun (B) laugh (C) suspend (D) scold

4. MASSIVE: (A) high (B) inferior (C) huge (D) ancient

5. DIN: (A) departure (B) clamor (C) code (D) supper

6. SCARCE: (A) delicious (B) afraid (C) thin (D) rare

7. DECEIT: (A) civility (B) trickery (C) rudeness (D) despair

8. HALLOWED: (A) carved (B) distinguished (C) empty (D) sacred

9. APPREHENSION: (A) appreciation (B) worry (C) aggravation (D) elevation

10. BLEAK: (A) charming (B) warm (C) drowsy (D) dreary

11. OFFEND: (A) divulge (B) betray (C) soothe (D) insult

12. VIGOROUS: (A) robust (B) hungry (C) destructive (D) lovely

13. DESPONDENT: (A) heightened (B) annoyed (C) relaxed (D) depressed

14. SATIATE: (A) prolong (B) elongate (C) seal (D) satisfy

15. SPONTANEOUS: (A) impulsive (B) excitable (C) ingenious (D) dazzling

16. WAN: (A) short (B) pale (C) foreign (D) insincere

17. ABHOR: (A) despise (B) horrify (C) avoid (D) deny

18. APPARITION: (A) clothing (B) ghost (C) guard (D) wall

19. BENEVOLENT: (A) disobedient (B) charitable (C) sensitive (D) widespread

20. TOLERANT: (A) open-minded (B) friendly (C) grave (D) ambitious

21. CONSISTENT: (A) effective (B) uniform (C) irregular (D) incisive

22. VELOCITY: (A) speed (B) direction (C) distance (D) weight

23. PREMISE: (A) remark (B) evidence (C) response (D) assumption

24. ACCESSIBLE: (A) empty (B) convenient (C) undefeated (D) ancient

GO ON TO THE NEXT PAGE ➡

DIRECTIONS: Select the word(s) that best fit the meaning of each sentence.

25. Except for periods where they function as "loners," wolves are generally ____ animals, living in packs.

   (A) carnivorous   (B) fearsome
   (C) social   (D) wild

26. The company employed many unproductive employees who had a ____ approach to their work.

   (A) creative   (B) discontented
   (C) independent   (D) lackadaisical

27. The recent forest fire which ____ the mountains of Indonesia was the most severe ____ disaster the region has ever experienced.

   (A) destroyed .. inflammable
   (B) devastated .. environmental
   (C) singed .. intangible
   (D) burned .. scientific

28. Despite his ____ beginnings as the son of a minor tribal chieftain, the warrior became one of the greatest ____ in Asia.

   (A) humble .. rulers
   (B) luxurious .. leaders
   (C) innocent .. monarchs
   (D) regal .. kings

29. Although Angela was an interior decorator, her home was ____ decorated.

   (A) sufficiently
   (B) impressively
   (C) modestly
   (D) amply

30. Beneath the calm surface of the lake, marine creatures ____ continually for food.

   (A) qualified
   (B) survived
   (C) contested
   (D) gathered

31. The captain demonstrated his ____ for the crew by bellowing his commands in a harsh voice.

   (A) admiration
   (B) contempt
   (C) reverence
   (D) affinity

32. The ballet dancers performed with a grace and ____ that left the audience breathless.

   (A) hilarity
   (B) ineptitude
   (C) elegance
   (D) reserve

33. Due to ____ weather, the school closed and ____ all classes.

   (A) cold .. continued
   (B) inclement .. canceled
   (C) humid .. alleviated
   (D) shoddy .. rescheduled

34. The volunteer association ____ people with a wide range of ____ to staff their offices.

   (A) recruited .. attributes
   (B) fired .. skills
   (C) rejected .. experiences
   (D) hired .. tendencies

35. In spite of her ____ work, Joanne did not receive a promotion.

   (A) tardy
   (B) industrious
   (C) irate
   (D) occasional

GO ON TO THE NEXT PAGE ➡

36. The sky jumper was ____ to survive after his parachute operated ____ .

    (A) unable .. perfectly
    (B) anxious .. instinctively
    (C) surprised .. adequately
    (D) fortunate .. improperly

37. The puppy was ____ to discipline, and whined when reprimanded by its new owner.

    (A) anxious
    (B) unaccustomed
    (C) jovial
    (D used

38. The old ____ hated parties and refused to ____ in the festivities.

    (A) actor .. direct
    (B) curmudgeon .. partake
    (C) mediator .. take
    (D) surgeon .. place

39. Jeremy has a(n) ____ personality and is very uncomfortable in social situations.

    (A) jolly
    (B) introverted
    (C) outgoing
    (D) gregarious

40. The ____ agreement had never been written down but was understood and upheld by the governments of both countries.

    (A) tacit
    (B) public
    (C) distinguished
    (D) illegal

IF YOU FINISH BEFORE TIME IS CALLED, YOU MAY CHECK YOUR WORK ON THIS SECTION ONLY. DO NOT TURN TO ANY OTHER SECTION IN THE TEST.

STOP

	In this section there are 4 possible answers after each problem. Look at each answer and choose which one is best. You may use the blank space at the right of the page for scratchwork.
Section 2 Time—35 Minutes 40 Questions	

Note: Figures provided with the problems are drawn with the greatest possible accuracy, UNLESS a specific problem states that its figure is not drawn to scale.

1. Two radii of a circle combine to form a diameter if they meet at an angle whose measure in degrees is

   (A) 90   (B) 120   (C) 180   (D) 240

2. The price of a stock doubled from Monday to Tuesday. What is the percent increase in the price of the stock from Monday to Tuesday?

   (A) 50%   (B) 100%   (C) 150%   (D) 200%

3. Which of the following is true?

   (A) $0.2 \times 0.2 = 0.4$ (B) $0.2 \times 2 = 0.04$

   (C) $\frac{0.2}{2} = 0.1$ (D) $\frac{0.2}{0.1} = 0.01$

4. A square has a perimeter of 8. What is the length of one of its sides?

   (A) 2   (B) 4   (C) 8   (D) 16

5. All of the following are equal to $\frac{1}{3}$ EXCEPT

   (A) $\frac{6}{18}$ (B) $\frac{10}{30}$ (C) $\frac{11}{33}$ (D) $\frac{7}{24}$

USE THIS SPACE FOR FIGURING.

GO ON TO THE NEXT PAGE ➡

KAPLAN

USE THIS SPACE FOR FIGURING.

6. If N is an integer, which of the following must be odd?

   (A) $2N$ (B) $N + 1$ (C) $2N + 1$ (D) $3N + 1$

7. If $\frac{700}{x} = 35$, then $x =$

   (A) 2   (B) 5   (C) 20   (D) 200

8. Which of the following is closest to 15% ?

   (A) $\frac{1}{7}$ (B) $\frac{1}{5}$ (C) $\frac{1}{4}$ (D) $\frac{1}{3}$

9. When A is divided by 5 it leaves a remainder of 3. What is the remainder when $A + 2$ is divided by 5 ?

   (A) 0   (B) 1   (C) 2   D) 3

10. The difference between 30% of 400 and 15% of 400 is

    (A) 200   (B) 150   (C) 60   (D) 30

11. If $\frac{x}{3} = \frac{y}{6} = 3$, what is the value of x + y ?

    (A) 27   (B) 21   (C) 18   (D) 9

12. In the triangle in Figure 1, $x =$

    (A) 50   (B) 60   (C) 80   (D) 100

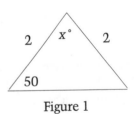

Figure 1

GO ON TO THE NEXT PAGE ➡

13. In Figure 2, if triangle ABC and triangle CED are equilateral, then the measure in degrees of angle BCE is

    (A) 60   (B) 90   (C) 120   (D) 180

USE THIS SPACE FOR FIGURING.

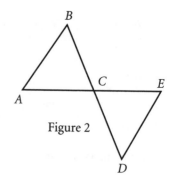

Figure 2

14. If 9 is added to the product of 12 and 4, the result is

    (A) 17   (B) 25   (C) 57   (D) 84

15. If 45 is divided by the product of 3 and 5, the result is

    (A) 3   (B) 5   (C) 9   (D) 15

16. Joe shoveled snow for $2\frac{1}{3}$ hours in the morning, and then for another $1\frac{3}{4}$ hours in the afternoon.

    How many hours did he shovel in total?

    (A) $3\frac{1}{6}$ (B) $3\frac{5}{6}$ (C) $4\frac{1}{12}$ (D) 7

17. All of the following are factors of 27 EXCEPT

    (A) 1   (B) 3   (C) 7   (D) 27

18. Greg has 50 cents and Margaret has $5.00. If Margaret gives Greg 75 cents, how much money will Greg have?

    (A) $1.00   (B) $1.25   (C) $1.50   (D) $5.50

19. $\frac{1}{2} + \frac{1}{6} =$

    (A) $\frac{1}{3}$ (B) $\frac{2}{3}$ (C) $\frac{5}{6}$ (D) $\frac{1}{12}$

20. How many integers are there from 1,960 to 1,980, inclusive?

    (A) 10   (B) 20   (C) 21   (D) 30

Directions: In questions 21–40, note the given information, if any, and then compare the quantity in Column A to the quantity in Column B. Next to the number of each question write:

A if the quantity in Column A is greater

B if the quantity in Column B is greater

C if the two quantities are equal

D if the relationship cannot be determined from the information given

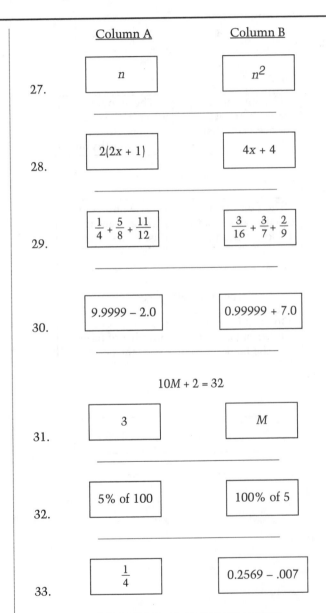

Column A · Column B

21.
$3 + 4$ · 3×4

22.
$1{,}000 - 3.45002$ · $1{,}000 - 3.45601$

The ages of the 5 members of a certain family are 8, 12, 16, 20, and 24.

23.
The average (arithmetic mean) age of the 5 family members · 16

The price of one grapefruit is $0.45 and the price of a bag of oranges is $2.45.

24.
The price of a grapefruit · The price of an orange

25.
Area of a triangle with a base of 6 and a height of 10 · Area of a triangle with a base of 12 and a height of 5

26.
$\frac{1}{4}$ of 12,948 · 25% of 12,948

Column A · Column B

27.
n · n^2

28.
$2(2x + 1)$ · $4x + 4$

29.
$\frac{1}{4} + \frac{5}{8} + \frac{11}{12}$ · $\frac{3}{16} + \frac{3}{7} + \frac{2}{9}$

30.
$9.9999 - 2.0$ · $0.99999 + 7.0$

$$10M + 2 = 32$$

31.
3 · M

32.
5% of 100 · 100% of 5

33.
$\frac{1}{4}$ · $0.2569 - .007$

Column A   Column B

A sweater sells for $60.00.

34.

| The price of the sweater after a 10% discount | $50.00 |

35.

| 4.23×8 | 37.2×8 |

36.

| The amount of water in an eight-ounce glass that is half full | The amount of water in a six-ounce glass that is three-fourths full |

37.

| The number of equal angles in an isosceles triangle | The number of equal sides in an isosceles triangle |

A book has 600 pages.

38.

| One-third of the number of pages in the book | Two-fifths of the number of pages in the book |

39.

| $\frac{1}{2} \times \frac{2}{3} \times \frac{3}{4}$ | $\frac{1}{3} \times \frac{3}{5} \times \frac{5}{7}$ |

40.

| 20% of $90.00 | $20.00 |

IF YOU FINISH BEFORE TIME IS CALLED, YOU MAY CHECK YOUR WORK ON THIS SECTION ONLY. DO NOT TURN TO ANY OTHER SECTION IN THE TEST. STOP

Section 3
Time—35 Minutes
40 Questions

Read each passage carefully and then answer the questions about it. For each question, decide on the basis of the passage which one of the choices best answers the question.

The reading passages in this test are brief excerpts or adaptations of excerpts from published material. To make the text suitable for testing purposes, we may in some cases have altered the style, contents or point of view of the original. The passages do not necessarily reflect the opinions of Kaplan, Inc.

Line
        The word "chocolate" is a generic term used to describe a variety of foods made from the seeds or beans of the cacao tree. The first people known to have consumed chocolate were the Aztecs, who
(5)   used cacao seeds to brew a bitter, aromatic drink. It was not until the Mexican expedition of Hernan Cortes in 1519, however, that Europeans first learned of cacao. Cortes came to the New World primarily in search of gold, but his interest was
(10) apparently also piqued by the Aztec's peculiar beverage, for when he returned to Spain, his ship's cargo included three chests of cacao beans. It was from these beans that Europe experienced its first taste of what seemed a very exotic beverage. The
(15) drink soon became popular among those wealthy enough to afford it, and over the next century cafes specializing in chocolate drinks began to spring up throughout Europe.

1. As used in line 1, the word "generic" means

(A) scientific
(B) technical
(C) general
(D) obscure

2. The passage suggests that chocolate foods can be

(A) unhealthy if consumed in excessive quantities
(B) one of the staples of a society's diet
(C) made from various parts of the cacao tree
(D) made from ingredients other than the cacao tree

3. It can be inferred from the passage that Cortes journeyed to Mexico mainly in order to

(A) conquer the Aztecs
(B) increase his personal wealth
(C) claim new land for Spain
(D) gain personal glory

4. The author implies in lines 9-14 that Cortes found the Aztecs' chocolate drink to be

(A) sweet
(B) relaxing
(C) stimulating
(D) strange

5. The passage suggests that most of the chocolate consumed by Europeans in the 1500s was

(A) expensive
(B) candy
(C) made by Aztecs
(D) made by Cortes

GO ON TO THE NEXT PAGE ➡

Line   It has been known for some time that wolves live and hunt in hierarchically structured packs, organized in a kind of "pecking order" similar to that found in flocks of birds. At the top of the
(5)   hierarchy in any wolf pack are the senior males, dominating the others in all matters of privilege and leadership. As many as three other distinct subgroups may exist within a pack: mature wolves with subordinate status in the hierarchy;
(10)   immature wolves (who will not be treated as adults until their second year); and outcast wolves rejected by the rest of the pack. Each individual wolf, moreover, occupies a specific position within these subgroups, taking precedence over wolves of
(15)   lower rank in the selection of food, mates, and resting places, and holding a greater share of the responsibility for protecting the pack from strange wolves and other dangers.

6. According to the passage, wolves and birds are similar in that they both

   (A)   mate for life
   (B)   become adults at two years of age
   (C)   defer to senior females
   (D)   live in structured groups

7. The passage suggests that our knowledge of the social hierarchies of wolves is

   (A)   mostly theoretical
   (B)   not a recent discovery
   (C)   based on observations of individual wolves
   (D)   in need of long-range studies

8. What is implied in the passage about outcast wolves?

   (A)   They never share the pack's food.
   (B)   They sometimes kill the pack's young.
   (C)   Their status is lower than that of immature wolves.
   (D)   They are incapable of protecting the pack from strange wolves.

9. According to the passage, the structure of a wolf pack is determined by each wolf's share of all of the following EXCEPT:

   (A)   food
   (B)   water
   (C)   resting place
   (D)   mate

10. The author's attitude toward her subject may best be described as

   (A)   admiring
   (B)   critical
   (C)   informative
   (D)   indifferent

GO ON TO THE NEXT PAGE ➡

Line   The Romantic poets in nineteenth-century
Britain prided themselves on their rejection of
many of the traditional practices of English poetry.
William Wordsworth, one of the leaders of the
(5)   Romantic movement, wished to avoid what he
considered the emotional insincerity and
affectation characteristic of much earlier poetry;
instead he attempted to achieve spontaneity and
naturalness of expression in his verse. According
(10)   to Wordsworth, a poet should be "a man speaking
to men" rather than a detached observer delivering
pronouncements from an ivory tower. John Keats,
Wordsworth's younger contemporary, brought a
similar attitude to his poetry. Keats tried to make
(15)   even the structure of his sentences seem
unpremeditated. "If poetry," he claimed, "comes
not as naturally as the leaves to a tree, it had better
not come at all."

11. The passage is primarily concerned with

  (A)   describing an artistic movement
  (B)   detailing the achievements of William
        Wordsworth
  (C)   criticizing traditional English poetry
  (D)   providing information about John
        Keats

12. As used in line 3, the word "traditional"
    means

  (A)   conservative
  (B)   formal
  (C)   boring
  (D)   standard

13. It is implied by the passage that

  (A)   the Romantic poets wrote better poetry
        than their predecessors did
  (B)   Keats imitated Wordsworth's poetry
  (C)   Keats is considered a Romantic poet
  (D)   Keats only wrote poetry about nature

14. By the statement that a poet should be "a
    man speaking to men," Wordsworth probably
    meant that poetry should

  (A)   be written in the form of a dialogue
  (B)   always be read aloud to an audience
  (C)   not be written by women
  (D)   have the directness and spontaneity of
        real speech

GO ON TO THE NEXT PAGE ➡

Line   The Alps are becoming victims of their own grandeur. In a strange twist of fate, this vast and beautiful European mountain chain is being destroyed by the very tourists it attracts. 20
(5)   million skiers visit the Alps every year. The Alpine roads are clogged by endless streams of vacationers in traffic jams 80 miles long. Off the roads, the Alpine terrain is threatened by the onslaught of ear-shattering dirt bikes, souped-up
(10)   off-road vehicles, snowmobiles and helicopters. Snow cannons that create artificial surfaces for skiers smother the fragile Alpine flora and fauna, adding to the damage caused by factories belching out nitrous and sulfur dioxide and pouring PCBs,
(15)   lead and mercury into the rivers.

15. The primary focus of the passage is

   (A)   the stunning beauty of the Alps
   (B)   the damage being done to the Alps each year by snowmobiles
   (C)   the irony of the Alps' gradual destruction by admiring visitors
   (D)   the fragile nature of the Alpine flora and fauna

16. As used in line 2, the word "grandeur" means

   (A)   size
   (B)   location
   (C)   magnificence
   (D)   significance

17. It can be inferred from the passage that snowmobiles and other vehicles

   (A)   help to relieve congestion on Alpine roads
   (B)   damage the land they travel on
   (C)   kill more Alpine animals than predatory animals do
   (D)   should not be allowed anywhere in the Alps

18. The passage implies that animals living in the Alps are threatened by

   (A)   various forms of human transportation
   (B)   the construction of roads and houses
   (C)   an increase in noise levels
   (D)   the spread of industrial pollutants

GO ON TO THE NEXT PAGE ➡

Line   Reconstructing extinct animals from their fossil bones is a challenging and exacting science. Fossil skeletons almost never survive intact. The bones of one animal may be scattered far and wide
(5)   by scavengers or by water. Fragments of several animals may come to rest in the same streambed or sandbar, and careful pains must be take not to mismatch them. As a result, paleontologists must spend years studying the skeletons of living
(10)   animals, documenting form and function and comparing anatomical details of related creatures before attempting to assemble a museum display. A collection of fossils, however fascinating, reveals its true worth only when assembled by an
(15)   informed anatomist.

19. As used in line 3, the word "intact" means

   (A) indefinitely
   (B) whole
   (C) without impurities
   (D) above ground

20. The passage suggests that finding a complete fossil skeleton is

   (A) a rare occurrence
   (B) easier in arid climates
   (C) dependent on skill rather than luck
   (D) possible only if the animal died of natural causes

21. The passage suggests that a fossil skeleton may be incorrectly assembled if

   (A) the bones are recovered by an informed anatomist
   (B) the assembly is done over a long period of time
   (C) the animal's carcass was attacked by a scavenger
   (D) the species is not yet extinct

22. It can be inferred from the passage that scientists who work with fossils

   (A) are employed only by museums
   (B) frequently make mistakes
   (C) also study geology
   (D) learn their craft from living species

23. The author's attitude toward paleontologists who assemble fossil collections can best be described as

   (A) skeptical
   (B) courteous
   (C) respectful
   (D) uninterested

Line   Edward Stratmeyer, the creator of the Hardy
Boys, Nancy Drew and Bobbsey Twins, did not
gain enormous commercial success through luck
alone.   His books, in which young amateur
(5)   detectives had fantastic adventures and always
saved the day, had a particular appeal in the time
they were written. When Stratmeyer himself was
a boy, the harsh economics of an industrializing
America quickly forced children to become adults.
(10)   By 1900, however, prosperity began to prolong
childhood, creating a new stage of life—
adolescence. From 1900 to 1930, the heyday of
Stratmeyer's career, adolescence came of age.
Child labor laws made schooling compulsory until
(15)   the age of sixteen. Young Americans, with more
free time than the working youth of the previous
century, looked to fiction and fantasy for
adventure. Stratmeyer, writing under a variety of
pseudonyms, responded to the needs of his readers
(20)   with a slew of heroic super-teens.

24. The passage primarily serves to explain

    (A)   the universal appeal of Stratmeyer's
          characters
    (B)   the benefits of mandatory schooling for
          teenagers
    (C)   the underlying reason for a writer's
          popularity
    (D)   the economic boom created by child
          labor laws

25. The passage suggests that the appeal of
Stratmeyer's fictional heroes lay partly in
the fact that

    (A)   they worked long hours in industrial
          jobs
    (B)   their activities were not restricted by
          fictional parents
    (C)   they were the same age as his readers
    (D)   they were based on young people
          Stratmeyer actually knew

26. According to the passage children under
sixteen during the 1930s

    (A)   led lives of fun and adventure
    (B)   were better off financially than ever
          before
    (C)   began to lose interest in Stratmeyer's
          books
    (D)   were legally required to attend school

27. According to the passage, Stratmeyer wrote
his books

    (A)   in a single thirty-year span
    (B)   using a series of pseudonyms
    (C)   to pay off family debts
    (D)   without ever gaining commercial
          success

GO ON TO THE NEXT PAGE ➡

Line   The ventriloquist's "dummy," the wooden figure that a ventriloquist uses to create the illusion of "throwing" his or her voice, was first developed in the 1880's. On the outside, the first
(5)   dummies looked very much like those used today—with much the same exaggerated mouth and range of movement. On the inside, however, the best of these wooden figures were a curious fusion of engineering feats and sculpture.
(10)   Underneath the wig, the back of the dummy's head opened up, revealing tangled innards of metal and wire, screws and levers. Arguably the most mechanically complex figures were made by the McElroy brothers, who together created one
(15)   hundred figures in the ten years prior to the Second World War. The mechanical brain of the McElroy dummy was assembled from some 300 different springs, pieces of metal, typewriter keys and bicycle spokes—a synergistic effort comparable to
(20)   the work of the Wright Brothers.

28. The primary purpose of the passage is to

(A) compare the achievements of two different families of inventors
(B) relate the history of the ventriloquist's art
(C) compare the ventriloquists' dummies of the 19th century with those produced today
(D) describe the complex craftsmanship behind early ventriloquists' dummies

29. It can be inferred from the passage that the outward appearance of ventriloquists' dummies

(A) is meant to seem as lifelike as possible
(B) has not changed much since they were invented
(C) depends on what mechanical devices are inside them
(D) changed after the work of the McElroy brothers

30. The passage suggests that the most complex dummies are

(A) created using scientific and artistic craftsmanship
(B) able to fool the most discerning observer
(C) those with the widest range of movement
(D) those made since the end of the Second World War

31. The author probably argues that the McElroy brothers' dummies were "a synergistic effort" (line 19) because

(A) the McElroys were related to the Wright Brothers
(B) the McElroys borrowed design concepts from other inventors
(C) the McElroys worked together on the design
(D) their dummies required so much energy to operate

32. The author's attitude toward the McElroy brothers can best be described as

(A) skeptical
(B) puzzled
(C) elated
(D) appreciative

GO ON TO THE NEXT PAGE ➡

Line   A jellyfish is only two thin layers of cells, covering the inner and outer surfaces of a saucer-shaped mass of nonliving gelatinous material. Equipped with an arsenal of viciously stinging
(5)   tentacles, the jellyfish, though considered primitive, is one of the few species that continue to hold the human predator at bay. Every attempt to control jellyfish on swimming beaches—nets, jellyfish-specific poisons, even biological
(10) controls—has failed. The Chrysaora, or stinging nettle, for example, appears to thrive in waters overenriched by sewage pollution, so much that stinging nettle congregations have clogged the intake pipes and the cooling systems of power
(15) plants. Another nuisance is Cassiopea, the mangrove jellyfish, a stinger whose population has exploded in the polluted canals of the Florida Keys, to the detriment of the tourist industry there.

33. The main focus of the passage is on

(A) the physical structure of the jellyfish
(B) the ability of the jellyfish to foil its predator
(C) problems in Florida tourism caused by the jellyfish
(D) the positive effects of pollution on the jellyfish

34. It can be inferred from the passage that the jellyfish is considered "primitive" because of its

(A) simple physical structure
(B) stinging tentacles
(C) lack of mobility
(D) preference for warm water

35. Which of the following can be inferred from the passage about the stinging nettle?

(A) It is an especially primitive form of jellyfish.
(B) It generally avoids swimming beaches and canals.
(C) It survives conditions that might kill other marine species.
(D) It is rarely found in the Florida Keys.

36. As used in line 18, the word "detriment" means

(A) delight
(B) harm
(C) fault
(D) cause

GO ON TO THE NEXT PAGE ➡

Line   In 1916, James VanDerZee opened a photography studio in New York City's Harlem. It was the eve of the Harlem Renaissance—the decade-long flowering of art and culture that
(5)   established Harlem as the most artistically vigorous African-American community in the nation. For some 40 years, VanDerZee captured the life and spirit of that burgeoning community, producing thousands of portraits, not only of
(10)   notables, but of ordinary citizens—parents and children, brides and grooms, church groups and women's clubs. Critics consider these images important today not only for their record of Harlem life, but for their reflection of their
(15)   subjects' keen sense of the importance of their culture. VanDerZee's carefully staged photographs spotlighted his subjects' pride and self-assurance. His unique vision recorded a time, place and culture that might otherwise have slipped away.

37. This passage focuses primarily on

   (A)   the cultural achievements of the Harlem Renaissance
   (B)   the history of African-American photography
   (C)   the creative influences that shaped one photographer's career
   (D)   the cultural record left by a Harlem photographer

38. It can be inferred from the passage that VanDerZee opened his studio

   (A)   just before the Harlem Renaissance began
   (B)   in order to photograph African-American celebrities
   (C)   without having previous photographic experience
   (D)   with financial support from his community

39. The passage most likely describes the subjects of VanDerZee's photographs (lines 7-13) in order to

   (A)   demonstrate the artist's flair for composition
   (B)   show that his work represented the whole community
   (C)   highlight the self-assurance of Harlem residents
   (D)   reflect upon the nature of photography

40. The author's attitude toward VanDerZee can best be described as

   (A)   neutral
   (B)   condescending
   (C)   admiring
   (D)   generous

IF YOU FINISH BEFORE TIME IS CALLED, YOU MAY CHECK YOUR WORK ON THIS SECTION ONLY. DO NOT TURN TO ANY OTHER SECTION IN THE TEST.

STOP

Section 4 Time—40 Minutes 50 Questions	In this section there are 4 possible answers after each problem. Look at each answer and choose which one is best. You may use the blank space at the right of the page for scratchwork. Note: Figures provided with the problems are drawn with the greatest possible accuracy, UNLESS a specific problem states that its figure is not drawn to scale.

USE THIS SPACE FOR FIGURING.

1. Ralph is twice as old as Howie. If Ralph is x years old, how many years old is Howie, in terms of x ?

    (A) $0.5x$ (B) $2x$ (C) $x + 2$ (D) $x - 2$

2. A bag contains only blue and red marbles. If there are three blue marbles for every red marble, what fraction of all the marbles are red?

    (A) $\frac{1}{4}$ (B) $\frac{1}{3}$ (C) $\frac{1}{2}$ (D) $\frac{3}{4}$

3. On Monday the temperatures of four different cities were 55°, –18°, 25° and –15°. What was the average (arithmetic mean) temperature on Monday for these four cities?

    (A) 103°   (B) 20°   (C) 12°   (D) 11.75°

Questions 4 – 5 refer to the graph in Figure 1.

4. Approximately how many medium-sized shirts were sold?

    (A) 300   (B) 400   (C) 500   (D) 600

5. If each shirt sells for $5.95, approximately how much was spent on small-sized shirts?

    (A) $300   (B) $900   (C) $1,800   (D) $3,600

September Sales
for Ace T-Shirt Co.

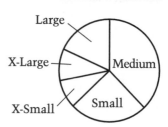

Total Sales: 1,200 shirts

Figure 1

6. How many seconds are there in $\frac{1}{20}$ of a minute?

    (A) 2   (B) 3   (C) 20   (D) 30

7. What is the greatest number of squares, each measuring two centimeters by two centimeters, that can be cut from a rectangle with a length of eight centimeters and a width of six centimeters?

    (A) 48   (B) 12   (C) 8   (D) 6

GO ON TO THE NEXT PAGE ➡

8. Five percent of the guests at a Halloween party were dressed as witches. If there were eight witches at the party, how many guests were at the party?

(A) 40   (B) 80   (C) 160   (D) 200

Questions 9 – 10 refer to the following definition.

For all real numbers a and b, $a@b = (a \times b) - (a + b)$

(Example: $6@5 = (6 \times 5) - (6 + 5) = 30 - 11 = 19$.)

9. $9@8 =$

(A) 73   (B) 72   (C) 71   (D) 55

10. If $10@N = -1$, then $N =$

(A) 0   (B) 1   (C) 9   (D) 11

11. A record collection was divided among six people so that each received the same number of records. Which of the following could be the number of records in the collection?

(A) 10   (B) 15   (C) 21   (D) 24

12. At which of the following times is the smaller angle formed by the minute hand and the hour hand of a clock less than 90 degrees?

(A) 1:30   (B) 3:00   (C) 4:30   (D) 6:00

13. Carol spent $\frac{1}{2}$ of her day at work, and $\frac{2}{3}$ of her time at work in meetings. What fraction of her entire day did Carol spend in meetings?

(A) $\frac{1}{2}$ (B) $\frac{1}{3}$ (C) $\frac{1}{5}$ (D) $\frac{1}{6}$

14. If $\frac{1}{2} \times S = 0.2$, then $S =$

(A) $\frac{2}{5}$ (B) $\frac{1}{4}$ (C) $\frac{1}{5}$ (D) $\frac{1}{10}$

GO ON TO THE NEXT PAGE ➡

USE THIS SPACE FOR FIGURING.

15. If 50% of a number equals 75, then 10% of the number equals

   (A) 15   (B) 30   (C) 60   (D) 150

16. If $\frac{1}{2} + \frac{1}{3} = \frac{M}{12}$, then $M =$

   (A) 8   (B) 9   (C) 10   (D) 11

17. The perimeter of a rectangle is 32. If its length is three times as long as its width, what is its width?

   (A) 12   (B) 8   (C) 6   (D) 4

$$2,955 \times A = 35,460$$
$$11,820 \times B = 35,460$$
$$3,940 \times C = 35,460$$
$$7,092 \times D = 35,460$$

18. If each of the above equations is correctly solved, which of the following has the greatest value?

   (A) A (B) B (C) C (D) D

19. In a certain garage, 3 out of every 10 cars are foreign. If there are 180 cars at the garage, how many of them are foreign?

   (A) 27   (B) 45   (C) 54   (D) 60

20. If $N_i = N \times 10$, then $30_i + 2_i =$

   (A) 32   (B) 302   (C) 320   (D) 3,200

21. Patricia began reading from the beginning of page 42 of a book, and stopped at the end of page 83. How many pages did she read?

   (A) 40   (B) 41   (C) 42   (D) 43

22. In Figure 2, if $AB = 8$ and $AC = 14$, how far is the midpoint of AB from the midpoint of BC ?

   (A) 3   (B) 4   (C) 7   (D) 8

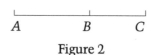

Figure 2

GO ON TO THE NEXT PAGE ➡

23. Judy has six more baseball cards than her brother. How many would she have to give him so that they would have an equal number of cards?

    (A) 6   (B) 4   (C) 3   (D) 2

24. Fred averaged 168 on the first three games he bowled. What must he score on his fourth game in order to raise his average 5 points?

    (A) 158   (B) 163   (C) 178   (D) 188

25. Which of the following equations could NEVER be true?

    (A) $N \times 0 = N$ (B) $1 \times N = N$
    (C) $N \times N = N$ (D) $N - 1 = N$

26. If X is the set of numbers greater than 6 and Y is the set of numbers less than 11, how many whole numbers are in both sets?

    (A) 4   (B) 5   (C) 6   (D) infinitely many

27. Mary has 30% more money than June has. If June has $65.00, how much money does Mary have?

    (A) $84.50   (B) $80.00
    (C) $50.00   (D) $45.50

28. If 9 is x percent of 90, what is 50 percent of x ?

    (A) 5   (B) 10   (C) 15   (D) 18

29. A certain machine caps 5 bottles every 2 seconds. At this rate, how many bottles will be capped in 1 minute?

    (A) 75   (B) 150   (C) 225   (D) 300

USE THIS SPACE FOR FIGURING.

GO ON TO THE NEXT PAGE ➡

30. What is five percent of twenty percent of one hundred?

    (A) 1   (B) 5   (C) 20   (D) 25

31. If an exam had 10 questions and Keith answered 2 questions incorrectly, what percent of the questions did he answer incorrectly?

    (A) 2%   (B) 10%   (C) 12%   (D) 20%

32. The difference between 6,985 and 3,001 is approximately

    (A) 3,000   (B) 3,500   (C) 4,000   (D) 4,500

33. One and one-third minus five-sixths equals

    (A) $\frac{1}{4}$ (B) $\frac{1}{3}$ (C) $\frac{1}{2}$ (D) $\frac{3}{4}$

34. Patty and Liza went out for lunch. Patty paid $3.30 for a drink and two hot dogs. Liza paid $2.15 for a drink and one hot dog. How much did a hot dog cost?

    (A) $0.90   (B) $1.15   (C) $1.30   (D) $1.65

35. If one fourth of a number is 3, what is one third of the same number?

    (A) 1   (B) 2   (C) 3   (D) 4

36. $2 \times 4 \times 7 \times 9$ is equal to the product of 18 and

    (A) 8   (B) 14   (C) 28   (D) 36

37. If $12 + P = 20 - 2 \times 3$, then $P =$

    (A) 2   (B) 14   (C) 36   (D) 42

38. One-tenth of 99 is

    (A) .99   (B) 9.9   (C) 99.0   (D) 99.9

39. Twenty percent of 30 is

    (A) 6   (B) 8   (C) 10   (D) 12.5

40. $\frac{64}{2 \times 4} =$

    (A) 8   (B) 24   (C) 42   (D) 128

USE THIS SPACE FOR FIGURING.

GO ON TO THE NEXT PAGE ➡

USE THIS SPACE FOR FIGURING.

41. $\frac{81}{9} + 2 =$

(A) 3   (B) 6   (C) 8   (D) 11

42. In a certain class, there are 6 girls for every 2 boys. What is the ratio of the number of girls to the entire class?

(A) 12:1   (B) 8:6   (C) 6:2   (D) 3:4

43. If $\frac{28}{a} = \frac{48}{12}$, then $a =$

(A) 7   (B) 8   (C) 9   (D) 10

44. If Set A contains all integers greater than 8, and Set B contains all integers less than 30, which of the following numbers could be in both sets?

(A) 0   (B) 2   (C) 4   (D) 9

45. $\frac{18 + 16}{4}$ equals

(A) 8   (B) 8.5   (C) 9   (D) 22

46. $\frac{1}{16} + \frac{3}{4} + \frac{8}{8} =$

(A) $\frac{3}{4}$ (B) $\frac{15}{16}$ (C) $1\frac{7}{8}$ (D) $1\frac{13}{16}$

47. If 12 of 16 cherries have pits, what fraction of the cherries do NOT have pits?

(A) $\frac{1}{4}$ (B) $\frac{1}{2}$ (C) $\frac{3}{4}$ (D) $\frac{5}{6}$

48. Nine hundred ninety-eight plus two times four equals

(A) 4,000   (B) 3,659   (C) 1,987   (D) 1,006

49. $4 + \frac{16}{4} =$

(A) 5   (B) 6   (C) 7   (D) 8

50. On Monday, Jennifer worked from 12:45 P.M. to 4:30 P.M. How many hours did she work?

(A) 3   (B) 3.5   (C) 3.75   (D) 4.75

IF YOU FINISH BEFORE TIME IS CALLED, YOU MAY CHECK YOUR WORK ON THIS SECTION ONLY. DO NOT TURN TO ANY OTHER SECTION IN THE TEST.

STOP

Section 5
Time—30 Minutes

DIRECTIONS: Write an essay on the following prompt on the paper provided. Your essay should NOT exceed 2 pages and must be written in ink. Erasing is not allowed.

Prompt: <u>You can't teach an old dog new tricks.</u>

Do you agree or disagree with this statement? Use examples from history, literature, or your own personal experience to support your point of view.

DO NOT TURN THE PAGE UNTIL TIME IS CALLED. ANSWER EXPLANATIONS
ARE AVAILABLE ON THE FOLLOWING PAGES.

STOP

KAPLAN 309

Answer Explanations

Section 1: Verbal

Synonyms

1. **B** An **excess** is an extra amount of something—a **surplus**.

2. **C** To **reimburse** someone is to pay him back or to **compensate** him.

3. **A** When you **astound** someone, you greatly surprise them or **stun** him.

4. **C** Something that is **massive** is extremely large or **huge**.

5. **B** **Din** refers to a large and distracting sound or a **clamor**.

6. **D** When something is **scarce** there is not a lot of it; it is very **rare**.

7. **B** If you accuse someone of **deceit**, you are accusing him of being untruthful or of **trickery**.

8. **D** You often hear the expression "**hallowed** ground" which means **sacred** ground.

9. **B** If you have **apprehension** about something, you have an acute concern or **worry** about it.

10. **D** When something is **bleak**, like the weather, it is very harsh or **dreary**.

11. **D** To **offend** someone is to be extremely rude to them or to **insult** them.

12. **A** Someone who is **vigorous** is very lively and healthy—**robust**.

13. **D** A **despondent** person feels very hopeless and **depressed**.

14. **D** If you are very hungry, and then eat a large meal, you can say that your appetite has been **satiated** or **satisfied**.

15. **A** **Spontaneous** actions or behavior occur with no apparent reason or cause—they are **impulsive**.

16. **B** Someone whose face is very **wan** is sickly and **pale**.

17. **A** If you **abhor** liver or brussels sprouts, you dislike them immensely—you **despise** them.

18. **B** If you see an **apparition** on Halloween, you are seeing something resembling a **ghost**.

19. **B** A person who is **benevolent** is kind and giving—**charitable**.

20. **A** A **tolerant** person does not become angry or intimidated by new and strange ideas because he is **open-minded**.

21. **B** Things which are **consistent** occur in a regular and predictable pattern: they are **uniform**.

22. **A** The **velocity** of something is how fast it is going—its **speed**.

23. **D** A **premise** is the presumed basis of something. The premise of a detective show on TV, for example, is that people know what a detective is. Another word for premise is **assumption**.

24. **B** Something or someone that is **accessible** is easy to approach—it is **convenient**.

Sentence Completions

25. **C** The clue "except for" indicates that you're looking for the opposite of "loners"—**social**, choice C.

26. **D** "Unproductive" is the clue here—it suggests that the company employs people who don't work hard. In other words, they have a **lackadaisical** approach to their work.

27. **B** Choice (B) **environmental** is the only word that fits the second blank—a forest fire "**devastated** the region" fits the first blank.

28. **A** "Despite" is a clue that indicates contrast—in spite of his **humble** beginnings, the chieftain became one of the greatest **rulers**.

29. **C** Another contrast question—in spite of Angela's job as an interior decorator, her home might be **modestly** decorated.

30. **C** **Contested** is the only word that fits the context here—you can't **gather**, **qualify** or **survive** for food if you're a marine creature.

31. **B** You're looking for a negative word here—(B)'s **contempt** fits the captain's attitude best.

32. **C** Which word goes best with grace? Grace and (C) **elegance** are the two words that best describe a ballet dancer.

33. **B** A logical structure here—predict words like "bad" and "closed" for the two blanks here—(B)'s **inclement** and **canceled** work best.

34. **A** The word "staff" indicates that the volunteer organization are either (A) **recruiting** or (D) **hiring**. (A)'s **attributes** is the word that best fits the idea of job qualifications.

35. **B** The phrase "in spite of" indicates a contrast or paradox—you can tell that Joanne didn't get the promotion even though she worked hard. (B) **industrious** is the only word that works.

36. **D** The sky diver's reaction has to be consistent with his parachute—if it opened **improperly**, then he would be **fortunate** to survive.

37. **B** The logic of the sentence suggests that the puppy would only whine if **unaccustomed** or unused to discipline.

38. **B** Only (B) **take** and (C) **partake** make sense in the second blank; only **curmudgeon** meaning grumpy old man fits blank number one.

39. **B** Another word for "uncomfortable in social situations" is (B), **introverted**.

40. **A** If something is not written down, but understood, it is described as **tacit**, choice A.

Section 2: Math

1. **C** A diameter is a chord that runs straight through the center of a circle. Two radii will form a diameter if they form a straight line, as shown in the figure below:

A straight angle has 180°, so **C** is correct.

2. **B** If the price of the stock doubled, it increased by its full price, or 100%, **B**. If this isn't clear, pick a number for the original price of the stock, say $100. On Tuesday it would be twice this, or $200. So the increase is $200 – $100 = $100; $100 is 100% of $100, so again **B** is correct.

3. **C** Evaluate each choice to see which is true:
A: $0.2 \times 0.2 = 0.04$, not 0.4, so **A** is false
B: $0.2 \times 2 = 0.4$, not 0.04, so **B** is false
C: $0.2 \div 2 = 0.1$, so **C** is true
D: $0.2 \div 0.1 = 2$, not 0.01, so **D** is false

4. **A** A square has 4 equal sides, so its perimeter is equal to $4s$, where s represents the length of one of its sides. So $4s = 8$, and a side of the square has length 2.

5. **D** Evaluate each choice to see which is not equal to $\frac{1}{3}$:

A: $\frac{6}{18} = \frac{1}{3}$ (when you factor out a 6)

B: $\frac{10}{30} = \frac{1}{3}$ (when you factor out a 10)

C: $\frac{11}{33} = \frac{1}{3}$ (when you factor out an 11)

D: $\frac{7}{24} \neq \frac{1}{3}$

6. **C** Pick numbers for N and see which of the choices must be odd. The question says must, not can, so the correct choice will be the one that is odd no matter what number you pick. Start with $N = 1$:
A: $2N = 2$; even so eliminate **A**
B: $N + 1 = 2$; even so eliminate **B**
C: $2N + 1 = 3$; odd. To see if this is always the case, try $N = 2$:
$2N + 1 = 5$; odd, so **C** is correct.
D: If $N = 1$, $3N + 1 = 4$; even so eliminate **D**.

7. **C** $\frac{700}{x} = 35$ so $35x = 700$ and $x = 20$.

8. **A** $15\% = \frac{15}{100} = .15$. Convert each choice to a decimal to see which comes closest to .15.

A: $\frac{1}{7} = .142...$

B: $\frac{1}{5} = .2$

C: $\frac{1}{4} = .25$

D: $\frac{1}{3} = 0\overline{33}$

Of the choices, .142 is closest to .15, so **A** is correct.

9. **A** Pick a number for A. Since A leaves a remainder of 3 when divided by 5, let $A = 5 + 3 = 8$. You're asked for the remainder when $A + 2$, or 10 is divided by 5. 10 is divisible by 5, so it leaves a remainder of 0, choice **A**.

10. **C** You could figure out 30% of 400, then figure out 15% of 400, and then find their difference, but it's not necessary. The difference between 30% of a number and 15% of that same number is 30% – 15% = 15% of that number. 15% of 400 is 60, so **C** is correct.

11. **A** Since $\frac{x}{3}$ and $\frac{y}{6}$ both equal 3, $\frac{x}{3}$ = 3, and

    $x = 3 \times 3 = 9$ and $\frac{y}{6} = 3$, so

    $y = 3 \times 6 = 18$. So $x + y = 9 + 18 = 27$.

12. **C** The triangle in Figure 1 is isosceles, since it has two sides of length 2. Therefore, the angles opposite these sides are also equal, and the unidentified base angle must equal 50°. The interior angles of a triangle sum to 180°, so $50 + 50 + x = 180$, $100 + x = 180$, and $x = 80$.

13. **C** Since triangle ABC is equilateral, it has three 60° angles. Therefore, $\angle BCA$ is 60°. $\angle BCE$ is supplementary to $\angle BCA$, so $60 + \angle BCE = 180$ and $\angle BCE = 120$.

14. **C** The product of two numbers is the result of multiplying them together, so the product of 12 and 4 is $12 \times 4 = 48$. Adding 9 to 48 gives you 57, choice **C**.

15. **A** The product of 3 and 5 is equal to $3 \times 5 = 15$. $45 \div 15 = 3$, choice **A**.

16. **C** Joe shoveled for a total of $2\frac{1}{3} + 1\frac{3}{4}$ hours.

    To add, first convert to improper fractions:

    $\frac{7}{3} + \frac{7}{4}$. Then find a common denominator:

    $\frac{28}{12} + \frac{21}{12} = \frac{49}{12}$. Lastly, convert to a mixed

    number: $\frac{49}{12} = 4\frac{1}{12}$.

17. **C** Evaluate each choice to see whether it is a factor of 27:
    A: $1 \times 27 = 27$, so 1 is a factor
    B: $3 \times 9 = 27$, so 3 is a factor
    C: 7 is <u>not</u> a factor of 27
    D: $27 \times 1 = 27$, so 27 is a factor

18. **B** Greg has $0.50 and is given $0.75, for a total of $1.25, choice **B**.

19. **B** $\frac{1}{2} + \frac{1}{6} = \frac{3}{6} + \frac{1}{6} = \frac{4}{6} = \frac{2}{3}$, choice **B**.

20. **C** To find the number of integers in an inclusive range, subtract the first integer from the last integer, and then add 1: $1,980 - 1,960 = 20$; $20 + 1 = 21$, choice **C**.

21. **B** In Column A, $3 + 4 = 7$. In Column B, $3 \times 4 = 12$, so **B** is correct.

22. **A** You don't need to figure out the differences to answer this QC. In both cases you're subtracting some number from 1,000. Since you're subtracting more from 1,000 in Column B, the difference in Column B will be smaller than the difference in Column A.

23. **C** Average = $\frac{\text{Sum of terms}}{\text{Number of terms}}$, so here:

    average age $= \frac{8 + 12 + 16 + 20 + 24}{5}$

    $= \frac{80}{5}$

    $= 16$

    You could have saved time if you remembered that the average of a group of consecutive integers is equal to the middle value. The ages of the family happen to be consecutive multiples of 4, so their average is the middle value, or 16.

24. **D** You're told that a grapefruit costs $0.45, so that's the value in Column A. You're told that a bag of oranges costs $2.45, but you're given no information about the number of oranges in the bag. If there were 2 oranges in the bag, each would cost about $1.25 and Column B would be greater. But if there were 10 oranges in the bag, each would cost about $0.25, and Column A would be greater. As it stands, you are not given enough information to determine which column is larger, so **D** is correct.

25. **C** Area of a triangle is equal to $\frac{1}{2}$(base)(height). In Column A you have $\frac{1}{2}$ (6)(10) = 30. In Column B you have $\frac{1}{2}$ (12)(5) = 30. The columns are equal, so **C** is correct.

26. **C** In Column A you have $\frac{1}{4}$ of 12,948 and in Column B you have 25% of 12,948. Since $\frac{1}{4}$ = 25%, the columns will be equal. Notice that you didn't need to do any calculation to solve this problem—in fact doing so would be wasting time you could use to answer other.

27. **D** Pick numbers for n. If $n = 1$, Column A is 1 and Column B is $1^2 = 1$, and the columns are equal. But if $n = 2$, Column A is 2, and Column B is $2^2 = 4$, and Column B is greater. Since there is more than one possible relationship between the columns, **D** is correct.

28. **B** Multiplying through Column A gives you $4x + 2$. Comparing piece by piece, while you may not know the value of $4x$, it will be the same in both columns. Looking at the second piece in each column, 4 is greater than 2, so Column B is greater.

29. **A** It's not necessary—and is actually a waste of time—to find common denominators and calculate the sum in each column. Compare piece by piece. The first piece in Column A is $\frac{1}{4}$ and the first piece in Column B is $\frac{3}{16}$; $\frac{1}{4} = \frac{4}{16}$, so the first piece in A is bigger. The second piece in A is $\frac{5}{8}$, which is a little more than $\frac{1}{2}$, and the second piece in B is $\frac{3}{7}$, which is a little less than $\frac{1}{2}$. Therefore the second piece in A is greater. The third piece in A is $\frac{11}{12}$, which is greater than $\frac{1}{2}$, and the third piece in B is $\frac{2}{9}$, which is less than $\frac{1}{2}$. So the third piece in A is also greater, and Column A is greater.

30. **B** The value in Column A is 7.9999, and the value in Column B is 7.99999. Column A only shows four places to the right of the decimal place, so any other places are understood to be zeros. Therefore Column A is actually 7.99990. So Column B is 0.00009 greater than Column A.

31. **C** $10M + 2 = 32$, so $10M = 30$ and $M = 3$. Therefore the columns are equal.

32. **C** This question is a breeze if you remember that $a\%$ of $b = b\%$ of a. If not, work it out. In Column A, 5% of 100 is 5. In Column B, 100% of 5 is 5. The columns are equal, so **C** is correct.

33. **A** Put the columns in the same form so that they're easier to compare. In Column A, $\frac{1}{4} = .25$. In Column B, $0.2569 - .007 = 0.2499$, but it's enough to just see that it will be less than .25 in Column A.

34. **A** A 10 percent discount on a price of $60.00 is $6.00, so the sale price is $60 - $6.00 = $54.00. This is greater than $50.00 in Column B.

35. **B** Comparing piece by piece you see that the second pieces in both columns are equal. Since $4.23 < 37.2$, the first piece in B is greater, so Column B is greater.

36. **B** An eight ounce glass that is half full will contain $\frac{1}{2} \times 8 = 4$ ounces of water. A six ounce glass that is three-fourths full will contain $\frac{3}{4} \times 6 = \frac{9}{2} = 4\frac{1}{2}$ ounces of water. Column B is greater.

37. **C** By definition, an isosceles triangle has two equal angles and two equal sides. Therefore the columns are equal, and **C** is correct.

38. **B** In Column A you have $\frac{1}{3} \times 600$ and in Column B you have $\frac{2}{5} \times 600$. You can figure out the value of each column, or you can see that since $\frac{1}{3} < \frac{2}{5}$, Column B must be greater. If this isn't clear, solve for the number of pages. In Column A you have 200, and in Column B you have 240, so again B is greater.

39. **A** Note that in Column A, $\frac{1}{2} \times \frac{2}{3} \times \frac{3}{4}$, you can cancel the 2's and the 3's before you multiply. This leaves $\frac{1}{1} \times \frac{1}{1} \times \frac{1}{4} = \frac{1}{4}$. In Column B, $\frac{1}{3} \times \frac{3}{5} \times \frac{5}{7}$, you can cancel the 3's and the 5's before you multiply. This leaves $\frac{1}{1} \times \frac{1}{1} \times \frac{1}{7} = \frac{1}{7}$. When two fractions have the same numerator, the one with the smaller denominator is greater, so Column A is greater.

40. **B** In Column A, 20% of $90.00 is $18.00, so $20 in Column B is greater. You might also have realized that since 20% of $100 is $20, 20% of something less than $100 would have to be less than $20.00.

Section 3: Reading Comprehension

Chocolate passage

The first passage is about chocolate, which comes from the seed or beans of the cacao tree. You're told that chocolate was first known to have been consumed (in drink form) by the Aztec people of Mexico, that the Spanish explorer Cortes learned of chocolate in 1519 on his expedition among the Aztec, and that he brought three chests of cacao beans back to Spain. Over the next century, the passage concludes, the chocolate drink became popular with the wealthy throughout Europe.

1. **C**   "Chocolate," we learn, is a "generic" term that describes "a variety of foods." In other words, "chocolate" is a general term, and choice (C) is correct.

2. **C**   The passage's first sentence says that chocolate can be "made from the seeds or beans of the cacao tree." Since seeds and beans are two different parts of the tree, (C) is correct. The healthiness of chocolate (A) is not mentioned; we don't know whether it's a main food or staple of any society (B); and we don't know what other ingredients, if any, go into making chocolate (D).

3. **B**   Stick to what the passage actually says. "Cortes came to the New World primarily in search of gold..." Therefore, (B) is correct: he came to amass wealth—i.e., to get rich.

4. **D**   We learn that Cortes' "interest was...piqued by the Aztec's peculiar beverage." The word "peculiar" suggests that Cortes found the Aztec's chocolate drinks strange, choice (D). Several lines earlier, we learn that the drink was bitter, so (A) is ruled out. And the passage doesn't say whether the drink was relaxing (B) or stimulating (C).

5. **A**   This question points you to the passage's final sentence. It says there that, in the century after its introduction to Europe, the chocolate drink "became popular among those wealthy enough to afford it," which implies that chocolate was very expensive in Europe at that time, choice (A). This early European chocolate was a drink, not a candy (B). As far as we know, Aztecs were not imported to make the drink (C), only the cacao beans were. And the passage never suggests that Cortes himself made most of the chocolate consumed in Europe during the entire 16th century (D).

Wolves passage

The next passage is about the structured packs that wolves live in. These packs are described as hierarchies similar to the "pecking order" of birds. Senior male wolves are at the top of the hierarchy, followed by mature wolves, young or immature wolves, and outcast wolves. We learn that a wolf's place in the hierarchy determines its selection of "food, mates and resting places," and how much responsibility each wolf is given in terms of protecting the pack from danger.

6. **D**   Wolves are compared with birds only in the first sentence, where the wolfpack structure is compared to the pecking order of a bird flock. So both species live in structured groups, and (D) is correct. We don't learn whether birds or wolves mate for life (A), when birds become "adults" (B), or whether either species defers to senior females (C).

7. **B**   The passage's opening sentence notes that "it has been known for some time" that wolves live in structured packs; therefore, our knowledge of such packs is not a recent discovery (B). (A) is wrong because the information given is not theoretical. (C) is presumably wrong because information about wolf packs must come from observations of the packs themselves, not individual wolves. And (D) is never suggested.

8. **C**   Outcast wolves are only mentioned in the third sentence, where we learn that they are fourth in order of importance, behind senior males, mature wolves and immature wolves. So (C) is correct: the status of outcast wolves is lower than that of immature wolves. (A), (B) and (D) are all plausible statements, but none of them is implied in the passage.

9. **B**   The passage's final sentence says that the order of the pack determines the selection of "food, mates and resting places," which eliminates choices (A), (C) and (D). It's plausible that a wolf's share of water (B) would also be determined by the pack structure, but this is never mentioned, so (B) is correct.

10. **C**   The author's attitude toward wolf packs may best be described as informative, choice (C). She simply tells you several facts about wolf pack structure, without signaling admiration (A), criticism (B), or indifference (D).

Romantics passage

The third passage is about the Romantic poets, a group of writers in 19th-century England who "prided themselves on their rejection of" earlier English poetry. In other words, the Romantic poets tried to write differently than their predecessors. In support of this thesis, you're told about how two major Romantic poets, Wordsworth and Keats, rejected pre-Romantic poems as insincere and affected, and tried to write more spontaneous-seeming poems.

11. **A** The main idea question. The best choice is (A): the passage describes an artistic movement, the Romantic movement in British poetry. (B) and (D) are equally wrong as each focuses on only one Romantic poet. And while (C) describes how the Romantics felt about earlier English poetry—they were critical of it—it doesn't sum up the passage, which also describes the kind of poetry the Romantics themselves tried to write.

12. **D** The word "traditional" is used here to describe earlier British poetry. The Romantics rebelled against what they saw as the usual or standard practices of earlier poets, so (D) is correct. (A), (B) and (C) are all fairly plausible in context, but don't have the equivalent meaning of "traditional."

13. **C** Which of these statements is implied in the passage? Choice (C): since Keats was Wordsworth's contemporary, and brought a similar attitude to his poetry as this leader of the Romantic movement did, Keats must also be a Romantic poet. (A) isn't implied; all we know about Romantic poetry is that it was different than earlier poetry, not that it was better (even if the Romantics themselves thought it was). Similarly, (B) is wrong because we only know that Keats brought an attitude to his writing that was similar to Wordsworth's—we don't know if the younger man actually imitated his older contemporary or not. And while Keats said that poetry should be written "as naturally as the leaves to a tree," this is a comment about spontaneity—it doesn't imply that Keats's poems are actually about nature (D).

14. **D** In the sentence just before the quoted one, we learn that Wordsworth "attempted to achieve spontaneity and naturalness of expression" in his poems. Therefore, (D) is correct. (A), (B) and (C) all interpret Wordsworth's statement too literally. Wordsworth meant that poetry should SEEM like spontaneous speech, not that it should actually be written in dialogue form, or always read aloud, or only be written by men.

Alps passage

The next passage is about the Alps, a European mountain chain that is "being destroyed by the very tourists it attracts." After stating this thesis, the author goes on to describe some of the factors involved in the destruction: millions of visitors, traffic jams, off-road vehicles, and the artificial snow for skiers and chemical pollution from factories that harm plants and animals alike.

15. **C** The primary focus of the passage is on the destruction of the Alps by tourists, making (C) correct. (C) also nicely points out the irony ("a strange twist of fate" in the author's words) of this destruction coming at the hands of the very people who admire the Alps. (A) leaves out the main point, that the beautiful Alps are being damaged. (B) and (D) each focus too narrowly on one element of the problem.

16. **C** "Grandeur" is the quality of being grand or magnificent, which means that (C) is correct here.

17. **B** The fifth sentence says that snowmobiles and other off-road vehicles threaten the Alpine terrain. So these vehicles damage the land they travel on, and (B) is correct. (A) and (C) are never suggested. And while (D) may sound like a pretty good idea, the author never calls for an outright ban on such vehicles.

18. **D** The phrase "flora and fauna" in the passage's final sentence is another way of saying "plants and animals." So the sentence says that plants and animals alike are threatened by artificial snow-makers, and by damage from factories "belching" pollutants "into the rivers." If the pollutants are going into the rivers, then at least one major element of the animals' water supply is being destroyed, which makes (D) correct. Tricky choice (A)'s phrase "forms of transportation" refers to the vehicles jamming the roads and threatening the terrain. "Terrain" refers to the land, which includes plants, but not animals—they aren't of the land, they just live on it. Neither road nor home construction (B) is mentioned, and the author doesn't speculate about the effects of noise pollution on animals (C).

Fossils passage

The fifth passage is about reconstructing extinct animals from their fossil bones. Basically, the author says it's a tough job, best done by experts. In the first place, it's difficult to find good fossil specimens. Experts who do so must then spend years studying the anatomy of living and/or extinct related creatures, if they want to succeed in assembling the fossils correctly.

19. **B**   Sentence 2 says that fossil skeletons are rarely found "intact," and sentence 3 goes on to explain why: one animal's bones may be "scattered far and wide." So "intact," is the opposite of "scattered"; something intact is together, complete, or whole, choice (B).

20. **A**   If fossil skeletons almost never survive intact—that is, in one piece—then to find a complete one is probably a rare occurrence, choice (A). The author does not cite climate (B) or how the animal died (D) as determining factors in finding a complete skeleton. And the opposite of (C) is the case: even for experts, finding a complete fossil skeleton is more a matter of luck than skill.

21. **C**   The third sentence indicates that the attack of a scavenger makes fossil bones hard to match. (A) contradicts the last line of the passage. (B) also contradicts the passage, which suggests that it takes a long time to correctly—not incorrectly—assemble a skeleton. As for (D), there's no reason to incorrectly assemble the skeleton of a living species, because the assembly can be checked against other members of the species. So (A) is best.

22. **D**   The passage says that paleontologists "must spend years studying" the skeletons and anatomy of living animals. You can infer, then, that scientists who work with fossils learn from living species, choice (D). The author never suggests that these scientists are employed only by museums (A). (B) is tricky, since the entire passage seems a warning that scientists can make mistakes if they're not careful. But this doesn't imply that they frequently do make mistakes. (C) is plausible—since you get fossils from the earth, it helps to know something about that earth, which is the subject of geology—but it's never suggested in the passage.

23. **C**   The author calls fossil reconstruction "challenging and exacting" work, requiring "careful pains" and years of study. It's safe to say, then, that the author has respect for paleontologists, and (C) is correct. Skeptical (A) means doubtful of, as in: "I'm skeptical that you really did your homework." Courteous (B) means polite; it's close to but not as good as respectful. Indifferent (D) means having

little feeling one way or the other—neither positively nor negatively.

Stratmeyer passage

The sixth passage is about Edward Stratmeyer, a writer who created those fictional teen heroes and heroines the Hardy Boys, Nancy Drew and the Bobbsey Twins. The author gives some biographical information about Stratmeyer, but the passage's main thrust is that he was so successful because his career coincided with the growth of a new population segment—adolescents. Labor laws passed early in this century required children to stay in school until the age of 16, which gave them more free time than they'd ever had before. Wanting adventure, they read Stratmeyer's books.

24. **C**   As noted above, the main thrust of the passage is not the universal appeal of Stratmeyer's characters (A), how mandatory schooling benefited teenagers (B), or the boom created by labor laws (D). Instead, the author is interested in telling us why Stratmeyer was so popular—a point echoed in correct choice (C).

25. **C**   The second sentence describes the adventurous young heroes of Stratmeyer's books as having particular appeal; the final sentence notes that Stratmeyer satisfied his readers' needs with a "slew of heroic super-teens." Since Stratmeyer's readers were mostly teenagers, you can infer that his fictional heroes appealed to them at least partly because readers and heroes were the same age, choice (C). (A), (B) and (D) are not mentioned in the passage.

26. **D**   The passage states that, by 1930, adolescence had come of age, because labor laws required children to be in school until the age of sixteen, which makes (D) correct. (A) distorts the passage: by 1930, adolescents had more free time, but it was Stratmeyer's heroes who led lives of fun and adventure. (B) distorts the fourth sentence, which notes that, by 1900, the nation was more prosperous—not that teens themselves were. (C) is tricky. 1930 is described as the end of the heyday of Stratmeyer's career, but that doesn't necessarily mean his reading audience started to drop. It may just as well mean he stopped writing so many books. So (D) is best for question 26.

27. **B**   Another factual detail question. (A) is wrong because the thirty-year span was the heyday, or best part, of Stratmeyer's career. This doesn't mean he wrote all his books within that span. The passage doesn't mention that his family was in debt (C), and we know from the

first sentence that, contrary to (D), he enjoyed enormous commercial success. This leaves correct choice (B): as the final sentence describes in passing, Stratmeyer wrote his books "under a variety of pseudonyms," or false names.

Dummies passage

The seventh passage is about ventriloquist's dummies. The author tells you when dummies were first developed, and that early dummies looked much like those of today on the outside, but on the inside were a complicated mixture of "engineering feats and sculpture." The passage goes on to describe the inside of early dummy heads, especially the dummies made by the McElroy brothers, whose creations are said to have rivaled those of the Wright Brothers—inventors of the airplane—in complexity.

28. **D** The author's primary purpose here is to describe early ventriloquists' dummies—the care and craft that went into making them. This point is restated in correct choice (D). The two inventing families mentioned in (A)—the McElroy and Wright Brothers—are only compared briefly in the passage's last sentence, making this a poor choice for a primary purpose question. (B) is too general: the passage focuses on only one historical aspect of ventriloquism, the craftsmanship of early dummies. As for (C), the passage compares early dummies with today's dummies only to tell us that both had similar exteriors. But the bulk of the passage is about the interiors of early dummies, and we learn nothing about the insides of today's dummies, so (D) remains best.

29. **B** As described in the last question, the outsides of dummies are only mentioned in the sentence 2: the outsides of early ones "looked very much like those used today." So you can infer choice (B), that outwardly, dummies haven't changed much since they were invented. (A) is not indicated, since at least one feature, the mouth, has always been "exaggerated." (C) is wrong because the outward appearance has remained the same even though the insides have changed over the years. And while the McElroy brothers obviously made wonderful dummies, the author never says that their innovations were used by other makers of dummies (D).

30. **A** Correct choice (A) restates sentence 3: the interiors of the best dummies "were a curious fusion of engineering feats and sculpture"—that is, a mix of science and art. With their exaggerated features, even the best-made

dummies aren't meant to fool the observer (B); it's the "throwing" of the ventriloquist's voice that does the fooling. (C) distorts the point, in sentence 2, that dummies from all eras have similar range of movement. And the McElroy brothers' dummies, arguably the best ever made, were constructed before World War II, not after (D).

31. **C** A "synergistic effort" describes two things working together so that the effect of the whole is more than the effect of the parts working separately. We know that the McElroy brothers worked together on their puppets, making (C) the correct answer. There's no evidence for choice (A). (B) and (D) are never mentioned in the passage.

32. **D** The author clearly admires the work of the McElroy brothers, so skeptical (A) and puzzled (B) are easily eliminated. Elated (C) means extremely happy, which doesn't seem fitting in the context of what is essentially a dry, expository passage. (D) is best: the author appreciates the effort and ingenuity that the McElroy brothers put into their dummies.

Jellyfish passage

The eighth passage is about jellyfish. The opening sentence describes the physical make-up of jellyfish, but the rest of the passage is about something else: how all our efforts to control jellyfish have been unsuccessful. Even human pollution, it turns out, creates aquatic environments that jellyfish thrive in. The author ends with examples of two species of jellyfish whose populations have continued to grow despite the presence of sewage or pollution in their water supply.

33. **B** As pointed out above, the author spends only a sentence and a half on the physical structure of the jellyfish. The rest of the passage, its main focus, is on how jellyfish defeat our attempts to control them. This is what correct choice (B) says—"foil" means to defeat, and humans are, of course, the jellyfish's "predator." (C) and (D) are only mentioned at the end of the passage, as examples of the larger premise accurately described in (B).

34. **A** Sentence 1 describes the jellyfish as only "two thin layers of cells" covering a mass of "nonliving" material. Sounds primitive, doesn't it? So the jellyfish is primitive because of its simple physical structure, and (A) is correct. The tentacles of the jellyfish (B) are only one aspect of its physical structure, so (A) remains the better, more comprehensive choice. (C) suggests that jellyfish are primitive because

they lack mobility, a claim the passage never makes and, indeed, seems to contradict (since some jellyfish can infiltrate power plants and canals). We're also never told that jellyfish prefer water of a particular temperature (D).

35. **C** Sentence 4 discusses the stinging nettle jellyfish, so hardy that it thrives in sewage-polluted waters and has even clogged up power plants. We can infer, then, that such waters would be harmful, perhaps even fatal, to other, less durable species of marine life, and (C) is correct. The author calls all jellyfish primitive just once, way back in sentence 2. You can't infer from this lone statement that the stinging nettle is an especially primitive species (A). The passage neither states or suggests that any species of jellyfish avoids swimming beaches or canals (B). Similarly, just because one species, the mangrove jellyfish, is known to thrive in the Florida Keys, you can't infer that other species such as the stinging nettle are rarely found there (D).

36. **B** Re-read the final sentence for a sense of context. The exploding population of mangrove jellyfish is a nuisance and a detriment to the local tourist industry. So "detriment" probably means something bad, which means you're looking for a word that sounds negative. Cross off "delight" (A) as too positive; "cause" (D) is too neutral, and besides, it doesn't make sense in context. The mangrove jellyfish is the "cause" of the tourist industry? We doubt it. Plugging (C) into the sentence doesn't make sense either. So choice (B) is correct: the exploding mangrove population has harmed the tourist industry.

Photography passage

The ninth and last passage on this test is about James VanDerZee, a photographer who worked in Harlem. We learn that VanDerZee's career started in 1916, just before an African-American cultural boom known as the Harlem Renaissance, and that, in a career spanning 40 years, he took thousands of photographs of Harlem residents. The passage states that these photographs—of celebrities and unknown citizens alike—are now considered an important cultural record of a proud community.

37. **D** The main focus of this passage is clearly on the work of VanDerZee, how he created an important cultural record. (D), which restates this idea, is thus the correct answer. (A) is too broad in scope and too narrow in time frame: VanDerZee was just one artist among many who made up the Harlem Renaissance, and that "decade-long flowering" spanned

only one-fourth of his productive career. (B) is similarly too broad, since VanDerZee is the only African-American photographer mentioned in the passage. And (C) is wrong because we're never told what creative influences shaped VanDerZee's career.

38. **A** The passage states that VanDerZee opened his studio in 1916, on "the eve of the Harlem Renaissance." As it does in "Christmas Eve," the word "eve" means, literally or figuratively, the night before. So we can infer that 1916 was, figuratively, the night before or just before the beginning of the Harlem Renaissance, and (A) is correct. (B) is unlikely, since the passage states that VanDerZee photographed thousands of non-celebrities. In fact, we really know nothing (and so can infer nothing) of his original intentions, of his experience prior to opening the studio (C), or of who bankrolled his studio (D).

39. **B** Sentence 3 describes VanDerZee's Harlem subjects as representing "the life and spirit of that burgeoning community." It also notes that they were not only "notables," or celebrities, but also "ordinary citizens." In other words, VanDerZee's subjects represented the entire Harlem community, and (B) is correct. The artist's flair for photographic composition (A) and the self-assurance of his subjects (C) are described further down in the passage, not in the lines in question. And (D) is too abstract and theoretical; the author wants to tell you whose pictures VanDerZee took, not to expound on the nature of photography in general.

40. **C** The author describes VanDerZee as capturing the life of a community, as an artist respected by critics who had a "unique vision." In other words, the author admires VanDerZee, and choice (C) is correct. Neutral (A) implies that the author doesn't feel one way or the other about VanDerZee, which clearly isn't the case. Condescending (B) is a negative word that means "looking down on," and it's also inappropriate. "Generous" (D) seems to imply that the author is somehow giving VanDerZee the benefit of the doubt, looking kindly on a career that really wasn't as great as the author says it was. No such attitude is hinted at in the passage, so (C) is best.

Section 4: Math

1. **A** Ralph's age is represented by x. Since Ralph is twice as old as Howie, Howie is half as old as Ralph, or $.5x$.

2. **A** If there are three blue marbles for every red marble, one out of every 4 marbles is red. Therefore, red marbles represent $\frac{1}{4}$ of all the marbles.

3. **D** Average $= \dfrac{\text{Sum of terms}}{\text{Number of terms}}$, so the average temperature on Monday was

   Average $= \dfrac{55° + (-18°) + 25° + (15°)}{4}$

   $= \dfrac{80° + (-33°)}{4}$

   $= 11\frac{3}{4}° = 11.75°$

4. **B** Looking at the pie chart, you can see that the slice that represents medium shirts represents about $\frac{1}{3}$ of the pie. The entire pie represents 1,200 shirts, so $\frac{1}{3}$ represents 400 shirts, (B).

5. **C** The slice that represents small shirts represents about $\frac{1}{4}$ of the pie. Since the whole pie is 1,200 shirts, there were 300 small shirts sold. Each shirt sold for $5.95. The question asks approximately how much was spent on the small shirts, so estimate the price of a shirt to be $6.00 to make calculation easier. The choices are pretty far apart, so it's O.K. to do this. $300 \times \$6.00 = \$1,800$, so (C) is correct.

6. **B** There are 60 seconds in a minute, so in $\frac{1}{20}$ of a minute there are $60 \times \frac{1}{20} = \frac{60}{20} = 3$ seconds.

7. **B** Sketch yourself a diagram:

	2	2	2	2
2				
2				
2				

   The 8 inch length can be divided into 4 2-inch segments and the 6 inch width can be

divided into 3 2-inch segments, which gives you a total of $4 \times 3 = 12$ squares.

8. **C** Five percent of the guests at the party were witches. There were 8 witches, so 8 represents five percent $= \frac{5}{100} = \frac{1}{20}$ of the guests. The total number of guests is $20 \times 8 = 160$.

9. **D** Just plug into the formula:
   $9@8 = (9 \times 8) - (9 + 8)$
   $= 72 - 17 = 55$

10. **B** Plug into the formula and solve for N:
    $$10@N = -1$$
    $$(10 \times N) - (10 + N) = -1$$
    $$10N - 10 - N = -1$$
    $$9N - 10 = -1$$
    $$9N = 9$$
    $$N = 1$$

11. **D** If a record collection can be evenly divided among 6 people, the number of records must be a multiple of 6. Only (D), 24, is a multiple of 6, since $6 \times 4 = 24$.

12. **C** Make yourself a few quick sketches:

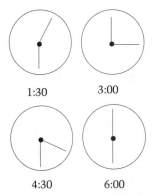

Only at 4:30 is the smaller angle less than 90°, so (C) is correct.

13. **B** Carol spent $\frac{1}{2}$ of her day at work, and $\frac{2}{3}$ of that time in meetings. So the amount of time she spent in meetings was $\frac{1}{2} \times \frac{2}{3} = \frac{2}{6} = \frac{1}{3}$ of her day.

14. **A** If $\frac{1}{2}S = 0.2$, S is twice that, or $2 \times 0.2 = 0.4$. The answer choices are all given as fractions, so convert .4 to a fraction. .4 is four-tenths, or $\frac{4}{10}$, which reduces to $\frac{2}{5}$, (A).

15. **A** 10% is one-fifth of 50%, so if 50% of a number is 75, 10% of that same number is $\frac{1}{5} \times 75 = 15$.

16. **C** $\frac{1}{2} + \frac{1}{3} = \frac{M}{12}$

$\frac{6}{12} + \frac{4}{12} = \frac{10}{12}$

So $M = 10$.

17. **D** Let w = the width of the rectangle. Its length is three times its width, or $3w$. Perimeter is equal to $2(l + w)$, where l and w represent length and width respectively. The perimeter is 32, so $2(l + w) = 32$. Plug in $3w$ for l: $2(3w + w) = 32$, $8w = 32$, $w = 4$.

18. **A** It is possible to solve for each of the four variables, but it is really a waste of time. Note that each of the equations is equal to 35,460. Therefore, the largest variable will be the one with the smallest coefficient, because it takes fewer of a larger number to come up with the same product. Looking at the equations, you see that since 2,955 is the smallest coefficient, A must have the greatest value.

19. **C** Let x = the number of foreign cars, and set up a proportion.

$\frac{3}{10} = \frac{x}{180}$

$(3)(180) = 10x$

$540 = 10x$

$54 = x$

20. **C** Plug in and solve. If $N_i = N \times 10$,

$30_i + 2_i = 30 \times 10 + 2 \times 10$

$= 300 + 20$

$= 320$

21. **C** To find the number of integers in an inclusive range, subtract the smaller integer from the larger and then add one: $83 - 42 = 41 + 1 = 42$, choice (C).

22. **C** Looking at the figure you can see that $AB + BC = AC$. Therefore, $8 + BC = 14$, and $BC = 6$. The midpoint of AB divides it into two segments of length 4, and the midpoint of BC divides it into two segments of length 3. Therefore the distance between their midpoints is $4 + 3 = 7$.

23. **C** Judy has 6 cards more than her brother. For each to have an equal number, she would have to split her 6 extra cards between them, that is, give him 3 while keeping 3 for herself.

If this isn't clear, pick numbers. Say Judy's brother had 4 cards. That would mean Judy had $4 + 6 = 10$ cards. If she gave him 3 she'd have $10 - 3 = 7$, and he would have $4 + 3 = 7$.

24. **D** Since Average = $\frac{\text{Sum of terms}}{\text{Number of terms}}$, Average $\times$ Number of terms = Sum of terms. If Fred averaged 168 for his first three games, that means he scored a total of $3 \times 168 = 504$ points. With his last game Fred wants to score enough to raise his average by 5 points, bringing it up to $168 + 5 = 173$. That means he needs to score a total of $173 \times 4 = 692$ for all four games. Since he scored 504 in the first three games, he'd need to score $692 - 504 = 188$ in his last game.

25. **D** Evaluate each statement. If you can come up with even one value for N that makes the statement true, eliminate it.
A: If $N = 0$, $0 \times 0 = 0$, and the statement is true—eliminate.
B: If $N = 1$, $1 \times 1 = 1$, and the statement is true—eliminate.
C: If $N = 1$, $1 \times 1 = 1$, and the statement is true—eliminate.
D: $N - 1 = N$, so $N = N + 1$. There is no value of N for which adding 1 to it will result in a sum of N, so this statement can never be true.

26. **A** To find the numbers that are in both sets, start listing the integers greater than 6, but stop before you hit 11: 7, 8, 9, 10. There are 4, so (A) is correct.

27. **A** If June has $65.00, Mary has
$65.00 + 30\%(\$65.00) = \$65.00 + \$19.50$
$= \$84.50$

28. **A** 9 is $\frac{1}{10}$ or 10% of 90, so $x = 10$. 50% or $\frac{1}{2}$ of $10 = 5$.

29. **B** Let x = the number of bottles capped in 1 minute, and set up a proportion. Be sure to convert 1 minute into 60 seconds.

$\frac{5}{2} = \frac{x}{60}$

$(5)(60) = 2x$

$300 = 2x$

$150 = x$

30. **A** Take this problem in steps: 20% of 100 is 20; 5% of 20 is 1.

31. **D** Keith answered 2 out of 10 questions, or $\frac{2}{10}$ incorrectly. $\frac{2}{10} = \frac{1}{5}$, or 20%, choice (D).

32. **C** 6,985 is approximately 7,000 and 3,001 is approximately 3,000. Therefore the difference between 6,985 and 3,001 is approximately 7,000 – 3,000 = 4,000, choice (C).

33. **C** Convert to improper fractions: $1\frac{1}{3} - \frac{5}{6} = \frac{4}{3} - \frac{5}{6}$ Find a common denominator: $\frac{16}{12} - \frac{10}{12} = \frac{6}{12} = \frac{1}{2}$

34. **B** Patty bought 2 hot dogs and a soda, and Liza bought 1 hot dog and a soda. Therefore the difference in what they paid, or $3.30 – $2.15 = $1.15, is the price of one hot dog.

35. **D** If one-fourth of a number is 3, the number is $4 \times 3 = 12$. One-third of 12 is 4, choice (D).

36. **C** $2 \times 4 \times 7 \times 9$ can be rewritten as $(2 \times 9)(4 \times 7)$ or 18×28. Choice (C) is correct.

37. **A** $12 + P = 20 - 2 ¥ 3$
$12 + P = 20 - 6$
$12 + P = 14$
$P = 2$

38. **B** One tenth or 0.1 of 99 is 9.9, choice (B).

39. **A** Twenty percent or $\frac{1}{5}$ of 30 is 6, choice (A).

40. **A** $\frac{64}{2 \times 4} = \frac{64}{8}$, = 8 choice (A).

41. **D** $\frac{81}{9} + 2 = 9 + 2 = 11$, choice (D).

42. **D** If there are 6 girls for every 2 boys, the ratio of girls to the entire class is 6:(6 + 2) or 6:8, which reduces to 3:4, choice (D).

43. **A** $\frac{48}{12} = \frac{4}{1}$, so $\frac{28}{a} = \frac{4}{1}$ $28 = 4a$, and $a = 7$, choice (A).

44. **D** For a number to be in both sets, it must be greater than 8 and less than 30. The only choice that falls in this range is 9, (D).

45. **B** $\frac{18 + 16}{4} = \frac{34}{4} = 8\frac{1}{2} = 8.5$, choice (B).

46. **D** $\frac{1}{16} + \frac{3}{4} + \frac{8}{8} = \frac{1}{16} + \frac{12}{16} + \frac{16}{16}$
$= 1\frac{13}{16}$

47. **A** If 12 of the 16 cherries have pits, 16 – 12 = 4 do not. So $\frac{4}{16} = \frac{1}{4}$ do not have pits.

48. **D** $998 + 2(4) = 998 + 8 = 1,006$, choice (D).

49. **D** $4 + \frac{16}{4} = 4 + 4 = 8$, choice (D).

50. **C** If Jennifer had worked from 12:45 P.M. to 4:45 P.M., she would have worked for 4 hours. She only worked until 4:30, though, so she worked for 4 hours minus 15 minutes, or 3 hours and 45 minutes. Since there are 60 minutes in an hour, $\frac{45}{60} = \frac{3}{4} = .75$, so she worked 3.75 hours, choice (C).

18

**ISEE Upper Level
Practice Test 2**

HOW TO TAKE THIS PRACTICE TEST

Before taking this practice test, find a quiet room where you can work uninterrupted for two-and-a-half hours. Make sure you have a comfortable desk, your calculator, and several No. 2 pencils.

Use the answer sheet provided to record your answers. (You can cut it out or photocopy it.)

Once you start this practice test, don't stop until you've finished. Remember—you can review any questions within a section, but you may not go back or forward a section.

You'll find an answer key, score conversion charts, and explanations following the test.

Good luck.

ISEE Practice Test 2
Answer Sheet

Remove (or photocopy) this answer sheet and use it to complete the practice test.

Start with number 1 for each section. If a section has fewer questions than answer spaces, leave the extra spaces blank.

SECTION 1

1 Ⓐ Ⓑ Ⓒ Ⓓ	9 Ⓐ Ⓑ Ⓒ Ⓓ	17 Ⓐ Ⓑ Ⓒ Ⓓ	25 Ⓐ Ⓑ Ⓒ Ⓓ	33 Ⓐ Ⓑ Ⓒ Ⓓ
2 Ⓐ Ⓑ Ⓒ Ⓓ	10 Ⓐ Ⓑ Ⓒ Ⓓ	18 Ⓐ Ⓑ Ⓒ Ⓓ	26 Ⓐ Ⓑ Ⓒ Ⓓ	34 Ⓐ Ⓑ Ⓒ Ⓓ
3 Ⓐ Ⓑ Ⓒ Ⓓ	11 Ⓐ Ⓑ Ⓒ Ⓓ	19 Ⓐ Ⓑ Ⓒ Ⓓ	27 Ⓐ Ⓑ Ⓒ Ⓓ	35 Ⓐ Ⓑ Ⓒ Ⓓ
4 Ⓐ Ⓑ Ⓒ Ⓓ	12 Ⓐ Ⓑ Ⓒ Ⓓ	20 Ⓐ Ⓑ Ⓒ Ⓓ	28 Ⓐ Ⓑ Ⓒ Ⓓ	36 Ⓐ Ⓑ Ⓒ Ⓓ
5 Ⓐ Ⓑ Ⓒ Ⓓ	13 Ⓐ Ⓑ Ⓒ Ⓓ	21 Ⓐ Ⓑ Ⓒ Ⓓ	29 Ⓐ Ⓑ Ⓒ Ⓓ	37 Ⓐ Ⓑ Ⓒ Ⓓ
6 Ⓐ Ⓑ Ⓒ Ⓓ	14 Ⓐ Ⓑ Ⓒ Ⓓ	22 Ⓐ Ⓑ Ⓒ Ⓓ	30 Ⓐ Ⓑ Ⓒ Ⓓ	38 Ⓐ Ⓑ Ⓒ Ⓓ
7 Ⓐ Ⓑ Ⓒ Ⓓ	15 Ⓐ Ⓑ Ⓒ Ⓓ	23 Ⓐ Ⓑ Ⓒ Ⓓ	31 Ⓐ Ⓑ Ⓒ Ⓓ	39 Ⓐ Ⓑ Ⓒ Ⓓ
8 Ⓐ Ⓑ Ⓒ Ⓓ	16 Ⓐ Ⓑ Ⓒ Ⓓ	24 Ⓐ Ⓑ Ⓒ Ⓓ	32 Ⓐ Ⓑ Ⓒ Ⓓ	40 Ⓐ Ⓑ Ⓒ Ⓓ

right in section 1

wrong in section 1

SECTION 2

1 Ⓐ Ⓑ Ⓒ Ⓓ	9 Ⓐ Ⓑ Ⓒ Ⓓ	17 Ⓐ Ⓑ Ⓒ Ⓓ	25 Ⓐ Ⓑ Ⓒ Ⓓ	33 Ⓐ Ⓑ Ⓒ Ⓓ
2 Ⓐ Ⓑ Ⓒ Ⓓ	10 Ⓐ Ⓑ Ⓒ Ⓓ	18 Ⓐ Ⓑ Ⓒ Ⓓ	26 Ⓐ Ⓑ Ⓒ Ⓓ	34 Ⓐ Ⓑ Ⓒ Ⓓ
3 Ⓐ Ⓑ Ⓒ Ⓓ	11 Ⓐ Ⓑ Ⓒ Ⓓ	19 Ⓐ Ⓑ Ⓒ Ⓓ	27 Ⓐ Ⓑ Ⓒ Ⓓ	35 Ⓐ Ⓑ Ⓒ Ⓓ
4 Ⓐ Ⓑ Ⓒ Ⓓ	12 Ⓐ Ⓑ Ⓒ Ⓓ	20 Ⓐ Ⓑ Ⓒ Ⓓ	28 Ⓐ Ⓑ Ⓒ Ⓓ	36 Ⓐ Ⓑ Ⓒ Ⓓ
5 Ⓐ Ⓑ Ⓒ Ⓓ	13 Ⓐ Ⓑ Ⓒ Ⓓ	21 Ⓐ Ⓑ Ⓒ Ⓓ	29 Ⓐ Ⓑ Ⓒ Ⓓ	37 Ⓐ Ⓑ Ⓒ Ⓓ
6 Ⓐ Ⓑ Ⓒ Ⓓ	14 Ⓐ Ⓑ Ⓒ Ⓓ	22 Ⓐ Ⓑ Ⓒ Ⓓ	30 Ⓐ Ⓑ Ⓒ Ⓓ	38 Ⓐ Ⓑ Ⓒ Ⓓ
7 Ⓐ Ⓑ Ⓒ Ⓓ	15 Ⓐ Ⓑ Ⓒ Ⓓ	23 Ⓐ Ⓑ Ⓒ Ⓓ	31 Ⓐ Ⓑ Ⓒ Ⓓ	39 Ⓐ Ⓑ Ⓒ Ⓓ
8 Ⓐ Ⓑ Ⓒ Ⓓ	16 Ⓐ Ⓑ Ⓒ Ⓓ	24 Ⓐ Ⓑ Ⓒ Ⓓ	32 Ⓐ Ⓑ Ⓒ Ⓓ	40 Ⓐ Ⓑ Ⓒ Ⓓ

right in section 2

wrong in section 2

SECTION 3

1 Ⓐ Ⓑ Ⓒ Ⓓ	9 Ⓐ Ⓑ Ⓒ Ⓓ	17 Ⓐ Ⓑ Ⓒ Ⓓ	25 Ⓐ Ⓑ Ⓒ Ⓓ	33 Ⓐ Ⓑ Ⓒ Ⓓ
2 Ⓐ Ⓑ Ⓒ Ⓓ	10 Ⓐ Ⓑ Ⓒ Ⓓ	18 Ⓐ Ⓑ Ⓒ Ⓓ	26 Ⓐ Ⓑ Ⓒ Ⓓ	34 Ⓐ Ⓑ Ⓒ Ⓓ
3 Ⓐ Ⓑ Ⓒ Ⓓ	11 Ⓐ Ⓑ Ⓒ Ⓓ	19 Ⓐ Ⓑ Ⓒ Ⓓ	27 Ⓐ Ⓑ Ⓒ Ⓓ	35 Ⓐ Ⓑ Ⓒ Ⓓ
4 Ⓐ Ⓑ Ⓒ Ⓓ	12 Ⓐ Ⓑ Ⓒ Ⓓ	20 Ⓐ Ⓑ Ⓒ Ⓓ	28 Ⓐ Ⓑ Ⓒ Ⓓ	36 Ⓐ Ⓑ Ⓒ Ⓓ
5 Ⓐ Ⓑ Ⓒ Ⓓ	13 Ⓐ Ⓑ Ⓒ Ⓓ	21 Ⓐ Ⓑ Ⓒ Ⓓ	29 Ⓐ Ⓑ Ⓒ Ⓓ	37 Ⓐ Ⓑ Ⓒ Ⓓ
6 Ⓐ Ⓑ Ⓒ Ⓓ	14 Ⓐ Ⓑ Ⓒ Ⓓ	22 Ⓐ Ⓑ Ⓒ Ⓓ	30 Ⓐ Ⓑ Ⓒ Ⓓ	38 Ⓐ Ⓑ Ⓒ Ⓓ
7 Ⓐ Ⓑ Ⓒ Ⓓ	15 Ⓐ Ⓑ Ⓒ Ⓓ	23 Ⓐ Ⓑ Ⓒ Ⓓ	31 Ⓐ Ⓑ Ⓒ Ⓓ	39 Ⓐ Ⓑ Ⓒ Ⓓ
8 Ⓐ Ⓑ Ⓒ Ⓓ	16 Ⓐ Ⓑ Ⓒ Ⓓ	24 Ⓐ Ⓑ Ⓒ Ⓓ	32 Ⓐ Ⓑ Ⓒ Ⓓ	40 Ⓐ Ⓑ Ⓒ Ⓓ

right in section 3

wrong in section 3

SECTION 4

1 Ⓐ Ⓑ Ⓒ Ⓓ	11 Ⓐ Ⓑ Ⓒ Ⓓ	21 Ⓐ Ⓑ Ⓒ Ⓓ	31 Ⓐ Ⓑ Ⓒ Ⓓ	41 Ⓐ Ⓑ Ⓒ Ⓓ
2 Ⓐ Ⓑ Ⓒ Ⓓ	12 Ⓐ Ⓑ Ⓒ Ⓓ	22 Ⓐ Ⓑ Ⓒ Ⓓ	32 Ⓐ Ⓑ Ⓒ Ⓓ	42 Ⓐ Ⓑ Ⓒ Ⓓ
3 Ⓐ Ⓑ Ⓒ Ⓓ	13 Ⓐ Ⓑ Ⓒ Ⓓ	23 Ⓐ Ⓑ Ⓒ Ⓓ	33 Ⓐ Ⓑ Ⓒ Ⓓ	43 Ⓐ Ⓑ Ⓒ Ⓓ
4 Ⓐ Ⓑ Ⓒ Ⓓ	14 Ⓐ Ⓑ Ⓒ Ⓓ	24 Ⓐ Ⓑ Ⓒ Ⓓ	34 Ⓐ Ⓑ Ⓒ Ⓓ	44 Ⓐ Ⓑ Ⓒ Ⓓ
5 Ⓐ Ⓑ Ⓒ Ⓓ	15 Ⓐ Ⓑ Ⓒ Ⓓ	25 Ⓐ Ⓑ Ⓒ Ⓓ	35 Ⓐ Ⓑ Ⓒ Ⓓ	45 Ⓐ Ⓑ Ⓒ Ⓓ
6 Ⓐ Ⓑ Ⓒ Ⓓ	16 Ⓐ Ⓑ Ⓒ Ⓓ	26 Ⓐ Ⓑ Ⓒ Ⓓ	36 Ⓐ Ⓑ Ⓒ Ⓓ	46 Ⓐ Ⓑ Ⓒ Ⓓ
7 Ⓐ Ⓑ Ⓒ Ⓓ	17 Ⓐ Ⓑ Ⓒ Ⓓ	27 Ⓐ Ⓑ Ⓒ Ⓓ	37 Ⓐ Ⓑ Ⓒ Ⓓ	47 Ⓐ Ⓑ Ⓒ Ⓓ
8 Ⓐ Ⓑ Ⓒ Ⓓ	18 Ⓐ Ⓑ Ⓒ Ⓓ	28 Ⓐ Ⓑ Ⓒ Ⓓ	38 Ⓐ Ⓑ Ⓒ Ⓓ	48 Ⓐ Ⓑ Ⓒ Ⓓ
9 Ⓐ Ⓑ Ⓒ Ⓓ	19 Ⓐ Ⓑ Ⓒ Ⓓ	29 Ⓐ Ⓑ Ⓒ Ⓓ	39 Ⓐ Ⓑ Ⓒ Ⓓ	49 Ⓐ Ⓑ Ⓒ Ⓓ
10 Ⓐ Ⓑ Ⓒ Ⓓ	20 Ⓐ Ⓑ Ⓒ Ⓓ	30 Ⓐ Ⓑ Ⓒ Ⓓ	40 Ⓐ Ⓑ Ⓒ Ⓓ	50 Ⓐ Ⓑ Ⓒ Ⓓ

right in section 4

wrong in section 4

Section 1
Time—20 Minutes
40 Questions

Each of the following questions consists of one word followed by four words or phrases. You are to select the one word or phrase whose meaning is closest to the word in capital letters.

1. DESECRATE: (A) defend (B) deny
   (C) describe (D) defile

2. LAUD: (A) touch (B) praise
   (C) insult (D) hear

3. AVERT: (A) vindicate (B) prevent
   (C) explain (D) dislike

4. PIETY: (A) rarity (B) smell
   (C) faith (D) meal

5. AMORAL: (A) unethical (B) lovable
   (C) transparent (D) imaginary

6. CANDOR: (A) odor (B) honesty
   (C) ability (D) wealth

7. HAUGHTINESS: (A) heat (B) height
   (C) rudeness (D) arrogance

8. VERIFY: (A) complete (B) prove
   (C) violate (D) consume

9. DECEIVE: (A) trick (B) empty
   (C) dye (D) view

10. FICTION: (A) presumption (B) growth
    (C) falsehood (D) wound

11. HARDY: (A) healthy (B) mysterious
    (C) firm (D) obese

12. LYRICAL: (A) mythical (B) bright
    (C) musical (D) wet

13. METAMORPHOSIS: (A) change (B) compliment
    (C) rejection (D) meeting

14. LAMENT: (A) support (B) decline
    (C) solidify (D) grieve

15. ARID: (A) light (B) clean
    (C) worried (D) dry

16. PERCEPTIVE: (A) confused (B) round
    (C) observant (D) imbued

17. ADAMANT: (A) thin (B) enlarged
    (C) admiring (D) stubborn

18. NEUTRAL: (A) inventive (B) foreign
    (C) unbiased (D) detailed

19. DOCILE: (A) old (B) tame
    (C) active (D) rare

20. WARINESS: (A) extremity (B) caution
    (C) superiority (D) mobility

21. RATIONAL: (A) logical (B) extraneous
    (C) spare (D) complete

22. DARING: (A) courageous (B) risky
    (C) impractical (D) inevitable

23. DONATE: (A) contribute (B) control
    (C) teach (D) conduct

24. TRANQUILITY: (A) fatigue (B) calm
    (C) warmth (D) origin

DIRECTIONS: Select the word(s) that best fit the meaning of each sentence.

25. Raccoons are ____ : they come out at night to look for food and sleep during the day.

   (A) nocturnal   (B) friendly
   (C) precocious   (D) monolithic

26. Normally ____ , Jenny lacked her usual ____ when I called her and invited her to a movie.

   (A) absurd .. severity
   (B) scornful .. predilection
   (C) amiable .. enthusiasm
   (D) distraught .. cheeriness

27. The soap opera regularly dwells on the ____ aspects of life; just last week two characters died.

   (A) morbid   (B) presumptuous
   (C) exciting   (D) expensive

28. Once a ____ gathering, the Greek festival has, in recent times, become highly ____ .

   (A) urban .. contemporary
   (B) religious .. commercialized
   (C) mournful .. gloomy
   (D) parallel .. transformed

29. The candidate changed his positions on so many issues that people began to think he was ____ .

   (A) reliable   (B) dependent
   (C) aloof   (D) flighty

30. Melanie danced with such ____ , that no one could ____ her talent any longer.

   (A) speed.. ascertain
   (B) grace .. affirm
   (C) agility .. question
   (D) melancholy .. deny

31. Sandy showed genuine ____ when she was caught: she cried and promised never to hurt anyone again.

   (A) remorse   (B) melodrama
   (C) wit   (D) enthusiasm

32. The ____ journey ____ us all; even my dog sat down to take a rest.

   (A) panoramic .. exhausted
   (B) tortuous .. invigorated
   (C) strenuous .. fatigued
   (D) arduous .. rejuvenated

33. Relying on every conceivable gimmick and stereotype, the latest Hollywood movie is not only ____ but ____ .

   (A) dull .. ambivalent
   (B) predictable .. absurd
   (C) complete .. erudite
   (D) boring .. enlightening

34. Lara not only respected her grandfather, she ____ him.

   (A) feared   (B) retired
   (C) resembled   (D) revered

35. That Chinese pieces of silk dating over 1500 years old have been found in Egypt is ____ since the landscape between these two countries includes arid deserts and several ____ mountain ranges.

   (A) known .. required
   (B) impressive .. reduced
   (C) predictable .. steep
   (D) incredible .. massive

36. At first the empty house seemed frightening with all its cobwebs and creaking shutters, but we soon realized that it was quite ____ .

   (A) benign   (B) deceptive
   (C) affluent   (D) obliterated

37. Once a ____ propagated only by science fiction movies, the possibility of life on Mars has recently become more ____ .

   (A) wish .. doubtful
   (B) myth .. plausible
   (C) story .. impossible
   (D) hypothesis .. empty

38. Many writers of the 20th century were influenced by Hemingway's ____ writing style and consequently discontinued the ____ language characteristic of the 19th century novel.

   (A) sparse .. verbose
   (B) dull .. insipid
   (C) peaceful .. descriptive
   (D) complete .. florid

GO ON TO THE NEXT PAGE ➡

39. Dave never failed to charm listeners with his ____ stories.

    (A) lethargic   (B) wan
    (C) insufferable   (D) engaging

40. Screaming and laughing, the students were ____ by their ____ experience on the white-water raft.

    (A) amused .. tepid
    (B) irritated .. continued
    (C) exhilarated .. first
    (D) frightened .. secure

IF YOU FINISH BEFORE TIME IS CALLED, YOU MAY CHECK YOUR WORK ON THIS SECTION ONLY. DO NOT TURN TO ANY OTHER SECTION IN THE TEST.   **STOP**

Section 2	In this section there are 4 possible answers after each problem. Look at each answer and choose which one is best. You may use the blank space at the right of the page for scratchwork.
Time—35 Minutes 40 Questions	Note: Figures provided with the problems are drawn with the greatest possible accuracy, UNLESS a specific problem states that its figure is not drawn to scale.

1. If $Q + 7 - 8 + 3 = 23$, what is the value of Q ?

    (A) 19
    (B) 20
    (C) 21
    (D) 22

2. A kilogram is equal to how many grams?

    (A) −1,000
    (B) −100
    (C) 100
    (D) 1,000

3. What is the value of $\frac{1}{9} + \frac{7}{12} + \frac{5}{6}$?

    (A) $\frac{9}{13}$

    (B) $1\frac{19}{36}$

    (C) $1\frac{2}{3}$

    (D) 2

4. What is 15% of 60 ?

    (A) 6
    (B) 9
    (C) 12
    (D) 15

5. If $a + 2 > 5$ and $q - 4 < 1$, which of the following is a possible value for a ?

    (A) 2
    (B) 3
    (C) 4
    (D) 5

6. If $2x + 4 = 26$, then $x + 4 =$

    (A) 9
    (B) 11
    (C) 13
    (D) 15

7. If the perimeter of an equilateral hexagon is 42, what is the sum of the lengths of 2 sides?

    (A) 6
    (B) 7
    (C) 12
    (D) 14

USE THIS SPACE FOR FIGURING.

GO ON TO THE NEXT PAGE ➡

8. If Angelo earns $2,000 per month and spends 30% of his monthly earnings on rent, how much does he pay for rent each month?

(A) $510
(B) $600
(C) $610
(D) $680

9. A farmer pays $58.00 for 6 new chickens. How many eggs must the farmer sell at 16 cents apiece in order to pay for the chickens?

(A) 360
(B) 361
(C) 362
(D) 363

10. A certain moped needs 12 gallons of fuel to go 48 miles. At this rate, how many gallons of fuel are needed to go 60 miles?

(A) 4
(B) 5
(C) 15
(D) 24

11. $1\frac{6}{11} + 1\frac{7}{22}$

(A) $2\frac{13}{33}$

(B) $2\frac{19}{22}$

(C) $2\frac{10}{11}$

(D) $2\frac{21}{22}$

12. If the average of 6 numbers is 9, what is the sum of those numbers?

(A) 15
(B) 30
(C) 54
(D) 96

13. If $\frac{1}{2} > x > 0$ and $\frac{1}{3} > x > \frac{1}{10}$, which of the following is a possible value for x ?

(A) $\frac{2}{3}$

(B) 0.47

(C) $\frac{1}{5}$

(D) $\frac{1}{20}$

GO ON TO THE NEXT PAGE ➡

USE THIS SPACE FOR FIGURING.

14. If $3a + 6a = 36$, what is the value of a?

    (A) 1
    (B) 2
    (C) 3
    (D) 4

15. What is $\frac{1}{4}$ of 0.72 ?

    (A) 0.018
    (B) 0.18
    (C) 1.8
    (D) 18

16. In the diagram to the right, what is the total area?

    (A) 10
    (B) 24
    (C) 28
    (D) 45

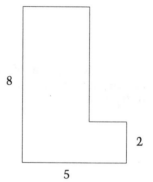

17. How many different prime factors are there of 48 ?

    (A) 1
    (B) 2
    (C) 3
    (D) 4

18. Which of the following is a factor of 36 but not of 48 ?

    (A) 3
    (B) 6
    (C) 12
    (D) 18

19. If the figure to the right is a cube, what is its volume?

    (A) 125
    (B) 100
    (C) 50
    (D) 25

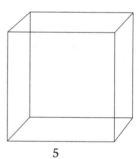

20. While studying for a history test, it took Jake 1 hour 15 minutes to review the first 30 pages. If he continues to study at the same pace, how long will it take him to review the remaining 70 pages?

    (A) 2 hours 30 minutes
    (B) 2 hours 37 minutes
    (C) 2 hours 45 minutes
    (D) 2 hours 55 minutes

GO ON TO THE NEXT PAGE ➡

Directions: In questions 21-40, note the given information, if any, and then compare the quantity in Column A to the quantity in Column B. Next to the number of each question write

A if the quantity in Column A is greater

B if the quantity in Column B is greater

C if the two quantities are equal

D if the relationship cannot be determined from the information given

	Column A	Column B
21.	$\frac{1}{2} + \frac{3}{4} + \frac{7}{8}$	$\frac{2}{5} + \frac{3}{4} + \frac{7}{9}$
22.	$\frac{4}{5} \times \frac{15}{45} \times \frac{3}{16}$	.05
23.	$\frac{4}{9} \times \frac{19}{6} \times \frac{12}{20}$	$\frac{5}{4}$

$3x - 12 = 3x - 6x$

	Column A	Column B
24.	$x + 2$	2

$x > 0$
$y > 0$

	Column A	Column B
25.	$x + 1$	y
26.	5% of $(3 + 4)$	4% of (3×4)
27.	0.46	$\frac{9}{20}$

	Column A	Column B
28.	The number of 32-cent stamps that can be purchased with $5.00	The number of 29-cent stamps that can be purchased with $5.00

$\frac{8}{9} > x > \frac{1}{2}$

	Column A	Column B
29.	x	$\frac{2}{3}$

$x < 0$

	Column A	Column B
30.	$2x$	$(2x)(1x)$
31.	Perimeter of an octagon with sides of equal length	8
32.	The number of prime factors of 21	3

$\frac{5}{7}$ of x is 35

	Column A	Column B
33.	x	48

GO ON TO THE NEXT PAGE ➡

Column A	Column B

34.

| 98% of 51 | 51% of 98 |

35.

| 20% of $42.00 | $9.00 |

A bag contains 3 green marbles, 4 white marbles, and 2 red marbles only.

36.

| The ratio of green to white marbles the total number of marbles in the bag | The ratio of white marbles and red marbles to |

$x > 0$

37.

| $\left(\dfrac{157}{x}\right) \times 2$ | $314x$ |

---

a is a member of the set {4, 7, 8}.
b is a member of the set {3, 6}.

38.

| Number of different values for $a + b$ | 5 |

39.

| $-(2x - 5)$ | $-(2x + 5)$ |

$x + y > 11$
$x < 5.5$

40.

| x | y |

IF YOU FINISH BEFORE TIME IS CALLED, YOU MAY CHECK YOUR WORK ON THIS SECTION ONLY. DO NOT TURN TO ANY OTHER SECTION IN THE TEST. **STOP**

Section 3
Time—35 Minutes
40 Questions

Read each passage carefully and then answer the questions about it. For each question, decide on the basis of the passage which one of the choices best answers the question.

Line   Porcupines have justifiable confidence in their defensive armament. Adult porcupines have upwards of 30,000 quills, spiny hairs strong and sharp enough to pierce the hide of any predator.

(5)   These quills have tiny barbs just below the tip, and are so loosely set in the skin that if they are touched with any force they pull out of the porcupine and stick into the porcupines' attacker. The longest quills, up to four inches long, are on

(10)   the porcupine's back and flanks, but the shorter ones that stud its muscular tail often do the most damage. With a few well-timed lashes, a porcupine can drive so many quills so quickly into an attacker as to give the erroneous impression

(15)   that it can throw the spines like darts.

1. According to the passage, porcupines use their quills to

   (A) capture food
   (B) protect their young
   (C) defend themselves
   (D) retain heat

2. As used in line 1, the word "justifiable" means

   (A) intellectual
   (B) understandable
   (C) unreasonable
   (D) defiant

3. Porcupine quills are most nearly comparable in function to

   (A) shark teeth
   (B) bear claws
   (C) a rhinocerous horn
   (D) cactus needles

4. The passage suggests that the porcupine's longest quills are

   (A) less important for protection than its tail quills
   (B) too loosely set in the skin to harm potential predators
   (C) less numerous than the quills on other parts of its body
   (D) sharper than the quills on its stomach, legs and tail

GO ON TO THE NEXT PAGE ➡

Line   The heyday of the log cabin occurred between
        1780 and 1850, when a great number of settlers
        forged westward.   While early cabins were
        primitive, with dirt floor and sod roofs, later
(5)   settlers built fine, two-story, log-hewn farmhouses
        with rooms for entertaining.   By the 1840's,
        though, the log cabin began fading out. Factors
        contributing to its decline included sawmills,
        nails, and the rising popularity of the Greek
(10)   Revival-style house, with its democratic roots in
        ancient Greece and its templed front facing the
        street. Trains brought hardware, manufactured
        goods, and an end to geographic isolation. Climate
        and the proximity of the local forest no longer set
(15)   architectural limits. In hundreds of towns, log
        homes were gradually sheathed with clapboard or
        brick, or, in many instances, were simply burned.
        Logs continued to house livestock, but after the
        1850's, fewer and fewer people.

5. As used in line 3, the word "forged" means

    (A)   fled
    (B)   wandered
    (C)   moved
    (D)   returned

6. The passage suggests that the origins of the
    Greek Revival style

    (A)   arose out of a general desire to replace
           log cabins
    (B)   widely influenced contemporary Greek
           architects
    (C)   were popular with devoutly religious
           Americans
    (D)   appealed to democratic-minded
           Americans

7. It can be inferred from the passage that,
    unlike Greek Revival homes, log cabins

    (A)   did not always face the street
    (B)   lacked indoor plumbing
    (C)   could not have glass windows
    (D)   were built near lakes and rivers

8. It can be inferred from the passage that a
    limiting factor in the construction of a
    settler's log cabin was often

    (A)   the availability of nails
    (B)   the location of the nearest forest
    (C)   the opinions of other settlers
    (D)   the laws of the local government

9. According to the passage, most log
    structures after 1850 were built

    (A)   in wilderness areas
    (B)   in frontier towns
    (C)   as railroad depots
    (D)   to shelter animals

GO ON TO THE NEXT PAGE ➡

Line   The plague, or Black Death, struck Europe in a
series of outbreaks in the 13th and 14th centuries,
killing an estimated one-third of the continent's
population. The epidemic wrought enormous
(5)   changes in European society, some of which,
ironically, were beneficial. Reform in the medical
profession, which had mostly failed to relieve the
suffering, was one of the most immediate benefits.
A great many doctors died or simply ran away
(10)   during the plague. By the 1300's, many
universities were lacking professors of medicine
and surgery. Into this void rushed people with new
ideas. In addition, ordinary people began acquiring
medical guides and taking command of their own
(15)   health. Gradually, more medical texts began to
appear in everyday languages rather than in Latin,
making medical knowledge more accessible.

10. The passage focuses primarily on

(A) the enormous loss of life caused by the
     plague
(B) the lack of qualified doctors during the
     plague
(C) one positive result of a catastrophic event
(D) the translation of medical texts into
     everyday language

11. As used in line 5, the word "wrought" means

(A) caused
(B) needed
(C) accelerated
(D) offered

12. The passage suggests that, prior to the
     plague outbreaks, European medicine was

(A) hampered by a shortage of doctors
(B) available only to university students
(C) in need of sweeping changes
(D) practiced mainly in Latin-speaking
     countries

13. It can be inferred from the passage that after
     the 1300's, medical texts

(A) included information on how to cure
     the plague
(B) were more easily available to the
     general population
(C) were no longer written in Latin
(D) were not written by university
     professors

GO ON TO THE NEXT PAGE ➡

Line   In the sport of orienteering, competitors use a
map and compass to navigate their way cross-
country along an unfamiliar course. The novice
quickly finds, however, that the most important
(5)   question in orienteering is not compass bearing
but choice of route. There are almost always
several different ways to get from one point to
another, and the beeline on a direct compass
bearing over a mountain is seldom the best.
(10)   Indeed, orienteers tend to disdain beelining over
obstacles as a crude approach; they aspire to
intellectual finesse.   If climbing 20 feet in
elevation requires the time and energy it would
take to travel 250 feet on level ground—the sort of
(15)   quick calculation orienteers are always making —
then it may be better to follow a prominent
contour along one flank of the mountain, or even
to stick to the safety of a trail looping around the
base.

14. The passage suggests that a hiker with a map
and compass is NOT orienteering if she

(A)   climbs more than one mountain per route
(B)   travels over a known, familiar route
(C)   takes more than one route per day
(D)   follows a direct path over an obstacle

15. According to the passage, an orienteer places
greatest importance on

(A)   maintaining a single compass bearing
(B)   avoiding hazardous terrain
(C)   overcoming obstacles as fast as possible
(D)   choosing the best route available

16. It can be inferred from the passage that most
orienteers would consider a competitor who
climbs a mountain in order to take the most
direct route to be

(A)   gaining a major advantage
(B)   lacking sophistication
(C)   breaking the rules
(D)   endangering other competitors

17. The passage suggests that one skill
orienteers require is the ability to

(A)   run while carrying a backpack
(B)   swim long distances
(C)   set up a campsite
(D)   make rapid calculations

GO ON TO THE NEXT PAGE ➡

Line Researchers have identified two phenomena that in previous literature were confounded under the category of nightmares. On the one hand, there is the true nightmare, which is an actual,
(5) detailed dream. On the other there is the "night terror," from which the sleeper, often a child, suddenly awakes in great fright with no memory of a dream, often screaming and sometimes going off in a sleepwalking trance. Night terrors are seldom
(10) of serious consequence, no matter how horrifying they may appear to anxious parents. Outside of taking commonsense precautions—such as making sure a sleepwalker does not go to bed near an open window or on a balcony—there is nothing
(15) much to do about them. A child's night terrors can be reduced somewhat with a consistent sleep schedule and by avoiding excessive fatigue. Excessive concern or medication should usually be avoided.

18. As used in line 3, the word "confounded" means

    (A) entitled
    (B) confused
    (C) written
    (D) underappreciated

19. The passage suggests that, until recently, sleep researchers

    (A) knew very little about the nature of dreams
    (B) studied only adult sleeping habits, not those of children
    (C) did not differentiate between nightmares and night terrors
    (D) prescribed medication for children suffering from night terrors

20. According to the passage, a nightmare is a

    (A) full-fledged dream
    (B) dream fragment
    (C) hallucination
    (D) trancelike state

21. The passage implies that parents of children who experience night terrors

    (A) tend to dismiss them as inconsequential
    (B) also suffered night terrors when they were children
    (C) find their occurrence nearly as frightening as the children themselves do
    (D) should consult a doctor as soon as possible

22. Which of the following questions is NOT answered in the passage?

    (A) What is the difference between nightmares and night terrors?
    (B) What are some precautions parents can take to ensure the safety of children who experience night terrors?
    (C) Does a child who is frightened upon waking from a night terror remember dreaming?
    (D) Why does a consistent sleep schedule reduce the incidence of night terrors?

GO ON TO THE NEXT PAGE ➡

Line   The Neanderthal was an early human that flourished throughout Europe and western Asia between 35,000 and 85,000 years ago. Physically, Neanderthals differed from modern humans in
(5) many important ways. They had massive limb bones, a barrel chest, thick brow ridges, a receding forehead and a bunlike bulge on the back of the skull. Yet despite Neanderthals' reputation for low intelligence, there is nothing that clearly
(10) distinguishes a Neanderthal's brain from that of modern humans—except for the fact that, on average, Neanderthal versions were slightly larger. Combining enormous physical strength with manifest intelligence, Neanderthals appeared to be
(15) supremely well adapted. Nevertheless, around 35,000 years ago, they vanished from the face of the earth. The question of what became of the Neanderthals still baffles paleontologists, and is perhaps the most talked-about issue in human
(20) origins research today.

23. It can be inferred from the passage that most Neanderthals probably had

(A) big arms
(B) wide-set eyes
(C) bowed legs
(D) narrow feet

24. According to the passage, Neanderthals lived

(A) in caves and mud dwellings
(B) by hunting in packs
(C) in Europe and Asia
(D) on all the continents

25. Based on information in the passage, modern humans, when compared with Neanderthals, probably have

(A) superior eyesight
(B) a better sense of smell
(C) less physical strength
(D) more body hair

26. The passage suggests that modern humans tend to think of Neanderthals as

(A) peaceful
(B) skilled artists
(C) farmers
(D) unintelligent

27. According to the passage, one question paleontologists are still trying to solve is

(A) what constituted the basic Neanderthal diet
(B) what were the Neanderthals' migratory patterns
(C) why the Neanderthal species became extinct
(D) where the Neanderthals originally came from

GO ON TO THE NEXT PAGE ➡

Line While the art of magic has always relied upon certain mechanics—angled mirrors, carefully concealed trapdoors—it is the art of deception that ultimately creates the illusion. The most

(5) important skill in any conjurer's repertoire is misdirection, the fine art of prompting an audience to look elsewhere at a critical moment. Presentation and timing are everything; when a magician makes an extravagant gesture with one

(10) hand, he is generally trying to divert your attention from the other. Misdirection is not always as subtle as snapping fingers or waving. One performer, wishing to distract his audience while he spirited an assistant offstage, arranged for

(15) a gorilla to ride a unicycle across the stage at the crucial moment. Whatever the gimmick, the mechanics of magic are almost beside the point; most magical effects owe their success to pure

(20) stagecraft.

28. It can be inferred from the passage that angled mirrors and trapdoors are

 (A) devices used by most magicians only in recent years

 (B) always activated by the magician's assistant, not the magician himself

 (C) less important for a successful illusion than presentation and timing

 (D) gimmicks that perceptive audience members can observe

29. As used in line 7, the word "prompting" means

 (A) telling
 (B) attending
 (C) entertaining
 (D) persuading

30. The primary focus of the passage is on the

 (A) various gimmicks used in magic shows

 (B) necessity of using mechanical effects to create an illusion

 (C) different ways in which a magician deceives an audience

 (D) ways in which an audience can figure out a magician's tricks

31. The passage suggests that, when a magician waves his hand grandly, he is

 (A) signaling an assistant to enter onstage

 (B) diverting attention from his other hand

 (C) announcing the start of a new illusion

 (D) warming up in order to perform a trick

Line   The American colonists were no less infatuated with wigs than were their European contemporaries. While cheaper wigs made from horse hair, goat hair or duck feathers were
(5)   available, the wealthy chose expensive wigs crafted from real human hair. Initially, most wigs worn in the New World were imported from England, although by the start of the Revolution numerous wigmakers were plying their trade in
(10) the Colonies. But the American War of Independence—and, even more so, the subsequent French Revolution—brought the wig's giddy heyday to an abrupt end. As the heads of bigwigs began to roll from the guillotines, extravagance,
(15) ostentation and anything that smacked of class distinction or the depredations of royalty fell quickly out of fashion.

32. The primary focus of this passage is on

(A)   the elaborate construction of wigs in the American colonies

(B)   the importance of English imports to the American colonies

(C)   the effect of historical events on a particular fashion

(D)   the influence of the War of Independence on commerce between England and the New World

33. The passage implies that wigs made of human hair were

(A)   more easily maintained than horse hair wigs

(B)   considered fashionable in England but not in France

(C)   made from the heads of guillotine victims

(D)   rarely worn by poor people

34. What is suggested in the passage about wigmakers who worked in the Colonies?

(A)   Their numbers had grown considerably by the start of the American Revolution.

(B)   They were specialists in goat hair and duck feather wigs.

(C)   They designed wigs that looked very different from European wigs.

(D)   They remained loyal to the British during the War of Independence.

35. As used in lines 1-2, the phrase "infatuated with" means

(A)   dependent on
(B)   fond of
(C)   critical of
(D)   repelled by

GO ON TO THE NEXT PAGE ➡

Line   Coyotes are one of the most primitive of living dogs. According to the fossil record, a close relative of the contemporary coyote existed here two to three million years ago. It in turn seems to
(5)   have descended from a group of small canids that was widely dispersed throughout the world and that also gave rise to the jackals of Eurasia and Africa. One to two million years ago, a division occurred in North America between the coyote
(10)   and the wolf. Time passed, and glaciers advanced and receded. Mammoths, saber-toothed tigers and dire wolves (canids with enormous heads) came and went. Native horses left the continent over land bridges, and others returned on galleons.
(15)   Through it all, coyotes remained basically the same—primitive in evolutionary terms but marvelously flexible, always progressive and innovative—riding out, adjusting to and exploiting the changes.

36. The primary focus of the passage is on

   (A)   the ability of the coyote species to survive unchanged
   (B)   the unfortunate extinction of many prehistoric life forms
   (C)   the changing nature of animal life in prehistoric times
   (D)   the evolutionary division between coyotes and wolves

37. The passage suggests that modern dogs are

   (A)   direct descendants of dire wolves
   (B)   native to North America but not to Eurasia
   (C)   genetically related to coyotes
   (D)   lacking in evolutionary flexibility

38. According to the passage, a close relative of the coyote existed in North America

   (A)   ten million years ago
   (B)   seven million years ago
   (C)   five million years ago
   (D)   two million years ago

39. The author probably mentions mammoths and saber-toothed tigers in order to give examples of

   (A)   the coyote's more distant relatives
   (B)   animals that did not leave North America by land bridge
   (C)   species that the jackal hunted into extinction
   (D)   species that failed to adapt as the coyote did

40. When the passage states that "others returned on galleons" (lines 15-16), it most probably means that

   (A)   some species of horse became extinct, then others appeared
   (B)   horses were re-introduced to North America when Europeans brought them by ship
   (C)   some coyotes were introduced into Africa and Eurasia
   (D)   prehistoric horses and dire wolves became extinct at roughly the same time

IF YOU FINISH BEFORE TIME IS CALLED, YOU MAY CHECK YOUR WORK ON THIS SECTION ONLY. DO NOT TURN TO ANY OTHER SECTION IN THE TEST.   STOP

Section 4	In this section there are 4 possible answers after each problem. Look at each answer and choose which one is best. You may use the blank space at the right of the page for scratchwork.
Time—40 Minutes 50 Questions	**Note:** Figures provided with the problems are drawn with the greatest possible accuracy, UNLESS a specific problem states that its figure is not drawn to scale.

1. What are all the values of x for which $(x-2)(x+5) = 0$?

    (A) −5
    (B) −2
    (C) 2 and −5
    (D) −2 and −5

2. Patty uses 2 gallons of paint to cover 875 square feet of surface. At this rate, how many gallons will she need to cover 4,375 square feet of surface?

    (A) 4
    (B) 5
    (C) 8
    (D) 10

3. What is the area of a triangle with a base of 4 inches and a height of 6 inches?

    (A) 10
    (B) 12
    (C) 20
    (D) 24

4. An equilateral triangle has sides of lengths $3x + 1$ and $x + 7$. What is the length of one side?

    (A) 3
    (B) 5
    (C) 8
    (D) 10

5. $(65 \times 10^2) + (31 \times 10^3) + 12 =$

    (A) 375,120.00
    (B) 37,512.00
    (C) 3,751.20
    (D) 375.12

6. Mr. Richman purchased a boat for $120,000. If the boat loses 20% of its value when placed in the water, how much did Mr. Richman lose in the value of his boat?

    (A) $2,400
    (B) $9,600
    (C) $24,000
    (D) $96,000

USE THIS SPACE FOR FIGURING.

GO ON TO THE NEXT PAGE ➡

7. A dog is chained by a flexible leash to a stake in the ground in the center of his yard. If the leash is 8 meters long, what is the area in square meters in which he is able to run?

   (A) 8
   (B) 16
   (C) 8π
   (D) 64π

8. If Megan needs to drive 328 miles in 4 hours, at what rate of speed must she drive?

   (A) 92 miles per hour
   (B) 82 miles per hour
   (C) 72 miles per hour
   (D) 67 miles per hour

9. If a jet travels at a constant rate of 270 miles per hour, approximately how many hours will it take to reach its destination 3,300 miles away?

   (A) 23.68
   (B) 18.91
   (C) 15.38
   (D) 12.22

10. If $a = 3$ and $b = 4$, what is the value of $a^2 + 2ab + b^2$?

    (A) 14
    (B) 24
    (C) 49
    (D) 144

11. If $x - y = 5$ and $4x + 6y = 20$, then $x + y =$

    (A) 3
    (B) 4
    (C) 5
    (D) 6

12. How many distinct prime factors are there of 726 ?

    (A) 2
    (B) 3
    (C) 4
    (D) 5

13. If n is an odd number, which of the following must be even?

    (A) $-2n - 1$
    (B) $2n + 1$
    (C) $2n - 1$
    (D) $4n$

14. If Jamie is in school for 6 hours per day, 5 days per week, how many seconds does Jamie spend in school in one week?

    (A) 1,108,000
    (B) 180,000
    (C) 108,000
    (D) 18,000

15. If it is snowing at a rate of 3.5 inches per hour and the storm is expected to continue at the same rate for the next 4 days. How many inches of snow accumulation can be expected?

    (A) 84
    (B) 168
    (C) 226
    (D) 336

16. Nicholas is x years old and Billy is three times as old as Nicholas. What was the sum of their ages, in years, 5 years ago?

    (A) $x - 5$
    (B) $2x + 2$
    (C) $3x - 10$
    (D) $4x - 10$

17. In a certain class, there are twice as many boys as girls. If the total number of students in the class is 36, how many boys are there?

    (A) 24
    (B) 18
    (C) 12
    (D) 9

18. At a party, $\frac{1}{3}$ of the guests drank only soda and $\frac{2}{5}$ of the guests drank only juice. If the remaining 16 guests had nothing to drink, then how many guests were at the party?

    (A) 60
    (B) 50
    (C) 45
    (D) 30

USE THIS SPACE FOR FIGURING.

GO ON TO THE NEXT PAGE ➡

19. If x and y are consecutive integers such that $xy = 6$ and y is greater than x, which of the following statements must be true?

   I. $x + y = 5$
   II. x is less than 6.
   III. $\dfrac{x}{y} = \dfrac{2}{3}$

   (A)   I only
   (B)   II only
   (C)   I and II
   (D)   I and III

20. Jenny has y baseball cards. She gives 5 cards to each of three different friends, and in return receives 2 cards from each friend. How many cards does Jenny have after the exchange?

   (A) $y - 9$
   (B) $y - 5$
   (C) $y + 3$
   (D) $y + 5$

21. If two fair coins are tossed simultaneously, what is the probability that two tails are thrown?

   (A) 1
   (B) $\dfrac{1}{2}$
   (C) $\dfrac{1}{4}$
   (D) $\dfrac{1}{8}$

22. A duplicating machine makes copies at a constant rate of 15 copies per minute. A certain copy job requires 600 copies. What fraction of the job will the machine finish in 5 minutes?

   (A) $\dfrac{1}{200}$
   (B) $\dfrac{1}{40}$
   (C) $\dfrac{1}{8}$
   (D) $\dfrac{1}{5}$

USE THIS SPACE FOR FIGURING.

GO ON TO THE NEXT PAGE ➡

23. Which of the following is a possible value of z if $2(z - 3) > 6$ and $z + 4 < 15$?

    (A)   3
    (B)   6
    (C)   7
    (D)   11

24. In a certain library there are 3 fiction books for every 8 nonfiction books. If the library has 600 nonfiction books, how many books does it have?

    (A)   2,200
    (B)   1,400
    (C)   825
    (D)   800

25. If $x + y$ equals an odd number and $x + z$ equals an even number, each of the following could be true EXCEPT

    (A) x is even and y is odd.
    (B) y is even and z is odd.
    (C) x and z are even and y is odd.
    (D) x and y are even and z is odd.

26. On the first test, Ted scored 7 points above the passing grade. On the second test he scored 12 points lower than he did on his first test. His score on the second test was

    (A)   19 points below the passing grade
    (B)   12 points below the passing grade
    (C)   5 points below the passing grade
    (D)   2 points above the passing grade

27. In a class, 70 percent of the students are right-handed, and the rest are left handed. If 70 percent of the left-handed students have brown eyes, then left handed students with brown eyes make up what percent of the entire class?

    (A)   14%
    (B)   21%
    (C)   30%
    (D)   49%

Questions 28 and 29 refer to the following definition:
For all real numbers q and r, let $q//r = (qr) - (q - r)$.

28. $8//2 =$

    (A)   6
    (B)   8
    (C)   10
    (D)   16

29. If $P//3 = 11$, then $P =$

    (A)   3
    (B)   4
    (C)   6
    (D)   7

GO ON TO THE NEXT PAGE ➡

30. If the product of integers a and b is 16 and a is greater than 4, then which of the following must be true?

   I. $b = 2$
   II.   The sum of a and b is greater than zero.
   III. a is greater than b.

(A) II only
(B) III only
(C) I and II
(D) II and III

31. In the figure to the right, what is the value of x ?

(A) 20
(B) 30
(C) 45
(D) 90

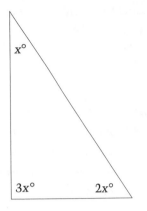

32. In the figure to the right, the distance from B to C is twice the distance from A to B and the distance from C to D is equal to half the distance from A to C. If the distance from B to C is 12, what is the distance from A to D ?

(A) 18
(B) 24
(C) 27
(D) 32

33. What is the greatest number of squares with sides of 2 centimeters that can be cut from a square with an area of 36 square centimeters?

(A) 4
(B) 9
(C) 18
(D) 36

34. If $x = 4y + 3$, then what does $x - 5$ equal?

(A) $4y - 8$
(B) $4y - 2$
(C) $4y + 5$
(D) $5y - 8$

35. A grocer buys oranges at a price of 4 for $1.00 and then sells them in his store for 40 cents each. How many oranges must he sell to earn a profit of $3.00 ?

(A) 2
(B) 10
(C) 15
(D) 20

GO ON TO THE NEXT PAGE ➡

USE THIS SPACE FOR FIGURING.

36. A wool sweater is on sale for $63 and a cotton sweater is on sale for $45. If the sale price for each sweater is 10% less than the original price, how much less did the cotton sweater cost than the wool sweater before either went on sale?

(A) $23.50
(B) $20.00
(C) $19.80
(D) $18.00

37. John finished $\frac{1}{3}$ of his homework assignment between 6:00 pm and 7:30 pm. He needs to finish the assignment by 11:00 pm. If he works at the same rate, what is the latest time that he can return to his homework?

(A) 7:45 pm
(B) 8:00 pm
(C) 8:30 pm
(D) 9:30 pm

38. There are twice as many men as women on a track team. Medals were given to $\frac{1}{3}$ of the women. If there are 45 men and women on the team, how many women received medals?

(A) 5
(B) 6
(C) 10
(D) 11

39. If m is greater than n, and n is greater than 4, which of the following is LEAST?

(A) $\frac{1}{4m}$

(B) $\frac{1}{4n}$

(C) $\frac{1}{4 + m}$

(D) $\frac{1}{4 + n}$

40. If $\frac{1}{5}$ of a number is less than 20, the number must be

(A) less than 4
(B) equal to 4
(C) greater than 4
(D) less than 100

GO ON TO THE NEXT PAGE ➡

USE THIS SPACE FOR FIGURING.

41. A 6-story apartment building has x apartments on each of its lower 3 floors and y apartments on each of its upper 3 floors. If 3 people live in each apartment, how many people live in the building?

(A) $3x + 3y$
(B) $3x + 3y + 3$
(C) $9x + 9y$
(D) $3x + 3y + 18$

42. Joe spent 20% of his allowance on tapes. Then he spent 10% of what was left on a movie. After the movie, he was left with what percent of his original allowance?

(A) 65%
(B) 70%
(C) 72%
(D) 75%

43. Each of the n members in an organization may invite up to 3 guests to a conference. What is the maximum number of members and guests who might attend the conference?

(A) $n + 3$
(B) $3n$
(C) $3n + 4$
(D) $4n$

44. A square rug with each side 4 meters long is placed on a square floor. If each side of the rug is one third the length of one side of the floor, what is the area, in square meters, of the floor?

(A) 144
(B) 96
(C) 64
(D) 16

45. The figure to the right is composed of six squares. How many rectangles are there in the figure?

(A) 20
(B) 18
(C) 15
(D) 12

GO ON TO THE NEXT PAGE ➡

46. If $-4a + 10 > 22$, then a must be

   (A) less than -3
   (B) less than -6
   (C) greater than -3
   (D) greater than 3

47. Package A weighs $1\frac{5}{6}$ kilograms and package B is $\frac{1}{2}$ kilogram lighter than package A. How many kilograms do the two packages weigh together?

   (A) $1\frac{1}{3}$

   (B) $2\frac{1}{3}$

   (C) $3\frac{1}{6}$

   (D) $3\frac{2}{3}$

48. The results of a census show that 15 out of every 50 people in City M live downtown. If City M has a population of 300,000, how many people live downtown?

   (A) 9,000
   (B) 20,000
   (C) 50,000
   (D) 90,000

49. Missy drives for 5 hours at an average speed of 50 kilometers per hour. She then travels for 3 more hours at an average speed of 40 kilometers per hour. What is the total distance, in kilometers, that she travels?

   (A) 290
   (B) 370
   (C) 380
   (D) 400

50. John has 3 quarters, 8 dimes, and 4 nickels in his pocket. He has no other coins in his pocket. If he reaches into his pocket and randomly pulls out one coin, what is the probability that he takes out a quarter?

   (A) $\frac{1}{5}$

   (B) $\frac{1}{4}$

   (C) $\frac{3}{8}$

   (D) $\frac{4}{5}$

IF YOU FINISH BEFORE TIME IS CALLED, YOU MAY CHECK YOUR WORK ON THIS SECTION ONLY. DO NOT TURN TO ANY OTHER SECTION IN THE TEST. **STOP**

Section 5
Time—30 Minutes

DIRECTIONS: Write an essay on the following prompt on the paper provided. Your essay should NOT exceed 2 pages and must be written in ink. Erasing is not allowed.

Prompt: <u>Technology makes the world smaller every day.</u>

Do you agree or disagree with this statement? Use examples from history, literature, or your own personal experience to support your point of view.

IF YOU FINISH BEFORE TIME IS CALLED, YOU MAY CHECK YOUR WORK ON THIS SECTION ONLY. DO NOT TURN TO ANY OTHER SECTION IN THE TEST. **STOP**

354 **KAPLAN**

Answer Explanations

Section 1: Verbal

Synonyms

1. **D** To **desecrate** is to commit a sacrilegious act—to **defile**.

2. **B** To **laud** is to **praise** in a lavish manner, e.g. "the spectators lauded the efforts of the competing athletes."

3. **B** To **avert** is to **prevent** something from occurring, e.g, "the disaster was averted by the air traffic controller."

4. **C** **Piety** is another word for religious **faith**.

5. **A** **Amoral** means without "without moral code." Ethics are a kind of moral code, so **unethical** is the best choice here.

6. **B** **Candor** means **honesty**—a "candid camera," for example, is one that shows real-life events.

7. **D** **Haughtiness** means excessive pride—**arrogance**. (C) **rudeness** was a tempting wrong answer choice, but haughty people aren't necessarily rude.

8. **B** To **verify** mean to **prove** something, e.g., "the existence of UFOs has never been verified."

9. **A** To **deceive** means to **trick**.

10. **C** Look for secondary definitions—a fiction is a story that is untrue, so one possible meaning for **fiction** is **falsehood**, e.g. "his reputation was largely based on the fiction that he had fought in WWII."

11. **A** Something that's **hardy** is **healthy**, e.g., "a hardy troop of soldiers."

12. **C** Something that's **lyrical** is like a singing voice—it's **musical**.

13. **A** Use roots here—META means change, and MORPH means shape. So the closest synonym is **change**.

14. **D** To **lament** for someone or something is to **grieve**.

15. **D** Something that's **arid** is **dry**, e.g. an arid desert. Word association could have worked here, if you'd thought of ARRID the deodorant.

16. **C** A **perceptive** person is **observant**—he or she is able to see perceive things quickly and understand them.

17. **D** An **adamant** person is convinced, resolute—**stubborn**, e.g,. "Dave was adamant about his decision to buy a Range Rover™."

18. **C** **Neutral** people or parties are impartial. They don't take sides—they're **unbiased**.

19. **B** **Docile** means **tame**, e.g., "the aggressive dog became docile in later life."

20. **B** **Wariness** means **caution**—if you're wary, you're apprehensive about a situation.

21. **A** **Rational** thinking means using the mind in a systematic manner—it's being **logical**, in other words.

22. **A** **Daring** is a word used to describe a **courageous** person or activity, e.g., "the daring scheme went disastrously wrong."

23. **A** To **donate** means to **contribute** money or possessions.

24. **B** **Tranquillity** is a state of **calm**.

Sentence Completions

25. **A** The clue words "come out at night" indicate that raccoons are **nocturnal**.

26. **C** The two clue words "normally" and "usual" suggest that both blanks mean more or less the same—(C) **amiable .. enthusiasm** works best here.

27. **A** Death is a **morbid** subject—making (A) the best choice here.

28. **B** You're looking for a contrast here; once a **religious** festival (B), the event is now **commercialized.**

29. **D** A person who is constantly changing his views, is described as **flighty**.

30. **C** You're looking for a positive word for the first blank, and a word meaning "deny" or "criticize" for the second blank. (C) **agility .. question** fits this description.

31. **A** Predict a synonym for "guilt" here—(A) **remorse** is the correct answer.

32. **C** The first blank should mean "tiring," so rule out choice (A). The only choice that means "tired" for the second blank is (C) **fatigued**. So **strenuous .. fatigued** is the correct answer.

33. **B** The phrase "not only..but.." indicates that the second word is slightly more extreme than the first. Since you're looking for negative-sounding words, (B) **predictable .. absurd** fits best.

34. **D** Predict a more extreme version of "respect" for the blank here; **revered** works best in this context.

35. **D** The first blank here should express the writer's incredulity—after all, it's pretty amazing that Chinese silk showed up in Egypt. (D)'s **incredible .. massive** best explains why this fact is so amazing.

36. **A** "At first" should have clued you into the contrast here—the house **seemed** frightening, but later proved **benign**, or friendly.

37. **B** You're looking for a contrast—once just a **myth**, UFO stories are now thought **plausible** or believable.

38. **A** Again, should be a contrast here—(A) **sparse** means terse, brief, minimal, and **verbose** means excessively wordy.

39. **D** The clues "charm his listeners" suggest a positive word here, such as (D) **engaging**.

40. **C** **Exhilarated** best captures the mixture of fear and enjoyment suggested by the sentence—consistent with a **first** trip on a raft.

Section 2: Math

1. **C**
$$Q + 7 - 8 + 3 = 23$$
$$Q + 2 = 23$$
$$Q = 21$$

2. **D** A kilogram is equal to 1,000 grams. Remember, "kilo" means 1,000. So a kilometer, for example, equals 1,000 meters.

3. **B** To solve this problem, you need to find a common denominator. In this case, the lowest common denominator is 36.
$$\frac{1}{9} + \frac{7}{12} + \frac{5}{6} = \frac{4}{36} + \frac{21}{36} + \frac{30}{36}$$
$$= \frac{55}{36}$$
$$= 1\frac{19}{36}$$

4. **B**
$$15\% \text{ of } 60 = (15\%)(60)$$
$$= (0.15)(60)$$
$$= 9$$

5. **C** To solve this problem, you first need to determine the limits of possible values for a:
$$a + 2 > 5$$
$$q > 3$$
$$a - 4 < 1$$
$$a < 5$$

So a is between 3 and 5. The only value from the answer choices that fits in the limits is (C) 4.

6. **D** To solve this equation, we first need to find the value of x.
$$2x + 4 = 26$$
$$2x = 30, \text{ so } x = 15$$

7. **D** The key to solving this problem is to take in the information one piece at a time. We're told that we have an equilateral hexagon. Equilateral means that all sides are equal: a hexagon has 6 sides. If we divide 6 into 42, we have the measure of one side: 7, so two sides would total 14.

8. **B** Angelo earns $2,000. Of this money, he spends 30% on rent. We can easily turn this information into an equation.

rent = 30% of $2,000
= (0.30)($2,000)
= $600

9. **D** The eggs cost 16 cents apiece. We need to figure out how many eggs can make up for the cost of 6 new chickens or 58 dollars. In other words, how many times does 16 cents divide into 58. Set this problem up as you would any division problem, paying attention to decimal places.

$$0.16\overline{)58.00}$$

$$16\overline{)5800} \quad 363$$

10. **C** Notice the use of the word "rate" in this problem. Don't be fooled by the terms "fuel" and "miles"—this is a straightforward rate problem and you want to set it up as such. Twelve gallons of fuel for 48 miles is the same as how many gallons for 60 miles?

$$\frac{12}{48} = \frac{x}{60}$$

$$48x = 12 \times 60$$

$$x = \frac{720}{48} = 15$$

11. **B** To add mixed numbers, add the whole number parts and add the fraction parts. (Sometimes the sum of the fraction parts will be greater than 1, in which case you would need to make some adjustments.) To add the fraction parts, find a common denominator.

$$1\frac{6}{11} + 1\frac{7}{22} = 1 + 1 + \frac{6}{11} + \frac{7}{22}$$

$$= 2 + \frac{12}{22} + \frac{7}{22}$$

$$= 2\frac{19}{22}$$

12. **C** Use the average formula:

$$\text{Average} = \frac{\text{Sum of the terms}}{\text{Number of terms}}$$

$$9 = \frac{\text{Sum}}{6}$$

$$\text{Sum} = 9 \times 6 = 54$$

13. **C** Let's consider each answer choice. (A) gives us the value $\frac{2}{3}$. But we know that x must be smaller than $\frac{1}{2}$, and $\frac{2}{3}$ is not so we an eliminate it. (B) proposes 0.47, but x must be smaller than $\frac{1}{3}$, and 0.47 is not. (C) gives us $\frac{1}{5}$, which is smaller than $\frac{1}{3}$, but larger than $\frac{1}{10}$ — it fits the given criteria. Since there can only be one correct answer there is no reason to check the last answer choice. (Choice (D) is wrong because $\frac{1}{20}$ is less than $\frac{1}{10}$ and x can not be less than $\frac{1}{10}$.

14. **D** The best way to solve this problem is to solve for a.

$$3a + 6a = 36$$
$$9a = 36$$
$$a = 4$$

15. **B** The easiest way to solve this problem is to convert $\frac{1}{4}$ to a decimal, 0.25, and then multiply. Again, make sure that you remember to count your decimal places.

$$(0.72) \times (0.25) = 0.18$$

16. **C** The easiest way to solve this problem is to break the diagram on the right into two rectangles. Then solve for each area and add them together.

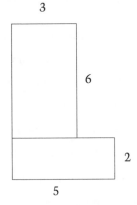

The area of the rectangle on top is $3 \times 6 = 18$. The area of the rectangle on bottom is $5 \times 2 = 10$. The total area is $18 + 10 = 28$.

17. **B** First you need to break down 48 into its prime factors, and then determine how may *different* ones there are.

$$48 = 2 \times 24$$
$$= 2 \times 2 \times 12$$
$$= 2 \times 2 \times 2 \times 6$$
$$= 2 \times 2 \times 2 \times 2 \times 3$$

There are only two different prime factors for 48; 2 and 3

18. **D** Again, the easiest way to solve this problem is to consider each factor individually. (A) cannot be the answer because 3 is a factor of 36 and also 48. Ditto for (B) 6 and (C) 12. The answer must be (D) 18. Remember as you do this problem that a factor is a number that divides evenly into another number.

19. **A** The formula for a cube is the length of a side cubed. We are told that the length of one side is 5. 5 cubed equals 125, or choice (A).

20. **D** Doubling the rate that we are given, we have 2 hours and 30 minutes for Jake to review 60 pages. We know that the answer cannot be letter (A). But, we need to figure out how long it will take Jack to review those final 10 pages. To do that, we can divide the rate it takes Jake to review 30 pages by 3; that should give us the rate it takes to read 10 pages. 1 hour and 15 minutes is the same as 75 minutes. A third of 75 is 25—we know it will take Jake 25 minutes to read ten pages. Put it all together and we have 2 hours and 55 minutes for Jack to read his history book.

21. **A** Remember to compare, not calculate: There is no reason to look for common denominators and solve here. The $\frac{1}{2}$ in column A is just slightly larger than the $\frac{2}{5}$ in column B. Both columns contain $\frac{3}{4}$, and are therefore equal. The $\frac{7}{8}$ in column A is also larger than the $\frac{7}{9}$ in column B, so overall, whatever the total value, Column A is larger than Column B.

22. **C** Put the expressions in Column A and Column B in the same form so they are easy to compare. First, simplify the value under Column A. It's easy to multiply these fractions together because they cancel easily, giving us a final value of $\frac{1}{20}$, which in decimal form is .05. The columns are equal.

23. **B** This problem is similar to the one above. First simplify the value under Column A, making sure that you cancel whenever possible. Under Column A we end up with the value $\frac{4}{5}$ which is less than 1. The value under Column B is $\frac{5}{4}$ which is greater than 1. So, the answer must be (B).

24. **A** The fastest way to solve this problem is to determine the value of x.

$$3x - 12 = 3x - 6x$$
$$-12 = = -6x$$
$$2 = x$$

So x equals 2. If you add 2 to x, you get 4, a value larger than the 2 in Column B. So Column A is larger.

25. **D** The answer to this problem is (D). All we know about x and y, is that both are positive. But we don't know their relative values: we don't know if x is greater than y or visa versa. Consequently, we can't determine if adding the number 1 to the value of x would make Column A greater, less than or equal to the value under Column B. The answer here must therefore be (D).

26. **B** Find the value of each column:

$$5\% \text{ of } (3 + 4) = 5\% \text{ of } 7$$
$$= (.05)(7)$$
$$= 0.35$$
$$4\% \text{ of } (3 \times 4) = 4\% \text{ of } 12$$
$$= (.04)(12)$$
$$= 0.48$$

27. **A** The easiest way to solve this problem is to change the value under Column B, a fraction, into a decimal. $\frac{9}{20}$ is the same as $\frac{45}{100}$ or .45. Clearly Column A, with a value of .46, is larger than Column B.

28. **B** This problem requires no math at all. You are given a certain amount of money—5 dollars. Can you buy more expensive items (32-cent stamps) or more cheaper items (29-cent stamps) with this money? You can buy more of the cheaper items, so the answer must be Column B.

29. **D** You're given that x is between $\frac{8}{9}$ and $\frac{1}{2}$, and you're asked to compare x to $\frac{2}{3}$. $\frac{2}{3}$ is between $\frac{8}{9}$ and $\frac{1}{2}$, but so are lots of other fractions, some less than $\frac{2}{3}$ and others greater than $\frac{2}{3}$. Column A could be greater than, equal to, or less than Column B, so the answer is (D).

30. **B** This is another problem that takes no math at all. We are told that x is negative. Before you start plugging in values for x, you should take a look at the expression under Column B; $(2x)(1x)$. If you multiply these xs together, whatever the value, the result would be positive. the value under Column A, however, would remain negative. Since a positive is always greater than a negative, the answer has to be (B).

31. **D** Don't be fooled by the number 8 under Column B. Column A asks you to find the perimeter of an octagon with sides of equal length. The problem is, we don't know what those lengths are. One side could equal 1, in which case the answer would be (C). One side could be 2, in which case the answer would be (A). We already have two possibilities, which tells us that the correct answer must be (D).

32. **B** The factors of 21 are 1, 3, 7, and 21. Of these only two are prime. Compare that to the value under Column B, 3, and the answer is clearly (B).

33. **A** Translate the expression into an equation.

$$\frac{5}{7} \text{ of } x \text{ is } 35.$$

$$\frac{5}{7}x = 35$$

$$x = 35 \times \frac{7}{5}$$

$$x = 49$$

34. **C** Remember the saying "A percent of B is equal to B percent of A"? If you did, then this question was a breeze. If not, you want to commit that rule to memory. In this case, 98% of 51 is $0.98 \times 51 = 49.98$, and 51% of 98 is $0.51 \times 98 = 49.98$. The columns are equal.

35. **B** There are a few ways to solve this problem. The first is to actually calculate the math. 20% of 42 is the same as (.20)(42) or 8.4. The other way to do this problem is to realize that 20% of 42 is the same as taking $\frac{1}{5}$ of 42. We know that $\frac{1}{5}$ of 45 is 9, the value under Column B. But we want $\frac{1}{5}$ of 42 which will be less than 9. In either case, the answer must be (B).

36. **A** Ratios when expressed as fractions have value. The ratio of green to white marbles is 3 to 4, or $\frac{3}{4}$. The ratio of white and red marbles to the total number of marbles is 6 to 9 or $\frac{6}{9}$, which can be reduced to $\frac{2}{3}$. Since $\frac{3}{4}$ is larger than $\frac{2}{3}$, the answer is (A).

37. **D** Don't bother actually solving for x. This is another case where we are not given enough information about a variable to determine the relative values of Column A or Column B. We can determine that $\frac{157}{x} \times 2$ equals $\frac{314}{x}$. We also know that x is positive, but that's all. We don't know if x equals 1, or if it is a fraction. The relative values of Column A and Column B would vary depending on that information. Since we don't know anything else, the answer must be (D).

38. **C** Be careful here. The problem asks for the number of different <u>sums</u> of a and b, not the number of different combinations. Some combinations yield the same sums. Let's go over them:
4 + 3 = 7: That's one sum.
4 + 6 = 10: That's two.
7 + 3 = 10: This value is the same as the one above, so we are still at two.
7 + 6 = 13: That's three.
8 + 3 = 11: That's four.
8 + 6 = 14: That's five.

39. **A** These two values are almost exactly the same, with the exception of the positive and negative signs. To determine which one is larger, we first need to simplify both sides. Column A simplifies to –2x + 5. Column B simplifies –2x – 5. We can now see that these two expressions are identical, except that Column A has a positive 5 and Column B has a negative 5. It doesn't matter what -2x equals; whatever it equals, Column A is still larger than Column B because it has a positive value added to it. The answer is (A).

40. **A** We know that the value under Column A must be less than 5.5. The only important question we need to answer is the value of y, or Column B. Since x + y must be greater than 11, and since x must be less than 5.5, we know that y must be greater than 5.5. For example, let's say that x is just barely less than 5.5 – say x equals 5.4. In this case, y would have to equal 5.6, and Column B would be greater than Column A.

Section 3: Reading Comprehension

Porcupines passage

The first passage on this test is about the porcupine, an animal whose fur consists of thousands of tough, sharp quills. The author gives several facts about the quills — that they're barbed, how long they are, and what kind of damage they can do. The passage ends with a description of how the porcupine uses its tail as a defensive weapon, lashing out at attackers in a way that makes it seem as if the quills have been thrown like darts, even though they haven't been.

1. **C** The passage's first sentence calls a porcupine's quills its "defensive armament." The last sentence talks about how the porcupine uses its tail to fight off attackers. So porcupines use their quills to defend themselves, and choice (C) is correct. (A) and (B) are plausible reasons why a porcupine would attack another animal, but the passage only describes the porcupine as taking defensive action. The heat-conserving properties, if any, of the porcupine's quills (D) are never mentioned.

2. **B** The passage opens with the statement that porcupines have "justifiable confidence" in the defensive capabilities of their quills. Another word for justifiable is understandable, choice (B), the correct answer. "Intellectual" (A) implies that porcupines have mental powers comparable to humans, which we know isn't true. "Unreasonable" (C) and "defiant (D) suggest the opposite of "understandable," implying that porcupines have no reason to be so confident—when, as we see, they do have good reason.

3. **D** Porcupine quills are long sharp spines that, when touched, stick in the attacker. In the same way, cactus needles are long sharp spines that, when touched, stick in the attacker, so (D) is correct here. Teeth, claws and horns (choices A, B and C) are not outward coverings; they're also shaped differently than quills and needles, and can be used for other things than for defense. So (D) remains the best answer.

4. **A** Sentence 4 says that the porcupine's longest quills are on its back and flank, but that the shorter quills on its tail "do the most damage." You can infer, then, that the longest quills aren't as important for defense as the shorter quills on the porcupine's tail; choice (A),

which restates this idea, is correct. (B) implies that the longest quills are incapable of harming attackers. But this contradicts the previous sentence, which says that the quills are so loosely set in the skin that any forceful touch will cause them to stick into the attacker. The passage says that each porcupine has up to 30,000 quills, but not that quills of a certain length are less numerous (C) or sharper (D) than quills of any other length.

Log Cabins passage

The second passage is about log cabins, and the era of their greatest popularity—a period from 1780 to 1850. The author describes early simple cabins and grand later ones, and then discusses the factors that led to a decline in the log cabin's popularity, factors like the greater availability of hardware and building materials, the rising popularity of the Greek Revival style of house, and the spread of the railroads. The passage ends with a brief description of what happened to most log cabins as their heyday ended.

5. **C** The first sentence says that "a great number of settlers forged westward." What word plugs in best for "forged"? Choice (C)'s "moved." "Fled" (A) incorrectly implies that the settlers were running away from something, "wandered" (B) that their movements were aimless, without purpose. "Returned" (D) suggests that the settlers had already been out west, which makes little sense in context.

6. **D** A tough question. The Greek Revival style is described as becoming increasingly popular, "with [i.e., because of] its democratic roots in ancient Greece..." So the origins of the new style lay in the ancient democracy of Greece —a fact that might well have appealed to the citizens of a young democratic nation like the U.S.—and (D) is the best answer. The passage never suggests that there had been a general desire to replace log cabins (A), and never mentions contemporary Greek architects (B) or devoutly religious Americans (C).

7. **A** The author indicates that Greek Revival houses became more popular than log cabins for two reasons: the democratic roots of the Greek Revival style, and the templed fronts of these houses, which faced the street. This last feature—that the fronts of Greek Revival houses faced the street—suggests that log cabins became less popular because they didn't always face the street, which makes choice (A) correct. The passage doesn't suggest that either style of house had indoor plumbing (B),

or that log cabins could not have glass windows (C). And while log cabins may well have been built near lakes and rivers (D), there's no suggestion that Greek Revival homes were not. So (A) is best here.

8. **B** The question stem's reference to limiting factors in the architecture of log cabins recalls sentence 6: "Climate and the proximity of the local forest no longer set architectural limits." What does this mean? It means that, with the new railroads bringing lumber and hardware to formerly isolated regions, a settler's choice of which house to build was no longer dictated by local weather and the distance to the nearest forest. Choice (B) restates this latter point, and it's correct. Choice (A) is wrong because, unlike logs from the local forest, nails were not widely available. Choices (C) and (D) bring up issues that aren't mentioned at all in the passage, and so cannot be inferred.

9. **D** The passage's final sentence notes that, after the 1850's, log structures housed livestock but "fewer and fewer people." So most log structures built after 1850 housed animals, choice (D).

Plague passage

Next up is a passage about the plague, an epidemic which killed one-third of the people in Europe in 13th and 14th centuries. The author says that, ironically, the plague created some beneficial changes in European society. One of these changes—the focal point of the passage—was in the medical profession. The plague created a shortage of doctors, allowing people with new ideas to enter the profession. In addition, having been failed by the old doctors with their Latin medical texts, ordinary people began clamoring for medical texts printed in everyday languages. These were eventually published, making medical knowledge more accessible to everyone.

10. **C** As noted above, the primary focus of the passage is how at least one good thing came out of the terrible tragedy of the plague. Choice (C) correctly restates this idea. (A) and (B) focus too narrowly on details mentioned in sentences 1 and 4. (D) is closer to the mark, but it too is a detail in the larger focus of the passage.

11. **A** Plug the choices into the sentence in question, and (A) is clearly best: the epidemic caused enormous changes in European society. The changes were needed (B), but needed by the society, not by the plague itself.

"Accelerated" (C) means moved faster, which implies that the changes were already occurring before the plague. But the passage never suggests that this was so. "Offered" (D) doesn't work at all.

12. **C** Sentence 6 says that, when the plague created a shortage of doctors, "people with new ideas" rushed in to fill the void, bringing needed reform (sentence 3) to the medical profession. This suggests that, prior to the plague, the medical profession was in need of new ideas—sweeping changes—which makes choice (C) correct. The shortage of doctors (A) occurred during and after the plague, not before it. As for (B), while sentence 5 says that universities were short on medical professors, there's no evidence that medical care was available only to students in the pre-plague years. And (D) distorts the final sentence, which says that people demanded medical texts printed in their own languages, not the language of Latin. This doesn't mean that, before the plague, medicine was only practiced in Latin-speaking countries. (Latin is, in fact, and was even then, a "dead" language, the language of the long-vanquished Roman Empire.)

13. **B** Take another look at the last sentence of the passage. It says that medical texts gradually began to be published in everyday languages instead of in Latin, "making medical knowledge more accessible." You can infer from this that, after the 1300s, easy-to-read medical texts were probably more available to the general public, an idea restated in correct choice (B). The passage never indicates that a cure for the plague (A) would soon be found (in fact, it would not be found for several centuries). As for (C), just because more medical texts were published in everyday languages after the plague doesn't mean that, a hundred years later, none were written in Latin. Finally, (D) is completely unsupported by the passage.

Orienteering passage

The fourth passage is about the sport of orienteering, in which competitors make their way across unfamiliar terrain using only a map and a compass. The author focuses on the notion that the most important element of orienteering is choosing a good route. Why? Because the shortest route from point A to point B is rarely the fastest or easiest way.

14. **B** What defines orienteering, if not having a compass and a map? Orienteers have to "nav-

igate their way cross-country along an unfamiliar course." Therefore, a hiker with a map and compass is NOT orienteering if she travels over a known, familiar route, and (B) is correct. Choices (A) and (B) propose rules that are never mentioned in the passage. (D) describes an orienteer who takes the "crude" approach.

15. **D** As sentence 2 puts it, "the most important question in orienteering is not compass bearing but choice of route," which eliminates choice (A) and makes choice (D) correct. While it is no doubt important to avoid hazardous terrain, (B), and to overcome obstacles quickly, (C), the passage places the highest priority on the choice of route.

16. **B** The competitor in question climbs a mountain to take the most direct route, but sentences 3 and 4 say that this is "seldom the best," and that orienteers "tend to disdain" competitors who do so as crude and lacking intellectual finesse, or sophistication, choice (B). (A) is wrong because the competitor's beeline approach will probably put him at a disadvantage in terms of both time and energy. The beeline approach may be stupid, but the author never says it's against the rules (C), or that it can endanger other competitors (D). So (B) is best.

17. **D** The passage never mentions running or backpacks (A), swimming (B), or setting up campsites (C). So (D) must be correct. And in fact, the final sentence of the passage notes that orienteers "are always making" quick calculations of the times and distances involved in various possible routes.

Night Terrors passage

Next up is a passage about two psychological phenomena: first, nightmares, and second, something called night terrors, where the sleeper, usually a child, wakes up in great fright with no memory of having dreamed. The passage begins with the statement that, while nightmares and night terrors used to be confused one with the other, researchers now know they are two different phenomena. The rest of the passage focuses on night terrors, noting that they're not really dangerous, that parents should use common sense, taking precautions and not worrying unduly. Let's take a look at the questions.

18. **B** Two phenomena, long "confounded" under one heading, are now known to be separate things. The word in question, then, should

mean confused, or mixed-up, choice (B). None of the other words means anything remotely similar to "confounded."

19. **C** The correct answer, (C), restates the first sentence of the passage. None of the other choices is suggested, even (D), which is a distorted echo of the passage's final sentence. The author says there that children suffering from night terrors should usually not be medicated. This is a far cry from saying that sleep researchers used to prescribe medication for such children, but have recently stopped.

20. **A** Sentence 2 says that a nightmare "is an actual, detailed dream." Choice (A) correctly restates this fact. No mention is made of dream fragments (B), hallucinations (C), or trances (D).

21. **C** What do we know about the parents of children who suffer from night terrors? That these parents themselves sometimes find their child's experience "horrifying." That a child suffering from night terrors can make a parent "anxious." We can infer, then, that the parents find night terrors nearly as frightening as the children do, and (C) is correct. Choice (A) is the opposite of what the author says. (B) makes a hereditary leap; the passage never suggests that these parents also suffered night terrors when they were children. And the last sentence of the passage implies, if anything, that a doctor usually should not be consulted at all, rather than as soon as possible (D).

22. **D** The difference between nightmares and night terrors, choice (A), is defined in sentences 2 and 3. The question in (B) is answered in the second-to-last sentence of the passage. Sentence 3 notes that the child waking from a night terror does not remember dreaming, choice (C). This leaves (D) as correct, and indeed, the author merely advises a sleep schedule, never explaining why a sleep schedule helps reduce night terrors.

Neanderthals passage

This passage is about the Neanderthal, an early human that lived in Europe and Asia until about 35,000 years ago. The passage puts forth two ideas: first, that Neanderthals were physically very different from modern humans and second, that despite their reputation to the contrary, Neanderthals were probably quite intelligent. The passage concludes with a teaser: the disappearance of this capable creature mystifies and fascinates scientists, and is "perhaps the most talked-about issue in human origins research today."

23. **A** All four choices are physical attributes of the Neanderthal. In the author's description of Neanderthals, found in sentence 3, "massive limb bones" are the first item on the list. A "limb" is an arm or a leg, so you can infer from this that most Neanderthals had big arms, choice (A). You can't infer, however, that their legs were bowed, choice (C), because "bowed" implies shape, not size. The set of Neanderthal eyes, (A), and the breadth of their feet, (D), are never mentioned.

24. **C** The opening sentence says that Neanderthals lived "throughout Europe and western Asia," which makes (C) correct. The passage never says what kind of dwellings they lived in (A), how they hunted (B), or whether they lived on all the continents (D) and not just the two mentioned in the correct answer.

25. **C** The author says that Neanderthals, unlike modern humans, had "massive limb bones," and "enormous physical strength." Modern humans, then probably have less physical strength than their Neanderthal cousins, and choice (C) is correct. No information is given on either species' eyesight (A), sense of smell (B), or amount of body hair (D).

26. **D** The only reference to what modern humans think of Neanderthals comes at the beginning of sentence 4: "yet despite the Neanderthals' reputation for low intelligence..." Choice (D) is thus the correct inference.

27. **C** The word "question" appears only once in the passage, in the final sentence. We know from the previous sentence that Neanderthals vanished or died out around 35,000 years ago. "The question of what became of the Neanderthals..." Therefore, (C) is correct. The questions of the Neanderthals' diet (A), migratory patterns (B), and origins (D) are never raised in the passage.

Magic passage

The seventh passage is about magic. The author's big point is that, for a magician, the art of deception is more important than mechanical gimmicks such as trap doors or mirrors. Magicians depend above all else on timing and misdirecting the audience's attention. The author gives one example of how misdirection need not be small and subtle: a gorilla riding across the stage on a unicycle to distract the audience from noticing his assistant being

whisked offstage. That's it: deception, or stagecraft, is more important than the mechanics of magic.

28. **C** The question stem takes you back to the first sentence of the passage, where the author says that mirrors and trapdoors are less important than the art of deception. Two sentences later, the author, expanding on this point, says that "presentation and timing are everything." You can infer, then, that mirrors and trapdoors are less important than presentation and timing, choice (C). More recent devices (A) are not mentioned in the passage. (B) is never suggested, either. And (D) misses the point: a successful magician tries to conceal all such gimmicks from even the most perceptive audience members.

29. **D** The quoted word appears in sentence 2, which says a magician must be skilled in misdirection, "the fine art of prompting an audience to look elsewhere at the crucial moment." Plugging in the words in the choices, (D) works best: a magician must persuade an audience to look elsewhere at the crucial moment. (A) is wrong, since if the audience is told to look elsewhere, they will of course do nothing of the sort. (B) doesn't make sense in context. (C) is a little tempting, since a gorilla riding across the stage would no doubt be entertaining. But "entertaining" does not mean the same thing as "prompting," so (D) is best here.

30. **C** The main idea question. As noted above, the author's focus is on magic—specifically, the idea that misdirection is more important to a magician's success than mechanical gimmicks such as mirrors or trapdoors. This eliminates choices (A) and (B), which focus on the gimmicks, and points to choice (C) as correct. (D) focuses too narrowly on sentence 3, where the author tries to educate you about how a magician practices deception. But the deception, and not an audience's perception of it, is the point here, so (C) is best.

31. **B** Again, back to sentence 3. As the author says, when a magician waves his hand grandly, "he is generally trying to divert your attention from the other [hand]." Thus, choice (B) is correct.

Wigs passage

The eighth passage is about wigs, the wigs worn by American colonists in the years before the American Revolution. The author details what kinds of wigs were available, noting that those made of human hair were the most desirable and expensive. The passage ends with the point that, when the American and French Revolutions occurred, anything that seemed overly extravagant or status-conscious became very unpopular, and so wigs fell out of fashion.

32. **C** Let's take the choices one by one. (A) doesn't sound right; the author doesn't go into the "elaborate construction" of American wigs. (B) is too general. The passage focuses on one particular English import: wigs. Furthermore, as sentence 3 notes, by the time of the Revolution, most American colonies had their own wigmakers. Skipping to choice (D), we find it has the same problem as (B): too general. That of course leaves (C) as correct. And it's true: the author focuses primarily on a particular fashion—the wearing of wigs— and the effect that historical events such as the American and French Revolutions had on this fashion.

33. **D** Human-hair wigs are mentioned in sentence 2, which says that cheaper wigs were made of horse or goat hair or duck feathers, while "the wealthy chose expensive wigs" made of human hair. If these human-hair wigs were so expensive, then you can infer that poor people rarely wore them, making choice (D) correct. The relative ease of maintenance of human and horsehair wigs (A) is never discussed in the passage. Nor does the author mention which wigs were fashionable in France (B). And (C) is a particularly gruesome piece of fiction.

34. **A** The first half of sentence 3 says that, in the beginning of the wig craze, most Americans wore wigs imported from England. This means that there probably weren't a lot of wigmakers in the Colonies. The second half of sentence 3 says that, by the start of the Revolutionary War, "numerous wigmakers were plying their trade in the Colonies." So you can infer that the number of wigmakers living in the Colonies must have increased considerably by the time of the Revolution, and (A) is correct. Sentence 3 is the only information we get about Colonial wigmakers, so statements (B), (C) and (D) are never suggested in the passage.

35. **B** "Infatuated with" means having a crush on, being in love with or fond of someone or something. Therefore, (B) is correct. None of the phrases in choices (A), (C) and (D) has a meaning similar to "infatuated with."

Coyotes passage

The final passage on this test is about coyotes. The author's main focus is not on the behavioral habits of living coyotes, but rather on the evolution of the coyote as found in the fossil record. Both the coyote and the wolf, we learn, had a common ancestor living in North America as long as three million years ago. One or two million years ago, the coyote and the wolf became separate species. As time passed, other species such as the mammoth and the saber-tooth tiger lived and became extinct, but the coyote endured —basically the same primitive animal, but still marvelously adaptable to its environment.

36. **A** In most passages, the main idea is stated in the first or second sentence. Here the main idea becomes clear only at the end: that the coyote has endured for millions of years without evolving into a more advanced species—a point restated in correct choice (A). (B) focuses on a detail, how other species came and went. But these species are described in order to provide a contrast with the coyote, which not only avoided extinction, but did so without evolving. (C) has the same problem: the author's point is that, unlike other animals, the coyote did not change—it survived by staying the same. And (D) is a passing detail found in sentence 4—not significant enough to be the primary focus.

37. **C** "Modern" dogs are mentioned only in the first sentence, which says that coyotes are "one of the most primitive of living dogs." This suggests that modern dogs are relatives of coyotes, as stated in (C). Dire wolves are extinct "canids"; we don't know from the passage whether they're related to modern dogs or not, but it's a pretty safe bet that modern dogs are not "direct descendants of dire wolves, as (A) suggests. Where modern dogs live (B) is not mentioned, but again, common sense suggests they're found everywhere, not just in North America. The evolutionary flexibility of modern dogs (D) is not discussed in the passage.

38. **D** A fairly easy detail question. Sentence 2 says that "a close relative of the contemporary coyote existed here two to three million years ago." The choice closest to this estimate is (D), and it's correct.

39. **D** Why does the author mention mammoths and saber-tooth tigers? Because they lived and became extinct, while the ever-adaptable coyote endured. In other words, these species died out because they failed to adapt as the

coyote did, and choice (D) is correct. Neither animal in question is described as a relative of the coyote (A). Unlike wild horses, mammoths and tigers are not described as having left North America by land bridge (C), but that's beside the point. These species died out because they couldn't adapt—as the coyote did. And the author never says that jackals hunted any species into extinction (D).

40. **B** Here's a word-in-context question that really requires you to know the meaning of the word —the word, in this case, being "galleon." Maybe you've come across it in pirate stories; a galleon is a kind of ship. So the idea that other horses "returned on galleons" means that horses, who had left North America by land bridge, returned to the continent when brought by ship, making choice (B) correct. None of the other choices picks up on the proper meaning of "galleon."

Section 4: Math

1. **C** $(x - 2)(x + 5)$ will equal 0 when either factor $(x - 2)$ or $(x + 5)$ is 0. That's when x is 2 or –5.

2. **D** Set up a proportion. 2 gallons for 875 square feet is the same as x gallons for 4,375 square feet:

$$\frac{2}{875} = \frac{x}{4,375}$$
$$875x = 2 \times 4,375$$
$$875x = 8,750$$
$$x = \frac{8,750}{875} = 10$$

3. **B** Use the formula for the area of a triangle:

$$\text{Area} = \frac{1}{2} \text{(base)(height)}$$

$$= \frac{1}{2} \text{(4 in.)(6 in.)} = 12 \text{ sq. in.}$$

4. **D** The sides of an equilateral triangle are equal in length, so $3x + 1$ and $x + 7$ are equal:

$$3x + 1 = x + 7$$
$$3x - x = 7 - 1$$
$$2x = 6$$
$$x = 3$$

Plug $x = 3$ back into either of the expressions $3x + 1$ and $x + 7$ and you'll find that the length of each side is 10.

5. **B** 65 times 10^2 means 65 times 100, or 6,500. 31 times 10^3 means 31 times 1,000, or 31,000. Add 6,500 and 31,000 and 12 and you get 37,512.

6. **C** He lost 20% of $120,000, which is 0.20 times $120,000, or $24,000.

7. **D** Use the formula for the area of a circle:

$$\text{Area} = \pi \text{ (radius)}^2$$
$$= \pi \text{ (8 meters)}^2$$
$$= 64\pi \text{ square meters}$$

8. **B** Rate is distance divided by time. 328 miles divided by 4 hours is $\frac{328}{4} = 82$ miles per hour.

9. **D** If distance equals rate times time, then time equals distance divided by rate. Here the distance is 3,300 miles and the rate is 270 miles per hour. 3,300 miles divided by 270 miles per hour is $\frac{3,300}{270} = 12.22$ hours.

10. **C** Plug $a = 3$ and $b = 4$ into the expression:

$$a^2 + 2ab + b^2 = 3^2 + 2(3)(4) + 4^2$$
$$= 9 + 24 + 16$$
$$= 49$$

11. **C** Look what happens when you just add the equations as presented:

$$x - y = 5$$
$$\frac{4x + 6y = 20}{5x + 5y = 25}.$$

Now just divide both sides by 5 and you get $x + y = 5$.

12. B Break 726 down to its prime factorization step-by-step by factoring out any prime factor you see one at a time:

$$726 = 2 \times 363$$
$$= 2 \times 3 \times 121$$
$$= 2 \times 3 \times 11 \times 11$$

The distinct prime factors are 2, 3, and 11. That's 3 distinct prime factors.

13. D Plug any odd number in for n and evaluate the answer choices. If you take $n = 3$, you'll find that (A) is $-2(3) - 1 = -7$; (B) is $2(3) + 1 = 7$; (C) is $2(3) - 1 = 5$; and (D) is $4(3) = 12$. Only (D) is even.

14. C 6 hours a day for 5 days is 30 hours. 30 hours is $30 \times 60 = 1{,}800$ minutes, and 1,800 minutes is $1{,}800 \times 60 = 108{,}000$ seconds.

15. D There are $4 \times 24 = 96$ hours in 4 days. 96 hours of snow at 3.5 inches per hour is $96 \times 3.5 = 336$ inches.

16. D Today Nicholas is x years old and Billy is $3x$ years old. Five years ago Nicholas was $x - 5$ years old and Nicholas was $3x - 5$, so the sum of their ages was $(x - 5) + (3x - 5) = 4x - 10$.

17. A If there are twice as many boys as girls, then $\frac{2}{3}$ of them are boys and $\frac{1}{3}$ are girls. Two-thirds of 36 is 24.

18. A The $\frac{1}{3}$ who drank soda only and the $\frac{2}{5}$ who drank juice only account for $\frac{1}{3} + \frac{2}{5} = \frac{5}{15} + \frac{6}{15} = \frac{11}{15}$ of the guests. The 16 who drank nothing therefore account for the other $\frac{4}{15}$. So you want to find out what number multiplied by $\frac{4}{15}$ will give you 16:

$$\frac{4}{15}x = 16$$

$$x = 16 \times \frac{15}{4} = 4 \times 15 = 60$$

19. B You might think that x has to be 2 and y has to be 3, but in fact there's another pair of consecutive integers that have a product of 6: -3 and -2. So what you know is that either $x = 2$ and $y = 3$, or $x = -3$ and $y = -2$. All three statements are true in the first case (when x and y are positive), but only statement II is true in the second case (when x and y are negative).

20. A She starts with y cards. Giving away 5 to each of 3 friends means giving away $3 \times 5 = 15$, leaving her with $y - 15$. Receiving 2 from each of 3 friends means receiving $3 \times 2 = 6$, leaving her with $y - 15 + 6 = y - 9$.

21. C For each coin the probability of tails is $\frac{1}{2}$, The combined probability is the product of the separate probabilities: $\frac{1}{2} \times \frac{1}{2} = \frac{1}{4}$.

22. C Five minutes at 15 copies per minute is $5 \times 15 = 75$ copies. 75 out of 600 is:

$$\frac{75}{600} = \frac{1}{8}$$

23. C Simplify each inequality:

$$2(z - 3) > 6$$
$$2z - 6 > 6$$
$$2z > 6 + 6$$
$$2z > 12$$
$$z > 6$$

$$z + 4 < 15$$
$$z < 15 - 4$$
$$z < 11$$

So z is between 6 and 11. The only answer choice that qualifies is (C), 7.

24. C Three fiction books for every 8 nonfiction books means that 8 out of $3 + 8$, or $\frac{8}{11}$ of all the books are nonfiction. The 600 nonfiction books are $\frac{8}{11}$ of the number you're looking for, so:

$$\frac{8}{11}x = 600$$

$$x = 600 \times \frac{11}{8} = \frac{6{,}600}{8} = 825$$

25. D (D) is impossible because if x and y were even and z were odd, then $x + y$ would be even and $x + z$ would be odd.

26. C If you call the passing grade x, then his second score was $x + 7$, and his third score was $x + 7 - 12 = x - 5$, which is 5 less than x.

27. B If 70 percent are right-handed and the rest are left-handed, then $100 - 70 = 30$ percent are left-handed. Of that 30 percent, 70 percent have brown hair. Seventy percent of 30 percent is $(0.70)(0.30) = 0.21$, or 21 percent.

28. **C** Plug $q = 8$ and $r = 2$ into the definition:
$$q//r = (qr) - (q - r)$$
$$8//2 = (8 \times 2) - (8 - 2)$$
$$= 16 - 6 = 10$$

29. **B** Plug $q = P$ and $r = 3$ into the definition:
$$q//r = (qr) - (q - r)$$
$$P//3 = (P \times 3) - (P - 3)$$
$$= 3P - P + 3$$
$$= 2P + 3$$

Set that equal to 11, and solve for P:
$$2P + 3 = 11$$
$$2P = 11 - 3$$
$$2P = 8$$
$$P = 4$$

30. **D** Since a is anything greater than 4, a can be 8 pr 16, so b doesn't have to be 2—which eliminates statement I. But you do know that b has to be positive, because a is positive (it's greater than 4) and the product of a and b is positive (it's 16). Therefore the sum of a and b is positive, and statement II is true. And lastly, when $a = 8$, $b = 2$; and when $a = 16$, $b = 1$; so 16 has two square roots, a is greater than b, and statement III is true.

31. **B** The three angles have to add up to 180°, so:
$$x + 2x + 3x = 180$$
$$6x = 180$$
$$x = 30$$

32. **C** AB is half of BC, which is given as 12, so $AB = 6$, and $AC = 6 + 12 = 18$. CD is half of AC, so $CD = 9$, and thus $AD = AB + BC + CD = 6 + 12 + 9 = 27$.

33. **B** A square with an area of 36 square centimeters has sides of length 6 centimeters. Thus each side of the large square gets cut into thirds, and the whole large square gets divided into $3 \times 3 = 9$ smaller squares:

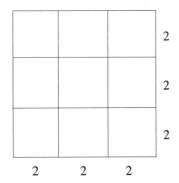

34. **B** Just subtract 5 from both sides of the given equation:
$$x = 4y + 3$$
$$x - 5 = 4y + 3 - 5$$
$$= 4y - 2$$

35. **D** Four for a dollar means 25 cents each. Selling them for 40 cents each means a profit of 15 cents on every orange sold. To get a total profit of \$3.00, he must sell $\frac{\$3.00}{\$0.15} = \frac{300}{15} = 20$ oranges.

36. **B** Each sale price is 90% of the original price. \$63 is 90% of what?
$$.90x = \$63$$
$$x = \$\frac{63}{.90} = \$70$$

The original price of the wool sweater was \$70. And \$45 is 90% of what?
$$.90y = \$45$$
$$y = \$\frac{45}{.90} = \$50$$

The original price of the cotton sweater was \$20. The difference was \$20.

37. **B** It took him a hour and a half to do the first one third, so it will take him twice that long—or 3 hours—to do the remaining two-thirds. To finish by 11:00 P.M., he must resume by 8:00 P.M.

38. **A** If there are twice as many men as women on the team, then two-thirds of the team members are men and one-third are women. One-third of 45 is 15, so there are 15 women. One-third of those 15 women received medals, so that's 5 women medal-winners.

39. **A** The four fractions you're comparing all have the same numerator (1) and they all have positive denominators, so the fraction with the least value be the one with the greatest denominator. m is greater than n, so $4m$ is greater than $4n$, and $4 + m$ is greater than $4 + n$. That eliminates (B) and (D). And since m is greater than 4, $4m$ is greater than $4 + m$. Thus (A) has the greatest denominator.

40. **D** Translate into algebra. If one-fifth of a number is less than 20, then:

$$\frac{1}{5}x < 20$$

$$x < 20 \times \frac{5}{1}$$

$$x < 100$$

41. **C** The lower three floors have a total of $3x$ apartments. The upper three floors have a total of $3y$ apartments. That's a total of $3x + 3y$ apartments in the building. If there are 3 people in each apartment, then the total number of people is 3 times $(3x + 3y)$, or $9x + 9y$.

42. **C** After spending 20% on tapes, Joe had 80% left. He then spent 10% of that, or 8%, leaving 72%.

43. **D** If every one of the n members invited 3 guests, that would be a total of $3n$ guests. n members plus $3n$ guests adds up to $n + 3n = 4n$ attendees.

44. **A** If each side of the 4-by-4 rug is one-third of the sides of the floor, then it's a 12-by-12 floor, which would have an area of 144 square meters.

45. **B** Each of the 6 squares is a rectangle. Plus there are these 3 rectangles:

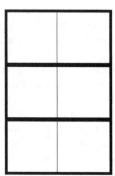

Plus there are these 2 rectangles:

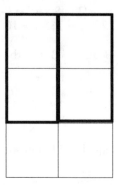

And these 2:

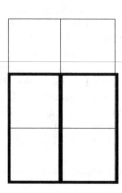

And these 2:

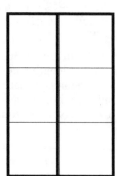

Plus this one:

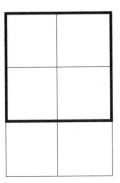

And this one:

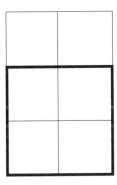

And lastly this one:

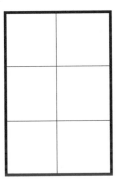

That's a total of 6 + 3 + 2 + 2 + 2 + 1 + 1 + 1 = 18

46. **A** Solve the inequality. First subtract 10 from both sides:

$$-4a + 10 > 22$$
$$-4a > 22 - 10$$
$$-4a > 12$$

Now divide both sides by -4, remembering to reverse the inequality sign:

$$-4a > 12$$
$$\frac{-4a}{-4} < \frac{12}{-4}$$
$$a < -3$$

47. **C** B weighs $1\frac{5}{6} - \frac{1}{2} = 1\frac{5}{6} - \frac{3}{6} = 1\frac{2}{6}$ kilograms, and the two together weigh $1\frac{5}{6} + 1\frac{2}{6} = 2\frac{7}{6} = 3\frac{1}{6}$ kilograms.

48. **D** Set up a proportion. 15 out of 50 is the same as how many out of 300,000 ?

$$\frac{15}{50} = \frac{x}{300,000}$$

$$50x = 15 \times 300,000$$

$$x = \frac{15 \times 300,000}{50} = 90,000$$

49. **B** Five hours at 50 kpm is (5 hours) × (50 kilometers per hour) = 250 kilometers. Three hours at 40 kpm is (3 hours) × (40 kilometers per hour) = 120 kilometers. The total distance, then, is 250 + 120 = 370 kilometers.

50. **A** Three quarters out of 15 coins means a probability of $\frac{3}{15} = \frac{1}{5}$.

19

Scoring Your ISEE
Practice Test

The ISEE calculates scores through a formula that compares each student's score against the scores of other students of the same grade level. The governing board of the ISEE does not release any information about how scores are actually calculated, so we are unable to provide you with a scaled score on your practice tests.

So, rather than worrying over what the numbers mean, just concentrate on improving your performance. Look over all the answers and explanations we have provided. Since you won't know how hard the actual test will be on test day, or how other students will do, simply focusing on performing your best in your practice will put you in the right frame of mind to do just that on Test Day.

Study Aids

20

Math Foundations Workshop

- Arithmetic
    Working with Fractions
    Exponents and Radicals

- Algebra
    The Fundamentals
    Intermediate Operations
    Working with Expressions
    Equations

- Geometry
    Lines and Angles
    Parallel Lines
    Area and Perimeter

ARITHMETIC

Working With Fractions

When you want to:	Here's how:	Examples:
Add fractions	*Get a common denominator and then add the numerators.*	$\frac{1}{4} + \frac{1}{3} = \frac{3}{12} + \frac{4}{12} = \frac{3+4}{12} = \frac{7}{12}$
Subtract fractions	*Get a common denominator and then subtract the numerators.*	$\frac{1}{4} - \frac{1}{3} = \frac{3}{12} - \frac{4}{12} = \frac{3-4}{12} = \frac{-1}{12} = -\frac{1}{12}$

1. $\frac{3}{5} + \frac{1}{3} =$

2. $\frac{1}{2} - \frac{1}{6} =$

3. $\frac{3}{4} - \frac{3}{8} =$

4. $\frac{5}{6} + \frac{4}{9} =$

When you want to:	Here's how:	Examples:
Multiply fractions	*Multiply the numerators and multiply the denominators.*	$\frac{1}{4} \times \frac{1}{3} = \frac{1 \times 1}{4 \times 3} = \frac{1}{12}$
Divide fractions	*Invert the second fraction and multiply.*	$\frac{1}{5} \div \frac{2}{3} = \frac{1}{5} \times \frac{3}{2} = \frac{1 \times 3}{5 \times 2} = \frac{3}{10}$

5. $\frac{1}{2} \times \frac{2}{3} =$

6. $\frac{3}{4} \div \frac{6}{7} =$

7. $\frac{3}{4} \times \frac{3}{8} =$

8. $\frac{\frac{5}{8}}{\frac{1}{2}} =$

When you want to:	Here's how:	Examples:
Convert a mixed number to an improper fraction	*Multiply the whole number part by the denominator. Then add the numerator and put the result over the same denominator.*	To convert $4\frac{2}{3}$ to an improper fraction, multiply 4 by 3, then add 2. Take the resulting 14 and put it over 3: $4\frac{2}{3} = \frac{4 \times 3 + 2}{3} = \frac{14}{3}$
Convert an improper fraction to a mixed number	*Divide the denominator into the numerator to get a whole number quotient and a remainder. The quotient becomes the whole number part and the remainder becomes the numerator of the fraction part.*	To convert $\frac{37}{7}$, divide 7 into 37. The whole number quotient is 5 and the remainder is 2, so: $\frac{37}{7} = \frac{35}{7} + \frac{2}{7} = 5 + \frac{2}{7} = 5\frac{2}{7}$
Find the reciprocal	*Switch the numerator and denominator.*	The reciprocal of $\frac{2}{9}$ is $\frac{9}{2}$.

Fill in the missing blanks:

Improper Fractions   **Mixed Number**

9. $\frac{15}{4}$ ⟶   _____

10.   _____   ⟵ $2\frac{1}{3}$

11. $\frac{29}{6}$ ⟶   _____

Fraction   **Reciprocal**

12. $\frac{6}{7}$ ⟶   _____

13. $\frac{17}{4}$ ⟶   _____

Mixed Number   **Improper Fraction**   **Reciprocal**

14. $4\frac{3}{5}$ ⟶   _____   ⟶   _____

Which of the following statements are false?

15. $2\frac{1}{2} + 3\frac{1}{4} = 5\frac{1}{3}$

16. $\frac{1}{4} + \frac{2}{3} = \frac{3}{7}$

17. $\frac{1}{2} + \frac{1}{2} = \frac{1}{2} \div \frac{1}{2}$

18. $\frac{2}{3} \times \frac{4}{9} < \frac{2}{3} \div \frac{4}{9}$

19. $2\frac{1}{4} > \frac{14}{5}$

20. $\dfrac{\frac{5}{6}}{6} = \frac{1}{6}$

21. The reciprocal of $1\frac{1}{4} = \frac{5}{4}$

22. $3\frac{3}{7} \times 1\frac{3}{4} = 3\frac{9}{28}$

23. $5\frac{1}{2} \div \frac{1}{2} > 10$

24. $\frac{1}{2}\left(4\frac{1}{2} + 3\frac{1}{3}\right) = 2\frac{1}{4} + 1\frac{2}{3}$

Exponents and Radicals

EXPONENT: the small, raised number written to the right of a variable or number, indicating the number of times that variable or number is to be used as a factor. In the expression 3^2, the exponent is 2, so $3^2 = 3 \times 3 = 9$. In the expression $3x^2$, the exponent is 2, so $3x^2 = 3 \times x \times x$.

1. $3 \times 3 =$ _____, so $3^2 =$ _____

2. $2 \times 2 \times 2 \times 2 =$ _____, so $2^4 =$ _____

3. $16 =$ _____

4. $(-1)^2 =$ _____

5. $5^2 + 2^2 =$ _____

6. $4^3 =$ _____

7. $(-1)^3 =$ _____

8. $(5 + 2)^2 =$ _____

SQUARE ROOT: a number which multiplied by itself produces the given quantity. The symbol "$\sqrt{4}$" is used to represent the positive square root of a number, so $\sqrt{25} = 5$, since $5 \times 5 = 25$. If $x > 0$, $\sqrt{x^2} = x$, because $x \times x = x^2$.

9. $\sqrt{81} = 9 \times 9$, so $\sqrt{81} =$ _____

10. $\sqrt{400} = \sqrt{2 \times 2 \times 10 \times 10}$, so $\sqrt{400}$ _____

11. $\sqrt{9} =$ _____

12. $\sqrt{64} =$ _____

13. $4 \times \sqrt{9} =$ _____

14. $\sqrt{900} =$ _____

15. $\sqrt{36} + \sqrt{16} =$ _____

16. $\sqrt{4 \times 9} =$ _____

This number line can help you estimate the values of radicals that are not perfect squares.

$\sqrt{0}$ $\sqrt{1}$ $\sqrt{4}$ $\sqrt{9}$ $\sqrt{16}$ $\sqrt{25}$ $\sqrt{36}$ $\sqrt{49}$ $\sqrt{64}$ $\sqrt{81}$ $\sqrt{100}$ $\sqrt{121}$ $\sqrt{144}$ $\sqrt{169}$

0   1   2   3   4   5   6   7   8   9   10   11   12   13

ALGEBRA

The Fundamentals

VARIABLE: a letter used in algebra to represent an unknown or unspecified quantity. (An algebraic expression made up of only one term is called a monomial.) Even though you don't know the value of the term, it is still essentially a number, and you can add to it, subtract from it, and multiply or divide it, following the rules below:

COEFFICIENT: the numerical or "constant" part of an algebraic term. In the monomial $-4x^2$, the coefficient is -4. In the expression $5x^2 + 12x + 3$, 5, 12, and 3 are the coefficients.

When you want to:	Here's how:	Examples:
Add or subtract monomials	Combine only "like terms." Add or subtract the coefficients of each term—leave the variable unchanged.	$4a + 5a = 9a$ $4a + 5a^2$ <u>cannot</u> be combined.
Multiply monomials	Multiply the coefficients of each term. Add the exponents of like variables. Multiply different variables together.	$(4a)(5b) = 20ab$ $(4a)(3a^4b) = 12a^5b$
Divide monomials	Divide the coefficients of each term. Subtract the exponents of like variables. Leave different variables as they are.	$8a \div 2a = 4$ $\dfrac{6a^2b}{3ab} = 2a$ $\dfrac{15a}{5b} = \dfrac{3a}{b}$

1. $n + n + n + n =$

2. $3r + r + 2r =$

3. $xy + 2xy =$

4. $4rs - rs =$

5. $8x - y - 4x - 2y =$

6. $12m - 2m - (-m) =$

7. $n \times n \times n \times n =$

8. $3r \times r \times 2r =$

9. $5a \times 3b \times a \times 4b =$

10. $xy \times 2xy =$

11. $\dfrac{6ab}{2ab} =$

12. $\dfrac{12mn}{-3n} =$

Intermediate Operations

The following examples use the fundamentals you just learned, but might be a bit trickier than the last group.

1. $3(p - r) =$

2. $2a(5b - 2a) =$

3. $-2r(s - r) =$

4. $(7 - z) - (1 - 3z) =$

5. $(-5c - d) + (c - 5d) =$

6. $2c(5c + 4d) =$

7. $9x(2x - 1) =$

8. $-5a(b + 3) =$

9. $-10(-x - 2) =$

10. $-2x(4x - 6) =$

11. $(4a + b) + (6a - b) =$

12. $(3a + b) - (2a + b) =$

13. $(6 + z) - (-5 - 3z) =$

14. $2(3a - b) + 4(2a + b) =$

15. $-3(x + y) - 4(-2x - y) =$

Working With Expressions

When you want to:	Here's how:	Examples:
Evaluate an expression	*Plug in the given values for the variables and follow the rules of PEMDAS—*	Find $x^2 - 4x - 3$ when $x = 5$.
	Parentheses, Exponents, Multiplication and Division from left to right, Addition and Subtraction from left to right.	$(5)^2 - (4)(5) - 3 =$ $25 - 20 - 3 = 2$

1.   If $x = 3$, $x + 4 =$

2.   If $y = 1$, $5y - 2 =$

3.   If $a = 2$, $a(a + 3) =$

4.   If $x = 5$ and $y = 1$, $x^2 + 2y =$

5.   If $a = 6$ and $b = -1$, $\dfrac{-9}{b} - \dfrac{a}{3} =$

6.   If $a = -5$ and $b = -1$, $ab(b - 1) =$

7.   If $b = 7$ and $a = -2$, $\dfrac{ab}{2b} =$

8.   If $c = 4$ and $d = 5$, $\dfrac{cd^2}{d} =$

9.   If $x = 2$, $(7 - x) + (4 + 3x) =$

10.   If $x = 2$, $3x^2 + 4x =$

Equations

When you want to:	Here's how:	Examples:
Solve an equation	Isolate the variable by getting it alone on one side of the equation and all the numbers on the other side of the equation.	$4a + 5 = 9a + 15$ $5 - 15 = 9a - 4a$ $-10 = 5a$ $-2 = a$

Solve for the variable in each of the following:

1. $8a - 3 = 6a - 1$

2. $10 - 4x = 10x + 3$

3. $\dfrac{15 + 2x}{3} = 10 - x$

4. $-6c + 2 = -5c - 1$

5. $2y + 4 = 4y - 6$

6. $10 - 2d = -(4d - 2)$

7. $\dfrac{4x - 4}{3} = 2x$

8. $\dfrac{10x}{4} = 2x + 5$

9. $-5x - 1 = -4x + 4$

10. $8x - 4 = 10x + 4$

11. $9x + 9 = 36x$

12. $\dfrac{x + 4}{3} = 3x - 4$

13. $24x - 4 = 4x + 1$

14. $2(x - 5) = 3x - 5$

15. $-3(x + 2) = -10x - 1$

GEOMETRY

Lines and Angles

Illustration:	Rule:
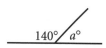	Angles that form a straight line add up to 180 degrees. In the figure to the left, **a + b + c = 180.**
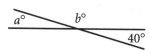	When two lines intersect, **adjacent angles are supplementary**, meaning they add up to 180 degrees. In the figure to the left, **x + y = 180**.

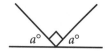

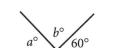

1. $a =$

5. $a =$
     $b =$

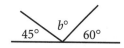

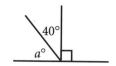

2. $a =$

6. $a + b =$

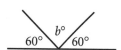

3. $b =$

7. $a =$

4. $b =$

Illustration:	Rule:
	Angles about a point add up to 360 degrees. In the figure to the left, $a + b + c + d + e = 360$.
	When two lines intersect, angles across the vertex from each other are called **vertical angles** and **are equal to each other.** To the left, $a = c$ and $b = d$.

8. $a =$

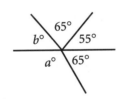

11. $a =$
      $b =$
      $c =$

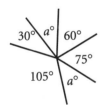

9. $a =$

12. $a =$
      $b =$

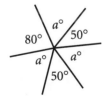

10. $a =$

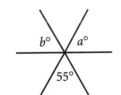

13. $a + b =$

Parallel Lines

Illustration:	Rule:
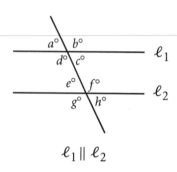	When parallel lines are crossed by a transversal: —Corresponding angles are equal (i.e., $a = e$). —Alternate interior angles are equal ($d = f$). —Same side interior angles are supplementary ($c + f = 180$). —All four acute angles are equal, as are all four obtuse angles.

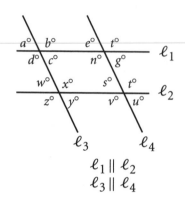

$$\ell_1 \parallel \ell_2$$

$$\ell_1 \parallel \ell_2$$
$$\ell_3 \parallel \ell_4$$

1. List all the angles equal to the angle marked $a°$:_____

    List all the angles equal to the angle marked $b°$:_____

3. If $a = 45$, $t = $ _____

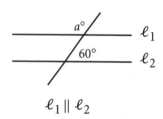

$$\ell_1 \parallel \ell_2$$

2. $a = $ _____

Area and Perimeter

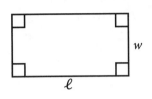

A **rectangle** is a parallelogram containing four right angles.
The formula for the area of a rectangle is:

Area = (length)(width)

In the diagram, ℓ = length and w = width, so Area = ℓw.

A **square** is a rectangle with four equal sides.
The formula for the area of a square is:

Area = (side)^2

In the diagram, s = the length of a side, so Area = s^2.

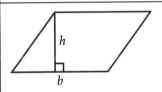

A **parallelogram** is a quadrilateral with two pairs of parallel sides.
The formula for the area of a parallelogram is:

Area = (base)(height)

In the diagram, h = height and b = base, so Area = bh.

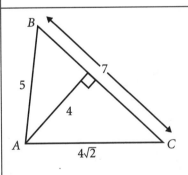

Area of triangle = $\frac{1}{2}$(base)(height)

The height is the perpendicular distance between the side that's chosen as the base and the opposite vertex. In this triangle, 4 is the height when the 7 is chosen as the base.

Area = $\frac{1}{2} bh = \frac{1}{2}(7)(4) = 14$

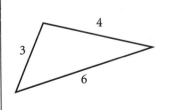

The **perimeter** of a polygon equals the sum of the lengths of its sides.
The perimeter of the triangle in the figure to the left is:

$3 + 4 + 6 = 13$

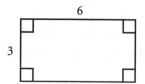

1.   Perimeter = _____

Area = _____

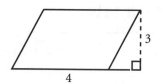

5.   Area = _____

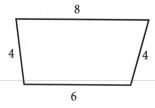

2.   Perimeter = _____

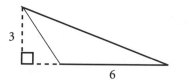

6.   Area = _____

3.   Perimeter = _____

Area = _____

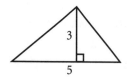

7.   Area = _____

4.   Area = _____

Practice Questions

1. $\left(\frac{1}{2}\right)^2 + \frac{3}{4} =$

   A. $\frac{3}{16}$

   B. $\frac{3}{8}$

   C. 1

   D. $1\frac{1}{4}$

   E. $4\frac{3}{4}$

2. $2\frac{1}{3}\left(\frac{5}{6} + \frac{1}{3}\right) =$

   F. $1\frac{1}{12}$

   G. $1\frac{1}{4}$

   H. $2\frac{3}{18}$

   J. $2\frac{13}{18}$

   K. $3\frac{1}{2}$

3. $\frac{7}{8} \div 3\frac{1}{2} =$

   A. $\frac{2}{24}$

   B. $\frac{1}{4}$

   C. $1\frac{1}{48}$

   D. $1\frac{1}{3}$

   E. $4\frac{3}{4}$

4. $\frac{8}{14} - \frac{1}{7} =$

   F. $\frac{3}{7}$

   G. $\frac{1}{2}$

   H. $\frac{9}{14}$

   J. $\frac{6}{7}$

   K. 1

5. $\frac{2}{3}\left(\frac{3}{8} - \frac{3}{4}\right) =$

   A. $-\frac{1}{2}$

   B. $-\frac{1}{4}$

   C. 0

   D. $\frac{1}{4}$

   E. $1\frac{7}{9}$

6. $\frac{5^2}{10^3} =$

   F. 0

   G. $\frac{1}{40}$

   H. $\frac{1}{8}$

   J. $\frac{1}{5}$

   K. $\frac{1}{4}$

7. $\left(1\frac{1}{3}\right)^2 =$

  A. $\frac{4}{9}$

  B. $1\frac{1}{9}$

  C. $1\frac{2}{3}$

  D. $1\frac{7}{9}$

  E. $2\frac{2}{9}$

8. $\sqrt{64} =$

  F. 2^3

  G. 4^2

  H. 4^3

  J. 8^2

  K. None of the above

9. $4\left(1\frac{1}{2} + \frac{1}{4}\right)^2 - \sqrt{81} =$

  A. $-8\frac{17}{81}$

  B. $-3\frac{5}{9}$

  C. $3\frac{1}{4}$

  D. $6\frac{5}{16}$

  E. 40

10. $5a + a =$

  F. 6

  G. $4a$

  H. $5 + 2a$

  J. $5a^2$

  K. $6a$

11. $5a(a)$

  A. $5 + 2a$

  B. $10a$

  C. $(5a)^2$

  D. $5a^2$

  E. $6a$

12. If $3x + 6 = \frac{7x}{3}$, then $x =$

  F. -9

  G. -3

  H. $1\frac{1}{9}$

  J. $4\frac{1}{2}$

  K. 9

13. If $n = 4$, then $\frac{1}{2}n - \sqrt{n} =$

  A. -14

  B. -4

  C. $-1\frac{7}{9}$

  D. 0

  E. 4

14. If $k = \frac{1}{3}$ and $2m + \frac{1}{3}k = \frac{1}{3}k^2$, then $m =$

   F. $-\frac{4}{81}$

   G. $-\frac{1}{27}$

   H. $\frac{2}{27}$

   J. $\frac{1}{9}$

   K. $1\frac{1}{2}$

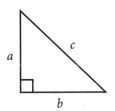

15. In the triangle above, $a^2 + b^2 = c^2$. All of the following sets of values could be correct EXCEPT:

   A. $a = 1, b = 1, c = \sqrt{2}$

   B. $a = 1, b = \sqrt{3}, c = 2$

   C. $a = 3, b = 4, c = 5$

   D. $a = \frac{1}{2}, b = 1\frac{1}{5}, c = 1\frac{3}{10}$

   E. None of the above

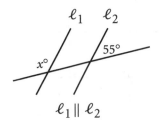

16. In the figure above, line ℓ_1 is parallel to line ℓ_2. What is the value of $2x$?

   F. 55

   G. 90

   H. 125

   J. 250

   K. 360

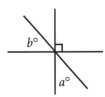

17. In the figure above, $a + b =$

   A. 30

   B. 45

   C. 90

   D. 180

   E. Cannot be determined from the information given.

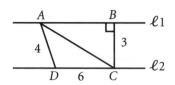

ℓ_1 is parallel to ℓ_2

18. What is the area of $\triangle ACD$?

 F. 3.5

 G. 6

 H. 9

 J. 12

 K. 24

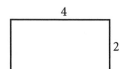

Figure 1
Rectangle

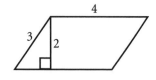

Figure 2
Parallelogram

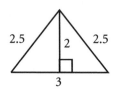

Figure 3
Triangle

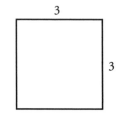

Figure 4
Square

19. Which figure is such that the number of square units in its area is greater than the number of units in its perimeter?

 A. Figure 1

 B. Figure 2

 C. Figure 3

 D. Figure 4

 E. None of the above

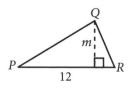

20. If the area of $\triangle PQR$ is 48, then $m =$

 F. 2

 G. 4

 H. 6

 J. 8

 K. 9

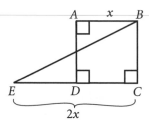

21. Based on the figure above, which of the following statements must be true?

 A. The area of square $ABCD$ is greater than the area of triangle BCE.

 B. The area of triangle BCE is greater than the area of square $ABCD$.

 C. The area of square $ABCD$ is equal to the area of triangle BCE.

 D. The perimeter of square $ABCD$ is equal to the perimeter of triangle BCE.

 E. The length of BC is half the length of BE.

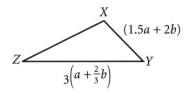

22. In triangle *XYZ*, *XY* = *XZ*. Which of the following is a correct expression for the perimeter of Δ*XYZ* ?

    F. $4a + 2\frac{2}{3}b$

    G. $4(a + b)$

    H. $4\frac{1}{2}a + 4\frac{2}{3}b$

    J. $5a + 4\frac{2}{3}b$

    K. $6(a + b)$

Exercise Answers

Arithmetic

Working with Fractions

1. $\dfrac{9}{15} + \dfrac{5}{15} = \dfrac{14}{15}$

2. $\dfrac{3}{6} - \dfrac{1}{6} = \dfrac{2}{6} = \dfrac{1}{3}$

3. $\dfrac{6}{8} - \dfrac{3}{8} = \dfrac{3}{8}$

4. $\dfrac{15}{18} + \dfrac{8}{18} = \dfrac{23}{18}$ or $1\dfrac{5}{18}$

5. $\dfrac{1}{2} \bullet \dfrac{2}{3} = \dfrac{2 \bullet 1}{2 \bullet 3} = \dfrac{2}{6} = \dfrac{1}{3}$

6. $\dfrac{3}{4} \bullet \dfrac{7}{6} = \dfrac{3 \bullet 7}{4 \bullet 6} = \dfrac{21}{24} = \dfrac{7}{8}$

7. $\dfrac{1}{4} \bullet \dfrac{1}{4} = \dfrac{1 \bullet 1}{4 \bullet 4} = \dfrac{1}{16}$

8. $\dfrac{5}{8} \bullet \dfrac{2}{1} = \dfrac{10}{8} = \dfrac{5}{4}$ or $1\dfrac{1}{4}$

9. $\dfrac{12}{4} + \dfrac{3}{4} = 3\dfrac{3}{4}$

10. $\dfrac{2 \bullet 3 + 1}{3} = \dfrac{7}{3}$

11. $\dfrac{29}{6} = 4\dfrac{5}{6}$

12. $\dfrac{7}{6}$ or $1\dfrac{1}{6}$

13. $\dfrac{4}{17}$

14. $\dfrac{4 \bullet 5 + 3}{5} = \dfrac{23}{5}, \dfrac{5}{23}$

15. F

16. F

17. T

18. T

19. F

20. T

21. F

22. F

23. T

24. T

Exponents and Radicals

1. 9

2. 16

3. 1

4. 1

5. 29

6. 64

7. −1

8. 49

9. 9

10. $2 \bullet 10 = 20$

11. 3

12. 8

13. $2 \bullet 3 = 6$

14. $\sqrt{9} \bullet \sqrt{100} = 3 \bullet 10 = 30$

15. $6 + 4 = 10$

16. $\sqrt{36} = 6$

Algebra

The Fundamentals

1. $4n$

2. $6r$

3. $3xy$

4. $3rs$

5. $4x - 3y$

6. $11m$

7. n^4

8. $6r^3$

9. $60a^2b^2$

10. $2x^2y^2$

11. 3

12. $-4m$

Intermediate Operations

1. $3p - 3r$

2. $10\,ab - 4a^2$

3. $-2rs + 2r^2$

4. $6 + 2z$

5. $-4c - 6d$

6. $10c^2 + 8cd$

7. $18x^2 - 9x$

8. $-5ab - 15a$

9. $10x + 20$

10. $-8x^2 + 12x$

11. $10a$

12. a

13. $11 + 4z$

14. $14a + 2b$

15. $5x + y$

Working With Expressions

1. 7

2. 3

3. 10

4. 27

5. 7

6. -10

7. -1

8. 20

9. 15

10. 20

Equations

1. $a = 1$

2. $x = \dfrac{1}{2}$

3. $x = 3$

4. $c = 3$

5. $y = 5$

6. $d = -4$

7. $x = -2$

8. $x = 10$

9. $x = -5$

10. $x = -4$

11. $x = \dfrac{1}{3}$

12. $x = 2$

13. $x = \dfrac{1}{4}$

14. $x = -5$

15. $x = \dfrac{5}{7}$

Geometry

Lines and Angles

1. $a = 40°$

2. $a = 45°$

3. $b = 60°$

4. $b = 75°$

5. $a = 40°$
   $b = 140°$

6. $a + b = 120°$

7. $a = 50°$

8. $a = 100°$

9. $a = 45°$

10. $a = 60°$

11. $a = 40°$
    $b = 140°$
    $c = 40°$

12. $a = 115°$
    $b = 60°$

13. $a + b = 125°$

Parallel Lines

1. $< a = < d, < e, < h$
   $< b = < c, < f, < g$

2. 120 degrees

3. 135 degrees

Area and Perimeter

1. Perimeter = 18, Area = 18

2. 22

3. Perimeter = 16, Area = 16

4. \f(15,2)

5. 12

6. 8

7. 9

Practice Question Answers

1. **C** $\left(\frac{1}{2}\right)^2 + \frac{3}{4} = \left(\frac{1}{2} \times \frac{1}{2}\right) + \frac{3}{4} =$

$\frac{1}{4} + \frac{3}{4} = 1$

2. **J** $2\frac{1}{3}\left(\frac{5}{6} + \frac{1}{3}\right) = \frac{7}{3}\left(\frac{5}{6} + \frac{2}{6}\right) =$

$\frac{7}{3} \cdot \frac{7}{6} = \frac{49}{18} = 2\frac{13}{18}$

3. **B** $\frac{7}{8} \div 3\frac{1}{2} = \frac{7}{8} \div \frac{7}{2}$

$\frac{7}{8} \cdot \frac{2}{7} = \frac{2}{8} = \frac{1}{4}$

4. **F** $\frac{8}{14} - \frac{1}{7} = \frac{8}{14} - \frac{2}{14} = \frac{6}{14} = \frac{3}{7}$

5. **B** $\frac{2}{3}\left(\frac{3}{8} - \frac{3}{4}\right) = \frac{2}{3}\left(\frac{3}{8} - \frac{6}{8}\right) =$

$\frac{2}{3} \cdot \left(\frac{-3}{8}\right) = \frac{-6}{24} = -\frac{1}{4}$

6. **G** $\frac{5^2}{10^3} = \frac{25}{1000} = \frac{1}{40}$

7. **D** $\left(1\frac{1}{3}\right)^2 = \left(\frac{4}{3}\right)^2 = \frac{4}{3} \cdot \frac{4}{3} = \frac{16}{9} = 1\frac{7}{9}$

8. **F** $\sqrt{64} = 8;\ 2^3 = 8,\ 4^2 = 16,$

$4^3 = 64,\ 8^2 = 64$

9. **C** $4\left(1\frac{1}{2} + \frac{1}{4}\right)^2 - \sqrt{81} =$

$4\left(\frac{3}{2} + \frac{1}{4}\right)^2 - \sqrt{81} =$

$4\left(\frac{6}{4} + \frac{1}{4}\right)^2 - \sqrt{81} = 4\left(\frac{7}{4}\right)^2 - \sqrt{81} =$

$4\left(\frac{49}{16}\right) - 9 = \left(\frac{4}{1} \cdot \frac{49}{16}\right) - 9$

$\frac{49}{4} - 9 = 12\frac{1}{4} - 9 = 3\frac{1}{4}$

10. **K** $5a + a = (5a + 1)a = 6a$

11. **D** $5a(a) = 5a(1a) = 5 \cdot 1)(a \cdot a) = 5a^2$

12. **F** $3x + 6 = \frac{7x}{3}$

$3(3x + 6) = \frac{3}{1}\left(\frac{7x}{3}\right)$

$9x + 18 = 7x$
$-9x + 9x + 18 = 7x - 9x$
$18 = -2x$
$x = -9$

13. **D** $\frac{1}{2}n - \sqrt{n} =$

$\frac{1}{2}(4) - \sqrt{4} =$

$\frac{4}{2} \cdot 2 = 2 \cdot 2 = 0$

$2 - 2 = 0$

14.　**G**　$2m + \frac{1}{3}k = \frac{1}{3}k^2$

$2m + \frac{1}{3}\left(\frac{1}{3}\right) = \frac{1}{3}\left(\frac{1}{3}\right)^2$

$2m + \frac{1}{9} = \frac{1}{3}\left(\frac{1}{9}\right)$

$2m + \frac{1}{9} = \frac{1}{27}$

$2m + \frac{1}{9} - \frac{1}{9} = \frac{1}{27} - \frac{1}{9}$

$2m = \frac{1}{27} - \frac{3}{27} = \frac{-2}{27}$

$m = \frac{1}{2}\left(-\frac{2}{27}\right)$

$m = \frac{-1}{27}$

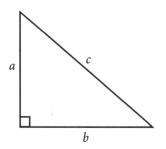

15.　**E**　$a^2 + b^2 = c^2$

(Pythagorean theorem for right triangles)
All of the answer choices make the equation
true when plugged in

A. $(1)^2 + (1)^2 = (\sqrt{2})^2$
　　$1 + 1 = 2$

B. $(1)^2 + (\sqrt{3})^2 = (2)^2$
　　$1 + 3 = 4$

C. $3^2 + 4^2 = 5^2$
　　$9 + 16 = 25$

D. $\left(\frac{1}{2}\right)^2 + \left(\frac{6}{5}\right)^2 = \left(\frac{13}{10}\right)^2$

　　$\frac{1}{4} + \frac{36}{25} = \frac{169}{100}$

　　$\frac{25}{100} + \frac{144}{100} = \frac{169}{100}$

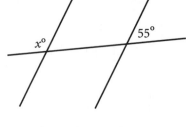

16.　**J**　　The angles supplementary to the 55°
(under or left) are = 125° (55 + 125 = 180).

The angle marked x° and the 125 degree angle
adjacent to and to the left of the angle marked
55° are corresponding angles. Corresponding
angles are equal, so x = 125.

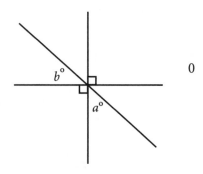

17.　**C**　　The angle adjacent to the angles
marked a° and b° is vertical to the angle
indicated to be a right angle. Vertical angles are
equal. So this angle is a right angle. Then
$a + b + 90 = 180$, and $a = b = 180 - 90 = 90$.

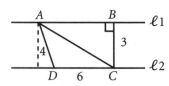

18.　**H**　　Area of $\triangle ABD = \frac{1}{2}bh$

$b = DC = 6$. h is the perpendicular to ℓ_2 from A.
Since ℓ_1 is parallel to ℓ_2, BC and the height are

equal, and $h = 3$. Area $= \frac{1}{2} \times 6 \times 3 = 9$

19. **E** Call the area A and the perimeter P.
Figure 1 is a rectangle.

$A = \ell \bullet w = 4 \times 2 = 8$
$P = 2(\ell + w) = 2(4 + 2) = 12$
So here, $A < P$.

Figure 2 is a parallelogram.

$A = b \bullet h = 4 \bullet 2 = 8$
$P = 2(\ell + w) = 2(4 + 3) = 14$
So here, $A < P$.

Figure 3 is a triangle.

$A = \frac{1}{2} b \bullet h = \frac{1}{2} 3 \bullet 2 = 3$

$P =$ Sum of the lengths of the sides
$2.5 + 2.5 + 3 = 8$.
So here, $A < P$.

Figure 4 is a square.
$A = 3^2 = 3 \times 3 = 9$
$P = 3 + 3 + 3 + 3 = 12$.
So here, $A < P$.

20. **J** $A = \frac{1}{2}bh$, $b = 12$, $h = m$, and $A = 48$.

$48 = \frac{1}{2} \bullet 12 \bullet m$

$48 = 6m$
$m = 8$

21. **C** You could either pick numbers or work with variables

Area of square $ABCD = x \bullet x = x^2$
Area of triangle $BCE =$

$\dfrac{x \bullet 2x}{2} = \dfrac{2x^2}{2} = x^2$

$x^2 = x^2$

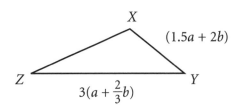

22. **K** Perimeter = sum of all the sides, or
Perimeter is $XY + XZ + YZ$. Since $XY = XZ$.

$(XY + XZ) = 2(XY)$.
So the perimeter is $2(XY) + YZ$.
Plug in and solve.

$2(1.5a + 2b) + 3\left(a + \dfrac{2}{3}b\right) =$

$(2 \bullet 1.5a) + (2 \bullet 2b) + (3 \bullet a) + \left(3 \bullet \dfrac{2}{3}b\right)$

$= 3a + 4b + 3a + 2b = 6a + 6b = 6(a + b)$

Question Bank

- Math

- Synonyms

- Analogies

- Reading Comprehension

- Sentence Completions

Math

Number Properties

1. Which of the following is a whole number?

   (A) $\sqrt{2}$
   (B) 5.5
   (C) 2π
   (D) 66.67
   (E) 1,001

2. How many distinct digits are in the number 123,345,567,789 ?

   (F) 9
   (G) 10
   (H) 11
   (J) 12
   (K) 13

3. What is the next number in the following sequence?

   16, 20, 24, 28,...

   (A) 29
   (B) 30
   (C) 31
   (D) 32
   (E) 33

4. How many whole numbers are there from 45 through 84, inclusive?

   (F) 38
   (G) 39
   (H) 40
   (J) 41
   (K) 42

5. $12 - 3 \times 5 + (7 - 10)^2 \div 3 =$

   (A) 0
   (B) 2
   (C) 4
   (D) 18
   (E) 48

6. What is the result when the product of 5 and 6 is subtracted from the sum of 7 and 8 ?

   (F) −45
   (G) −26
   (H) −15
   (J) −4
   (K) 4

7. W is a whole number between 4 and 11, and W is between 9 and 15. What is the value of W ?

   (A) 9
   (B) 9.5
   (C) 10
   (D) 11
   (E) 13

8. If the sum of x and y is an odd whole number and the sum of x and z is an even whole number, which of the following CANNOT be true?

   (F) x is even and y is odd.
   (G) y is even and z is odd.
   (H) x and z are even and y is odd.
   (J) x and y are even and z is odd.
   (K) z is even and y is odd.

9. If D is the difference of two consecutive whole numbers, which of the following must be true?

   (A) D is positive.
   (B) D is negative.
   (C) D is even.
   (D) D is odd.
   (E) D is less than either whole number.

10. If x and y are consecutive integers such that $xy = 6$ and y is greater than x, which of the following statements must be true?

    I. $x + y = 5$
    II. x is less than 6.
    III. $\frac{x}{y} = \frac{2}{3}$

    (F) I only
    (G) II only
    (H) I and II
    (J) I and III
    (K) II and III

Factors, Multiples, and Divisibility

11. Which of the following is a multiple of 5 but NOT a multiple of 10 ?

    (A) 390
    (B) 392
    (C) 393
    (D) 395
    (E) 399

12. Which of the following is a multiple of 3 but NOT a multiple of 9 ?

    (F)   133
    (G)   297
    (H)   333
    (J)   456
    (K)   567

13. Which of the following is a factor of both 24 and 36 but NOT of 54 ?

    (A)   1
    (B)   2
    (C)   3
    (D)   4
    (E)   5

14. Find the least common multiple of 15 and 18.

    (F)   1
    (G)   3
    (H)   33
    (J)   90
    (K)   270

15. What is the least prime number greater than 90 ?

    (A)   91
    (B)   93
    (C)   95
    (D)   97
    (E)   99

16. How many distinct prime factors does the number 36 have?

    (F)   2
    (G)   3
    (H)   4
    (J)   5
    (K)   6

17. Find the greatest common factor of 30 and 42.

    (A)   2
    (B)   3
    (C)   6
    (D)   84
    (E)   210

18. Dividing 87 by 6 leaves a remainder of

    (F)   6
    (G)   4
    (H)   3
    (J)   2
    (K)   1

19. When the positive whole number P is divided by 7, the remainder is 5. What is the remainder when $5P$ is divided by 7 ?

    (A)   0
    (B)   1
    (C)   2
    (D)   3
    (E)   4

20. If a whole number is divisible by 6 and by 9, then the number must be divisible by which of the following?

    I.   12

    II. 18

    III. 36

    (F) I only
    (G) II only
    (H) I and II only
    (J) II and III only
    (K) I, II, and III

Fractions

21. $\frac{1}{3} + \frac{2}{5} =$

    (A) $\frac{3}{8}$

    (B) $\frac{5}{8}$

    (C) $\frac{2}{15}$

    (D) $\frac{3}{15}$

    (E) $\frac{11}{15}$

22. $\frac{1}{3} \times \frac{1}{6} =$

    (F) $\frac{1}{18}$

    (G) $\frac{1}{9}$

    (H) $\frac{2}{9}$

    (J)   2

    (K)   3

23. $\frac{1}{3} \div \frac{1}{6} =$

    (A) $\frac{1}{18}$

    (B) $\frac{1}{9}$

    (C) $\frac{2}{9}$

    (D)   2

    (E)   3

24. What is the reciprocal of 4 ?

    (F) -4

    (G) $\frac{1}{4}$

    (H) $\frac{1}{2}$

    (J)   2

    (K)   16

25. Which of the following is the greatest?

    (A) $\frac{1}{2}$

    (B) $\frac{3}{4}$

    (C) $\frac{5}{8}$

    (D) $\frac{7}{8}$

    (E) $\frac{7}{16}$

26. Express $4\frac{3}{7}$ as an improper fraction.

    (F) $\frac{22}{7}$

    (G) $\frac{24}{7}$

    (H) $\frac{27}{7}$

    (J) $\frac{31}{7}$

    (K) $\frac{27}{14}$

27. $\left(\frac{1}{5} + \frac{1}{3}\right) \div \frac{1}{2} =$

    (A) $\frac{1}{8}$

    (B) $\frac{1}{4}$

    (C) $\frac{4}{15}$

    (D) $\frac{1}{2}$

    (E) $\frac{16}{15}$

28. $8\frac{1}{3} \div 6\frac{2}{3} =$

    (F) $1\frac{1}{4}$

    (G) $1\frac{2}{3}$

    (H) $2\frac{1}{2}$

    (J) $2\frac{2}{3}$

    (K) $55\frac{4}{9}$

29. If $\left(\frac{1}{2} + \frac{1}{6}\right) - \left(\frac{1}{12} + \frac{1}{3}\right)$ is calculated and the result is reduced to simplest terms, what is the numerator of this fraction?

    (A)   1
    (B)   2
    (C)   3
    (D)   4
    (E)   5

30. For how many whole number values of x will $\frac{7}{x}$ be greater than $\frac{1}{4}$ and less than $\frac{1}{3}$?
    (F)   6
    (G)   7
    (H)   12
    (J)   28
    (K)   infinitely many

Fractions and Decimals

31. Express $\frac{3}{5}$ as a decimal.
    (A)   0.035
    (B)   0.06
    (C)   0.35
    (D)   0.6
    (E)   3.5

32. Which of the following is the best decimal approximation of $\frac{4}{7}$?
    (F)   0.47
    (G)   0.57
    (H)   0.75
    (J)   1.75
    (K)   4.7

33. Express 0.875 as a fraction in lowest terms.
    (A) $\frac{5}{7}$
    (B) $\frac{5}{8}$
    (C) $\frac{7}{5}$
    (D) $\frac{7}{8}$
    (E) $\frac{87}{5}$

34. $0.215 \div 0.05 =$
    (F)   0.00043
    (G)   0.0043
    (H)   0.043
    (J)   0.43
    (K)   4.3

35. What is the sum of 3.4 and $\frac{3}{4}$?
    (A) $3\frac{3}{10}$
    (B) $3\frac{9}{10}$
    (C) $4\frac{3}{20}$
    (D) $4\frac{1}{5}$
    (E) $6\frac{4}{5}$

36. What is the product of 0.03 and $4\frac{1}{6}$?
    (F) $\frac{1}{8}$
    (G) $\frac{1}{4}$
    (H) $1\frac{1}{8}$
    (J) $6\frac{1}{4}$
    (K) $12\frac{1}{2}$

37. When $\frac{4}{11}$ is written as a decimal, what is the 100th digit after the decimal point?
    (A)   3
    (B)   4
    (C)   5
    (D)   6
    (E)   7

38. As a decimal, what is the sum of $\frac{2}{3}$ and $\frac{1}{12}$?
    (F)   0.2
    (G)   0.5
    (H)   0.75
    (J)   0.833
    (K)   0.875

39. Which of the following fractions is greater than 0.68 and less than 0.72 ?

    (A) $\frac{3}{5}$

    (B) $\frac{5}{7}$

    (C) $\frac{3}{4}$

    (D) $\frac{2}{3}$

    (E) $\frac{5}{8}$

40. At a party, $\frac{2}{3}$ of the guests drank only soda, $\frac{1}{4}$ of the guests drank only juice, and no guest drank both soda and juice. If the remaining 5 guests had nothing to drink, then how many guests were at the party?

    (F)   60
    (G)   50
    (H)   45
    (J)   30
    (K)   25

Percents

41. Express 84% as a fraction.

    (A) $\frac{7}{8}$

    (B) $\frac{11}{13}$

    (C) $\frac{4}{21}$

    (D) $\frac{21}{25}$

    (E) $\frac{41}{50}$

42. What is 20% more than 80 ?

    (F)   64
    (G)   84
    (H)   90
    (J)   96
    (K)   100

43. Express $\frac{9}{10}$ as a percent.

    (A)   0.9%
    (B)   1.1%
    (C)   9%
    (D)   11%
    (E)   90%

44. Express $\frac{5}{4}$ as a percent.

    (F)   1.25%
    (G)   12.5%
    (H)   80%
    (J)   125%
    (K)   800%

45. Express $\frac{2}{3}$ precisely as a percent.

    (A)   66%
    (B)   67%
    (C)   66.6%
    (D)   66.7%
    (E) $66\frac{2}{3}\%$

46. What is $\frac{1}{4}$% of 16 ?

    (F)   0.004
    (G)   0.04
    (H)   0.4
    (J)   4
    (K)   64

47. If 25% of x is 120, what is the value of x ?

    (A)   30
    (B)   90
    (C)   145
    (D)   150
    (E)   480

48. What percent of 100 gives the same number as 10 percent of 150 ?

    (F)   5%
    (G)   10%
    (H)   15%
    (J)   25%
    (K)   45%

49. What is 16 percent of 25 percent of 1,000,000 ?

    (A)   40
    (B)   400
    (C)   4,000
    (D)   40,000
    (E)   400,000

50. What percent of 75 is the same as 15 percent of 140 ?

    (F)   7%
    (G)   14%
    (H)   21%
    (J)   28%
    (K)   35%

Percent Word Problems

51. In a group of 25 students, 16 are female. What percentage of the group are female?

    (A)   16%
    (B)   40%
    (C)   60%
    (D)   64%
    (E)   75%

52. Pat deposited 15% of last week's take-home pay into a savings account. If she deposited $37.50, what was last week's take-home pay?

    (F) $ 25.00
    (G) $ 56.25
    (H) $112.50
    (J) $225.00
    (K) $250.00

53. For what price is a discount of 15 percent the same as a discount of $30 ?

    (A) $1
    (B) $15
    (C) $20
    (D) $100
    (E) $200

54. The population of country X increased by 30 percent one year and then decreased by 20 percent the following year. Over the 2-year period, the population of country X

    (F)   increased by 10%
    (G)   increased by 6%
    (H)   increased by 4%
    (J)   decreased by 5%
    (K)   decreased by 10%

55. After eating 25% of the jelly beans, Brett has 72 left. How many jelly beans did Brett have originally?

    (A)   90
    (B)   96
    (C)   97
    (D)   180
    (E)   288

56. In a class, 70 percent of the students are right-handed, and the rest are left-handed. If 70 percent of the left-handed students have brown eyes, then left-handed students with brown eyes make up what percent of the entire class?

    (F)   14%
    (G)   21%
    (H)   30%
    (J)   49%
    (K)   60%

57. At the end of the season, a team's ratio of wins to losses was 3:5. If there were no ties, what percentage of its games did the team win?

    (A) $33\frac{1}{3}\%$

    (B) $37\frac{1}{2}\%$

    (C)   40%

    (D)   60%

    (E) $62\frac{1}{2}\%$

58. The regular price for a certain bicycle is $125.00. If that price is reduced by 20%, what is the new price?

    (F) $100.00
    (G) $105.00
    (H) $112.50
    (J) $120.00
    (K) $122.50

59. A music store's everyday price for CDs is 10 percent less than the list price. If the everyday price of a particular CD is reduced by 30 percent, then the final price of that CD is what percent of the list price?

(A) 60%
(B) 63%
(C) 65%
(D) 70%
(E) 75%

60. From 1970 through 1980, the population of City Q increased by 20%. From 1980 through 1990, the population increased by 30%. What was the combined percent increase for the period 1970-1990 ?

(F) 25%
(G) 26%
(H) 36%
(J) 50%
(K) 56%

Ratios, Rates, and Proportions

61. If there are 15 women and 12 men in the room, what is the ratio of men to women?

(A) 2:5
(B) 3:5
(C) 4:5
(D) 5:4
(E) 5:3

62. After 30 games, a team's ratio of wins to losses is 2:3. If there were no ties, how many games did the team win?

(F) 12
(G) 15
(H) 18
(J) 20
(K) 24

63. How many kilometers would a person travel driving 5 hours at 75 kilometers per hour?

(A) 175
(B) 225
(C) 250
(D) 325
(E) 375

64. There are 4 blue ties for every 3 red ties in a drawer. If there are only blue ties and red ties in the drawer, which of the following could be the total number of ties in the drawer?

(F) 10
(G) 20
(H) 25
(J) 30
(K) 35

65. Water drips from a faucet at a rate of 40 drops per minute. At this rate, how many minutes will it take to fill a container that can hold 2,000 drops of water?

(A) 15
(B) 20
(C) 30
(D) 45
(E) 50

66. Ashley biked 32 miles uphill at 4 miles per hour and 32 miles downhill at 16 miles per hour. What was Ashley's average speed in miles per hour for the entire 64 miles?

(F) 6.4
(G) 9.6
(H) 10
(J) 12
(K) 20

67. If the ratio of males to females in a group of students is 3:5, which of the following COULD be the total number of students in the group?

(A) 148
(B) 150
(C) 152
(D) 154
(E) 156

68. A car travels 288 miles in 6 hours. At that rate, how many miles will it travel in 8 hours?

(F) 216
(G) 360
(H) 368
(J) 376
(K) 384

69. Vito read 96 pages in 2 hours and 40 minutes. What was Vito's average rate of reading in pages per hour?

   (A)   24
   (B)   30
   (C)   36
   (D)   42
   (E)   48

70. Jan types at an average rate of 12 pages per hour. At that rate, how long will it take Jan to type 100 pages?

   (F)   8 hours and 3 minutes
   (G)   8 hours and 15 minutes
   (H)   8 hours and 20 minutes
   (J)   8 hours and 30 minutes
   (K)   8 hours and $33\frac{1}{3}$ minutes

Averages

71. What is the average of 12, 12, 15, 37, and 44 ?

   (A)   15
   (B)   18
   (C)   24
   (D)   26
   (E)   29

72. If the largest of 5 consecutive whole numbers is 11, then the average of these numbers is

   (F)   5
   (G)   6
   (H)   7
   (J)   9
   (K)   10

73. If the average of 12 numbers is 3, what is the sum of the 12 numbers?

   (A)   36
   (B)   51
   (C)   72
   (D)   102
   (E)   144

74. The average of 5 numbers is 8. If the average of 4 of those numbers is 6, what is the fifth number?

   (F)   4
   (G)   8
   (H)   12
   (J)   14
   (K)   16

75. What is the average of all the whole numbers from 32 through 108, inclusive ?

   (A)   70
   (B)   71
   (C)   72
   (D)   73
   (E)   74

76. What is the average of $\frac{1}{20}$ and $\frac{1}{30}$?

   (F) $\frac{1}{25}$

   (G) $\frac{1}{24}$

   (H) $\frac{2}{25}$

   (J) $\frac{1}{12}$

   (K) $\frac{1}{6}$

77. Rachel's average score after 6 tests is 83. If Rachel earns a score of 97 on the 7th test, what is her new average?

   (A)   85
   (B)   86
   (C)   87
   (D)   88
   (E)   90

78. Martin's average score after 4 tests is 89. What score on the 5th test would bring Martin's average up to exactly 90 ?

   (F)   90
   (G)   91
   (H)   92
   (J)   93
   (K)   94

79. In a certain club, the average age of the male members is 35 and the average age of the female members is 25. If 20% of the members are male, what is the average age of all the club members?

   (A)   26
   (B)   27
   (C)   28
   (D)   30
   (E)   33

80. What is the average of $2x + 5$, $5x - 6$, and $-4x + 2$?

   (F) $x + \frac{1}{3}$

   (G) $x + 1$

   (H) $3x + \frac{1}{3}$

   (J) $3x + 3$

   (K) $3x + 3\frac{1}{3}$

Arithmetic Word Problems

81. On the first test, Ted scored 7 points above the passing grade. On the second test, he scored 12 points lower than he did on the first test. His score on the second test was

   (A) 19 points below the passing grade
   (B) 12 points below the passing grade
   (C) 5 points below the passing grade
   (D) 2 points above the passing grade
   (E) 7 points above the passing grade

82. Chris sold 4 times as many newspapers as magazines. Which of the following could be the total number of newspapers and magazines Chris sold?

   (F) 18
   (G) 24
   (H) 25
   (J) 27
   (K) 29

83. The price of a camera was first increased by $45 and then decreased by $68. If the original price of the camera was $200, what was the price after these changes?

   (A) $145
   (B) $168
   (C) $177
   (D) $213
   (E) $245

84. Four trucks are each carrying 250 crates. If each crate weighs 400 kilograms, how many kilograms are the 4 trucks carrying together?

   (F) 1,000
   (G) 4,000
   (H) 40,000
   (J) 100,000
   (K) 400,000

85. If the value of one share of stock X increased from $42 a share to $56 a share, what is the increase in value of 20 shares?

   (A) $420
   (B) $280
   (C) $140
   (D) $56
   (E) $28

86. Each worker received the same payment for a project. If the total amount paid to the workers was $200, which of the following CANNOT be the payment each worker received?

   (F) $20
   (G) $30
   (H) $40
   (J) $50
   (K) $100

87. Here are two addition methods:

   Abe's method: Round the numbers to the nearest whole number and add.

   Ben's method: Add the numbers, then round the result to the nearest whole number.

   What is the positive difference between the results of applying Abe's addition method and Ben's addition method to 3.3 and 6.4 ?

   (A) 0
   (B) 0.3
   (C) 0.7
   (D) 1.0
   (E) 9.7

88. The table below displays Jamie's income for each of the years 1989–1994. Which of the years 1990–1994 shows the greatest percent increase over the previous year?

Year	Income
1989	$20,000
1990	$25,000
1991	$30,000
1992	$33,000
1993	$36,000
1994	$44,000

   (F) 1990
   (G) 1991
   (H) 1992
   (J) 1993
   (K) 1994

89. In a group of 50 students, 28 speak English and 37 speak Spanish. If everyone in the group speaks at least one of the two languages, how many speak both English and Spanish?

   (A) 11
   (B) 12
   (C) 13
   (D) 14
   (E) 15

90. The toll for driving a segment of a certain freeway is $1.50 plus 25 cents for each mile traveled. Joy paid a $25.00 toll for driving a segment of the freeway. How many miles did she travel?

   (F) 10
   (G) 75
   (H) 94
   (J) 96
   (K) 100

Algebra Word Problems

91. In 1990, the population of Town A was 9,400 and the population of Town B was 7,600. Since then, each year, the population of Town A has decreased by 100, and the population of Town B has increased by 100. Assuming that in each case the rate continues, in what year will the two populations be equal?

   (A) 1998
   (B) 1999
   (C) 2000
   (D) 2008
   (E) 2009

92. If Noah earns $20 per hour of work, how many hours would he need to work to earn $580 ?

   (F) 91
   (G) 58
   (H) 42
   (J) 34
   (K) 29

93. The ratio of oil to vinegar in a salad dressing is 5 to 2. If 8 liters of vinegar is used, how many liters of oil is used?

   (A) 5
   (B) 10
   (C) 16
   (D) 20
   (E) 40

94. In a certain library there are 3 fiction books for every 8 nonfiction books. If the library has 600 nonfiction books, how many books does it have in all?

   (F) 225
   (G) 800
   (H) 825
   (J) 1,400
   (K) 2,200

95. Paul has d dollars and Robert has twice as many. If Paul gives 5 dollars to Robert, how many dollars, in terms of d, will Robert have then?

   (A) $d + 5$
   (B) $d + 7$
   (C) $2d + 2$
   (D) $2d + 5$
   (E) $5d + 2$

96. If the product of integers a and b is 16 and a is greater than 4, then which if the following must be true?

   I. $b = 2$
   II. $a + b > 0$
   III. $a > b$

   (F) II only
   (G) III only
   (H) I and II only
   (J) II and III only
   (K) I, II, and III

97. Joan has q quarters, d dimes, n nickels, and no other coins in her pocket. Which of the following represents the total number of coins in Joan's pocket?

   (A) $q + d + n$
   (B) $5q + 2d + n$
   (C) $0.25q + 0.10d + 0.05n$
   (D) $(25 + 10 + 5)(q + d + n)$
   (E) $25q + 10d + 5n$

98. One can determine a student's score S on a certain test by dividing the number of wrong answers (w) by 4 and subtracting the result from the number of right answers (r). This relation is expressed by which of the following formulas?

(F) $s = \dfrac{r - w}{4}$

(G) $s = r - \dfrac{w}{4}$

(H) $s = \dfrac{r}{4} - w$

(J) $s = 4r - w$

(K) $s = r - 4w$

99. The formula for the lateral surface area S of a right circular cone is $s = \pi r \sqrt{r^2 + h^2}$, where r is the radius of the base and h is the altitude. What is the lateral surface area, in square feet, of a right circular cone with base radius 3 feet and altitude 4 feet?

(A) $3\pi \sqrt{5}$

(B) $3\pi\sqrt{7}$

(C) 15π

(D) 21π

(E) $\dfrac{75\pi}{2}$

100. The formula for converting a Fahrenheit temperature reading to Celsius is

$C = \dfrac{5}{9}(F - 32)$, where C is the reading in degrees Celsius and F is the reading in degrees Fahrenheit. Which of the following is the Fahrenheit equivalent to a reading of 95° Celsius?

(F) 35° F
(G) 53° F
(H) 63° F
(J) 203° F
(K) 207° F

Exponents

101. $4^3 =$

(A) 12
(B) 24
(C) 48
(D) 64
(E) 96

102. $a^3 \times a^5 =$

(F) a^8
(G) a^9
(H) a^{10}
(J) a^{11}
(K) a^{15}

103. Which of the following numbers is greater than its square?

(A) -2
(B) -1
(C) -0.5
(D) 0
(E) 0.5

104. $(-1)^{13} =$

(F) -13
(G) -1
(H) $-\dfrac{1}{13}$
(J) 1
(K) 13

105. $(b^5)^2 =$

(A) b^7
(B) b^{10}
(C) b^{25}
(D) b^{32}
(E) b^{52}

106. What is the greatest of the numbers 1^{32}, 36^1, 3^6, 3^{12}, and 12^3 ?

    (F) 1^{32}

    (G) 36^1

    (H) 3^6

    (J) 3^{12}

    (K) 12^3

107. Which of the following is equal to

    $\dfrac{(3.0 \times 10^4)(8.0 \times 10^9)}{1.2 \times 10^6}$?

    (A) 2.0×10^6

    (B) 2.0×10^7

    (C) 2.0×10^8

    (D) 2.0×10^{30}

    (E) 2.0×10^{31}

108. Express 0.02718 in scientific notation.

    (F) 0.02718×10^2

    (G) 0.2718×10^{-1}

    (H) 0.2718×10^1

    (J) 2.718×10^{-2}

    (K) 2.718×10^2

109. For how many positive whole number values of n is 2^n greater than 10 and less than 1,000 ?

    (A)   5
    (B)   6
    (C)   7
    (D)   8
    (E)   9

110. If a and b are positive whole numbers and a^b is odd, which of the following must be true?

    I. a is odd.
    II. b is odd.

    (F) I only
    (G) II only
    (H) Neither I nor II
    (J) Either I or II, but not both.
    (K) Both I and II

Square Roots

111. $\sqrt{64} =$

    (A)   4
    (B)   8
    (C)   16
    (D)   32
    (E)   164

112. $\sqrt{54} =$

    (F) $6\sqrt{3}$
    (G) $3\sqrt{6}$
    (H) $18\sqrt{3}$
    (J) $27\sqrt{2}$
    (K)   27

113. $\dfrac{\sqrt{14}}{\sqrt{7}} =$

    (A) $\dfrac{1}{2}$

    (B)   2

    (C) $\sqrt{2}$

    (D) $\dfrac{\sqrt{2}}{2}$

    (E)   7

114. $\sqrt{\dfrac{16}{25}} =$

    (F) $\dfrac{2}{5}$

    (G) $\dfrac{4}{5}$

    (H) $\dfrac{8}{5}$

    (J) $\dfrac{16}{5}$

    (K) $\dfrac{2}{25}$

115. $\sqrt{0.0016} =$

    (A) 0.04
    (B) 0.08
    (C) 0.004
    (D) 0.0004
    (E) 0.0008

116. For all positive real numbers x, y, and z,
$\sqrt{8xy^2z^3} =$

    (F) $2yz\sqrt{2xz}$

    (G) $2yz^2\sqrt{2xyz}$

    (H) $4yz\sqrt{xz}$

    (J) $4yz\sqrt{2xz}$

    (K) $2yz^2\sqrt{xyz}$

117. $\sqrt{50} + \sqrt{8} + \sqrt{18} =$

    (A) 12

    (B) $10\sqrt{2}$

    (C) $4\sqrt{19}$

    (D) 20

    (E) 38

118. $(5\sqrt{3})^2 =$

    (F) 15

    (G) $10\sqrt{3}$

    (H) $25\sqrt{3}$

    (J) 30

    (K) 75

119. Which of the following is the reciprocal of $\sqrt{2}$?

    (A) $\sqrt{2}$

    (B) $-\sqrt{2}$

    (C) $2 - \sqrt{2}$

    (D) $\frac{1}{2}\sqrt{2}$

    (E) $2\sqrt{2}$

120. If the area of a square is 32, which of the following is the best approximation of the length of one side of the square?

    (F) 2.8

    (G) 5.7

    (H) 7.3

    (J) 8.0

    (K) 16.0

Algebraic Expressions

121. $3c + 4c =$

    (A) $5c$

    (B) $7c$

    (C) $12c$

    (D) $7c^2$

    (E) $12c^2$

122. $(2d^2 + 5d - 6) + (d^2 - 4d - 4) =$

    (F) $d^2 + d + 2$

    (G) $2d^2 + d + 2$

    (H) $2d^4 + 20d + 24$

    (J) $3d^2 + d - 10$

    (K) $3d^2 - 9d + 10$

123. For all x, $2x^2 + 3x + x^2 - 4x - x =$

    (A) x^3

    (B) $5x^2$

    (C) $3x^2 - 2x$

    (D) $3x^4 - x^2$

    (E) $5x^4 - x^2$

124. For all x, $3x^2 \times 5x^3 =$

    (F) $8x^5$

    (G) $8x^6$

    (H) $15x^5$

    (J) $15x^6$

    (K) $15x^8$

125. $(-2n)(-2n^2)(-2n^2) =$

    (A) $-8n^4$

    (B) $-8n^5$

    (C) $-64n^5$

    (D) $64n^4$

    (E) $64n^5$

126. Which of the following is equivalent to $(5x^2 + 6x - 7) - (6x^2 - 7x - 8)$?

    (F) $-x^2 - x - 1$

    (G) $-x^2 + 13x - 1$

    (H) $-x^2 - x + 1$

    (J) $-x^2 + 13x + 1$

    (K) $11x^2 - x - 15$

127. What is the value of $\frac{k^2 - k}{2}$ when $k = 10$?

    (A) 5
    (B) 15
    (C) 20
    (D) 25
    (E) 45

128. If $x = -5$, then $2x^2 - 6x + 5 =$

    (F) -15
    (G) 15
    (H) 25
    (J) 85
    (K) 135

129. What is the value of $x^2 - 2x$ when $x = -2$?

    (A) -8
    (B) -4
    (C) 0
    (D) 4
    (E) 8

130. The quantity m is equal to $\frac{x^2 y}{2xy^2}$. If $x = 2y$, and $xy \neq 0$, then $m =$

    (F) $\frac{1}{8}$

    (G) $\frac{1}{4}$

    (H) $\frac{1}{2}$

    (J) 1

    (K) 2

Equations

131. If $6m - 8 = 10 - 3m$, what is the value of m ?

    (A) 2
    (B) 3
    (C) 4
    (D) 5
    (E) 6

132. If $5n + 3p = 8n - 3p$, what is the value of n in terms of p ?

    (F) $\frac{p}{4}$

    (G) $\frac{p}{2}$

    (H) $2p$

    (J) $4p$

    (K) $5p$

133. If $x = y + 2$, what is the value of $3x - 4$, in terms of y ?

    (A) $y - 2$
    (B) $y + 6$
    (C) $2y + 6$
    (D) $4y - 4$
    (E) $3y + 2$

134. If $\frac{s}{1,000} = \frac{3}{5}$, what is the value of s ?

    (F) 6
    (G) 60
    (H) 600
    (J) 800
    (K) 6,000

135. If $n = 4p - 8$, then what is the value of $n - 4$ in terms of p ?

    (A) $2p - 4$
    (B) $4p - 4$
    (C) $4p - 8$
    (D) $2p - 12$
    (E) $4p - 12$

136. If $2r + 8 = 24$, then $2r + 2 =$

    (F) 8
    (G) 16
    (H) 18
    (J) 24
    (K) 32

137. Which of the following is a possible value of *z* if
    $2 \times (z - 3) > 6$ and $z + 4 < 15$?

    (A)   3
    (B)   6
    (C)   7
    (D)   11
    (E)   15

138. If $6 \times (C + D) = 48$, and *D* is less than 5, then *C*
    could be any of the following EXCEPT

    (F)   8
    (G)   7
    (H)   6
    (J)   4
    (K)   2

Questions 139–140 refer to the following definition.

    For all real numbers *q* and *r*, let
        $q//r = (q \times r) - (q - r)$.

139. $8//2 =$

    (A)   6
    (B)   8
    (C)   10
    (D)   16
    (E)   24

140. If $P//3 = 11$, then $P =$

    (F)   3
    (G)   4
    (H)   6
    (J)   7
    (K)   11

Lines and Angles

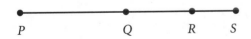

141. In the figure above, $PR = 16$, $QS = 11$, and
    $PS = 20$. What is the length of *QR* ?

    (A)   7
    (B)   8
    (C)   9
    (D)   10
    (E)   11

142. In the figure above, the distance from *B* to *C* is
    twice the distance from *A* to *B*, and the distance
    from *C* to *D* is equal to half the distance from *A*
    to *C*. If the distance from *B* to *C* is 12, what is
    the distance from *A* to *D* ?

    (A)   18
    (B)   24
    (C)   27
    (D)   32
    (E)   36

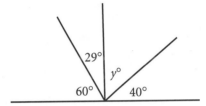

143. In the figure above, what is the value of *y* ?

    (A)   41
    (B)   49
    (C)   51
    (D)   59
    (E)   61

Triangles

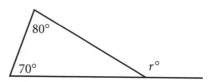

146. In the figure above, $r =$

    (F)   30
    (G)   70
    (H)   80
    (J)   110
    (K)   150

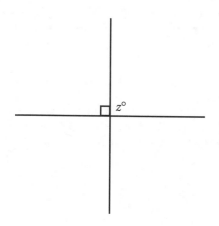

144. What is the value of z ?

    (F)   22.5
    (G)   45
    (H)   90
    (J)   180
    (K)   360

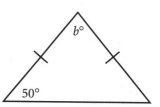

147. In the figure above, $b =$

    (F)   50
    (G)   70
    (H)   80
    (J)   100
    (K)   130

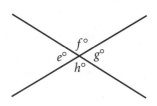

145. $e + f =$

    (F)   90
    (G)   135
    (H)   180
    (J)   270
    (K)   360

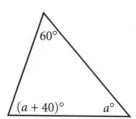

148. In the figure above, what is the value of a ?

    (F)   20
    (G)   40
    (H)   50
    (J)   60
    (K)   80

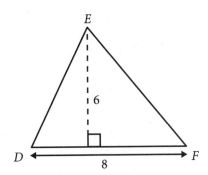

149. What is the area of triangle *DEF* in the figure above?

(A) 14
(B) 15
(C) 24
(D) 32
(E) 48

150. If the measure of one angle of an isosceles triangle is 80°, which of the following could be the measure of another angle of the triangle?

I. 20°
II. 50°
III. 80°

(F) I only
(G) II only
(H) III only
(J) I and III only
(K) I, II, and III

151. If the measure of one angle of an isosceles triangle is 100°, which of the following could be the measure of another angle of the triangle?

I. 40°
II. 50°
III. 100°

(A) I only
(B) II only
(C) III only
(D) I and III only
(E) I, II, and III

152. If the lengths of the sides of a triangle are 3, 4, and 5, what is the area of that triangle?

(F) 6
(G) 7.5
(H) 10
(J) 12
(K) 15

Rectangles, Squares, and Other Polygons

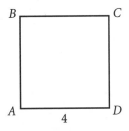

153. In the figure above, *ABCD* is a square. What is the length of *AB* ?

(F) 1
(G) 2
(H) 4
(J) 16
(K) 90

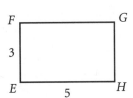

154. What is the perimeter of rectangle *EFGH* ?

(A) 8
(B) 15
(C) 16
(D) 30
(E) 32

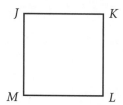

155. If the perimeter of square *JKLM* is 64, what is the length of side *JK* ?

(F)   4
(G)   8
(H)   16
(J)   32
(K)   90

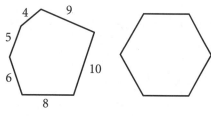

Polygon *A*   Polygon *B*

156. In the figure above, polygons *A* and *B* have the same perimeter. If all the sides of polygon *B* are of equal length, what is the length of one side of polygon *B* ?

(A)   4
(B)   5
(C)   6
(D)   7
(E)   8

157. The area of a rectangle is 15, and the lengths of all four sides are whole numbers. What is the greatest possible perimeter of the rectangle?

(A)   8
(B)   12
(C)   16
(D)   24
(E)   32

Circles

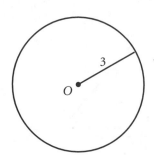

158. In the figure above, what is the diameter of the circle with center *O* ?

(F)   3
(G)   6
(H)   9
(J)   3π
(K)   6π

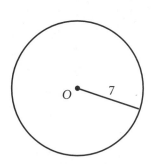

159. In the figure above, what is the area of the circle with center *O* ?

(F)   14
(G)   49
(H)   7π
(J)   14π
(K)   49π

160. What is the circumference of a circle with radius 5 ?

(A)   5π
(B)   10π
(C)   20π
(D)   25π
(E)   100π

161. What is the area of a circle with radius 5 ?

   (F) 5π
   (G) 10π
   (H) 20π
   (J) 25π
   (K) 100π

162. What is the radius of a circle with circumference 100π ?

   (A) 5
   (B) 10
   (C) 25
   (D) 50
   (E) 100

163. What is the radius of a circle with area 100π ?

   (F) 5
   (G) 10
   (H) 25
   (J) 50
   (K) 100

164. What is the diameter of a circle with circumference 36π ?

   (A) 3
   (B) 6
   (C) 12
   (D) 18
   (E) 36

165. What is the diameter of a circle with area 36π ?

   (F) 3
   (G) 6
   (H) 12
   (J) 18
   (K) 36

Quantitative Comparisons I

Directions: Note the given information, if any, and then compare the quantity in Column A to the quantity in Column B. Answer

   A if the quantity in Column A is greater
   B if the quantity in Column B is greater
   C if the two quantities are equal
   D if the relationship cannot be determined from the information given

Column A	Column B

166. 52% of 34 | 17

167. 0.76 | $\frac{3}{4}$

$0 < x < 1$

168. $3x$ | $2x$

169. x | $x - 1$

170. x | $-x$

$x < 0$

171. x | x^2

Column A   Column B

172.
$$\frac{1}{8} + \frac{1}{10}$$ $$\frac{1}{9} + \frac{1}{11}$$

$a > b > c > 0$

173.
$a - c$ $b - c$

174.
50×8.01 $\dfrac{801}{2}$

175.
$\dfrac{(-2)(-4)}{(-6)(-8)}$ $\dfrac{(-6)(-8)}{(-4)(-10)(-12)}$

Quantitative Comparisons II

Column A   Column B

176.
-2 -1

$14 < x < 16$
$18 < y < 20$

177.
34 $x + y$

178.
$4x + 5$ $5x$

Column A   Column B

179.
748 + 749 + 750 + 751 + 752   5(750)

180.
 $\sqrt{10} + \sqrt{65}$ $3 + 8$

$x > 0$

181.
$\dfrac{99x}{100}$ $\dfrac{100x}{99}$

The product of two whole numbers is 10.

182.
6   The sum of the whole numbers

183.
19(56) + 44(19)   1901

A   B   C   D

$AC = BD$

184.
AB BC

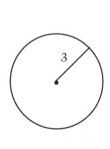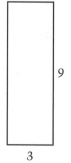

The radius of the circle above is 3 and the quadrilateral above is a rectangle

185.
The area of the circle   The area of the rectangle

Synonyms

1. CONVENE: (A) assemble (B) resume (C) depart (D) take over (E) confer

2. GLIB: (F) passionate (G) lengthy (H) articulate (J) timely (K) opportune

3. MARVEL: (A) scoff (B) recoil (C) wonder (D) point (E) shake

4. ULTIMATE: (F) correct (G) deplorable (H) torrid (J) despicable (K) final

5. FORMIDABLE: (A) imposing (B) proposed (C) eroded (D) picturesque (E) forbidden

6. QUENCH: (F) exaggerate (G) indicate (H) satisfy (J) ban (K) withdraw

7. ECCENTRIC: (A) exacting (B) apt (C) massive (D) absurd (E) peculiar

8. DEBRIS: (F) wreckage (G) evidence (H) detour (J) onlooker (K) condition

9. ALLOT: (A) collect (B) restrict (C) abolish (D) apportion (E) reimburse

10. TETHER: (F) muzzle (G) leash (H) license (J) collar (K) guard

11. MAR: (A) loosen (B) spoil (C) encircle (D) purify (E) camouflage

12. SAVOR: (F) prolong (G) verify (H) relish (J) boast (K) recall

13. ANTIDOTE: (A) effect (B) symptom (C) source (D) remedy (E) taste

14. TAUT: (F) aloft (G) tight (H) slack (J) frayed (K) inert

15. OBSOLETE: (A) outdated (B) dangerous (C) broken (D) noisy (E) inefficient

16. VEX: (F) prod (G) coerce (H) enrage (J) baffle (K) annoy

17. DIN: (A) aroma (B) pressure (C) noise (D) fumes (E) strife

18. INCENTIVE: (F) plan (G) space (H) threat (J) inducement (K) deadline

19. DEJECTED: (A) saddened (B) reported (C) fired (D) ruined (E) sickened

20. STAUNCH: (F) sympathetic (G) renowned (H) steadfast (J) flexible (K) vocal

21. PERJURY: (A) assault (B) blackmail (C) theft (D) insubordination (E) lying

22. PETRIFY: (F) shock (G) entertain (H) edify (J) confuse (K) stimulate

23. IMMINENT: (A) huge (B) dangerous (C) insignificant (D) impending (E) abating

24. ABDUCT: (F) initiate (G) steal (H) kidnap (J) flatter (K) tutor

25. TORRID: (A) freezing (B) treacherous (C) pleasant (D) awful (E) sweltering

26. LURID: (F) ridiculous (G) dingy (H) hidden (J) clear (K) sensational

27. INCESSANT: (A) eventual (B) internal (C) influential (D) generous (E) unending

28. CIRCUMVENT: (F) ventilate (G) go around (H) accumulate (J) expose to (K) cut into

29. CALLOUS: (A) illustrious (B) insensitive (C) passionate (D) withdrawn (E) impatient

30. NARRATIVE: (F) speaker (G) rodent (H) relative (J) story (K) addition

31. REIGN: (A) rule (B) remain (C) resign (D) continue (E) emerge

32. OPTION: (F) solution (G) hope (H) goal (J) inspiration (K) alternative

33. FATIGUED: (A) exhausted (B) pestered (C) irritated (D) bored (E) unnerved

34. FLIPPANT: (F) ingenious (G) weak (H) comical (J) sincere (K) frivolous

35. ADHERE: (A) cling (B) prefer (C) remember (D) revere (E) interpret

36. VEHEMENT: (F) overwhelming (G) immediate (H) unanimous (J) fiery (K) predictable

37. INFECTIOUS: (A) deadly (B) mysterious (C) embarrassing (D) common (E) contagious

38. INSOMNIA: (F) alienation (G) sleeplessness (H) mania (J) anxiety (K) depression

39. PUNGENT: (A) tempting (B) spicy (C) familiar (D) toxic (E) simmering

40. GRUESOME: (F) violent (G) awesome (H) sentimental (J) hideous (K) mediocre

41. MELANCHOLY: (A) perplexed (B) sad (C) tired (D) lonely (E) old-fashioned

42. NAUSEOUS: (F) palatable (G) novel (H) bland (J) sickening (K) surprising

43. CASCADE: (A) container (B) ton (C) volley (D) shower (E) wall

44. ABYSS: (F) pit (G) oasis (H) river (J) cascade (K) monastery

45. SEVER: (A) treat harshly (B) cut apart (C) segregate (D) scorch (E) signify

46. DOGGED: (F) obstinate (G) confident (H) rabid (J) fanatical (K) exhausted

47. ALLAY: (A) arise (B) adjust (C) soothe (D) increase (E) terrify

48. TUMULT: (F) twilight (G) hilarity (H) commotion (J) fall (K) darkness

49. SCATHING: (A) enthusiastic (B) indifferent (C) mixed (D) harsh (E) supportive

50. BEWILDER: (F) perplex (G) anger (H) amuse (J) surprise (K) horrify

51. MINUSCULE: (A) massive (B) invisible (C) tiny (D) lethal (E) precise

52. COLLUSION: (F) accident (G) brainstorm (H) fracture (J) evasion (K) conspiracy

53. DISSEMINATE: (A) spread (B) ignore (C) debate (D) analyze (E) scoff

54. PARADOX: (F) inconsistency (G) best (H) absurdity (J) pain (K) flaw

55. EXOTIC: (A) glamorous (B) tropical (C) foreign (D) exclusive (E) secret

56. ARMADA: (F) fleet (G) division (H) madness (J) view (K) weaponry

57. DEJECTED: (A) rejected (B) depressed (C) thrown (D) demolished (E) theorized

58. LADEN: (F) single (G) dense (H) loaded (J) buckled (K) liberated

59. INTIMATE: (A) frighten (B) time (C) interview (D) hint (E) learn

60. MALEVOLENCE: (F) humor (G) elevation (H) revolt (J) guilt (K) evil

61. DINGY: (A) crazy (B) dirty (C) expensive (D) noisy (E) cheap

62. ERA: (F) century (G) area (H) period (J) settlement (K) country

63. WRATH: (A) anger (B) insomnia (C) mood (D) sarcasm (E) acclaim

64. GLEE: (F) fear (G) indifference (H) interest (J) wrath (K) joy

65. MIMIC: (A) surrender (B) imitate (C) cure (D) limit (E) analyze

66. CUE: (F) salary (G) inspiration (H) script (J) prompt (K) style

67. FAUNA: (A) beer (B) cuisine (C) natives
(D) animals (E) fruits

68. AUXILIARY: (F) incidental (G) exotic
(H) secondary (J) military (K) rotating

69. AMOROUS: (A) urgent (B) anonymous
(C) melancholy (D) romantic (E) fluent

70. BOULEVARD: (F) park (G) avenue
(H) boutique (J) intersection (K) bakery

71. WANE: (A) wander (B) blow (C) decrease
(D) measure (E) tumble

72. CACHE: (F) thief (G) shipment (H) brooch
(J) sack (K) stash

73. RANCOR: (A) bitterness (B) pleasure
(C) nostalgia (D) shock (E) exuberance

74. DECLAMATION: (F) announcement
(G) deputy (H) speech (J) proposal
(K) campaign

75. DISCLOSE: (A) expose (B) suffer (C) cover
(D) commit (E) believe

76. SINISTER: (F) cryptic (G) jovial
(H) threatening (J) odd (K) wise

77. LUNGE: (A) crash (B) topple (C) creep
(D) plunge (E) speed

78. CONDONE: (F) condemn (G) donate
(H) approve (J) conduct (K) soften

79. ZEALOUS: (A) scrupulous (B) original
(C) fanatical (D) optimistic (E) astute

80. REPARTEE: (F) pratfall (G) guess
(H) report (J) retort (K) ignorance

81. APPREHENSION: (A) anxiety (B) awe
(C) relief (D) excitement (E) hilarity

82. REALIZATION: (F) awareness (G) existence
(H) formation (J) projection (K)
truthfulness

83. OBSTINATE: (A) stubborn (B) fat
(C) intriguing (D) flippant (E) sociable

84. EBULLIENT: (F) fat (G) elated
(H) insecure (J) pious (K) gregarious

85. SCALD: (A) chastise (B) burn (C) hate
(D) injure (E) worry

86. AUDACITY: (F) boldness (G) intellect
(H) generosity (J) affectation (K) lunacy

87. MAGNANIMOUS: (A) amplified
(B) generous (C) magnified (D)
tremendous (E) unconcerned

88. TEMPERATE: (F) cranky (G) heated
(H) moderate (J) raised (K) temporary

89. COPIOUS: (A) duplicated (B) stagnant
(C) illegible (D) plentiful (E) serious

90. ENIGMA: (F) failure (G) attraction
(H) paradox (J) challenge (K) mystery

Analogies

1. Food is to famine as
   (A) drink is to thirst
   (B) canal is to irrigation
   (C) disease is to plague
   (D) river is to flood
   (E) water is to drought

2. Airplane is to pilot as car is to
   (F) fly (G) drive (H) travel
   (J) control (K) pass

3. Ample is to excessive as
   (A) desirable is to endurable
   (B) peaceful is to tranquil
   (C) timid is to brave
   (D) bold is to reckless
   (E) cowardly is to daunted

4. Cow is to calf as
   (F) hog is to pork
   (G) horse is to mule
   (H) sheep is to lamb
   (J) tiger is to stripe
   (K) ram is to ewe

5. Test is to study as
   (A) makeup is to apply
   (B) food is to prepare
   (C) play is to rehearse
   (D) course is to pass
   (E) opera is to sing

6. Banana is to peel as corn is to
   (F) husk (G) shell (H) ear
   (J) kernel (K) ground

7. Tactile is to touch as
   (A) deaf is to hearing
   (B) loud is to sound
   (C) acrid is to smell
   (D) visual is to sight
   (E) numb is to sense

8. Hour is to minute as dollar is to
   (F) money (G) time (H) cent
   (J) day (K) purchase

9. Tornado is to breeze as
   (A) storm is to drizzle
   (B) season is to monsoon
   (C) time is to weather
   (D) lightning is to thunder
   (E) rain is to water

10. Ship is to dock as
    (F) truck is to drive
    (G) wheel is to steer
    (H) horse is to ride
    (J) raft is to float
    (K) car is to park

11. Asparagus is to vegetable as
    (A) pea is to carrot
    (B) band is to polka
    (C) violin is to orchestra
    (D) waltz is to dance
    (E) dress is to ball

12. Time is to clock as direction is to
    (F) watch (G) compass (H) needle
    (J) hand (K) north

13. Light is to lamp as heat is to
    (A) bulb (B) electricity (C) radiator
    (D) valve (E) oil

14. Banal is to originality as
    (F) cured is to meat
    (G) clever is to invention
    (H) certain is to meaning
    (J) paltry is to worth
    (K) jamb is to door

15. Staircase is to step as
    (A) ladder is to rung
    (B) paper is to wall
    (C) brush is to paint
    (D) grass is to ground
    (E) success is to method

16. Throne is to king as
    (F) drawer is to desk
    (G) crown is to queen
    (H) chair is to table
    (J) gavel is to hammer
    (K) bench is to judge

17. Listen is to eavesdrop as watch is to
    (A) look   (B) observe   (C) spy
    (D) overhear   (E) interrupt

18. Biology is to life as
    (F) identity is to person
    (G) psychology is to mind
    (H) health is to doctor
    (J) medicine is to surgery
    (K) decay is to teeth

19. Generosity is to miser as
    (A) affluence is to money
    (B) ethics is to doctor
    (C) impiety is to saint
    (D) training is to engineer
    (E) ruthlessness is to criminal

20. Rabbit is to hutch as
    (F) tractor is to farm
    (G) chicken is to coop
    (H) bar is to cage
    (J) feed is to pen
    (K) hay is to stable

21. Volcano is to erupt as
    (A) lava is to flow
    (B) ball is to bounce
    (C) metal is to erode
    (D) bomb is to explode
    (E) army is to assault

22. Soldier is to regiment as student is to
    (F) class   (G) troops   (H) platoon
    (J) school   (K) teacher

23. Reveal is to conceal as
    (A) secrete is to hide
    (B) dig is to delve
    (C) trouble is to stir
    (D) affirm is to repudiate
    (E) suspect is to confirm

24. Shout is to whisper as guzzle is to
    (F) quiet   (G) sip   (H) forage
    (J) eat   (K) consume

25. Warm is to scorching as
    (A) polite is to insolent
    (B) friendly is to affable
    (C) unfriendly is to hostile
    (D) strong is to tough
    (E) hot is to humid

26. Grocer is to food as
    (F) carnivore is to meat
    (G) locksmith is to key
    (H) librarian is to book
    (J) apothecary is to medicine
    (K) writer is to pen

27. Score is to musician as script is to
    (A) playwright   (B) author
    (C) dancer   (D) sculptor   (E) actor

28. Line is to circle as
    (F) plane is to sphere
    (G) triangle is to pyramid
    (H) angle is to square
    (J) pentagon is to hexagon
    (K) point is to surface

29. Movement is to symphony as
    (A) note is to piano
    (B) act is to play
    (C) canvas is to painting
    (D) meter is to poem
    (E) frame is to film

30. Curtail is to length as constrict is to
    (F) width   (G) eternity   (H) condition
    (J) honor   (K) discomfort

31. Book is to library as
    (A) car is to garage
    (B) apple is to tree
    (C) cabinet is to kitchen
    (D) video is to television
    (E) shade is to window

32. Chapter is to book as scene is to
    (F) actor (G) play (H) director (J) stage
    (K) audience

33. Fastidious is to untidiness as
    (A) punctual is to lateness
    (B) unruly is to disorder
    (C) immortal is to saint
    (D) improbable is to story
    (E) dishonest is to falsehood

34. Trumpet is to brass as flute is to
    (F) percussion
    (G) woodwind
    (H) string
    (J) clarinet
    (K) harmony

35. Benefactor is to generous as skinflint is to
    (A) stingy
    (B) irritable
    (C) ancient
    (D) wealthy
    (E) popular

36. Reclusive is to isolation as
    (F) exclusive is to contract
    (G) amiable is to confrontation
    (H) difficult is to problem
    (J) quiet is to peace
    (K) sociable is to company

37. Shoal is to fish as herd is to
    (A) dogs (B) geese (C) sheep
    (D) elephants (E) horses

38. Entertain is to enthrall as
    (F) mock is to humiliate
    (G) attack is to defend
    (H) instruct is to teach
    (J) subvert is to suggest
    (K) employ is to resign

39. Umbrella is to rain as
    (A) ski is to snow
    (B) parasol is to sun
    (C) trenchcoat is to fog
    (D) sweater is to wind
    (E) water is to drought

40. Weak is to enervated as
    (F) sick is to tired
    (G) lethargic is to muscular
    (H) pristine is to chaotic
    (J) large is to colossal
    (K) old is to original

41. Abbreviate is to speech as
    (A) applaud is to performance
    (B) edit is to article
    (C) extend is to deadline
    (D) meet is to objective
    (E) cancel is to reservation

42. Witness is to testimony as
    (F) professor is to lecture
    (G) traitor is to accusation
    (H) accountant is to taxation
    (J) plumber is to faucet
    (K) mechanic is to garage

43. Month is to year as
    (A) scale is to ounce
    (B) hour is to mile
    (C) inch is to foot
    (D) spring is to season
    (E) minute is to time

44. Stationary is to motion as
    (F) abundant is to plenty
    (G) empty is to content
    (H) elementary is to education
    (J) careful is to error
    (K) capacious is to limit

45. Fresh is to hackneyed as original is to
    (A) ancient (B) dusty (C) copied
    (D) wasted (E) priceless

Reading Comprehension

Martha Graham

Line   The dancer and choreographer Martha Graham is regarded as one of the outstanding innovators in the history of dance. In a career that lasted over fifty years, Graham created more than 170 works ranging
(5) from solos to large-scale pieces, and danced in most of them herself. Trained in a variety of different international styles of dance, she set out in the mid-1920s to break away from the rigid traditions of classical ballet. She wanted to create new dance forms
(10) and movements that would reflect the changed atmosphere of the postwar period.

     Her early dances reflect this spirit. She rejected the extravagant stylization of classical ballet, using the natural breath pulse as the basis for movement, instead
(15) of formalized classical motions. She avoided decorative sets and costumes, and used an all-female dance troupe. Moreover, her productions used music purely as an accompaniment to dance rather than as an elaborate showpiece in itself. In fact, Graham's early
(20) work was so stark and severe that it was described by one critic as "uncompromisingly ugly." As the decades passed, however, Graham's work found wider acceptance. By the 1940s, it had already become the tradition against which a new avant-garde was
(25) rebelling—a fate common to all artistic revolutions.

1. Which of the following best tells what this passage is about?
   (A) changes in the art world during the 1920s
   (B) the revolution in classical ballet
   (C) Graham's ground-breaking role as a dancer and choreographer
   (D) the critical reception of Graham's early works
   (E) the experience of seeing Graham's dances performed

2. The passage suggests that Martha Graham introduced new dance techniques in order to
   (F) attract attention to her all-female troupe
   (G) visually dramatize the ugliness of life
   (H) express the changed mood of her time
   (J) strike a blow at the traditions of classical ballet

   (K) emphasize the rigidity of conventional dance movement

3. What can be inferred from the passage about the "formalized classical motions" (line 15) of ballet dancers prior to the 1920s?
   (A) They were originally developed to reflect the spirit of the times.
   (B) They expressed universal ideas and feelings.
   (C) They depicted characters from Greek mythology.
   (D) They were not based on natural breathing rhythms.
   (E) They were easier than the motions used by Graham's dancers.

4. It can be inferred that classical ballet of the early twentieth century generally
   (F) was loose and formless
   (G) was disliked by critics and the public
   (H) sought to dramatize ugliness
   (J) reflected the changing times
   (K) employed elaborate sets and costumes

5. The "fate common to all artistic revolutions" (line 25) is best illustrated by which of the following?
   (A) a revolutionary method of painting that is eventually accepted, but later rejected by innovative artists
   (B) a style of musical composition that ignores the rules of harmony and emphasizes dissonance and ugly sounds
   (C) a movement in fiction that focuses on the gritty aspects of everyday life rather than its beautiful aspects
   (D) a new trend in theatrical performance that becomes immensely popular but is soon forgotten
   (E) a technical innovation in cinematography that makes moviemaking much less expensive

Tunnels

Line   Tunnel construction is costly and dangerous, but new technologies are allowing tunnelers to work more quickly and safely than ever before. Today's rock tunnels are being drilled by modern full-face tunnel-
(5)   boring machines (TBMs). The drilling end of a TBM consists of a rotating cutterhead whose diameter covers the entire face of a tunnel. As the cutterhead turns, hard-steel blades cut steadily through the rock. The first successful hard-rock TBM was built in 1957,
(10)   and many improvements have been made in TBM design in subsequent years.

        Developments in TBM technology have helped spur ambitious new projects. Most notable is the 50-kilometer Eurotunnel (also known as the Chunnel)
(15)   which has been bored by modern TBMs beneath the English Channel. The tunneling was done by British and French teams that started on opposite sides of the Channel and eventually met underground, in the middle. Thus TBMs have contributed to building a
(20)   technological and cultural milestone. Trains can now travel between England and France in under an hour, and for the first time in history Britain and continental Europe are linked by land.

6. The passage suggests that, despite three decades' worth of technological improvement, tunnel construction is

    (F) rarely worth the risks involved

    (G) still expensive and dangerous

    (H) possible only with international cooperation

    (J) heavily reliant on geological guesswork

    (K) not as efficient as it should be

7. Which of the following best describes what this passage is about?

    (A) Why tunnel construction is expensive

    (B) The significance of the Eurotunnel

    (C) How TBMs operate

    (D) Tunnel construction with TBMs

    (E) Why the Eurotunnel was difficult to dig

8. The author most likely describes the Eurotunnel as a "cultural milestone" (line 20) because it

    (F) lifts travel restrictions among all European countries

    (G) connects Europe and Britain by land for the first time

    (H) harms the relationship between Britain and France

    (J) affects the way all future tunnels are dug

    (K) changes the political climate in Europe

9. As it is used in line 13, the word "notable" most nearly means

    (A) popular

    (B) legendary

    (C) remarkable

    (D) weighty

    (E) memorable

10. The attitude of the writer towards the subject is best described as

    (F) enthusiastic

    (G) uncertain

    (H) cautious

    (J) bitter

    (K) jubilant

Acoustics

Line   Almost everyone enjoys hearing some kind of
live music. But few of us realize the complex process
that goes into designing the acoustics of concert and
lecture halls. In the design of any building where
(5) audibility of sound is a major consideration, architects
have to carefully match the space and materials they
use to the intended purpose of the venue. One problem
is that the intensity of sound may build too quickly in
an enclosed space. Another problem is that only part
(10) of the sound we hear in any large room or auditorium
comes directly from the source. Much of it reaches us
a fraction of a second later after it has been reflected
off the walls, ceiling and floor as reverberated sound.
How much each room reverberates depends upon both
(15) its size, and the ability of its contents to absorb sound.
Too little reverberation can make music sound thin
and weak; too much can blur the listener's sense of
where one note stops and the next begins.
Consequently the most important factor in acoustic
(20) design is the time it takes for these reverberations to
die down altogether, called the reverberation time.

11. Which of the following is the main topic of this
passage?

    (A) the challenges of an architect's job

    (B) the differences between speech and music

    (C) the experience of hearing live music

    (D) the role of reverberation in acoustic design

    (E) the construction of large buildings

12. The passage suggests that the "complex process"
of acoustic design (line 2) is

    (F) not widely appreciated by the public

    (G) really a matter of listener sensitivity

    (H) wholly dependent on the choice of con-
struction materials

    (J) an engineer's problem, not an architect's

    (K) most difficult in concert hall construction

13. According to the passage, audibility of sound is
influenced by which of the following factors?

    I. the type of materials used to construct a
building

    II. the reflection of sound off a room's ceiling
or walls

    III. the size and purpose of a particular room
or space

    (A) I only

    (B) II only

    (C) I and II

    (D) II and III

    (E) I, II and III

14. According to the passage, too little reverberation
in a concert hall can result in

    (F) a rapid increase in the volume of sound

    (G) the blurring of details in a piece of musical

    (H) a quiet and insubstantial quality of sound

    (J) confusion among a listening audience

    (K) an inaccurate estimate of its reverberation
time

15. Which of the following does the author regard as
the most significant consideration in the design
of a concert hall?

    (A) an appreciation for music

    (B) an understanding of reverberation time

    (C) the choice of building materials

    (D) the purpose of the venue

    (E) the audience capacity

Termites

Line   Usually regarded as a pest, the termites of South
Florida provide an excellent illustration of nature at
work. In the natural world, when two or more different
organisms coexist to each other's benefit, it's called a
(5) symbiotic relationship. The dominant member of the
symbiotic pair or group is known as the "host," while a
smaller, less dominant member is a "parasite." A
classic symbiotic relationship of this kind takes place
in the digestive tract of Florida wood-eating termites.
(10) We think of a termite as being able to digest wood, but
it really cannot. The termite plays host to parasitic
protozoans, single-celled organisms that live in the
termite's gut. The protozoans provide the termite with
a service necessary to its survival: they digest the
(15) cellulose in the wood that it consumes.

16. Which of the following is suggested in the
passage about the protozoans?

    (F) They are essential to the continued exis-
tence of termites.

    (G) They are both a parasitic and a host organ-
ism.

    (H) They are roughly equal in size to bacteria.

    (J) They attach themselves to the membranes
of termites.

    (K) They can survive on their own when neces-
sary.

17. Which of the following best describes what this
passage is about?

    (A) Why most parasites perform a useful func-
tion

    (B) Why a termite cannot digest food

    (C) How symbiotic relationships have evolved

    (D) Why protozoans digest wood

    (E) How two organisms cooperate to survive

18. According to the passage, a "host" organism is
generally

    (F) found in South Florida

    (G) the dominant partner in a symbiotic rela-
tionship

    (H) unable to digest cellulose

    (J) able to survive on its own

    (K) associated with single-celled organisms

19. With which of the following statements about a
symbiotic relationship would the author most
likely agree?

    (A) It involves organisms that are alike.

    (B) It often involves harmful parasites.

    (C) It mostly involves tiny organisms.

    (D) It usually involves organisms that are simi-
lar.

    (E) It may be beneficial to both organisms.

20. The relationship between termites and
protozoans is best described as

    (F) cooperative

    (G) occasional

    (H) friendly

    (J) violent

    (K) improbable

Bogs

Line

A typical northern bog, also called a sphagnum bog, is a wetland ecosystem characterized by soggy, poorly drained soil. The dominant plants in bogs are various species of sphagnum mosses, which absorb

(5) and retain water like sponges. Bogs formed in old, shallow depressions, usually in areas that were covered with glaciers 25,000 to 2.5 million years ago. As glacial ice melted, these scooped-out depressions filled with water. If the water had a low mineral

(10) content, mosses colonized the depressions and converted them into bogs.

How do these conditions develop? The mineral content of the water remains low once a bog is formed because pure rainwater is usually the only source of

(15) new water. Furthermore, any minerals that are available in the water are absorbed by the mosses and replaced with acid. This means that bogs eventually become highly acidic, because the mosses prevent water from draining out. Bogs are, in fact, so water-

(20) soaked due to poor drainage that air cannot even pass through the plants to the soil. Except for the top layers of dead vegetation, the soil contains practically no oxygen.

21. This passage deals primarily with

   (A) the minerals provided by bogs
   (B) the development of bogs
   (C) how peat changes to coal
   (D) how glaciers reshape the land
   (E) various different kinds of wetlands

22. In line 2, the word "characterized" most nearly means

   (F) labelled
   (G) marked
   (H) portrayed
   (J) described
   (K) tagged

23. The passage suggests that which of the following conditions is necessary for the maintenance of bogs?

   (A) mineral-rich water
   (B) the presence of peat
   (C) an adequate oxygen supply
   (D) regular intervals of rain
   (E) above-average sunlight

24. According to the passage, bogs become highly acidic as they develop because

   (F) they are fed by melting ice
   (G) they are supplied with certain minerals
   (H) they support many organisms
   (J) they are frequently flooded by rainfall
   (K) they do not drain well

25. It can be inferred from the passage that pure rainwater is

   (A) possible to extract from bogs
   (B) low in mineral content
   (C) becoming increasingly difficult to obtain
   (D) available only in rural areas
   (E) low in oxygen content

Ozone

Line   The ozone layer of the atmosphere protects the
earth from harmful solar radiation. But the
ozonosphere is fragile, and evidence indicates that it is
thinning: since 1975, the amount of radiation reaching
(5)   the Earth has increased steadily. The implications of
this are not good. Solar radiation causes cancer and
contributes to other serious illnesses. Also, as radiation
increases, more and more warm air gets trapped near
the Earth, and hot, humid conditions like those in a
(10) greenhouse begin to prevail. Some scientists warn that
within 50 years people could be facing major climatic
changes and sea levels far above what they are now.
Public outcry about the issue has led to international
efforts to stop the release of CFCs and other pollutants
(15) harmful to the ozonosphere. Thanks to a global pact to
eliminate the production of CFCs by 1996, the ozone
layer should stop losing ozone around the turn of the
century. Total ozone recovery, however, is predicted to
take more than a century beyond that.

26. Which of the following is directly mentioned as
    evidence of ozone depletion?

    (F) an increase in unusual disturbances on the
        sun's surface
    (G) a decrease in the amount of sunlight reach-
        ing the Earth
    (H) a decline in skin cancers among people
    (J) an increase in solar radiation reaching the
        Earth's surface
    (K) gaps in the ozonosphere over North
        America

27. This passage deals primarily with

    (A) the reasons why solar radiation is damaging
    (B) the atmosphere over Antarctica
    (C) how pollutants are destroying the environ-
        ment
    (D) the discovery of the hole in the ozone layer
    (E) the loss of ozone from the ozone layer

28. Which of the following explains why ozone
    depletion has occurred?

    (F) Oxygen is disappearing from the atmos-
        phere.
    (G) Temperatures on earth are rising.

    (H) The ozone layer is being broken down by
        pollutants.
    (J) The sun's rays are becoming stronger.
    (K) Sea levels are falling.

29. The author most likely mentions a greenhouse
    (line 10) in order to

    (A) suggest a way to protect plants from harm-
        ful radiation
    (B) describe an effect of increasing solar radia-
        tion
    (C) explain how ozone forms in the atmosphere
    (D) explain that heat and humidity are destroy-
        ing the ozonosphere
    (E) describe a climate that would be healthier
        for people

30. The passage suggests that a full restoration of the
    ozonosphere

    (F) is the only way of saving Antarctica from
        destruction
    (G) will probably occur by the year 2000
    (H) depends on the frequency of future volcanic
        eruptions
    (J) remains an impossibility despite interna-
        tional efforts
    (K) is highly unlikely in the near future

Immigrants

Line   At the end of the nineteenth century, a new wave of immigration caused a massive population explosion in the United States. Between 1880 and 1910, 18 million immigrants flooded into the U.S. from
(5)   southern and eastern Europe, attracted by economic opportunity, religious freedom and political democracy. Few immigrants of this period found life in America easy, however. Many of those who lacked professional skills and did not speak English found
(10)   themselves living in slum conditions in the sprawling cities of the northeast, exploited by their employers and trapped at poverty level.

Around the turn of the century a number of different organizations made efforts to help these
(15)   newly-arrived immigrants adapt to American life. In 1889, the reformer Jane Addams founded a volunteer organization in Chicago called Hull House that attempted to improve conditions in the city's poor immigrant neighborhoods. Addams' organization
(20)   sought to ease the immigrants' adjustment to an unfamiliar society by offering whatever social services were not provided by local governments, including medical care, legal assistance, and adult education. Also fundamental to the settlement house philosophy
(25)   was a respect for the cultural heritage of the new arrivals.

31. Which of the following best describes what this passage is about?

(A) the story of immigration to the U.S.
(B) the cultural contributions offered by immigrants
(C) turn-of-the-century immigrants and Addams' efforts to help them
(D) how immigrants changed life in U.S. cities
(E) different concepts of helping immigrants assimilate

32. Which of the following is NOT mentioned as a characteristic of the life that awaited immigrants to the U.S. between 1890 and 1910?

(F) poor housing
(G) harsh working conditions
(H) religious persecution
(J) lack of opportunity for advancement
(K) political democracy

33. Which of the following would most likely be source of the passage?

(A) a speech at a conference for historians
(B) a biography of Jane Addams
(C) a newspaper article on social work
(D) a history book about immigration to the U.S. in the 19th century
(E) a proposal for a new welfare program

34. The services provided by the Hull House were intended to

(F) supplement the services provided by local government
(G) discourage the use of foreign languages in schools
(H) enable immigrants to open similar settlement houses elsewhere
(J) instruct immigrants in the beliefs of the reformers
(K) teach immigrants to conform to rigid standards

35. Which of the following would most probably have been supported by reformers such as Jane Addams?

(A) a language course to help immigrants lose their accents
(B) a law that would require all immigrants to leave the country after five years
(C) a program to relocate immigrant populations out of the cities
(D) a requirement that all immigrants pledge absolute loyalty to their adopted country
(E) a program to provide legal advice to uninformed new immigrants

Coral Reefs

Line   The environment of the coral reef is formed over thousands of years by the life cycle of vast numbers of coral animals. The main architect of the reef is the stony coral, a relative of the sea anemone that lives in
(5)   tropical climates and secretes a skeleton of almost pure calcium carbonate. Its partner is the green alga, a tiny unicellular plant, which lives within the tissues of the coral. The two organisms coexist in a mutually beneficial relationship, with the algae consuming
(10)   carbon dioxide given off by the corals, and the corals thriving in the abundant oxygen produced photosynthetically by the algae. When the coral dies, its skeleton is left, and other organisms grow on top of it. Over the years, the sheer mass of coral skeletons,
(15)   together with those of associated organisms, combines to form the petrified underwater forest that divers find so fascinating.

36. According to the passage, the skeleton of the stony coral is mostly composed of

    (F) cartilage
    (G) stone
    (H) calcium carbonate
    (J) carbon dioxide
    (K) sediment

37. This passage primarily deals with

    (A) different forms of marine life
    (B) the contribution of the stony coral to reef formation
    (C) the interaction between two inhabitants of coral reefs
    (D) the physical beauty of coral reefs
    (E) the geological origins of reef islands

38. It can be inferred from the passage that divers are primarily interested in which aspect of reefs?

    (F) the biological cycles of reef animals
    (G) the visual appeal of a mass of coral skeletons
    (H) the fertile growing environment that reefs provide
    (J) the historical implications of reef development
    (K) the actual number of dead animals required to form a reef

39. The relationship between the coral and the algae is best described as

    (A) unfriendly
    (B) competitive
    (C) predatory
    (D) collaborative
    (E) mysterious

40. All of the following are mentioned in the passage as part of the life cycle of reef organisms EXCEPT:

    (F) the coral lives within the tissues of the alga
    (G) algae consumes carbon dioxide emitted by corals
    (H) the skeleton of the coral provides an environment for other organisms
    (J) corals secrete a calcium carbonate skeleton
    (K) corals consume oxygen produced by algae

Smallpox

Line   For thousands of years, smallpox was one of the
world's most dreaded diseases. An acutely infectious
disease spread by a virus, smallpox was the scourge of
medieval Europe, where it was known by its
(5)   symptoms of extreme fever and disfiguring rash as
"the invisible fire." In many outbreaks, mortality rates
were higher than 25 percent. Ancient Chinese medical
texts show that the disease was known as long ago as
1122 BC. But as recently as 1967, more than 2 million
(10)   people died from the disease annually.
       A method of conferring immunity from smallpox
was discovered in 1796 by an English doctor named
Edward Jenner. It was not until 1966, however, that
the World Health Organization was able to marshal the
(15)   resources to launch a worldwide campaign to wipe out
the disease. In an immense project involving
thousands of health workers, WHO teams moved from
country to country, locating every case of active
smallpox and vaccinating all potential contacts. In
(20)   1977, the last active case of smallpox was found and
eliminated. Since there are no animal carriers of
smallpox, the WHO was able to declare in 1980 that
the dreaded killer had been conquered. For the first
time in the history of medicine, a disease had been
(25)   completely destroyed.

41. Which of the following best tells what this
    passage is about?

    (A) how to treat viral diseases
    (B) the purpose of the World Health
        Organization
    (C) the tragic symptoms of smallpox
    (D) the history of the fight against smallpox
    (E) early efforts at controlling infectious dis-
        eases

42. In line 2, the word "acutely" most nearly means

    (F) painfully
    (G) extremely
    (H) unnaturally
    (J) sensitively
    (K) partly

43. It can be inferred from the passage that the
    earliest recorded cases of smallpox were located
    in

    (A) China
    (B) Europe
    (C) The Middle East
    (D) North America
    (E) Africa

44. The passage implies that smallpox was not
    eliminated before 1966 because

    (F) vaccination did not prevent all forms of the
        disease
    (G) not enough was known about immunity to
        disease
    (H) there was no effective protection against
        animal carriers
    (J) there had never been a coordinated world-
        wide vaccination campaign
    (K) the disease would lie dormant for many
        years and then reappear

45. According to the passage, the WHO's fight
    against smallpox was a unique event because

    (A) it involved a worldwide campaign of vacci-
        nation
    (B) a disease had never before been utterly
        wiped out
    (C) animals carriers had to be isolated and vac-
        cinated
    (D) doctors were uncertain as to whether
        Jenner's methods would work
    (E) it was more expensive than any other single
        vaccination campaign

Steamboats

Line   My father was a justice of the peace, and I supposed he possessed the power of life and death over all men and could hang anybody that offended him. This was distinction enough for me as a general

(5)   thing; but the desire to be a steamboatman kept intruding, nevertheless. I first wanted to be a cabin boy, so that I could come out with a white apron on and shake a tablecloth over the side, where all my old comrades could see me. Later I thought that I would

(10)   rather be the deck hand who stood on the end of the stage plank with a coil of rope in his hand, because he was particularly conspicuous.

      But these were only daydreams—too heavenly to be contemplated as real possibilities. By and by one of

(15)   the boys went away. He was not heard of for a long time. At last he turned up as an apprentice engineer or "striker" on a steamboat. This thing shook the bottom out of all my Sunday-school teachings. That boy had been notoriously worldly and I had been just the

(20)   reverse—yet he was exalted to this eminence, and I was left in obscurity and misery. There was nothing generous about this fellow in his greatness. He would always manage to have a rusty bolt to scrub while his boat was docked at our town, and he would sit on the

(25)   inside guard and scrub it, where we could all see him and envy him and loathe him.

46. The author makes the statement that "I supposed he...offended him" (lines 1-4) primarily to suggest the

    (F) power held by a justice of peace in a frontier town

    (G) naive view that he held of his father's importance

    (H) respect in which the townspeople held his father

    (J) possibility of miscarriages of justice on the American frontier

    (K) harsh environment in which he was brought up

47. As used in line 4, the word "distinction" most nearly means

    (A) difference

    (B) variation

    (C) fame

    (D) desperation

    (E) clarity

48. The author decides he would rather become a deck hand than a cabin boy primarily because

    (F) the job offers higher wages

    (G) he believes that the work is easier

    (H) he wants to avoid seeing his old friends

    (J) deck hands often later become pilots

    (K) the job is more visible to passersby

49. The author most likely mentions his "Sunday-school teachings" in line 18 in order to emphasize

    (A) the influences of his early education in later life

    (B) his sense of injustice at the engineer's success

    (C) his disillusionment with long-standing religious beliefs

    (D) his determination to become an engineer at all costs

    (E) the unscrupulous nature of the engineer's character

50. The author most likely concludes that the engineer is not "generous" (line 22) because he

    (F) has no respect for religious beliefs

    (G) refuses to share his wages with his friends

    (H) shows off his new position in public

    (J) takes a pride in material possessions

    (K) ignores the disappointment of other people's ambitions

Animal Coloring

Line   Animals that use coloring to safeguard
themselves from predators are said to have "protective
coloration." One common type of protective
coloration is called cryptic resemblance, where an
(5)   animal adapts in color, shape and behavior in order to
blend into its environment. The camouflage of the pale
green tree frog is a good example of cryptic
resemblance. The tree frog blends so perfectly into its
surroundings that when it sits motionless it is all but
(10) invisible against a background of leaves.
       Many animals change their protective
pigmentation with the seasons. The caribou sheds its
brown coat in winter, replacing it with white fur. The
stoat, a member of the weasel family, is known as the
(15) ermine in winter, when its brown fur changes to the
white fur prized by royalty. The chameleon, even more
versatile than these, changes color in just a few
minutes to match whatever surface it happens to be
lying on or clinging to. Some animals use protective
(20) coloration not for camouflage but to stand out against
their surroundings. The skunk's brilliant white stripe is
meant to be seen, as a warning to predators to avoid
the animal's stink. Similarly, the hedgehog uses its
"salt and pepper" look to loudly announce its identity,
(25) since it depends on its evil stench and unpleasant
texture to make it unpalatable to the predators around
it.

51. The author uses the caribou and the stoat as
    examples of animals that

    (A) change their color according to the time of
        year
    (B) are protected by disruptive coloring
    (C) possess valuable white fur
    (D) have prominent markings to warn predators
    (E) protect themselves by constantly changing
        their coloring

52. Which of the following best describes what the
    passage is about?

    (F) how animals blend into their surroundings
    (G) several types of protective coloration
    (H) a contrast between the tree frog, the zebra,
        the caribou, and the skunk
    (J) a description of predators in the animal
        kingdom
    (K) the difference between cryptic resemblance
        and disruptive coloring

53. The feature of the chameleon discussed in this
    passage is its ability to

    (A) camouflage itself despite frequent changes
        in location
    (B) cling to surfaces that are hidden from
        attackers
    (C) adapt easily to seasonal changes
    (D) use disruptive coloring to confuse predators
    (E) change the colors of surfaces it is resting on

54. It can be inferred from the passage that which of
    the following animals employ cryptic
    resemblance?

    I.   the green tree frog

    II. the chameleon

    III. the skunk

    (F) I only
    (G) II only
    (H) I and II
    (J) I and III
    (K) I, II and III

55. The passage suggests that the hedgehog is
    primarily different from the chameleon in that

    (A) it changes its skin color less frequently
    (B) it makes its presence known to potential
        predators
    (C) it has fewer predators to avoid
    (D) its predators find it unpleasant to eat
    (E) it skin is almost devoid of color

Poetry

Line   Being out of heart with government
I took a broken root to fling
Where the proud, wayward squirrel went,
Taking delight that he could spring;
(5)   And he, with that low whinnying sound
That is like laughter, sprang again
And so to the other tree at a bound.
Nor the tame will, nor timid brain,
Nor heavy knitting of the brow
(10)   Bred that fierce tooth and cleanly limb
And threw him to laugh on the bough;
No government appointed him.

(From *An Appointment*, Responsibilities, W.B. Yeats, 1914)

56. The author's attitude towards the government in this poem would best be described as

    (F) amused

    (G) disenchanted

    (H) furious

    (J) melancholy

    (K) neutral

57. Which of the following does the author admire about the squirrel?

    I. His independence.

    II. His faith in systems of government.

    III. His ability to spring from tree to tree.

    (A) I only

    (B) III only

    (C) I and II

    (D) I and III

    (E) I, II and III

58. The passage implies that the squirrel most resembles humans in

    (F) the timidity of his intellect

    (G) the sounds that he makes

    (H) the fierce expression on his face

    (J) his contempt for the world of politics

    (K) his concentration in moving from tree to tree

59. The author most likely regards the squirrel's laugh as

    (A) a warning about the future

    (B) a reflection of his own happiness

    (C) a symbol of his freedom

    (D) a sign of friendliness towards the poet

    (E) an unexplained natural phenomenon

60. In line 9, the phrase "heavy knitting of the brow" most likely refers to

    (F) the movement towards political reform

    (G) the seriousness of government officials

    (H) the expression on the squirrel's face

    (J) the poet's attitude towards politicians

    (K) the beauty of the natural world

Sentence Completions

1. George concealed his true _____ under a guise
   of _____ .
   (A) passions . . instability
   (B) humility. . modesty
   (C) concern . . indifference
   (D) generosity . . altruism

2. Though normally quite _____, the grizzly can
   become _____ when disturbed by a human.
   (A) enormous . . frightened
   (B) affectionate . . happy
   (C) harmless . . ferocious
   (D) voracious . . appeased

3. Many people _____ that owls are intelligent ,
   but this claim is nothing more than a _____.
   (A) assume. . fact
   (B) agree . . rebuttal
   (C) refute . . tale
   (D) believe . . myth

4. The teacher tried to _____ the student's _____
   use of grammar and vocabulary.
   (A) replace . . remarkable
   (B) distort . . uncomplimentary
   (C) approve . . perfect
   (D) correct . . faulty

5. After its engine _____, the boat drifted _____
   for days.
   (A) started . . swiftly
   (B) raced . . slowly
   (C) died . . aimlessly
   (D) broke . . briefly

6. Roberta was _____ for cheating, though she
   believed that her _____ use of encyclopedia
   entries was not deceitful.
   (A) censured . . fraudulent
   (B) reprimanded . . extensive
   (C) honored . . primitive
   (D) chastised . . treacherous

7. The newspaper editorial argued that allowing
   violence to pass without _____ gives the
   appearance of _____ it.
   (A) comment . . condoning
   (B) incident . . provoking
   (C) activity . . soothing
   (D) agitation . . pacifying

8. Cowbirds _____ their eggs in the nests of other
   birds, who _____ raise the chicks as their own.
   (A) deposit . . unwittingly
   (B) steal . . enthusiastically
   (C) exchange . . debatably
   (D) ignore . . unanimously

9. The politician's thoughtful _____ helped to
   ____ the skeptical public.
   (A) beliefs . . warn
   (B) service . . justify
   (C) presence . . betray
   (D) argument . . convince

10. The author's first novel was critically
    acclaimed for its originality and _____, but its
    _____ appeal was limited.
    (A) repartee . . individual
    (B) suspensefulness . . vital
    (C) obscurity. . . lasting
    (D) sophistication . . popular

11. Investigators believe that the rash of fires was
    not the work of a(n) _____ but a _____ of
    unfortunate accidents.
    (A) a pyromaniac . . factor
    (B) an accomplice . . consequence
    (C) a criminal . . premonition
    (D) an arsonist . . series

12. Archaeologists _____ the documents while
    _____ the remains of a I,000-year-old Roman
    fort in what is now northern England.
    (A) attached . . marring
    (B) unearthed . . excavating
    (C) diverted . . mourning
    (D) construed . . surmising

13. The lake was in serious jeopardy, it was being contaminated and _____ by human beings faster than nature could _____ and replenish it.
    (A) endangered . . flow
    (B) drained . . purify
    (C) modified . . improve
    (D) impelled . . filter

14. At his concert debut, the young violinist tossed off the most difficult passages without any apparent effort, _____ the audience with his _____ .
    (A) enraging . . timorousness
    (B) impressing . . prestige
    (C) enthralling . . stolidity
    (D) dazzling. . . virtuosity

15. Except for a few _____ shrubs, the frozen, windswept tundra provides little _____ for the herds of caribou that migrate across it seasonally.
    (A) stunted . . nourishment
    (B) harmful . . credit
    (C) formless . . refuge
    (D) premature . . privacy

16. Because it features many _____ actors, the new film is _____ to be a major box office success.
    (A) important . . doomed
    (B) prominent . . expected
    (C) unknown . . certain
    (D) talented . . unlikely

17. Rats mature very quickly and _____ prolifically, facilitating the _____ of disease.
    (A) run . . control
    (B) hide . . prevention
    (C) breed . . spread
    (D) mutate . . obstruction

18. Because Joel did not _____ his homework assignment on time, the teacher _____ his grade.
    (A) submit . . accepted
    (B) notify . . ignored
    (C) understand . . contradicted
    (D) complete . . lowered

19. The shrewd private investigator noticed several _____ clues that the police had failed to _____.
    (A) significant . . detect
    (B) irrelevant . . pursue
    (C) crucial . . scan
    (D) spurious . . find

20. The writing process is _____ for most, but she is able to compose poems without much _____.
    (A) repugnant . . skill
    (B) amusing . . pain
    (C) tedious . . excitement
    (D) arduous . . effort

21. After being unfairly _____ by the chairperson Luis _____ out of the meeting room.
    (A) upbraided . . stormed
    (B) burdened . . sauntered
    (C) scrutinized . . strolled
    (D) heckled . . strutted

22. Through years of _____, the once _____ cathedral was allowed to become shabby, dirty and increasingly unappealing.
    (A) renovation . . impressive
    (B) adornment . . decrepit
    (C) neglect . . majestic
    (D) improvement . . towering

23. Although the game was _____ in its early stages, it later turned into a _____.
    (A) unfair . . debacle
    (B) close . . rout
    (C) uneven . . trouncing
    (D) uncontested . . stalemate

24. The news wire service _____ information so _____ that events are reported all over the world shortly after they happen.
    (A) records . . precisely
    (B) falsifies . . deliberately
    (C) verifies . . painstakingly
    (D) disseminates . . rapidly

25. Given the _____ in today's market, our sale predictions may have been a little _____.
    (A) upturn . . inexact
    (B) boom . . audacious
    (C) instability . . reckless
    (D) stagnation . . optimistic

26. Nearly everyone has seen photographs of the Grand Canyon, but its _____ topography cannot be fully _____ through two-dimensional images.
    (A) spectacular . . appreciated
    (B) copious . . decorated
    (C) dingy . . screened
    (D) peripheral . . saturated

27. The farmers continued to work long hours throughout the fall and winter, _____ their _____ and repairing buildings and equipment.
    (A) clearing . . crop
    (B) reaping . . fauna
    (C) securing . . debris
    (D) tending . . livestock

28. The ancient stone carvings are wonderfully _____, depicting in intricate detail the _____ in battle of thousands of soldiers.
    (A) fragmentary . . .succumbing
    (B) beautiful . . lunging
    (C) worn . . enacting
    (D) ornate . . clashing

29. Tory painted a(n) _____ view of the city, starting at the lakefront and _____ inland for several males.
    (A) impressionistic . . burnishing
    (B) ascetic . . eddying
    (C) intrinsic . . embellishing
    (D) panoramic . . ranging

30. Faced with such a paucity of _____ information about the millionaire's new husband, the newspaper has _____ printing unsubstantiated rumors.
    (A) paramount . . balked at
    (B) reliable . . resorted to
    (C) wealthy . . refrained from
    (D) immediate . . wavered about

31. Once _____ across the continent, wolves had been _____ almost to extinction by the 1950s.
    (A) nonexistent . . propelled
    (B) numerous . . hunted
    (C) garrulous . . abducted
    (D) captive . . secured

32. Despite the _____ predictions of noted meteorologists, the damage caused by the storm was _____
    (A) accurate . . foreseen
    (B) ominous . . minimal
    (C) dire . . terrible
    (D) encouraging . . slight

33. A public official who accepts _____ is guilty of _____.
    (A) aid . . abuse
    (B) awards . . dishonesty
    (C) bribes . . corruption
    (D) advice . . misbehavior

34. The hostess invited relatively _____ guests, making the party seem less _____ than it had last year.
    (A) eccentric . . unique
    (B) talkative . . lengthy
    (C) ordinary . . banal
    (D) undistinguished . . exclusive

35. Tony and Marcia spent an _____ afternoon _____ hand in hand through the sun-dappled park.
    (A) untimely . . traipsing
    (B) ebullient . . recurring
    (C) exhaustive . . persevering
    (D) idyllic . . strolling

36. The best archaeological evidence _____ that the gigantic structures were _____ by a lost extinct aboriginal people.
    (A) indicates . . erected
    (B) specifies . . registered
    (C) replies . . built
    (D) imagines . . drafted

37. Cockroaches are one of the most _____ of all creatures because they can _____ in almost any situation.
    (A) adaptable . . thrive
    (B) disgusting . . reside
    (C) frail . . survive
    (D) versatile . . die

38. The violinist gave an _____ performance in the final movement and left the audience _____.
    (A) extended . . early
    (B) accomplished . . astounded
    (C) exquisite . . afflicted
    (D) absorbing . . distracted

39. Since Ricky's college interview had gone well, his counselor was _____ to learn that he was _____ about applying for college.
    (A) relieved . . ambivalent
    (B) troubled . . decisive
    (C) disappointed . . unenthusiastic
    (D) delighted . . aghast

40. Deirdre was _____ as a leader in student government, even though she would have been just as happy to play a(n) _____ role.
    (A) questioned . . minor
    (B) applauded . . pivotal
    (C) hailed . . integral
    (D) recognized . . supporting

41. The film has a _____ effect on viewers, leaving them emotionally _____ and physically spent.
    (A) flippant . . relaxed
    (B) normal . . intact
    (C) stern . . laconic
    (D) cathartic . . drained

42. Later that evening, the snow _____ in huge drifts, making driving _____ difficult and finally impossible.
    (A) melted . . continually
    (B) accumulated . . increasingly
    (C) amassed . . conversely
    (D) evaporated . . starkly

43. Because the astronomy textbook was so difficult to _____, she had to rely on the physics professor's lectures to explain the more _____ concepts.
    (A) consider . . intricate
    (B) orbit . . essential
    (C) repudiate . . basic
    (D) follow . . complicated

44. Though Elena had received the company's _____ possible service award, her supervisor felt it necessary to _____ her for arriving ten minutes late.
    (A) highest. . admonish
    (B) poorest . . vex
    (C) best . . commend
    (D) finest . . extol

45. The 16th-century chateau is _____ decorated with delicately wrought tapestries, hand-crafted _____, and leaded stained glass windows.
    (A) sumptuously . . furnishings
    (B) artistically . . accompaniments
    (C) concisely . . cadences
    (D) imprudently . . trappings

46. As the supply of fresh water _____, the castaways were forced to _____ the remainder.
    (A) dwindled . . ration
    (B) stabilized . . waste
    (C) grew . . preserve
    (D) drained . . distribute

47. Somehow, in spite of her _____ study habits, Mary always received _____ grades on her history exams.
    (A) atrocious . . failing
    (B) lackadaisical . . mediocre
    (C) careful . . outstanding
    (D) excellent . . poor

48. At the mercy of his _____ appetite, Henry was _____ to stay on his diet.
    (A) light . . unwilling
    (B) moderate . . free
    (C) massive . . sure
    (D) healthy . . unable

49. Having seen the film before, Mark was _____ to be as _____ as we who were viewing it for the first time.
    (A) prone . . bewildered
    (B) predicted . . critical
    (C) flagrant . . blissful
    (D) unlikely . . shocked

50. A born pessimist, Lisa was _____ when her favorite team _____ in the final quarter of the last regular season game.
    (A) impartial . . tied
    (B) forgiven . . forfeited
    (C) depressed . . conceded
    (D) stunned . . triumphed

51. Having procrastinated far too long, he attacked the project so _____ that he made many _____ errors.
    (A) hastily . . inadvertent
    (B) learnedly . . noticeable
    (C) methodically . . fundamental
    (D) weakly . . trivial

52. Most of the opinions expressed in her book are _____, but it does contain a few _____ insights.
    (A) sensible . . intelligent
    (B) absurd . . brilliant
    (C) useless . . ambitious
    (D) sound . . practical

53. He was an _____ art collector and had _____ several fine paintings by such artists as Picasso and Matisse.
    (A) unsuccessful . . bought
    (B) active . . released
    (C) avid . . acquired
    (D) enthusiastic . . destroyed

54. The politician _____ his position and _____ a proposal he had previously opposed.
    (A) changed . . criticized
    (B) reversed . . supported
    (C) modified . . blocked
    (D) upheld . . defended

55. Most of those polled seemed _____ a change and _____ that they would vote to re-elect the mayor.
    (A) wary of . . stated
    (B) cautious about . . denied
    (C) afraid of . . disputed
    (D) open to . . asserted

56. Moviegoers were thrilled by the hero's daring _____ and amused by his sidekicks madcap _____.
    (A) feats . . tribulations
    (B) escapades . . ordeals
    (C) tedium . . zaniness
    (D) exploits . . antics

57. Randy's grandmother could have _____ half a dozen small children under her _____ old fashioned skirts.
    (A) sheltered . . voluminous
    (B) spliced . . formal
    (C) ensnared . . perched
    (D) revealed . . colorful

58. Before rolling out the pie crust, the chef _____ the counter with flower to _____ the dough from sticking.
    (A) drenched . . halt
    (B) baked . . banish
    (C) kneaded . . alleviate
    (D) dusted . . prevent

59. Some claim that the new educational project _____ to gifted pupils while _____ the needs of average students, who constitute a clear majority.
    (A) adapts . . emulating
    (B) salutes . . effecting
    (C) objects . . implying
    (D) caters . . ignoring

60. Weighted down with heavy armor, medieval knights _____ their broadswords too _____ to fight for more than a few minutes at a time.
    (A) wielded . . awkwardly
    (B) parried . . perversely
    (C) hoisted . . obdurately
    (D) swung . . actively

61. The bears that frequent the campground are bold and occasionally _____ in their _____ for food.
    (A) abundant . . capacity
    (B) emphatic . . inclination
    (C) aggressive . . quest
    (D) unbalanced . . pressure

62. Despite the _____ price of the car, Jose's parents were _____ to permit him to buy it.
    (A) affordable . . willing
    (B) outrageous . . hesitant
    (C) usual . . afraid
    (D) reasonable . . reluctant

63. Brett brought Vicky's horse back to the stable by improvising a harness that _____ the mare to his own _____.
    (A) hitched . . zenith
    (B) motivated . . goal
    (C) spurred . . steed
    (D) yoked . . mount

64. To his admirers, the Prime Minister was _____; to his _____, merely stubborn.
    (A) eminent . . imitators
    (B) remarkable . . adherents
    (C) tenacious . . detractors
    (D) complimentary . . endorsers

65. The speaker _____ on for hours, repeating herself at length and _____ her audience to tears.
    (A) prated . . frightening
    (B) simpered . . forcing
    (C) whined . . provoking
    (D) droned . . boring

66. The whale shark is _____ encountered by divers because of its low numbers and _____ habits.
    (A) successfully . . congenial
    (B) anxiously . . unfortunate
    (C) constantly. . . indifferent
    (D) rarely . . solitary

67. The _____ deposited tons of mineral-rich volcanic ash, restoring to the soil nutrients _____ decades of farming.
    (A) eruption . . depleted by
    (B) abyss . . harvested during
    (C) tumult . . alien to
    (D) barrier . . entrenched in

68. Members of the sect _____ from before sun-up until long after dusk, _____ the sin of sloth.
    (A) fasted . . savoring
    (B) sanctified . . tainting
    (C) concealed . . deploring
    (D) toiled . . avoiding

69. Meteorologists _____ storm systems in order to give shoreline residents adequate _____ of hurricanes, floods, and other disasters.
    (A) track . . forewarning
    (B) study . . almanacs
    (C) record . . barometers
    (D) design . . pretense

70. In his _____ to eliminate clutter, Terry discarded old files and documents _____, heedless of their potential future importance.
    (A) zeal . . indiscriminately
    (B) agitation . . persuasively
    (D) bravado . . competitively
    (D) insomnia . . tactfully

QUESTION BANK ANSWERS

Math

Number Properties

1. **E**   Only (E) is a whole number.

2. **F**   "Distinct" means "different." The number has 12 digits, but the 3, 5, and 7 are repeated. There are only 9 distinct digits.

3. **D**   Each term in the sequence is 4 more than the preceding term. The next term after 28, then, will be 28 + 4 = 32.

4. **H**   To count the number of integers from one integer to another, inclusive, subtract and **then add 1**. The positive difference in this case is 84 − 45 = 39. Add 1 and you get 39 + 1 = 40.

5. **A**   Simplify $12 - 3 \times 5 + (7 - 10)^2 \div 3$ using PEMDAS.

    Do what's in parentheses first:
    $12 - 3 \times 5 + (7 - 10)^2 \div 3$
    $= 12 - 3 \times 5 + (-3)^2 \div 3$

    Next do the exponent:
    $= 12 - 3 \times 5 + 9 \div 3$

    Then multiplication and division:
    $= 12 - 15 + 3$

    Finally addition and subtraction:
    $= 0$

6. **H**   The product of 5 and 6 is 5 × 6 = 30. The sum of 7 and 8 is 7 + 8 = 15. When 30 is subtracted from 15, the result is 15 − 30 = −15.

7. **C**   Eliminate the answer choices that can't be right. You can eliminate (B) because 9.5 is not a whole number. You can eliminate (A) because it's too small—9 is not between 9 and 15. And

you can eliminate (D) and (E) because they're too big. The only choice left is (C).

8. **J**   Since you know that the rules about addition, subtraction, and multiplication for even and odd numbers can be determined from a single example of each of these rules (for example, 4 + 8 = 12 shows that the sum of two even integers is always even), the easiest way to approach this question is to pick integer values for x, y, and z for each answer choice to find out which one cannot be true.

    (F) Say $x = 2$ and $y = 3$. In this case $x + y$ is definitely odd, and $x + z$ is possibly even (depending on whether or not z is even). This choice could be true.

    (G) Say $y = 2$ and $z = 3$. In this case $x + y$ is possibly odd (depending on whether or not x is odd), and $x + z$ is possibly even (again depending on whether or not x is odd). This choice could be true.

    (H) Say $x = 2$, $y = 3$, and $z = 4$. In this case $x + y$ is definitely odd, and $x + z$ is definitely even. This choice could be true.

    (J) Say $x = 2$, $y = 4$, and $z = 3$. In this case $x + y$ is definitely even, and $x + z$ is definitely odd. This is the choice that **cannot** be true, so it's the answer.

    (K) Say $z = 2$ and $y = 3$. In this case $x + y$ is possibly odd (depending on whether or not x is even), and $x + z$ is possibly even (again depending on whether or not x is even). This choice could be true.

9. **D**   When you subtract consecutive integers, you get either 1 or −1, depending on the order. So D can be either positive or negative. D cannot be even; it has to be odd. D doesn't have to be less than either integer—the integers could be negative.

10. **G**   You're looking for statements that must be true, so if you can find just one case where a statement is not true, you can cross it off. You're given that x and y are consecutive integers (and that x is less than y) whose product is 6, but that doesn't necessarily mean they're 2

and 3. They could just as well be –3 and –2. Now you can see that Statement I doesn't have to be true: it could be that $x + y = -5$.

Statement II is definitely true: x has to be either –3 or 2, both of which are less than 6. Finally, Statement III doesn't have to be true. If $x = -3$ and $y = -2$, then $\frac{x}{y} = \frac{-3}{-2} = \frac{3}{2}$. Statement II is the only one that has to be true.

Factors, Multiples, and Divisibility

11. **D**   Multiples of 5 all end in 5 or 0. Multiples of 10 end in 0. A number that's a multiple of 5 but not a multiple of 10 will end in 5, like (D), 395.

12. **J**   If the sum of the digits is a multiple of 3, then the original number is a multiple of 3. Similarly, if the sum of the digits is a multiple of 9, then the original number is a multiple of 9. So you're looking for the choice where the digits add up to a multiple of 3, but not to a multiple of 9. You can eliminate (F) because it's not a multiple of 3. And you can eliminate (G), (H), and (K) because they **are** multiples of 9.

13. **D**   Eliminate choices (A), (B), and (C) because they are all factors of 54. Eliminate (E) because it's not a factor of either 24 or 36. The answer is (D) because 4 goes into 24 and 36, but not into 54.

14. **J**   One quick way to find the least common multiple is to check out the multiples of the larger number until you find one that's also a multiple of the smaller number. Here you check out the multiples of 18: 18. . . 36. . . 54. . . 72. . . 90. That's it: 90 is the smallest multiple of 18 that's also a multiple of 15.

15. **D**   After 90, the first odd number is 91, which is not prime because it's equal to 7×13. The next odd number is 93, which is not prime because it's equal to 3×31. The next odd number is 95, which is not prime because it's

equal to 5×19. The next odd number is 97, and try as you might, you won't find any factors other than 1 and 97.

16. **F**   The prime factorization of 36 is $2 \times 2 \times 3 \times 3$. That factorization includes 2 distinct factors, 2 and 3.

17. **C**   The prime factorization of 30 is $2 \times 3 \times 5$. The prime factorization of 42 is $2 \times 3 \times 7$. The two factorizations share a 2 and a 3, so the greatest common factor is $2 \times 3 = 6$.

18. **H**   Long division shows that 6 goes into 87 fourteen times with a remainder of 3:

$$
\begin{array}{r}
14 \\
6{\overline{\smash{\big)}\,87}} \\
\underline{6} \\
27 \\
\underline{24} \\
3
\end{array}
$$

19. **E**   If P divided by 7 leaves a remainder of 5, you can say that $P = 7n + 5$, where n represents some integer. Multiply both sides by 5 to get $5P = 35n + 25$. The remainder when you divide $35n$ by 7 is 0. The reminder when you divide 7 into 25 by 7 is 4, so the remainder when you divide $5P$ by 7 is $0 + 4 = 4$.

For most people this one's a lot easier to do by picking numbers. Think of an example for P and try it out. P could be 12, for example, because when you divide 12 by 7, the remainder is 5. (P could also be 19, 26, 33, or any of infinitely many more possibilities.) Now multiply your chosen P by 5: $12 \times 5 = 60$. Divide 60 by 7 and see what the remainder is: $60 \div 7 = 8$, remainder 4.

20. **G**   An integer that's divisible by 6 has at least one 2 and one 3 in its prime factorization. An integer that's divisible by 9 has at least two 3's in its prime factorization. Therefore, an integer that's divisible by both 6 and 9 has at least one

2 and two 3's in its prime factorization. That means it's divisible by 2, 3, $2 \times 3 = 6$, $3 \times 3 = 9$, and $2 \times 3 \times 3 = 18$. It's **not** necessarily divisible by 12 or 36, each of which includes **two** 2's in its prime factorization.

You could also do this one by **picking numbers**. Think of a common multiple of 6 and 9 and use it to eliminate some options. $6 \times 9 = 54$ is an obvious common multiple—and it's not divisible by 12 or 36, but it is divisible by 18. The **least** common multiple of 6 and 9 is 18, which is also divisible by 18. It looks like every common multiple of 6 and 9 is also a multiple of 18.

Fractions

21. **E**   To add fractions, you need a common denominator:

$$\frac{1}{3} + \frac{2}{5} = \frac{1 \times 5}{3 \times 5} + \frac{2 \times 3}{5 \times 3} = \frac{5}{15} + \frac{6}{15} = \frac{11}{15}$$

22. **F**   To multiply fractions, multiply the numerators and multiply the denominators:

$$\frac{1}{3} \times \frac{1}{6} = \frac{1 \times 1}{3 \times 6} = \frac{1}{18}$$

23. **D**   To divide fractions, flip the second one and multiply:

$$\frac{1}{3} \div \frac{1}{6} = \frac{1}{3} \times \frac{6}{1} = \frac{6}{3} = 2$$

24. **G**   To find the reciprocal, switch the numerator and denominator. A whole number like 4 has an implied denominator of 1 (that is, $4 = \frac{4}{1}$), so the reciprocal of 4 is $\frac{1}{4}$.

25. **D**   The easiest way to compare these fractions is to give them all a common denominator of 16. (A) becomes $\frac{8}{16}$, (B) becomes $\frac{12}{16}$, (C)

becomes $\frac{10}{16}$, (D) becomes $\frac{14}{16}$, and (E) already is $\frac{7}{16}$. Now you can see that (D) is the greatest because it has the greatest numerator.

26. **J**   To convert a mixed number to an improper fraction, multiply the whole number part by the denominator, add the numerator, and put the result over the original denominator. Here 4 times 7 plus 3 is 31. Put that over 7 and you get $\frac{31}{7}$.

27. **E**   Do what's in parentheses first:

$$\left(\frac{1}{5} + \frac{1}{3}\right) \div \frac{1}{2} = \left(\frac{3}{15} + \frac{5}{15}\right) \div \frac{1}{2} = \frac{8}{15} \div \frac{1}{2}$$

Then, to divide fractions, invert the one after the division sign and multiply:

$$\frac{8}{15} \div \frac{1}{2} = \frac{8}{15} \times \frac{2}{1} = \frac{16}{15}$$

28. **F**   Before you can divide mixed numbers, you should convert them to improper fractions:

$$8\frac{1}{3} \div 6\frac{2}{3} = \frac{25}{3} \div \frac{20}{3}$$

Then, to divide fractions, invert the one after the division sign and multiply:

$$\frac{25}{3} \div \frac{20}{3} = \frac{25}{3} \times \frac{3}{20} = \frac{25}{20} = \frac{5}{4} = 1\frac{1}{4}$$

29. **A**   Do what's in parentheses first:

$$\left(\frac{1}{2} + \frac{1}{6}\right) - \left(\frac{1}{12} + \frac{1}{3}\right)$$
$$= \left(\frac{3}{6} + \frac{1}{6}\right) - \left(\frac{1}{12} + \frac{4}{12}\right)$$
$$= \frac{4}{6} - \frac{5}{12} = \frac{8}{12} - \frac{5}{12} = \frac{3}{12} = \frac{1}{4}$$

The numerator of $\frac{1}{4}$ is 1.

30. **F**   For $\frac{7}{x}$ to be greater than $\frac{1}{4}$, the denominator x has to be less than 4 times the numerator, or 28. And for $\frac{7}{x}$ to be less than $\frac{1}{3}$, the denominator x has to be greater than 3 times the numerator, or 21. Thus x could be any of the integers 22 through 27, of which there are 6.

Fractions and Decimals

31. **D**   To turn a fraction into a decimal, divide the bottom into the top:

$$5\overline{)3.0} \quad .6$$

32. **G**   To turn a fraction into a decimal, divide the bottom into the top. You can stop when you get three digits:

$$7\overline{)4.00000} \quad .571\ldots$$

(G) is the best approximation.

33. **D**   Put the 875 over 1,000 and reduce:

$$\frac{875}{1,000} = \frac{25 \times 35}{25 \times 40} = \frac{35}{40} = \frac{5 \times 7}{5 \times 8} = \frac{7}{8}$$

In fact, this is a decimal-fraction equivalence many people just know.

34. **K**   To divide decimals, move the decimal points in both numbers enough spaces to the right to turn the number after the division sign—that is, the number you're dividing by, in this case 0.05—into a whole number:

$$0.05\overline{)0.21.5} \quad 4.3$$

35. **C**   To begin, you should convert 3.4 to a fraction or convert $\frac{3}{4}$ to a decimal. Since the answer choices are all fractions, convert 3.4 to a fraction. Just convert 0.4 to a fraction and then add it to the integer part, 3. Then

$0.4 = \frac{4}{10} = \frac{2 \times 2}{2 \times 5} = \frac{2}{5}$. So $3.4 = 3\frac{2}{5}$. Then, add the fractions $3\frac{2}{5}$ and $\frac{3}{4}$. Find a common denominator for the fractional part $\frac{2}{5}$ of $3\frac{2}{5}$ and $\frac{3}{4}$. Use the common denominator $5 \times 4 = 20$. Then

$$3\frac{2}{5} + \frac{3}{4} = 3 + \frac{2}{5} + \frac{3}{4}$$
$$= 3 + \frac{2 \times 4}{5 \times 4} + \frac{3 \times 5}{4 \times 5}$$
$$= 3 + \frac{8}{20} + \frac{15}{20}$$
$$= 3 + \frac{23}{20}$$
$$= 3 + 1\frac{3}{20}$$
$$= 4\frac{3}{20}$$

36. **F**   The answer choices are all fractions, so convert 0.03 to a fraction, convert $4\frac{1}{6}$ to an improper fraction, and multiply. First, $0.03 = \frac{3}{100}$. To convert a mixed number to an improper fraction, multiply the whole number part by the denominator, add the numerator, and put the result over the original denominator. In this instance you have

$4\frac{1}{6} = \frac{4 \times 6 + 1}{6} = \frac{24 + 1}{6} = \frac{25}{6}$. Finally,

$$0.03 \times 4\frac{1}{6} = \frac{3}{100} \times \frac{25}{6} = \frac{3}{4} \times \frac{1}{6} = \frac{1}{4} \times \frac{1}{2} = \frac{1}{8}.$$

37. **D**   To convert a fraction to a decimal, you divide the denominator into the numerator. Clearly you don't have time to take the division out to 100 places after the decimal point. There must be a pattern you can take advantage of.

Start dividing and continue just until you see what the pattern is:

```
      .363636…
11)4.000000…
```

The 1st, 3rd, 5th, etc. digits are 3; and the 2nd, 4th, 6th, 8th, etc. digits are 6. In other words, every digit in an odd-numbered place after the decimal point is a 3 and every digit in an even-numbered place after the decimal point is a 6. The 100th digit is in an even-numbered place after the decimal point, so that digit is a 6.

38. **H** Normally you would have a choice: Either convert the fractions to decimals first and then add, or add the fractions first and then convert the sum to a decimal. In this case, however, both fractions would convert to endlessly repeating decimals, which might be a bit unwieldy when adding. In this case it seems to make sense to add first, then convert:

$$\frac{2}{3} + \frac{1}{12} = \frac{8}{12} + \frac{1}{12} = \frac{9}{12} = \frac{3}{4} = 0.75.$$

39. **B** To convert a fraction to a decimal, you divide the denominator into the numerator.

Choice (A), $\frac{3}{5}$, is equal to 0.6. This is less than 0.68, so eliminate choice (A). Choice (B), $\frac{5}{7}$, is equal to 0.714.... This is greater than 0.68 and less than 0.72, so choice (B) is correct, and there is no need to look at the other choices.

40. **F** First figure out what fraction of all the guests the 5 remaining guests are. $\frac{2}{3}$ of all the guests drank only soda, $\frac{1}{4}$ of the guests drank only juice, and no guest drank both soda and juice. Together, the guests who drank either soda or juice made up

$$\frac{2}{3} + \frac{1}{4} + 0 = \frac{2}{3} \times \frac{4}{4} + \frac{1}{4} \times \frac{3}{3} = \frac{8}{12} + \frac{3}{12} = \frac{11}{12}$$

of all the guests. So the remaining 5 guests made up $\frac{1}{12}$ of all the guests. If you call the total number of guests at the party T, then $\frac{1}{12}T = 5$, and $T = 12 \times 5 = 60$.

Percents

41. **D** The symbol "%" means $\frac{1}{100}$. So $84\% = \frac{84}{100}$. This fraction can be reduced by dividing the numerator and denominator by 4. So $\frac{84}{100} = \frac{21}{25}$.

42. **J** 20% more than 80 means 20% of 80 added to 80. First find 20% of 80. Then add this on to 80. 20% of $80 = \frac{1}{5} \times 80 = 16$. Then 20% more than 80 is $80 + 16 = 96$.

43. **E** To convert to a percent, multiply by 100%. Then $\frac{9}{10} = \frac{9}{10} \times 100\% = 9 \times 10\% = 90\%$.

44. **J** To convert to a percent, multiply by 100%. Then $\frac{5}{4} = \frac{5}{4} \times 100\% = 5 \times 25\% = 125\%$.

45. **E** To convert to a percent, multiply by 100%. Then $\frac{2}{3} = \frac{2}{3} \times 100\% = \frac{200}{3}\% = 66\frac{2}{3}\%$.

46. **G** Be careful. The question is not asking: "What is $\frac{1}{4}$ of 16 ?" It's asking, what is $\frac{1}{4}$ **percent** of 16 ?" One-fourth of 1 percent is 0.25%, or 0.0025: $\frac{1}{4}\%$ of $16 = 0.0025 \times 16 = 0.04$.

47. **E** Translate. "25% of x is 120" translates to: $0.25x = 120$. Multiply both sides of this equation by 4 and you get: $4(0.25x) = 4(120)$
$$x = 480$$

48. **H** Remember that a percent is a fraction, so just find what fraction of 100 gives the same number as 10 percent of 150 and then convert that fraction to a percent. Also remember that the word "of" means times. First find 10% of 150. 10% is $\frac{1}{10}$, so 10% of 150 is $\frac{1}{10} \times 150 = 15$. So the question is now what fraction of 100 gives 15? Call the fraction x. Then $x(100) = 15$. So $x = \frac{15}{100}$. There is no need to reduce this fraction. It is apparent that this fraction is equal to 15%.

49. **D** Remember that the word "of" means times. Then 16% of 25% of 1,000,000 is $\frac{16}{100} \times \frac{25}{100} \times 1,000,000 =$

$\frac{16}{100} \times \frac{25}{100} \times 100 \times 100 \times 100 =$

$16 \times 25 \times 100 = 400 \times 100 = 40,000$.

50. **J** You are looking for that percent of 75 which equals 15 percent of 140. Remember that a percent is a fraction, so just find what fraction of 75 is the same as 15 percent of 140 and then convert that fraction to a percent. Also remember that the word "of" means times. First find 15 percent of 140. 15 percent of 140 is $\frac{15}{100} \times 140 = \frac{3}{20} \times 140 = 3 \times 7 = 21$. So the question is now what fraction of 75 is 21? Call the fraction x. Then $x(75) = 21$. Then $x = \frac{21}{75}$. Divide the top and bottom by 3. Then $x = \frac{7}{25}$. Finally convert this fraction to a percent. $\frac{7}{25} = \frac{7}{25} \times 100\% = 7 \times 4\% = 28\%$.

That is, the unknown percent is 28%; 28% of 75 is the same as 15 percent of 140.

Percent Word Problems

51. **D** Percent times Whole equals Part:

(Percent) $\times 25 = 16$

Percent $= \frac{16}{25} = 0.64 = 64\%$

52. **K** Percent times Whole equals Part:

(15%) $\times$ (take-home pay) = $37.50

(0.15) $\times$ (take-home pay) = $37.50

(take-home pay) $= \frac{\$37.50}{0.15}$

$= \$250.00$

53. **E** Call the price P dollars. Then 15% of P dollars is equal to 30 dollars. Then $\frac{15}{100} P = 30$. So $P = \frac{100}{15} \times 30 = 100 \times 2 = 200$.

54. **H** This question has no actual number for any population given, so this is a good question for solving by picking numbers. With percents questions like this one, it is good to use 100. Use 100 for the original population. It doesn't matter if 100 does not seem like a realistic number to choose for the population. What's important is that 100 is easy to work with in percents questions. The population increased by 30 percent one year. During this year the population increased by

$30\% \times 100 = \frac{30}{100} \times 100 = 30$. So at the end of this year the population was $100 + 30$ or 130. The following year the population decreased by 20 percent. So the following year the decrease was $20\% \times 130 = \frac{20}{100} \times 130 = \frac{1}{5} \times 130 = 26$. At the end of the second year the population was $130 - 26 = 104$. The population increased from 100 to 104. This is an increase of 4. In terms of a percent increase, it is a percent increase of $\frac{4}{100}$ or 4 percent over the original population of 100.

55. **B** Be careful with a question like this one. You're given the percent decrease (25%) and the **new** number (72), and you're asked to reconstruct the original number. Don't just take 25% of 72 and add it on. That 25% is based not on the new number, 72, but on the

original number—the number you're looking for. The best way to do a problem like this is to set up an equation:

(Orig. #) − (25% of Orig. #) = New #

$$x - 0.25x = 72$$
$$0.75x = 72$$
$$x = 96$$

56. **G** This question has no actual number for any group of students given, so this is a good question for solving by picking numbers. With percents questions like this one, it is good to use 100. Use 100 for the number of students in the class. Also remember that the word "of" means times. Since 70 percent of the students are right-handed, the remaining 30 percent are left-handed. So 30 percent of the 100 students are left-handed. 30 percent of 100 is

$30\% \times 100 = \dfrac{30}{100} \times 100 = 30$. So 30 students are left-handed. Of these 30 left-handed students, 70 percent have brown eyes. So the number of left-handed students with brown eyes is

$70\% \times 30 = \dfrac{70}{100} \times 30 = \dfrac{7}{10} \times 30 = 7 \times 3 = 21$.

21 is 21 percent of 100, which is what the number of students in the class was chosen to be.

57. **B** When you know that the given parts add up to the whole, then you can turn a part-to-part ratio into 2 part-to-whole ratios—put each term of the ratio over the sum of the terms. In this case, there were no ties, so the wins and losses account for all the games (i.e., the parts add up to the whole). The sum of the terms in the ratio 3:5 is 8, so the 2 part-to-whole ratios are 3:8 (the ratio of wins to total games) and 5:8 (the ratio of losses to total games):

$$\frac{\text{wins}}{\text{total games}} = \frac{3}{8} = \frac{3}{8} \times 100\% = \frac{300\%}{8} = 37.5\%$$

58. **F** To reduce a number by 20%, you could take 20% of the original number and subtract the result, or you could just take 80% of the original number:

New price = 80% of Original price

$$= (0.80)(\$125)$$
$$= \$100$$

59. **B** This question has no actual number given for the any type of price of a CD, so this is a good question for solving by picking numbers. With percents questions like this one, it is good to use 100. Use 100 for the list price of a CD. The everyday price is 10 percent less than the list price, or 90 percent of the list price. So the

everyday price is $\dfrac{90}{100} \times 100 = 90$. The everyday price is reduced by 30 percent to get the final price, so the final price is 70 percent of the everyday price. So the final price is

$\dfrac{70}{100} \times 90 = \dfrac{7}{10} \times 90 = 7 \times 9 = 63$. Since the final price is 63 and the list price is 100, the final price is 63 percent of the list price.

60. **K** Be careful with combined percent increase. You generally cannot just add the 2 percents, because they're generally percents of different bases. In this instance, the 20% increase is based on the 1970 population, but the 30% increase is based on the larger 1980 population. If you just added 20% and 30% to get 50%, you fell into the test maker's trap.

The best way to do a problem like this one is to **pick a number** for the original whole and just see what happens. And, as usual, the best number to pick here is 100. (That may be a small number for the population of a city, but verisimilitude is not important—all that matters is the math.)

If the 1970 population was 100, then a 20% increase would put the 1980 population at 120. Now, to figure the 30% increase, multiply 120 by 130% (now 120 is the original whole):

New # = (Orig. #) + (30% of Orig. #)

New # = 130% of Orig. #

$$x = 1.3(120)$$
$$= 156$$

Since the population went from 100 to 156, that's a 56% increase.

Ratios, Rates, and Proportions

61. **C** The ratio of men to women is 12:15. By dividing both members of the ratio 12:15 by 3, this ratio can be reduced to 4:5. Notice that the ratio 12:15 is the same as the fraction $\frac{12}{15}$. This fraction can be reduced by dividing the top and bottom by 3 to get the fraction $\frac{4}{5}$, which is the same as the ratio 4:5.

62. **F** When you know that the given parts add up to the whole, then you can turn a part-to-part ratio into 2 part-to-whole ratios—put each term of the ratio over the sum of the terms. In this case, there were no ties, so the wins and losses account for all the games (i.e., the parts add up to the whole). The sum of the terms in the ratio 2:3 is 5, so the 2 part-to-whole ratios are 2:5 (the ratio of wins to total games) and 3:5 (the ratio of losses to total games): $\frac{\text{wins}}{\text{total games}} = \frac{2}{5}$. Since the total number of games was 30, $\frac{\text{wins}}{30} = \frac{2}{5}$. So the number of wins was $30 \times \frac{2}{5} = 6 \times 2 = 12$.

63. **E** Remember the formula Distance = Rate × Time. Here, the distance traveled would be $75 \frac{\text{kilometers}}{\text{hours}} \times 5 \text{ hours} = 375 \text{ kilometers}$.

64. **K** The number of red ties and the number of blue ties must both be whole numbers. The only way you can have blue and red ties in a 4-to-3 ratio is if the total number of ties is a multiple of 4 + 3 = 7. Only multiples of 7 can be split into parts in a 4-to-3 ratio such that both parts are whole numbers. The only choice that's a multiple of 7 is (K), 35.

65. **E** Set up a proportion. Use the units to keep things straight. 40 drops in 1 minute is the same as 2,000 drops in how many minutes?

$$\frac{40 \text{ drops}}{1 \text{ minute}} = \frac{2,000 \text{ drops}}{x \text{ minutes}}$$

$$\frac{40}{1} = \frac{2,000}{x}$$

$$40x = 2,000$$

$$x = 50$$

66. **F** To solve this question, use the formula Average speed = $\frac{\text{Total distance}}{\text{Total time}}$. Here Ashley went 32 miles uphill and 32 miles downhill, so the Total distance was 32 + 32, or 64 miles. To find the Total time, you need the time going uphill and the time going downhill. Since you always have that Distance = Speed × Time,

Time = $\frac{\text{Distance}}{\text{Speed}}$. The time uphill was

$\frac{32 \text{ miles}}{4 \text{ miles per hour}} = 8 \text{ hours}$. The time downhill

was $\frac{32 \text{ miles}}{16 \text{ miles per hour}} = 2 \text{ hours}$. So the Total

time was 8 + 2 or 10 hours. Since the Total distance was 64 miles, Ashley's average speed for

the entire 64 miles was $\frac{64 \text{ miles}}{10 \text{ hours}} = 6.4$ miles per hour.

67. **C** When you're given a ratio (in lowest terms) of quantities that come only in whole-number amounts—like students—you can narrow down the possibilities for the quantities to multiples of the given terms. In this instance, you're given a male-to-female ratio of 3:5. From that ratio you know that the number of males has to be a multiple of 3, the number of females has to be a multiple of 5, and the total number of students has to be a multiple of 3 + 5 = 8. The correct answer is the only choice that's a multiple of 8, and that's 152.

68. **K** Set up a proportion:

$$\frac{288 \text{ miles}}{6 \text{ hours}} = \frac{x \text{ miles}}{8 \text{ hours}}$$

$$6x = 288(8)$$
$$6x = 2{,}304$$
$$x = 384$$

69. **C** To get Vito's rate in pages per hour, take the 96 pages and divide by the time **in hours**. The time is given as "2 hours and 40 minutes." Forty minutes is $\frac{2}{3}$ of an hour, so you can express Vito's time as $2\frac{2}{3}$ hours, or $\frac{8}{3}$ hours:

$$\text{Pages per hour} = \frac{96 \text{ pages}}{\frac{8}{3} \text{ hours}}$$

$$= 96 \times \frac{3}{8} \text{ pages per hour}$$

$$= 36 \text{ pages per hour}$$

70. **H** Set up a proportion:

$$\frac{12 \text{ pages}}{1 \text{ hour}} = \frac{100 \text{ pages}}{x \text{ hours}}$$

$$12x = 100$$

$$x = 8\frac{1}{3}$$

One-third of an hour is 20 minutes, so the time is 8 hours and 20 minutes.

Averages

71. **C** To find the average of 5 numbers, add them up and divide by 5. Here the sum is $12 + 12 + 15 + 37 + 44 = 120$. So the average is $120 \div 5 = 24$.

72. **J** The five consecutive whole numbers are 7, 8, 9, 10, and 11. The average of consecutive whole numbers is the middle number, which in this case is 9.

73. **A** The average of 12 numbers is their sum divided by 12, so the sum of the numbers is equal to the average times 12. $3 \times 12 = 36$.

74. **K** If the average of 5 numbers is 8, then those 5 numbers add up to $5 \times 8 = 40$. Similarly, the 4 numbers whose average is 6 add up to $4 \times 6 = 24$. The fifth number, then, is $40 - 24 = 16$.

75. **A** The average of consecutive integers is simply the average of the smallest and largest of the integers. To find the average of 32 and 108, add them up ($32 + 108 = 140$) and divide by 2 ($140 \div 2 = 70$).

76. **G** Don't jump to hasty conclusions—don't just average the denominators. Do it right—add the fractions and divide by 2:

Average of 2 numbers

$$= \frac{\text{Sum}}{2} = \frac{\frac{1}{20} + \frac{1}{30}}{2} = \frac{\frac{3}{60} + \frac{2}{60}}{2}$$

$$= \frac{\frac{5}{60}}{2} = \frac{\frac{1}{12}}{2} = \frac{1}{12} \times \frac{1}{2} = \frac{1}{24}$$

77. **A** Don't just average the old average and the last score—that would give the last score as much weight as all previous scores combined. The best way to deal with changing averages is to go by way of the sums. Use the old average to figure out the total of the first 6 scores:

Sum of first 6 scores = $6 \times 83 = 498$

Then add the 7th score and divide by 7:

New average $= \frac{498 + 97}{7} = \frac{595}{7} = 85$

78. **K** The best way to deal with changing averages is go by way of the sums. Use the old average to figure out the total of the first 4 scores:

Sum of the first four scores = $4 \times 89 = 356$

And use the new average to figure out the total he needs after the 5th score:

Sum of 5 scores = 5 × 90 = 450

To get his sum up from 356 to 450, Martin needs to score 450 − 356 = 94.

79. **B**   The overall average is not simply the average of the 2 average ages. Because there are a lot more women than men, women carry more weight, and the overall average will be a lot closer to 25 than to 35.

This problem's easiest to deal with if you pick particular numbers for the females and males. The best numbers to pick are the smallest: Say there are 4 females and 1 male. Then the ages of the 4 females total 4 times 25, or 100, and the age of the 1 male totals 35. The average, then, is (100 + 35) divided by 5, or 27.

80. **F**   To find the average of three numbers—even if they're algebraic expressions—add them up and divide by 3:

$$\text{Average} = \frac{\text{Sum of the terms}}{\text{Number of terms}}$$

$$= \frac{(2x + 5) + (5x - 6) + (-4x + 2)}{3}$$

$$= \frac{3x + 1}{3} = x + \frac{1}{3}$$

Arithmetic Word Problems

81. **C**   Say the passing grade is 50. Seven points higher than that is 57. Twelve points lower than 57 is 45, which is **five** points lower than the passing grade of 50.

82. **H**   For every magazine sold, there were 4 newspapers sold. Since the number of magazines is a whole number, the number of newspapers is 4 times a whole number, and is therefore a multiple of 4, and the number of magazines and newspapers combined is therefore a multiple of 5. The only choice that's a multiple of 5 is (H), 25.

83. **C**   After the 45-dollar increase, the price was 200 + 45 = 245 dollars. Then, after the 68-dollar decrease, the final price was 245 − 68 = 177 dollars.

84. **K**   The 4 trucks together are carrying 4 × 250 = 1,000 crates. Since each crate weighs 400 kilograms, the 1,000 crates combined weigh 400 × 1,000 = 400,000 kilograms.

85. **B**   The value of one share increased by 56 − 42 = 14 dollars. The value of 20 shares increased by 20 × 14 = 280 dollars.

86. **G**   If you divide the total $200 by the amount given to each worker, you'll get the number of workers. Since the number of workers has to be a whole number, the correct answer is the choice that's not a factor of 200. Only 30 is not a factor of 200.

87. **D**   Abe's method yields: 6 + 3 = 9. Ben's method yields 6.4 + 3.3 = 9.7, rounded to 10. The positive difference is 1.0

88. **F**   The greatest dollar increase came in 1993-94, but that's not necessarily the greatest **percent** increase. The $5,000 increase for 1989-90 is an increase of $\frac{1}{4}$, or 25%. The $5,000 increase the following year is an increase of just $\frac{1}{5}$, or 20%. You don't even have to give much thought to the $3,000 increases of the next 2 years—but what about the $8,000 increase in 1993-94 ? $8,000 out of $36,000 is less than $\frac{1}{4}$, so there's no need to calculate the percent—the 1989-90 increase wins.

89. **E**   If you add the number of English-speakers and the numbers of Spanish-speakers, you get 28 + 37 = 65. But there are only 50 students, so 65 − 50 = 15 of them are being counted twice—because those 15 speak both languages.

90. **H** Everyone pays $1.50, and the rest of the toll is based on the number of miles traveled. Subtract $1.50 from Joy's toll to see how much is based on distance traveled: $25.00 − $1.50 = $23.50. Then divide that amount by 25 cents per mile:

$$\frac{\$23.50}{\$0.25 \text{ per mile}} = 94 \text{ miles}$$

Algebra Word Problems

91. **B** The difference between the populations in 1990 was 9,400 − 7,600 = 1,800. Each year, as the larger population goes down by 100 and the smaller population goes up by 100, the difference decreases by **200**. Thus it will take 1,800 ÷ 200 = 9 years to erase the difference.

92. **K** Let N be the number of hours that Noah must work. Then

$$20 \frac{\text{dollars}}{\text{hour}} \times N \text{ hours} = 580 \text{ dollars}.$$

So $20N = 580$ and $N = \frac{580}{20} = 29$.

93. **D** Set up a proportion. 5 parts of oil is to 2 parts of vinegar as how many liters of oil is to 8 liters of vinegar? Call the number of liters of oil x. Then

$$\frac{5}{2} = \frac{x}{8}$$
$$2x = 40$$
$$x = 20$$

94. **H** The ratio of fiction to nonfiction is 3 to 8, so the ratio of non-fiction to total books is 8 to 11. Set up a proportion:

$$\frac{8}{11} = \frac{600}{x}$$

Cross multiply:

$$8x = 600 \times 11$$
$$x = \frac{6,600}{8} = 825$$

95. **D** Just translate from English to math. Paul has d dollars and Robert has twice as many dollars as Paul. So Robert has $2d$ dollars. If Paul then gives 5 dollars to Robert, then Robert will have $2d + 5$ dollars.

96. **J** Think about what pairs of integers have a product of 16. There aren't that many; the pairs are 16 and 1, 8 and 2, 4 and 4, −16 and −1, −8 and −2, and −4 and −4. Regarding the last three pairs listed, don't forget that the product of two negative numbers is a positive number. Since the question says that a is greater than 4, a must be either 8 or 16. Therefore b must be either 2 or 1. Statement I says that $b = 2$. It was determined that b could be either 1 or 2, so statement I does not have to be true. (H) and (K) can be eliminated because they both contain statement I. Statement II says that $a + b > 0$. When $a = 8$, $b = 2$ and when $a = 16$, $b = 1$. These are the only possibilities for the values of a and b, and with each of these possibilities, $a + b > 0$. So statement II must be true. (G) can be eliminated because it doesn't contain statement II. Statement III says that $a > b$. As we said when considering statement II, the only possibilities for the values of a and b are that when $a = 8$, $b = 2$ and when $a = 16$, $b = 1$. With each of these possibilities, $a > b$. So statement III must be true. So only statements II and III must be true.

97. **A** Read carefully. This question's a lot easier than you might think at first. It's asking for the total **number** of coins, not the total value. q quarters, d dimes, and n nickels add up to a total of $q + d + n$ coins.

98. **G** When you divide w by 4, you get $\frac{w}{4}$. When you subtract that result from r, you get $r - \frac{w}{4}$.

99. **C** This looks like a solid geometry question, but in fact it's just a "plug-in-the-number-and-see-what-you-get" question.

$$S = \pi r \sqrt{r^2 + h^2}$$

$$= \pi(3)\sqrt{3^2 + 4^2}$$

$$= 3\pi\sqrt{9 + 16}$$

$$= 3\pi\sqrt{25}$$

$$= 3\pi \times 5$$

$$= 15\pi$$

100. **J** This looks like a physics question, but in fact it's just a "plug-in-the-number-and-see-what-you-get" question. Be sure you plug 95 in for C (not F):

$$C = \frac{5}{9}(F - 32)$$

$$95 = \frac{5}{9}(F - 32)$$

$$\frac{9}{5} \times 95 = F - 32$$

$$171 = F - 32$$

$$F = 171 + 32 = 203$$

Exponents

101. **D** 4^3 means $4 \times 4 \times 4$, which equals 64.

102. **F** To multiply powers with the same base, just add the exponents:

$$a^3 \times a^5 = a^{3+5} = a^8$$

103. **E** When you square a negative number, you get a positive result, so you can eliminate (A), (B), and (C). When you square 0, you get 0, so you can eliminate (D). All that's left is (E). When you square 0.5, you get 0.25. All numbers between 0 and 1 are greater than their squares.

104. **G** -1 to an even power is $+1$, and -1 to an odd power is -1.

105. **B** To raise a power to an exponent, multiply the exponents:

$$(b^5)^2 = b^{5 \times 2} = b^{10}$$

106. **J** Compare the numbers in pairs that are easy to compare. 1^{32} is simply 1, and 36^1 is 36, so eliminate the first from contention. It's easy to compare the third and fourth numbers, too: 3^6 is clearly less than 3^{12}, so 3^6 can be eliminated. You don't have to multiply too many 3's to get more than 36, so 3^{12} is certainly greater than 36^1. That narrows the choice down to 3^{12} or 12^3. Rather than multiplying both of these out, you could facilitate comparison by re-expressing 3^{12}:

$$3^{12} = 3^{4 \times 3} = \left(3^4\right)^3 = 81^3$$

In this form it's clear that 3^{12} is greater than 12^3.

107. **C** Be careful with the decimal points and exponents:

$$\frac{(3.0 \times 10^4)(8.0 \times 10^9)}{1.2 \times 10^6}$$

$$= \frac{(3.0 \times 8.0) \times (10^4 \times 10^9)}{1.2 \times 10^6}$$

$$= \frac{24.0 \times 10^3}{1.2 \times 10^6} = \frac{24.0}{1.2} \times \frac{10^{13}}{10^6}$$

$$= \frac{24.0 \times 10^{13}}{1.2 \times 10^6} = \frac{24.0}{1.2} \times \frac{10^{13}}{10^6}$$

$$= 20 \times 10^{(13-6)} = 20 \times 10^7 = 2.0 \times 10^8$$

108. **J** Move the decimal point to get a number between 1 and 10, which here means moving the decimal point 2 places to the right. Because you moved the decimal point 2 places to the right, the exponent you need to attach to the 10 is -2.

109. **B** Just use trial and error as much as you need to in order to find the integers. $2^3 = 2 \times 2 \times 2 = 8$ and $2^4 = 2 \times 2 \times 2 \times 2 = 16$, so the smallest integer n such that $10 < 2^n < 1000$ is 4. $2^5 = 32$, $2^6 = 64$, $2^7 = 128$, $2^8 = 256$, $2^9 = 512$, and $2^{10} = 1{,}024$. So when n is any of the integers 4, 5, 6, 7, 8, or 9, then 2^n is

greater than 10 and less than 1,000. There are 6 such integers.

110. **F** Whenever you have a product of integers, if any one of the integers is even, the product is even. For example, $3 \times 4 \times 5 = 60$, which is even. So since a^b is the product $a \times a \times a \times a \times \ldots \times a$, with b factors of a, a must be odd. So Statement I must be true. Statement II on the other hand does not have to be true. a^b can be odd when b is even, just as long as a is odd. For example, let $a = 3$ and $b = 4$. Then $a^b = 3^4 = 3 \times 3 \times 3 \times 3 = 9 \times 9 = 81$. Only statement I must be true and choice (F) is correct.

Square Roots

111. **B** In mathematics, by definition, the radical symbol, "$\sqrt{}$," means the non-negative square root of a number. 64 has two square roots, 8 and -8, since $8^2 = 64$ and $(-8)^2 = 64$. However, since $\sqrt{}$ means the non-negative square root, $\sqrt{64} = 8$.

112. **G** To rewrite a radical, look for a factor of the number under the radical sign which is a perfect square. A perfect square is an integer which is the square of another integer. For example, 49 is a perfect square because $49 = 7^2$. To rewrite $\sqrt{54}$, look for a factor of 54 which is a perfect square. 9 is a factor of 54 since $54 = 9 \times 6$, and 9 is a perfect square since $9 = 3^2$. Then use the law of radicals which says that $\sqrt{ab} = \sqrt{a}\sqrt{b}$. Here, $\sqrt{54} = \sqrt{9 \times 6} = \sqrt{9} \times \sqrt{6} = 3\sqrt{6}$.

113. **C** Here, you use the law of radicals which says that $\sqrt{\dfrac{a}{b}} = \dfrac{\sqrt{a}}{\sqrt{b}}$. Here, $\dfrac{\sqrt{14}}{\sqrt{7}} = \sqrt{\dfrac{14}{7}} = \sqrt{2}$.

114. **G** Here, you use the law of radicals which says that $\sqrt{\dfrac{a}{b}} = \dfrac{\sqrt{a}}{\sqrt{b}}$. You then write

$$\sqrt{\frac{16}{25}} = \frac{\sqrt{16}}{\sqrt{25}} = \frac{4}{5}$$

115. **A** You're looking for the choice which squared yields 0.0016:

$$\sqrt{0.0016} = \sqrt{\frac{16}{10,000}}$$
$$= \frac{\sqrt{16}}{\sqrt{10,000}} = \frac{4}{100} = 0.04$$

116. **F** Find all the perfect squares you can under the radical, factor them out, unsquare them, and put them in front of the radical:

$$\sqrt{8xy^2z^3} = \sqrt{(4 \times 2)(x)(y^2)(z^2 \times z)}$$
$$= \sqrt{4 \times y^2 \times z^2} \cdot \sqrt{2 \times x \times z}$$
$$= 2yz\sqrt{2xz}$$

117. **B** Simplify the square roots first. Then, if any have like radicals, you can add:

$$\sqrt{50} + \sqrt{8} + \sqrt{18} = \sqrt{25 \times 2} + \sqrt{4 \times 2} + \sqrt{9 \times 2}$$
$$= 5\sqrt{2} + 2\sqrt{2} + 3\sqrt{2}$$
$$= 10\sqrt{2}$$

118. **K** Square the coefficient and square the radical:

$$\left(5\sqrt{3}\right)^2 = 5^2 \times (\sqrt{3})^2 = 25 \times 3 = 75$$

119. **D** The reciprocal of any non-zero number x is $\dfrac{1}{x}$. So the reciprocal of $\sqrt{2}$ is $\dfrac{1}{\sqrt{2}}$. However, none of the answer choices is $\dfrac{1}{\sqrt{2}}$. Rearrange $\dfrac{1}{\sqrt{2}}$ by rationalizing the denominator. This is done by multiplying the numerator and the denominator by $\sqrt{2}$. Then $\dfrac{1}{\sqrt{2}} = \dfrac{1 \times \sqrt{2}}{\sqrt{2} \times \sqrt{2}} = \dfrac{\sqrt{2}}{2} = \dfrac{1}{2}\sqrt{2}$.

120. **G** The area of a square is its side squared. So if you're given the area of a square, you can

find its side length by taking the non-negative square root of the area. Since the area of this square is 32, the length of a side is œ32w. Then $\sqrt{32} = \sqrt{16 \times 2} = \sqrt{16} \times \sqrt{2} = 4\sqrt{2}$. $\sqrt{2}$ is approximately 1.4, so $\sqrt{32}$ is approximately $4(1.4) = 5.6$. Looking at the answer choices, this is closest to choice (G), 5.7.

Algebraic Expressions

121. **B**   To add monomials (when, as here, they're like terms), add the coefficients and keep the variable parts unchanged.

122. **J**   To add polynomials, combine like terms. $2d^2$ and d^2 are like terms that add up to $3d^2$. $5d$ and $-4d$ are like terms that add up to d. Finally, -6 and -4 are like terms that add up to -10. Put them all together and you get $3d^2 + d - 10$.

123. **C**   Combine like terms:

$2x^2 + 3x + x^2 - 4x - x$

$= (2x^2 + x^2) + (3x - 4x - x)$

$= 3x^2 - 2x$

124. **H**   Multiply the coefficients and add the exponents:

$3x^2 \times 5x^3 = 3 \times 5 \times x^{2+3} = 15x^5$

125. **B**   Multiply the coefficients and add the exponents:

$(-2n)(-2n^2)(-2n^2)$

$= (-2)(-2)(-2)\left(n^{1+2+2}\right) = -8n^5$

126. **J**   Distribute the minus sign over the second polynomial and combine like terms:

$(5x^2 + 6x - 7) - (6x^2 - 7x - 8)$

$= 5x^2 + 6x - 7 - 6x^2 + 7x + 8$

$= -x^2 + 13x + 1$

127. **E**   Plug $k = 10$ into the expression:

$$\frac{k^2 - k}{2} = \frac{10^2 - 10}{2}$$

$$= \frac{100 - 10}{2}$$

$$= \frac{90}{2}$$

$$= 45$$

128. **J**   Plug in $x = -5$ and see what you get:

$$2x^2 - 6x + 5 = 2(-5)^2 - 6(-5) + 5$$

$$= 2 \times 25 - (-30) + 5$$

$$= 50 + 30 + 5$$

$$= 85$$

129. **E**   Plug in $x = -2$ and see what you get:

$$x^2 - 2x = (-2)^2 - 2(-2)$$

$$= 4 - (-4)$$

$$= 4 + 4$$

$$= 8$$

130. **J**   Plug in a $2y$ wherever you see an x:

$$\frac{x^2y}{2xy^2} = \frac{(2y)^2y}{2(2y)y^2} = \frac{4y^3}{4y^3} = 1$$

Equations

131. **A**   Solve the equation $6m - 8 = 10 - 3m$. Add 8 to both sides: $6m = 18 - 3m$. Add $3m$ to both sides: $9m = 18$. Divide both sides by 2: $m = 2$.

132. **H**   Solve for n in terms of p by getting n by itself on one side of the equation. The equation is $5n + 3p = 8n - 3p$. Subtract $3p$ from both sides of the equation: $5n = 8n - 6p$. Subtract $8n$ from both sides: $-3n = -6p$. Divide both sides by -3: $\frac{-3n}{-3} = \frac{-6p}{-3}$, so $n = 2p$.

133. **E**   Just plug $y + 2$ for x into the expression $3x - 4$ and then simplify the expression that results:

$$3x - 4 = 3(y + 2) - 4$$

$$= 3y + 6 - 4$$
$$= 3y + 2$$

134. **H**   Just solve the equation $\frac{S}{1,000} = \frac{3}{5}$ for S:

$$S = \frac{3}{5} \times 1,000 = 3 \times 200 = 600$$

135. **E**   You want to find the value of $n - 4$ in terms of p. Notice that n is on the left side of the equation $n = 4p - 8$. So subtract 4 from both sides of this equation: $n - 4 = 4p - 8 - 4$. Finally, simplify the right side of the equation and you have that $n - 4 = 4p - 12$.

136. **H**   You want to find the value of $2r + 2$. Notice that $2r + 8$ is on the left side of the equation $2r + 8 = 24$. So subtract 6 from both sides of this equation: $2r + 8 - 6 = 24 - 6$, and $2r + 2 = 18$. You could also have solved the equation for the value of r and then plugged this value into the expression $2r + 2$:

$$2r + 8 = 24$$
$$2r = 16$$
$$r = 8$$

Finally, $2r + 2 = 2(8) + 2 = 16 + 2 = 18$.

137. **C**   To find a possible value for z, solve the two inequalities.

$$2 \times (z - 3) > 6$$
$$2z - 6 > 6$$
$$2z > 12$$
$$z > 6$$
$$z + 4 < 15$$
$$z < 11$$

So z must be greater than 6 and less than 11. That is, $6 < z < 11$. The only answer choice which is in this range is choice (C), 7, which is correct. Notice that choice (B), 6, is not greater than 6, and choice (D), 11, is not less than 11.

138. **K**   Begin by dividing both sides of the equation $6 \times (C + D) = 48$ by 6. Then $C + D = 8$. Since D is less than 5, C must be greater than 3

in order for the sum of C and D to equal 8. The correct choice will be a choice which is not greater than 3. Only choice (K), 2, is not greater than 3 and is correct.

139. **C**   Just plug 8 for q and 2 for r into the defining equation. Then
$8//2 = (8 \times 2) - (8 - 2) = 16 - 6 = 10$.

140. **G**   Use the equation given in the definition to set $P//3$ equal to 11 and solve for P:

$$P \times 3 - (P - 3) = 11$$
$$3P - P + 3 = 11$$
$$2P + 3 = 11$$
$$2P = 8$$
$$P = 4$$

Lines and Angles

141. **A**   Notice that $QS = QR + RS$. So the length of QR can be found by subtracting from the length of QS the length of RS. The length of QS is given to be 11. The length of RS can be found by subtracting the length of PR from the length of PS, because $PS = PR + RS$. Both the length of PR and the length of PS are given. It is given that $PR = 16$ and $PS = 20$. So $RS = PS - PR = 20 - 16 = 4$. Then, $QR = QS - RS = 11 - 4 = 7$.

142. **C**   It is given that the distance from B to C is 12. This means that $BC = 12$. It is given that the distance from B to C is twice the distance from A to B. This means that $BC = 2AB$. Then $AB = \frac{1}{2}BC = \frac{1}{2}(12) = 6$. It is given that the distance from C to D is equal to half the distance from A to C. This means that $CD = \frac{1}{2}AC$. Now $AC = AB + BC = 6 + 12 = 18$. So $CD = \frac{1}{2}AC = \frac{1}{2}(18) = 9$. Finally, the distance from A to D is the length of segment AD.

$$AD = AC + CD = 18 + 9 = 27.$$

143. **C** The four marked angles in the figure add up to a straight line, or 180 degrees. So $60 + 29 + y + 40 = 180$. Then $129 + y = 180$ and $y = 180 - 129 = 51$.

144. **H** When a pair of lines intersect, angles which are opposite each other are equal. The angle marked z degrees and the angle indicated with a little box to be a right angle are opposite each other. So $z = 90$.

145. **H** The angles marked $e°$ and $f°$ make up a straight line, or 180°. So $e + f = 180$.

Triangles

146. **K** The angle marked $r°$ is an exterior angle of the triangle, so it's equal to the sum of the remote interior angles—that is, not the adjacent angle, but the other two. Here the remote interior angles measure 70° and 80°, so $r = 70 + 80 = 150$.

147. **H** The hatch marks tell you that this is an isosceles triangle, so the other base angle measures 50°: Now you know 2 of the 3 angles. The two 50° angles add up to 100°, which leaves $180 - 100 = 80$ degrees for the third angle.

148. **G** Use the fact that the interior angles of a triangle add up to 180 degrees to write an equation:

$$60 + (a + 40) + a = 180$$
$$2a + 100 = 180$$
$$2a = 180 - 100$$
$$2a = 80$$
$$a = 40$$

149. **C** The area of a triangle is $\frac{1}{2}$ times base times height, that is, $\frac{1}{2}bh$. The base of this triangle can be called side DF, which is 8. Then the height is 6. So the area is $\frac{1}{2} \times 8 \times 6 = 4 \times 6 = 24$.

150. **K** An isosceles triangle has two equal sides and the angles opposite the two equal sides have equal measure. In this question, what's important to consider is the measure of angles. Suppose that the 80° angle is one of the two equal angles in the isosceles triangle. Then one of the other angles of this triangle has a measure of 80°. The sum of the angles of any triangle is 180°. So the third angle of this triangle has a measure of $180° - 80° - 80° = 20°$. Thus 20° and 80° can both be the measure of another angle of the triangle when the three angles of the triangle are 80°, 80°, and 20°. So options I and III are both part of the correct answer. Eliminate choices (F), (G), and (H). Now suppose that the other two angles of the triangle each have a measure of $x°$, so that the angle of measure 80° is not equal to the other two equal angles. The three angles of the triangle have measures of $x°$, $x°$, and 80°. The sum of the angles of any triangle is 180°. So $x + x + 80 = 180$, $2x + 80 = 180$, $2x = 100$, and $x = 50$. Thus, 50° could be the measure of another angle of the triangle when the three angles of the triangle are 80°, 50°, and 50°. So option II is also part of the correct answer. So options I, II, and III could all be the measure of another angle of the triangle and choice (K) is correct.

151. **A** An isosceles triangle has two equal sides and the angles opposite the two equal sides have equal measure. In this question, what's important to consider is the measure of angles. One of the angles of this isosceles triangle is 100°. This angle cannot be one of the two equal angles because two equal angles each having a measure of 100° would have a sum of $100° + 100° = 200°$ and the sum of all three angles of any triangle is 180°. You can eliminate choices (C), (D), and (E), which all include option III. Now suppose that the other two angles of the triangle each have a measure of $x°$, so that the angle of measure 100° is not equal to the other two equal angles. The three angles of the triangle have measures of $x°$, $x°$, and 100°. The sum of the angles of any triangle is 180°. So $x + x + 100 = 180$, $2x + 100 = 180$,

$2x = 80$, and $x = 40$. Thus, 40° could be the measure of another angle of the triangle when the three angles of the triangle are 100°, 40°, and 40°. This is the only possible measure of another angle of the triangle. So the correct answer is (A), I only.

152. **F** The key to solving this question is realizing that the triangle is a right triangle; you have the very well known 3-4-5 Pythagorean triplet. The area of any triangle is $\frac{1}{2}$ times base times height. The area of a right triangle is $\frac{1}{2}$ the product of the legs, or $\frac{1}{2} \times \text{leg}_1 \times \text{leg}_2$, because one leg can be considered to be the base and the other leg can be called the height. The legs of this right triangle are 3 and 4. So the area of this right triangle is $\frac{1}{2} \times 3 \times 4 = \frac{1}{2} \times 12 = 6$.

Rectangles, Squares, and Other Polygons

153. **H** All sides of a square are equal. One side is given as 4, so side AB is also 4.

154. **C** The perimeter of a rectangle is equal to twice the width plus twice the length. Twice 3 plus twice 5 is $3 + 3 + 5 + 5 = 16$.

155. **H** Since the four sides of a square are equal, you can say that each side of a square is one-fourth of the perimeter. Here the perimeter is given as 64, so one side is one-fourth of that, or 16.

156. **D** The perimeter of any polygon is the sum of the lengths of its sides. The perimeter of polygon A is $5 + 4 + 9 + 10 + 8 + 6 = 42$. The perimeters of polygons A and B are equal. So the perimeter of polygon B is also 42. Polygon B has 6 sides of equal length. So 6 times the length of a side of polygon B is 42. So the length of one side of polygon B must be $42 \div 6$, or 7.

157. **E** The area of a rectangle is length times width. Think about what pairs of positive integers have a product of 15. There are not that many pairs. The pairs, not including the order, are 15 and 1, and 5 and 3. The perimeter of a rectangle is twice the length plus twice the width. If the rectangle has the dimensions 15 and 1, its perimeter is $2(15) + 2(1) = 30 + 2 = 32$. If the rectangle has the dimensions 5 and 3, its perimeter is $2(5) + 2(3) = 10 + 6 = 16$. The greatest possible perimeter of the rectangle is 32.

Circles

158. **G** The figure shows the radius to be 3, so the diameter is twice that, or 6.

159. **K** The figure shows the radius to be 7. Plug $r = 7$ into the formula for the area of a circle:

$$\text{Area} = \pi r^2$$
$$= \pi (7)^2$$
$$= 49\pi$$

160. **B** Plug $r = 5$ into the formula for the circumference of a circle:

$$\text{Circumference} = 2\pi r$$
$$= 2\pi (5)$$
$$= 10\pi$$

161. **J** Plug $r = 5$ into the formula for the area of a circle:

$$\text{Area} = \pi r^2$$
$$= \pi (5)^2$$
$$= 25\pi$$

162. **D** Use the formula for the circumference of a circle to find the radius:

$$2\pi r = 100\pi$$
$$2r = 100$$
$$r = 50$$

163. **G** Use the formula for the area of a circle to find the radius:

$$\pi r^2 = 100\pi$$
$$r^2 = 100$$
$$r = 10$$

164. **E**   Use the formula for the circumference of a circle to find the radius:

$$2\pi r = 36\pi$$
$$2r = 36$$
$$r = 18$$

The radius is 18, so the diameter is twice that, or 36.

165. **H**   Use the formula for the area of a circle to find the radius:

$$\pi r^2 = 36\pi$$
$$r^2 = 36$$
$$r = 6$$

The radius is 6, so the diameter is twice that, or 12.

Quantitative Comparisons I

166. **A**   Don't calculate. Compare Column A to a percent of 34 that's easy to find. Think of 52% as just a bit more than 50%, or $\frac{1}{2}$. 52% of 34, then, is just a bit more than half of 34, so it's more than 17.

167. **A**   If you know your standard fraction-decimal equivalents, you know that $\frac{3}{4}$ is the same as 0.75, which is less than 0.76.

168. **A**   Tripling x doesn't necessarily give you more than doubling x, but it does when x is positive.

169. **A**   Subtract x from both columns to get 0 in Column A and –1 in Column B. Column A is greater.

170. **D**   At first glance you might think that x is greater than $-x$ because a positive is greater than a negative, but nothing says that x has to

be positive or that $-x$ has to be negative. If x is negative to start with, then $-x$ is positive, and the relationship is reversed. And if $x = 0$, the columns are equal, so the answer is (D).

171. **B**   Since x is negative, Column A is negative. But, because a negative number squared is positive, Column B is positive and therefore greater than Column A.

172. **A**   Don't calculate. Compare piece by piece. The first fraction in Column A is greater than the first fraction in Column B, and the second fraction in Column A is greater than the second fraction in Column B. Therefore the sum in Column A is also greater.

173. **A**   Add c to both columns and you end up comparing a and b. The centered information tells you straight out that a is greater.

174. **C**   Multiply both columns by 2 and you end up with 100×8.01, or 801, in Column A, and you also end up with 801 in Column B.

175. **A**   Just look at the number of negative signs in each column, use what you know about numbers, and you won't have to evaluate the two expressions. In Column A you have a positive over a positive, which is positive, and in Column B you have a positive over a negative, which is negative. There's no need to calculate to see that Column A is greater.

Quantitative Comparisons II

176. **B**   –1 is further to the right on the number line than –2, so –1 is greater.

177. **D**   Use what you know about x and y to figure out how big and how small the value of $x + y$ can be. Don't assume that x and y are integers. That would make $x = 15$ and $y = 19$, and then the columns would be equal. But x might be less than 15, perhaps 14.5, and y

might be less than 19, perhaps 18.5. In that case Column A would be greater. (It's also possible for $x + y$ to be <u>greater</u> than 34.) More than one relationship is possible, so the answer is (D).

178. **D**   If you tried to do this one by picking numbers and all you picked was the small integers 1, 2, 3 you'd think the answer was (A). Try taking a value for x that's greater than 5. When $x = 6$, for example, Column A is 29 and Column B is 30. More than one relationship is possible, so the answer is (D).

179. **C**   There's no need to calculate. The sum of the five consecutive integers in Column A will be simply 5 times the middle number, exactly what you have in Column B.

180. **A**   Compare piece by piece. You know that $\sqrt{9}$ is 3, so $\sqrt{10}$ is something more than 3. By similar reasoning, you know that $\sqrt{65}$ is something more than 8. Each piece of Column A is greater than the corresponding piece of Column B, so the sum of the pieces in Column A will be greater than the sum of the pieces in Column B.

181. **D**   These two quantities are reciprocals, so when Column A is greater than 1, Column B is less than 1, and vice versa. Column A will be greater than 1, and consequently greater than Column B, when $99x$ is greater than 100—in other words, when x is greater than $\frac{100}{99}$. On the other hand, Column A will be less than 1, and consequently less than Column B, when x is **less** than $\frac{100}{99}$. And of course the columns will be equal when $x = \frac{100}{99}$. More than one relationship is possible, so the answer is (D).

182. **D**   There are several pairs of integers that have a product of 10. You don't need to find every pair. Just try to find a pair that has a sum

greater than 6 and another pair that has a sum less than 6. An example of the former is 5 and 2. An example of the latter is –5 and –2. Thus the answer is (D).

183. **B**   Note that if you factor 19 out of Column A, you end up with 19 times 100, which is just one less than 1901.

184. **D**   It looks at first glance like B and C divide the segment into three equal pieces. But check the mathematics of the situation to be sure. You're given that $AC = BD$:

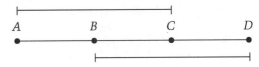

What can you deduce from that? You can subtract BC from both equal lengths and you'll end up with another equality: $AB = CD$. But what about BC? Does it have to be the same as AB and CD? No. The diagram could be resketched like this:

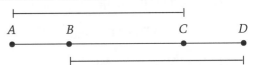

Now you can see that it's possible for AC and BD to be equal but for BC to be longer than AB. It's also possible for BC to be shorter:

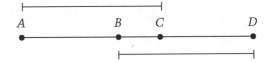

More than one relationship is possible, so the answer is (D).

185. **A**   The area of the circle is $\pi r^2 = \pi(3)^2 = 9\pi$. The area of the rectangle is 9×3. Don't think of it as 27; it's easier to compare in the form 9×3. π is more than 3, so 9π is more than 9×3.

Synonyms

1.	A	CONVENE = assemble
2.	H	GLIB = articulate
3.	C	MARVEL = wonder
4.	K	ULTIMATE = final
5.	A	FORMIDABLE = imposing
6.	H	QUENCH = satisfy
7.	E	ECCENTRIC = peculiar
8.	F	DEBRIS = wreckage
9.	D	ALLOT = apportion
10.	G	TETHER = leash
11.	B	MAR = spoil
12.	H	SAVOR = relish
13.	D	ANTIDOTE = remedy
14.	G	TAUT = tight
15.	A	OBSOLETE = outdated
16.	K	VEX = annoy
17.	C	DIN = noise
18.	J	INCENTIVE = inducement
19.	A	DEJECTED = saddened
20.	H	STAUNCH = steadfast
21.	E	PERJURY = lying
22.	F	PETRIFY = shock
23.	D	IMMINENT = impending
24.	H	ABDUCT = kidnap
25.	E	TORRID = sweltering
26.	K	LURID = sensational
27.	E	INCESSANT = unending

28.	G	CIRCUMVENT = go around
29.	B	CALLOUS = insensitive
30.	J	NARRATIVE = story
31.	A	REIGN = rule
32.	K	OPTION = alternative
33.	A	FATIGUED = exhausted
34.	K	FLIPPANT = frivolous
35.	A	ADHERE = cling
36.	J	VEHEMENT = fiery
37.	E	INFECTIOUS = contagious
38.	G	INSOMNIA = sleeplessness
39.	B	PUNGENT = spicy
40.	J	GRUESOME = hideous
41.	B	MELANCHOLY = sad
42.	J	NAUSEOUS = sickening
43.	D	CASCADE = shower
44.	F	ABYSS = pit
45.	B	SEVER = cut apart
46.	F	DOGGED = obstinate
47.	C	ALLAY = soothe
48.	H	TUMULT = commotion
49.	D	SCATHING = harsh
50.	F	BEWILDER = perplex
51.	C	MINUSCULE = tiny
52.	K	COLLUSION = conspiracy
53.	A	DISSEMINATE = spread
54.	F	PARADOX = inconsistency
55.	C	EXOTIC = foreign
56.	F	ARMADA = fleet

57.	**B**	DEJECTED = depressed
58.	**H**	LADEN = loaded
59.	**D**	INTIMATE = hint
60.	**K**	MALEVOLENCE = evil
61.	**B**	DINGY = dirty
62.	**H**	ERA = period
63.	**A**	WRATH = anger
64.	**K**	GLEE = joy
65.	**B**	MIMIC = imitate
66.	**J**	CUE = prompt
67.	**D**	FAUNA = animals
68.	**H**	AUXILIARY = secondary
69.	**D**	AMOROUS = romantic
70.	**G**	BOULEVARD = avenue
71.	**C**	WANE = decrease
72.	**K**	CACHE = stash
73.	**A**	RANCOR = bitterness

74.	**H**	DECLAMATION = speech
75.	**A**	DISCLOSE = expose
76.	**H**	SINISTER = threatening
77.	**D**	LUNGE = plunge
78.	**H**	CONDONE = approve
79.	**C**	ZEALOUS = fanatical
80.	**J**	REPARTEE = retort
81.	**A**	APPREHENSION = anxiety
82.	**F**	REALIZATION = awareness
83.	**A**	OBSTINATE = stubborn
84.	**G**	EBULLIENT = elated
85.	**B**	SCALD = burn
86.	**F**	AUDACITY = boldness
87.	**B**	MAGNANIMOUS = generous
88.	**H**	TEMPERATE = moderate
89.	**D**	COPIOUS = plentiful
90.	**K**	ENIGMA = mystery

Analogies

1. **E**   The relationship between **FOOD** and **FAMINE** is that a *famine* is a severe lack of *food*. Now for the answer choices. Choice (E) is correct because a **DROUGHT** is a severe lack of **WATER**. You might have fallen for choice (A) here, but *thirst* refers to a single person; a *drought* or *famine* refers to an entire area.

2. **G**   Note that **PILOT** is used here as a verb, since all the answer choices are verbs. To *pilot* an **AIRPLANE** is to do what a pilot does; that is, to control or steer it. So we want something that means to control or steer a **CAR**. Of course, the correct answer here is (G) **DRIVE**. (J) *control* may seem like a possibility, but *control* doesn't refer specifically to the act of driving a *car*. In fact, you rarely say that you *control* a *car*; you often say that you *drive* a *car*.

3. **D**   **AMPLE** means "large or abundant." **EXCESSIVE** goes beyond *ample*; it means "too ample." It's good to be **BOLD**, but to be **RECKLESS** is to take boldness too far. So the words in choice (D) have the same relationship as *ample* does to *excessive*.

4. **H**   A **CALF** is a young or immature **COW**. And the word for a young **SHEEP** is **LAMB**, so choice (H) is the correct answer. (F) *pork* is the meat that comes from a *hog*. A (G) *mule* is a cross between a *horse* and a *donkey*. A (K) *ram* is a male sheep, and a *ewe* is a female sheep.

5. **C**   In order to prepare for a **TEST**, you need to **STUDY**. In order to prepare for a **PLAY**, you have to **REHEARSE**, so (C) is the correct answer here.

6. **F**   A **BANANA** is covered by a **PEEL**. **CORN** is covered by a **HUSK**, so choice (F) is the correct answer.

7. **D**   **TACTILE** means "having to do with **TOUCH**." Choice (D) is the correct answer here, since **VISUAL** means "having to do with **SIGHT**."

8. **H**   An **HOUR** is a unit of time, as is a **MINUTE**. A *minute* is a part of an *hour*: it's a smaller unit. A **DOLLAR** is a unit of money, so we need something that represents some fraction of a *dollar*. The only answer choice that fits this requirement is (H) **CENT**.

9. **A**   A **TORNADO** is a violent windstorm, and a **BREEZE** is a light, pleasant wind, so the relationship between a *tornado* and a *breeze* is one of degree. A *tornado* and a *breeze* are at the opposite ends of the wind spectrum. The only choice that can be right here is (A), since a **DRIZZLE** is a very light rain, while a **STORM** is much more severe. A (B) *monsoon* is a violent rainstorm.

10. **K**   When a **SHIP** stops in a port to unload, it's said to **DOCK** there. In the same way, when you stop a **CAR** to unload it, you **PARK** it, so choice (K) is the answer here.

11. **D**   **ASPARAGUS** is a kind of **VEGETABLE**. A **WALTZ** is a kind of **DANCE**, so choice (D) is the correct answer here. A (B) *polka* is another kind of dance, and an (E) *ball* is a kind of formal party, at which there is dancing.

12. **G**   **TIME** is measured or registered by a **CLOCK**, so we want an instrument that measures or registers **DIRECTION**. That's what you use a **COMPASS** for, so (G) is the answer. The (H) *needle* of a *compass* is analogous to the hands of a *clock*, not to the *clock* itself.

13. **C**   **LIGHT** is provided by a **LAMP**, so the right answer to this question is something that provides **HEAT**. A **RADIATOR** provides *heat*; that's the function of a *radiator*. So choice (C) is the correct answer here.

14. **J**   Something that is **BANAL** is commonplace and ordinary; something *banal* lacks **ORIGINALITY**. Something **PALTRY** lacks **WORTH**, so choice (J) is the answer. (F) *meat* that's been *cured* has been treated (by salting or smoking) to prevent spoilage. A (K) *jamb* is one of the side pieces of the frame of a *door*.

15. **A**   A **STAIRCASE** is made up of a series of **STEPS**. In the same way, a **LADDER** is made up of a series of **RUNGS**, so choice (A) is the right answer.

16. **K**   A **THRONE** is the seat of a **KING**. A **BENCH** is the seat of a **JUDGE**, so choice (K) is the correct answer. A *throne* can also be the symbol of a *king*'s authority, and a (G) *crown* can be a symbol of a *queen*'s authority, but both *throne* and *crown* go equally well

with either *king* or *queen*. Consequently, (G) is not as good an answer as (K) is. A (J) *gavel* is a kind of *hammer*.

17. **C** To **EAVESDROP** is to **LISTEN** secretly. Now we need to find something that means to **WATCH** secretly. (C) **SPY** is what we want here: to *spy* means to *watch* secretly. (A) *look* and (B) *observe* both mean to *watch*, but they don't mean to watch <u>secretly</u>.

18. **G** **BIOLOGY** is the science of **LIFE**. The best choice here is (G), because **PSYCHOLOGY** is the science of the **MIND**.

19. **C** A **MISER**, or stingy person, is without **GENEROSITY**. **IMPIETY** means a lack of reverence for sacred things, so it's correct to say that a **SAINT** is without *impiety*. Choice (C) is therefore the best answer. (A) *affluence* is wealth, an abundance of *money*. (B) *ethics* are rules of correct conduct; a particular *doctor* might or might not be lacking in *ethics*. (E) *ruthlessness* is lack of pity.

20. **G** A **RABBIT** is kept in a **HUTCH** (a *hutch* is a pen for small animals). A **CHICKEN** is kept in a **COOP**, so choice (G) is the correct answer.

21. **D** A **VOLCANO** is a hole in the earth's crust. When it **ERUPTS**, molten rock, called *lava*, comes out of it. So *erupt* is just the verb that we use to describe the violent action of a *volcano*. Choice (D) is correct because what a **BOMB** does is **EXPLODE**. *Explode* is the verb that we use to describe the violent action of a *bomb*. In fact, the eruption of a *volcano* can be a kind of explosion, so this is a good analogy. (A) *lava* <u>does</u> *flow*, and a (B) *ball* <u>does</u> *bounce*, but these are not violent, explosive actions, so they aren't good matches for the stem pair. An (E) *army* does *assault* or attack, and this is a violent action, but it is not the kind of physical explosion suggested both in the stem pair and in choice (D).

22. **F** A **REGIMENT** is a group of **SOLDIERS** (it's a part of an army). What do you call a group of **STUDENTS**? A **CLASS**. In the same way that a *regiment* is a group of *soldiers*, and several *regiments* together make up an army, a *class* is a group of *students*, with many *classes* making up a *school*. That's why (J) *school*

isn't as good an answer. (G) *troops* and (H) *platoon* are groups of *soldiers*.

23. **D** To **REVEAL** something is to show or display it. To **CONCEAL** something is to hide it. So *reveal* and *conceal* are opposites. The best choice here is (D), because to **REPUDIATE** something is to *disown* or *renounce* it. It's the opposite of **AFFIRM**. In (A), *secrete* is a synonym for *hide*, and in (B), *dig* is a synonym for *delve*.

24. **G** To **SHOUT** and to **WHISPER** are to do the same thing in opposite ways. To *shout* is to speak very loudly, and to *whisper* is to speak very quietly. To **GUZZLE** means to drink quickly or greedily. The opposite of *guzzle* must mean to drink slowly or sparingly. The best answer is (G) **SIP**.

25. **C** The adjectives **WARM** and **SCORCHING** represent different degrees of the same basic thing. That is, *warm* means "slightly hot," and *scorching* means "very hot." Choice (C) is the best answer. **UNFRIENDLY** and **HOSTILE** mean roughly the same thing, but *hostile* connotes a much stronger state of antagonism than *unfriendly* does. (A) *polite* and *insolent* are opposite in meaning. (B) *friendly* and *affable* mean the same thing at about the same level of strength; the same is true of (D) *strong* and *tough*.

26. **J** A **GROCER** is a person who sells **FOOD**. Choice (J) is the correct answer, because a **APOTHECARY** or pharmacist is a person who sells **MEDICINE**. An (F) *carnivore* is an animal that eats *meat*. A (G) *locksmith* makes (and sells) both locks and *keys*, but a *grocer* doesn't so much make *food* as sell *food* that others have made, so this isn't as good a match for the stem pair as (J) is. An (H) *librarian* doesn't <u>sell</u> books.

27. **E** A **SCORE** is a written or printed copy of a piece of music which a **MUSICIAN** reads and follows. A **SCRIPT** is a written or printed copy of a **PLAY**. It's an **ACTOR** who reads and follows a *script* in the way that a *musician* reads and follows a *score*, so (E) is the answer.

28. **F** This one is easier to grasp intuitively than it is to explain. A **LINE** is a one-dimensional form, and a **CIRCLE** is a round two-dimensional figure whose outer edge is a curved *line* (that's not correct mathe-

matical terminology, but you get the point). A **PLANE** is a two-dimensional form, and a **SPHERE** is a round three-dimensional figure whose outer edge is a curved *plane*, so choice (F) is the best answer. A (G) *triangle* is one of the two-dimensional figures that make up a *pyramid*. An (H) *angle* is a corner of a *square* or any other geometrical figure. A (J) *pentagon* is a five-sided geometrical figure, and a *hexagon* is a six-sided one.

29. **B**   A **MOVEMENT** is one of the sections that make up a **SYMPHONY** (a typical *symphony* has three or four *movements*, though some have more). In the same way, an **ACT** is one of the sections that make up a **PLAY** (a typical *play* has anywhere from one to five *acts*). An (E) *film* is made up of *frames*, but a *frame* is a tiny segment of the film. A *movement* or an *act* is a much longer structural unit.

30. **F**   To **CURTAIL** something is to cut it short, to reduce its **LENGTH**. To **CONSTRICT** something means to make it more narrow, to reduce its (F) **WIDTH**.

31. **A**   A **BOOK** is stored in a **LIBRARY**, just as a *car* is stored in a *garage*.

32. **G**   A **CHAPTER** is a part of a **BOOK**, just as a *scene* is a part of a *play*.

33. **A**   A **FASTIDIOUS** person is almost obsessively tidy—he or she tries to avoid **UNTIDINESS**, just as a **punctual** person strives to avoid **lateness**.

34. **G**   A **TRUMPET** is a **BRASS** instrument; a *flute* is a *woodwind* instrument.

35. **A**   A **BENEFACTOR** is by definition a **GENEROUS** person—a *skinflint* is *characteristically* stingy.

36. **K**   A **RECLUSIVE** person is like a hermit—he or she seeks **ISOLATION** from other people. Choice K has a similar bridge—a *sociable* person seeks out human *company*.

37. **D**   A **SHOAL** is a group of **FISH**, just as a *herd* is a group of *elephants*.

38. **F**   This is a bridge where one word is an extreme of the other—to **ENTHRALL** is to thoroughly **ENTERTAIN** some person or group of people. Similarly, to *ridicule* is to *mock* a person or group of people in an extreme fashion.

39. **B**   An **UMBRELLA** protects someone from the **RAIN**; a *parasol* protects someone from the *sun*.

40. **J**   Another "extremes" bridge—someone who is **ENERVATED** is extremely **WEAK**. Likewise, something *colossal* is extremely *large*.

41. **B**   To **ABBREVIATE** a **SPEECH** is to make it shorter. Likewise, to *edit* an *article* is to make it shorter.

42. **F**   **TESTIMONY** is a speech given by a **WITNESS**. In similar fashion, a *lecture* is a speech given by a *professor*.

43. **C**   A **MONTH** is a part of a **YEAR**, as an *inch* is a part of a *foot*.

44. **G**   Something that's **STATIONARY** does not have **MOTION**, just as something *empty* has no *content*.

45. **C**   Something that's **HACKNEYED** is not **FRESH**, just as something that's a *copied* is not *original*.

Reading Comprehension

Martha Graham passage

The first paragraph of this passage introduces us to Martha Graham, the dancer and choreographer who wanted to break away from the traditions of classical ballet. The second paragraph describes the ways in which her work, especially the early pieces, differed from classical ballet.

1.   **C**   The passage focuses on Martha Graham's work as an innovator in dance, so (C) is correct.

2.   **H**   Choice (H) is correct because it accurately paraphrases the last sentence of the first paragraph.

3.   **D**   Since the author says that Graham used the natural breath pulse as the basis for movement "instead of formalized classical motions," you can infer that formalized classical motions were not based on natural breathing.

4.   **K**   Choice (K) is correct because the author mentions decorative sets and costumes as one of the features of classical ballet that Graham rejected.

5.   **A**   Choice (A) captures the author's idea that all artistic revolutions eventually become the traditions against which a new avant-garde rebels.

Tunnels passage

This passage discusses full-face tunnel boring machines, which were recently used to dig the Eurotunnel beneath the English channel.

6.   **G**   In the very first sentence the author says that tunnel construction is costly and dangerous, and nowhere does he say that TBMs have made tunnel construction less expensive or less dangerous, so (G) is correct.

7.   **D**   Choice (D) is a better answer than (C) because (D) covers the entire passage whereas (C) is only discussed in the first passage.

8.   **G**   Choice (G) echoes the final couple of lines of the passage.

9.   **C**   In the context of the sentence in which the word "notable" appears, it has the meaning "remarkable."

10.   **F**   The author certainly thinks highly of TBMs, so "enthusiastic" is correct. "Jubilant" (K) is too strong a word, however.

Acoustics passage

This passage is a discussion of the challenge of proper acoustic design of concert and lecture halls. The author pays special attention to the problem of fine-tuning reverberated sound, which is the sound that comes to the listener after it has been reflected off the walls, ceiling and floor.

11.   **D**   Lines 14-26 focus on reverberation, which the author describes as the "most important factor in acoustic design" at the end of the passage.

12.   **F**   Choice (F) is the correct answer because the author says that "few of us realize the complex process that goes into designing the acoustics of concert and lecture halls."

13.   **E**   All three options are mentioned in the passage as factors that affect the acoustics of a building, so (E) is the right answer.

14.   **H**   According to the passage, too little reverberation can make sound thin and weak.

15.   **B**   The final sentence of the passage says that the important factor in acoustic design is the reverberation time, which makes (B) correct.

Termites passage

This is a brief discussion of the symbiotic relationship between the termite and the parasitic protozoans that live in the termite's gut. The presence of the protozoans benefits the termite in that they digest the cellulose in the wood the termite consumes.

16.   **F**   The last sentence of the passage says that the protozoans provide the termite with a service necessary to its survival, so (F) is correct.

17.   **E**   The passage is about the symbiotic relationship between termites and protozoans, two

organisms that cooperate to survive. (E) is the correct answer.

18.   **G**   According to the passage, the host organism is the dominant member of the symbiotic pair or group (G).

19.   **E**   The author defines a symbiotic relationship as one in which two organisms coexist to each other's benefit, so (E) is correct.

20.   **F**   "Cooperative" is the proper word here. "Friendly" (H) would imply that termites and protozoans have feelings, which is going a little bit too far.

Bogs passage

This rather dry passage explains how bogs were formed as mosses moved into old glacial depressions. The second paragraph explains why bog water has a low mineral content and is so acidic.

21.   **B**   Choice (B) is the best answer because the entire passage is an explanation of how bogs form and develop.

22.   **G**   "Marked" is the word that can replace "characterized" in the first sentence without changing the sentence's meaning.

23.   **D**   Without regular intervals of rain, a bog could not easily maintain its water-soaked state (D). All of the other choices are either not mentioned in the passage at all or would in fact be detrimental to the maintenance of a bog.

24.   **K**   The author says that since mosses prevent acidic water from draining out, bogs eventually become highly acidic (K).

25.   **B**   Choice (B) is correct. The author says that the mineral content of bog water remains low because pure rainwater is usually the only source of new water. This means that rainwater must be low in mineral content.

Ozone passage

This passage is about a problem you may have heard something about before: the thinning of the Earth's ozone layer. After laying out the various consequences of ozone loss, the author discusses some of the steps

that have been taken by the international community to combat the problem.

26.   **J**   The second sentence of the passage supports (J) as the correct answer.

27.   **E**   Choice (E) is the one that captures the central focus of the passage without being too narrow or too broad.

28.   **H**   The way the international community responded to the ozone problem was to ban CFCs and other pollutants; this is supposed stop ozone loss by the turn of the century. From this you can infer that ozone loss was due to pollutants (H).

29.   **B**   The author uses the greenhouse image to describe the effect of increased radiation on the climate of the Earth.

30.   **K**   Choice (K), although pessimistic, is correct because the last sentence of the passage says that "total ozone recovery" will not occur for more than a hundred years.

Immigrants passage

The first paragraph of this passage describes the wave of immigrants that came into the US from southern and eastern Europe at the end of the nineteenth century. The second paragraph is about the work of Jane Addams, who attempted to improve the living and working conditions of the immigrants who settled in Chicago.

31.   **C**   Choice (A) is too broad; (B) is never discussed in detail; (D) and (E) were not discussed either. (C) covers both paragraphs adequately.

32.   **H**   Nowhere in this passage does the author say that the immigrants met with religious persecution.

33.   **D**   Choice (D) is better than choice (C) because the author never delves into Addams's personal life as a biographer would. Also, the focus of the passage is more on nineteenth-century immigration than on Addams.

34.   **F**   Hull House was meant to provide the immigrants with social services that were not provided by local governments. Thus (F) is correct.

35. **E** Choice (E) is correct because the author says that Hull House offered legal assistance to immigrants.

Coral Reefs passage

This passage explains that coral reefs are formed by the skeletal remains of stony coral. We also learn that when stony coral are alive, they coexist in a mutually beneficial relationship with green algae.

36. **H** The stony coral secretes a skeleton of calcium carbonate.

37. **C** Choice (B) may look tempting but it's too narrow—the passage is about how <u>both</u> the stony coral and the green alga interact to help form coral reefs.

38. **G** You can infer from the final sentence that diver are primarily interested in the visual appeal of the coral reef.

39. **D** Choice (D) is correct because the passage states that the coral and the algae have a mutually beneficial relationship.

40. **F** Choice (F) has things backwards; the algae live within the tissues of the coral.

Smallpox passage

The first paragraph of this passage describes the once-dreaded disease smallpox, while the second paragraph discusses the massive (and successful) global effort in the 1960s and 70s to wipe smallpox out through immunization.

41. **D** Choice (D) is better than (C) because (C) only covers the first paragraph whereas (D) is broad enough to cover the whole passage.

42. **G** In the context of the second sentence, "acutely" means "extremely."

43. **A** "China" is the correct answer, judging from the fourth sentence of the first paragraph.

44. **J** The problem before 1966 was not that there was no smallpox immunization; the problem was that no worldwide campaign had been launched to wipe out the disease.

45. **B** Choice (B) paraphrases the final sentence of the passage and is correct.

Steamboats passage

This amusing fiction passage is a man's description of his youthful desire to gain status among his boyhood comrades by becoming a steamboatman, and his chagrin when another boy fulfills this dream and he does not.

46. **G** Clearly a justice of the peace cannot hang anybody who offends him, so the fact that the boy believed this indicates his naivete.

47. **C** Beware of obvious synonyms such as "difference." In the context of the sentence, "distinction" means "fame."

48. **K** Choice (K) is correct because the author says that he would rather be a deck hand because the deck hand was "particularly conspicuous."

49. **B** Choice (B) reflects the author's entire feeling in the second paragraph. It just didn't seem fair—and it was certainly counter to Sunday-school teaching—that the other boy had been worldly and the author had been good, and yet the other boy had been "exalted."

50. **H** The engineer is described in the final sentence of the passage as a show-off, so (H) is correct.

Animal Coloring passage

This passage discusses different types of "protective coloration" that animals employ to camouflage themselves or to make themselves stand out.

51. **A** The caribou and the stoat are examples of animals that change their   or with the change of seasons, so (A) is correct.

52. **G** As we mentioned in the passage summary, this passage is a discussion of different types of protective coloration.

53. **A** Choice (A), the correct answer, is just another way of saying, as the author does, that the chameleon changes colors rapidly to match whatever surface it happens to be on.

54.   **H**   Cryptic resemblance is when an animal adapts in color, shape and behavior in order to blend into its environment. The green tree frog (I) and the chameleon (II) blend into their environment, but the skunk (III) definitely does not.

55.   **B**   The hedgehog, unlike the chameleon, "loudly announces its identity" to predators, so (B) is correct.

Poetry passage

This poem expresses the poet's dissatisfaction with government in a roundabout way: he praises the "fierce tooth...cleanly limb," and quick movement of a squirrel, and then says ironically "no government appointed him."

56.   **G**   "Disenchanted" expresses the poet's sentiment well; "furious" (H) is too strong to be correct.

57.   **D**   Option II you can throw out right away because the poet dislikes government. Option III is taken right from the poem. Option I is also correct but is not as evident as Option III; you have to infer that the poet likes the squirrel's independence from the overall description of the squirrel and its movement.

58.   **G**   Choice (G) is correct because the most human aspect of the squirrel is its low whinnying sound "that is like laughter."

59.   **C**   The squirrel's laughter is an expression, in the poet's eyes, of its freedom. None of the other choices matches the overall message of the poem.

60.   **G**   "Heavy knitting of the brow" is an expression a serious government official would have, not the squirrel.

Sentence Completions

1. **C**   The clue words "true" and "guise" indicate a contrast between the two words—George concealed his **concern** under a guise of **indifference**.

2. **C**   Again, the clues indicate a contrast—the grizzly is "normally" **harmless** but can become **ferocious**.

3. **D**   "But this claim" suggests that people's ——s about owls are false—**believe** and **myth** fit the assumption-reality structure here.

4. **D**   What's a likely scenario between a teacher and student here? **Correct** and **faulty** make the best sense in this sentence.

5. **C**   "Drifted" is the clue word here—a boat would drift **aimlessly** if its engine **died**.

6. **A**   The second blank should suggest cheating—it's her **fraudulent** use of encyclopedia entries that gets Roberta in trouble. **Censured** means scolded, reprimanded.

7. **A**   Tricky vocabulary here. **Condoning** means approving—if (A) a newspaper editorial didn't offer any **comment** on a violent incident, it might seem like they were **condoning** violence.

8. **A**   Here it's hard to predict the blanks—you have to plug in each answer choice. Only (A) makes sense—other birds would **unwittingly** (without realizing it) raise cowbird chicks as their own if the eggs were **deposit**ed in their nests.

9. **D**   The clue words "thoughtful" and "helped" indicate positive words for both blanks here—with a thoughtful **argument**, a politician might **convince** a skeptical public.

10. **D**   Positive word for the first blank—originality and **sophistication**. "Limited in **popular** appeal" is another way of saying the book did not appeal to a broad range of people.

11. **D**   "**Arsonist**" and "pyromaniac" are both words for people who start fires—but **series** is the only word that fits the second half of the sentence.

12. **B**   When archeologists dig things up, they **excavate**, sometimes **unearthing** treasures.

13. **B**   Only **purify** fits the second blank here—**purify** describes the natural process by which a lake replenishes itself.

14. **D**   **Virtuosity** is the word that best describes **dazzling** musical ability here.

15. **A**   The clue words "except for" indicate a contrast here—except for **stunted** shrubs, the tundra provides little **nourishment** for the caribou.

16. **B**   A typical cause-and-effect sentence here—because x, then y. (B) fits the structure of the sentence—a film with **prominent** or famous actors would be **expected** to be successful.

17. **C**   "Mature quickly and **breed** prolifically" (meaning a lot) describes why rats contribute to the **spread** of disease.

18. **D**   Cause and effect again—if Joel did not **complete** his homework on time, you would expect his teacher to **lower** his grade.

19. **A**   The clues are obviously either (A) **significant** or (C) crucial here. Only **detect** fits the first blank however.

20. **D**   Contrast between most people's experience and that of the poet's here—most people find writing **arduous** (hard work), but she does it without **effort**.

21. **A**   "After" indicates cause and effect. "Unfairly" tells us that Luis was not treated kindly - he was either (A) **upbraided** or (D) **heckled**. But only (A) **stormed** shows the effect we are looking for.

22. **C**   Cause and effect again. The cathedral has become "shabby, dirty and increasingly unappealing." So the cathedral was once (A) **impressive** or (C) **majestic**. But only (C) **neglect** fits the first blank.

23. **B**   You are looking for opposites. The game was **close** but became a **rout**.

24. **D**   Events are reported "shortly" or **rapidly** after they happen, because the news wire service is able to **disseminate** or "spread out" information.

25.   **D**   "Given" and "may have been" tell us that whatever the market is doing, the "predictions" were the opposite. Given the **stagnation** or sloth in the market, predictions were **optimistic** or positive.

26.   **A**   "But" tells us that "photographs" and "two-dimensional images" don't give us the full impact of the real Grand Canyon. Its **spectacular** topography cannot be fully **appreciated** through pictures alone.

27.   **D**   Only (D) makes sense here. While "repairing buildings and equipment", farmers are also **tending** their **livestock**.

28.   **D**   The stone carvings depict a battle scene "in intricate detail". While both (B) **beautiful** and (D) **ornate** seem like possibilities for the first blank, the answer clearly must be (D) because **clashing** is the only appropriate word to describe a battle scene.

29.   **D**   Tory's painting depicts the "lakefront" and the "inland." Such a broad view is summed up in the word **panoramic** for the first blank. **Ranging** is also the only word to fit into the second blank.

30.   **B**   "Paucity" means scarcity. "Unsubstantial" means unproven. So, we can assume that the newspaper has very little proven or **reliable** information, and has relied on or **resorted to** rumors.

31.   **B**   The word "once" tells us that while wolves are now "extinct" they were **numerous** at one point. The only word to logically fit into the second blank is **hunted**.

32.   **B**   "Despite" indicates that the predictions of the meteorologists were the opposite of what damage the storm actually caused. **Ominous** and **minimal** are the opposites that we are looking for.

33.   **C**   This is a clear cause and effect statement: A public official who accepts **bribes** by definition is guilty of **corruption**.

34.   **D**   The hostess has done something to make this year's guests less ____ than last years. In other words, we want opposites. **Undistinguished** and **exclusive** fit the bill.

35.   **D**   The phrases "hand in hand" and "sun-dappled" suggest that Tony and Marcia's walk was pleasant or **idyllic**. Also, only **strolling** fits in with the kind of meandering action we are looking for.

36.   **A**   What would a "lost extinct aboriginal people" have done with a "gigantic structure"? Either (A) **erected** it or (C) **built** it. But only (A) **indicates** fits into the first blank.

37.   **A**   The two words we are looking for relate closely to each other. Cockroaches are ____ and consequently can ____. **Adaptable** and **thrive** are the only words which relate to each other in this way.

38.   **B**   The audience reacted in a particular way as the direct result of how the violinist played. Again, we need words that relate to each other strongly. Only **accomplished** and **astounded** fit the bill.

39.   **C**   "Since" is the key word here. Ricky's interview went well, but his counselor was **disappointed** to learn Ricky was **unenthusiastic** about going to college.

40.   **D**   "Even though" tells us that we have a contrast. While Deidre was a clear leader, or **recognized** as a leader, she was just as happy to play a secondary role, or to be **supportive**.

41.   **D**   "And physically spent" clues us that the viewers were also emotionally spent or **drained**. Being **cathartic** would accomplish this state.

42.   **B**   Driving must go from one state of difficulty to being "finally impossible". Logically, only **increasingly** difficult fits here. Also, the fact that the snow **accumulated** in big drifts accounts for the worsening driving conditions.

43.   **D**   The textbook was so difficult, so it logically follows that the professor's lectures would have to help her with the more difficult or more (A) **intricate** or (D) **complicated** concepts. However, only (D) **follow** logically fits in the first blank.

44.   **A**   Elena was "ten minutes late", so we can assume her supervisor would **admonish** her. This admonishment stands in direct opposition to the fact that she received the **highest** service award.

45.   **A**   What would be hand-crafted? A strong case can be made for (A) **furnishings**, and a weaker case made for (D) **trappings**. Looking at the first blank, however, only (A) **sumptuously** makes sense.

46.   **A**   We are looking for a logical connection here. Because _____ happened to the water, the castaways had to _____ the water. Only (A) **dwindled** and **rationed** make sense.

47.   **D**   "Somehow" tells us that Mary's study habits and grades are opposite each other. The answer must be (D) since **excellent** and **poor** are opposites.

48.   **D**   "At the mercy of" is the clue here— Henry has a **healthy** appetite, which renders him **unable** to stay on his diet.

49.   **D**   Mark has already seen the film, while everyone else is seeing it for the first time. Both parties reactions will be opposite each other. Mark is **unlikely** to be as **shocked** as everyone else.

50.   **D**   The sentence is set up as a subtle contrast type. While Lisa is a "pessimist", or someone who looks on the down side, her team did well. So, she was **stunned** when her team **triumphed**.

51.   **A**   He "procrastinated", or waited until the last minute to do his work. It follows that he would have to attack the project in a big hurry or **hastily**. As a result of this haste, it follows that he would make careless or **inadvertent** errors.

52.   **B**   "But" tells us that most of her "opinions" stand in contrast to a "few....insights". **Absurd** and **brilliant** oppose each other in the way that we want.

53.   **C**   What kind of an art collector would have paintings by Picasso and Matisse? Someone either (C) **avid** or (D) **enthusiastic**. However, only (C), "acquired" paintings makes any sense.

54.   **B**   "Previously" tells us that what the politician is now doing with the proposal stands in opposition to what he did formerly. In other words he **reversed** his position on a proposal that he had **supported** earlier.

55.   **A**   Voters who say they would "vote to re-elect the mayor" are not in favor of change. They are **wary** of change.

56.   **D**   A hero would perform either daring (B) **escapades** or (D) **exploits**. However, only **antics** would amuse an audience.

57.   **A**   What would six children be able to do under a skirt? Hide or be **sheltered**. And the only kind of skirt that would accomplish this, would be a skirt that is very large or **voluminous**.

58.   **D**   What would the chef do to the counter? And would he want the pie crust to stick? He'd probably want to **prevent** it from sticking, and he'd do this by making sure that he'd **dusted** the counter.

59.   **D**   "While" tells us that the "new educational project" appears one way to some, and another way to "others". In other words, it **caters** to some people while **ignoring** others.

60.   **A**   The knights are "weighted down with heavy armor". It follows logically that fighting or **wielding** a sword with all that armor would be very uncomfortably or **awkwardly** performed.

61.   **C**   If the bears are bold, it follows logically that they would be **aggressive** in their search or **quest** for food.

62.   **D**   "Despite" tells us that the cost of the car and Jose's parents response to buying a car stood in opposition to each other. While the cost was **reasonable**, his parents were **reluctant**.

63.   **D**   Brett improvised a harness - he had to make one up. (A) **hitched** or (D) **yoked** make sense for the first blank, but only (D) **mount** fits the second blank.

64.   **C**   The semi colon indicates that we need words which are opposites. His admirers found the Prime Minister tough or **tenacious**, but his enemies or **detractors** found him merely stubborn.

65.   **D**   The speaker repeated herself at length - in other words she **droned** on for hours, consequently **boring** her audience to tears.

66.   **D**   "Low numbers" tells us that there aren't many sharks. In other words, they are **rarely** encountered by divers due to their lonely or **solitary** habitats.

67.   **A**   We know that soil nutrients were restored. This must mean that the soil nutrients were at one time taken away or **depleted** from the earth. A catastrophic event such as an **eruption** is a logical explanation as to how the minerals were restored.

68.   **D**   What would a sect do from "sun-up until long after dark"? Logically, they would work or **toil**, thus **avoiding** laziness or the "sin of sloth".

69.   **A**   Meteorologists would either (A) **track**, or (B) **study** storm systems. But only (A) **forewarning** fits in her logically.

70.   **A**   "Heedless" tells us that Terry was a little careless, and a little over eager to clean up his mess. In other words, he had too much **zeal** and carelessly or **indiscriminately** "discarded old files and documents."

22

Vocabulary Reference

QUICK STUDY LIST

Word Groups

Don't learn words one-by-one. Learning words in **groups** helps you remember:

- common roots and prefixes.

- the "word charge" of certain word groups.

- synonyms and antonyms.

Example:

MALEDICTION   *n., a curse or the utterance of a curse.*

Synonyms (*words with similar meanings*)	Antonyms (*opposite words*)	MAL words (*bad, harmful*)	DICT words (*to say*)
curse	benediction	malediction	benediction
oath	blessing	malady	contradiction
anathema	encomium	malice	dictate
imprecation	endorsement	malign	predict
condemnation	eulogy	malfunction	diction
execration			

Exercises

Match the right word to the context.

Exercise 1:

malady	malice	malevolent
malign	malignant	malfunction

1. The satellite launch was delayed by a _____ of the booster rocket.

2. The tumor is _____ and may result in death.

3. The criticism was given without _____, and so I did not feel angered by it.

4. The _____ dictator meted out harsh punishments to those whom he disliked.

5. Sea-sickness is a kind of _____.

6. She tends to _____ people behind their backs.

MAL = _____

Exercise 2:

benign	beneficial	benefit
benefactor	benediction	
beneficiary	benevolence	

1. The tumor is _____, so there is no danger.

2. The _____ of the insurance policy is the spouse of the deceased.

3. Some experts believe that oat bran is _____ to your health, while others argue that it is useless or even detrimental.

4. The leader was noted for her _____: she believed more in kindness and compassion than in brutally exercising her power.

5. A _____ said at a wedding blesses not only the happy couple, but all the guests as well.

6. The _____ of this job is shorter hours; the disadvantage is lower pay.

7. The young orphan has a _____ who is paying for his college education.

> BENE = _____

Exercise 3:

transcend	transient	transit
transport	transitory	
intransigent	transgress	

1. Every day I take two buses and a train, so I really rely on mass _____ .

2. Feelings of infatuation are usually _____ and will pass after a brief period of time.

3. The Senators are _____ regarding this issue, and refuse to change their votes.

4. Migrant workers typically lead a _____ life, moving from place to place to find work.

5. If one _____ the bounds of acceptable behavior, one must expect some negative consequences as a result.

6. It is often difficult to _____ a troubled childhood and become an emotionally healthy adult.

7. In order to _____ the goods from there to here, we will need a van.

> TRANS = _____

Exercise 4:

dialogue   circumlocution
loquacious   monologue
elocution   eloquent
locution   interlocutor

1. A witness with something to hide may evade the point of his interrogators' questions, resorting to _____ and indirect answers.

2. The actor was a ready speaker, but not a good conversationalist; people who tried to speak with him couldn't break into his _____.

3. It is usually unwise to confide important secrets to extremely open and _____ friends.

4. When people begin with a difference of opinion on some issue, often meaningful _____ can resolve their disagreement.

5. By the end of her speech, the councilwoman had persuaded even her most doubtful listeners with her _____ description of the housing project.

6. The professional public speaker was fully trained in the fine art of _____.

7. One _____ in the conversation disagreed with the other participants.

8. The dialogue written by this novelist successfully portrays the particular _____ of the residents of his urban neighborhood.

LOC/LOG/LOQ = _____

Exercise 5:

international   intersect
intersperse   intervene
interject   interact
intermission   interlude

1. The United Nations was created in hopes of promoting _____ understanding.

2. Because negotiations between labor and management seemed hopelessly deadlocked, a mediator was asked to _____ in the talks between the two sides.

3. The two roads _____ at the crossroads.

4. The play had only one ten-minute _____ between Act One and Act Two.

5. The audience was primarily composed of the Senator's supporters with only a few hecklers _____ (d) throughout the crowd.

6. The hermit had no idea how to _____ with other people.

7. The one-day truce provided only a brief _____ between long periods of fighting.

8. My friend is always interrupting the teacher during class; he can't let ten minutes go by without feeling the need to _____ his comments into the discussion.

INTER = _____

Exercise 6:

vivid	vitality	convivial
vivacious	vitamin	revival
viva	voce	

1. Novelists who depict children's experiences and viewpoints in striking detail rely on unusually _____ memories of their own childhoods.

2. Since the early 20th century, when a biochemist discovered that food contains _____ (s), our attitudes toward nutrition have gradually but fundamentally changed.

3. The historical period following the Dark Ages is called the Renaissance (which means "rebirth") because a _____ of classical literature took place then.

4. Since this restaurant draws many regulars who enjoy each other's company, it is known for its informal and _____ atmosphere.

5. The comedian energized the audience with his quick delivery of jokes and his _____ manner.

6. Consistently good nutrition and habits of vigorous exercise can preserve a person's health and _____ even into old age.

7. Many poets believe that poetry should be read _____ in order to appreciate its sound as well as its visual imagery and sense.

VIV/VIT = _____

Exercise 7:

transcribe	scribble	script
circumscribe	descriptive	
inscription	proscribe	conscription

1. His English teacher commended the short story Laurence had written and especially praised its vividly _____ passages.

2. Instead of taking notes in potentially informative lectures, inattentive students may _____ all over the margins of their notebooks.

3. Before a movie director can cast her film, she must send a copy of her movie's _____ to an actor she hopes will fill an important role.

4. The pedestal that supports the statue of Columbus carries a(n) _____ in honor of Italian immigrants to America.

5. At the end of every day she conducted experiments in the laboratory, the genetic biologist used a personal computer to _____ her handwritten notes into typed records.

6. A tutor at the Writing Workshop advised me to narrow the topic of my term paper and to _____ the subject area I covered.

7. Codes of police conduct _____ undue force in the handling of suspects under arrest.

8. During the American Civil War, the leaderships of the North and South used _____ as a means of bolstering their armed forces.

SCRIB/SCRIPT = _____

Exercise 8:

vocation	revoke	convocation
evocative	invoke	vociferous
vocal	provoke	

1. A person who works in a helping profession like social work or teaching often views his or her work as a _____ rather than a mere job.

2. The sense of smell is thought to be the sense most _____ of distant memories: the aroma of a particular cookie can bring back long-forgotten childhood indulgences.

3. The college's administration, faculty, students and their families came together to celebrate seniors' graduation at the school's spring _____.

4. Warnings of an approaching hurricane _____ a flurry of precautions along the shorelines: boats are beached, windows are reinforced, every outdoor movable is secured.

5. In the recent history of popular music, _____ recordings have usually sold much better than instrumental ones.

6. To increase participation in local government, this suburban town has agreed to _____ the law requiring five years' residency for service on the town council.

7. Last night at the music club, when the master of ceremonies announced that the featured band would not be playing, the audience became _____ in its protests.

8. Poems written before the 19th century often began with a prayer for inspiration; a poet would commonly _____ the Muses for guidance.

VOC/VOK = _____

Exercise 9:

general	gender	generic
generation	homogenous	
heterogeneous	engender	progeny
congenital		

1. Latin has three _____ (s), masculine, feminine, and neuter.

2. Since all the students came from the same town and had similar backgrounds, the class was _____.

3. Widespread poverty and rampant government corruption _____ (ed) dissatisfaction among the people.

4. Something was wrong with the baby's heart at birth; it had a _____ defect.

5. The ice age affected the climate all over the world and caused a _____ change in temperature.

6. With representation by countries from all over the world, the United Nations is a _____ political body.

7. Grandmother looked at all her children and grandchildren and realized she was surrounded by her _____.

8. When filling a prescription, many people prefer _____ drugs, which are chemically the same as brand names but often much cheaper.

9. Because of their supposed selfishness and lack of concern for others, those who came of age in the 80's have sometimes been labeled the "Me _____."

GEN = _____

In the following exercises, identify whether each word is **positive** *(+) or* **negative** *(–) in connotation, then match each word to a definition:*

Exercise 10: Intelligence words

ingenuity	( )
astute	( )
befuddled	( )
obtuse	( )
vacuous	( )
profound	( )
addle	( )
competent	( )
penetrate	( )
acute	( )

1. _____ *wise, deep*

2. _____ *empty-headed, inane*

3. _____ *capable, having enough skill for a task*

4. _____ *to understand, arrive at a meaning*

5. _____ *to make or become confused*

6. _____ *sharp, perceptive*

7. _____ *shrewd, discerning*

8. _____ *confused, baffled*

9. _____ *dull, slow to understand*

10. _____ *inventiveness, cleverness*

Exercise 11: Sad/happy words

ebullient	( )
despondent	( )
ecstatic	( )
affable	( )
dismal	( )
felicity	( )
glee	( )
melancholy	( )
mourn	( )
revel	( )
savor	( )
wretched	( )

1. _____ *gloomy, cheerless*

2. _____ *sorrow*

3. _____ *delight in*

4. _____ *pitiful*

5. _____ *sad*

6. _____ *bubbling with energy*

7. _____ *friendly*

8. _____ *happiness*

9. _____ *grieve*

10. _____ *celebrate*

In the following exercises, use the clues in each sentence to find the appropriate vocabulary word.

Exercise 12: Positive describers

eminent	tenacious	thrifty
erudite	gregarious	prolific
zealous	tactful	meticulous
ingenious		

1. The winning team was famous for its _____ defense.

2. The old man turned out to be an _____ professor.

3. The clerk was _____ in her attention to detail.

4. The inn was run by a _____ Scotsman.

5. The politician chose her words in a _____ manner.

6. The magazine featured an _____ article on Elizabethan drama.

7. The organization attracted many _____ volunteers.

8. All the _____ types were at the party.

9. Einstein was an _____ scientist.

10. The _____ writer was on her twelfth novel.

Exercise 13: Negative describers

irritable	miserly	reclusive
pompous	frivolous	taciturn
dogmatic	eccentric	officious
lethargic	congenital	

1. Amelia generally felt _____ at the height of the summer.

2. Leon was often _____ after a tough day at work.

3. Tim's strange habits were regarded as _____ by people who didn't know him well.

4. Nobody could tell what the _____ coach was thinking.

5. The shy composer became _____ in his later years.

6. Ronald read the announcement in a _____ voice.

7. The principal was notorious for his _____ views.

8. Jim was _____ when it came to contributing his share.

9. The tour operator annoyed us with his _____ manner.

10. The class reacted to the grave news with _____ remarks.

Exercise 14: Compliments

> sophisticated extraordinary
> commended incredible distinctive
> unprecedented essential acclaim
> innovative beneficial

1. The first album was greeted with enormous popular _____.

2. The response to the fundraising event was _____.

3. Troy led the team to an _____ third championship.

4. Considering her injury, the athlete's performance was _____.

5. The soldier was _____ for his bravery.

6. Carmella was wearing a _____ new coat.

7. The airplane engine was built using an _____ new technology.

8. Freshman students found the orientation talk a _____ experience.

9. Tara's observations were _____ to the project.

10. The poet displayed a _____ command of verse form.

Exercise 15: Insults

> impractical trite futile
> extravagant obscure convoluted
> obsolete unexceptional meager
> abominable

1. Though underfunded, the school made the best of its _____ resources.

2. The advent of the computer chip made Frank's job _____.

3. The film star gave an _____ performance in his latest role.

4. The service in the diner was just _____.

5. Kevin's explanation for his behavior was _____.

6. The plot of the thriller was too _____ for the late night audience to follow.

7. The countesses' party was an _____ affair.

8. Jessie's latest scheme was entertaining but _____.

9. The final episode of the TV series seemed a little _____.

10. All efforts to save the nature preserve proved _____.

Exercise 16: Science words

evolution	experimental	rigorous
hypothetical	conclusive	consistent
distinguish	tangible	analyzed
characteristic		

1. Scientists _____ the hair sample to determine the identity of the murderer.

2. The photographs gave astronomers _____ proof of the comet's existence.

3. The committee demanded _____ evidence to support Oppenheimer's claims.

4. The elusive otter left no _____ trace of its whereabouts.

5. The biologists were able to _____ three different species of bacteria.

6. The discussion about life on other planets was purely _____.

7. The _____ of the human being took many hundreds of thousands of years.

8. The scale of the earthquake was _____ with seismologists' predictions.

9. Prototypes of the vaccine are still in the _____ stage.

10. The bird's _____ blue stripe sets it apart from the other forest-dwellers.

Exercise 17: Social Science words

emphasize	reimbursed	exploited
allocated	depleted	conserve
relevant	acquired	eradicate
squandered		

1. The efficient new heating system was installed in order to _____ energy.

2. The scientists discovered that CFCs were _____ the ozone layer.

3. The interviewees were all _____ for their travel expenses.

4. The lawyer arrived at the office with all the _____ papers for the case.

5. The expanding company _____ some valuable assets.

6. The party _____ money on an expensive campaign.

7. Part of the government grant was _____ towards research.

8. The unexpected results _____ the need for more research.

9. The mining company shamelessly _____ the area's natural resources.

10. The pesticide was designed to _____ the locust problem.

Exercise 18: Positive attitudes

benevolent	attentive	responsible
intrigued	impartial	punctual
lenient	prudently	optimistic
endeavored		

1. While Rudy didn't participate in the demonstration, he attended as an _____ observer.

2. The lucky prize winner was in a _____ mood that morning.

3. The judge was inclined to be _____ with young offenders.

4. Joanne _____ remembered to fasten her seat belt.

5. Kenny was _____ by the new girl's foreign accent.

6. Louis seemed like the only _____ candidate for the job.

7. The _____ doctor invariably kept her appointments.

8. Hegel was _____ about his prospects for college.

9. Abbey _____ to level the score in the third quarter.

10. The nurse tried to be _____ to her patient's needs.

Exercise 19: Negative attitudes

indifferent	skeptical	reluctant
repelled	obstinately	despondent
apathetic	animosity	headstrong
subdued		

1. The diner _____ refused to pay for his check.

2. The team was _____ after their crushing defeat.

3. Rita was much too _____ to listen to advice.

4. The usually boisterous twins seemed quite _____.

5. Rolande was _____ about her chances of winning the lottery.

6. Colleagues admitted to being _____ by Billy's body odor.

7. Robbie was generally _____ to part with money.

8. The boxer regarded his opponent with _____.

9. Neil seemed surprisingly _____ about his suspension.

10. The part-time workers were _____ about their responsibilities.

Exercise Answers

Exercise 1:
1. malfunction
2. malignant
3. malice
4. malevolent
5. malady
6. malign

Exercise 2:
1. benevolent
2. beneficiary
3. beneficial
4. benevolence
5. benediction
6. benefit
7. benefactor

Exercise 3:
1. transit
2. transitory
3. intransigent
4. transient
5. transgress
6. transcend
7. transport

Exercise 4:
1. circumlocution
2. monologue
3. loquacious
4. dialogue
5. eloquent
6. elocution
7. interlocutor
8. locution

Exercise 5:
1. international
2. interlude
3. intersect
4. intermission
5. interspersed
6. interact
7. interlude
8. interject

Exercise 6:
1. vivid
2. vitamins
3. revival
4. vivacious
5. convivial
6. vitality
7. viva voce

Exercise 7:
1. descriptive
2. scribble
3. script
4. inscription
5. transcribe
6. circumscribe
7. proscribe
8. conscription

Exercise 8:
1. vocation
2. evocative
3. convocation
4. provoke
5. vocal
6. revoke
7. vociferous
8. invoke

Exercise 9:
1. gender
2. homogenous
3. engender
4. congenital
5. general
6. heterogeneous
7. generic
8. generation

Exercise 10:
1. profound (+)
2. vacuous (-)
3. competent (+)
4. penetrate (+)
5. addle (-)
6. acute (+)
7. astute (+)
8. befuddled (-)
9. obtuse (-)
10. ingenuity (+)

Exercise 11:
1. dismal (-)
2. melancholy (-)
3. savor (+)
4. wretched (-)
5. despondent (-)
6. ebullient (+)
7. affable (+)
8. felicity (+)
9. mourn (-)
10. revel (+)

Exercise 12:
1. tenacious
2. eminent
3. meticulous
4. thrifty
5. tactful
6. erudite
7. zealous
8. gregarious
9. ingenious
10. prolific

Exercise 13:
1. lethargic
2. irritable
3. eccentric
4. t aciturn
5. reclusive
6. pompous
7. dogmatic
8. miserly
9. officious
10. frivolous

Exercise 14:
1. acclaim
2. extraordinary
3. unprecedented
4. incredible
5. commended
6. distinctive
7. innovative
8. beneficial
9. essential
10. sophisticated

Exercise 15:
1. meager
2. obsolete
3. unexceptional
4. abominable
5. obscure

6. convoluted
7. extravagant
8. impractical
9. trite
10. futile

Exercise 16:
1. analyzed
2. conclusive
3. rigorous
4. tangible
5. distinguish
6. hypothetical
7. evolution
8. consistent
9. experimental
10. charactersitic

Exercise 17:
1. conserve
2. depleting
3. reimburse
4. relevant
5. acquire
6. squandered
7. allocated
8. emphasize
9. exploit
10. eradicate

Exercise 18:
1. impartial
2. benevolent
3. lenient
4. prudent
5. intrigue
6. responsible
7. punctual
8. optimistic
9. endeavored
10. attentive

Exercise 19:
1. obstinately
2. despondent
3. headstrong
4. subdued
5. skeptical
6. repelled
7. reluctant
8. animosity
9. indifferent
10. apathetic

ROOT LIST

ROOT	MEANING	EXAMPLES
A, AN	*not, without*	amoral, atrophy, asymmetrical, anarchy, anesthetic, anonymity, anomaly, annul
AB, A	*from, away, apart*	abnegate, abortive, abrogate, abscond, absolve, abstemious, abstruse, avert, aversion, abnormal, abdicate, aberration, abhor, abject, abjure, ablution
AC, ACR	*sharp, sour*	acid, acerbic, exacerbate, acute, acuity, acumen, acrid, acrimony
AD, A	*to, toward*	adhere, adjacent, adjunct, admonish, adroit, adumbrate, advent, abeyance, abet, accede, accretion, acquiesce, affluent, aggrandize, aggregate, alleviate, alliteration, allude, allure, ascribe, aspersion, aspire, assail, assonance, attest
ALI, ALTR	*another*	alias, alienate, inalienable, altruism
AM, AMI	*love*	amorous, amicable, amiable, amity
AMBI, AMPHI	*both*	ambiguous, ambivalent, ambidextrous, amphibious
AMBL, AMBUL	*walk*	amble, ambulatory, perambulator, somnambulist
ANIM	*mind, spirit, breath*	animal, animosity, unanimous, magnanimous
ANN, ENN	*year*	annual, annuity, superannuated, biennial, perennial
ANTE, ANT	*before*	antecedent, antediluvian, antebellum, antepenultimate, anterior, antiquity, antiquated, anticipate
ANTHROP	*human*	anthropology, anthropomorphic, misanthrope, philanthropy

ROOT	MEANING	EXAMPLES
ANTI, ANT	*against, opposite*	antidote, antipathy, antithesis, antacid, antagonist, antonym
AUD	*hear*	audio, audience, audition, auditory, audible
AUTO	*self*	autobiography, autocrat, autonomous
BELLI, BELL	*war*	belligerent, bellicose, antebellum, rebellion
BENE, BEN	*good*	benevolent, benefactor, beneficent, benign
BI	*two*	bicycle, bisect, bilateral, bilingual, biped
BIBLIO	*book*	Bible, bibliography, bibliophile
BIO	*life*	biography, biology, amphibious, symbiotic, macrobiotics
BURS	*money, purse*	reimburse, disburse, bursar
CAD, CAS, CID	*happen, fall*	accident, cadence, cascade, deciduous
CAP, CIP	*head*	captain, decapitate, capitulate, precipitous, precipitate, recapitulate
CARN	*flesh*	carnal, carnage, carnival, carnivorous, incarnate, incarnadine
CAP, CAPT, CEPT, CIP	*take, hold, seize*	capable, capacious, captivate, deception, intercept, precept, inception, anticipate, emancipate, incipient, percipient
CED, CESS	*yield, go*	cede, precede, accede, recede, antecedent, intercede, secede, cession, cease, cessation, incessant

ROOT	MEANING	EXAMPLES
CHROM	*color*	chrome, chromatic, monochrome
CHRON	*time*	chronology, chronic, anachronism
CIDE	*murder*	suicide, homicide, regicide, patricide
CIRCUM	*around*	circumference, circumlocution, circumnavigate, circumscribe, circumspect, circumvent
CLIN, CLIV	*slope*	incline, declivity, proclivity
CLUD, CLUS, CLAUS, CLOIS	*shut, close*	conclude, reclusive, claustrophobia, cloister, preclude, occlude
CO, COM, CON	*with, together*	coeducation, coagulate, coalesce, coerce, cogent, cognate, collateral, colloquial, colloquy, commensurate, commodious, compassion, compatriot, complacent, compliant, complicity, compunction, concerto, conciliatory, concord, concur, condone, conflagration, congeal, congenial, congenital, conglomerate, conjure, conjugal, conscientious, consecrate, consensus, consonant, constrained, contentious, contrite, contusion, convalescence, convene, convivial, convoke, convoluted, congress
COGN, GNO	*know*	recognize, cognition, cognizance, incognito, diagnosis, agnostic, prognosis, gnostic, ignorant
CONTRA	*against*	controversy, incontrovertible, contravene, contradict
CORP	*body*	corpse, corporeal, corpulence
COSMO, COSM	*world*	cosmopolitan, cosmos, microcosm, macrocosm
CRAC, CRAT	*rule, power*	democracy, bureaucracy, theocracy, autocrat, aristocrat, technocrat
CRED	*trust, believe*	incredible, credulous, credence

ROOT	MEANING	EXAMPLES
CRESC, CRET	*grow*	crescent, crescendo, accretion
CULP	*blame, fault*	culprit, culpable, inculpate, exculpate
CURR, CURS	*run*	current, concur, cursory, precursor, incursion
DE	*down, out, apart*	depart, debase, debilitate, declivity, decry, deface, defamatory, defunct, delegate, demarcation, demean, demur, deplete, deplore, depravity, deprecate, deride, derivative, desist, detest
DEC	*ten, tenth*	decade, decimal, decathlon, decimate
DEMO, DEM	*people*	democrat, demographics, demagogue, epidemic, pandemic, endemic
DI, DIURN	*day*	diary, diurnal, quotidian
DIA	*across*	diagonal, diatribe, diaphanous
DIC, DICT	*speak*	diction, interdict, predict, abdicate, indict, verdict, dictum
DIS, DIF, DI	*not, apart, away*	disaffected, disband, disbar, disburse, discern, discordant, discredit, discursive, disheveled, disparage, disparate, dispassionate, dispirit, dissemble, disseminate, dissension, dissipate, dissonant, dissuade, distend, differentiate, diffidence, diffuse, digress, divert
DOC, DOCT	*teach*	doctrine, docile, doctrinaire
DOL	*pain*	condolence, doleful, dolorous, indolent
DUC, DUCT	*lead*	seduce, induce, conduct, viaduct, induct
EGO	*self*	ego, egoist, egocentric

ROOT	MEANING	EXAMPLES
EN, EM	*in, into*	enter, entice, encumber, endemic, ensconce, enthrall, entreat, embellish, embezzle, embroil, empathy
ERR	*wander*	erratic, aberration, errant
EU	*well, good*	eulogy, euphemism, euphony, euphoria, eurythmics, euthanasia
EX, E	*out, out of*	exit, exacerbate, excerpt, excommunicate, exculpate, execrable, exhume, exonerate, exorbitant, exorcise, expatriate, expedient, expiate, expunge, expurgate, extenuate, extort, extremity, extricate, extrinsic, exult, evoke, evict, evince, elicit, egress, egregious
FAC, FIC, FECT, FY, FEA	*make, do*	factory, facility, benefactor, malefactor, fiction, fictive, beneficent, affect, confection, refectory, magnify, unify, rectify, vilify, feasible
FAL, FALS	*deceive*	false, infallible, fallacious
FERV	*boil*	fervent, fervid, effervescent
FID	*faith, trust*	confident, diffidence, perfidious, fidelity
FLU, FLUX	*flow*	fluent, flux, affluent, confluence, effluvia, superfluous
FORE	*before*	forecast, foreboding, forestall
FRAG, FRAC	*break*	fragment, fracture, diffract, fractious, refract
FUS	*pour*	profuse, infusion, effusive, diffuse
GEN	*birth, class, kin*	generation, congenital, homogeneous, heterogeneous, ingenious, engender, progenitor, progeny

ROOT	MEANING	EXAMPLES
GRAD, GRESS	*step*	graduate, gradual, retrograde, centigrade, degrade, gradation, gradient, progress, congress, digress, transgress, ingress, egress
GRAPH, GRAM	*writing*	biography, bibliography, epigraph, grammar, epigram
GRAT	*pleasing*	grateful, gratitude, gratis, ingrate, congratulate, gratuitous, gratuity
GRAV, GRIEV	*heavy*	grave, gravity, aggravate, grieve, aggrieve, grievous
GREG	*crowd, flock*	segregate, gregarious, egregious, congregate, aggregate
HABIT, HIBIT	*have, hold*	habit, inhibit, cohabit, habitat
HAP	*by chance*	happen, haphazard, hapless, mishap
HELIO, HELI	*sun*	heliocentric, helium, heliotrope, aphelion, perihelion
HETERO	*other*	heterosexual, heterogeneous, heterodox
HOL	*whole*	holocaust, catholic, holistic
HOMO	*same*	homosexual, homogenize, homogeneous, homonym
HOMO	*man*	Homo sapiens, homicide, bonhomie
HYDR	*water*	hydrant, hydrate, dehydration
HYPER	*too much, excess*	hyperactive, hyperbole, hyperventilate
HYPO	*too little, under*	hypodermic, hypothermia, hypochondria, hypothesis, hypothetical

ROOT	MEANING	EXAMPLES
IN, IG, IL, IM, IR	*not*	incorrigible, indefatigable, indelible, indubitable, inept, inert, inexorable, insatiable, insentient, insolvent, insomnia, interminable, intractable, incessant, inextricable, infallible, infamy, innumerable, inoperable, insipid, intemperate, intrepid, inviolable, ignorant, ignominious, ignoble, illicit, illimitable, immaculate, immutable, impasse, impeccable, impecunious, impertinent, implacable, impotent, impregnable, improvident, impassioned, impervious, irregular
IN, IL, IM, IR	*in, on, into*	invade, inaugurate, incandescent, incarcerate, incense, indenture, induct, ingratiate, introvert, incarnate, inception, incisive, infer, infusion, ingress, innate, inquest, inscribe, insinuate, inter, illustrate, imbue, immerse, implicate, irrigate, irritate
INTER	*between, among*	intercede, intercept, interdiction, interject, interlocutor, interloper, intermediary, intermittent, interpolate, interpose, interregnum, interrogate, intersect, intervene
INTRA, INTR	*within*	intrastate, intravenous, intramural, intrinsic
IT, ITER	*between, among*	transit, itinerant, reiterate, transitory
JECT, JET	*throw*	eject, interject, abject, trajectory, jettison
JOUR	*day*	journal, adjourn, sojourn
JUD	*judge*	judge, judicious, prejudice, adjudicate
JUNCT, JUG	*join*	junction, adjunct, injunction, conjugal, subjugate
JUR	*swear, law*	jury, abjure, adjure, conjure, perjure, jurisprudence
LAT	*side*	lateral, collateral, unilateral, bilateral, quadrilateral
LAV, LAU, LU	*wash*	lavatory, laundry, ablution, antediluvian

ROOT	MEANING	EXAMPLES
LEG, LEC, LEX	*read, speak*	legible, lecture, lexicon
LEV	*light*	elevate, levitate, levity, alleviate
LIBER	*free*	liberty, liberal, libertarian, libertine
LIG, LECT	*choose, gather*	eligible, elect, select
LIG, LI, LY	*bind*	ligament, oblige, religion, liable, liaison, lien, ally
LING, LANG	*tongue*	lingo, language, linguistics, bilingual
LITER	*letter*	literate, alliteration, literal
LITH	*stone*	monolith, lithograph, megalith
LOQU, LOC, LOG	*speech, thought*	eloquent, loquacious, colloquial, colloquy, soliloquy, circumlocution, interlocutor, monologue, dialogue, eulogy, philology, neologism
LUC, LUM	*light*	lucid, illuminate, elucidate, pellucid, translucent
LUD, LUS	*play*	ludicrous, allude, delusion, allusion, illusory
MACRO	*great*	macrocosm, macrobiotics
MAG, MAJ, MAS, MAX	*great*	magnify, majesty, master, maximum, magnanimous, magnate, magnitude
MAL	*bad*	malady, maladroit, malevolent, malodorous
MAN	*hand*	manual, manuscript, emancipate, manifest
MAR	*sea*	submarine, marine, maritime

ROOT	MEANING	EXAMPLES
MATER, MATR	*mother*	maternal, matron, matrilineal
MEDI	*middle*	intermediary, medieval, mediate
MEGA	*great*	megaphone, megalomania, megaton, megalith
MEMOR, MEMEN	*remember*	memory, memento, memorabilia, memoir
METER, METR, MENS	*measure*	meter, thermometer, perimeter, metronome, commensurate
MICRO	*small*	microscope, microorganism, microcosm, microbe
MIS	*wrong, bad, hate*	misunderstand, misanthrope, misapprehension, misconstrue, misnomer, mishap
MIT, MISS	*send*	transmit, emit, missive
MOLL	*soft*	mollify, emollient, mollusk
MON, MONIT	*warn*	admonish, monitor, premonition
MONO	*one*	monologue, monotonous, monogamy, monolith, monochrome
MOR	*custom, manner*	moral, mores, morose
MOR, MORT	*dead*	morbid, moribund, mortal, amortize
MORPH	*shape*	amorphous, anthropomorphic, metamorphosis, morphology
MOV, MOT, MOB, MOM	*move*	remove, motion, mobile, momentum, momentous
MUT	*change*	mutate, mutability, immutable, commute

ROOT	MEANING	EXAMPLES
NAT, NASC	*born*	native, nativity, natal, neonate, innate, cognate, nascent, renascent, renaissance
NAU, NAV	*ship, sailor*	nautical, nauseous, navy, circumnavigate
NEG	*not, deny*	negative, abnegate, renege
NEO	*new*	neoclassical, neophyte, neologism, neonate
NIHIL	*none, nothing*	annihilation, nihilism
NOM, NYM	*name*	nominate, nomenclature, nominal, cognomen, misnomer, ignominious, antonym, homonym, pseudonym, synonym, anonymity
NOX, NIC, NEC, NOC	*harm*	obnoxious, noxious, pernicious, internecine, innocuous
NOV	*new*	novelty, innovation, novitiate
NUMER	*number*	numeral, numerous, innumerable, enumerate
OB	*against*	obstruct, obdurate, obfuscate, obnoxious, obsequious, obstinate, obstreperous, obtrusive
OMNI	*all*	omnipresent, omnipotent, omniscient, omnivorous
ONER	*burden*	onerous, onus, exonerate
OPER	*work*	operate, cooperate, inoperable
PAC	*peace*	pacify, pacifist, pacific
PALP	*feel*	palpable, palpitation

ROOT	MEANING	EXAMPLES
PAN	*all*	panorama, panacea, panegyric, pandemic, panoply
PATER, PATR	*father*	paternal, paternity, patriot, compatriot, expatriate, patrimony, patricide, patrician
PATH, PASS	*feel, suffer*	sympathy, antipathy, empathy, apathy, pathos, impassioned
PEC	*money*	pecuniary, impecunious, peculation
PED, POD	*foot*	pedestrian, pediment, expedient, biped, quadruped, tripod
PEL, PULS	*drive*	compel, compelling, expel, propel, compulsion
PEN	*almost*	peninsula, penultimate, penumbra
PEND, PENS	*hang*	pendant, pendulous, compendium, suspense, propensity
PER	*through, by, for, throughout*	perambulator, percipient, perfunctory, permeable, perspicacious, pertinacious, perturbation, perusal, perennial, peregrinate
PER	*against, destruction*	perfidious, pernicious, perjure
PERI	*around*	perimeter, periphery, perihelion, peripatetic
PET	*seek, go toward*	petition, impetus, impetuous, petulant, centripetal
PHIL	*love*	philosopher, philanderer, philanthropy, bibliophile, philology
PHOB	*fear*	phobia, claustrophobia, xenophobia
PHON	*sound*	phonograph, megaphone, euphony, phonetics, phonics
PLAC	*calm, please*	placate, implacable, placid, complacent

ROOT	MEANING	EXAMPLES
PON, POS	*put, place*	postpone, proponent, exponent, preposition, posit, interpose, juxtaposition, depose
PORT	*carry*	portable, deportment, rapport
POT	*drink*	potion, potable
POT	*power*	potential, potent, impotent, potentate, omnipotence
PRE	*before*	precede, precipitate, preclude, precocious, precursor, predilection, predisposition, preponderance, prepossessing, presage, prescient, prejudice, predict, premonition, preposition
PRIM, PRI	*first*	prime, primary, primal, primeval, primordial, pristine
PRO	*ahead, forth*	proceed, proclivity, procrastinator, profane, profuse, progenitor, progeny, prognosis, prologue, promontory, propel, proponent, propose, proscribe, protestation, provoke
PROTO	*first*	prototype, protagonist, protocol
PROX, PROP	*near*	approximate, propinquity, proximity
PSEUDO	*false*	pseudoscientific, pseudonym
PYR	*fire*	pyre, pyrotechnics, pyromania
QUAD, QUAR, QUAT	*four*	quadrilateral, quadrant, quadruped, quarter, quarantine, quaternary
QUES, QUER, QUIS, QUIR	*question*	quest, inquest, query, querulous, inquisitive, inquiry
QUIE	*quiet*	disquiet, acquiesce, quiescent, requiem

ROOT	MEANING	EXAMPLES
QUINT, QUIN	*five*	quintuplets, quintessence
RADI, RAMI	*branch*	radius, radiate, radiant, eradicate, ramification
RECT, REG	*straight, rule*	rectangle, rectitude, rectify, regular
REG	*king, rule*	regal, regent, interregnum
RETRO	*backward*	retrospective, retroactive, retrograde
RID, RIS	*laugh*	ridiculous, deride, derision
ROG	*ask*	interrogate, derogatory, abrogate, arrogate, arrogant
RUD	*rough, crude*	rude, erudite, rudimentary
RUPT	*break*	disrupt, interrupt, rupture, erupt
SACR, SANCT	*holy*	sacred, sacrilege, consecrate, sanctify, sanction, sacrosanct
SCRIB, SCRIPT, SCRIV	*write*	scribe, ascribe, circumscribe, inscribe, proscribe, script, manuscript, scrivener
SE	*apart, away*	separate, segregate, secede, sedition
SEC, SECT, SEG	*cut*	sector, dissect, bisect, intersect, segment, secant
SED, SID	*sit*	sedate, sedentary, supersede, reside, residence, assiduous, insidious
SEM	*seed, sow*	seminar, seminal, disseminate
SEN	*old*	senior, senile, senescent

ROOT	MEANING	EXAMPLES
SENT, SENS	*feel, think*	sentiment, nonsense, assent, sentient, consensus, sensual
SEQU, SECU	*follow*	sequence, sequel, subsequent, obsequious, obsequy, non sequitur, consecutive
SIM, SEM	*similar, same*	similar, semblance, dissemble, verisimilitude
SIGN	*mark, sign*	signal, designation, assignation
SIN	*curve*	sine curve, sinuous, insinuate
SOL	*sun*	solar, parasol, solarium, solstice
SOL	*alone*	solo, solitude, soliloquy, solipsism
SOMN	*sleep*	insomnia, somnolent, somnambulist
SON	*sound*	sonic, consonance, dissonance, assonance, sonorous, resonate
SOPH	*wisdom*	philosopher, sophistry, sophisticated, sophomoric
SPEC, SPIC	*see, look*	spectator, circumspect, retrospective, perspective, perspicacious
SPER	*hope*	prosper, prosperous, despair, desperate
SPERS, SPAR	*scatter*	disperse, sparse, aspersion, disparate
SPIR	*breathe*	respire, inspire, spiritual, aspire, transpire
STRICT, STRING	*bind*	strict, stricture, constrict, stringent, astringent
STRUCT, STRU	*build*	structure, construe, obstruct

ROOT	MEANING	EXAMPLES
SUB	*under*	subconscious, subjugate, subliminal, subpoena, subsequent, subterranean, subvert
SUMM	*highest*	summit, summary, consummate
SUPER, SUR	*above*	supervise, supercilious, supersede, superannuated, superfluous, insurmountable, surfeit
SURGE, SURRECT	*rise*	surge, resurgent, insurgent, insurrection
SYN, SYM	*together*	synthesis, sympathy, synonym, syncopation, synopsis, symposium, symbiosis
TACIT, TIC	*silent*	tacit, taciturn, reticent
TACT, TAG, TANG	*touch*	tact, tactile, contagious, tangent, tangential, tangible
TEN, TIN, TAIN	*hold, twist*	detention, tenable, tenacious, pertinacious, retinue, retain
TEND, TENS, TENT	*stretch*	intend, distend, tension, tensile, ostensible, contentious
TERM	*end*	terminal, terminus, terminate, interminable
TERR	*earth, land*	terrain, terrestrial, extraterrestrial, subterranean
TEST	*witness*	testify, attest, testimonial, testament, detest, protestation
THE	*god*	atheist, theology, apotheosis, theocracy
THERM	*heat*	thermometer, thermal, thermonuclear, hypothermia
TIM	*fear, frightened*	timid, intimidate, timorous
TOP	*place*	topic, topography, utopia

ROOT	MEANING	EXAMPLES
TORT	*twist*	distort, extort, tortuous
TORP	*stiff, numb*	torpedo, torpid, torpor
TOX	*poison*	toxic, toxin, intoxication
TRACT	*draw*	tractor, intractable, protract
TRANS	*across, over, through, beyond*	transport, transgress, transient, transitory, translucent, transmutation, transpire, intransigent
TREM, TREP	*shake*	tremble, tremor, tremulous, trepidation, intrepid
TURB	*shake*	disturb, turbulent, perturbation
UMBR	*shadow*	umbrella, umbrage, adumbrate, penumbra
UNI, UN	*one*	unify, unilateral, unanimous
URB	*city*	urban, suburban, urbane
VAC	*empty*	vacant, evacuate, vacuous
VAL, VAIL	*value, strength*	valid, valor, ambivalent, convalescence, avail, prevail, countervail
VEN, VENT	*come*	convene, contravene, intervene, venue, convention, circumvent, advent, adventitious
VER	*true*	verify, verity, verisimilitude, veracious, aver, verdict
VERB	*word*	verbal, verbose, verbiage, verbatim

ROOT	MEANING	EXAMPLES
VERT, VERS	*turn*	avert, convert, pervert, revert, incontrovertible, divert, subvert, versatile, aversion
VICT, VINC	*conquer*	victory, conviction, evict, evince, invincible
VID, VIS	*see*	evident, vision, visage, supervise
VIL	*base, mean*	vile, vilify, revile
VIV, VIT	*life*	vivid, vital, convivial, vivacious
VOC, VOK, VOW	*call, voice*	vocal, equivocate, vociferous, convoke, evoke, invoke, avow
VOL	*wish*	voluntary, malevolent, benevolent, volition
VOLV, VOLUT	*turn, roll*	revolve, evolve, convoluted
VOR	*eat*	devour, carnivorous, omnivorous, voracious

VOCABULARY LIST

WORD	DEFINITION, CONTEXT, SYNONYMS
ABDICATE	to give up a position, right, or power. *With the angry mob clamoring outside the palace, the king abdicated his throne and fled with his mistress.* SYN: **quit**, **resign**, **renounce**, **step down**.
ABDUCT	forcefully and wrongfully to carry, take, or lead away. *The kidnappers planned to abduct the child and hold her for ransom.* SYN: **kidnap, carry off.**
ABHOR	to hate, to view with repugnance, to detest. *After repeated failure to learn the Pythagorean theorem,* Susan began to abhor geometry. SYN: **hate, loathe, abominate.**
ABSURD	ridiculously unreasonable, lacking logic. *Ironing one's underwear is* absurd. SYN: **ridiculous, ludicrous, preposterous, bizarre.**
ABYSS	deep hole; deep immeasurable space, gulf or cavity. *Looking down into the abyss was terrifying, for I could not see the bottom.* SYN: **chasm, pit.**
ACCELERATE	to increase in speed, cause to move faster. *The new disease has spread like wildfire, causing researchers to accelerate their search for a cure.* SYN: **speed up, hasten, expedite.**
ACCLAIM	(n) praise, enthusiastic approval. *The artist won international* acclaim; *critics and viewers all over the world were intrigued by the works.* SYN: **praise, approval.** (v) to approve, to welcome with applause and praise. *The critic was eager to acclaim the actress for her performance.* SYN: **cheer, applaud, praise, honor.**
ACUTE	sharp in some way (as in an acute angle) or sharp in intellect; crucial. *There is an acute shortage of food, which will ultimately result in a famine if something is not done soon to increase the food supply.* SYN: **perceptive, sharp, keen, shrewd; crucial.**
ADAGE	old saying, proverb. *"A penny saved is a penny earned" is a popular* adage. SYN: **proverb, maxim.**
ADHERE	to stick fast; to hold to. *After we put glue on his pants, John adhered to the chair. He was a strict Catholic who adhered to all the teachings of the Church.* SYN: **stick to** (like glue or adhesive tape); **follow.**
ADJOURN	to postpone; to suspend (a meeting) for a period of time. *Since it was late in the day, the prosecutor moved that the court adjourn for the day.* SYN: **suspend, recess, postpone.**
ADJUNCT	something or someone associated with another but in a defendant or secondary position. *An adjunct professor is one not given the same full-time status as other faculty members.* SYN: **additional, supporting, assisting, accessory.**
ADMONISH	to scold (sometimes in a good natured way); to urge to duty, remind; to advise against something. *My mother began to admonish me about my poor grades.* SYN: **warn, caution, scold.**

WORD	DEFINITION, CONTEXT, SYNONYMS
ADORN	to decorate or add beauty to, for instance with ornaments: to make pleasing, more attractive. *She adorned her hair with flowers.* SYN: **decorate, ornament, embellish.**
ADVERSARY	opponent or enemy. *Democrats and Republicans are usually adversaries in the political world.* SYN: **enemy, foe, opponent.**
AERONAUTIC	relating to aircraft. *The Air Force's Stealth plane is reported to be a masterpiece of* aeronautic *design.*
AFFABLE	pleasantly easy to get along with; friendly and warm. *He was an affable host and made us feel right at home.* SYN: **agreeable, amiable.**
AFFECTATION	attempt to appear to be what one is not for the purpose of impressing others (for instance, pretending to have a pretentiously cultured accent). *Justin once spent three months in France and has now acquired the silly affectation of using French phrases in casual conversation.* SYN: **pretension, unnaturalness, artificiality, mannerism, pretense, airs, sham, facade, pose, posture.**
AGHAST	overcome by surprise, disgust, or amazement; seized with terror; shocked. *The investigator was* aghast *at the horrible conditions in the nursing home.* SYN: **astounded, dismayed, appalled, astonished, shocked.**
AGILITY	condition of being able to move quickly and easily or being mentally alert. *Strength and agility are important for an athlete.* SYN: **skillfulness, dexterity, nimbleness.**
AGITATE	to shake or grow excited; to move around a lot, to disturb or excite emotionally. *The bat's flight into the classroom managed to* agitate *the teacher so much that he went home early.* SYN: **disturb, upset, stir up** (like a washing machine).
AIMLESS	lacking purpose or goals. *After its engine died, the boat drifted aimlessly for days.* SYN: **purposeless, haphazard, accidental.**
ALLEVIATE	to make easier to bear, lessen. *This medicine will help to* alleviate *the pain.* SYN: **relieve, allay, assuage, ease, decrease, lessen, mitigate.**
ALLURE	fascination, appeal. *Video games have an* allure *that some people find impossible to resist.* SYN: **temptation, attraction, fascination.**
ALOOF	distant in relations with other people. *The newcomer remained* aloof *from all our activities and therefore made no new friends.* SYN: **detached, cool, blase, remote.**
ALTRUISTIC	concerned for the welfare of others. *The altruistic woman gave out money to all who seemed needy.* SYN: **benevolent, charitable, compassionate, humane.**

WORD	DEFINITION, CONTEXT, SYNONYMS
AMATEUR	someone not paid to engage in a hobby, sport, art, etc. *Since professionals couldn't play, only* amateur *athletes were allowed to participate in the Olympics.* SYN: **devotee, dabbler, enthusiast, buff, non-professional.** (adj) like an amateur. *The brilliant author James Joyce was an* amateur *singer.*
AMEND	to improve; to alter, to add to, or subtract from by formal procedure. *Congress will* amend *the bill so that the President will sign it.* SYN: **alter, improve, repair, mend, make better, ameliorate.**
AMOROUS	having to do with love. *The love-sick young poet wrote many* amorous *poems about his girlfriend.* SYN: **romantic, erotic.**
AMORPHOUS	lacking a specific shape. *In the movie, "The Blob", the creature was an* amorphous *one that was constantly changing shape.* SYN: **shapeless, vague.**
AMPHIBIAN	animal at home on both land and in the water. *A frog, which lives both on land and in the water, is an* amphibian.
ANGULAR	having clear angles or thin and bony facial features. SYN: **lanky, gaunt. bony**.
ANIMOSITY	feeling of ill will, intense dislike for someone or something. *The deep-rooted* animosity *between them made it difficult for the brothers to work together.* SYN: **ill will, ill feeling, bitterness, rancor, acrimony.**
ANNIHILATE	to destroy completely. *The first troops to land on the beach during the invasion were* annihilated *by the powerful artillery of the enemy.* SYN: **destroy, devastate, demolish.**
ANTIDOTE	remedy to relieve the effects of poison. *The first aid kit included an* antidote *for snake bite.* SYN: **remedy, counteragent, neutralizer.**
APERTURE	opening. *The* aperture *of a camera lens is a circular opening of variable diameter that regulates the amount of light entering the lens.* SYN: **hole, gap, space, opening, crack.**
AQUEOUS	similar to, or composed of water. *The inside of an eyeball is filled with an* aqueous *substance.* SYN: **watery, aquatic, hydrous, liquid.**
ARDENT	characterized by passion or desire. *After a 25 game losing streak, even the Mets' most* ardent *fans realized the team wouldn't finish first.* SYN: **passionate, enthusiastic, fervent.**
ARID	very dry, lacking moisture; unproductive, unimaginative. *The* arid *farmland produced no crops.* SYN: **dry, parched, barren; dull, uninteresting, insipid.**
AROMA	pleasing fragrance; any odor or smell. *The* aroma *in the bakery made her mouth water.* SYN: **smell, fragrance, odor.**

WORD	DEFINITION, CONTEXT, SYNONYMS
ARTICULATE	(adj) well-spoken, lucidly presented. *Joe's* articulate *argument was so persuasive that we all agreed with him.* SYN: **eloquent, glib.** (v) to pronounce clearly. *The great actor articulated every word so clearly it was easy to understand him.* SYN: **enunciate**
ARTIFICE	(1) trickery, clever ruse. *Ralph's use of rubber masks proved to be a brilliant* artifice. SYN: **stratagem, trick, ploy, deception, ruse,** maneuver. (2) ability to create or imagine. *Many question the meaningfulness of Jamie's science fiction novel, but its fantastic images and ingenious plot cannot fail to impress one with his sheer* artifice. SYN: **creativity, inventiveness, innovation, resourcefulness, imagination, ingenuity.**
ASCERTAIN	to find out or discover by examination. *Try though he did, the archaeologist couldn't* ascertain *the correct age of the Piltdown man's skeleton.* SYN: **determine, discover, unearth, find out.**
ASSAILABLE	able to be attacked or assaulted by blows or words. *Carcassonne was widely thought to be an* unassailable *fortress after it resisted a siege by Charlemagne.* SYN: **vulnerable, exposed, unprotected.**
ASTOUND	to overwhelm with amazement. *The extent of his great knowledge never ceases to* astound *me.* SYN: **amaze, stupefy, stun.**
ASTUTE	shrewd and perceptive; able to understand clearly and quickly. *The novelist Judy Blume is an* astute *judge of human character.* SYN: **keen, discerning, penetrating, incisive, perceptive; crafty, foxy, wily, shrewd.**
ATROCITY	horrible, usually brutal, act. *During the Indian bid for freedom from British colonial rule, a British officer committed the* atrocity *of slaughtering a large congregation of peaceful Indian demonstrators.* SYN: **horror, barbarity, outrage.**
AUDACITY	boldness or daring, especially with disregard for personal safety. *He had the* audacity *to insult the President to his face.* SYN: **a lot of nerve: boldness, daring, impudence.**
AUTHORITATIVE	having great authority. *J.R.R. Tolkien, who had written many books about Old English poetry, was widely considered to be the most* authoritative *scholar in the field.* SYN: **masterful.**
BANAL	boringly predictable. *A boring conversation is likely to be full of* banal *statements like "Have a nice day."* SYN: **boring, dull, bland, insipid.**
BANISH	to send away, condemn to exile; drive or put away. *After the incident with the Jello, Arthur was* banished *from the lunchroom.* SYN: **send away, get rid of, expel, exile, deport.**

WORD	DEFINITION, CONTEXT, SYNONYMS
BARRIER	anything that makes progress harder or impossible; a limit or boundary. *The Pythagorean theorem has been a* barrier *to Donald's complete understanding of geometry. To discourage visitors, Janet built a* barrier *in front of the entrance to her room.* SYN: **something that blocks or limits: obstacle.**
BEGUILE	to delude, deceive by trickery. *Beguiled by the supernatural songs of the Sirens, Odysseus wanted to abandon all his men and forget his family.* SYN: **charm, allure, bewitch, captivate**.
BELLIGERENCE	aggressive hostility. *A soldier can be shocked by the* belligerence *of his enemy.* SYN: **aggressiveness, combativeness**.
BENEFACTOR	someone giving financial or general assistance. *A wealthy alumnus who gives 5 million to his old college would be considered a great* benefactor. SYN: **patron, backer, donor**.
BENEFICIAL	advantageous, helpful, conferring benefit. *Eating vegetables and getting 8 hours of sleep is* beneficial t*o your health, but it sure isn't much fun.* SYN: **has a good effect; advantageous, favorable.**
BENEVOLENCE	inclination to do good deeds. SYN: **largess**.
BEWILDERED	completely confused or puzzled, perplexed. *I was* bewildered *by the complex algebra problem.* SYN: **confused, puzzled, perplexed.**
BIAS	(n) prejudice, particular tendency. *Racial* bias *in employment is illegal in the United States.* SYN: **partiality.** (v) to cause prejudice in (a person); to influence unfairly. *The article is not completely accurate, and may* bias *some readers.* SYN: **show favor or prejudice.**
BILE	ill temper, irritability. *Mr. Watkins is very harsh when he grades essays; his comments reveal his* bile *and sharp tongue.* SYN: **bitterness, bad temper.**
BLISS	supreme happiness, utter joy or contentment; heaven, paradise. *For lovers of ice cream, this new flavor is absolute* bliss. SYN: **joy, delight, ecstasy.**
BOISTEROUS	loud and unrestrained. *The* boisterous *party make so much noise last night that I got no sleep.* SYN: **loud, noisy, raucous.**
BOTANIST	scientist specializing in study of plants. *A* botanist *is a scientist who studies plants.*
BOUNTY	generosity in giving; reward. *In the Old West,* bounty *hunters often pursued outlaws in hopes of reward.* SYN: **abundance, cornucopia, reward, loot**.
BRAVADO	showy and pretentious display of courage. *The coward's* bravado *quickly vanished when his captors threatened to hit him; he began to whine for mercy.* SYN: **bluster, bombast, swagger.**

WORD	DEFINITION, CONTEXT, SYNONYMS
BREVITY	state of being brief, of not lasting a long time. *The* brevity *of your visit to my home implied that you did not enjoy my family's company.* SYN: **shortness, fleetness, swiftness.**
BRIG	ship's prison. *Captain Bligh had the rebellious sailor thrown into the* brig. SYN: **jail, prison.**
BURNISH	(n) to make shine by rubbing, as with a cloth. *Mr. Frumpkin loved to stand in the sun and* burnish *his luxury car until it gleamed.* SYN: **shine, polish, buff, varnish.** (n) shininess produced by burnishing. *They all admired the* burnish *on the car.* SYN: **shine, luster, gleam, brilliance.**
CACHE	hiding place for treasures, etc.; anything in such a hiding place. *The secret panel hid a* cache *of jewels.* [It sounds like cash.] SYN: **stash.**
CAJOLE	to wheedle, persuade with promises or flattery, coax. *The spoiled girl could* cajole *her father into buying her anything.* SYN: **coax, wheedle.**
CAMOUFLAGE	(n) disguise worn in order to deceive an enemy; for instance, uniforms the color of trees and dirt. *The soldiers wore* camouflage *on their helmets.* SYN: **disguise.** (v) to deceive by means of camouflage. *They have* camouflaged *the missile silo in order to deceive enemy bombers.* SYN: **disguise, obscure, cloud, hide.**
CANDOR	frankness and sincerity; fairness. *The* candor *of his confession impressed his parents, and they gave him a light punishment as a result.* SYN: **honesty, sincerity.**
CANINE	relating to dogs. Canine *relates to dogs in the same way as feline relates to cats.*
CANTANKEROUS	quarrelsome and grouchy. *The old grouch was always in a* cantankerous *mood.* SYN: **grouchy, argumentative, ill-tempered.**
CAPRICE	sudden, unpredictable change. *With the* caprice *of an irrational man, he often went from rage to laughter.* SYN: **impulse, whim, fancy.**
CASCADE	(n) waterfall, as in a type of fireworks resembling a waterfall. SYN: **waterfall, torrent.** (v) to fall like a cascade. *The stream flowed over the cliff and* cascaded *down into the valley below.*
CATASTROPHE	disastrous event. *The eruption was truly a* catastrophe; *lava and ash buried several towns on the slopes of the volcano.* SYN: **disaster, ruin, devastation.**
CELESTIAL	relating to the heavens. *Venus is a* celestial *body sometimes visible form Earth.* SYN: **heavenly, divine, spiritual**.

WORD	DEFINITION, CONTEXT, SYNONYMS
CENSOR	to remove material from books, plays, magazines, etc. for moral, political, or religious reasons. *After they* censored *the "dirty" parts out of the book, all that was left was the dedication and half of the cover.* SYN: **suppress, delete.**
CHASM	gorge or deep canyon. *If you look down from the top floor of a New York City skyscraper, it seems as though you're looking into a deep* chasm. SYN: **ravine, canyon, abyss**.
CHOLERIC	bad-tempered. SYN: **bad-tempered.**
CHOREOGRAPHER	person creating and arranging dances for stage performances. *After being an innovative dancer, Martha Graham became a* choreographer *and arranged many innovative dance performances for her company.*
CHORUS	group acting together. *The* chorus *of over fifty people harmonized as one.* SYN: **group, band.**
CHRONIC	continuing over a long period of time, long-standing. *Joshua suffered from* chronic *tiredness; most days he slept straight through geometry class.* SYN: **continuous, constant, persistent, confirmed, settled.**
CIRCUMSCRIBE	to encircle with a line; to limit in any way. *The Howards' country estate is* circumscribed *by rolling hills.* SYN: **limit, outline, bound, define, encompass.**
COLLISION	crash, clash, or conflict. *The* collision *of the two cars made a terrible sound and tied up traffic for hours.* SYN: **crash, clash, impact.**
COMMUNICATIVE	talkative and likely to communicate. SYN: **talkative, articulate, vocal, expressive**.
COMPASSION	deep feeling of pity or sympathy for others. *The jury decided that the cold-hearted killer felt no* compassion *for his victims.* SYN: **pity, sympathy, mercy.**
COMPEL	to force someone or something to act. *Chinese water-torture couldn't* compel *the spy to reveal his secrets.* SYN: **force, coerce, goad, motivate**.
COMPETENT	having enough skill for some purpose; adequate but not exceptional. *He was not the most qualified candidate, but at least he was* competent. SYN: **qualified, capable, fit.**
CONCISE	brief and compact. *Barry gave a* concise *speech: he said everything he needed to and was finished in five minutes.* SYN: **brief, terse, succinct, compact.**
CONDONE	to pardon, to forgive, or overlook. *"We cannot* condone *your behavior," said Ben's parents after he missed his curfew. "You are grounded for two weeks."* SYN: **pardon, excuse, forgive, absolve, overlook, accept, tolerate, allow, permit, suffer, endure, bear, stomach.**

WORD	DEFINITION, CONTEXT, SYNONYMS
CONFIDENTIAL	done secretly or in confidence. *The confidential memorandum listed everyone's salary.* SYN: **secret, covert, off-the-record**.
CONSTRICT	to squeeze, make tighter. *As my chest became constricted, I found it difficult to breathe.* SYN: **choke, stifle, contract, smother.**
CONTEMPLATION	thoughtful observation. *When the philosopher studied complicated issues, he often became so lost in contemplation that he forget to eat or sleep.* SYN: **thought, deliberation, meditation, reflection.**
CONTEND	to fight or struggle against; to debate. *Some people contend that no boxer past or present would have been able to contend with Muhammad Ali for boxing's World Heavyweight Championship.* SYN: **combat, compete; argue, assert.**
CONTENTIOUS	eager to quarrel. *The contentious gentleman in the bar angrily ridiculed whatever anyone said.* SYN: **quarrelsome, cantankerous, feisty, combative, irascible, pugnacious.**
CONVENE	to assemble or meet. *The members of the board convene at least once a week.* SYN: **gather, assemble, meet.**
CONVENTIONAL	established or approved by general usage. *Conventional wisdom today says that a good job requires a college education.* SYN: **customary, well-established, habitual**.
COPIOUS	abundant, large in number or quantity, plentiful. *The hostess had prepared copious amounts of food.* SYN: **abundant, plentiful, profuse.**
COUNTENANCE	(n) face or facial expression, or the general appearance or behavior of something or someone. *Jeremy felt quite unsettled about the new Music Appreciation instructor; she seemed to have such an evil countenance.* SYN: **face, aspect, appearance, bearing, demeanor, air, visage.** (v) to approve or support. *When Dorothy and Irene started their nightly pillow fight, the babysitter warned them, "I will not countenance such behavior."* SYN: **sanction, approve, endorse, bless, favor, encourage, condone.**
COUPLET	unit of poetry with two rhyming lines. *Rub a dub, dub/Three men in a tub is an example of a couplet.*
COURIER	person who carries messages, news, or information. *The courier will deliver the document.* SYN: **messenger, runner, carrier.**
CUE	hint or guiding suggestion. *My mother cleared her throat loudly, which was my cue to be quiet and let her speak.* SYN: **hint, prompt, signal.**
CURVATURE	state of being curved. *Someone with curvature of the spine usually doesn't stand up straight.* SYN: **arc, arch. bow.**

WORD	DEFINITION, CONTEXT, SYNONYMS
DAWDLE	to waste time with idle lingering. *If you* dawdle *on your way to school, you'll be late.* SYN: **delay, linger, dally.**
DEADLOCK	standoff caused by opposition of two conflicting forces. *Despite days of debate, the legislature remained* deadlocked *at 50 votes "yea" and 50 votes "nay"* SYN: **stalemate, standoff, standstill**.
DEARTH	scarcity, lack. *The* dearth *of supplies in our city made it difficult to hold out for long against the attack of the aliens.* SYN: **shortage, lack, scarcity.**
DEBRIS	charred or spoiled remains of something that has been destroyed. *Scavengers searched for valuables amid the* debris. SYN: **trash, rubbish, wreckage, remains.**
DECADE	period of ten years. *The 60's are known as the* decade *of protest.* SYN: **ten years.**
DECEIT	deception or tricky falseness. *Morgan Le Fay, the sorceress, used spells and* deceit *to lure Merlin away from Camelot.* SYN: **dishonesty, fraudulence, deception, trickery.**
DECEIVE	to delude or mislead. *A liar often will try to* deceive *you by not telling the truth.* SYN: **mislead, delude, trick, dupe, lie.**
DECLAMATION	exercise in speech-giving; attack or protest. *The candidate made a* declamation *against the new tax law.* SYN: **long speech, harangue.**
DEFICIENT	defective, insufficient, or inadequate. *Failing to study will make you* deficient *in your readiness for the test.* SYN: **inadequate, defective, insufficient, failing, lacking**.
DEHYDRATE	to remove water from. *Too much time in the sun will* dehydrate *you.* SYN: **remove water from, dry out, parch.**
DEJECT	to depress or make sad. *He was too ambitious to become* dejected *by a temporary setback.* SYN: **sadden, depress, discourage, dishearten.**
DELUDE	to deceive, to mislead. *After three hours of pouring rain, we stopped* deluding *ourselves that the picnic could go on.* SYN: **deceive, dupe, hoax, trick.**
DELUGE	(n) flood, large overflowing of water. Or too much of anything. *The president's veto of the housing bill brought a* deluge *of angry calls and letters from people all over America.* SYN: **flood, overflow, inundation, torrent.** (v) to overflow, to inundate, to flood. *The actor was* deluged *with fan mail.* SYN: **inundate, engulf, flood, overwhelm.**
DEMOTE	to reduce to a lower grade or class. [Opposite of promote] *The army will* demote *any soldier who disobeys orders.* SYN: **downgrade.**

WORD	DEFINITION, CONTEXT, SYNONYMS
DEPLORE	to regard as deeply regrettable and hateful. *"I simply* deplore *your table manners," she told him, as he stuck his head into the bowl to lick the last of the oatmeal.* SYN: **regret, lament, bemoan, bewail, mourn, grieve for, denounce, condemn, protest, oppose, despise, loathe, abominate.**
DESOLATION	condition of being deserted and destroyed. *The terrible flood, which destroyed all the buildings and caused everyone to flee, left only* desolation *in its path.* SYN: **barrenness, desertion, bleakness.**
DESPICABLE	deserving contempt. *Stealing from poor people is* despicable. *In fact, stealing from anyone is* despicable. SYN: **hateful, contemptible, base, mean, vile, detestable, depraved.**
DESPONDENT	in a state of depression. *Mrs. Baker was* despondent *after her husband's death.* SYN: **depressed, morose, gloomy, sad, brooding, desolate, forlorn, woeful, mournful, dejected.**
DESTITUTE	bereft (of something), without or left without (something); poor. *Destitute of friends, Charlotte wandered the streets alone. "I have no money," Jerome said; "I am destitute."* SYN: **bereft, devoid, lacking; poor, impoverished.**
DEVASTATE	to lay waste, make desolate; to overwhelm. *News of the death of his beloved wife will* devastate *him.* SYN: **ruin, wreck.**
DEVOTEE	someone passionately devoted. *The opera* devotee *didn't mind standing on line for hours to get a ticket.* Synonym: **enthusiast, fan, admirer.**
DEVOUT	deeply religious. *Priests and nuns are known to be* devout *people.* SYN: **pious, religious, reverent.**
DEXTERITY	skill in using the hands or body, agility; cleverness. *The gymnast who won the contest demonstrated the highest level of* dexterity *of all the competitors. She was the only one who didn't fall off the balance beam.* SYN: **skill, agility.**
DIMINISH	to become or to make smaller in size, number, or degree. *He was once such a beautiful actor, but now his beauty has greatly* diminished! *As has his bank account.* SYN: **decrease, lessen, dwindle, shrink, contract, decline, subside, wane, fade, recede, weaken, moderate.**
DIN	loud, confused noise. *The* din *in the cafeteria made conversation difficult.* SYN: **noise, uproar, clamor.**
DINGY	dark or drab in color; dirty, shabby, squalid. *He lived alone in a depressing,* dingy *apartment.* SYN: **dirty, filthy, shabby, dark.**
DIPLOMATIC	tactful; skilled in the art of conducting negotiations and other relations between nations. *Our host had a very* diplomatic *nature which enabled her to bring together people who disagreed strongly on many points.* SYN: **polite, tactful.**

WORD	DEFINITION, CONTEXT, SYNONYMS
DISCLAIM	to deny ownership of or association with. *Francine's statement was so silly that she later* disclaimed *it, pretending that it had been made by someone who looked exactly like her.* SYN: **repudiate, reject, disown, disavow, renounce.**
DISCURSIVE	covering a wide area or digressing from a topic. *The professor, who was known for his* discursive *speaking style, covered everything from armadillos to zebras in his zoology lecture.* SYN: **digressive, rambling.**
DISMAL	causing gloom; cheerless. *Our team made a* dismal *showing in the play-offs; we lost every game.* SYN: **miserable, dreary**.
DISPUTE	(n) argument or quarrel. *The* dispute *between the United States and the Soviet Union arose in part as a result of disagreement over the occupation of Berlin.* (v) to argue or quarrel. SYN: **argue, disagree with.**
DISSEMINATE	to scatter or spread widely. *The news wire service* disseminates *information rapidly, so that events get reported all over the world shortly after they happen.* SYN: **spread (an idea or a message), broadcast, disperse.**
DIVERT	(1) to change the course of. *Emergency crews tried to* divert *the flood waters by building a wall of sandbags across the road.* SYN: **deflect, reroute, turn, detour.** (2) *to draw someone's attention by amusing them. While their mother napped, Dad* diverted *the twins by playing hide and seek.* SYN: **amuse, entertain, distract**.
DOFF	to remove or take off, as clothing. *Baseball players usually* doff *their hats during the National Anthem.* SYN: **take a piece of clothing off.**
DOGGED	persistent in effort; stubbornly tenacious. *He worked steadily with a* dogged *determination to finish the difficult task.* SYN: **stubborn (as a bulldog), obstinate.**
DOGMATIC	asserting without proof; stating opinion as if it were fact in a definite and forceful manner. *The* dogmatic *professor would not listen to the students' views; she did not allow debate in class.* SYN: **absolute, opinionated, dictatorial, authoritative, arrogant.**
DOZE	to nap or sleep lightly. *I was so tired from working all night that I kept* dozing *off during the next day.* SYN: **nap, sleep.**
DUNGEON	underground room in fortress often used to keep prisoners. *Henry VIII ordered that Anne Boleyn be kept in the* dungeon *of the Tower of London until she was beheaded.* SYN: **vault, cellar.**
EBULLIENT	overflowing with fervor, enthusiasm, or excitement; high-spirited. *The* ebullient *child exhausted the baby-sitter, who lacked the energy needed to keep up with her.* SYN: **bubbling, enthusiastic, exuberant.**

WORD	DEFINITION, CONTEXT, SYNONYMS
ECCENTRIC	(n) person who differs from the accepted norms in an odd way. *The old eccentric was given to burning hundred-dollar bills.* SYN: **freak, oddball, weirdo, nonconformist.** (adj) *deviating from accepted conduct. Her eccentric behavior began to worry her close friends.* SYN: **odd, unorthodox, unconventional, offbeat.**
ECSTATIC	deliriously overjoyed. *Mortimer was ecstatic when he learned of his 1600 SAT scores.* SYN: **delighted, overjoyed, euphoric.**
EDDY	small whirlpool or any similar current. *Eddies can be in the air or water. When water gets pulled down a drain, it forms a small whirlpool, or an eddy.* SYN: **swirling water, whirlpool.**
EFFECT	(n) result, impression. *The effect of the new policy will not be known for some time, as it often takes several years for new programs to have a noticeable impact.* SYN: **result, impression.** (v) *to produce, make or bring about. We are willing to make any sacrifice in order to effect lasting change for the better.* SYN: **produce, cause, bring about**.
ELUSIVE	hard to find or express. *The elusive nature of the platypus makes it difficult to sight platypus in the wild. Their ugliness makes it unpleasant.* SYN: **hard to catch; slippery, evasive.**
EMBELLISH	to add detail, make more complicated. *Sanjev's short story is too short: it needs to be embellished with more details about life among penguins.* SYN: **elaborate, expand, ornament.**
EMINENT	distinguished, high in rank or station. *They were amazed that such an eminent scholar could have made such an obvious error.* SYN: **prominent, well-known, famous, distinguished, noteworthy.**
EMULATE	to imitate or copy. *Hundreds of writers have emulated Stephen King, but the result is usually a poor imitation.* SYN: **imitate, simulate, copy, follow.**
ENACT	to make into law. *The government wishes to enact the new law in January.* SYN: **pass** (a law), **decree; act out.**
ENCOMPASS	to form a circle or a ring around. *In New York City, Manhattan is an island so it is completely encompassed by water.* SYN: **encircle, circumscribe.**
ENDORSE	to approve, sustain, support. *The principal refused to endorse the plan to put a video arcade in the cafeteria.* SYN: **accept, approve, authorize, accredit, encourage, advocate, favor, support.**
ENIGMA	mystery or riddle. *The source of the mysterious hole remained an enigma.* SYN: **mystery, riddle, puzzle.**

WORD	DEFINITION, CONTEXT, SYNONYMS
ENIGMATIC	unexplainable, mysterious. *The students found the new history teacher to be enigmatic; none of them could figure out what he was thinking.* SYN: **mysterious, unexplainable, inexplicable, incomprehensible, strange, puzzling, baffling, bewildering, perplexing, cryptic.**
ENSNARE	to capture in, or involve, as in a snare. *The investigators managed to* ensnare *the corrupt official when they offered him a bribe that he accepted.* SYN: **trap.**
ENTICE	to lure or attract by feeding desires. *Millions of dollars couldn't* entice *Michael Jordan to play basketball in Europe.* SYN: **tempt, lure, attract.**
ENTOURAGE	group of followers, attendants or assistants. *The movie star was always followed around by an* entourage *of flunkies and assistants.* SYN: **group, retinue, coterie.**
ERA	period of time. *The invention of the atomic bomb marked the beginning of a new* era *in warfare.* SYN: **period of time, age, epoch.**
ERR	to make a mistake (as in error). *To* err *is human; we have all made mistakes.* SYN: **make a mistake or error; go wrong, sin.**
ERUDITE	knowledgeable and learned. *We were not surprised to read the praises of Mario's history of ancient Greece, for we had expected an* erudite *work from him.* SYN: **wise, learned, knowledgeable, informed.**
ESSENTIAL	of the innermost nature of something; basic, fundamental; of great importance. *Eating vegetables is* essential *to your well-being.* SYN: **basic, central, fundamental, important, crucial, necessary, urgent.**
ETIQUETTE	code of social behavior. *Some people think that* etiquette *forbids eating with your elbows on the table.* SYN: **manners, propriety, decorum.**
EVACUATE	to empty out, remove, or withdraw. *The National Guard had to* evacuate *thousands of people following the catastrophe.* SYN: **expel, empty, vacate, remove.**
EXOTIC	of foreign origin or character: strange, exciting. *The atmosphere of the restaurant was* exotic, *but the food was pedestrian.* SYN: **foreign, alien, unfamiliar.**
EXPAND	to make greater, broader, larger, or more detailed. *Friedrich now sells only scary plastic fangs, but he plans to* expand *his business to include rubber vampire bats with glowing eyes.* SYN: **enlarge, increase, augment, extend, broaden, widen, stretch, spread, swell, inflate, dilate, bloat.**
EXPUNGE	to delete or omit completely. *The censor wanted to* expunge *all parts of Joyce's Ulysses he thought were obscene.* SYN: **erase, obliterate, strike out.**

WORD	DEFINITION, CONTEXT, SYNONYMS
EXTRACTION	process of removal or something removed *My toothache meant I had to undergo the* extraction *of my wisdom teeth.* SYN: **removal**.
EXTRICATE	to release from difficulty or an entanglement. *The fly was unable to* extricate *itself from the flypaper.* SYN: **disengage, release, withdraw.**
EXTROVERTED	outgoing or interested in people. *An* extrovert *wouldn't think twice about going to a party of strangers.* SYN: **outgoing, gregarious.**
FANATIC	someone with excessive enthusiasm, especially in politics or religion. *Unable to listen to differing opinions, the* fanatic *politician screamed at his opponent and ran out of the debate.* SYN: **zealous**.
FATAL	causing, or capable of causing, death or ruin. *The racer driver suffered a* fatal *accident when his car hit a patch of oil on the roadway.* SYN: **lethal, deadly, killing, mortal, malignant.**
FATIGUE	(v) to exhaust the strength of. *The energetic baby* fatigued *me.* SYN: **tire out, weary, enervate.** (n) weariness, tiredness from exertion. *The recruits suffered from* fatigue *after the twenty-mile march.* SYN: **exhaustion, weariness.**
FAUNA	animals of a given area. *Darwin studied the* fauna *of the Galapagos Islands.* SYN: **animals, creatures, beasts.**
FELICITY	happiness, bliss. *She was so good, she deserved nothing but* felicity *her whole life.* SYN: **happiness, contentment, bliss.**
FEROCIOUS	savage and fierce. *Ferocious Arctic wolves will hunt and kill much larger animals in pursuit of food.* SYN: **fierce.**
FERVENT	showing great warmth, intensity, feeling, enthusiasm; hot, burning, glowing. *I am a* fervent *admirer of that author's works; I think she is a genius.* SYN: **warm, eager, enthusiastic.**
FICKLE	easily changeable, especially in emotions SYN: **inconstant.**
FIDELITY	faithfulness to duties; truthfulness. *A traitor is someone whose* fidelity *is questioned.* SYN: **loyalty, allegiance, faithfulness, devotion; truthfulness, accuracy.**
FINALE	the final part of some entertainment, often music. *The* finale *of the 1812 Overture is often accompanied by fireworks.* SYN: **end, finish, conclusion, wind-up.**
FLAGRANT	outrageously glaring, noticeable or evident; notorious, scandalous. *His* flagrant *disregard for the rules has resulted in his dismissal from the job.* SYN: **obvious, glaring.**

WORD	DEFINITION, CONTEXT, SYNONYMS
FLIPPANT	not serious, playful; irreverent. *John was* flippant *to the teacher, so she sent him to the principal's office.* SYN: **frivolous, flip, playful.**
FLOW	to move along in a stream or like a stream; to proceed continuously. (As in a computer flowchart, which shows how a program flows.) *People* flowed *out of the crowded department store through the main doors.* SYN: **run, stream** (like water).
FORETELL	to predict the future. *Some prophets claim to* foretell *the future.* SYN: **forecast, prophesy, auger.**
FORMIDABLE	able to inspire awe or wonder because of outstanding power, size, etc. *The steep face of rock we were directed to climb was indeed* formidable. SYN: **impressive, awe-inspiring, impregnable, invincible.**
FOUNDATION	basis or groundwork of anything: whether a building or idea. *The claim that the sun revolves around the earth has no* foundation, *because scientific evidence disproves this claim.* SYN: **bottom, groundwork, basis.**
FRAGILE	easily broken, or damaged. *The Ming dynasty porcelain vase was* fragile *and needed to be handled carefully.* SYN: **breakable, frail, brittle, delicate.**
FREQUENT	(adj) happening or occurring at short intervals. *He travels so much he's a member of five* frequent *flyer plans.* SYN: **repeated, regular, habitual, common.** (v) to visit often. My friend loves antique-hunting and frequents the local antique shops.
FUTILE	ineffective, useless: unimportant. *Our attempt to reach the shore before the storm was* futile; *the wind blew us back into the middle of the lake.* SYN: **useless, hopeless, pointless.**
GARRULOUS	talkative and likely to chatter. *My* garrulous *friend often talks on the telephone for hours at a time.* SYN: **talkative, loquacious.**
GERMINATE	to bud or sprout. *Three weeks after planting, the seeds will* germinate. SYN: **sprout, grow.**
GLEE	joy, pleasure, happiness. *The child was filled with* glee *at the sight of so many presents.* SYN: **joy, elation.**
GLIB	able to speak profusely; having a ready flow of words. It often implies <u>lying</u> or <u>deceit</u>. *The politician was a* glib *speaker.* SYN: **flip, fluent, verbose, smooth, smug.**
GREGARIOUS	fond of company. *For the* gregarious *person, dormitory life is a pleasure.* SYN: **sociable, companionable, amiable, convivial.**
GROTESQUE	odd or unnatural in some way. *The minotaur is a* grotesque *creature out of mythology: part man and part bull.* SYN: **bizarre, outlandish, ugly.**

WORD	DEFINITION, CONTEXT, SYNONYMS
GROVEL	to humble oneself, to beg. *The dog* groveled *at his owner's feet.* SYN: **crawl, beg.**
GRUESOME	grisly, horrible. *The horror film was filled with* gruesome *scenes.* SYN: **frightful, shocking, ghastly.**
HALLOWED	regarded as holy; sacred. *The Constitution is a* hallowed *document in the United States.* SYN: **holy, sacred.**
HARBINGER	omen, precursor, forerunner. *The groundhog's appearance on February 2 is a* harbinger *of spring.* SYN: **precursor, forerunner, omen, messenger.**
HARSH	stern or cruel; physically uncomfortable; unpleasant to the ear. Harsh *words were exchanged during their argument. They barely survived the* harsh *winter nights.* SYN: **rough, strict, severe.**
HASTY	done quickly (often too quickly); rushed, sloppy. *Henry was too* hasty *in completing his research paper, and forgot to put his name on it.* SYN: **rushed, sloppy, shoddy, careless.**
HEED	(n) careful attention, notice, observation. *Pay* heed *to his warnings about that place; he's been there enough times to know the dangers.* (v) to listen to and obey. SYN: **listen to, obey.**
HERBIVOROUS	feeding on plants. *A cow is a* herbivorous *animal.* SYN: **plant-eating.**
HETEROGENEOUS	not uniform; made up of different parts that remain separate. (Its opposite is homogeneous). *The United Nations is a* heterogeneous *body.* SYN: **mixed, unlike, diverse, dissimilar, various.**
HEXAGON	polygon having six sides. *A* hexagon *has six sides and an octagon has eight.*
HIBERNATE	to spend the winter in a sleep-like, dormant state. *During winter, bears* hibernate *in caves.* SYN: **sleep.**
HIVE	structure where bees live. *My friend, Les, is so interested in bees that he'll watch them going into and out of one of their* hives *for hours.*
HORRID	something that causes horror, or is at least pretty bad. *The weather has been just* horrid; *we've had three storms in a week.* SYN: **dreadful, horrible, shocking.**
HOVEL	small, miserable shack. *In Charles Dickens' novels poor people often live in terrible, dirty* hovels. SYN: shack, **shanty.**
HUMID	moist or damp. *It is so* humid *in the jungle that it is advisable to wear light, loose clothing.* SYN: **moist, damp, sultry**.

WORD	DEFINITION, CONTEXT, SYNONYMS
IGNITE	(literally) to set on fire; (figuratively) to stir emotionally, (light a fire under someone). *If you* ignite *that match, you might burn the whole house down. Through his speaking ability, the speaker was able to* ignite *the people who attended his speeches.* SYN: **light, kindle, inflame; rouse, excite, agitate, stir, provoke, prod, inspire.**
ILLITERACY	inability to read and write. *If everyone learned how to read and write,* illiteracy *wouldn't be a problem.*
IMMACULATE	spotless; free from error. *After I cleaned my apartment for hours, it was finally* immaculate. SYN: **errorless, faultless; unblemished, impeccable.**
IMMINENT	about to happen, on the verge of occurring. *Joan was becoming nervous about her* imminent *wedding.* SYN: **impending, approaching, near.**
IMMORTAL	never-dying. *Someone who never grows old and never dies is* immortal. SYN: **undying, eternal.**
IMPASSE	road having no exit or a dilemma with no solution. *A rock slide produced an* impasse *so we could proceed no further on the road.* SYN: **deadlock, standoff, stalemate, standstill.**
IMPERVIOUS	incapable of being penetrated; unable to be influenced. *Superman was* impervious *to bullets.* SYN: **impenetrable.**
IMPIOUS	lacking piety or respect for religion. SYN: **irreverent, sacrilegious.**
IMPLY	to suggest without stating directly. *Although Jane did not state that she loved Mr. Rochester, it was clearly* implied *in her look.* SYN: **hint, suggest, intimate.**
INADVERTENT	unintentional. *I wrote my paper in such a hurry that I made many* inadvertent *errors.* SYN: **accidental, unintentional.**
INCENTIVE	motivation or drive to do a particular task or to go in a given direction. *His father's encouragement gave him the* incentive *to try again.* SYN: **motive, inducement, stimulus.**
INCREDULOUS	not believing. *I was* incredulous *about Ismael's wild fishing story about 'the one that got away.'* SYN: **skeptical, disbelieving.**
INDICATE	to point out or make known with a good degree of certainty. *Recent polls* indicate *that the Democrats will probably be victorious.* SYN: **disclose, show, reveal, imply, signify.**
INERT	having no power to move or act; resisting motion or action. *In the heat of the desert afternoon, lizards are* inert. SYN: **sluggish, passive, inactive, dormant, lethargic, lifeless.**

WORD	DEFINITION, CONTEXT, SYNONYMS
INFECTIOUS	able to be passed from one person to another (such as an infection); contagious. *Her laughter was* infectious, *and soon we were all laughing.* SYN: **catching, contagious.**
INGENIOUS	possessing or displaying great creativity and resourcefulness. *Luther found an* ingenious *way to solve the math problem.* SYN: **brilliant, inspired, imaginative, shrewd, crafty, cunning, resourceful.**
INGENUITY	inventive skill or cleverness. *Use your* ingenuity *to come up with a new solution to the problem.* SYN: **creativity, cleverness, inventiveness.**
INHABIT	to reside or live in. *Arboreal creatures, such as monkeys,* inhabit *the trees.* SYN: **live, occupy, reside, dwell, stay.**
INNATE	present at birth. *The plan was doomed from the start; there was an* innate *problem in it.* SYN: **natural, inborn, inherent, instinctive.**
INNOCENT	pure, not guilty. Someone with the simplicity of a baby. *Those accused of practicing witchcraft in Salem were clearly* innocent *of any such act.* SYN: **pure, harmless, guiltless, naïve, chaste.**
INSINUATION	devious hint or sly suggestion made to cause suspicion or doubts. *During the last election, the* insinuation *that the Congressman had taken kickbacks cost him thousands of votes.* SYN: **hint, suggestion, reference, implication.**
INSOMNIA	inability to fall sleep. *No matter how tired I am, I continue to suffer from* insomnia. SYN: **sleeplessness.**
INSURGENT	(adj) rebel. (adj) rising in revolt, starting a revolution. *The* insurgent *crew staged a mutiny and threw the captain overboard.* SYN: **rebellious.**
IRATE	full of anger, wrathful, incensed. *He was* irate *at being wrongly accused of the crime.* SYN: **angry, indignant, infuriated, enraged.**
JEER	to mock in an abusive way; taunting remark. *As the foolish political candidate stumbled through his poorly written speech, the crowd began to* jeer. SYN: **ridicule, mock, scoff; gibe, taunt.**
JUBILANT	feeling joy or happiness. *We were* jubilant *after our victory in the state championships.* SYN: **very happy, exultant, gleeful, joyful, ecstatic.**
JUDICIOUS	having wise judgment. *The wise and distinguished judge was well-known for having a* judicious *temperament.* SYN: **wise, sage, sagacious.**
KINETIC	relating to motion. *A* kinetic *sculpture is one that moves.* SYN: **animated, energetic, spirited, moving.**

WORD	DEFINITION, CONTEXT, SYNONYMS
LAGOON	shallow body of water connected to a much larger one, as a lake or sea. *The pirates anchored their ship offshore and rowed into the* lagoon, *where they went ashore.* SYN: **inlet, pool.**
LENIENT	merciful, not strict. *When the Commissioner only fined the pitcher fifty dollars for throwing a baseball at a batter, many fans thought the punishment was too* lenient. SYN: **merciful, indulgent.**
LETHARGY	drowsiness, tiredness, inability to do anything much. *A feeling of* lethargy *came over me, and I wanted nothing more than a nice long nap.* SYN: **sluggishness, fatigue.**
LIMBER	bending and moving easily. *The gymnast warmed up for thirty minutes so that she would be* limber *before her routine.* SYN: **agile, supple.**
LUNGE	(n) sudden forward movement, plunge. (v) to thrust something forward. *The toboggan* lunged *forward at the point where the slope became quite steep.* SYN: **thrust, plunge.**
MAGNANIMOUS	having a great or noble spirit, acting generously, patiently, or kindly. *Although at first he seemed cold, Uncle Frank turned out to be a very* magnanimous *fellow.* SYN: **big-hearted, generous, noble, princely, forgiving, patient, tolerant, indulgent, ungrudging, unresentful.**
MALFUNCTION	to fail to function; an instance of failing to function. *The* malfunction *of the main booster rocket meant that the space capsule wasn't launched on schedule.* SYN: **failure.**
MALLEABLE	can be molded or shaped. *Gold is so* malleable *that it can be beaten into a thin foil.* SYN: **soft, flexible, yielding.**
MAR	to damage something and make it imperfect. *Telephone poles* mar *the beauty of the countryside.* SYN: **deform, impair, spoil, disfigure, damage.**
MARVEL	(n) amazing thing; something astonishing or marvelous. *It was a* marvel *that they survived the crash.* SYN: **miracle, prodigy, wonder.** (v) to be surprised or full of wonder. I marvel at your ability to remain calm. SYN: **wonder.**
MEAGER	very small or insufficient. *He rented an expensive apartment and dined at fine restaurants, but he earned a* meager *wage and soon ran out of money.* SYN: **slight, trifling, skimpy, puny, scant, inadequate, insufficient, insubstantial.**
MEEK	humble and submissive. *People who are too* meek *won't stand up for themselves.* SYN: **passive, unassertive, docile, compliant.**
MELANCHOLY	very sad or depressing. *The rainy weather made James feel* melancholy. SYN: **gloomy, mournful, somber.**

WORD	DEFINITION, CONTEXT, SYNONYMS
METEOROLOGIST	scientist dealing with weather and weather conditions. *Although the* meteorologist *predicted a heat wave, the temperature remained below freezing.*
MIMIC	imitate, copy not always in a complimentary way. *Mary got in trouble for* mimicking *the teacher.* SYN: **mock, impersonate, simulate, counterfeit.**
MINUSCULE	tiny, miniature. *Dave needed a magnifying glass to read the* minuscule *print on the lease.* SYN: **microscopic, minute.**
MISBEGOTTEN	poorly conceived, poorly planned, based on false assumptions or false reasoning. *It came as no surprise when Fred's* misbegotten *scheme proved an utter failure.* SYN: **illegitimate, ill-conceived.**
MOURN	feel sad for, regret. *The family gathered to* mourn *for the dead.* SYN: **lament, grieve.**
MURKY	dark, dim. *Jill groped her way down the* murky *hallway.* SYN: **obscure, gloomy.**
NAUSEOUS	sickening, makes you feel sick, or turns your stomach. *The cook mixed skim milk with green eels, and produced a concoction that was truly* nauseous. SYN: **revolting, disgusting, nauseating.**
NEBULOUS	hazy, not well-defined. *During the campaign, the candidate promised to fight crime. But when reporters asked for details, his plan was* nebulous -- *he could not say whether he would hire more police or support longer jail sentences.* SYN: **hazy, cloudy, ill-defined, unclear, shapeless, vague, unspecific.**
NIMBLE	quick and agile in movement or thought. *A* nimble *athlete is a well-coordinated one.* SYN: **agile, active, quick, clever, cunning.**
NOMAD	someone who has no permanent home and wanders. *The Berbers are a tribe of* nomads *who travel from place to place searching for grassland for their herds.* SYN: **wanderer, vagrant.**
NOTIFY	to tell, let know, give notice. *The landlord failed to* notify *the tenants of the planned demolition of the building.* SYN: **tell, inform, apprise.**
OBESE	very fat. *Some* obese *people suffer from anxiety-induced overeating.* SYN: **fat, corpulent, portly.**
OBNOXIOUS	offensive and very disagreeable. *The last time I went to the movies, an* obnoxious *person sitting beside me talked loudly during the entire movie.* SYN: **offensive, repugnant, repellant.**
OBSCURE	(v) to hide or make difficult to find. (adj) *hard to see; unknown, uncertain. The speaker's style was so confusing that it* obscured *his main point rather than clarified it.* SYN: **confuse, becloud; vague, unclear, dubious.**

WORD	DEFINITION, CONTEXT, SYNONYMS
OBSERVATION	(1) examination, as in the observation deck at the World Trade Center. *Close observation of Arnold led Anne to believe that he was hiding something.* SYN: **attention, watching.** (2) remark, comment. *Damon amused the class with his witty* observation *about the teacher's methods.* SYN: **pronouncement, opinion.**
OBSOLETE	no longer in use; discarded or outmoded. *It's as* obsolete *as black-and-white television.* SYN: **outdated, passé, old-fashioned.**
OBSTINATE	stubborn. *Hal's mother tried to get him to eat his spinach, but he remained* obstinate. SYN: **mulish, dogged.**
OBSTRUCT	to get in the way of; to block; to hamper. *He removed his hat so as not to* obstruct *another's view of the stage.* SYN: **block, check, clog, impede.**
OBTUSE	not acute; someone who is not smart; thick, dull. *Alfred was too* obtuse *to realize that the sum of the angles of a triangle is 180 degrees.* SYN: **slow, stupid.**
OLFACTORY	relating to the sense of smell. *In human beings,* olfactory *sensations are perceived with the nose.*
OMINOUS	threatening, menacing, having the character of an evil omen. *The sky filled with* ominous *dark clouds before the storm.* SYN: **foreboding.**
OPPORTUNE	appropriate to time or circumstances: timely, lucky. *Dalbert's investment in plastics, made just before the demand for plastics began to rise, was* opportune. SYN: **timely, appropriate, lucky.**
OPTION	choice, selection, preference. *Donna carefully considered every* option *before making her final decision.* SYN: **alternative, election**.
ORBIT	to move around some object, as a planet; to circle. *The moon* orbits *the earth, which in turn orbits the sun.* SYN: **circle, revolve, circuit.** (n) the actual route the thing takes when it goes around the other thing, as in the orbit of the moon around the earth. *The German shepherd dog approached the intruder cautiously, circled him and sniffed, made two more* orbits, *and then walked away.* SYN: **circuit, revolution.**
ORCHID	purple (as in the flower). *The vice-principal turned* orchid *with rage.* SYN: **lavender.**
OSTENTATIOUS	pretentious and flashy. *Some think Donald Trump's Taj Mahal casino, which he proudly calls the Eighth Wonder of the World, is really an* ostentatious *display of wealth and poor taste.* SYN: **conspicuous, flashy, flamboyant, showy.**
PALATABLE	good tasting. *Her cooking is quite* palatable. SYN: **savory, agreeable, appetizing, delicious, acceptable.**

WORD	DEFINITION, CONTEXT, SYNONYMS
PARADOX	contradiction, something that doesn't fit: something that shouldn't be true because it seems to offend common sense, yet is true anyway. *The* paradox *of government is that the person who most desires power is the person who least deserves it.* SYN: **contradiction.**
PASSIVE	not active; someone who lets things happen rather than himself taking action. *Ned portrayed himself as the* passive *victim of external forces.* SYN: **submissive.**
PEDDLE	sell (although usually used in a somewhat bad way. *People* peddle *rags or junk; not Tiffany jewelry or Gucci luggage.) Bill got a job going door to door to* peddle *vacuum cleaners.* SYN: **hawk, vend.**
PEDESTRIAN	(adj) common, everyday, usual. *The critics called the new restaurant's food* pedestrian; *it never had many customers, and eventually closed.* SYN: **plodding, prosaic, commonplace, ordinary, plain, mundane, humdrum, trite, banal, drab, colorless, boring, barren, unimaginative, uninspired, undistinguished, unremarkable, unexceptional.** (n) one who does not ride but walks. *With the way the taxis speed, it can be dangerous to be a* pedestrian *in New York. Of course, it's dangerous to be in the cab too, which leaves little choice but to stay home in bed.* SYN: **walker, hiker, stroller.**
PERJURY	making deliberately false statements when under oath. *Mr. Mason accused the witness of* perjury. SYN: **falsehood, fraud, lies.**
PERSEVERE	to continue in some course of action despite setbacks and opposition. *Although at first the problems looked difficult, Wendy* persevered, *and found that she could answer almost all of them.* SYN: **continue, struggle, endure, persist.**
PETRIFY	literally, to turn to stone; figuratively, to paralyze with fear or with surprise. *The movie is so frightening that it would* petrify *even the bravest viewer.* SYN: **shock, stun, stiffen, paralyze, fossilize.**
PIOUS	religiously devout or moral. *Saul, a* pious *man, walks, to the synagogue on the Sabbath and prays daily.* SYN: **devout, religious, God-fearing, reverent, moral, upstanding, scrupulous.**
PLAGIARISM	copying of someone else's work and claiming it as your own. *The notable scientist lost his job when his* plagiarism *was revealed; years before, he had copied a research paper from a magazine.* SYN: **copying, stealing.**
PLAUSIBLE	seeming to be true. *Joachim's excuse for lateness to class sounded* plausible *at the time, but I later learned that it had been a lie.* SYN: **credible, believable, likely, probable, conceivable.**
POMPOUS	characterized by stiff, unnatural formality. *Gerald began his speech to the class with a* pompous *quote from Julius Caesar.* SYN: **stuffy, stiff, affected, mannered, unnatural, pretentious, self-important, conceited.**

WORD	DEFINITION, CONTEXT, SYNONYMS
PROCRASTINATE	to postpone; to put something off to a later time. *Don't procrastinate; do your homework now.* SYN: **delay, postpone, defer.**
PROFOUND	deep, wise, serious. *Both the Book of Ecclesiastes and the Tao Te Ching contain* profound *observations about human life.* SYN: **wise, deep, sagacious.**
PROLIFIC	producing great amounts; fertile. *Stephen King, a* prolific *writer, seems to write new books as fast as they are published.* SYN: **productive, fertile.**
PROPEL	to move, make something go forward. *An ill-timed push on the gas pedal* propelled *the car through the plate glass window of the dealership.* SYN: **compel, project, drive.**
PROPHESY	**to predict the future using divine guidance.** *The ancient Greek oracles at Delphi were supposed to be able to* prophesy *the future.* SYN: **predict. foretell, forecast, auger.**
PUNGENT	sharp, flavorful (sometimes too flavorful). *The soup was so* pungent *that it brought tears to Alice's eyes.* SYN: **peppery, hot, piquant, biting, acrid.**
PURSUE	to chase, go after. *The cat* pursued *the squirrel up the tree.* SYN: **trail, tail, dog, follow.**
QUELL	to quiet something raucous (often a rebellion); crush, defeat, conquer. *The dictator dispatched troops to* quell *the rebellion.* SYN: **quash, overpower, overcome, quench, suppress.**
QUENCH	to satisfy a need or desire. *After coming in from the desert, Ezra needed gallons of water to* quench *his thirst.* SYN: **satisfy, extinguish, subdue, sate.**
RABBLE	large, disorderly, and easily excited mob. *The* rabble *waited anxiously below the king's window for news of the tax decree.* SYN: **crowd, mob, multitude, horde.**
RABID	(literally) afflicted with rabies, a disease of the nervous system that causes convulsions and wildly irrational behavior. (figuratively) acting fanatically or madly, as if afflicted by rabies. Rabid *animals can sometimes be identified by saliva dripping from their jaws and by frantic behavior. [Sounds pleasant, doesn't it?] The first speaker was calm, but the second--a wild-eyed man advocating the destruction of all tractors--was positively* rabid. SYN: **fanatical, mad, crazy, irrational, wild-eyed, maniacal, lunatic, incoherent.**
RANCOR	bad feeling, bitterness. *Herbert was so filled with* rancor *that he could think of nothing but taking revenge on those who had humiliated him.* SYN: **animosity, resentment, hatred, malice, spite.**
RANDOM	lacking order, free from order or bias. *She conducted a* random *survey of garage mechanics by drawing their names from a hat.* SYN: **chance, haphazard, unordered, unbiased.**

WORD	DEFINITION, CONTEXT, SYNONYMS
RANSACK	to search thoroughly and messily. *Did the burglars* ransack *your entire house?* SYN: **plunder, pillage, search, loot, pilfer, steal.**
RATIFY	to approve formally. *The Senate* ratified *treaty after only a brief debate.* SYN: **confirm, affirm, endorse, approve, sanction.**
RAVENOUS	(literally) wildly eager to eat; (figuratively) hungry for anything. *The homeless man had not had a bite of food in two days and was* ravenous. *The abandoned puppy was* ravenous *for affection and tenderness.* SYN: **hungry, famished, voracious, starved.**
RAZE	to destroy (a building, city, etc.) utterly. *The house had been* razed: *where once it had stood there was nothing but splinters and bricks.* SYN: **demolish, destroy, wreck, level, flatten.**
RECLUSE	someone who lives far away from other people. *Anthony left the city and lived as a* recluse *in the desert.* SYN: **hermit, loner.**
RECUR	to return; to occur again. *The problem is bound to* recur *if you don't solve it now.* SYN: **return, repeat.**
REEK	(literally) giving off a strong, offensive odor; strong smell *"Boy! Something really* reeks *in here. Did you bring a dead skunk with you or something?"* SYN: **stink.** (figuratively) to be pervaded by something unpleasant. The city government reeks of corruption.
REFRAIN	to stop or avoid doing something, quit. *The librarian insisted that everyone* refrain *from making any noise.* SYN: **abstain, cease, desist.**
REGAL	royal, splendid. *Prince Charles was married with full* regal *ceremony.* SYN: **kingly, majestic.**
REIGN	rule over, govern, dominate. [Pronounced like rain.] *The British monarch used to* reign *over the entire British Empire.* SYN: **rule, prevail.**
REIMBURSE	to repay someone for their expenses. *If you buy me lunch today, I'll* reimburse *you tomorrow.* SYN: **repay, compensate.**
REINFORCE	strengthen, add to. *The purpose of the homework is to* reinforce *what's taught in class.* SYN: **support.**
REMINISCENCE	memory or act of recalling the past. *The old timer's* reminiscence *of his childhood was of a time when there were no cars.* SYN: **collection, recall, memory, nostalgia.**
RENOWNED	well-known, famous, celebrated. *Having spent her whole childhood banging on things, Jane grew up to be a* renowned *drummer.* SYN: **famed, distinguished, notable.**

WORD	DEFINITION, CONTEXT, SYNONYMS
REPARTEE	witty conversation, retort. *As a master of* repartee, *Bob was the hit of every party he attended.* SYN: **banter.**
REPUDIATE	to reject what one was once associated with. *After Grace discovered that her friends had been spreading false rumors about her, she* repudiated *them and made new friends.* SYN: **disown, reject, renounce.**
REPUGNANT	something gross, repulsive, or revolting. *Bill liked his macaroni and cheese with jelly, a combination that many of his friends found* repugnant. SYN: **distasteful, objectionable, offensive.**
RESIDUE	something that remains after a part is taken. *The fire burned everything leaving only a* residue *of ash and charred debris.* SYN: **remainder, remnant, leftover.**
REVEAL	show, divulge, expose. *Wendy cut through the frog's abdominal wall to* reveal *the internal organs.* SYN: **unveil, disclose.**
REVEL	celebrate noisily, have a party. *The whole school got together to* revel *in the football team's victory.* SYN: **celebrate, indulge, enjoy.**
ROUT	conquer, defeat, and chase off. *The renewed onslaught* routed *the enemy.* SYN: **overwhelm, overcome, subdue, scatter.**
SATELLITE	moon, a small thing going around a bigger thing. [Well, you try to define it!] *A spy* satellite *can take pictures of the people and things that it passes above as it circles the globe.* SYN: **moon.**
SATURATE	to fill something to the point where it can hold no more. *Reading the entire encyclopedia will* saturate *your mind with facts.* SYN: **soak, fill, drench, permeate.**
SAUCY	impudent, impertinent, flippant. *She always got in trouble with her parents for her* saucy *remarks.* SYN: **pert, lively, rude, insolent.**
SAVOR	to enjoy something with relish or delight. *I* savored *every bite of my father's chocolate cream pie.* SYN: **taste, relish, enjoy, appreciate.**
SCALD	burn with hot liquid or steam. *Sharon was* scalded *when she bumped into a pot of boiling water.* SYN: **burn, scorch, boil.**
SCARCE	rare, uncommon. *Water is* scarce *in the Sahara Desert.* SYN: **sparse, infrequent.**
SCATHING	overly critical. *Walter was depressed by the* scathing *reviews that his play received.* SYN: **searing, crushing, harmful.**

WORD	DEFINITION, CONTEXT, SYNONYMS
SCHISM	division or separation between groups of members within an organization. *Because half of the student council wanted the jukebox in the cafeteria, and the other half wanted it in the library, the council suffered a* schism. SYN: **disunity, break, division, conflict, clash.**
SCRUPULOUS	acting in accordance with a strict moral code; thorough in the performance of a task. *David could not have stolen Sheila's money; he was too* scrupulous *to carry out the threat. Roger is a* scrupulous *editor who checks every word his reporters write.* SYN: **moral, upstanding, virtuous, principled, ethical, careful, conscientious, thorough, diligent.**
SECURE	(v) to fasten, make secure. *I had* secured *my suitcase in the overhead luggage rack at the beginning of the journey.* SYN: **fasten, bind, clamp.** (adj) well-fastened, not likely to fall or come loose. *My suitcase seemed* secure *in the luggage rack. But then it fell on me.* SYN: **fastened, fixed, bound, safe, stable.**
SEETHE	to heave or bubble from great inner turmoil, as a volcano; to boil. *Immediately after learning of Roger's gossip about me, I began to boil with anger, and by the time I reached his house I was* seething. SYN: **boil, bubble, steam, foam, surge, heave, swell.**
SENTRY	guard, sentinel, watchman. *Mitchell stood as* sentry *while the other boys were in the boys room smoking.* SYN: **watch, lookout.**
SEQUEL	addition or result; story that continues a previous one. *I hear they're making another* sequel *to the Friday the 13th movies.* SYN: **aftermath, outcome, continuation, consequence.**
SHREWD	clever, keen-witted, cunning, sharp in practical affairs. *He was a* shrewd *businessman and soon parlayed his meager savings into a fortune.* SYN: **clever, keen, astute, cunning, wily, sharp, discerning.**
SIGNIFICANT	meaningful, important, relevant. *A good detective knows that something that hardly seems worth noticing may be highly* significant. SYN: **consequential, momentous, weighty.**
SINISTER	threatening, evil, menacing. *His friendly manner concealed* sinister *designs.* SYN: **ominous, wicked.**
SLACK	(n) lack of tautness or tension; a time of little activity or dullness. *There was no wind; the sails hung* slack *and the boat was motionless.* SYN: **lull, relaxation.** (adj) sluggish, idle, barely moving, loose, relaxed. *The* slack *atmosphere made it unlikely that anyone would work efficiently.* SYN: **lax, negligent, remiss, careless, inactive, slow, loose, relaxed.**
SOCIABLE	friendly, companionable. *Although they maintain their independence, cats are* sociable *creatures.* SYN: **gregarious, companionable, friendly, affable, amiable.**

WORD	DEFINITION, CONTEXT, SYNONYMS
SOLICIT	to seek (something) from another; to make a request of someone. *The tennis player disagreed with the first judge's decision, so he* solicited *the opinion of the second judge. I* solicited *my parents for money. But they said no.* SYN: **request, seek, petition, beg.**
SPECIFY	to mention, name or require specifically or exactly. *The report* specified *the steps to be taken in an emergency.* SYN: **detail, identify, stipulate, itemize, define, state.**
SPLICE	to join, bind, attach; in film editing, to join two pieces of film. *The editor removed all the scenes with the troublesome actress and* spliced *the remainder together.* SYN: **join, bind, connect, attach, link, unite.**
SPURN	reject with scorn, turn away. *When Harvey proposed to Harriet, she* spurned *him; she loved another man.* SYN: **refuse, snub.**
SQUALID	very dirty or foul; wretched. *The* squalid *living conditions in the tenement building outraged the new tenants.* SYN: **filthy, sordid, poor, foul.**
SQUANDER	to waste (often money) on some worthless purchase or practice. *While I have carefully saved money to buy the piano I have always wanted, my friend Sean has* squandered *his earnings on thousands of lottery tickets.* SYN: **waste, fritter away, consume, exhaust.**
STAUNCH	steady, loyal. *A dog is a* staunch *friend.* SYN: **firm, sturdy, stable, solid, established, substantial, steadfast, faithful, unfailing.**
STEALTHY	sneaky, secret. *The children made a* stealthy *raid on the refrigerator during the night.* SYN: **sneaky, furtive, clandestine.**
STRESS	emphasize, point out. *Vanessa wrote on the blackboard the main points that she was going to* stress *in her lecture.* SYN: **highlight.**
SUAVE	smooth, graceful, and confident in speech and behavior (sometimes insincerely). *Nina was a* suave *young woman who knew exactly how to act in any situation.* SYN: **smooth, gracious, courtly, worldly, sophisticated, urbane, cosmopolitan, cultivated, cultured, refined.**
SUBDUE	to bring under control; to decrease the intensity of (as in the adjective subdued). *The king's army attempted to* subdue *the rebellious peasants, who were threatening to storm the castle.* SYN: **control, vanquish, suppress, repress, master, overcome, tame.**
SUCCEED	(1) to follow, come after. *George Bush* succeeded *Ronald Reagan as President.* SYN: **follow, replace.** (2) to prosper, do well. *Valerie was resolved to* succeed *in her new school.* SYN: **flourish, thrive.**
SUCCUMB	to give in, to submit. *Don't* succumb *to temptation.* SYN: **yield, surrender, give in, submit, die, expire.**

WORD	DEFINITION, CONTEXT, SYNONYMS
SUFFICE	to be adequate or enough. *"A light dinner should* suffice *the average person,"* said the thin man, eating his lettuce sandwich. SYN: **satisfy.**
SUMMIT	highest level or point. *The first people to reach the* summit *of Mt. Everest were Tenzing Norgay and Edmund Hillary.* SYN: **apex, peak, top, pinnacle.**
SUPERB	wonderful, superior, excellent. *The main course was merely adequate, but the dessert was* superb. SYN: **splendid, magnificent, grand.**
SUPPRESS	Scrush, hold in, hide. *The students could hardly* suppress *their excitement on the last day of school.* SYN: **quell, contain.**
SURFEIT	overly abundant supply, an excess. *There certainly is no* surfeit *of gasoline this year.* SYN: **excess, glut, overabundance.**
SURMISE	(v) to guess, to infer. *From his torn pants and bloody nose I* surmised *that he had been in a fight.* SYN: **guess, conjecture, speculate, hypothesize, infer.** (n) instance of surmising. *My* surmise *was correct; he had been in a fight.*
SURROGATE	person or thing substituted for another. *When I was ill, my friend agreed to act as my* surrogate *and give my speech for me.* SYN: **proxy, substitute, alternate.**
SUSCEPTIBLE	vulnerable, liable to be affected by something. *Because of her weakened state, Valerie was* susceptible *to infection.* SYN: **vulnerable, open, exposed.**
SUSPENSE	fear or anticipation of waiting for something. Something having to do with fear or mystery, as in a suspense novel. *Joe was in an agony of* suspense *waiting to find out if he'd gotten the lead part in the school play.* SYN: **apprehension, anxiety.**
SYNOPSIS	short summary, outline. *Oren wrote a one-page* synopsis *of a 55-page book.* SYN: **summary, outline.**
TACITURN	quiet, tending not to speak. *Lyle is a* taciturn *boy who plays by himself and rarely says a word.* SYN: **quiet, shy, reserved, guarded.**
TACTFUL	acting with sensitivity to others' feelings. *I sent Eva to explain our sudden departure to our smelly hosts, for she is the most* tactful *person I know.* SYN: **diplomatic, discreet, judicious, sensitive, considerate, thoughtful, politic, delicate.**
TAINT	to poison, as a drink; to corrupt, as a person. *"I have* tainted *the princess's wine with a potion that will age her horribly in a few short weeks!" the witch proclaimed gleefully.* SYN: **poison, contaminate, infect, spoil; corrupt, debase, pervert, stain, blemish.**

WORD	DEFINITION, CONTEXT, SYNONYMS
TAMPER	bother, interfere, meddle. *Dan* tampered *with the thermostat and raised the temperature in the room to 85 degrees.* SYN: **tinker, manipulate.**
TANGIBLE	can be felt by touching; having actual substance. *The storming of the castle didn't bring the soldiers* tangible *rewards, but it brought them great honor. They would have preferred the rewards.* SYN: **material, real, touchable, palpable, concrete, perceptible.**
TAUT	stretched tightly; tense. *The tightrope was* taut. SYN: **tight, stretched, tense, strained.**
TEMPERATE	denying oneself too much pleasure; avoiding extreme positions; moderate, sensible; a mild climate. *Lloyd is the most* temperate *student I have ever met; even on Friday night he goes to bed early. The* temperate *weather of California is a welcome change from the harsh winters and muggy summers of New York.* SYN: **self-denying; sensible, level-headed, rational, moderate, restrained, mild.**
TENACIOUS	steadily pursuing a goal, unwilling to give up; stubborn. *For years, against all odds, women* tenaciously *fought for the right to vote.* SYN: **persistent, persevering, untiring, tireless.**
TEPID	neither hot nor cold, lukewarm; lacking character or spirit, bland. *Roxanne refused to take a bath in the* tepid *water, fearing that she would catch a cold. Neither liking nor disliking Finnegan's film, the critics gave it tepid reviews.* SYN: **lukewarm, mild, temperate; unenthusiastic, halfhearted, indifferent.**
TERMINATE	to stop, end. *Amy and Zoe* terminated *their friendship, and never spoke to each other again.* SYN: **cease, finish, conclude.**
TERSE	concise, brief, using few words. *Kate was noted for her* terse *replies, rarely going beyond "yes" or "no."* SYN: **concise, succinct, compact.**
TETHER	(n) chain or rope tied to an animal to keep it within specific bounds. *The cheetah chewed through its* tether *and wandered off.* SYN: **rope, chain.** (v) to fasten or confine. *I have to tether my dog to the fence to keep it out of the neighbor's yard.* SYN: **tie, fasten.**
TOKEN	(n) sign or symbol. *I offered him a chocolate bar as a* token *of my gratitude for his help.* SYN: **symbol, expression, representation.** (adj) existing in name or appearance only, without depth, or significance. *He offered me a* token *handshake, but I knew that we were in fact still enemies.* SYN: **nominal, superficial, meaningless.**
TORRID	extremely hot, scorching. *The* torrid *weather destroyed the crops.* SYN: **hot, parched, sizzling.**
TREPIDATION	fear, apprehension. *Mike approached the door of the principal's office with* trepidation. SYN: **fright, anxiety, trembling, hesitation.**

WORD	DEFINITION, CONTEXT, SYNONYMS
TRITE	lacking originality, inspiration, and interest. *Lindsay's graduation speech was the same* trite *nonsense we've heard a hundred times in the past.* SYN: **tired, banal, unoriginal, common, stale, stock.**
TUMULT	noise and confusion. *The* tumult *of the No Nukes demonstrators drowned out the president's speech.* SYN: **racket, disorder.**
TYRANNY	harsh exercise of absolute power, as in the deadly dinosaur **Tyrannosaurus Rex.** *The students accused Mrs. Morgenstern of* tyranny *when she assigned them seats instead of letting them choose their own.* SYN: **oppression, repression.**
ULTIMATE	marking the highest point; cannot be improved upon; final. *The new fashions from Paris are the* ultimate *in chic.* SYN: **maximum, remotest, final, conclusive, last, elemental, primary, fundamental.**
UNANIMOUS	approved by everyone concerned. *The Student Council voted* unanimously; *not one person opposed the plan.* SYN: **unchallenged, uncontested, unopposed, united, harmonious.**
UNKEMPT	messy, sloppily maintained. *Sam's long hair and wrinkled shirt seemed* unkempt *to his grandmother; she told him he looked like a bum.* SYN: **sloppy, slovenly, ruffled, disheveled, messy, untidy, ragged.**
USURP	to seize, take by force (most often used of abstract nouns like "power" rather than concrete nouns like "bathrobe"). *The vice-principal was power-hungry, and tended to* usurp *the principal's power.* SYN: **seize, grab, steal, snatch.**
VACATE	leave as in a vacation. *The police ordered the demonstrators to* vacate *the park.* SYN: **depart, go.**
VACUOUS	silly, empty-headed, not serious. *The book that Victor loved when he was six struck him as utterly* vacuous *when he was twenty. But he still liked the pictures.* SYN: **shallow, vapid.**
VAGUE	not clear or certain. *It took us a while to find John's house because the directions were* vague. SYN: **nebulous, imprecise.**
VEHEMENT	with deep feeling. *Susanne responded to the accusation of cheating with a* vehement *denial.* SYN: **passionate, earnest, fervent.**
VEND	to sell goods. *Every Saturday in the Summer, craftsmen* vend *their products in the park.* SYN: **sell, peddle, merchandise.**
VEX	to irritate to a great degree, to annoy. *Your constant sniveling is beginning to* vex *me.* SYN: **tease, irritate, provoke, torment, pester, harass, bother, annoy.**

WORD	DEFINITION, CONTEXT, SYNONYMS
VITALIZE	make something come alive. *The government's flagrant acts of injustice* vitalized *the opposition.* SYN: **animate, vivify.**
VIVACIOUS	lively, full of spirit. *Quiet and withdrawn at first, Joan became increasingly* vivacious. SYN: **animated, sprightly, spirited.**
WAN	unnaturally pale, lacking color. *The sick child had a* wan *face.* SYN: **pale, ashen, bloodless.**
WANTONLY	without a reason. *Instead of singling out appropriate targets for his anger, the crazed robot struck out* wantonly. SYN: **randomly, indiscriminately.**
WRATH	extreme anger. *He denounced the criminals in a speech filled with righteous* wrath. SYN: **ire, fury, rage.**
WRETCHED	miserable, pathetic. *Steve felt* wretched *when he failed the test.* SYN: **dejected, woebegone, forlorn.**
WRITHE	to squirm or twist as if in pain. *After the being hit by a car, the pedestrian was* writhing *in pain.* SYN: **squirm, twitch, twist.**
ZEALOUS	enthusiastic, eager. *Serge was a* zealous *supporter of the cause who never missed a rally.* SYN: **fervent, fervid, intense, passionate.**

23

Math Reference

Number Properties

1. Integer/Noninteger

Integers are **whole numbers**; they include negative whole numbers and zero.

2. Adding/Subtracting Signed Numbers

To **add a positive and a negative**, first ignore the signs and find the positive difference between the number parts. Then attach the sign of the original number with the larger number part. For example, to add 23 and –34, first we ignore the minus sign and find the positive difference between 23 and 34—that's 11. Then we attach the sign of the number with the larger number part—in this case it's the negative sign from the –34. So, 23 + (–34) = –11.

Make **subtraction** situations simpler by turning them into addition. For example, think of –17 – (–21) as –17 + (+21).

To **add or subtract a string of positives and negatives**, first turn everything into addition. Then combine the positives and negatives so that the string is reduced to the sum of a single positive number and a single negative number.

3. Multiplying/Dividing Signed Numbers

To multiply and/or divide positives and negatives, treat the number parts as usual and **attach a minus sign if there were originally an odd number of negatives**. For example, to multiply –2, –3, and –5, first multiply the number parts: $2 \times 3 \times 5 = 30$. Then go back and note that there were three—an odd number—negatives, so the product is negative: $(–2) \times (–3) \times (–5) = –30$.

4. Prime Numbers

A prime number is an integer greater than 1 that has no positive factor other than one and itself. 2 is the only even prime number.

5. Counting Consecutive Integers

To count consecutive integers, **subtract the smallest from the largest and add 1**. To count the integers from 13 through 31, subtract: $31 – 13 = 18$. Then add 1: $18 + 1 = 19$.

6. PEMDAS

When performing multiple operations, remember **PEMDAS**, which means **Parentheses** first, then **Exponents**, then **Multiplication and Division** (left to right), and lastly, **Addition and Subtraction** (left to right). In the expression $9 – 2 \times (5 – 3)^2 + 6 \div 3$, begin with the parentheses: $(5 – 3) = 2$. Then do the exponent: $2^2 = 4$. Now the expression is: $9 – 2 \times 4 + 6 \div 3$. Next do the multiplication and division to get: $9 – 8 + 2$, which equals 3. If you have difficulty remembering PEMDAS, use this sentence to recall it: **P**lease **E**xcuse **M**y **D**ear **A**unt **S**ally.

7. Rounding

Look at the number to the right of the digit in question. If it is 4 or less, leave the digit in question as it is and replace all the digits to the right with zeros. If it is 5 or more, increase the digit in question by 1 and replace all the digits to its right with zeros. To round 654,321 to the nearest hundred, look at the digit in the hundreds' place: 3. Since the number to its right is 2, the 3 remains: 654,300.

Divisibility

8. Factor/Multiple

The **factors** of integer n are the positive integers that divide into n with no remainder. The **multiples** of n are the integers that n divides into with no remainder. For example, 6 is a factor of 12, and 24 is a multiple of 12. 12 is both a factor and a multiple of itself, since $12 \div 12 = 1$ and $12 \times 1 = 12$.

9. Common Multiple

A common multiple is a number that is a multiple of two or more integers. You can always get a common multiple of two integers by **multiplying** them, but, unless the two numbers are relative primes, the product will not be the *least* common multiple. For example, to find a common multiple for 12 and 15, you could just multiply: $12 \times 15 = 180$.

10. Least Common Multiple (LCM)

To find the least common multiple, check out the **multiples of the larger integer** until you find one that's **also a multiple of the smaller**. To find the LCM of 12 and 15, begin by taking the multiples of 15: 15 is not divisible by 12; 30 is not; nor is 45. But the next multiple of 15, 60, *is* divisible by 12, so it's the LCM.

11. Greatest Common Factor (GCF)

To find the greatest common factor, break down both integers into their prime factorizations and multiply **all the prime factors they have in common**. $36 = 2 \times 2 \times 3 \times 3$, and $48 = 2 \times 2 \times 2 \times 2 \times 3$. What they have in common is two 2s and one 3, so the GCF is $2 \times 2 \times 3 = 12$.

12. Even/Odd

To predict whether a sum, difference, or product will be even or odd, just **take simple numbers such as 1 and 2 and see what happens**. There are rules—"odd times even is even," for example—but there's no need to memorize them. What happens with one set of numbers generally happens with all similar sets.

13. Multiples of 2 and 4

An integer is divisible by 2 (which is even) if the **last digit is even**. An integer is divisible by 4 if the **last two digits form a multiple of 4**. The last digit of 562 is 2, which is even, so 562 is a multiple of 2. The last two digits form 62, which is *not* divisible by 4, so 562 is not a multiple of 4. The integer 512, however, is divisible by four because the last two digits form 12, which is a multiple of 4.

14. Multiples of 3 and 9

An integer is divisible by 3 if the **sum of its digits is divisible by 3**. An integer is divisible by 9 if the **sum of its digits is divisible by 9**. The sum of the digits in 957 is 21, which is divisible by 3 but not by 9, so 957 is divisible by 3 but not by 9.

15. Multiples of 6

An integer is divisible by 6 if it meets the divisibility requirements of 2 and 3, that is, if its last digit is even and the sum of its digits is divisible by 3. The last digit of 456 is even, and the sum of its digits is 15, which is divisible by 3, so 456 is divisible by 6.

16. Multiples of 5 and 10

An integer is divisible by 5 if the **last digit is 5 or 0**. An integer is divisible by 10 if the **last digit is 0**. The last digit of 665 is 5, so 665 is a multiple of 5 but *not* a multiple of 10.

17. Remainders

The remainder is the **whole number left over after division**. 487 is 2 more than 485, which is a multiple of 5, so when 487 is divided by 5, the remainder will be 2.

Fractions and Decimals

18. Reducing Fractions

To reduce a fraction to lowest terms, **factor out and cancel** all factors the numerator and denominator have in common.

$$\frac{28}{36} = \frac{4 \times 7}{4 \times 9} = \frac{7}{9}$$

19. Adding/Subtracting Fractions

To add or subtract fractions, first find a **common denominator**, then add or subtract the numerators.

$$\frac{2}{15} + \frac{3}{10} = \frac{4}{30} + \frac{9}{30} = \frac{4+9}{30} = \frac{13}{30}$$

20. Multiplying Fractions

To multiply fractions, **multiply** the numerators and **multiply** the denominators.

$$\frac{5}{7} \times \frac{3}{4} = \frac{5 \times 3}{7 \times 4} = \frac{15}{28}$$

21. Dividing Fractions

To divide fractions, **invert** the second one and **multiply**.

$$\frac{1}{2} \div \frac{3}{5} = \frac{1}{2} \times \frac{5}{3} = \frac{1 \times 5}{2 \times 3} = \frac{5}{6}$$

22. Converting a Mixed Number to an Improper Fraction

To convert a mixed number to an improper fraction, **multiply** the whole number part by the denominator, then **add** the numerator. The result is the new numerator (over the same denominator). To convert $7\frac{1}{3}$, first multiply 7 by 3, then add 1, to get the new numerator of 22. Put that over the same denominator, 3, to get $\frac{22}{3}$.

23. Converting an Improper Fraction to a Mixed Number

To convert an improper fraction to a mixed number, divide the denominator into the numerator to get a **whole number quotient with a remainder**. The quotient becomes the whole number part of the mixed number, and the remainder becomes the new numerator—with the same denominator. For example, to convert $\frac{108}{5}$, first divide 5 into 108, which yields 21 with a remainder of 3. Therefore, $\frac{108}{5} = 21\frac{3}{5}$.

24. Reciprocal

To find the reciprocal of a fraction, **switch the numerator and the denominator**. The reciprocal of $\frac{3}{7}$ is $\frac{7}{3}$. The reciprocal of 5 is $\frac{1}{5}$. The product of reciprocals is 1.

25. Comparing Fractions

One way to compare fractions is to **re-express them with a common denominator**. $\frac{3}{4} = \frac{21}{28}$ and $\frac{5}{7} = \frac{20}{28}$. $\frac{21}{28}$ is greater than $\frac{20}{28}$, so $\frac{3}{4}$ is greater than $\frac{5}{7}$. Another way to compare fractions is to **convert them both to decimals**. $\frac{3}{4}$ converts to 0.75 , and $\frac{5}{7}$ converts to approximately 0.714.

26. Converting Fractions to Decimals

To convert a fraction to a decimal, **divide the top by the bottom**. To convert $\frac{5}{8}$, divide 5 by 8, yielding 0.625.

27. Converting Decimals to Fractions

To convert a decimal to a fraction, set the decimal over 1 and **multiply the numerator and denominator by ten raised to the number of digits to the right of the decimal point**. For instance, to convert 0.625 to a fraction, you would multiply $\frac{0.625}{1}$ by $\frac{10^3}{10^3}$, or $\frac{1,000}{1,000}$. Then simplify: $\frac{625}{1,000} = \frac{5 \times 125}{8 \times 125} = \frac{5}{8}$.

28. Repeating Decimal

To find a particular digit in a repeating decimal, note the **number of digits in the cluster that repeats**. If there are 2 digits in that cluster, then every second digit is the same. If there are three digits in that cluster, then every third digit is the same. And so on. For example, the decimal equivalent of $\frac{1}{27}$ is .037037037..., which is best written $0.\overline{037}$. There are three digits in the repeating cluster, so every third digit after a given digit is the same: 0, 3, or 7, depending on what dgit you are looking at. To find the 50th digit, look for the multiple of three just less than 50—that's 48. The 48th digit is 7, and with the 49th digit the pattern repeats with 0. The 50th digit is 3.

29. Identifying the Parts and the Whole

The key to solving most fractions and percents story problems is to identify the part and the whole. Usually you'll find the **part** associated with the verb *is/are* and the **whole** associated with the word *of*. In the sentence, "Half of the boys are blonds," the whole is the boys ("of the boys"), and the part is the blonds ("are blonds").

Percents

30. Percent Formula

Whether you need to find the part, the whole, or the percent, use the same formula:

$$\text{Part} = \text{Percent} \times \text{Whole}$$

Example: What is 12% of 25?
Setup: Part $= 0.12 \times 25$

Example: 15 is 3% of what number?
Setup: $15 = 0.03 \times$ Whole

Example: 45 is what percent of 9?
Setup: 45 = Percent × 9

31. Percent Increase and Decrease

To increase a number by a percent, **add the percent to 100 percent**, convert to a decimal, and multiply. To increase 40 by 25 percent, add 25 percent to 100 percent, convert 125 percent to 1.25, and multiply by 40. 1.25 × 40 = 50.

32. Finding the Original Whole

To find the **original whole before a percent increase or decrease, set up an equation**. Think of the result of a 15 percent increase over x as $1.15x$.

Example: After a 5 percent increase, the population was 59,346. What was the population before the increase?
Setup: $1.05x = 59{,}346$

33. Combined Percent Increase and Decrease

To determine the combined effect of multiple percent increases and/or decreases, **start with 100 and see what happens**.

Example: A price went up 10 percent one year, and the new price went up 20 percent the next year. What was the combined percent increase?
Setup: First year: 100 + (10 percent of 100) = 110. Second year: 110 + (20 percent of 110) = 132. That's a combined 32 percent increase.

Average, Median, and Mode

34. Average Formula

To find the average of a set of numbers, **add them up and divide by the number of numbers**.

$$\text{Average} = \frac{\text{Sum of the terms}}{\text{Number of terms}}$$

To find the average of the five numbers 12, 15, 23, 40, and 40, first add them: 12 + 15 + 23 + 40 + 40 = 130. Then divide the sum by 5: 130 ÷ 5 = 26.

35. Average of Consecutive Numbers

The average of a group of consecutive numbers is always the middle value. The average of 21, 22, 23, 24, and 25 is 23. You can also find the average of consecutive numbers by averaging the smallest and the largest. So the average of the group of numbers above is the same as the average of 21 and 25:

$$\frac{21 + 25}{2} = \frac{46}{2} = 23$$

36. Using the Average to Find the Sum

Sum = (Average) × (Number of terms)

If the average of ten numbers is 50, then they add up to 50 × 10, or 500.

37. Finding the Missing Number

To find a missing number when you're given the average, **use the sum**. If the average of four numbers is 7, then the sum of those four numbers is 7 × 4, or 28. Suppose that three of the numbers are 3, 5, and 8. These three numbers add up to 16 of that 28, which leaves 12 for the fourth number.

38. Median

The median of a set of numbers is the **value that falls in the middle of the set**. If you have five test scores, and they are 88, 86, 57, 94, and 73, you must first list the scores in increasing or decreasing order:

57, 73, 86, 88, 94

The median is the middle number, or 86. If there is an even number of values in a set (six test scores, for instance), simply take the average of the two middle numbers.

39. Mode

The mode of a set of numbers is the **value that appears most often**. If your test scores were 88, 57, 68, 85, 99, 93, 93, 84, and 81, the mode of the scores would be 93 because it appears more often than any other score. If there is a tie for the most common value in a set, the set has more than one mode.

Ratios, Proportions, and Rates

40. Setting up a Ratio

To find a ratio, put the number associated with the word *of* **on top** and the quantity associated with the word *to* **on the bottom** and reduce. The ratio of 20 oranges to 12 apples is $\frac{20}{12}$, which reduces to $\frac{5}{3}$.

41. Part-to-Part Ratios and Part-to-Whole Ratios

If the parts add up to the whole, a part-to-part ratio can be turned into two part-to-whole ratios by putting **each number in the original ratio over the sum of the numbers.** If the ratio of males to females is 1 to 2, then the males-to-people ratio is $\frac{1}{1+2} = \frac{1}{3}$ and the females-to-people ratio is $\frac{2}{1+2} = \frac{2}{3}$. In other words, $\frac{2}{3}$ of all the people are female.

42. Solving a Proportion

To solve a proportion, **cross-multiply:**

$$\frac{x}{5} = \frac{3}{4}$$
$$4x = 3 \times 5$$
$$x = \frac{15}{4} = 3.75$$

43. Rate

To solve a rates problem, set up a proportion:

Example: A certain machine produces 50 pencils in 30 minutes. How many pencils will this machine produce in 75 minutes?

Set-up: $\frac{50 \text{ pencils}}{30 \text{ minutes}} = \frac{x \text{ pencils}}{75 \text{ minutes}}$

$$30x = 50 \times 75$$
$$x = 125$$

Sometimes you'll need to **use the units** to keep things straight.

Example: If snow is falling at the rate of one foot every four hours, how many inches of snow will fall in seven hours?

Setup: $\frac{1 \text{ foot}}{4 \text{ hours}} = \frac{x \text{ inches}}{7 \text{ hours}}$

$$\frac{12 \text{ inches}}{4 \text{ hours}} = \frac{x \text{ inches}}{7 \text{ hours}}$$
$$4x = 12 \times 7$$
$$x = 21$$

Possibilities and Probability

44. Counting the Possibilities

The fundamental counting principle: If there are *m* **ways** one event can happen and *n* **ways** a second event can happen, then there are *m* × *n* **ways** for the two events to happen. For example, with five shirts and seven pairs of pants to choose from, you can put together 5 × 7 = 35 different outfits.

45. Probability

$$\text{Probability} = \frac{\textbf{Favorable outcomes}}{\textbf{Total possible outcomes}}$$

For example, if you have 12 shirts in a drawer and nine of them are white, the probability of picking a white shirt at random is $\frac{9}{12} = \frac{3}{4}$. This probability can also be expressed as 0.75 or 75%.

Exponents and Radicals

46. Multiplying and Dividing Powers

To multiply powers with the same base, **add the exponents and keep the same base:**

$$x^3 \times x^4 = x^{3+4} = x^7$$

To divide powers with the same base, **subtract the exponents and keep the same base:**

$$y^{13} \div y^8 = y^{13-8} = y^5$$

47. Raising Powers to Exponents

To raise a power to an exponent, **multiply the exponents:**

$$(x^3)^4 = x^{3 \times 4} = x^{12}$$

48. Simplifying Square Roots

To simplify a square root, **factor out the perfect squares** under the radical, unsquare them and put the result in front.

$$\sqrt{12} = \sqrt{4 \times 3} = \sqrt{4} \times \sqrt{3} = 2\sqrt{3}$$

49. Adding and Subtracting Roots

You can add or subtract radical expressions **when the part under the radicals is the same:**

$$2\sqrt{3} + 3\sqrt{3} = 5\sqrt{3}$$

Don't try to add or subtract when the radical parts are different. There's not much you can do with an expression like:

$$3\sqrt{5} + 3\sqrt{7}$$

50. Multiplying and Dividing Roots

The product of non-negative square roots is equal to the non-negative **square root of the product:**

$$\sqrt{3} \times \sqrt{5} = \sqrt{3 \times 5} = \sqrt{15}$$

The quotient of square roots is equal to the **square root of the quotient:**

$$\frac{\sqrt{6}}{\sqrt{3}} = \sqrt{\frac{6}{3}} = \sqrt{2}$$

Algebraic Expressions

51. Substitution

Replace the variables with the given values and follow the rules of PEMDAS—Parentheses, Exponents, Multiplication and Division from left to right, Addition and Subtraction from left to right. To find the value of $5x - 6$ when $x = -2$, plug in -2 for x:
$5(-2) - 6 = -10 - 6 = -16$.

52. Adding and Subtracting Monomials

To combine like terms, **keep the variable part unchanged while adding or subtracting the coefficients:**

$$2a + 3a = (2 + 3)a = 5a$$

53. Adding and Subtracting Polynomials

To add or subtract polynomials, **combine like terms**.

$$(3x^2 + 5x - 7) - (x^2 + 12) =$$
$$(3x^2 - x^2) + 5x + (-7 - 12) =$$
$$2x^2 + 5x - 19$$

54. Multiplying Monomials

To multiply monomials, **multiply the coefficients and the variables separately:**

$$2a \times 3a = (2 \times 3)(a \times a) = 6a^2$$

Solving Equations

55. Solving a Linear Equation

To solve an equation, do whatever is necessary to both sides to **isolate the variable**. To solve the equation $5x - 12 = -2x + 9$, first get all the xs on one side by adding $2x$ to both sides: $7x - 12 = 9$. Then add 12 to both sides: $7x = 21$. Then divide both sides by 7: $x = 3$.

56. Solving "in Terms of"

To solve an equation for one variable **in terms of** another means to **isolate the one variable on one side of the equation**, leaving an expression containing the other variable on the other side of the equation. To solve the equation $3x - 10y = -5x + 6y$ for x in terms of y, isolate x:

$$3x - 10y = -5x + 6y$$
$$3x + 5x = 6y + 10y$$
$$8x = 16y$$
$$x = 2y$$

57. Translating from English into Algebra

To translate from English into algebra, **look for the key words and systematically turn phrases into algebraic expressions and sentences into equations**. Be careful about order, especially when subtraction is called for.

Example: The charge for a phone call is r cents for the first three minutes and s cents for each minute thereafter. What is the cost, in cents, of a phone call lasting exactly t minutes? $(t > 3)$

Setup: The charge begins with r, and then something more is added, depending on the length of the call. The amount added is s times the number of minutes past three minutes. If the total number of minutes is t, then the number of minutes past three is $t - 3$. So the charge is $r + s(t - 3)$.

58. Solving an Inequality

To solve an inequality, do whatever is necessary to both sides to **isolate the variable**. Just remember that when you **multiply or divide both sides by a negative number**, you must **reverse the sign**. To solve $-5x + 7 < -3$, subtract 7 from both sides to get: $-5x < -10$. Now divide both sides by -5, remembering to reverse the sign: $x > 2$.

59. Symbolism

When a problem supplies you with an unfamiliar symbol, it will always define this symbol for you, and indicate the operation you are to perform. Simply plug in to the prescribed definition and solve.

Example: Let $a\spadesuit$ be defined for all positive integers a by the equation $a\spadesuit = \frac{a}{4} - \frac{a}{6}$. What is $12\spadesuit$?

Set-up: Just plug in and solve.

$12\spadesuit = \frac{12}{4} - \frac{12}{6} = 3 - 2 = 1.$

Lines and Angles

60. Line Segments

A line segment is a piece of a line and has an exact measurable length. That length is the distance between the two endpoints. The midpoint is the point exactly in the middle of the line segment. The midpoint divides the line segment into two equal parts.

61. Intersecting Lines

When two lines intersect, **adjacent angles are supplementary and vertical angles are equal**.

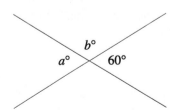

In the figure above, the angles marked $a°$ and $b°$ are adjacent and supplementary, so $a + b = 180$. Furthermore, the angles marked $a°$ and $60°$ are vertical and equal, so $a = 60$.

62. Perpendicular Lines

Lines that intersect to form right angles are said to be perpendicular. When two lines are perpendicular, they intersect to form four right angles.

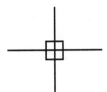

Right angles are generally indicated by small boxes, as shown in the figure above.

63. Supplementary Angles

Two angles that add up to 180 degrees are supplementary. When two lines intersect, the adjacent angles are supplementary.

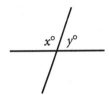

In the figure above, angles x and y are adjacent and supplementary.

64. Complementary Angles

Two angles whose measure sum to 90 degrees are said to be complementary. A 30° angle and a 60° angle are complementary.

65. Right Angles

A right angle is an angle that **measures 90 degrees**. In right triangle ABC below, angle BAC is a right angle.

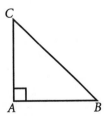

As shown in the figure above, a right angle is usually indicated by a small box.

Triangles—General

66. Interior Angles of a Triangle

The three angles of any triangle add up to 180°.

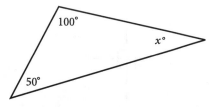

In the figure above, $x + 50 + 100 = 180$, so $x = 30$.

67. Exterior Angles of a Triangle

An exterior angle of a triangle is equal to the **sum of the remote interior angles**.

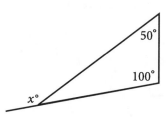

In the figure above, the exterior angle labeled $x°$ is equal to the sum of the remote inferior angles:
$x = 50 + 100 = 150$.

The three exterior angles of a triangle add up to 360°.

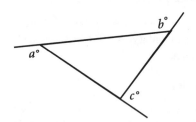

In the figure above, $a + b + c = 360$.

68. Area of a Triangle

$$\text{Area of Triangle} = \frac{1}{2}(\text{base})(\text{height})$$

The height is the perpendicular distance between the side that's chosen as the base and the opposite vertex.

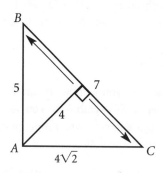

In the triangle above, 4 is the height when the 7 is chosen as the base.

$\text{Area} = \frac{1}{2}bh = \frac{1}{2}(7)(4) = 14$

69. Similar Triangles

Similar triangles have the same shape; **corresponding angles are equal and corresponding sides are proportional.**

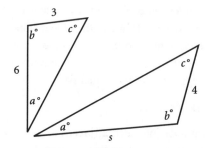

The triangles above are similar because they have the same angles. The 3 corresponds to the 4 and the 6 corresponds to the s.

$$\frac{3}{4} = \frac{6}{s}$$

$$3s = 24$$

$$s = 8$$

70. Isosceles Triangles

An isosceles triangle is a triangle that has **two equal sides**. Not only are two sides equal, but the angles opposite the equal sides, called base angles, are also equal.

71. Equilateral Triangles

Equilateral triangles are triangles in which **all three sides are equal**. Since all the sides are equal, all the angles are also equal. All three angles in an equilateral triangle measure 60 degrees, regardless of the lengths of sides.

Right Triangles

72. Pythagorean Theorem

For all right triangles:

$$(\text{leg}_1)^2 + (\text{leg}_2)^2 = (\text{hypotenuse})^2$$

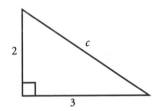

If one leg is 2 and the other leg is 3, then:

$$2^2 + 3^2 = c^2$$
$$c^2 = 4 + 9$$
$$c = \sqrt{13}$$

73. The 3-4-5 Triangle

If a right triangle's leg-to-leg ratio is 3:4, or if the leg-to-hypotenuse ratio is 3:5 or 4:5, it's a 3-4-5 triangle and you don't need to use the Pythagorean theorem to find the third side. Just figure out what multiple of 3-4-5 it is.

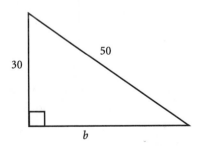

In the right triangle shown, one leg is 30 and the hypotenuse is 50. This is 10 times 3-4-5. The other leg is 40.

74. The 5-12-13 Triangle

If a right triangle's leg-to-leg ratio is 5:12, or if the leg-to-hypotenuse ratio is 5:13 or 12:13, then it's a 5-12-13 triangle. You don't need to use the Pythagorean theorem to find the third side. Just figure out what multiple of 5-12-13 it is.

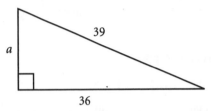

Here one leg is 36 and the hypotenuse is 39. This is 3 times 5-12-13. The other leg is 15.

75. The 30-60-90 Triangle

The sides of a 30-60-90 triangle are in a ratio of $x : x\sqrt{3} : 2x$; the Pythagorean theorem is not necessary.

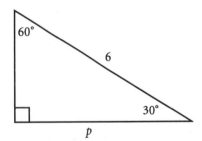

If the hypotenuse is 6, then the shorter leg is half that, or 3; and then the longer leg is equal to the short leg times $\sqrt{3}$, or $3\sqrt{3}$.

76. The Isosceles Right Triangle

An isosceles right triangle has a right angle and two 45-degree angles. The legs of an isosceles right triangle are equal. The sides of a 45-45-90 triangle are in a ratio of $x : x : x\sqrt{2}$.

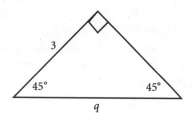

If one leg is 3, then the other leg is also 3, and the hypotenuse is equal to a leg times $\sqrt{2}$, or $3\sqrt{2}$.

Quadrilaterals

77. Characteristics of a Rectangle

A rectangle is a **four-sided figure with four right angles**. Opposite sides are equal. Diagonals are equal.

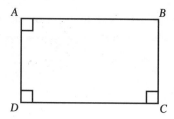

Quadrilateral *ABCD* above is shown to have three right angles. The fourth angle therefore also measures 90°, and *ABCD* is a rectangle. The perimeter of a rectangle is equal to the sum of the lengths of the four sides, which is equivalent to 2(length + width).

78. Area of a Rectangle

Area of a Rectangle = Length × Width

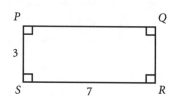

The area of a 7-by-3 rectangle is $7 \times 3 = 21$.

79. Characteristics of a Parallelogram

A parallelogram has **two pairs of parallel sides**. Opposite sides are equal. Opposite angles are equal. Consecutive angles add up to 180°.

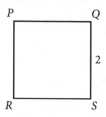

In the figure above, *s* is the length of the side opposite the 3, so *s* = 3.

80. Area of a Parallelogram

Area of a Parallelogram = base × height

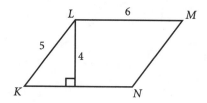

In parallelogram *KLMN* above, 4 is the height when *LM* or *KN* is used as the base. Base × height = $6 \times 4 = 24$.

81. Characteristics of a Square

A square is a **rectangle with four equal sides**.

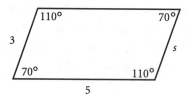

If *PQRS* is a square, all sides are the same length as *QR*. The perimeter of a square is equal to four times the length of one side.

82. Area of a Square

Area of a Square = (Side)²

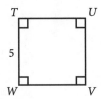

The square above, with sides of length 5, has an area of $5^2 = 25$.

Circles

83. Circumference of a Circle

$$\text{Circumference} = 2\pi r$$

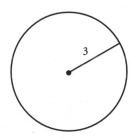

In the circle above, the radius is 3, and so the circumference is $2\pi(3) = 6\pi$.

84. Area of a Circle

$$\text{Area of a Circle} = \pi r^2$$

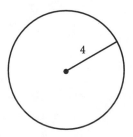

The area of the circle above is $\pi(4)^2 = 16\pi$.

How Did We Do? Grade Us.

Thank you for choosing a Kaplan book. Your comments and suggestions are very useful to us. Please answer the following questions to assist us in our continued development of high-quality resources to meet your needs.

The title of the Kaplan book I read was: _____

My name is: _____

My address is: _____

_____

My e-mail address is: _____

What overall grade would you give this book?	(A)	(B)	(C)	(D)	(F)
How relevant was the information to your goals?	(A)	(B)	(C)	(D)	(F)
How comprehensive was the information in this book?	(A)	(B)	(C)	(D)	(F)
How accurate was the information in this book?	(A)	(B)	(C)	(D)	(F)
How easy was the book to use?	(A)	(B)	(C)	(D)	(F)
How appealing was the book's design?	(A)	(B)	(C)	(D)	(F)

What were the book's strong points? _____

How could this book be improved? _____

Is there anything that we left out that you wanted to know more about?

Would you recommend this book to others?   ☐ YES   ☐ NO

Other comments: _____

_____

_____

Do we have permission to quote you?   ☐ YES   ☐ NO

Thank you for your help.
Please tear out this page and mail it to:

> Managing Editor
> Kaplan, Inc.
> 888 Seventh Avenue
> New York, NY 10106

Thanks!

KAPLAN®

Paying for graduate school just got easier...

The Kaplan/American Express Student Loan Information Program.

Get free information on the financial aid process before you apply.

When you request your student loan applications through Kaplan/American Express, we'll send you our free Financial Aid Handbook. With the Kaplan/American Express Student Loan Information Program, you'll have access to some of the least expensive educational loans available.

■ The Federal Stafford Loan—Eligible students may borrow up to $18,500 each year toward the cost of education.

■ A Private Loan—If the federal Stafford Loan does not fully meet educational financing needs, additional funds may be available under a private loan program.

Make the most of your financial aid opportunities. Contact us today!

www.kaploan.com

Educational Loans

1-888-KAP-LOAN

*Kaplan is not a lender and does not participate in the determination of loan eligibility.
Telephone inquiries to 1-888-KAP-LOAN will be answered by a representative of a provider of federal and certain private educational loans.

Kaplan, Inc. is one of the nation's leading providers of education and career services. Kaplan is a wholly owned subsidiary of The Washington Post Company.

KAPLAN TEST PREPARATION & ADMISSIONS

Kaplan's nationally recognized test prep courses cover more than 20 standardized tests, including secondary school, college and graduate school entrance exams, as well as foreign language and professional licensing exams. In addition, Kaplan offers a college admissions course, private tutoring, and a variety of free information and services for students applying to college and graduate programs. Kaplan also provides information and guidance on the financial aid process. Students can enroll in online test prep courses and admissions consulting services at www.kaptest.com.

Kaplan K12 Learning Services partners with schools, universities, and teachers to help students succeed, providing customized assessment, education, and professional development programs.

SCORE! EDUCATIONAL CENTERS

SCORE! after-school learning centers help K–10 students build confidence along with academic skills in a motivating, sports-oriented environment.

SCORE! Prep provides in-home, one-on-one tutoring for high school academic subjects and standardized tests.

eSCORE.com is the first educational services Web site to offer parents and kids newborn to age 18 personalized child development and educational resources online.

KAPLANCOLLEGE.COM

KaplanCollege.com, Kaplan's distance learning platform, offers an array of online educational programs for working professionals who want to advance their careers. Learners will find nearly 500 professional development, continuing education, certification, and degree courses and programs in Nursing, Education, Criminal Justice, Real Estate, Legal Professions, Law, Management, General Business, and Computing/Information Technology.

KAPLAN PUBLISHING

Kaplan Publishing produces retail books and software. Kaplan Books, published by Simon & Schuster, include titles in test preparation, admissions, education, career development, and life skills; Kaplan and *Newsweek* jointly publish guides on getting into college, finding the right career, and helping children succeed in school.

KAPLAN PROFESSIONAL

Kaplan Professional provides assessment, training, and certification services for corporate clients and individuals seeking to advance their careers. Member units include:

- Dearborn, a leading supplier of licensing training and continuing education for securities, real estate, and insurance professionals

- Perfect Access/CRN, which delivers software education and consultation for law firms and businesses

- Kaplan Professional Call Center Services, a total provider of services for the call center industry

- Self Test Software, a world leader in exam simulation software and preparation for technical certifications

- Schweser's Study Program/AIAF, which provides preparation services for the CFA examination

KAPLAN INTERNATIONAL PROGRAMS

Kaplan assists international students and professionals in the United States through a series of intensive English language and test preparation programs. These programs are offered at campus-based centers across the United States. Specialized services include housing, placement at top American universities, fellowship management, academic monitoring and reporting, and financial administration.

COMMUNITY OUTREACH

Kaplan provides educational career resources to thousands of financially disadvantaged students annually, working closely with educational institutions, not-for-profit groups, government agencies and grass roots organizations on a variety of national and local support programs. These programs help students and professionals from a variety of backgrounds achieve their educational and career goals.

BRASSRING

BrassRing Inc., the premier business-to-business hiring management and recruitment services company, offers employers a vertically integrated suite of online and offline solutions. BrassRing, created in September 1999, combined Kaplan Career Services, Terra-Starr, Crimson & Brown Associates, thepavement.com, and HireSystems. In March 2000, BrassRing acquired Career Service Inc./Westech. Kaplan is a shareholder in BrassRing, along with Tribune Company, Central Newspapers, and Accel Partners.

Want more information about our services, products, or the nearest Kaplan center?

 Call our nationwide toll-free numbers:

1-800-KAP-TEST for information on our courses, private tutoring and admissions consulting
1-800-KAP-ITEM for information on our books and software

 Connect with us in cyberspace:

On the World Wide Web, go to:
1. www.kaplan.com
2. www.kaptest.com
3. www.eSCORE.com
4. www.dearborn.com
5. www.BrassRing.com
6. www.concordlawschool.com
7. www.KaplanCollege.com
Via e-mail: info@kaplan.com

 **Write to:**

 Kaplan, Inc.
888 Seventh Avenue
New York, NY 10106